Seventh Edition

A Framework for Human Resource Management

Gary Dessler
Florida International University

PEARSON

Boston   Columbus   Indianapolis   New York   San Francisco   Upper Saddle River
Amsterdam   Cape Town   Dubai   London   Madrid   Milan   Munich   Paris
Montreal   Toronto   Delhi   Mexico City   São Paulo   Sydney
Hong Kong   Seoul   Singapore   Taipei   Tokyo

Editor-in-Chief: Stephanie Wall
Acquisitions Editor: April Cole
Editorial Project Manager: Sarah Holle
Editorial Assistant: Bernard Ollila
Director of Marketing: Maggie Moylan
Senior Marketing Manager:
   Nikki Ayana Jones
Marketing Assistant: Gianna Sandri
Senior Managing Editor: Judy Leale
Production Project Manager:
   Kelly Warsak
Senior Operations Supervisor:
   Arnold Vila
Operations Specialist: Cathleen Petersen
Creative Director: Blair Brown
Senior Art Director: Kenny Beck

Cover Designer: Suzanne Behnke
Cover Photo: iStockphoto
Permission Specialist:
   Brooks Hill-Whilton
Media Project Manager:
   Lisa Rinaldi
Media Assistant Editor:
   Denise Vaughn
Full-Service Project Management:
   Jennifer Welsch/Bookmasters
Composition: Integra Software Services
Printer/Binder: Courier/Westford
Cover Printer:
   Lehigh-Phoenix Color/
   Hagerstown
Text Font: 11/12 Minion Pro

Credits and acknowledgments borrowed from other sources and reproduced, with permission, in this textbook appear on appropriate page within text.

Microsoft® and Windows® are registered trademarks of the Microsoft Corporation in the U.S.A. and other countries. Screen shots and icons reprinted with permission from the Microsoft Corporation. This book is not sponsored or endorsed by or affiliated with the Microsoft Corporation.

Library of Congress Cataloging-in-Publication Data
Dessler, Gary
   A framework for human resource management/Gary Dessler—7th ed.
      p. cm.
   Includes bibliographical references and index.
   ISBN-13: 978-0-13-257614-7 (pbk. : alk. paper)
   ISBN-10: 0-13-257614-7
   1. Personnel management.   I. Title.
HF5549.D43788 2013   2012008792
658.3—dc23

10 9 8 7 6 5 4 3 2 1   V013

PEARSON

ISBN-10:   0-13-257614-7
ISBN-13: 978-0-13-257614-7

To my mother

BRIEF CONTENTS

CONTENTS

PREFACE

A Framework for Human Resource Management provides students and practicing managers with a concise but thorough review of essential human resource management concepts and techniques in a highly readable and understandable form. Most books in this market (including my *Human Resource Management,* 13th edition, and *Fundamentals of Human Resource Management*, 2nd edition) contain 14–18 chapters and 450–800 large-trim-size pages. In contrast, writing *Framework* is like building a boat in a bottle: My aim is to create a precise and complete but dramatically downsized model of the human resource management body of knowledge by stripping away repetition, long research reviews, and extraneous content such as long company-based chapter openers. The people reading this book are busy, and I want them to be able to focus on learning the core concepts and tools of human resource management.

Adopters use this book in many ways. Many use it as the basic textbook for the human resource management course, sometimes supplementing it with extra cases or human resource management exercises. Others use it with other textbooks in courses that blend several topics (such as HR and organizational behavior), or in specialized courses (such as "HR for Entrepreneurial Companies"). Because *Framework* contains a practical and up-to-date review of essential human resource management concepts and techniques, practicing human resource and line managers use it to update their HR skills and to help prepare for certification exams.

WHAT'S NEW IN THE 7TH EDITION

Given its gratifying acceptance and the 6th edition reviewers' comments, *Framework 7*'s themes, approach, and outline continue largely unchanged from *Framework 6*. All managers have personnel responsibilities, so I again wrote this book for all managers and management students, not just those who are or will be human resource managers. The book's basic idea—to provide a concise but thorough review of HR concepts and techniques—is the same. The table of contents is about the same, as is the topic coverage. Adopters can again order a Human Resource Certification Institute guide. There are again *five comprehensive cases* that I wrote at the end of the book, in addition to the end-of-chapter case incidents. However, I also made seven main changes to this 7th edition, as follows.

1. **Dozens of new topics.** For example, you'll find expanded treatments of reliability, validity, generalizability, utility, person-job fit, and bias. Dozens of other new topics appear throughout the book, including using the standard deviation rule in equal employment compliance, retaliation, job satisfaction and withdrawal, managing voluntary turnover, management's willingness to take a strike, cross training, and job hazard analysis.
2. **Expanded coverage of strategic human resource management in Chapter 1,** including discussions of HR Scorecards and strategy maps.
3. **A new boxed feature,** *HR as a Profit Center*, in most chapters. These *HR as a Profit Center* features present actual examples of how human resource managers added measurable value to their companies. In addition, continuing their use from the 6th edition, the separate *HR in Practice* features provide all managers—not just HR managers—with actionable HR tools and guidelines.

4. **A completely revised Chapter 8,** now titled **Managing Employee Ethics, Engagement, Retention, and Fair Treatment,** which includes discussions of employee engagement, withdrawal, and retention, as well as managing ethics, and a **new presentation (in Chapter 7) of how to create a market-competitive pay structure**.

5. **Expanded treatment of Career Management** in Chapter 6 (Performance Management, Appraisals, and Careers) **and of the ADDIE training process** in Chapter 5 (Training and Developing Employees).

6. **A new end-of-book module on Practical HR Tools for Managers,** focusing on nuts-and-bolts human resource management tools, guidelines, and systems all managers can use, for instance, to comply with EEOC interview question guidelines. This module replaces the 6th edition's *International HR module*, with international HR issues still covered in special boxed features in most chapters.

7. **Nine new videos** with discussion questions and a synopsis for each video included at the end of each part of the textbook.

Websites to which we refer in the text sometimes change or are discontinued because companies change names, are bought or sold, merge, or fail. They were accurate when we put the book into production. We apologize in advance for any inconvenience.

ACKNOWLEDGMENTS

No book ever reaches the light of day without the dedicated efforts of many people, and *Framework* is no exception. I am grateful to past and present reviewers:

Mark Barnard, *Edgewood College*

Kathleen Barnes, *East Stroudsburg University*

Gerald Baumgardner, *Penn College*

Jerry Bennett, *Western Kentucky University*

Stephen Betts, *William Paterson University*

Genie Black, *Arkansas Tech University*

David Lawrence Blum, *Moraine Park Technical College*

Michael Bochenek, *Elmhurst College*

Henry Bohleke, *Owens Community College*

Frank Bosco, *University of Memphis*

Richard Brocato, *Mount Saint Mary's University*

Patricia Buhler, *Goldey-Beacom College*

Jackie Bull, *Immaculata University*

Melissa Cardon, *Pace University*

Martin Carrigan, *The University of Findlay*

Yvonne Chandler, *Seattle Community Colleges*

Charlie Cook, *University of West Alabama*

Roger Dean, *Washington and Lee University*

Karen Dielmann, *Lebanon Valley College and Elizabethtown College*

Michael Dutch, *Greensboro College*

Dale Dwyer, *University of Toledo*

William Ferris, *Western New England College*

John Fielding, *Mount Wachusett Community College*

Michael Frew, *Oklahoma City University*

Eugene Garaventa, *College of Staten Island, CUNY*

Alyce Giltner, *Shawnee Community College*

Armand Giroux, *Mitchell College*

Caren Goldberg, *American University*

John Golden, *Slippery Rock University*

John Gronholt, *Modesto Junior College*

Janet Henquinet, *Metropolitan State University, St. Paul, MN*

William Hodson, *Indiana University*

Peter Hughes, *Cambridge College, Lawrence, MA*

John Kachurick, *College Misericordia*

Dennis Kimble, *Central Michigan University*

Jacqueline Landau, *Salem State College*

Cheryl Macon, *Butler County Community College*

Dan Morrell, *Middle Tennessee State University*

Patricia Morrow, *Middlesex Community College*

Arlene Nicholas, *Salve Regina University*

Kay Nicols, *Texas State University–San Marcos*

Jacquelyn Palmer, *Wright State University*

Rich Patterson, *Western Kentucky University*

Diana Peaks, *Jacksonville University*

Jane Philbrick, *Savannah State University*

Larry Phillips, *Indiana University South Bend*

Jonathan Phillips, *North Carolina State University*

Tracy Porter, *Cleveland State University*

Luanne Powel, *Union University*

Chris Osuanah, *J. Sargeant Reynolds Community College and University of Phoenix*

David Radosevich, *Montclair State University*

Carlton R. Raines, *Lehigh Carbon Community College*

Pramila Rao, *Marymount University–Arlington*

Dr. Michael J. Renahan, *College of Saint Elizabeth*

Fritz Scherz, *Morrisville State College*

Biagio Sciacca, *Penn State University*

Dan Scotti, *Providence College*

Robert W. (Bill) Service, *Samford University*

John Shaw, *Mississippi State University*

Walter Siganga, *Southern Illinois University Edwardsville*

Deanna Smith, *Missouri State University*

Marjorie Smith, *Mountain State University*

Chester Spell, *Rutgers University*

Jerry Stevens, *Texas Tech University*

Susan Stewart, *University of Puget Sound*

Michele Summers, *Purdue University*

Vicki Talor, *Shippensburg University*

Rebecca Thacker, *Ohio University*

Jeff Walls, *Indiana Institute of Technology*

Carol Williams, *Pearl River Community College*

Angela Willson, *Yuba College*

Jenell Wittmer, *University of Toledo*

I am grateful to the professors, students, managers, and Prentice Hall sales and marketing associates who have helped make this a top-selling book, not only in English but also in several languages world-wide, including Chinese. At Pearson, I appreciate the efforts of all the professionals on the 7th edition team, including Stephanie Wall, editor-in-chief; Judy Leale, senior managing editor; Kelly Warsak, production project manager; Nikki Jones, senior marketing manager; Linda Albelli, editorial supervisor; and Sarah Holle, editorial project manager.

For many years senior project director Jennifer Welsch has managed the actual day-day-to-day production of *Framework* and my other Pearson books. I am and will always be grateful to her for the major role she has played in making these books successful.

At home, I appreciate all my wife Claudia's support, and my son Derek's support, assistance, and practical suggestions.

One

Managing Strategic Human Resources Today

When you finish studying this chapter you should be able to:

- Answer *the question "What is human resource management?"*
- Discuss *the trends affecting human resource management.*
- Describe *important competencies human resource managers need today.*
- Explain *and give examples of strategic human resource management.*
- Discuss *three strategic management tools managers use.*

OVERVIEW

If you've eaten at a restaurant where the food is overcooked or the wait staff seems inept, then you already know something about human resource management. Human resource management includes tasks like selecting, training, and appraising employees. The main purpose of this chapter is to explain what human resource management is, and why it is important to all managers. We will see that human resource management—activities like recruiting, hiring, training, appraising, and compensating employees—is both a separate management function as well as part of every manager's job. The main topics we cover here are What Is Human Resource Management, Trends Influencing Human Resource Management, The New Human Resource Managers, Strategic Human Resource Management, and The Plan of This Book.

WHAT IS HUMAN RESOURCE MANAGEMENT?

Human resource management refers to the practices and policies you need to carry out the personnel aspects of your management job, specifically, acquiring, training, appraising, rewarding, and providing a safe, ethical, and fair environment for your company's employees. These practices and policies include, for instance:

- Conducting job analyses (determining the nature of each employee's job)
- Planning labor needs and recruiting job candidates
- Selecting job candidates
- Orienting and training employees
- Appraising performance
- Managing wages and salaries (how to compensate employees)
- Providing incentives and benefits
- Communicating and managing employee relations (interviewing, counseling, disciplining)

And what a manager should know about:

- Equal opportunity, ethics, and affirmative action
- Employee health, safety, and ethical treatment
- Grievances and labor relations

Why Is HR Management Important to All Managers, and Why Should I Study This Book?

Why are these concepts and techniques important to all managers?

AVOID PERSONNEL MISTAKES   Perhaps the best way to answer that is to start by listing the sorts of personnel mistakes you *don't* want to make while managing. For example, no manager wants:

- To have your employees not performing at peak capacity
- To hire the wrong person for the job
- To experience high turnover
- To find employees not doing their best
- To have your company taken to court because of your discriminatory actions
- To have your company cited under federal occupational safety laws for unsafe practices
- To allow a lack of training to undermine your department's effectiveness
- To commit any unfair labor practices

Carefully studying this book can help you avoid mistakes like these. More important, it can help ensure that you get results—through people. Remember that you could do everything else right as a manager—lay brilliant plans, draw clear organization charts, set up modern assembly lines, and use sophisticated accounting controls—but still fail, for instance, by hiring the wrong people.

IMPROVE PROFITS AND PERFORMANCE   On the other hand, many managers—from presidents to supervisors—have been successful without adequate plans, organizations, or controls. They were successful because they had the knack for hiring the right people and motivating, appraising, and developing them. Remember as you read this book that getting results is the bottom line of managing and that, as a manager, you will have to get these results through people. That fact hasn't changed from the dawn of management. As one company president summed it up,

> For many years it has been said that capital is the bottleneck for a developing industry. I don't think this any longer holds true. I think it's the workforce and the company's inability to recruit and maintain a good workforce that does constitute the bottleneck for production. I don't know of any major project backed by good ideas, vigor, and enthusiasm that has been stopped by a shortage of cash. I do know of industries whose growth has been partly stopped or hampered because they can't maintain an efficient and enthusiastic labor force, and I think this will hold true even more in the future.[1]

YOU MAY SPEND SOME TIME AS AN HR MANAGER   Here is a third reason to study this book. You may well make a career stopover as a human resource manager. For example, Pearson Corporation (which publishes this book) recently promoted the head of one of its publishing divisions to chief human resource executive at its corporate headquarters. One survey found that about one-fourth of large U.S. businesses appointed managers with no human resource management experience as their top human resource executives. Reasons given include the fact that these people may be better equipped to integrate the firm's human resource efforts with the rest of the business.[2] However, about 80% of top human resource executives in one survey did work their way up within HR.[3] SHRM— the Society for Human Resource Management—offers a brochure describing alternative career paths within human resource management. Find it at www.shrm.org/Communities/StudentPrograms/Documents/07-0971%20Careers%20HR%20Book_final.pdf.

HR FOR ENTREPRENEURS   And here is another reason to study this book. You may well end up as your own human resource manager. More than half the people working in the United States work for small firms. Therefore, most people graduating in the next few years will either work for small businesses or create new small businesses of their own. Most of these firms are too small to have their own human resource managers. Especially if you are managing your own small firm, you'll have to be skilled at human resource management.[4]

Line and Staff Aspects of HRM

All managers are in a sense human resource managers, because they all get involved in recruiting, interviewing, selecting, and training their employees. Yet most firms also have human resource departments with their own top HR managers. How do the duties of this human resource manager and department relate to the human resource duties of sales and production and other managers? Answering this requires a short definition of line versus staff authority.

   Authority is the right to make decisions, to direct the work of others, and to give orders. Managers usually distinguish between line authority and staff authority.

   In organizations, having what managers call **line authority** traditionally gives managers the right to *issue orders* to other managers or employees. Line authority therefore creates a superior (order giver)–subordinate (order receiver) relationship. When the vice president of sales tells her sales director to "get the sales presentation ready by

Tuesday" she is exercising her line authority. **Staff authority** gives a manager the right to *advise* other managers or employees. It creates an advisory relationship. When the human resource manager suggests that the plant manager use a particular selection test, the HR manager is exercising his staff authority.

On the organization chart, managers with line authority are **line managers.** Those with staff (advisory) authority are **staff managers.** In popular usage, people tend to associate line managers with managing departments (like sales or production) that are crucial for the company's survival. Staff managers generally run departments that are advisory or supportive, like purchasing, and human resource management. Human resource managers are usually staff managers. They assist and advise line managers in areas like recruiting, hiring, and compensation.

LINE–STAFF HR COOPERATION   HR and line managers share responsibility for most human resource activities. For example, human resource and line managers in about two-thirds of the firms in one survey shared responsibility for skills training.[5] (Thus the supervisor might describe what training the new employee needs, HR might design the training, and the supervisor might then do the actual training.) Figure 1-1 illustrates the typical HR–line partnership. For example, HR alone typically handles interviewing in about 25% of firms. But in about 60% of firms, HR and the other hiring departments are both involved in interviewing.

Line Managers' Human Resource Management Responsibilities

In any case, the direct handling of people always has been part of every line manager's responsibility, from president to first-line supervisor. All managers therefore spend much of their time on HR-type tasks.

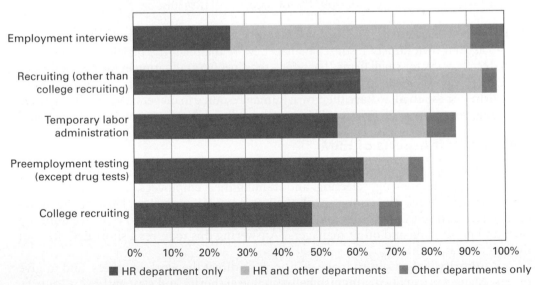

Note: Length of bars represents prevalence of activity among all surveyed employers.

FIGURE 1-1 Employment and Recruiting—Who Handles It? (Percentage of All Employers).   *Source:* Reproduced with permission from HR Department Benchmarks and Analysis 2004, p. 17, Figure 2.1, "Employment and Recruiting—Who Handles It?", p. 17 by The Bureau of National Affairs, Inc. (800-372-1033) http://www.bna.com.

For example, one company outlines its line supervisors' responsibilities for effective human resource management under the following general headings:

1. Placing the right person in the right job
2. Starting new employees in the organization (orientation)
3. Training employees for jobs that are new to them
4. Improving the job performance of each person
5. Gaining cooperation and developing smooth working relationships
6. Interpreting the company's policies and procedures
7. Controlling labor costs
8. Developing the abilities of each person
9. Creating and maintaining departmental morale
10. Protecting employees' health and physical conditions

In small organizations, line managers may carry out all these personnel duties unassisted. But as the organization grows, line managers need the assistance, specialized knowledge, and advice of a separate human resource staff.

Organizing the Human Resource Department's Responsibilities

The human resource department provides this specialized assistance. Figure 1-2 shows typical human resource management jobs. These include compensation and benefits manager, employment and recruiting supervisor, and employee relations executive. Examples of job duties include:

Recruiters: Maintain contact within the community and publicize openings to search for qualified job applicants.[6]

Equal employment opportunity (EEO) representatives or affirmative action coordinators: Investigate and resolve EEO grievances, examine organizational practices for potential violations, and compile and submit EEO reports.

Job analysts: Collect and examine detailed information about job duties to prepare job descriptions.

Compensation managers: Develop compensation plans and handle the employee benefits program.

Training specialists: Plan, organize, and direct training activities.

At the other extreme, the human resource team for a small company may contain just five or six (or fewer) staff. There is *generally* about one human resource employee per 100 company employees.

NEW WAYS TO ORGANIZE THE HUMAN RESOURCES FUNCTION   Employers are also delivering human resource services in new ways. For example, many employers now organize how they deliver their HR services via the following groups:[7]

- The *transactional HR* group uses call centers and outsourced vendors (such as outside benefits advisors) to deliver day-to-day HR support on matters such as changing benefits plans and employee assistance programs to all the company's employees.[8]
- The *corporate HR* group focuses on giving top management advice on "top level" matters, such as explaining the personnel aspects of the company's long-term strategic plan.

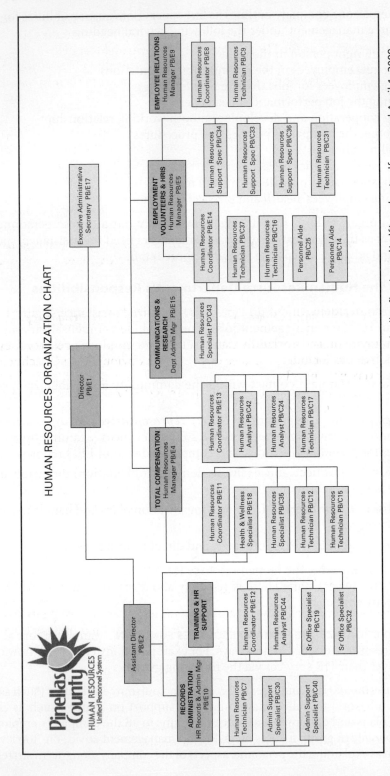

FIGURE 1-2 Human Resource Department Organization Chart. *Source:* www.co.pinellas.fl.us/persnl/pdf/orgchart.pdf, accessed April 1, 2009.

- The *embedded HR* group places ("embeds") HR professionals (also known as "relationship managers" or "HR business partners") in departments like sales and production to provide the HR assistance these departments need.
- *Centers of expertise* groups are like specialized HR consulting firms within the company. For example, they offer specialized assistance in areas such as organizational change.

IBM EXAMPLE   Randall MacDonald, IBM's head of human resources, says the traditional human resource organization isolates HR functions into "silos" such as recruitment, training, and employee relations. He says this silo approach means there's no one team of human resource selection, training, and compensation specialists focusing on the needs of specific groups of employees. MacDonald therefore segmented IBM's 330,000 employees into executive and technical employees, managers, and rank and file. Separate human resource management teams (consisting of recruitment, training, and compensation specialists, for instance) now focus on each employee segment. These specialized teams help the employees in each segment get precisely the talent, learning, and compensation they require.[9]

TRENDS INFLUENCING HUMAN RESOURCE MANAGEMENT

As the IBM example suggests, what human resource managers do and how they do it is changing.[10] Some of the reasons for these changes are obvious. One is technology. For example, employers now use their intranets to let employees modify their own benefits plans, something they obviously couldn't do years ago.[11] Other trends shaping human resource management include globalization of competition, deregulation, changes in demographics and the nature of work, and economic challenges.

We'll see that trends like these pressure employers to lower costs and to boost performance through the efforts of highly engaged and well-trained employees. They rely on their human resource managers to put in place the HR practices that will produce such highly engaged and trained "human resources." The transformation of *personnel* into *human resource management* reflects this. Several trends brought human resource management to this point.[12]

Globalization

Globalization refers to the propensity of firms to extend their sales, ownership, and/or manufacturing to new markets abroad. Thus, Mercedes produces its M-class cars in Alabama, while Dell produces PCs in China. Free trade areas—agreements that reduce tariffs and barriers among trading partners—further encourage international trade. NAFTA (the North American Free Trade Agreement) and the EU (European Union) are examples. So, for example, the total sum of U.S. imports and exports rose from $47 billion in 1960, to $562 billion in 1980, to about $4.7 *trillion* in 2011.[13]

More globalization means more competition, and more competition means more pressure to be "world class"—to lower costs, to make employees more productive, and to do things better and less expensively. This pressures employers and their HR teams to institute practices that get the best from their employees.

HR AS A PROFIT CENTER

Boosting Customer Service

A bank installed special software that made it easier for its customer service representatives to handle customers' inquiries. However, the bank did not otherwise change the service reps' jobs in any way. Here, the new software system did help the service reps handle more calls. But otherwise, this bank saw no big performance gains.[14]

A second bank installed the same software. But, seeking to capitalize on how the new software freed up customer reps' time, this bank also had its human resource team upgrade the customer service representatives' jobs. This bank taught them how to sell more of the bank's services, gave them more authority to make decisions, and raised their wages. Here, the new computer system dramatically improved product sales and profitability, thanks to the newly trained and empowered customer service reps.[15]

Technological Advances

Managers increasingly use technology for many human resource management–type applications. *Facebookrecruiting* is one example.[16] According to Facebook's *Facebookrecruiting* site, employers start the process by installing the "Careers Tab" on their Facebook page. Once installed, "companies have a seamless way to recruit and promote job listings from directly within Facebook."[17] Then, after creating a job listing, the employer can advertise its job link using Facebook Advertisements. The accompanying HR as a Profit Center offers another example.

The Nature of Work

Technology is also changing the nature of work. Skilled machinist Chad Toulouse illustrates this. After an 18-week training course, he now works as a team leader in a plant where about 40% of the machines are automated. Chad and his team type commands into computerized machines that create precision parts for products like water pumps.[18] Human resource managers recently listed "critical thinking/problem solving" and "information technology application" as the two skills most likely to increase in importance over the next 5 years.[19]

Service Jobs

Technology is not the only trend driving this change from "brawn to brains." Today over two-thirds of the U.S. workforce is employed in producing and delivering services, not products. Between 2004 and 2014, almost all the new 19 million new jobs added in the United States will be in services, not in goods-producing industries.[20]

Human Capital

For employers, this all means a growing need for "knowledge workers" and human capital. *Human capital* refers to the knowledge, education, training, skills, and expertise of a firm's workers.[21] This places a big premium on having effective selection, training, and compensation practices.

Offshoring

The search for greater efficiencies prompts employers to export more jobs abroad. For example, Bank of America's Merrill Lynch has some of its security analysis work done abroad. Some American hospitals have radiologists abroad, for example in India, read their patients' X-rays through a process they call teleradiology.[22] By one estimate, between 2005 and 2015, about 3 million U.S. jobs, ranging from office support and computer jobs to management, sales, and even legal jobs, will likely move offshore.[23]

Demographic Trends

The U.S. workforce is becoming older and more multi-ethnic (Table 1-1).[24] For example, between 1998 and 2018, the percent of the workforce that Table 1-1 classifies as "white, non-Hispanic" will drop from 83.8% to 79.4%, and the percent that is black will rise from 11.6% to 12.1%. Those classified Asian will rise from 4.6% to 5.6%, and those of Hispanic origin will rise from 10.4% to 17.6%. The percentages of younger workers will fall, while those over 55 will leap from 12.4% of the workforce in 1998 to 23.9% in 2018.[25]

Such demographic trends are making finding and hiring employees more challenging. In the United States, labor force growth is not expected to keep pace with job growth, with an estimated shortfall of about 14 million college-educated workers by 2020.[26]

"GENERATION Y"   Also called "Millennials," Gen Y employees are roughly those born 1977 to 2002. They take the place of the labor force's previous new entrants, Generation X, those born roughly 1965–1976 and who themselves were the children of, and followed into the labor force, the baby boomers, born just after the Second World War (born roughly 1944–1960.) Although every generation obviously has its own new generation of labor force entrants, Gen Y employees are different. Says one expert, they have "been pampered, nurtured, and programmed with a slew of activities since they were toddlers, meaning they are both high-performance and high-maintenance…"[27] They seek out creative challenges and want to make an important impact on Day 1.[28] As the first generation raised on e-mail, their capacity for using information technology may make them history's most high-performing employees.[29]

TABLE 1-1 Demographic Groups as a Percent of the Workforce, 1998–2018			
Age, race, ethnicity	1998	2008	2018
Age: 16–24	15.9%	14.3	12.7
25–54	71.7	67.7	63.5
55+	12.4	18.1	23.9
White, non-Hispanic	83.8	81.4	79.4
Black	11.6	11.5	12.1
Asian	4.6	4.7	5.6
Hispanic Origin	10.4	14.3	17.6

Source: Data from U.S. Department of Labor, Bureau of Labor Statistics, accessed May 10, 2010.

RETIREES   Many call "the aging workforce" the biggest demographic threat affecting employers. The basic problem is that there aren't enough younger workers to replace the baby boom era older workers retiring.[30] One survey found that 41% of surveyed employers are bringing retirees back into the workforce.[31]

NONTRADITIONAL WORKERS   There is also a shift to nontraditional workers. These workers hold multiple jobs, or are "contingent" or part-time workers, or have alternative work arrangements (like a mother and daughter sharing one clerical job). Today, almost 10% of American workers—13 million people—fit this nontraditional workforce category.

Technology facilitates alternative work arrangements. For example, online websites such as LinkedIn (www.linkedin.com) enable free agent professionals to promote their services. Seeking the collaboration that's often missing when one works alone, "co-working sites" offer freelance workers and consultants office space and access to office equipment for fees of perhaps $200 or $300 per month.[32]

WORKERS FROM ABROAD   With retirements triggering projected workforce shortfalls, many employers are hiring foreign workers for U.S. jobs. The country's H-1B visa program lets U.S. employers recruit skilled foreign professionals to work in the United States when they can't find qualified U.S. workers. U.S. employers bring in about 181,000 foreign workers per year under these programs. Particularly with high unemployment, such programs face opposition. For example, one study concluded that many workers brought in under the programs filled jobs that didn't actually demand highly specialized skills, many paying less than $15 an hour.[33]

Economic Challenges and Trends

All these trends are occurring within the context of economic turmoil. Deregulation was one reason. Around the world, the rules that prevented commercial banks from expanding into new businesses such as stock brokering were relaxed. Giant multinational "financial supermarkets" such as Citibank quickly emerged. As economies boomed, more businesses and consumers went deeply into debt. Homebuyers bought homes, often with little money down. Banks freely lent money to developers to build more homes. For almost 20 years, U.S. consumers spent more than they earned. On a grander scale, the United States became a debtor. Its balance of payments (exports minus imports) went from a healthy positive $3.5 billion in 1960, to a not-so-healthy *minus* $19.4 billion in 1980 (imports exceeded exports), to a huge $497 billion deficit in 2011.[34] The only way the country could keep buying more from abroad than it sold was by borrowing money. So, much of the boom was built on debt.

As you can see in Figure 1-3, gross national product (GNP)—a measure of U.S. total output—boomed between 2001 and 2007. During this period, home prices leaped as much as 20% per year. Unemployment remained docile at about 4.7%.[35] Then, a few years ago, all these measures fell off a cliff. GNP fell. Home prices dropped by 20% or more (depending on city). Unemployment nationwide rose to more than 10%.

Why did all this happen? All those years of accumulating debt seem to have run their course. Banks and other financial institutions (such as hedge funds) owned trillions of dollars of worthless loans. Governments stepped in to try to prevent their collapse. Lending dried up. Many businesses and consumers stopped buying. The economy tanked.

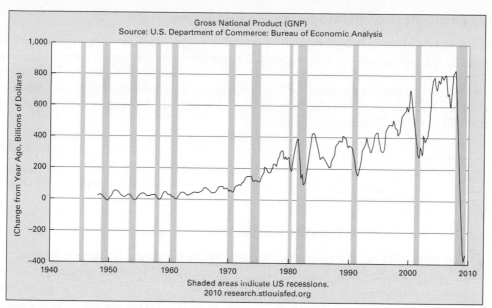

FIGURE 1-3 Changes in Gross National Product (GNP).   *Source:* Data from U.S. Department of Commerce and Bureau of Economic Analysis.

Economic trends will turn positive again, perhaps as you read these pages. However, after what the world went through, it's doubtful that the deregulation, leveraging, and globalization that drove economic growth will continue unabated. That may mean slower growth, perhaps for years. The challenging times mean that employers will have to be more frugal and creative in managing their human resources.[36]

THE NEW HUMAN RESOURCE MANAGERS

Trends like these mean changes in human resource management practices, and in what employers expect from their human resource managers. We'll look at some specifics.

Human Resource Management Yesterday and Today

For much of the twentieth century, personnel/HR managers focused on "day-to-day" transactional sorts of activities. In the earliest firms, they first took over hiring and firing from supervisors, ran the payroll department, and administered benefit plans. As expertise in areas like testing began to appear, the personnel department began to play an expanded role in employee selection and training.[37] The emergence of union legislation in the 1930s added dealing with unions to its list of duties. Then, as Congress passed new equal employment legislation in the 1960s and 1970s, employers began leaning on their human resource managers' expertise for avoiding and managing discrimination claims.[38]

Today, we've seen that trends like globalization, competition, and technology confront employers with new challenges. Employers expect their human resource managers to have what it takes to address these challenges. We can list 10 characteristics of today's human resource professionals.

They Focus More on Strategic, Big Picture Issues

First, reflecting their increased influence, human resource managers are *more involved in strategic, "big picture" issues.* For example, Wisconsin-based Signicast Corp.'s president, Terry Lutz, and his board decided to build a new, computerized plant. Mr. Lutz and his team understood that "in the real world, new automation technology requires a new kind of employee." The computerized plant would be useless without computer-literate employees who could work in self-managing teams.

Lutz and his management team relied on their human resource management team to select and train the tech-friendly employees the new plant required.[39] By putting in place the hiring and other personnel practices that Signicast needed to make the new plant function effectively, the HR team helped top management implement Signicast's new strategy.[40] We discuss strategic human resource management later in this chapter.

They Use New Ways to Provide Transactional Services

While focusing more on strategic issues, today's human resource managers must be skilled at offering HR's traditional HR services in innovative ways.[41] For example, they *outsource* more benefits administration and safety training to outside *vendors.*[42] They use technology, for instance, in the form of *company portals* to let employees self-administer benefits plans, *Facebookrecruiting* to recruit job applicants, *online testing* services to prescreen job applicants, and *centralized call centers* to answer HR-related inquiries from supervisors. As another example, IBM calls its internal social network site w3. IBM's employees use w3 to "create personal profiles similar to those on LinkedIn, bookmark websites and news stories of interest, comment on company blogs, contribute to wikis, share files, and gain knowledge from white papers, videos, and podcasts."[43]

Table 1-2 lists some other examples of how employers use technology to support human resource management activities.[44]

They Take an Integrated, "Talent Management" Approach to Managing Human Resources

With employers competing vigorously, no one wants to fail to attract or fully utilize top-caliber employees.[45] One survey of human resource executives found that "talent management" issues were among the most pressing ones they faced.[46]

TABLE 1-2	Some Other Technology Applications to Support Human Resource Activities
Technology	**How Used by HR**
Streaming desktop video	Used, for instance, to facilitate distance learning and training or to provide corporate information to employees quickly and inexpensively
Internet- and network-monitoring software	Used to track employees' Internet and e-mail activities or to monitor their performance
Data warehouses and computerized analytical programs	Used to help HR managers monitor their HR systems. For example, they make it easier to assess things like cost per hire, and to compare current employees' skills with the firm's projected strategic needs

WHAT IS TALENT MANAGEMENT?   **Talent management** is the *goal-oriented* and *integrated* process of *planning, recruiting, developing, managing, and compensating* employees.[47] It means putting in place a coordinated process for identifying, recruiting, hiring, and developing high-potential employees.

What does this mean in practice? For one thing, talent management means being proactive about how you manage your company's talent (employees). For example, we saw that IBM segmented its employees into three groups. Now it can fine-tune the way it hires, trains, and rewards the employees in each segment. As another example, many employers pinpoint their most "mission-critical" employees, and manage their development and rewards separately from the firms' other employees. We'll look more closely at talent management starting in Chapter 3.

They Manage Employee Engagement

In today's environment, no employer can afford to have its employees present but "checked out" mentally. The Institute for Corporate Productivity defines engaged employees "as those who are mentally and emotionally invested in their work and in contributing to an employer's success." Unfortunately, studies suggest that less than one-third of the U.S. workforce is engaged.[48] One Gallup study estimated that $350 billion is lost annually in the United States alone on damage done by disengaged workers.[49] Today's human resource managers must know how to foster employee engagement.

They Measure HR Performance and Results

With today's emphasis on controlling costs and boosting profits, employers expect their human resource managers to take action based on measurable performance-based criteria. For example, IBM's Randall MacDonald needed $100 million from IBM to reorganize its HR operations. He told top management, "I'm going to deliver talent to you that's skilled and on time and ready to be deployed. I will be able to measure the skills, tell you what skills we have, what [skills] we don't have [and] then show you how to fill the gaps or enhance our training."[50]

SAMPLE METRICS   To make claims like these, human resource managers need performance measures (or "metrics"). For example, median HR expenses as a proportion of companies' total operating costs average just under 1%. There tends to be between 0.9 and 1.0 human resource staff persons per 100 employees.[51] To see how they're doing compared to others, employers obtain customized benchmark comparisons from services such as the Society for Human Resource Management's Human Capital Benchmarking Service.[52]

They Add Value

This focus on performance and measurement reflects another trait of today's human resource managers. HR management must *add value*, particularly by boosting profitability and performance in measurable ways. Professors Dave Ulrich and Wayne Brockbank explain this in terms of "The HR Value Proposition."[53] They say the human resource manager's programs (such as screening tests and training tools) are just a means to an end. The ultimate aim must be to add value. "Adding value" means helping the firm and its employees gain in a measurable way from the human resource manager's actions.

We'll see in this book how human resource selection, training, rewards, and other practices improve profitability and performance. We use HR as a Profit Center features in each chapter to highlight such efforts.

They Build High-Performance Work Systems

With today's focus on *productivity and performance* improvement, employers seek to install what they call high performance work systems.[54] A *high-performance work system* is a set of human resource management policies and practices that together produce superior employee performance. For example, in one study, the high-performance plants paid more (median wages of $16 per hour compared with $13 per hour for all plants); trained more (83% offered more than 20 hours of training per year, compared with 32% for all plants); used more sophisticated recruitment and hiring practices (tests and validated interviews, for instance); and used more self-managing work teams. These plants also had the best overall performance, in terms of higher profits, lower operating costs, and lower turnover.[55] We discuss such high-performance methods in this book.

They Practice Evidence-Based Human Resource Management

Saying you have a "high-performance" organization assumes that you can back up what you're doing with measurable evidence.[56] For example, "How much will that new testing program save us in reduced employee turnover?"[57]

Providing evidence such as this is the heart of *evidence-based human resource management*. This is the use of data, facts, analytics, scientific rigor, critical evaluation, and critically evaluated research/case studies to support human resource management proposals, decisions, practices, and conclusions.[58] Put simply, evidence-based human resource management means using the best available evidence in making decisions about the human resource management practices you are focusing on.[59] The evidence may come from *actual measurements* (such as, how did the trainees like this program?). It may come from *existing data* (such as, what happened to company profits after we installed this training program?). Or it may come from published *research studies* (for instance, median HR expenses as a proportion of companies' total operating costs average about 0.8%[60]). As an example, BASF Corp. analyzed the relationship between its employees' stress and productivity. It discovered that stress-reduction programs would more than pay for themselves in increased productivity.[61] We present examples of such evidence throughout this book.

They Manage Ethics

Ethics refers to the standards someone uses to decide what his or her conduct should be. Ethical decisions always involve *morality*, matters of serious consequence to society's well-being, such as murder, lying, or stealing (as via financial Ponzi schemes).

One survey found that 6 of the 10 most serious ethical issues—workplace safety, security of employee records, employee theft, affirmative action, comparable work, and employee privacy rights—were human resource management related.[62] We will explain ethics in human resource management more fully in Chapter 8.

They Have New Proficiencies[63]

In turn, activities such as evidence-gathering and dealing with technology demand *new human resource management proficiencies.* Human resource managers still need skills in subjects such as employee selection and training. But now they also require broader *business knowledge and competencies.* For example, to assist top management in formulating strategic plans, the human resource manager needs to understand strategic planning, marketing, production, and finance.[64] He or she must also be able to "speak the CFO's language," by explaining human resource activities in financially measurable terms.[65]

THE HUMAN RESOURCE MANAGER'S COMPETENCIES   The accompanying Figure 1-4 provides one view of the competencies today's HR managers need.[66] They need the knowledge, skills, and competencies to be:

Strategic Positioners, for instance by helping to craft the firm's strategy.[67]

Capability Builders, for instance by creating a meaningful work environment and aligning strategy, culture, practices, and behavior.

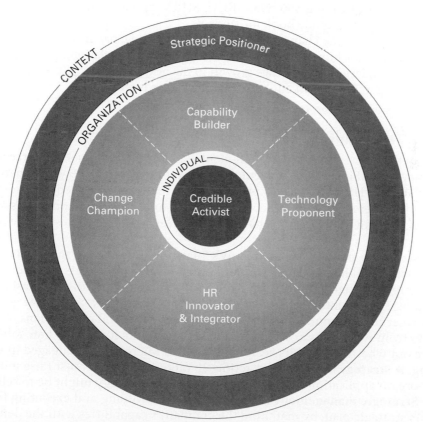

FIGURE 1-4 The Human Resource Manager's Competencies.   *Source:* The RBL Group, copyright 2012.

Change Champions, for instance by initiating and sustaining change.

HR Innovators and Integrators, for instance by developing talent, and optimizing human capital through workforce planning and analytics.

Technology Proponents, for instance by connecting people through technology.

Credible Activists, by exhibiting the leadership and other competencies that make them "both *credible* (respected, admired, listened to) and *active* (offers a point of view, takes a position, challenges assumptions.)"[68]

HR Certification

As the human resource manager's job becomes more demanding, human resource managers are becoming more professional. More than 100,000 have already passed one or more of the Society for Human Resource Management's (SHRM) HR professional certification exams. SHRM's Human Resource Certification Institute offers these exams. Exams test the professional's knowledge of all aspects of human resource management, including ethics, management practices, staffing, development, compensation, labor relations, and health and safety. Those who successfully complete all requirements earn the SPHR (Senior Professional in HR), GPHR (Global Professional in HR), or PHR (Professional in HR) certificate. Managers can take an online HRCI assessment exam at *www.HRCI.org* (or by calling 866-898-HRCI). SHRM provides an assurance of learning assessment preparation guide book for students.[69]

Finally, with all the changes taking place, the U.S. Department of Labor projects that employment for human resource, training, and labor relations professionals will experience much faster than average growth in the next few years.[70] Top-ranked human resource managers earn multi-million dollar total take home pay.[71]

STRATEGIC HUMAN RESOURCE MANAGEMENT

We've seen that exercising strategic judgment is an important human resource manager proficiency. As at Signicast Corp., employers want their human resource managers to put in place the HR policies and practices that the company needs to produce the employee competencies and behaviors required to achieve the company's strategic objectives. Human resource managers therefore need a command of strategic planning methods.

A **strategic plan** is the company's plan for how it will match its internal strengths and weaknesses with external opportunities and threats in order to maintain a competitive advantage. The essence of strategic planning is to ask, "Where are we now as a business, where do we want to be, and how should we get there?" The manager then formulates specific (human resources and other) plans to take the company from where it is now to where he or she wants it to be. When Yahoo! tries to figure out whether to sell its search business to Microsoft, it's engaged in strategic planning. A **strategy** is a course of action. If Yahoo! decides it must raise money and focus more on applications like Yahoo! Finance, one strategy might be to sell Yahoo! Search. **Strategic management** is the process of identifying and executing the organization's strategic plan, by matching the company's capabilities with the demands of its environment.

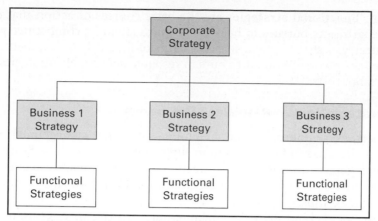

FIGURE 1-5 Three Levels of Strategies in Multiple-Business Firms. *Source:* Gary Dessler, Ph.D.

Strategic Planning Basics

Managers engage in three levels of strategic planning (see Figure 1-5).[72]

CORPORATE STRATEGY   Many firms consist of several businesses. For instance, PepsiCo includes Frito-Lay North America, PepsiCo Beverages North America, PepsiCo International, and Quaker Oats North America. PepsiCo therefore needs a *corporate-level strategy.* A company's **corporate-level strategy** identifies the rationale for the portfolio of businesses that, in total, comprise the company as well as the ways in which these businesses relate to each other. For example, a *diversification* strategy implies that the firm will expand by adding new products. A *vertical integration* strategy means the firm expands by, perhaps, producing its own raw materials or selling its products directly. *Consolidation*—reducing the company's size—and *geographic expansion*—for instance, taking the business abroad—are some other corporate strategy possibilities.

COMPETITIVE STRATEGY   At the next level down, each of these businesses (such as Quaker Oats) needs a *business-level/competitive strategy.* A **competitive strategy** identifies how to build and strengthen the business's long-term competitive position in the marketplace. It identifies, for instance, how Pizza Hut will compete with Papa John's. Companies try to achieve competitive advantages for each of their businesses. We can define **competitive advantage** as any factors that allow an organization to differentiate its product or service from those of its competitors to increase market share.[73]

There are three basic ways to achieve competitive advantage. *Cost leadership* means the company aims to become the low-cost leader in an industry. Walmart is a typical example.

With a *differentiation* competitive strategy, a business seeks to be unique in its industry in ways valued by buyers.[74] Thus, Volvo stresses safety, and Papa John's Pizza stresses fresh ingredients. Still other firms compete as *focusers.* They carve out a market niche (as for Rolls-Royce cars) and compete by providing something their customers can get in no other way.

FUNCTIONAL STRATEGY   Each of the firm's individual businesses (such as PepsiCo's Frito-Lay) has departments, such as manufacturing, sales, and human resource management. **Functional strategies** are the basic courses of action that each of the business's departments pursues to help the business attain its competitive goals. These functional strategies should make sense in terms of the business/competitive strategy. Thus (for better or worse) Walmart's human resource department strategies emphasize minimizing labor costs.

What Is Strategic Human Resource Management?

As at Walmart, every company wants its human resource management policies and practices to make sense in terms of and to support its strategic aims. **Strategic human resource management** means formulating and executing human resource policies and practices that produce the employee competencies and behaviors the company needs to achieve its strategic aims.

The basic idea behind strategic human resource management is this: In formulating human resource management policies and practices, the manager's aim must be to produce the employee skills and behaviors that the company needs to achieve its strategic aims.

Figure 1-6, The Practices Behaviors Strategy Pyramid, graphically outlines this idea. Management formulates a *strategic plan*. That strategic plan implies certain *workforce behaviors and competencies*. (For example, do we need more computer-literate employees for our new machines?) Given these workforce requirements, human resource management formulates *HR strategies (policies and practices)* to produce the desired workforce skills, competencies, and behaviors.

As part of that last step, the human resource manager may choose measures to gauge the extent to which the new policies and practices are actually producing the required employee skills and behaviors. These measures might include, for instance, "hours of computer training per employee," "productivity per employee," and (via customer surveys) "customer satisfaction."

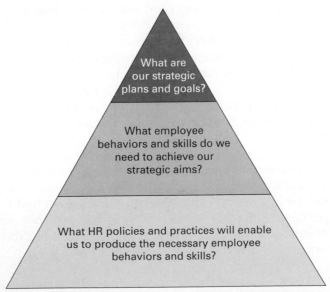

FIGURE 1-6 The Practices Behavior Strategy Pyramid.   *Source:* Gary Dessler, Ph.D.

Human Resource Strategies and Policies

Managers call the human resource management policies and practices they use to support their strategic aims *human resource strategies.*[75] For example, the Ritz-Carlton Portman Hotel in Shanghai aimed to cultivate service-oriented employee behaviors, so as to boost the hotel's level of service. Its new HR policies included installing the Ritz-Carlton Company's human resource selection/training/compensation system, having top management interview each job candidate, and selecting only employees who cared for and respected others. The accompanying HR as a Profit Center feature presents another example.

Strategic Human Resource Management Tools

Managers use several tools to translate strategic goals such as "superior service" into human resource management policies and activities. Three important tools include the strategy map, the HR Scorecard, and the digital dashboard.

STRATEGY MAP   The **strategy map** provides an overview of how each department's performance contributes to achieving the company's overall strategic goals. It helps the manager understand the role his or her department plays in helping to execute the company's strategic plan.

Figure 1-7 presents a strategy map example, in this case for Southwest Airlines. Southwest has a low-cost leader strategy. The strategy map for Southwest succinctly lays out the hierarchy of main activities required for Southwest Airlines to get costs down and profits up. At the top of the map is achieving company-wide, strategic financial goals. Beneath that, the strategy map shows the chain of activities that help Southwest Airlines achieve these goals. For example, to boost revenues and profitability Southwest needs to fly fewer planes (to keep costs down), maintain low prices, and maintain on-time flights.

In turn (further down the strategy map), on-time flights and low prices require fast turnaround. And, fast turnaround requires motivated ground and flight crews.

HR AS A PROFIT CENTER

Albertsons Example

Several years ago, Albertsons Markets had to improve performance, and fast. With 2,500 stores and 230,000 workers, it faced competition not only from grocery chains, but also from Walmart and online sites. Albertsons' overall strategy included reducing costs, maximizing financial returns, becoming more customer-focused, and energizing employees. Albertsons turned to its human resource managers to help achieve these strategic aims. Its new human resource strategy entailed new screening, training, pay, and other human resources policies and practices, and using more technology to reduce its HR activities' costs.[76] The Albertsons human resource team's steps helped Albertsons to cut costs, and to boost customer service by hiring and motivating customer-focused applicants.

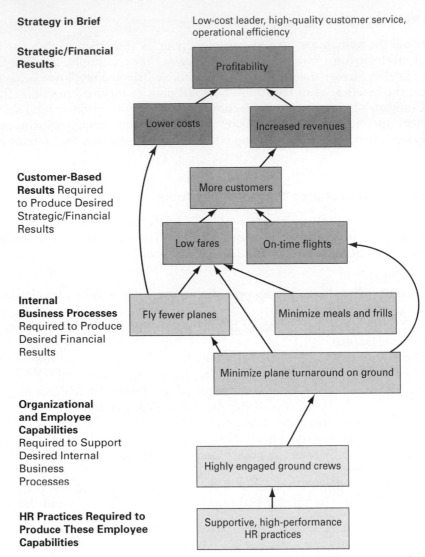

Strategy in Brief — Low-cost leader, high-quality customer service, operational efficiency

Strategic/Financial Results
- Profitability
- Lower costs
- Increased revenues

Customer-Based Results Required to Produce Desired Strategic/Financial Results
- More customers
- Low fares
- On-time flights

Internal Business Processes Required to Produce Desired Financial Results
- Fly fewer planes
- Minimize meals and frills
- Minimize plane turnaround on ground

Organizational and Employee Capabilities Required to Support Desired Internal Business Processes
- Highly engaged ground crews

HR Practices Required to Produce These Employee Capabilities
- Supportive, high-performance HR practices

FIGURE 1-7 Example of Strategy Map.   *Sources:* Based on TeamCHRYSALIS.com, accessed July 2006; http://mcknightkaney.com/Strategy_Maps_Primer.html, accessed August 3, 2011; http://www.strategy map.com.au/ home/StrategyMapOverview.htm, accessed August 3, 2011.

The strategy map helps each department visualize what it needs to do to support Southwest's low-cost strategy. Thus its HR policies aim to produce motivated crews, for instance through exceptional benefits and pay. Then, Engaged and Motivated Flight Crews > Fast Turnaround > Lower Costs > Profitability.

THE HR SCORECARD   Many employers quantify and computerize the strategy map's activities. The HR Scorecard helps them to do so. The **HR Scorecard** is not a scorecard. It refers to a process for *assigning financial and nonfinancial goals or metrics* to the human resource management–related chain of activities required for achieving the

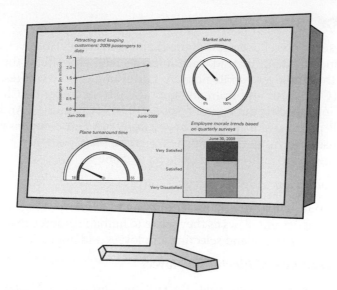

company's strategic aims.[77] (Metrics for Southwest might include airplane turnaround time, percent on-time flights, and ground crew productivity.) Simply put, the idea is to take the strategy map and to quantify it.

Managers use special scorecard software to facilitate this. The computerized scorecard process helps the manager quantify the relationships between (1) the HR activities (amount of testing, training, and so forth), (2) the resulting employee behaviors (customer service, for instance), and (3) the resulting firm-wide strategic outcomes and performance (such as customer satisfaction and profitability).[78]

DIGITAL DASHBOARDS   The saying "a picture is worth a thousand words" explains the purpose of the digital dashboard. A **digital dashboard** presents the manager with desktop graphs and charts, showing a computerized picture of where the company stands on all those metrics from the HR Scorecard process. As in the illustrated PC screen above, a top Southwest Airlines manager's dashboard might display real-time trends for various strategy map activities. These might include fast turnaround, attracting and keeping customers, and on-time flights. This gives the manager time to take corrective action. For example, if ground crews are turning planes around slower today, financial results tomorrow may decline unless the manager takes action. Figure 1-8 summarizes the three tools.

Strategy Map	HR Scorecard	Digital Dashboard
Graphical tool that summarizes the chain of activities that contribute to a company's success, and so shows employees the "big picture" of how their performance contributes to achieving the company's overall strategic goals.	A process for managing employee performance and for aligning all employees with key objectives, by assigning financial and nonfinancial goals, monitoring and assessing performance, and quickly taking corrective action.	Presents the manager with desktop graphs and charts, so he or she gets a picture of where the company has been and where it's going, in terms of each activity in the strategy map.

FIGURE 1-8 Three Important Strategic HR Tools.

THE PLAN OF THIS BOOK

This section presents a brief overview of the chapters to come. However, do not think of these topics as independent. Instead, each interacts with and affects the others, and all should fit with the employer's strategic plan. For example, how you test and interview job candidates (Chapter 4) and train and appraise job incumbents (Chapters 5 and 6) depends on the job's specific duties and responsibilities (Chapter 3). And, as we've seen, each of your HR policies—for instance, how you recruit and compensate employees—should make sense in terms of the company's strategic plan.

The following is an outline of the chapters to come:

Part I: Introduction

Chapter 2: Managing Equal Opportunity and Diversity What you need to know about equal opportunity laws as they relate to human resource management activities such as interviewing and selecting employees and managing diversity

Part II: Recruiting and Placing Employees

Chapter 3: Personnel Planning, Recruiting, and Talent Management How to analyze a job to determine the job's specific duties and responsibilities and what sorts of people to hire

Chapter 4: Testing and Selecting Employees Techniques such as testing that you can use to ensure that you're hiring the right people

Chapter 5: Training and Developing Employees Providing the training and development necessary to ensure that your employees have the knowledge and skills required to accomplish their tasks

Part III: Appraising and Compensating Employees

Chapter 6: Performance Management, Appraisals, and Careers Techniques for managing and appraising performance and managing careers

Chapter 7: Compensating Employees How to develop equitable pay plans, including incentives and benefits

Part IV: Employee Rights and Safety

Chapter 8: Managing Employee Ethics, Engagement, Retention, and Fair Treatment Ensuring ethical and fair treatment through discipline and grievance management; tools for improving employee engagement and retention

Chapter 9: Managing Labor Relations and Collective Bargaining Concepts and techniques concerning the relations between unions and management, including the union-organizing campaign, and negotiating a collective bargaining agreement

Chapter 10: Protecting Safety and Health The causes of accidents, how to make the workplace safe, and laws governing your responsibilities in regard to employee safety and health

Module A: Practical HR Tools, Guidelines, and Systems for Managers Practical human resource management interview questions and other tools for first-line supervisors, managers, and small business owners

REVIEW

Summary

1. Staffing, personnel management, or human resource management includes activities such as recruiting, selecting, training, compensating, appraising, and developing employees.

2. HR management is a part of every line manager's responsibilities. It includes placing the right person in the right job and then orienting, training, and compensating the person to improve his or her job performance.

3. The human resource manager and his or her department provide various staff services to line management; for example, the HR manager or department assists in the hiring, training, evaluating, rewarding, promoting, and disciplining of employees at all levels.

4. Changes in the environment of human resource management are requiring HR to play a strategic role in organizations. These changes include growing workforce diversity, rapid technological change, globalization, and changes in the nature of work, such as the movement toward a service society and a growing emphasis on education and human capital.

5. One consequence of changes in the work environment is that HR management must be involved in both the formulation and the implementation of a company's strategies, given the need for the firm to use its employees as a competitive advantage.

6. We defined strategic human resource management as "formulating and executing HR systems—HR policies and practices—that produce the employee competencies and behaviors the company needs to achieve its strategic aims." HR is a strategic partner in that it works with other top managers to formulate the company's strategy as well as to execute it.

Key Terms

human resource management *2*
authority *3*
line authority *3*
staff authority *4*
line manager *4*
staff manager *4*

talent management *13*
ethics *14*
strategic plan *16*
strategy *16*
strategic management *16*
corporate-level strategy *17*
competitive strategy *17*

competitive advantage *17*
functional strategy *18*
strategic human resource management *18*
strategy map *19*
HR Scorecard *20*
digital dashboard *21*

Discussion Questions

1. Explain what HR management is and how it relates to line management.

2. Give several examples of why all managers should have human resource management knowledge and skills.

3. Compare the work of line and staff managers. Give examples of each.
4. What skills and competencies do today's human resource managers need, and why?
5. What is strategic human resource management, and what is HR's role in the strategic planning process?

Individual and Group Activities

1. Working individually or in groups, contact the HR manager of a local bank. Ask the person how he or she is working as a strategic partner to manage human resources, given the bank's strategic goals and objectives. Back in class discuss the responses of the different HR managers.
2. Working individually or in groups, interview an HR manager. Based on that interview, write a short presentation regarding HR's role today in building competitive organizations.
3. Working individually or in groups, bring business publications such as *Bloomberg Businessweek* and the *Wall Street Journal* to class. Based on their contents, compile a list entitled "What HR Managers and Departments Do Today."
4. Based on your personal experiences, list 10 examples showing how you used (or could have used) human resource management techniques at work or school.
5. Laurie Siegel, senior vice president of human resources for Tyco International, took over her job just after numerous charges forced the company's previous executives to leave the firm. Hired by new CEO Edward Breen, Siegel had to tackle difficult problems. For example, she had to help hire a new management team. She had to do something about what the outside world viewed as questionable ethics at her company. And she had to revamp the company's top management compensation plan, which many felt contributed to the allegations by some that some former company officers had used the company as a sort of private ATM.

   Working individually or in groups, conduct an Internet search and library research to answer the following questions: What human resource management–related steps did Siegel take to help get Tyco back on the right track? Do you think she took the appropriate steps? Why or why not? What, if anything, do you suggest she do now?
6. Working individually or in groups, develop a list showing how trends such as workforce diversity, technological trends, globalization, and changes in the nature of work have affected the college or university you are now attending or the organization for which you work.
7. Working individually or in groups, develop several examples showing how the new HR management practices mentioned in this chapter (using technology, for instance) have or have not been implemented to some extent in the college or university you are now attending or in the organization for which you work.

APPLICATION EXERCISES

CASE INCIDENT

Jack Nelson's Problem

As a new member of the board of directors for a local bank, Jack Nelson was being introduced to all the employees in the home office. When he was introduced to Ruth Johnson, he was curious about her work and asked her what her machine did. Johnson replied that she really did not know what the machine was called or what it did. She explained that she had been working there for only 2 months. She did, however, know precisely how to operate the machine. According to her supervisor, she was an excellent employee.

At one of the branch offices, the supervisor in charge spoke to Nelson confidentially, telling him that "something was wrong," but she didn't know what. For one thing, she explained, employee turnover was too high, and no sooner had one employee been put on the job than another one resigned. With customers to see and loans to be made, she explained, she had little time to work with the new employees.

All branch supervisors hired their own employees without communication with the home office or other branches. When an opening developed, the supervisor tried to find a suitable employee to replace the worker.

After touring the 22 branches and finding similar problems in many of them, Nelson wondered what the home office should do or what action he should take. The banking firm was generally regarded as a well-run institution that had grown from 27 to 191 employees during the past 8 years. The more he thought about the matter, the more puzzled Nelson became. He couldn't put his finger on the problem, and he didn't know whether to report his findings to the president.

QUESTIONS

1. What do you think is causing some of the problems in the bank's home office and branches?
2. Do you think setting up an HR unit in the main office would help?
3. What specific functions should an HR unit carry out? What HR functions would then be carried out by supervisors and other line managers?

Source: George, *Supervision in Action: Art Managing Others,* 4th, © 1985. Printed and Electronically reproduced by permission of Pearson Education, Inc., Upper Saddle River, New Jersey.

CONTINUING CASE

Carter Cleaning Company

Introduction

A main theme of this book is that human resource management activities like recruiting, selecting, training, and rewarding employees is not just the job of a central HR group but rather a job in which every manager must engage. Perhaps nowhere is this more apparent than in the typical small service business. Here the owner/manager usually has no HR staff to rely on. However, the success of his or her enterprise (not to mention his or her family's peace of mind) often depends largely on the effectiveness through which workers are recruited, hired, trained, evaluated, and rewarded. Therefore, to help illustrate and emphasize the front-line manager's HR role, throughout this book we will use a continuing case based on an actual small business in the southeastern

(continued)

United States. Each chapter's segment of the case will illustrate how the case's main player—owner/manager Jennifer Carter—confronts and solves personnel problems each day at work by applying the concepts and techniques of that particular chapter. Here is background information you will need to answer questions that arise in subsequent chapters. (We also present a second, unrelated "application case" case incident in each chapter.)

Carter Cleaning Centers

Jennifer Carter graduated from State University in June 2009, and, after considering several job offers, decided to do what she always planned to do—go into business with her father, Jack Carter.

Jack Carter opened his first laundromat in 1999 and his second in 2002. The main attraction of these coin laundry businesses for him was that they were capital- rather than labor-intensive. Thus, once the investment in machinery was made, the stores could be run with just one unskilled attendant and none of the labor problems one normally expects from being in the retail service business.

The attractiveness of operating with virtually no skilled labor notwithstanding, Jack had decided by 2003 to expand the services in each of his stores to include the dry cleaning and pressing of clothes. He embarked, in other words, on a strategy of "related diversification" by adding new services that were related to and consistent with his existing coin laundry activities. He added these for several reasons. He wanted to better utilize the unused space in the rather large stores he currently had under lease. Furthermore, he was, as he put it, "tired of sending out the dry cleaning and pressing work that came in from our coin laundry clients to a dry cleaner 5 miles away, who then took most of what should have been our profits." To reflect the new, expanded line of services, he renamed each of his two stores Carter Cleaning Centers and was sufficiently satisfied with their performance to open four more of the same type of stores over the next 5 years. Each store had its own on-site manager and, on average, about seven employees and annual revenues of about $500,000. It was this six-store chain that Jennifer joined after graduating.

Her understanding with her father was that she would serve as a troubleshooter/consultant to the elder Carter with the aim of both learning the business and bringing to it modern management concepts and techniques for solving the business's problems and facilitating its growth. She needs your advice.

QUESTIONS

1. Jennifer asks that you make a list of five specific HR problems you think Carter Cleaning will have to grapple with.
2. And she asks, what would you do first if you were me, Jennifer Carter?

EXPERIENTIAL EXERCISE

Helping "The Donald"

Purpose: The purpose of this exercise is to provide practice in identifying and applying the basic concepts of human resource management by illustrating how managers use these techniques in their day-to-day jobs.

Required Understanding: Be thoroughly familiar with the material in this chapter, and with at least several episodes of *The Celebrity Apprentice*, the TV show in which developer Donald Trump starred.

How to Set Up the Exercise/Instructions:
1. If so desired, divide the class into teams.
2. Read this: As you know by watching "The Donald" as he organizes his business teams

for *The Celebrity Apprentice*, human resource management plays an important role in what Donald Trump and the participants on his separate teams need to do to be successful. For example, Donald Trump needs to be able to appraise each of the participants. And, for their part, the leaders of each of his teams need to be able to staff his or her teams with the right participants and then provide the sorts of training, incentives, and evaluations that help their companies succeed and that therefore make the participants themselves (and especially the team leaders) look like "winners" to Mr. Trump.

3. Watch several of these shows (or reruns of the shows), and then meet with your team and answer the following questions:

   a. What specific HR functions (recruiting, interviewing, and so on) can you identify Donald Trump using on this show? Make sure to give specific examples based on the show.

   b. What specific HR functions (recruiting, selecting, training, and so on) can you identify one or more of the team leaders using to help manage their teams on the show? Again, please give specific answers.

   c. Provide a specific example of how HR functions (such as recruiting, selecting, interviewing, compensating, appraising, and so on) contributed to one of the participants coming across as particularly successful to Mr. Trump. Can you provide examples of how one or more of these functions contributed to Mr. Trump telling a participant "You're fired"?

   d. Present your team's conclusions to the class.

Two

Managing Equal Opportunity and Diversity

When you finish studying this chapter you should be able to:

- Summarize *the basic equal employment opportunity laws regarding age, race, sex, national origin, religion, and handicap discrimination.*
- Explain *the basic defenses against discrimination allegations.*
- Present *a summary of what managers can and cannot do with respect to illegal recruitment, selection, and promotion and layoff practices.*
- Describe *the Equal Employment Opportunity Commission enforcement process.*
- Explain *important ways to manage diversity.*

OVERVIEW

A federal court in New York recently approved a $175 million settlement by Novartis Pharmaceuticals to pay current and former female sales representatives to settle their sex discrimination suit.[1] As you'll see at http://eeoc.gov/eeoc/newsroom/index.cfm, hardly a day goes by without equal opportunity–related lawsuits at work. The main purpose of this chapter is to provide you with the knowledge you'll need to do a better job dealing with equal employment issues at work. The main topics we cover include: Selected Equal Employment Opportunity Laws, Defenses against Discrimination Allegations, Illustrative Discriminatory Employment Practices, The EEOC Enforcement Process, and Diversity Management and Affirmative Action Programs.

SELECTED EQUAL EMPLOYMENT OPPORTUNITY LAWS

Hiring or transferring employees without understanding equal employment law is fraught with peril. One survey of corporate general counsels found that employment lawsuits were their biggest litigation fears.[2]

Background

Legislation barring discrimination against minorities in the United States is nothing new.[3] For example, the Fifth Amendment to the U.S. Constitution (ratified in 1791) states, "no person shall…be deprived of life, liberty, or property, without due process of the law."[4] Other laws made discrimination against minorities illegal by the early 1900s, at least in theory.[5] But as a practical matter, Congress and presidents avoided dramatic action on equal employment until the early 1960s. At that point, civil unrest among minorities and women and changing traditions prompted them to act. Congress passed a multitude of new civil rights laws.

Equal Pay Act of 1963

The **Equal Pay Act of 1963** (amended in 1972) was one of the first new laws. It made it unlawful to discriminate in pay on the basis of sex when jobs involve equal work—equivalent skills, effort, and responsibility—and are performed under similar working conditions. However, differences in pay do not violate the act if the difference is based on a seniority system, a merit system, a system that measures earnings by quantity or quality of production, or a differential based on any factor other than sex.

Title VII of the 1964 Civil Rights Act

WHAT THE LAW SAYS   **Title VII of the 1964 Civil Rights Act** was another of these new laws. Title VII (amended by the 1972 Equal Employment Opportunity Act) says an employer cannot discriminate based on race, color, religion, sex, or national origin. Specifically, it states that it shall be an unlawful employment practice for an employer:[6]

1. *To fail or refuse to hire or to discharge an individual or otherwise to discriminate against any individual* with respect to his or her compensation, terms, conditions, or privileges of employment, because of such individual's race, color, religion, sex, or national origin.
2. *To limit, segregate, or classify his or her employees or applicants for employment* in any way that would deprive or tend to deprive any individual of employment opportunities or otherwise adversely affect his or her status as an employee, because of such individual's race, color, religion, sex, or national origin.

The **Equal Employment Opportunity Commission (EEOC)** was instituted by Title VII. It consists of five members, appointed by the president with the advice and consent of the Senate. Each member of the EEOC serves 5 years. The EEOC has a staff of thousands to assist it in administering the civil rights law.

The EEOC receives and investigates job discrimination complaints. When it finds reasonable cause that the charges are justified, it attempts to reach an agreement. If this fails, the EEOC can go directly to court to enforce the law. Discrimination charges may be filed by the EEOC on behalf of an aggrieved individual, as well as by the individuals themselves. We explain this procedure later in this chapter.

Executive Orders

Under executive orders that U.S. presidents issued years ago, most employers who do business with the U.S. government have an obligation beyond that imposed by Title VII. Executive Orders 11246 and 11375 don't just ban discrimination; they require that contractors take **affirmative action** to ensure equal employment opportunity (we also explain affirmative action later in this chapter). These orders also established the **Office of Federal Contract Compliance Programs (OFCCP)** within the Labor Department. It is responsible for ensuring the compliance of federal contracts.[7] President Obama directed more funds and staffing to the OFCCP.[8]

Age Discrimination in Employment Act of 1967

The **Age Discrimination in Employment Act (ADEA) of 1967,** as amended, makes it unlawful to discriminate against employees or applicants for employment who are 40 years of age or older, effectively ending most mandatory retirement.[9]

Vocational Rehabilitation Act of 1973

The **Vocational Rehabilitation Act of 1973** requires employers with federal contracts over $2,500 to take affirmative action for the employment of handicapped persons. The act does not require hiring an unqualified person. It does require that an employer take steps to accommodate a handicapped worker unless doing so imposes an undue hardship on the employer.

Pregnancy Discrimination Act of 1978

Congress passed the **Pregnancy Discrimination Act (PDA)** in 1978 as an amendment to Title VII. The act broadened the definition of sex discrimination to encompass pregnancy, childbirth, or related medical conditions. It prohibits using these for discrimination in hiring, promotion, suspension or discharge, or any other term or condition of employment. For example, if an employer offers its employees disability coverage, then the employer must treat pregnancy and childbirth like any other disability.[10] Pregnancy discrimination claims to the EEOC rose about 50% from 2000 to 2010, to 6,119 charges in fiscal year 2010.[11]

Progressive human resource thinking notwithstanding, several years ago an auto dealership fired an employee after she told them she was pregnant. The reason? Allegedly, "in case I ended up throwing up or cramping in one of their vehicles. They said pregnant women do that sometimes, and I could cause an accident."[12] Managers therefore should base "…any [such] decision on whether an employee can do the job on medical documentation, not on a manager's interpretation."[13]

Federal Agency Guidelines

The federal agencies charged with ensuring compliance with these laws and executive orders issue their own implementing guidelines. The overall purpose of these **federal agency guidelines** is to specify the procedures these agencies recommend employers follow in complying with the equal opportunity laws.

UNIFORM GUIDELINES ON EMPLOYEE SELECTION PROCEDURES   The EEOC, Civil Service Commission, Department of Labor, and Department of Justice have approved uniform guidelines for employers.[14] They set forth "highly recommended" guidelines regarding matters such as record keeping, preemployment inquiries, and affirmative action. The OFCCP has its own *Manual of Guidelines.* The American Psychological Association published its own (nonlegally binding) *Standards for Educational and Psychological Testing.*

Historically, all these guidelines have fleshed out the procedures to use in complying with equal employment laws. For example, they lay out acceptable procedures for validating—determining the accuracy and usefulness of—selection tools such as tests.[15]

Selected Court Decisions Regarding Equal Employment Opportunity (EEO)

Several early (pre-1980s) court decisions helped to form the interpretive foundation for EEO laws such as those involving sexual harassment. We summarize some important decisions in this section.

GRIGGS v. DUKE POWER COMPANY   *Griggs* v. *Duke Power Company* (1971) was a landmark case because the Supreme Court used it to define unfair discrimination. In this case, a suit was brought against the Duke Power Company on behalf of Willie Griggs, an applicant for a job as a coal handler. The company required its coal handlers to be high school graduates. Griggs claimed that this requirement was illegally discriminatory because it wasn't related to success on the job and because it resulted in more blacks than whites being rejected.

Griggs won the case. The decision of the Court was unanimous, and in his written opinion, Chief Justice Burger laid out three guidelines affecting equal employment legislation. First, the court ruled that discrimination on the part of the employer *need not be overt*; in other words, the employer does not have to be shown to have intentionally discriminated against the employee or applicant—it need only be shown that discrimination took place. Second, the court held that an employment practice (in this case requiring the high school diploma) must be shown to be *job related* if it has an unequal impact on members of a **protected class.** In the words of Justice Burger,

> The act proscribes not only overt discrimination but also practices that are fair in form, but discriminatory in operation. The touchstone is business necessity. If an employment practice which operates to exclude Negroes cannot be shown to be related to job performance the practice is prohibited.[16]

Third, Burger's opinion placed the burden of proof on the employer to show that the hiring practice is job related. Thus the *employer* must show that the employment practice (in this case, requiring a high school diploma) is needed to perform the job satisfactorily if it has a disparate impact on (unintentionally discriminates against) members of a protected class.

ALBEMARLE PAPER COMPANY v. MOODY   In the *Griggs* case, the Supreme Court decided that a screening tool (such as a test) had to be job related or valid—that is, performance on the test must relate to performance on the job. The 1975 *Albemarle Paper Company* **v.** *Moody* case is important because it helped to clarify what the employer must do to prove that the test or other screening tool is related to performance on the job. For example, the Court said that before using a test to screen job candidates, the performance standards for the job in question should be clear and unambiguous. That way, the employer can identify which employees were performing better than others were (and thus whether the tests were effective). The Court here also cited the EEOC guidelines concerning acceptable selection procedures, and made these guidelines the "law of the land."[17]

The Civil Rights Act of 1991

Subsequent Supreme Court rulings in the 1980s had the effect of limiting the protection of women and minority groups under equal employment laws (for instance, by placing more burden for showing discrimination on the employee); this prompted Congress to pass a new Civil Rights Act. The first President George Bush signed the **Civil Rights Act of 1991 (CRA 1991)** into law in November 1991.

First, CRA 1991 addressed the issue of *burden of proof.* We'll discuss filing and responding to a discrimination charge later in this chapter, but assume for a moment that the plaintiff (say, a rejected applicant) demonstrates that an employment practice (such as a test) has a disparate (or "adverse") impact on a particular group.[18] Requiring a college degree for a job would have an adverse impact on some minority groups, for instance.[19]

Then, once the plaintiff shows such disparate impact, the *employer* now has the *burden of proving* that the challenged practice is job related for the position in question. For example, the employer has to show that lifting 100 pounds is actually required for the position in question—that it is a business necessity.

CRA 1991 also makes it easier to sue for *money damages.* It provides that an employee who is claiming *intentional discrimination* (which is called **disparate treatment**) can ask for both compensatory damages and punitive damages, if he or she can show the employer engaged in discrimination "with malice or reckless indifference to the federally protected rights of an aggrieved individual." (See also the Global Issues in HR feature.)

Finally, under CRA 1991, an employer generally can't avoid liability by proving it would have taken the same action—such as terminating someone—even without the discriminatory motive. If there is any such motive, the practice may be unlawful.[20]

GLOBAL ISSUES IN HR

Enforcing Equal Employment Laws with International Employees

Most employers' workforces are increasingly international, and this complicates applying equal employment laws. Illustrative guidelines for applying EEO laws when foreign workers (or work abroad) are involved follow.[21]

- U.S. EEO laws generally *do* apply inside the United States when the employer is a U.S. entity and the employee is *not* a U.S. citizen.[22]
- U.S. EEO laws generally *do* apply to jobs located inside the United States when the employer is a foreign entity *not* exempted by a treaty.
- U.S. EEO laws generally *do* apply to jobs located outside the United States when the employer is a U.S. entity and the employee is a U.S. citizen, if compliance with U.S. laws would *not* violate foreign laws.

Sexual Harassment

Sexual harassment is a violation of Title VII when such conduct has the purpose or effect of substantially interfering with a person's work performance or creating an intimidating, hostile, or offensive work environment. The EEOC guidelines further assert that employers have a duty to maintain workplaces free of sexual harassment and intimidation. The Civil Rights Act of 1991 added teeth to this by permitting victims of intentional discrimination, including sexual harassment, to have jury trials and to collect compensatory damages in cases in which the employer acted with "malice or reckless indifference" to the individual's rights.[23]

The EEOC guidelines define **sexual harassment** as unwelcome sexual advances, requests for sexual favors, and other verbal or physical conduct of a sexual nature that takes place under any of the following conditions:

1. Submission is explicitly or implicitly a term or condition of an individual's employment.
2. Submission to or rejection of such conduct is the basis for employment decisions affecting such individual.
3. Such conduct has the purpose or effect of unreasonably interfering with an individual's work performance or creating an intimidating, hostile, or offensive work environment.

Sexual harassment laws also cover occasions when women harass men and when there is same-sex harassment.[24] Again, sexual harassment is a violation of Title VII when such conduct has the purpose or effect of substantially interfering with a person's work performance or creating an intimidating, hostile, or offensive work environment. The EEOC guidelines further assert that employers have a duty to maintain workplaces free of sexual harassment and intimidation. In 2011, the EEOC received 11,364 sexual harassment charges, about 15% of which were filed by men.[25]

Proving Sexual Harassment

An employee can prove sexual harassment in three main ways:

QUID PRO QUO   The most direct is to prove that rejecting a supervisor's advances adversely affected a "tangible employment action" such as hiring, firing, promoting, or compensating. Thus in one case the employee showed that continued job success and advancement were dependent on her agreeing to her supervisor's sexual demands.

HOSTILE ENVIRONMENT CREATED BY SUPERVISORS   One need not show that the harassment had tangible consequences such as a demotion. For example, in one case, the court found that a male supervisor's sexual harassment had substantially affected a female employee's emotional and psychological ability to the point that she felt she had to quit her job. Even though no direct threats or promises were made in exchange for sexual advances, the fact that the advances interfered with the woman's performance and created an offensive work environment were enough to prove that sexual harassment had occurred. However, U.S. Supreme Court Justice Antonin Scalia has said courts must carefully distinguish between "simple teasing" and truly abusive behavior.[26]

HOSTILE ENVIRONMENT CREATED BY COWORKERS OR NONEMPLOYEES   An employee's coworkers or customers can also cause the employer to be held responsible for sexual harassment. In one case, the court held that a sexually provocative server's uniform that the employer required led to lewd customer comments. When she complained she was fired. Because the employer could not show a job-related necessity for requiring such a uniform, the court ruled that the employer, in effect, was responsible for the sexually harassing behavior. Such abhorrent client behavior is more likely when the clients are in positions of power, and when they have less reason to think they'll be penalized.[27]

SEXUAL HARASSMENT COURT DECISIONS   The U.S. Supreme Court used a case called *Meritor Savings Bank, FSB* v. *Vinson* case to endorse the EEOC's guidelines on sexual harassment. Then two other U.S. Supreme Court decisions, *Burlington Industries* v. *Ellerth* and *Faragher* v. *City of Boca Raton,* further clarified the law on sexual harassment. The upshot of these cases is that an employer can defend itself against harassment allegations by showing two things. First, "that the employer exercised care to prevent and correct promptly any sexually harassing behavior."[28] Second, that the plaintiff "unreasonably failed to take advantage of any preventive or corrective opportunities provided by the employer." The Supreme Court said that the employee's failing to use formal organizational reporting systems would satisfy the second component.

Sensible employers promptly promulgated strong harassment policies, trained managers and employees regarding their responsibilities, instituted reporting processes, investigated charges promptly, and then took corrective actions promptly, as required.[29]

Sexual Harassment Causes

Sexual harassment is more likely to occur under certain circumstances. The most important factor is a permissive social climate, one where employees conclude there's a risk to victims for complaining, that complaints won't be taken seriously, and that there's a lack of sanctions against offenders.[30] Minority women are particularly at risk.[31]

Furthermore, women react differently to possible harassment than do men. In one study, about 58% of employees reported experiencing at least some potentially harassment-type behaviors at work. Of these, about 25% found it fun and flattering and about half viewed it as benign. But on closer examination, about four times as many men as women found the behavior flattering or benign.[32] "Women perceive a broader range of socio-sexual behaviors as harassing."[33]

Most people assume that sexual motives drive sexual harassment, but that's not always so. **Gender harassment** is "a form of hostile environment harassment that appears to be motivated by hostility toward individuals who violate gender ideals." Thus in one case, her bosses told a high-performing female accountant to "walk more femininely [and] dress more femininely."[34]

Adding to the causes is the unfortunate fact that most victims don't sue or complain. "The few women who do formally complain do so only after encountering frequent, severe sexual harassment; at that point, considerable damage may have already occurred."[35] The harassers sometimes don't even realize that their abominable behavior is offending others.[36]

HR IN PRACTICE

What Managers and Employers Should Do to Minimize Liability in Sexual Harassment Claims

- Take all complaints about harassment seriously.
- Issue a strong policy statement condemning such behavior. It should describe the prohibited conduct, ensure protection against retaliation, describe a confidential complaint process, and provide impartial investigation and corrective action.
- Take steps to prevent sexual harassment from occurring. For example, communicate to employees that the employer will not tolerate sexual harassment, and take immediate action when someone complains.
- Establish a management response system that includes an immediate reaction and investigation.
- Discipline managers and employees involved in sexual harassment.

What the Manager/Employer Should Do[37]

Given this, employers should take several steps, as we summarize in the accompanying HR in Practice feature.[38]

Unfortunately, taking what courts call "reasonable" steps to prevent harassment may not be enough. In one study, researchers surveyed about 6,000 U.S. military employees. Their findings showed that reporting incidents of harassment often triggered retaliation. Under such conditions, it's no wonder that for many of these employees, the most "reasonable" thing to do was to avoid reporting. Managers therefore must ensure that the organization's culture supports employees who feel harassed.[39]

What the Employee Can Do

Courts generally look at whether the conduct is frequent or severe, whether it is physically threatening or humiliating or a mere offensive utterance, and whether it unreasonably interferes with an employee's work performance. They also look at whether an employee welcomed the conduct, or instead immediately made it clear that the conduct was unwelcome, and at whether the harassed employee used the employer's reporting procedures to file a complaint.[40] The steps an employee can take include:

1. Follow the employer's reporting polices and procedures. In the absence of such policies:
2. File a verbal contemporaneous complaint with the harasser and the harasser's boss stating that the unwanted overtures are unwelcome and should cease.
3. If the unwelcome conduct does not cease, file verbal and written reports with the harasser's manager and/or the human resource director.
4. If the letters and appeals to the employer do not suffice, the accuser should turn to the local office of the EEOC to file the necessary claim. In very serious cases, the employee can also consult an attorney about suing the harasser for assault and battery, intentional infliction of emotional distress, injunctive relief, and to recover compensatory and punitive damages.

The Americans with Disabilities Act

WHAT IS THE ADA?   The **Americans with Disabilities Act (ADA)** of 1990 prohibits employment discrimination against qualified disabled individuals.[41] It also requires that employers make "reasonable accommodations" for physical or mental limitations, unless doing so imposes an "undue hardship" on the business.

Under the ADA, "impairment" includes any physiological disorder or condition, cosmetic disfigurement, or anatomical loss affecting one or more of several body systems, or any mental or psychological disorder.[42] However, the act doesn't list specific disabilities. Instead, the EEOC's regulations provide that an individual is disabled if he or she has a physical or mental impairment that substantially limits one or more major life activities. The act does set forth certain conditions that it does not regard as disabilities, including homosexuality, voyeurism, compulsive gambling, pyromania, and certain disorders resulting from the person's currently using illegal drugs.[43]

Simply being disabled does not qualify someone for a job, of course. Instead, the act prohibits discrimination against qualified individuals—those who, with (or without) a reasonable accommodation, can carry out the essential functions of the job. This means that the individual must have the requisite skills, educational background, and experience to do the job's essential functions. A job function is essential when it is the reason the position exists, or because the function is so specialized, the employer hires the person doing the job for his or her expertise or ability to perform that particular function.[44]

REASONABLE ACCOMMODATION   If the individual can't perform the job as currently structured, the employer is required to make a reasonable accommodation, unless doing so would present an undue hardship. *Reasonable accommodation* might include redesigning the job, modifying work schedules, or modifying or acquiring equipment.[45]

Court cases illustrate what "reasonable accommodation" means. For example, when an Iowa County highway worker had an on-the-job seizure, his driver's license was suspended and the state fired him. The court ruled that he had no ADA claim because he couldn't perform the essential functions of the job.[46]

THE ADA IN PRACTICE[47]   Until recently, employers tended to prevail in ADA lawsuits. A main reason is that employees failed to show that they were disabled under the ADA.[48] Doing so is more complicated than proving that one is of a particular age, race, or gender.

A U.S. Supreme Court decision typifies what plaintiffs faced. An assembly-line worker sued Toyota, arguing that carpal tunnel syndrome and tendonitis prevented her from doing her job (*Toyota Motor Manufacturing of Kentucky, Inc. v. Williams*). The Court ruled that the ADA covers carpal tunnel syndrome and tendonitis if impairments affect not only job performance but also daily living activities. Here, the employee admitted that she could perform personal tasks and chores such as washing her face and doing laundry. The court said she wasn't disabled because the disability must be central to the employee's daily living (not just job) to qualify under the ADA.[49]

THE "NEW" ADA   The era in which employers prevail in most ADA claims probably ended January 1, 2009, when the ADA Amendments Act (ADAAA) of 2008 became effective. The new Act makes it much easier for employees to show that their disability is influencing one of their "major life activities." It does this by adding examples like reading, concentrating, thinking, sleeping, and communicating to the list of ADA major life activities. Employers will henceforth have to redouble their efforts to ensure they're complying with the ADA.[50]

ADA IMPLICATIONS FOR MANAGERS AND EMPLOYERS All this distills down to several basic ADA legal obligations and implications for employer and managers. We can summarize examples as follows.

- *Do not* deny a job to a disabled individual if the person is qualified and able to perform the essential job functions.
- *Make* a reasonable accommodation unless doing so would result in undue hardship.
- *Know* what you can ask applicants. In general, you may *not* make preemployment inquiries about a person's disability before making an offer. However, you *may* ask questions about the person's ability to perform essential job functions.
- *Itemize* essential job functions on the job descriptions. In virtually any ADA legal action, a central question will be, what are the essential functions of the job?
- *Do not* allow misconduct or erratic performance (including absences and tardiness), even if that behavior is linked to the disability.

Many employers simply take a progressive approach. Common employer concerns about people with disabilities (for instance, that they have more accidents) are generally baseless.[51] So, for example, Walgreens has a goal of filling at least one-third of the jobs at its distribution centers with people with disabilities.[52]

IMPROVING PRODUCTIVITY THROUGH HRIS: ACCOMMODATING DISABLED EMPLOYEES Technology makes it easier for employers to accommodate disabled employees. For example:

- Employees with *mobility or vision impairments* may benefit from voice recognition software.
- Word prediction software suggests words based on context with just one or two letters typed.
- Real-time translation captioning enables employees to participate in meetings.
- Vibrating text pagers notify employees when messages arrive.
- Arizona created a disability friendly website to help link prospective employees and others to various agencies.

Genetic Information Non-Discrimination Act of 2008 (GINA)

GINA prohibits discrimination by health insurers and employers based on people's genetic information. Specifically, it prohibits the use of genetic information in employment, prohibits the intentional acquisition of genetic information about applicants and employees, and imposes strict confidentiality requirements.[53]

The Federal Employment Non-Discrimination Act (ENDA)

ENDA would prohibit workplace discrimination based on sexual orientation and gender identity if Congress passes it.[54] Many states bar discrimination at work based on sexual orientation.[55]

State and Local Equal Employment Opportunity Laws

In addition to the federal laws, all states and many local governments also prohibit employment discrimination.

Most state and local laws cover employers not covered by federal legislation (such as those with fewer than 15 employees). For example, one State of Florida statute prohibits wage rate discrimination based on sex in employer and labor organizations not subject to the federal Fair Labor Standards Act.[56]

State and local equal employment opportunity agencies (often called *human resources commissions,* or *fair employment commissions*) also play a role in the equal employment compliance process. When the EEOC receives a discrimination charge, it usually defers it for a time to the relevant state and local agencies. If these agencies don't achieve satisfactory remedies, the charges are referred back to the EEOC for resolution.

SUMMARY   Table 2-1 summarizes selected equal employment opportunity legislation, executive orders, and agency guidelines.

TABLE 2-1	Summary of Important Equal Employment Opportunity Actions
Action	**What It Does**
Title VII of 1964 Civil Rights Act, as amended	Bars discrimination because of race, color, religion, sex, or national origin; instituted EEOC
Executive orders	Prohibit employment discrimination by employers with federal contracts of more than $10,000 (and their subcontractors); require affirmative action programs
Federal agency guidelines	Indicate policy covering discrimination based on sex, national origin, and religion, as well as on employee selection procedures; for example, require validation of tests
Supreme Court decisions: *Griggs* v. *Duke Power Company, Albemarle Paper Company* v. *Moody*	Ruled that job requirements must be related to job success; that discrimination need not be overt to be proved; that the burden of proof is on the employer to prove the qualification is valid
Equal Pay Act of 1963	Requires equal pay for men and women for performing similar work
Age Discrimination in Employment Act of 1967	Prohibits discriminating against a person aged 40 or over in any area of employment because of age
State and local laws	Often cover organizations too small to be covered by federal laws
Vocational Rehabilitation Act of 1973	Requires affirmative action to employ and promote qualified handicapped persons and prohibits discrimination against handicapped persons
Pregnancy Discrimination Act of 1978	Prohibits discrimination in employment against pregnant women, or related conditions

TABLE 2-1	Continued
Action	**What It Does**
Vietnam Era Veterans' Readjustment Assistance Act of 1974	Requires affirmative action in employment for veterans of the Vietnam War era
Wards Cove v. Atonio, and Patterson v. McLean Credit Union	Made it more difficult to prove a case of unlawful discrimination against an employer
Americans with Disabilities Act of 1990	Requires most employers to make reasonable accommodations for disabled employees at work; prohibits discrimination
Civil Rights Act of 1991	Places burden of proof back on employer and permits compensatory and punitive money damages for discrimination
Genetic Information Non-Discrimination Act of 2008 (GINA)	Prohibits discrimination by health insurers and employers based on people's genetic information

DEFENSES AGAINST DISCRIMINATION ALLEGATIONS

What Is Adverse Impact?

To understand how employers defend themselves against employment discrimination claims, we should first briefly review some basic legal concepts.

DISPARATE TREATMENT, DISPARATE IMPACT, AND ADVERSE IMPACT   Title VII prohibits both "disparate treatment" and "disparate impact" discrimination. *Disparate treatment* refers to intentional discrimination. For example, grossly biased statements (such as "we don't hire Asians") exemplify disparate treatment. *Disparate impact* refers to unintentional discrimination. For example, the EEOC says that Title VII prohibits employers from using apparently neutral selection tests that have the *effect* of disproportionately excluding persons based on race, color, religion, sex, or national origin, unless the tests or selection procedures are "job-related and consistent with business necessity." With disparate treatment, the discrimination is obvious. For disparate impact cases, one measures the *effect* of the employer's actions by analyzing their adverse impact on the employer's actual hiring results. The question in assessing adverse impact is, is the effect of the action substantial? (We will see in a moment that tools for measuring an action's adverse impact include the 4/5ths rule, and the McDonnell-Douglas test.) Proving that there was a business necessity for the practice is usually the defense for disparate impact claims.

Adverse impact therefore plays a central role in discriminatory practice allegations. Under the Civil Rights Act of 1991, a person who believes he or she has been unintentionally discriminated against need only establish a prima facie case of discrimination; this means showing that the employer's selection procedures had an adverse impact on a protected minority group. *Adverse impact* "refers to the total employment process that results in a significantly higher percentage of a protected group in the candidate population being rejected for employment, placement, or promotion."[57] "Employers may not institute an employment practice that causes a disparate [adverse] impact on a particular class of people unless they can show that the practice is job related and necessary."[58]

What does this mean? If a minority or other "protected group"[59] applicant for the job feels he or she has been discriminated against, the applicant need only show that the selection procedures resulted in a substantial adverse impact on his or her minority group. There are several ways to do this; we look at two.[60]

DISPARATE REJECTION RATES: THE "4/5THS RULE"   One is by showing that 80% (4/5ths) of the nonminority applicants passed the test, but only 20% (or less) of the minority applicants passed; if this is the case, a minority applicant has a prima facie case proving adverse impact. Then, it becomes the employer's burden to prove that its test, application blank, interview, or the like is a valid predictor of performance on the job and that it was applied fairly and equitably to both minorities and nonminorities.[61] For example, suppose the employer hires 60% of male applicants, but only 30% of female applicants. Four-fifths of the 60% male hiring rate would be 48%. Because the female hiring rate of 30% is less than 48%, adverse impact exists as far as these federal agencies are concerned.[62]

McDONNELL-DOUGLAS TEST   This test grew out of a case at the former McDonnell-Douglas Corporation. The applicant was qualified but the employer rejected the person and continued seeking applicants. Did this show that the hiring company intentionally discriminated against the female or minority candidate? The U.S. Supreme Court set four rules for applying the McDonnell-Douglas test:

1. That the person belongs to a protected class;
2. that he or she applied and was qualified for a job for which the employer was seeking applicants;
3. that, despite this qualification, he or she was rejected; and
4. that, after his or her rejection, the position remained open and the employer continued seeking applications from persons with the complainant's qualifications.

WORKFORCE ANALYSIS   Employers use **workforce analysis** to obtain and to analyze the data regarding the firm's use of protected versus non-protected employees in various job classifications. The process of *comparing* the percentage of minority employees in a job (or jobs) at the company with the number of similarly trained minority employees available in the relevant labor market is **utilization analysis.**

BRINGING A CASE OF DISCRIMINATION: SUMMARY   Assume that an employer rejects someone for a job based on a test score (or some other employment practice, such as interview questions or application blank responses). Further, assume that the person believes that he or she was discriminated against due to being in a protected class and decides to sue the employer.

All he or she has to do is show (to the court's satisfaction) that the employer's test had an adverse impact on members of his or her minority group. Then, the burden of proof shifts to the employer, which then has the burden of defending itself against the charges of discrimination.

The employer can then use two defenses. These are the **bona fide occupational qualification (BFOQ)** defense and the business necessity defense. Either can justify an employment practice that has been shown to have an adverse impact on the members of a minority group. (A third defense is that the decision was made on the basis of legitimate nondiscriminatory reasons, such as poor performance, having nothing to do with the alleged prohibited discrimination.)

Bona Fide Occupational Qualification

One approach an employer can use is to claim that the employment practice is a bona fide occupational qualification for performing the job. Specifically, Title VII provides that

> it should not be an unlawful employment practice for an employer to hire an employee...on the basis of religion, sex, or national origin in those certain instances where religion, sex, or national origin is a bona fide occupational qualification reasonably necessary to the normal operation of that particular business or enterprise.

For example, an employer can use age as a BFOQ to defend itself against a disparate treatment (intentional discrimination) charge when federal requirements impose a compulsory age limit, such as age 65 for pilots.[63] Actors required for youthful or elderly roles suggest other instances when age may be a BFOQ. However, the courts set the bar high: The reason for the discrimination must go to the essence of the business. The BFOQ defense is not explicitly allowed for race or color.

A Texas man filed a complaint against Hooters of America, alleging that one of its franchisees would not hire him as a waiter because it "merely wishes to exploit female sexuality as a marketing tool to attract customers and insure profitability" and so was limiting hiring to females.[64] Hooters argued a BFOQ defense before reaching a confidential settlement with him.

Business Necessity

The **business necessity** defense requires showing that there is an overriding business purpose for the discriminatory practice and that the practice is therefore acceptable.

It's not easy to prove that a practice is a business necessity. The Supreme Court has made it clear that business necessity does not encompass such matters as avoiding inconvenience. One Court of Appeals held that *business necessity* means an "irresistible demand" and that to be retained the practice "must not only directly foster safety and efficiency" but be essential to these goals.[65]

Thus it is not easy to prove that a practice is required for business necessity. For example, an employer cannot generally discharge employees whose wages have been garnished merely because garnishment (requiring the employer to divert part of the person's wages to pay his or her debts) creates an inconvenience. On the other hand, many employers have used this defense successfully. Thus, in *Spurlock* v. *United Airlines,* a minority candidate sued United Airlines, stating that its requirements that a pilot candidate have 500 flight hours and a college degree were unfairly discriminatory. The

Court agreed that these requirements did have an adverse impact on members of the person's minority group. However, the Court held that in light of the cost of the training program and the tremendous human and economic risks involved in hiring unqualified candidates, the selection standards were a business necessity.[66]

Attempts by employers to show that their selection tests or other screening practices are valid are an example of the business necessity defense. Where such validity can be established, the courts have often supported the use of the test or other practice as a business necessity. Used in this context, the word *validity* means the degree to which the test or other employment practice is related to or predicts performance on the job. We discuss validation in Chapter 4.

Retaliation

To paraphrase the EEOC, "all of the laws we enforce make it illegal to fire, demote, harass, or otherwise 'retaliate' against people because they filed a charge, complained to their employer or other covered entity (such as the EEOC) about discrimination, or because they participated in a discrimination investigation or lawsuit."[67]

ILLUSTRATIVE DISCRIMINATORY EMPLOYMENT PRACTICES

A Note on What You Can and Cannot Do

In this section, we present several illustrations of what managers can and cannot do under equal employment laws. But before proceeding, keep in mind that most federal laws, such as Title VII, do not expressly ban preemployment questions about an applicant's race, color, religion, sex, age, or national origin.[68] For example, it's not illegal to ask a job candidate about her marital status. But, in practice, there are two reasons to avoid such questionable practices. First, although federal law may not bar such questions, many state and local laws do. Second, the EEOC has said that it disapproves of such practices as asking women their marital status. Employers who use such practices thus increase their chances of having to defend themselves.

Recruitment

WORD OF MOUTH   You cannot rely on word-of-mouth dissemination of information about job opportunities when your workforce is substantially all white or all members of some other class such as all female or all Hispanic. Doing so might reduce the likelihood that others will become aware of the jobs.

MISLEADING INFORMATION   It is unlawful to give false or misleading information to members of any group or to fail to advise them of work opportunities and the procedures for obtaining them.

HELP WANTED ADS   "Help wanted—male" and "Help wanted—female" advertising classifieds are violations of laws forbidding sex discrimination in employment unless sex is a BFOQ for the job advertised.[69] Also, you cannot advertise in any way that suggests that the employer discriminates against applicants based on age (as in "young" man or woman).

Selection Standards

EDUCATIONAL REQUIREMENTS   An educational requirement (such as a high school degree) may be held illegal when (1) it can be shown that minority groups are less likely to possess the educational qualification, *and* (2) such qualifications are not job related.[70]

TESTS   According to a former U.S. Supreme Court Chief Justice, "Nothing in the [Title VII] act precludes the use of testing or measuring procedures; obviously they are useful. What Congress has forbidden is giving these devices and mechanisms controlling force unless they are demonstrating a *reasonable measure of job performance.*" The employer must be prepared to show that the test results are job related—for instance, that test scores relate to on-the-job performance.

PREFERENCE TO RELATIVES   You cannot give preference to relatives of your current employees with respect to employment opportunities if your current employees are substantially nonminority.

HEIGHT, WEIGHT   Few applicants or employees can demonstrate weight-based disability (in other words that they are 100% above their ideal weight and there is a physiological or psychological cause for their obesity). Few are thus entitled to reasonable accommodations under the ADA.

Managers still must be vigilant against stigmatizing obese people. Obese individuals are less likely to be hired, less likely to receive promotions, more likely to get less-desirable sales assignments, and more likely to receive poor customer service as customers.[71] One study compared the wages of women whose weights ranged from very thin to average with men's wages and salaries. The very thin women received the most severe "wage punishment" for adding their first few pounds.[72]

APPEARANCE   *Tattoos and body piercings* are an issue at work. For example, about 38% of millennials in one survey had tattoos as compared with 15% of baby boomers. About 23% of millennials had body piercings as compared with 1% of baby boomers. One case involved a waiter with religious tattoos on his wrists at a Red Robin Gourmet Burgers store. The company insisted he cover his tattoos at work; he refused. Red Robin subsequently settled a lawsuit after the waiter claimed that covering the tattoos would be a sin based on his religion.[73]

HEALTH QUESTIONS   Under the ADA, employers generally cannot ask questions about applicants' medical history or require preemployment physical examinations. They can, however, once a formal job offer is made (to ensure the person can do the job.)

ARREST RECORDS   You cannot ask about or use a person's arrest record to disqualify him or her for a position because there is always a presumption of innocence until proof of guilt.[74] In addition, arrest records in general have not been valid for predicting job performance, and a higher percentage of minorities than nonminorities have arrest records.

APPLICATION FORMS   Employment applications generally shouldn't contain questions pertaining, for instance, to applicants' disabilities, workers' compensation history, age, arrest record, marital status, or U.S. citizenship. Personal information required for legitimate reasons (such as who to contact in case of emergency) are best collected after you've hired the person.

Promotion, Transfer, and Layoff Procedures

Any employment practices regarding pay, promotion, termination, discipline, or benefits that (1) the employer applies differently to different classes of persons, (2) have the effect of adversely affecting members of a protected group, and (3) cannot be shown to be required as a BFOQ or business necessity may be illegally discriminatory.[75] For example, employers may not discriminate against employees in connection with their benefits plans.[76]

UNIFORMS   When it comes to discriminatory uniforms and suggestive attire, courts frequently side with the employee. For example, requiring waitresses to wear sexually suggestive attire as a condition of employment has been ruled as violating Title VII in many cases.[77] However, Alamo Rent-A-Car lost a case when it tried to prevent a Muslim woman employee from wearing a head scarf.

THE EEOC ENFORCEMENT PROCESS

Processing a Charge

The EEOC enforcement process begins with someone filing a claim.[78]

FILE CLAIM   Under CRA 1991, the discrimination claim must be filed within 300 days (when there is a similar state law) or 180 days (where there is no similar state law) after the alleged incident took place (2 years for the Equal Pay Act). In 2007, the U.S. Supreme Court, in *Ledbetter* v. *Goodyear Tire & Rubber Company*, held that employees claiming Title VII pay discrimination must file their claims within 180 days of when they first receive the allegedly discriminatory pay. In 2009, Congress formulated and the president signed the so-called "Ledbetter" Act enabling employees to file claims anytime, as long as the person is still receiving a paycheck.[79] Any filing (not just for Ledbetter claims) must be in writing and under oath, by (or on behalf of) the aggrieved person or by a member of the EEOC who has reasonable cause to believe that a violation occurred. In practice, the EEOC typically defers a person's charge to the relevant state or local regulatory agency; if the latter waives jurisdiction or cannot obtain a satisfactory solution to the charge, it is referred back to the EEOC. In fiscal year 2010, individuals filed 99,922 charges with the EEOC; the two largest categories were for race discrimination (36% of total charges), and sex discrimination (29%).[80] Insofar as it reflects national origin or religious discrimination, discrimination against Muslim employees is prohibited under Title VII.[81]

After a charge is filed (or the state or local deferral period has ended), the EEOC has 10 days to serve notice of the charge on the employer. The EEOC then investigates the charge to determine whether there is reasonable cause to believe it is true; it is supposed to make this determination within 120 days. If it finds no reasonable cause, the EEOC must dismiss the charge, in which case the person who filed the charge has 90 days to file a suit on his or her own behalf. If it does find reasonable cause, the EEOC must attempt to conciliate. If this conciliation is not satisfactory, the EEOC may bring a

1. Exactly what is the charge and is your company covered by the relevant statutes? (For example, Title VII and the Americans with Disabilities Act generally apply only to employers with 15 or more employees; the Age Discrimination in Employment Act applies to employers with 20 or more employees; but the Equal Pay Act applies to virtually all employers with one or more employees.) Did the employee file his or her charge on time, and was it processed in a timely manner by the EEOC?

2. What protected group does the employee belong to? Is the EEOC claiming disparate impact or disparate treatment?

3. Are there any obvious bases upon which you can challenge and/or rebut the claim? For example, would the employer have taken the action if the person did not belong to a protected group? Does the person's personnel file support the action taken by the employer?

4. If it is a sexual harassment claim, are there offensive comments, calendars, posters, screensavers, and so forth on display in the company?

5. In terms of the practicality of defending your company against this claim, who are the supervisors who actually took the allegedly discriminatory actions and how effective will they be as potential witnesses? Have you received an opinion from legal counsel regarding the chances of prevailing? Even if you do prevail, what do you estimate will be the out-of-pocket costs of taking the charge through the judicial process? Would you be better off settling the case, and what are the prospects of doing so in a way that will satisfy all parties?

FIGURE 2-1 Questions to Ask When an Employer Receives Notice that EEOC Has Filed a Bias Claim.   *Sources:* Based on Fair Employment Practices Summary of Latest Developments, January 7, 1983, p. 3, Bureau of National Affairs, Inc. (800-372-1033); Kenneth Sovereign, *Personnel Law* (Upper Saddle River, NJ: Prentice Hall, 1999), pp. 36–37; "EEOC Investigations—What an Employer Should Know," Equal Employment Opportunity Commission (http://www.eeoc.gov/policy/docs/medfin5.pdf), accessed May 18, 2010.

civil suit in a federal district court or issue a notice of right to sue to the person who filed the charge. Figure 2-1 summarizes important questions an employer should ask upon receiving notice from the EEOC of a bias complaint.

VOLUNTARY MEDIATION   The EEOC refers about 10% of its charges to a voluntary mediation mechanism. If the plaintiff agrees to mediation, the employer is asked to participate. If no agreement is reached or one of the parties rejects participation, the charge is then processed through the EEOC's usual mechanisms.

Faced with an offer to mediate, three responses are generally possible: agree to mediate, make a settlement offer without participating in mediation, or prepare a "position statement" for the EEOC. If the employer does not mediate or make an offer, the position statement is required. It should include information relating to the company's business and the charging party's position, a description of any rules or policies and procedures that are applicable, and the chronology of the offense that led to the adverse action.[82]

The EEOC is expanding its mediation program. Under this program, the EEOC refers all eligible discrimination charges filed against these employers to the commission's mediation unit, rather than to the usual charge processing system.[83] (Note that many employers have their own **alternative dispute resolution (ADR) programs**; these programs require employees to pursue mediation prior to pressing a claim.) The accompanying HR in Practice feature summarizes how to deal with EEOC charges.

HR IN PRACTICE

Management Guidelines for Dealing with EEOC Charges[84]

During the EEOC Investigation:

- *Conduct your own investigation* to get the facts.
- Ensure that there is information in the EEOC's file *demonstrating lack of merit* of the charge.
- *Limit the information supplied* to only those issues raised in the charge itself.
- *Meet with the employee* who made the complaint to clarify all the relevant issues.
- Remember that *the EEOC can only ask (not compel) employers* to submit documents and ask for the testimony of witnesses.
- Give the EEOC a *position statement.* It should contain words to the effect that "the company has a policy against discrimination and would not discriminate in the manner charged in the complaint." Support the statement with documentation.

During the Fact-Finding Conference:

- Because the only official record is the notes the EEOC investigator takes, *keep your own records.*
- Bring an *attorney.*
- Make sure you are *fully informed* of the charges and facts of the case.
- Before appearing, *witnesses (especially supervisors) need to be aware* of the legal significance of the facts they will present.

During the EEOC Determination and Attempted Conciliation:

- If there is a finding of cause, *review it carefully*, and point out inaccuracies in writing.
- *Conciliate prudently.* It is likely that no suit will be filed by the EEOC. If you have properly investigated the case, there may be no real advantage in settling at this stage.

DIVERSITY MANAGEMENT AND AFFIRMATIVE ACTION PROGRAMS

To some extent, demographic changes and globalization are rendering moot the goals of equitable and fair treatment driving equal employment legislation. Today, white males no longer dominate the labor force, and women and minorities will account for most labor force growth over the near future. Employers are therefore often striving for demographic balance, not just because the law says they must, but due to self-interest.[85]

Because many American workplaces are already diverse, the focus increasingly is on managing diversity.[86] **Diversity** at work means having a workforce comprised of two or more groups of employees with various racial, ethnic, gender, cultural, national origin, handicap, age, and religious backgrounds.[87]

Diversity's Potential Pros and Cons

Workforce diversity produces both benefits and threats for employers.

SOME DOWNSIDES   Demographic differences can produce behavioral barriers that undermine collegiality and cooperation. Potential problems include these:

- **Stereotyping** is a process in which someone ascribes specific behavioral traits to individuals based on their apparent membership in a group.[88] For example, "older people can't work hard." *Prejudice* means a bias toward prejudging someone based on that person's traits. For example, "we won't hire him because he's old."

- **Discrimination** means taking specific actions toward or against the person based on the person's group.[89]

  In the United States and many countries, we've seen that it's generally illegal to discriminate at work based on a person's age, race, gender, disability, or country of national origin. But in practice, discrimination is often subtle. For example, many argue that a "glass ceiling," enforced by an "old boys' network" (friendships built in places like exclusive clubs), effectively prevents women from reaching top management. Equal opportunity laws aim to prohibit and eliminate discrimination.

- **Tokenism** occurs when a company appoints a small group of women or minorities to high-profile positions, rather than more aggressively seeking full representation for that group. Tokenism is a diversity barrier when it slows the process of hiring or promoting more members of the minority group.[90]

- **Ethnocentrism** is the tendency to view members of other social groups less favorably than one's own. For example, one study found that managers attributed the performance of some minorities less to their abilities and effort and more to help they received from others.[91]

- Discrimination against women goes beyond glass ceilings. Working women also confront **gender-role stereotypes**, the tendency to associate women with certain (frequently nonmanagerial) jobs. In one study, attractiveness was advantageous for female interviewees when the job was nonmanagerial. When the job was managerial, there was a tendency for a woman's attractiveness to reduce her chances of being hired.[92]

SOME DIVERSITY BENEFITS   The key is properly managing these potential threats. In one study, researchers examined the diversity climate in 654 stores of a large U.S. retail chain. They defined diversity climate as the extent to which employees in the stores reported believing that the firm promotes equal opportunity and inclusion. They found the greatest sales growth in stores with the highest pro-diversity climate, and the lowest in stores that reported less-hospitable diversity climates.[93] The following HR as a Profit Center feature provides another example.

HR AS A PROFIT CENTER

Boosting Sales at IBM

IBM created several minority task forces focusing on groups such as women and Native Americans. One effect of these teams has been internal: In the 10 or so years since forming them, IBM boosted the number of U.S.-born ethnic minority executives by almost 2 1/2 times.[94]

   The teams also supported IBM's sales plans. For example, one team focused on expanding IBM's market among multicultural and women-owned businesses, providing "much-needed sales and service support to small and midsize businesses, a niche well populated with minority and female buyers."[95] As a result, this market grew from $10 million to more than $300 million in revenue in just 3 years.

Managing Diversity

Managing diversity means maximizing diversity's potential advantages while minimizing the potential barriers—such as prejudices and bias—that can undermine the functioning of a diverse workforce. In practice, diversity management involves both compulsory (legal) and voluntary actions. We've seen there are many compulsory legal actions employers must take to minimize discrimination.

However, compulsory actions won't guarantee a close-knit and thriving community. *Diversity management* therefore also relies on taking steps to encourage all employees to work together productively.[96]

TOP–DOWN PROGRAMS   This starts at the top. The employer institutes a diversity management program. One aim here is to make employees more sensitive to and better able to adapt to individual cultural differences. One diversity expert concluded that five sets of voluntary organizational activities are at the heart of the typical company-wide diversity management program. We can summarize these as follows:

Provide strong leadership. Companies with exemplary reputations in managing diversity have CEOs who champion diversity. Leadership means, for instance, becoming a role model for the behaviors required for the change.

Assess the situation. Common tools for measuring a company's diversity include equal employment hiring and retention metrics, employee attitude surveys, management and employee evaluations, and focus groups.[97]

Provide diversity training and education. The most common starting point for a diversity management effort is usually an employee education program.

Change culture and management systems. Combine education programs with other concrete steps aimed at changing the organization's culture. For example, appraise supervisors based partly on their success in reducing intergroup conflicts.

Evaluate the diversity management program. For example, do employee attitude surveys indicate any improvement in employees' attitudes toward diversity?

"AGEM"   Another writer advocates a four-step "AGEM" diversity training process: *Approach, Goals, Executive commitment,* and *Mandatory attendance.* First, determine if diversity training is the solution or if other approaches (such as revised selection processes) are more advisable. If training is the solution, then set measurable program goals, for instance, based on having trainees evaluate their units' diversity efforts. Next, make sure a high-visibility executive commits to the program. Finally, consider making participation in the training mandatory.[98]

Encouraging Inclusiveness

A big part of managing diversity involves overcoming barriers to inclusion—to bringing all employees "under the same tent," in a matter of speaking. Figure 2-2 illustrates strategies for overcoming barriers to inclusion, such as learning about other cultures and helping all employees to better understand the causes of prejudice.

Inclusive strategies that overcome barriers to inclusion.	
Inclusive Strategies	**Barriers to Inclusion**
Personal Level	
Become aware of prejudice and other barriers to valuing diversity	Stereotypes, prejudices
Learn about other cultures and groups	Past experiences and influences
Serve as an example, walk the talk	Stereotyped expectations and perceptions
Participate in managing diversity	Feelings that tend to separate, divide
Interpersonal Level	
Facilitate communication and interactions in ways that value diversity	Cultural differences
Encourage participation	Group differences
Share your perspective	Myths
Facilitate unique contributions	Relationship patterns based on exclusion
Resolve conflicts in ways that value diversity	
Accept responsibility for developing common ground	
Organizational Level	
All employees have access to networks and focus groups	Individuals who get away with discriminating and excluding
All employees take a proactive role in managing diversity and creating a more diverse workplace culture	A culture that values or allows exclusion
All employees are included in the inner circle that contributes to the bottom-line success of the company	Work structures, policies, and practices that discriminate and exclude
All employees give feedback to teams and management	
All employees are encouraged to contribute to change	

FIGURE 2-2 What the Manager Can Do to Overcome Barriers to Inclusion.   *Source:* Norma Carr-Ruffino, *Making Diversity Work*, © 2005. Printed and Electronically reproduced by permission of Pearson Education, Inc., Upper Saddle River, New Jersey.

Boosting Workforce Diversity

Employers use various means to increase workforce diversity. Many companies, such as Baxter Healthcare Corporation, start by adopting *strong company policies* advocating the benefits of a culturally, racially, and sexually diverse workforce: "Baxter International believes that a multi-cultural employee population is essential to the company's leadership in healthcare around the world." Baxter then *publicizes* this philosophy throughout the company.

Next, Baxter takes *concrete steps* to foster diversity at work. These include recruiting minority members to the board of directors, interacting with representative minority groups, and diversity training. The latter aims at sensitizing all employees about the need to value differences, build self-esteem, and generally create a more hospitable environment for the firm's diverse workforce.

Equal Employment Opportunity versus Affirmative Action

Equal employment opportunity aims to ensure that anyone, regardless of race, color, disability, sex, religion, national origin, or age, has an equal chance for a job based on his or her qualifications. *Affirmative action* goes beyond equal employment opportunity by requiring the employer to make an extra effort to hire and promote those in a protected group. Affirmative action thus includes specific actions (in recruitment, hiring, promotions, and compensation) to eliminate the present effects of past discrimination.

Steps in an Affirmative Action Program

According to the EEOC, the employer ideally takes nine steps in an affirmative action program:

1. Issue a written equal employment policy indicating that the firm is an equal employment opportunity employer and the employer's commitment to affirmative action.
2. Demonstrate top-management support for the equal employment policy—for instance, appoint a high-ranking EEO administrator.
3. Publicize internally and externally the equal employment policy and affirmative action commitment.
4. Survey current minority and female employment by department and job classification to determine where affirmative action programs are especially desirable.
5. Carefully analyze employer human resources practices to identify and eliminate hidden barriers.
6. Review, develop, and implement specific HR programs to improve female and minority utilization.
7. Use focused recruitment to find qualified applicants from the target group(s).
8. Establish an internal audit and reporting system to monitor and evaluate progress.
9. Develop support for the affirmative action program, inside the company and in the community.

AFFIRMATIVE ACTION TODAY   Affirmative action is still a significant workplace issue today. The incidence of major court-mandated programs is down. However, many employers still engage in voluntary programs. Executive Order 11246 (issued in 1965) requires federal contractors to take affirmative action to improve employment opportunities for women and racial minorities. It covers about 26 million workers—about 22% of the U.S. workforce.

VOLUNTARY PROGRAMS   In implementing voluntary affirmative action programs, the employer should ensure that its program does not conflict with the Civil Rights Act of 1991, which two experts say may "bar employers from giving any consideration whatsoever to an individual's status as a racial or ethnic minority or as a woman when making an employment decision."[99] Employers should emphasize the external recruitment and internal development of better-qualified minority and female employees "while basing employment decisions on legitimate criteria."[100]

RICCI* v. *DESTEFANO   Avoiding an employee backlash to affirmative action programs is important. In 2009, the U.S. Supreme Court decided an important "reverse discrimination" suit brought by Connecticut firefighters. In *Ricci* v. *DeStefano*, 19 white firefighters and one Hispanic firefighter said the city of New Haven should have promoted them based on their successful scores. The city argued that certifying the tests would have left them vulnerable to lawsuits by minorities for violating Title VII.[101] The Court decided in favor of the white firefighters.

As here, nonminorities may object to what they see as "reverse discrimination" if the employer seems to favor minorities. Current employees need to see that the program is fair. *Transparent selection procedures* help in that regard. *Communication* is crucial. Make clear that the program doesn't involve preferential selection standards. Provide details on the qualifications of all new hires (both minority and nonminority). *Justifications* for the program should emphasize redressing past discrimination and the practical value of diversity, not underrepresentation.[102]

IMPROVING PRODUCTIVITY THROUGH HRIS   The manager who wants to assess his or her company's equal employment and diversity efforts has numerous measures or metrics from which to choose. These might include, for example, the number of EEOC claims per year, the cost of HR-related litigation, and various measures for analyzing the survival and loss rate among new diverse employee groups.

Even for a company with just several hundred employees, keeping track of metrics like these is expensive. The HR manager may therefore want to rely on various computerized solutions. One package, called *Measuring Diversity Results,* provides several diversity-related software options. This vendor's packages let the manager more easily calculate the cost-per-diversity hire, a workforce profile index, and the numeric impact of voluntary turnover among diverse employee groups.

REVIEW

Summary

1. Legislation barring discrimination is not new. For example, the Fifth Amendment to the U.S. Constitution (ratified in 1791) states that no person shall be deprived of life, liberty, or property without due process of law.
2. Legislation barring employment discrimination includes Title VII of the 1964 Civil Rights Act (as amended), which bars discrimination because of race, color, religion, sex, or national origin; various executive orders; federal guidelines (covering procedures for validating employee selection tools, etc.); the Equal Pay Act of 1963; and the Age Discrimination in Employment

Act of 1967. In addition, various Court decisions (such as *Griggs* v. *Duke Power Company*) and state and local laws bar various aspects of discrimination.

3. Title VII of the Civil Rights Act created the EEOC. It has the power to go directly to court to enforce the law.

4. The Civil Rights Act of 1991 placed the burden of proof back on employers and held that a nondiscriminatory reason was insufficient to let an employer avoid liability for an action that also had a discriminatory motive.

5. The Americans with Disabilities Act prohibits employment discrimination against the disabled. Specifically, the firm cannot discriminate against qualified persons if the firm can make reasonable accommodations without undue hardship to the business.

6. A person who believes he or she has been discriminated against must prove either that he or she was subjected to unlawful disparate treatment (intentional discrimination) or that the procedure in question has a disparate impact (unintentional discrimination) on members of his or her protected class. Once a prima facie case of disparate treatment is established, an employer must produce evidence that its decision was based on legitimate reasons (such as BFOQ).

7. An employer should avoid various specific discriminatory human resource management practices. For example:
   a. *In recruitment.* An employer usually should not rely on word-of-mouth advertising or give false or misleading information to minority-group members.
   b. *In selection.* An employer should avoid using any educational or other requirements where (1) it can be shown that minority-group members

are less likely to possess the qualification and (2) such requirement is also not job related.

8. In practice, a person's charge to the EEOC is often first referred to a state agency. When the EEOC finds reasonable cause to believe that discrimination occurred, it has 30 days to try to conciliate. Important points for the employer to remember include (1) EEOC investigators can only make recommendations, (2) you cannot be compelled to submit documents without a court order, and (3) limit the information you do submit. Also, make sure you clearly document your position (as the employer).

9. An employer can use three basic defenses in the event of a discriminatory practice allegation. One is *business necessity.* Attempts to show that tests or other selection standards are valid are one example of this defense. *Bona fide occupational qualification* applies when, for example, religion, national origin, or sex is a bona fide requirement of the job (such as for actors or actresses). A third is that the decision was made on the basis of legitimate nondiscriminatory reasons (such as poor performance) having nothing to do with the prohibited discrimination alleged.

10. There are nine steps in an affirmative action program, based on suggestions from the EEOC. These are (1) issue a written equal employment policy, (2) appoint a top official, (3) publicize the policy, (4) survey present minority and female employment, (5) develop goals and timetables, (6) develop and implement specific programs to achieve goals, (7) establish an internal audit and reporting system, and (8) develop support of in-house and community programs.

11. Recruitment is one of the first activities to which EEOC laws and procedures are applied. We turn to this in Chapter 3.

Key Terms

Equal Pay Act of 1963 *29*
Title VII of the 1964 Civil
Rights Act *29*
Equal Employment
Opportunity Commission
(EEOC) *29*
affirmative action *30*
Office of Federal Contract
Compliance Programs
(OFCCP) *30*
Age Discrimination in
Employment Act (ADEA)
of 1967 *30*
Vocational Rehabilitation Act
of 1973 *30*
Pregnancy Discrimination
Act (PDA) *30*

federal agency
guidelines *30*
Griggs v. *Duke Power
Company 31*
protected class *31*
Albemarle Paper Company v.
Moody 31
Civil Rights Act of 1991
(CRA 1991) *32*
disparate
impact *39*
disparate treatment *32*
sexual harassment *33*
gender harassment *34*
Americans with Disabilities
Act (ADA) *36*
adverse impact *39*

workforce
analysis *40*
utilization
analysis *40*
bona fide occupational
qualification (BFOQ) *41*
business necessity *41*
alternative dispute
resolution (ADR)
program *45*
diversity *46*
stereotyping *46*
discrimination *47*
tokenism *47*
ethnocentrism *47*
gender-role
stereotypes *47*

Discussion Questions

1. What is Title VII? What does it state?
2. What important precedents were set by the *Griggs* v. *Duke Power Company* case? The *Albemarle* v. *Moody* case?
3. What is adverse impact? How can it be proven?
4. Assume that you are a supervisor on an assembly line; you are responsible for hiring subordinates, supervising them, and recommending them for promotion. Compile a list of discriminatory management practices that you should avoid.
5. Explain the defenses and exceptions to discriminatory practice allegations.
6. What is the difference between affirmative action and equal employment opportunity?
7. Explain how you would set up an affirmative action program.

Individual and Group Activities

1. Working individually or in groups, respond to these three scenarios based on what you learned in this chapter. Under what conditions (if any) do you think the following constitute sexual harassment? (a) A female manager fires a male employee because he refuses her requests for sexual favors. (b) A male manager refers to female employees as "sweetie" or "baby." (c) A female employee overhears two male employees exchanging sexually oriented jokes.
2. Working individually or in groups, discuss how you would set up an affirmative action program.
3. Compare and contrast the issues presented in recent court rulings on affirmative action. Working individually or in groups, discuss the current direction of affirmative action.
4. Working individually or in groups, write a paper entitled "What the Manager Should Know about How the EEOC Handles a Person's Discrimination Charge."

5. Explain the difference between affirmative action and equal employment opportunity.
6. Assume you are the manager in a small restaurant; you are responsible for hiring employees, supervising them, and recommending them for promotion. Working individually or in groups, compile a list of potentially discriminatory management practices you should avoid.

APPLICATION EXERCISES

CASE INCIDENT

A Case of Racial Discrimination?

John Peters was a 44-year-old cardiologist on the staff of a teaching hospital in a large city in the southeastern United States. Happily married with two teenage children, he had served with distinction for many years at this same hospital.

Alana Anderson was an African American registered nurse on the staff at the same hospital with Peters. Unmarried and without children, she lived in a hospital-owned apartment on the hospital grounds and devoted almost all her time to her work at the hospital or to taking additional coursework to further improve her already excellent nursing skills.

The hospital's chief administrator, Gary Chapman, took enormous pride in what he called the extraordinary professionalism of the doctors, nurses, and other staff members at his hospital. Although he took a number of rudimentary steps to guard against blatant violations of equal employment opportunity laws, he believed that most of the professionals on his staff were so highly trained and committed to the highest professional standards that "they would always do the right thing," as he put it.

Chapman was therefore upset to receive a phone call from Peters, informing him that Anderson had (in Peters's eyes) "developed an unwholesome personal attraction" to him and was bombarding the doctor with Valentine's Day cards, affectionate personal notes, and phone calls—often to the doctor's home. Concerned about hospital decorum and the possibility that Peters was being sexually harassed, Chapman met privately with Anderson, explained that Peters was very uncomfortable with the personal attention she was showing to him, and asked that she please not continue to exhibit her show of affection for the doctor.

Chapman assumed that the matter was over. Several weeks later, when Anderson resigned her position at the hospital, Chapman didn't think much of it. He was therefore shocked and dismayed to receive a registered letter from a local attorney, informing him that both the hospital and Peters and Chapman personally were being sued by Anderson for racial discrimination. Her claim was that Chapman, in their private meeting, had told her, "We don't think it's right for people of different races to pursue each other romantically at this hospital." According to the lawyer, his preliminary research had unearthed several other alleged incidents at the hospital that apparently supported the idea that racial discrimination at the hospital was widespread.

QUESTIONS

1. What do you think of the way Chapman handled the accusations from Peters and his conversation with Anderson? How would you have handled them?
2. Do you think Peters had the basis for a sexual harassment claim against Anderson? Why or why not?
3. What would you do now if you were Chapman to avoid further incidents of this type?

CONTINUING CASE

Carter Cleaning Company

A Question of Discrimination

One of the first problems Jennifer faced at her father's Carter Cleaning Centers concerned the inadequacies of the firm's current HR management practices and procedures.

One problem that particularly concerned her was the lack of attention to equal employment matters. Each store manager independently handled virtually all hiring; the managers had received no training regarding such fundamental matters as the types of questions they should not ask of job applicants. It was therefore not unusual—in fact, it was routine—for female applicants to be asked questions such as "Who's going to take care of your children while you are at work?" and for minority applicants to be asked questions about arrest records and credit histories. Nonminority applicants—three store managers were white males and three were white females, by the way—were not asked these questions, as Jennifer discerned from her interviews with the managers. Based on discussions with her father, Jennifer deduced two reasons for the laid-back attitude toward equal employment: (1) her father's lack of sophistication regarding the legal requirements and (2) the fact that, as Jack Carter put it, "Virtually all our workers are women or minority members anyway, so no one can really come in here and accuse us of being discriminatory, can they?"

Jennifer decided to mull that question over, but before she could, she was faced with two serious equal rights problems. Two women in one of her stores privately confided to her that their manager was making unwelcome sexual advances toward them, and one claimed he had threatened to fire her unless she "socialized" with him after hours. And during a fact-finding trip to another store, an older gentleman—he was 73 years old—complained of the fact that although he had almost 50 years of experience in the business, he was being paid less than people half his age who were doing the very same job. Jennifer's review of the stores resulted in the following questions that she would like you to answer.

QUESTIONS

1. Is it true, as Jack Carter claims, that "we can't be accused of being discriminatory because we hire mostly women and minorities anyway"?
2. How should she and her company address the sexual harassment charges and problems?
3. How should she and her company address the possible problems of age discrimination?
4. Given the fact that each of its stores has only a handful of employees, is her company covered by equal rights legislation?
5. And finally, aside from the specific problems, what other personnel management matters (application forms, training, and so on) have to be reviewed given the need to bring them into compliance with equal rights laws?

EXPERIENTIAL EXERCISE

Too Informal?

Dan Jones had run his textile plant in a midsize southern town for many years without a whiff of trouble with the EEOC. In fact, a professor from a local college had once told him to be more careful about how applicants were recruited and screened and employees were treated. However,

Jones's philosophy was "If it ain't broke, don't fix it," and because he'd never had any complaints, he assumed that his screening process wasn't "broke."

For many years Jones had no problems. If he needed a new employee, he simply asked his current employees (most of whom were Hispanic) if they had any friends. Sometimes, he would also ask the local state employment office to list the open jobs and send over some candidates. He then had

(continued)

his sewing supervisor and plant manager (both also Hispanic) interview the applicants. No tests or other background checks were carried out, in part, said Jones, because "most of these applicants are friends and relatives of my current employees, and they wouldn't send me any lemons."

Now Jones is being served with a formal notice from the county's Equal Rights Commission. It seems that of the 20 or so non-Hispanic applicants sent to Jones's firm last year from the state employment office, none had received a job offer. In fact, Jones's supervisor had not even returned the follow-up card to the employment office to verify that each applicant had shown up and been interviewed. Jones was starting to wonder if his HR process was too informal.

Purpose: The purpose of this exercise is to provide practice in analyzing and applying knowledge of equal opportunity legislation to a realistic problem.

Required Understanding: Be thoroughly familiar with the material presented in this chapter. In addition, read "Too Informal?" the case on which this experiential exercise is based.

How to Set Up the Exercise/Instructions:
1. If so desired, divide the class into groups.
2. Each group should develop answers to the following:
   a. How could the EEOC prove *adverse impact*?
   b. Cite specific discriminatory personnel practices at Dan Jones's company.
   c. How could Jones's company defend itself against the allegations of discriminatory practice?
3. If time permits, a spokesperson from each group can present his or her group's findings. Would it make sense for this company to try to defend itself against the discrimination allegations?

VIDEO CASE

HUMAN RESOURCE MANAGEMENT (AT PATAGONIA)

Synopsis

The mission at Patagonia is to build the best product possible, cause no unnecessary environmental harm, and inspire solutions to the environmental crisis. The benefits to employees working for Patagonia are considerable. Although the pay is slightly below the industry average, employees are given time off from work to try out the wetsuits the company produces, and employees are encouraged to put the needs of their families first. Workers can work flexible hours to accommodate this company value. Employees are also offered a period of 60 days in which they can work for a nonprofit environmental organization and still receive their full pay. Much thought goes into

hiring new employees at Patagonia; ambitious, mission-driven people, with whom the core values of Patagonia resonate, are selected to fill open positions within this unique company.

DISCUSSION QUESTIONS

1. How does the strategy of Patagonia differ from most other companies?
2. Patagonia has often been selected as one of the country's best places to work. What Patagonia HR practices and employee benefits do you think help Patagonia earn this honor?
3. What characteristics would you use to describe a candidate likely to be hired by Patagonia? How do these characteristics reflect and support Patagonia's strategy?

VIDEO CASE

EQUAL EMPLOYMENT (UPS)

Synopsis

A former HR director for UPS, now the president of "The Virtual HR Director," gives some perspective on what diversity means, and what its value can be to a company. Employees of a wide variety of backgrounds can help a company find creative solutions to new problems that it has not encountered before.

But where employees come from a variety of backgrounds and ethnicities, there is always the possibility of harassment between employees. The video addresses the value of diversity training in its capacity to help prevent employee harassment.

DISCUSSION QUESTIONS

1. What kinds of things does Gary Wheeler think a diverse workforce can contribute to a company?
2. What avenues are open to an employee who feels he or she is being harassed? Do you see any room for improvement based on our discussion in Chapter 2?
3. What does Gary Wheeler report is most often the basis of reported claims of harassment, and how are these cases dealt with?
4. What else would you do to deal with employees who are hostile to diversity?
5. To what extent do you believe that harassment, such as sexual harassment, is usually primarily a communications problem? Why?

Three

Personnel Planning, Recruiting, and Talent Management

When you finish studying this chapter you should be able to:

- Define *and list the main components of talent management.*
- Describe *the basic methods of collecting job analysis information.*
- Conduct *a job analysis.*
- Explain *the process of forecasting personnel requirements.*
- Compare *eight methods for recruiting job candidates.*
- Explain *how to use application forms to predict job performance.*

OVERVIEW

Even with the recession, employers are having trouble finding and hiring employees. The main purpose of this chapter is to explain the tools employers use to build a pool of hirable job candidates. The main topics we cover include The Talent Management Framework, The Basics of Job Analysis, The Recruitment and Selection Process, Workforce Planning and Forecasting, Recruiting Job Candidates, and Developing and Using Application Forms.

THE TALENT MANAGEMENT FRAMEWORK

This is the first chapter of those chapters (Chapters 3–7) which for many embody the heart of human resource management—staffing, training, appraisal, career development, and compensation. The traditional way to view these topics is as a series of steps:

1. Decide what positions to fill, through *job analysis* and *personnel planning and forecasting.*
2. Build a pool of job candidates, by *recruiting* internal or external candidates.
3. Have candidates complete *application forms* and perhaps undergo initial screening interviews.
4. Use *selection tools* such as tests, interviews, background checks, and physical exams to identify viable candidates.
5. Decide to whom to *make an offer.*
6. *Orient, train, and develop employees* to provide them with the competencies they need to do their jobs.
7. *Appraise employees* to assess how they're doing.
8. *Reward and compensate* employees to maintain their motivation.

This linear view makes sense; for example, you need to recruit applicants before selecting whom you'll hire. However, this view also masks the topics' interrelatedness. For example, employers don't just train employees and then appraise how they're doing; the appraisal also loops back to shape the employee's subsequent training. Therefore, employers increasingly view all these staff–train–reward activities as part of a single integrated *talent management* process.

What Is Talent Management?

We can define **talent management** as the *goal-oriented* and *integrated* process of *planning, recruiting, developing, managing, and compensating* employees.[1] When a manager takes a talent management perspective, he or she:

1. **Understands that the talent management tasks** (such as recruiting, training, and paying employees) are components in a single talent management process. For example, having employees with the right skills depends as much on recruiting, training, and compensation as it does on applicant testing.
2. **Makes sure talent management decisions such as staffing, training, and pay are goal-directed.** Managers should always be asking, "What recruiting, testing, or other actions should I take *to produce the employee competencies we need to achieve our strategic goals?*"
3. **Consistently uses the same "profile" of competencies, traits, knowledge, and experience for formulating recruitment plans for a job as for making selection, training, appraisal, and payment decisions for it.** For example, ask selection interview questions to determine if the candidate has the knowledge and skills to do the job. Then train and appraise the employee based on whether he or she shows mastery of that knowledge and skills.
4. **Actively segments and manages employees.** A talent management approach requires that employers *proactively manage* their employees' recruitment, selection, development, and rewards. For example, these employers pinpoint their

"mission-critical" employees, and manage their development and rewards separately from the firms' other employees.

5. **Integrates/coordinates all the talent management functions.** Finally, an effective talent management process *integrates the underlying talent management activities* such as recruiting, developing, and compensating employees. HR managers can simply meet as a team to visualize and discuss how to coordinate activities such as testing, appraising, and training. (For instance, making sure the firm uses the same skills profile to recruit, select, train, and appraise employees for a particular job.) Or, they can use information technology. As one example, Talent Management Solutions' (www.talentmanagement101.com) talent management suite includes e-recruiting software, employee performance management, a learning management system, and compensation management. This suite of programs ensures "that all levels of the organization are aligned—all working for the same goals."[2]

THE BASICS OF JOB ANALYSIS

Talent management begins with understanding what jobs need to be filled, and the human traits and competencies employees need to do those jobs effectively. **Job analysis** is the procedure through which you determine the duties of the positions and the characteristics of the people to hire for them.[3] Job analysis produces information for writing **job descriptions** (a list of what the job entails) and **job specifications** (what kind of people to hire for the job). Virtually every personnel-related action you take—interviewing applicants, and training and appraising employees, for instance—depends on knowing what the job entails and what human traits one needs to do the job well.[4] A supervisor or HR specialist normally does the job analysis, perhaps using a questionnaire like the one on pages 95–96, Figure A3-2.[5]

Job analysis information is crucial for several human resource management activities.[6] For example, you'll use information regarding the job's duties to decide what sort of people to recruit and hire, and to select workers for the job.

Methods of Collecting Job Analysis Information

Employers usually collect job analysis data from several job incumbents, using questionnaires and interviews. They then average data from different departments to determine how much time a typical employee (say, a sales assistant) spends on each task (such as interviewing).[7] Job analysis data reported by job incumbents display the lowest reliability, while those collected independently by job analysts are usually more reliable.[8] The process might include these steps:[9]

1. Greet participants;
2. Briefly explain the job analysis process and reason, and the participants' roles in this process;
3. Spend about 15 minutes getting agreement on the job's basic summary;
4. Identify the job's broad functional areas, such as "administrative" and "supervisory";
5. Identify specific tasks within each functional area; and,
6. Print the task list and get the group to sign it.

Managers use various techniques to do a job analysis (to collect information on the job's duties, responsibilities, and activities).

INTERVIEWS   Job analysis interviews involve interviewing job incumbents or one or more supervisors who know the job. Typical questions include "What are the major duties?" and "What exactly do you do?"

Interviewing is simple and lets workers report activities that might not otherwise surface. For example, the interview could unearth important activities that occur only occasionally, or informal communication (between, say, a production supervisor and sales manager).

Interviewing's main problem is distortion of information. Employers often use job analysis before changing a job's pay rate. Employees therefore sometimes exaggerate some responsibilities and minimize others.[10]

QUESTIONNAIRES   Employees can also use questionnaires to collect information on duties and responsibilities.

Some questionnaires are structured checklists. Each lists perhaps hundreds of specific duties or tasks (such as "change and splice wire"). Each employee must indicate whether he or she performs each task and, if so, how much time is spent on each. Alternatively, the questionnaire may simply ask the employee to "describe the major duties of your job."

As in Figure A3-2 (pages 95–96), a typical questionnaire might combine several open-ended questions ("Is the incumbent performing duties he/she considers unnecessary?") with structured questions (concerning, for instance, previous experience required).

OBSERVATION   Direct observation is useful when jobs consist of observable activity. Jobs such as janitor and accounting clerk are examples. On the other hand, observation is usually not appropriate when the job entails mental activity (lawyer, design engineer). Nor is it useful if the employee engages in important activities that might occur only occasionally, such as a nurse who handles emergencies.

PARTICIPANT DIARY/LOGS   Here workers keep diary/logs or lists of what they do during the day (along with the time). The detailed, chronological nature of the log tends to mediate against exaggerating some duties. Some employees compile their logs by periodically listing what they're doing on iPads or by dictating them.

USING INTERNET-BASED DATA COLLECTION   Face-to-face interviews and observations can be time-consuming. Collecting any information from internationally dispersed employees is challenging.[11]

Internet-based job analysis is one solution.[12] The human resource department distributes standardized job analysis questionnaires to dispersed employees via their company intranets, with instructions to complete and return the forms.

OTHER JOB ANALYSIS METHODS   You may encounter several other job analysis methods, most notably those in this chapter's appendix.

Writing Job Descriptions

The job analysis should provide the basis for writing a job description. A job description (Figure 3-1) is a written statement of *what* the jobholder does, *how* he or she does it, and under *what conditions* the job is performed. The manager in turn uses this information to write a job specification that lists the knowledge, abilities, and skills needed to perform the job. As is usual, it contains several types of information.

JOB IDENTIFICATION   As in Figure 3-1, the job identification section contains the job title, such as marketing manager or inventory control clerk.

JOB SUMMARY   The job summary should describe the general nature of the job, listing only its major functions or activities.

JOB TITLE: Telesales Representative		**JOB CODE:** 100001	
RECOMMENDED SALARY GRADE:		**EXEMPT/NONEXEMPT STATUS:** Nonexempt	
JOB FAMILY: Sales		**EEOC:** Sales Workers	
DIVISION: Higher Education		**REPORTS TO:** District Sales Manager	
DEPARTMENT: In-House Sales		**LOCATION:** Boston	
		DATE: April 2010	

SUMMARY (Write a brief summary of job.)

The person in this position is responsible for selling college textbooks, software, and multimedia products to professors, via incoming and outgoing telephone calls, and to carry out selling strategies to meet sales goals in assigned territories of smaller colleges and universities. In addition, the individual in this position will be responsible for generating a designated amount of editorial leads and communicating to the publishing groups product feedback and market trends observed in the assigned territory.

SCOPE AND IMPACT OF JOB
Dollar responsibilities (budget and/or revenue)

The person in this position is responsible for generating approximately $X million in revenue, for meeting operating expense budget of approximately $X,XXX, and a sampling budget of approximately XX,XXX units.

Supervisory responsibilities (direct and indirect)

None

Other

REQUIRED KNOWLEDGE AND EXPERIENCE (Knowledge and experience necessary to do job)
Related work experience

Prior sales or publishing experience preferred. One year of company experience in a customer service or marketing function with broad knowledge of company products and services is desirable.

Formal education or equivalent
Bachelor's degree with strong academic performance or work equivalent experience.

Skills
Must have strong organizational and persuasive skills. Must have excellent verbal and written communications skills and must be PC proficient.

Other

Limited travel required (approx 5%)

FIGURE 3-1 Sample Job Description, Pearson Education.   *Source:* Used by permission of Pearson Education, Inc.

PRIMARY RESPONSIBILITIES (List in order of importance and list amount of time spent on task.)

Driving Sales (60%)
- Achieve quantitative sales goal for assigned territory of smaller colleges and universities.
- Determine sales priorities and strategies for territory and develop a plan for implementing those strategies.
- Conduct 15–20 professor interviews per day during the academic sales year that accomplishes those priorities.
- Conduct product presentations (including texts, software, and Website); effectively articulate author's central vision of key titles; conduct sales interviews using the PSS model; conduct walk-through of books and technology.
- Employ telephone selling techniques and strategies.
- Sample products to appropriate faculty, making strategic use of assigned sampling budgets.
- Close class test adoptions for first edition products.
- Negotiate custom publishing and special packaging agreements within company guidelines.
- Initiate and conduct in-person faculty presentations and selling trips as appropriate to maximize sales with the strategic use of travel budget. Also use internal resources to support the territory sales goals.
- Plan and execute in-territory special selling events and book-fairs.
- Develop and implement in-territory promotional campaigns and targeted e-mail campaigns.

Publishing (editorial/marketing) 25%
- Report, track, and sign editorial projects.
- Gather and communicate significant market feedback and information to publishing groups.

Territory Management 15%
- Track and report all pending and closed business in assigned database.
- Maintain records of customer sales interviews and adoption situations in assigned database.
- Manage operating budget strategically.
- Submit territory itineraries, sales plans, and sales forecasts as assigned.
- Provide superior customer service and maintain professional bookstore relations in assigned territory.

Decision-Making Responsibilities for This Position:
Determine the strategic use of assigned sampling budget to most effectively generate sales revenue to exceed sales goals.
Determine the priority of customer and account contacts to achieve maximum sales potential.
Determine where in-person presentations and special selling events would be most effective to generate most sales.

Submitted By: Jim Smith, District Sales Manager	Date: April 10, 2007
Approval:	Date:
Human Resources:	Date:
Corporate Compensation:	Date:

FIGURE 3-1 Continued

RELATIONSHIPS   A relationships statement may show the jobholder's relationships with others inside and outside the organization and might look like this for a human resource manager:

Reports to: Vice president of employee relations

Supervises: Human resource clerk, test administrator, labor relations director, and one secretary

Works with: All department managers and executive management

Outside the company: Employment agencies, executive recruiting firms, union representatives, state and federal employment offices, and various vendors

FIGURE 3-2 Marketing Manager Description from Standard Occupational Classification. *Source:* From U.S. Department of Labor, Bureau of Labor Statistics.

RESPONSIBILITIES AND DUTIES   This is the heart of the job description. Here, list and describe in several sentences each of the job's major duties. For instance, supplement the duty "selects, trains, and develops subordinate personnel" with "develops spirit of cooperation and understanding."

Human resource managers formerly used the Department of Labor's bulky *Dictionary of Occupational Titles* to find and itemize a job's duties and responsibilities. Today, the U.S. Department of Labor's *Occupational Information Network*, or O*NET (and its Standard Occupational Classification, as in Figure 3-2), has largely replaced the *Dictionary of Occupational Titles.* The O*NET site (http://online.onetcenter.org/) enables users to see the most important characteristics of an occupation, as well as the training, experience, and education it requires.[13] O*NET also lists the occupation's skills, including *basic skills* such as reading, *process skills* such as critical thinking, and *transferable skills* such as persuasion.[14]

AUTHORITY   This section details the job's authority. For example, the jobholder might have authority to approve purchase requests up to $5,000, and recommend salary increases.

STANDARDS OF PERFORMANCE   If present, this lists standards the employee is expected to achieve in each of the job's main duties and responsibilities.

WORKING CONDITIONS AND PHYSICAL ENVIRONMENT   The job description also lists the job's general working conditions, such as noise level, hazardous conditions, and heat.

INTERNET-BASED JOB DESCRIPTIONS   Employers are turning to the Internet to write their job descriptions. One site, www.jobdescription.com, illustrates why. Search by alphabetical title, keyword, category, or industry to find the desired job title. This leads you to a generic job description for that title—say, "Computers & EDP systems sales representative." You can then add specific information about your organization, such as job title, job codes, department, and preparation date.[15] Others use O*NET (see the chapter appendix) to create job descriptions.

COMPLYING WITH THE AMERICANS WITH DISABILITIES ACT (ADA)   The EEOC does not require job descriptions. However, most ADA lawsuits involve the question: What are the essential functions of the job? (Essential job functions are those duties that employees must be able to perform, with or without reasonable accommodation.)[16] Without a job description listing these functions as "essential," it's difficult to prove that the functions are essential.[17]

Writing Job Specifications

The job specification answers the question: What human traits and experience are required to do this job well? It shows for what qualities to test the applicants. It may be a section on the job description (as at the end of the first page of Figure 3-1) or a separate document.

Writing job specifications for trained employees is straightforward. Thus, for a trained bookkeeper, your job specifications might focus mostly on traits such as length of previous service, or relevant training. So, it's usually not too difficult to determine the human requirements for placing already trained people on a job.

It's more complicated when you're filling jobs with untrained people. Here you must specify qualities such as physical traits, personality, or sensory skills that imply some potential for performing the job or for being trainable. Your goal here, in other words, is to identify those personal traits (say, finger dexterity) that predict which candidate would do well on the job (say, assembler.) Employers identify the job's required human traits using either a judgmental approach or statistical analysis.

Common sense is required when listing a job's human requirements. Certainly job-specific human traits such as manual dexterity and education are important. However, it's important not to ignore work behaviors (such as conscientiousness) that apply to most jobs but might not normally be unearthed through a job analysis.[18]

The Role of Competencies and Profiles

WHY USE PROFILES?   Traditionally, a *job* is a set of closely related tasks, but the concept of a job is changing. Employers are instituting high-performance work practices. These include practices (such as using work teams) that require multiskilled employees to tackle multiple jobs.

The problem here is that each employee's job may change constantly, so describing job requirements as a list of duties can backfire.[19] Often, it's preferable to use profiles or models that list the sets of competencies, traits, knowledge, and skills that someone would need to do the team's multiple jobs. The managers then use the list of attributes in each job's profile as the standard for recruitment, selection, training, and evaluation plans for each job.[20] Figure 3-3 illustrates one such profile, in this case a "competency model." We look next at how to produce such competencies models.

Competency-Based Job Analysis

We can define *competencies* as demonstrable characteristics of the person that enable performance (one *technical competency* for a systems engineer might be "have a command of processor structure"). *Competency-based job analysis* means describing the job in terms of the observable competencies (knowledge, skills, and/or behaviors)

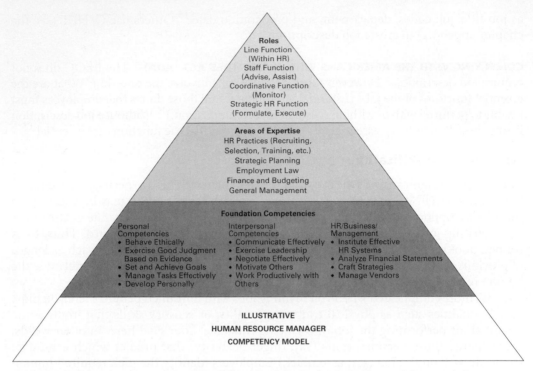

FIGURE 3-3 Example of Competency Model Summarizing Roles, Expertise, and Competencies of Human Resource Manager.

that an employee doing that job must have to do the job. This contrasts with describing the job in terms of job duties and responsibilities (splice wires, answer phones).[21] *Traditional job analysis* focuses on the job's duties and responsibilities. *Competency analysis* focuses on what competencies or skills the worker must have to do the work.[22]

BP EXAMPLE   British Petroleum's (BP's) exploration division decided its unit needed a faster-acting organization.[23] To help accomplish this, it felt it had to shift employees from a job duties–oriented "that's-not-my-job" attitude to one that motivated them to obtain the skills required to accomplish their broader responsibilities.

BP created skills matrices (Figure 3-4) for each job or job family (such as drilling managers). As in Figure 3-4, each matrix listed (1) the basic skills required to do that job (such as technical expertise) and (2) the minimum level of each skill required for that job or job family. Now, with these matrices, the exploration division's focus is on recruiting, hiring, and developing people with the skills employees need. Talent management in this BP unit now involves recruiting, hiring, training, appraising, and rewarding employees based on the competencies they need to perform their ever-changing jobs, with the overall aim of creating a faster-acting, more flexible organization.

THE RECRUITMENT AND SELECTION PROCESS

Employers use job analysis and job descriptions for several things—for example, to develop training programs. But the most familiar use for job descriptions is for deciding what types of people to recruit and select for the company's jobs.

H	H	H	H	H	H	H
G	G	G	G	G	G	G
F	F	F	F	F	F	F
E	E	E	E	E	E	E
D	D	D	D	D	D	D
C	C	C	C	C	C	C
B	B	B	B	B	B	B
A	A	A	A	A	A	A
Technical Expertise	Business Awareness	Communi-cation and Interpersonal	Decision Making and Initiative	Leadership and Guidance	Planning and Organizational Ability	Problem Solving

FIGURE 3-4 The Skills Matrix for One Job at BP.   *Note:* The shaded boxes (D, C, B, E, D, D, C) indicate the minimum level of skill required for the job.

This *recruiting and selecting process* is a series of steps, as follows:

1. Do workforce planning and forecasting to determine the positions to fill.
2. Build a pool of candidates for these jobs by recruiting internal or external candidates.
3. Have the applicants fill out application forms and perhaps undergo an initial interview.
4. Utilize various selection techniques such as tests, background investigations, and physical exams to choose job candidates.
5. Send one or more job candidates to the supervisor responsible for the job.
6. Have the candidate go through selection interviews, and determine to which candidate(s) to make an offer.

Workforce planning and recruiting (steps 1 through 3) are the subjects of the remainder of this chapter. Chapter 4 then discusses employee selection techniques including tests (steps 4 through 6).

WORKFORCE PLANNING AND FORECASTING

Recruitment and selection ideally start with workforce planning. After all, if you don't know what your employment needs will be, why should you be hiring?

Workforce (or *employment* or *personnel*) **planning** is the process of deciding what positions the firm will have to fill, and how to fill them. Most firms use the term *succession planning* to refer to planning how to fill the company's most important top executive positions.

Strategy and Workforce/Personnel Planning

Personnel planning should be an integral part of a firm's strategic planning. For example, IBM has been transitioning from mostly supplying computers, to supplying software and consulting services. Therefore, in terms of IBM's strategic workforce needs, "in three years, 22 percent of our workforce will have obsolete skills. Of the 22 percent, 85 percent have fundamental competencies that we can build on to get them ready for skills we'll need years from now."[24] IBM needs plans for building these skills.

The heart of personnel planning involves predicting the skills the employer will need to execute its strategy. In the short term, there's not much employers can do to overcome recessions or housing bubbles. However, the manager should control his or her strategy. So, knowing that the firm plans, say, to expand abroad, means making plans for ramping up hiring in the firm's international division. At IBM, human resource executives discuss with other executives the personnel ramifications of their company's strategic plans, including the employee skills the firm will need to achieve its goals.[25]

INSIDE OR OUTSIDE CANDIDATES?   One big question is always whether to fill projected openings with current employees or by recruiting from outside. Each option produces its own set of HR plans. Current employees may require training, development, and coaching before they're ready to fill new jobs. Going outside requires deciding what recruiting sources to use and what the availability will be.

The basic workforce planning process is to (1) forecast the employer's demand for labor (needs) and supply of labor (supply), (2) identify supply–needs gaps, and (3) develop action plans to fill the projected gaps.

How to Forecast Personnel Needs (Labor Demand)

A firm's staffing needs reflect demand for its products or services, adjusted for changes the firm plans to make in its strategic goals and for changes in its turnover rate and productivity. Forecasting workforce demand therefore starts with estimating what the demand will be for your products or services.[26] Managers will follow industry publications and economic forecasts, for instance, from the *Conference Board*. Predicting a rise or fall in business activity a year of two off won't be precise. However, the process may help identify problem areas and options.

Traditional personnel planning involves using tools such as *ratio analysis* or *trend analysis* to estimate staffing needs based on sales projections and on historical sales to personnel relationships. The usual process is to forecast revenues first. Then estimate the size of the staff required to achieve this volume, for instance, by using historical ratios. In addition to expected demand, the manager may adjust projected staffing needs to reflect:

1. Projected turnover (resignations or terminations)
2. Quality and skills of your employees (in relation to your company's changing needs)
3. Strategic decisions to upgrade the quality of products or services or enter into new markets
4. Technological and other changes resulting in increased productivity
5. The financial resources available

Larger employers computerize the workforce planning process. *Computerized forecasts* enable the manager to build more variables into his or her personnel projections.[27] For example, newer workforce planning systems enable managers to factor in specific goals, such as reducing inventory on hand.[28]

TREND ANALYSIS   Computerized planning aside, there are simple ways to estimate future personnel needs. **Trend analysis** involves studying your firm's employment levels over the past 5 years or so to predict future needs. Thus, you might compute the number of employees in your firm at the end of each of the past 5 years, or the number in each subgroup (such as salespeople, engineers, and administrative). Carefully studying employment history, demographics. and voluntary withdrawals can help reveal impending labor force needs.

RATIO ANALYSIS   Another approach, **ratio analysis,** means making forecasts based on the ratio between some causal factor (such as sales volume) and the number of employees required (for instance, number of salespeople). For example, suppose a salesperson usually generates $500,000 in sales. Then, if the sales revenue-to-salespeople ratio remains the same, you would require six new salespeople next year (6 × $500,000 in sales) to produce, say, the desired extra $3 million in sales.

SCATTER PLOTS   The **scatter plot** shows graphically how two variables (such as a measure of business activity and your firms' staffing levels) are related. If they are, then if you can forecast the level of business activity, you should also be able to estimate your personnel requirements.

For example, assume a 500-bed hospital expects to expand to 1,200 beds over the next 5 years. The director of nursing and the human resource director want to forecast the requirement for registered nurses. The human resource director decides to determine the relationship between size of hospital (in terms of number of beds) and number of nurses required. She calls several hospitals of various sizes and obtains the following figures:

Size of Hospital (Number of Beds)	Number of Registered Nurses
200	240
300	260
400	470
500	500
600	620
700	660
800	820
900	860

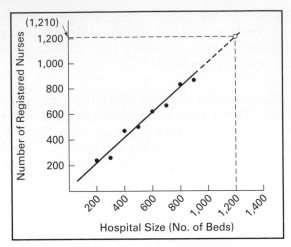

FIGURE 3-5 Determining the Relationship Between Hospital Size and Number of Nurses.   *Note:* After fitting the line, you can extrapolate—project—how many nurses you'll need, given your projected volume.

Figure 3-5 shows the hospital size (in beds) on the horizontal axis. The number of nurses is shown on the vertical axis. If the two factors are related, then the points will tend to fall along a line, as here. If you draw in a line to minimize the distances between the line and each of the plotted points, you will be able to estimate (forecast) the number of nurses needed for each given hospital size. Thus, for a 1,200-bed hospital, the human resource director would assume she needs about 1,210 nurses.[29]

Managerial judgment is important in employment planning. It's rare that any historical trend will continue unchanged. Important factors that may influence your forecast include decisions to upgrade product quality or enter into new markets, financial resources, and technological changes resulting in increased productivity.

IMPROVING PRODUCTIVITY THROUGH HRIS: COMPUTERIZED PERSONNEL FORECASTING
As noted, *computerized forecasts* enable managers to build more variables into their personnel projections.[30] Thus, at Chelan County Public Utility District, the development manager built a statistical model encompassing such things as age, tenure, turnover rate, and time to train new employees. This model helped them quickly identify five employment "hotspots" among 33 occupational groups at their company. This in turn prompted them to focus more closely on creating plans to retain and hire, for instance, more systems operators.[31]

Forecasting the Supply of Inside Candidates

The preceding personnel needs forecast provides half the staffing equation, by answering the question: How many employees will we need? Next, the manager must try to assess the projected *supply* of both internal and external candidates.

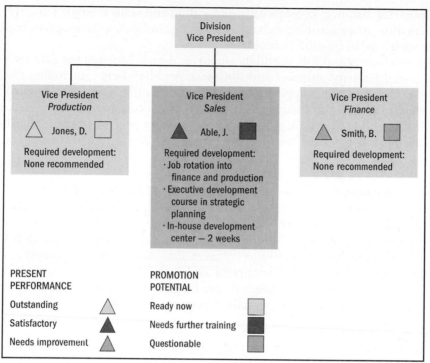

FIGURE 3-6 Management Replacement Chart Showing Development Needs of Potential Future Divisional Vice Presidents.

We'll see that forecasting external labor supply depends first on the manager's own sense of what's happening in his or her industry and locale. He or she then supplements these observations with more formal labor market analyses, for instance from the U.S. Bureau of Labor Statistics and from O*NET. A qualifications inventory can help facilitate forecasting the supply of inside candidates. **Qualifications inventories** contain summary data, such as each current employee's performance record, educational background, and promotability, compiled manually or in a computerized system. **Personnel replacement charts** (Figure 3-6) show the present performance and promotability for each potential replacement for important positions. As an alternative, you can develop a *position replacement card* for each position, showing possible replacements as well as present performance, promotion potential, and training required by each possible candidate.

COMPUTERIZED INFORMATION SYSTEMS   Employers can't maintain qualifications inventories on hundreds or thousands of employees manually. Many firms computerize this information, and there are a number of packaged systems available for accomplishing this task.

Typically, employees fill out a Web-based survey in which they describe their background and experience. The system also maintains records of performance appraisals and training. When a manager needs a qualified person, he or she describes the position (for instance, in terms of the education and skills it entails) and then enters this information. After scanning its bank of possible candidates, the program presents the manager with a list of qualified candidates.

The employer should secure all its employee data.[32] Much of the data are personal (such as Social Security numbers and illnesses). And legislation, including the Federal Privacy Act of 1974 (which applies to federal workers), the New York Personal Privacy Act of 1985, and the Health Insurance Portability and Accountability Act (HIPAA), gives legal rights regarding access. A growing problem is that peer-to-peer file sharing applications jump firewalls. Pfizer Inc. lost personal data on about 17,000 current and former employees this way.[33]

SUCCESSION PLANNING   Forecasting the availability of inside candidates is particularly important in succession planning. In brief, *succession planning* means the plans a company makes to fill its most important executive positions. The basic process is to identify key needs, develop candidates, and assess and choose those to fill the key positions.[34] A comprehensive definition of *succession planning* is "the process of ensuring a suitable supply of successors for current and future key jobs arising from business strategy, so that the careers of individuals can be planned and managed to optimize the organization's needs and the individuals' aspirations."[35] Succession planning includes these activities:

- Analysis of the future demand for managers and professionals by company level, function, and skill
- Audit of existing executives and projection of likely future supply from internal and external sources
- Planning of individual career paths based on objective estimates and assessments of potential and career interests
- Training and development to prepare individuals for future expected roles
- Accelerated promotions
- Planned strategic recruitment, to fill short-term needs and to provide people to develop to meet future needs[36]

Succession planning should conform to basic talent management practices. In particular, the key is to list the competencies that the firm's evolving strategy will require the new CEO or other executive to have; then use that profile as the benchmark for formulating an integrated set of selection, training, appraisal, and compensation standards for the job.

Forecasting the Supply of Outside Candidates

If there are not enough qualified inside candidates to fill anticipated openings, employers turn to projecting supplies of outside candidates—those not currently employed by your organization. This may require forecasting general economic conditions, local market conditions, and occupational market conditions. For example, unemployment rates of about 9% in the United States in 2012 signaled to HR managers that finding good candidates would be easier.[37]

The first step is to forecast general economic conditions and, for instance, the expected prevailing rate of unemployment. Usually, the lower the rate of unemployment, the more difficult it is to recruit personnel. Look for economic projections online, for example, from the U.S. Congressional Budget Office (CBO), www.cbo.gov/topics/economy/economic-projections and the "Employment Situation Summary" from the U.S. Bureau of Labor Statistics (BLS), www.bls.gov.

Local labor market conditions are also important. For example, the growth of computer and semiconductor firms recently prompted lower unemployment in cities like Seattle, quite aside from general economic conditions in the country.

Finally, you may want to forecast the availability of potential job candidates in specific occupations. For example, information technology–related jobs, such as for network systems and data communications analysts, are among the most in-demand occupations for the period 2006–2016.[38] Sources such as *Occupational Outlook Quarterly* from the U.S. Labor Department can be useful here.

Talent Management and Predictive Workforce Monitoring

Traditionally, employers engage in formal workforce planning perhaps every year or so. However, this may not always provide enough time. For instance, having failed to do much such employment planning for years, one firm, Valero Energy, discovered that many of its most crucial employees would soon be retiring, and had to be replaced.

In contrast, the talent management philosophy to workforce planning requires *paying continuous attention* to workforce planning issues. Managers call this newer workforce planning approach **predictive workforce monitoring.**

INTEL CORPORATION EXAMPLE   For example, Intel conducts semiannual "Organization Capability Assessments." The staffing department works with the firm's business heads twice a year to assess workforce needs—immediate and up to 2 years out.[39]

AMERADA HESS EXAMPLE   Amerada Hess's Organizational Capability (OC) group monitors workforce attrition (such as retirement age, experience with Hess, education, etc.) and prospective talent requirements. It "then works with the lines of business to better prepare them for meeting changing global talent demands. The group considers how each line of business is evolving, examines what jobs at Hess will look like in the future, identifies sources for procuring the best talent, and assists in developing current and newly hired employees."[40]

VALERO ENERGY EXAMPLE   Valero created a *labor supply chain* for monitoring steps in recruiting and hiring. It includes an analytic tool that predicts Valero's labor needs based on past experience. It also includes computer screen "dashboards" that show how components in the chain, such as ads placed on job boards, are performing according to cost, job-placement speed, and quality.[41]

Developing an Action Plan to Match Projected Labor Supply and Labor Demand

Workforce planning should culminate in a workforce action plan. This lays out the employer's projected workforce demand–supply gaps, as well as staffing plans for filling the necessary positions. The staffing plan should identify the positions to be filled; potential internal and external sources for these positions; the required training, development, and promotional activities moving people into the positions will entail; and the resources that implementing the staffing plan will require. Resources might include, for instance, advertising costs, recruiter fees, relocation costs, and travel and interview expenses.[42]

RECRUITING JOB CANDIDATES

Once authorized to fill a position, the next step is to develop an applicant pool, either from internal or external sources. Recruiting is important because the more applicants you have, the more selective you can be in your hiring. By several estimates, the shortage of workers will grow from almost nothing today to about 20 million workers by 2020.[43] Effective recruitment is important because the more qualified applicants you have, the more selective you can be in whom you hire.

The Complex Job of Recruiting Employees

Recruiting does not just involve placing ads or calling employment agencies. For one thing, we just saw that your recruitment efforts should make sense in terms of your company's strategic plans. Filling a large number of anticipated openings also implies that you've carefully thought through when and how you will do your recruiting—the sources you will use, for instance.

Second, we'll see that some recruiting methods are superior to others, depending on whom you're recruiting and what your resources are.

Third, the success you have with your recruiting depends on nonrecruitment issues and policies. For example, deciding to pay 10% more than most firms in your locale should, other things equal, help you build a bigger applicant pool faster.[44] Similarly, employers who send effective recruiters to campus and build relationships with opinion leaders such as career counselors and professors have better recruiting results.[45]

Then there are the legal considerations. For example, with a nondiverse workforce, the EEOC may view word-of-mouth referrals as a barrier to equal employment.[46] It's also becoming more difficult to hire workers from abroad. Security concerns and rising resistance from Congress are making it more difficult to obtain the coveted work visas permitting work in the United States.[47] The HR in Practice feature provides another factor to consider.

HR IN PRACTICE

The Hiring Manager's Obligations

The recruiting manager should take care not to interfere with the applicant's obligations to his or her current employer. In general, even without a written contract, courts hold that employees have a duty of loyalty to their current employers during their employment.[48] For example, they should maintain the confidentiality of customer lists. In general, the hiring manager has both an ethical and legal obligation to respect the prospective employee's duty of loyalty. To the extent that the hiring manager participates in any breach of that loyalty—for instance, inquiring about customers' buying patterns or about new products—the hiring manager may share in the liability for the breach. Make it clear at the outset that you expect applicants to honor their duty of loyalty to their current employers.[49]

HR AS A PROFIT CENTER

GE Medical Example

GE Medical has cut its hiring costs by 17%, reduced time to fill the positions by 20% to 30%, and cut in half the percentage of new hires who don't work out.[50]

GE Medical's HR team accomplished this by applying purchasing techniques to its recruiters. For example, it told 20 recruiters that it would work with only the 10 best. To measure "best," the company created measurements such as "percentage of résumés that result in interviews." Similarly, GE Medical interviews just 1% of applicants whose résumés it receives, while 10% of employee referrals result in actual hires. So GE Medical took steps to double the number of employee referrals.

Recruiting Effectiveness

Given all this, it's also important to assess how effectively the employer is spending its recruiting dollars. Should we use this employment agency or that one? One survey found that only about 44% of the 279 firms surveyed make formal attempts to evaluate the outcomes of their recruitment efforts.[51] The accompanying HR as a Profit Center feature illustrates one solution.

Internal Sources of Candidates

Although *recruiting* may bring to mind job boards and classified ads, filling jobs with current employees (internal recruiting) is often an employer's best bet. To be effective, this approach requires using job posting and personnel records.[52] **Job posting** means "posting the open job—on company bulletin boards and/or Intranet—and listing its attributes, such as qualifications, supervisor, working schedule, and pay scale" (as in Figure 3-7). Some union contracts require postings. Yet posting is also good practice in nonunion firms, as it facilitates promoting qualified inside candidates. Personnel records are also useful here. An examination of personnel records (including qualifications inventories) may reveal individuals who have potential for further training or who already have the background for the open job.

Recruiting via the Internet

You may not be able to (nor want to) fill all your recruiting needs with internal candidates. In that case, one turns to outside sources, often starting with the Internet.[53]

Many firms use their company websites. For example, GE's home page (www.ge.com) includes a link to http://jobs.gecareers.com/. Others, of course, post positions on Internet job boards such as Careerbuilder.com, on the sites of professional associations (such as the American Institute of Chemical Engineers), or the sites of their local newspapers. Other employers simply screen through job boards' résumé listings.[54] E-recruiting has potential legal pitfalls. For example, fewer minorities use the Internet, so employers may inadvertently exclude minority applicants.[55]

Whether using one's own site or a job board, it's important to capitalize on the Web's advertising strengths. For example, the Cheesecake Factory doesn't just post short help wanted ads on the Web. Instead, it usually includes the whole job description.[56]

JOB POSTING FORM

Please complete all applicable areas and return via e-mail (JobForm@bigCo.com) or FAX (123-456-7890)

Date Posted _____

Reply no later than _____

Type of Employment   Summer _____   Part-Time _____   Full-Time _____

Job Title of Open Position _____

Employer _____   Department _____

Location Address _____

Website _____

Pay Scale _____   Shifts/Hours _____   # of Vacancies _____

Brief Job Description _____
_____
_____
_____
_____
_____
_____

Qualifications: Required Skills and Abilities _____
_____
_____
_____
_____
_____
_____

Desired Skills and Abilities _____
_____
_____
_____
_____
_____
_____

How to Apply: By FAX or e-mail as above, no later than _____ . Please ensure HR has updated copy of your résumé. Selections will be made by _____ .

FIGURE 3-7 Job Posting Form.

Ideally, you should also include a way (such as a checklist of the job's human requirements) for potential applicants to gauge the extent to which the job is a good fit.[57] More information is usually better than less. Job applicants view ads with more specific job information as more attractive and more credible.[58] Studies suggest that employers should probably include employee testimonials on their recruitment websites. Testimonials in the form of video and audio have the most impact.[59] In addition, make it easy to get from the home page to the career page in one or two clicks, allow job seekers to apply online and via fax or e-mail, and enable visitors to receive e-mail notices about new jobs.[60]

Job boards account for about 12.3% of recent hires. Other major sources include company website (20.1%); referrals (27.3%); plus others such as temp to hire, rehires, and employment agencies.

New sites capitalize on social networking. Users supply their name, location, and the kind of work they do on sites like LinkedIn.com. These sites help nurture personal relationships for networking, hiring, and employee referrals.[61] (If you're an applicant, note that U.S. laws generally *do not* prohibit job boards from sharing your data with other sources. One reportedly had personal information on over a million subscribers stolen.)[62]

Recruiting for professionals and managers is also shifting to social networking sites such as Facebook and LinkedIn. For example, Science Applications International Corp. cut the job boards it uses from 15 to 6 or so. Instead, its recruiters are searching for candidates on professional social networks.

One problem is that many applications received via job boards don't meet the job's qualifications. As one recruiter said, "recruiters had to put in all this extra time to read applications but we didn't get benefit from it." Instead, this company now hires recruiters who specialize in digging through social websites and competitors' publications to find applicants who may not even be looking for jobs.[63] McDonald's Corp. posted a series of employee testimonials on social networking sites like Second Life as a way to attract applicants.[64] Other employers simply skim through job boards' résumé listings.[65] Others use Twitter to announce job openings to job seekers who subscribe to their Twitter feeds.[66] ResumePal is an online standard job application. Jobseekers submit it to participating employers, who can then use the standardized application's keywords to identify viable candidates (www.resumepal.com/Site/Default.aspx).[67]

TEXTING   Some employers use text messaging to build an applicant pool. For example, at one conference, consultants Hewitt Associates displayed posters asking attendees to text message *hewdiversity* to a specific five digit number. Each person texting then became part of Hewitt's "mobile recruiting network," periodically receiving text messages regarding Hewitt openings.[68]

VIRTUAL JOB FAIRS   Virtual (fully online) job fairs are another option. At a virtual job fair, online visitors see a very similar setup to a regular job fair. They can listen to presentations, visit booths, leave résumés and business cards, participate in live chats, and get contact information from recruiters, HR managers, and even hiring managers.[69] As one writer pithily said, "virtual career fairs are appealing because they're a way to get your foot in the door without having to walk out the door."[70] The fairs last about 5 hours. Attendees might find 30 or more employers recruiting. Specialist virtual fair websites include Milicruit (for former military personnel) and Unicruit (for college students).

APPLICANT TRACKING SERVICES   The ease of responding to Internet job postings encourages large numbers of often unqualified job seekers. More firms today therefore install applicant-tracking systems. Popular applicant tracking systems help employers by screening, categorizing, keeping track of applicants, and matching them to jobs. They also help employers compile reports, such as "applicants by reject reason."[71] Application service providers (ASPs) process the applicants who go to your site, using their own servers. Other employers let job boards process the online applications.[72] Suppliers of e-recruiting tracking (and other) services include Automatic Data Processing (ADP.com), HRSmart (hrsmart.com), and recruitsoft.com.[73]

Advertising as a Source of Candidates

Placing a help wanted print ad begins with deciding where to place the ad. The best medium (such as your local paper, the *Wall Street Journal,* or a technical journal) depends on the job. The local newspaper or the Web is usually the best source of blue-collar help, clerical employees, and lower-level administrative employees. For professionals, you can advertise on the Web or in trade and professional journals such as the *American Psychologist, Sales Management,* and *American Banker.* Help wanted ads in papers such as the *Wall Street Journal* are good sources of middle- or senior-management personnel, but there may be a week or more between insertion of the ad and publication.

Employment Agencies as a Source of Candidates

There are three types of employment agencies: (1) those operated by federal, state, or local governments, (2) those associated with nonprofit organizations, and (3) privately owned agencies.

Public state employment agencies exist in every state, aided and coordinated by the U.S. Department of Labor. The latter also maintains a nationwide computerized job bank to which state employment offices connect. Public agencies are a major source of blue-collar and often white-collar workers. Beyond just filling jobs, counselors will visit an employer's work site, review the employer's job requirements, and even assist the employer in writing job descriptions. And most states have turned their local state employment service agencies into "one-stop" shops. Under a single roof, employers and job seekers can access an array of services such as recruitment services, employee training programs, and local and national labor market information.

Other employment agencies are associated with *nonprofit organizations*. For example, most professional and technical societies have units that help their members find jobs. Many public welfare agencies try to place people who are in special categories, such as those who are disabled.

Private employment agencies are important sources of clerical, white-collar, and managerial personnel. Their fees are usually set by state law and are posted in their offices. Most often, the employer pays the fees.

You might want to turn to an agency because:

- Your firm does not have its own human resource department.
- Your firm has found it difficult to generate a pool of qualified applicants.
- You must fill an opening quickly.

- There is a perceived need to attract a greater number of minority or female applicants.
- The recruitment effort aims to reach employed individuals who might feel more comfortable dealing with employment agencies than with competing companies.

But, employment agencies are no panacea. For example, the employment agency's screening may let unqualified applicants go directly to the supervisors doing the hiring, who then naively hire the unscreened candidates.

TEMPORARY WORKERS   Many employers supplement their permanent employee base by hiring contingent or temporary workers, often through temporary help agencies. Also called *part-time* or *just-in-time* workers, the *contingent workforce* is big, growing, and not limited to clerical or maintenance staff. Recently, about 26% of all jobs private-sector employers added were temporary positions.

Several things contribute to the trend toward using more temporary employees. One is continuing weak economic confidence. Another is outsourcing. For example, Makino, which manufactures machine tools, now outsources the installation of large machines to contract firms, who in turn hire temps to do the installations. Flexibility is another concern, with more employers wanting to quickly reduce employment levels if necessary.[74]

Employers can hire such workers either directly or through temporary staff agencies. The employer usually pays direct-hire temps directly, as it does all its employees. However, it classifies them separately from regular employees, usually as casual, seasonal, or temporary employees.[75] Temporary employees typically receive few if any benefits (such as pensions).

If you hire temps through agencies, the agency usually pays the employees' salaries and (any) benefits. For instance, Nike Inc. signed a multimillion-dollar deal with Kelly Services to manage Nike's temporary hires.[76] However, using agencies requires care. Several years ago, federal agents rounded up illegal "contract" workers in 60 Walmart stores cleaning after-hours, under the auspices of contingent staffing firms.[77]

ALTERNATIVE STAFFING   Temporary employees are examples of alternative staffing—basically, the use of nontraditional recruitment sources. Other alternative staffing arrangements include "contract technical employees" (highly skilled workers like engineers, who are supplied for long-term projects under contract from an outside technical services firm). The use of alternative staffing sources is widespread and growing. About 1 of 10 U.S. employees is employed in some type of alternative work arrangement.

Executive Recruiters as a Source of Candidates

Executive recruiters (also called *headhunters*) are special employment agencies that employers retain to seek out top-management talent. They fill jobs in the $80,000 and up category, although $120,000 is often the lower limit. The percentage of your firm's positions filled by these services might be small. However, these jobs include the most crucial executive and technical positions. For top executive positions, headhunters may be your only source. The employer pays their fees.[78]

Many (but not all) of these firms are specialized, a fact that facilitates quickly finding candidates when, for instance, an academic recruiter is asked to fill a university president's spot. But even specialists will need to advertise for candidates. And most of these firms are also adept at using Internet-linked databases to create a list of potential candidates.

PROS AND CONS   Headhunters have many contacts and are especially adroit at contacting qualified employed candidates who are not actively seeking jobs. They can also keep your firm's name confidential until late in the search process. The recruiter can save top management time by doing the preliminary work of advertising for and screening applicants. The recruiter's fee might actually be insignificant compared to the cost of the executive time saved.

But there are drawbacks. As an employer, you must carefully explain the candidate you require and why. Some recruiters may be more interested in persuading you to hire a candidate than in finding one who will do the best job. Sometimes, what clients think they want isn't really what they need. Therefore, be prepared for dissecting of your request.[79] Also, meet the person who will handle your search, and get exact charges. Make sure the recruiter checks candidates' references, but double-check the final candidate's references yourself.[80]

CANDIDATES' CAVEATS   As a job candidate, keep several things in mind. Some of these firms may present an unpromising candidate to a client just to make their other candidates look better. Some eager clients may also jump the gun, undermining your present position. Finally, do not confuse executive search firms with the many executive assistance or coaching firms that help out-of-work executives find jobs. The latter charge the job seekers handsome fees to assist with things like résumé preparation and interview skills. They rarely actually reach out to prospective employers to find their clients jobs. Also, know that recruiters are usually coy about revealing the full amount they're willing to pay.[81]

College Recruiting and Interns as Sources of Candidates

College recruiting is an important source of management trainees and of professional and technical employees. GE hires 800 to 1,000 students each year from about 40 schools, and uses teams of employees and interns to build GE's brand at each school. Similarly, IBM has 10 recruiting staff who focus on improving the results of IBM's on-campus recruiting efforts.[82]

Campus recruiting has two main problems. First, it's expensive. Schedules must be set well in advance, company brochures printed, and much recruiting time spent on campus. Second, even more than usual, the recruiter must be personable and effective.[83] Students complain that some recruiters are unprepared, show little interest, act superior, and don't know what to ask.

Campus recruiters should have two goals. The main goal is determining whether a candidate is worthy of further consideration. Exactly which traits you look for depends on your specific recruiting needs. However, the checklist in Figure 3-8 is typical. Traits to assess include motivation, communication skills, education, appearance, and attitude.

The second aim is to attract ("recruit") good candidates to your firm. A sincere and informal attitude, respect for the applicant, and prompt follow-up letters can help here.

INTERNSHIPS   Many college students get their jobs through college internships, a recruiting approach that has grown dramatically.

Internships can be win-win. For students, an internship may mean being able to hone business skills, check out potential employers, and learn more about their career

Candidate Evaluation Form

Interviewer _____   Date _____
Candidate
Name _____   Position _____

Scoring

Candidate evaluation forms are to be completed by the interviewer to rank the candidate's overall qualifications for the position to which they have applied. Under each heading the interviewer should give the candidate a numerical rating and write specific job-related comments in the space provided. The numerical rating system is based on the following.

5 - Exceptional	4 - Above Average	3 - Average	2 - Satisfactory	1 - Unsatisfactory

Educational Background - Does the candidate have the appropriate educational qualifications or training for this position?

Rating: 1 2 3 4 5

Comments:

Prior Work Experience - Has the candidate acquired similar skills or qualifications through past work experiences?

Rating: 1 2 3 4 5

Comments:

Technical Qualifications/Experience - Does the candidate have the technical skills necessary for this position?

Rating: 1 2 3 4 5

Comments:

Verbal Communication - How were the candidate's communication skills during the interview (i.e. body language, answers to questions)?

Rating: 1 2 3 4 5

Comments:

Candidate Enthusiasm - How much interest did the candidate show in the position and the company?

Rating: 1 2 3 4 5

Comments:

Knowledge of Company - Did the candidate research the company prior to the interview?

Rating: 1 2 3 4 5

Comments:

FIGURE 3-8 Candidate Evaluation Form for On/Off Campus Use.   *Source:* "Interview: Candidate Evaluation Form #2" from SHRM Online: Sample HR Forms. © 2012 by SHRM. Reprinted with permission.

(continued)

Teambuilding/Interpersonal Skills - Did the candidate demonstrate, through their answers, good teambuilding/interpersonal skills?

Rating: 1 2 3 4 5

Comments:

Initiative - Did the candidate demonstrate, through their answers, a high degree of initiative?

Rating: 1 2 3 4 5

Comments:

Time Management - Did the candidate demonstrate, through their answers, good time management skills?

Rating: 1 2 3 4 5

Comments:

Customer Service - Did the candidate demonstrate, through their answers, a high level of customer service skills/abilities?

Rating: 1 2 3 4 5

Comments:

Salary Expectations - What were the candidate's salary expectations? Were they within the range for the position?

Rating: 1 2 3 4 5

Comments:

Overall Impression and Recommendation - Final comments and recommendations for proceeding with the candidate.

Rating: 1 2 3 4 5

Comments:

FIGURE 3-8 Continued

likes (and dislikes). Employers can use the interns to make useful contributions while evaluating them as possible full-time employees. A recent study found that about 60% of internships turned into job offers.[84]

Collaborating with a college or university's career center facilitates on-campus recruiting.[85] The Shell Group of companies reduced the schools its recruiters visit to 26, based on things such as academic program quality, number of students enrolled, and student body diversity.[86] Employers who send effective recruiters to campus and build relationships with opinion leaders such as career counselors and professors have better recruiting results.[87]

Outsourcing and Offshoring

Rather than bringing people in to do the company's jobs, outsourcing and offshoring send the jobs out. *Outsourcing* means having outside vendors supply services (such as benefits management) or perform jobs that the company's own employees previously did in-house. *Offshoring* is a narrower term. It means having outside employees *abroad* supply services that the company's own employees previously did in-house.

Outsourcing and offshoring are contentious. Particularly in challenging economic times, employees, unions, legislators, and even many business owners feel that "shipping jobs out" (particularly overseas) is ill-advised. That notwithstanding, employers are sending more jobs out, and not just blue-collar jobs. But rising overseas wages, higher oil prices, and quality issues are prompting more U.S. employers to bring their jobs home.[88]

Referrals and Walk-Ins as a Source of Candidates

With *employee referrals* campaigns, the firm posts announcements of openings and requests for referrals on its intranet and bulletin boards. It may offer prizes for referrals that culminate in hiring.

Employee referral programs have pros and cons. The biggest advantage is that referrals tend to generate "more applicants, more hires, and a higher yield ratio [hires/applicants]."[89] Current employees usually do provide accurate information about the applicants they refer, and those hired through referrals subsequently tend to be among the lower turnover employees.[90] The new employees may also come with a more realistic picture of the employer after speaking with friends who work there. Referral programs may also result in higher-quality candidates, insofar as employees are reluctant to refer less-qualified candidates. But the success of the campaign depends on morale. And the campaign can backfire if an employee's referral is rejected. Using referrals exclusively may also be discriminatory if most of your current employees (and their referrals) are, say, white.

Employee referral programs are popular. For example, health care giant Kaiser Permanente says, "Our employee referral program encourages you to introduce your talented friends, family members, or former colleagues to career opportunities at Kaiser Permanente." Referring someone can produces bonuses of $3,000 or more.[91] As one head of recruiting says, "Quality people know quality people."[92]

WALK-INS   Particularly for hourly workers, *walk-ins*—direct applications made at your office—are a major source of applicants, and you can even encourage them by posting "for hire" signs on your property. Treat all walk-ins courteously, for the sake of both common decency and your firm's reputation. Many employers thus give every walk-in a brief interview, even if it is only to get information in case a position should open in the future. If possible, all applicants should also receive a response, preferably a personalized one.[93]

Don't underestimate the importance of employee referrals. One review of recruitment sources concluded, for instance, "Referrals by current personnel, in-house job postings, and the rehiring of former employees are the most effective [recruiting] sources. Walk-ins have been slightly less effective, and the least effective sources are newspaper ads, school placement services, and employment agencies (government/private)."[94]

CUSTOMERS AS CANDIDATES   The Container Store uses a successful variant of the employee referrals campaign. They train their employees to recruit new employees from among the firm's customers. For example, if an employee sees that a customer seems interested in the Container Store, the employee might say, "If you love shopping here, you'd love working here."[95]

TELECOMMUTERS   Hiring "telecommuters" is another option. For example, JetBlue Airways uses at-home agents who are JetBlue employees to handle its reservation needs. These "crew members" all live in the Salt Lake City area, and work from their homes. They use JetBlue-assigned computers and technology.[96]

UNEMPLOYED PEOPLE   The Equal Employment Opportunity Commission has noted that many employers are discriminating against unemployed people. The EEOC refers to "[s]tories suggesting systematic exclusion, often blatant, of unemployed workers…").[97] Some employers seem to assume (based on little or no real evidence) that those out of work would not have been let go, or would already be working, if they were competent. In fact, this is not the case. For example, many employers are hiving off whole divisions for purely strategic reasons, and with them those units' employees. The bottom line is that employers should assess every applicant's fit for the job using defensible selection criteria, not baseless assumptions.

Military Personnel

Returning and discharged U.S. military personnel provide an excellent source of trained recruits. Several military branches have programs to facilitate soldiers finding jobs. For example, the U.S. Army's Partnership for Youth Success enables someone entering the army to select a post-army corporate partner for an employment interview, as a way to help soldiers find jobs after leaving the army.[98]

Recruiting a More Diverse Workforce

The composition of the U.S. workforce is changing. More employees will be older, minorities, and women. This means taking special steps to recruit older workers, minorities, and women.

Many factors contribute to successful diversity recruiting. For example, flexible hours make it easier to attract single parents. Overall, the important thing is to take steps that say, "This is a good place for diverse employees to work." This might include using diverse ads, emphasizing inclusiveness in policy statements, and using minority and female recruiters.[99]

The basic aim is to unearth diverse applicants with the desired qualities (such as cognitive ability and conscientiousness). So, for example, seek out candidates based on academic achievement information such as dean's lists. Google posted math puzzles on large signs in subway stations in major cities. When people who solved the puzzles followed a Web link, Google encouraged them to submit résumés.[100]

OLDER WORKERS AS A SOURCE OF CANDIDATES   Employers are looking to older workers as a source of recruits, for several reasons. Because of recessions, buyouts, and early retirements, many workers who retired early want to reenter the job market. Furthermore, the number of retirees is rising as the baby boom generation retires, and employers are having trouble replacing them with younger workers. A survey by the American Association of Retired Persons (AARP) and the Society for Human Resource

Management (SHRM) concluded that older workers actually tend to have lower absenteeism and more reliability than younger workers do.[101]

Recruiting and attracting older workers involve any or all of the usual recruiting sources but with one big difference.[102] The most effective ads here emphasize schedule flexibility.[103] For example, at one company, workers over age 65 can shorten their work schedules; another company uses "mini-shifts" to accommodate those interested in working less than full time.[104]

RECRUITING SINGLE PARENTS About two-thirds of all single parents are in the workforce, so they represent an important source of candidates.

Formulating an effective program for attracting single parents begins with understanding the problems that they face in balancing work and family life. In one survey, working single parents (most are single mothers) described as a no-win situation the challenge of having to both do a good job at work and be a good parent. However, most were hesitant to dwell on their single-parent status at work for fear that such disclosures would jeopardize their jobs.[105] Therefore the first step in attracting (and keeping) single parents is to make the workplace user-friendly. Many firms institute *flextime* programs (such as 1-hour windows at the beginning or end of the day), but these "may not be sufficient to really make a difference."[106] Accountants Deloitte and Touche instituted a "Career Customization Program." Employees periodically complete short surveys indicating whether they want to "maintain," "dial up," or "dial down" their hours and responsibilities. They then work with their managers to reformulate their responsibilities.[107]

Supervisor training is important: "Very often, the relationships which the single mother has with her supervisor and co-workers is a significant factor influencing whether the single-parent employee perceives the work environment to be supportive."[108]

RECRUITING MINORITIES AND WOMEN The same prescriptions apply to recruiting minorities and women. In other words, employers have to formulate plans for attracting minorities and women, including reevaluating personnel policies and developing flexible work options.

To the extent that some minority applicants may not meet the educational or experience standards for a job, many companies (such as Aetna Life & Casualty) offer remedial training in arithmetic and writing. Recruiting via online diversity data banks or minority-focused recruiting publications are other options. Checking with your own minority employees can also be useful. The *Global Issues* box provides an additional perspective.

Sometimes the easiest way to recruit women and minorities is to avoid losing them in the first place. For example, the accounting firm KPMG works to make sure female employees on maternity leave want to return. It sends expectant mothers a basket containing a description of its parental leave benefits as well as a baby bottle, a rattle, and a tiny "My mom works at KPMG" T-shirt.[109]

WELFARE-TO-WORK Employers also implement various "welfare-to-work" programs for attracting and assimilating as new employees former welfare recipients.

The key to such programs' success is the employer's pretraining assimilation program. During these, participants receive counseling and basic skills training spread

---

GLOBAL ISSUES IN HR

The Global Talent Search

You don't have to be a multinational to have to recruit abroad. Desperate for qualified nurses, many hospitals (such as Sinai and Northwest hospitals in Maryland) are recruiting in the Philippines and China.[110] Furthermore, today, employers recognize that with business increasingly multinational, "every employee needs to have a certain level of global awareness."[111]

For example, at the U.S. headquarters of Tetra PAK, Inc., the HR manager reportedly looks for expatriate potential every time she makes a hire: "We're interested in people who eventually could relocate internationally and handle that adjustment well."[112] International experience (including internships and travel abroad) as well as language proficiency are two of the things employers may look for.

---

over several weeks.[113] For example, Marriott hired 600 welfare recipients under its Pathways to Independence program. The heart of the program was a 6-week preemployment training program. This taught work and life skills and was designed to rebuild workers' self-esteem and instill positive attitudes about work.[114]

THE DISABLED   The disabled typically suffer relatively high unemployment rates. For example in January 2012, 12.9% of disabled were unemployed, compared to 8.7% of non-disabled. [115]

However, it doesn't have to be that way. Thousands of employers in the United States and elsewhere have found that disabled employees provide an excellent and largely untapped source of competent, productive labor for jobs ranging from information technology to creative advertising to receptionist.

DEVELOPING AND USING APPLICATION FORMS

Purpose of Application Forms

Once you have a pool of applicants, the selection process can begin, and for most employers the application form is the first step in this process. (Some firms first require a brief, prescreening interview.) The **application form** is a form for quickly collecting verifiable (and therefore reasonably accurate) historical data (education, prior work history, and so on) from the candidate.

A filled-in form provides five types of information. First are data on *substantive matters*, such as does the applicant have the required education? Second, you can draw some conclusions about the applicant's *career progress*. Third, you can draw tentative conclusions regarding the applicant's *employment stability*. (However, with recent recessions and downsizings, this is a dubious gauge.) Fourth, it provides information to *check references* and to assess the veracity of the applicant's answers.

Finally, employers use application information ("biodata") to *predict* employee tenure and performance. Thus in one study, researchers found that applicants who had longer tenure with previous employers were less likely to quit and had higher performance 6 months after hire.[116] Examples of biodata items include "quit a job without giving notice," and "graduated from college."[117]

Most employers need several application forms. For technical and managerial personnel, the form may require detailed answers concerning such areas as education. The form for hourly factory workers might focus on tools and equipment the applicant used.

APPLICANT EXAGGERATION   Job applicants often exaggerate their qualifications.[118] The most common exaggerations concern education and job experience. A majority of graduating seniors reportedly believe that employers expect a degree of exaggeration on résumés. Therefore, always ensure applicants complete the form and sign a statement on it indicating that the information is true. The court will almost always support a discharge for falsifying information when applying for work.[119] Some applicants simply scribble "see résumé attached" on the application. This is not acceptable. You need the signed, completed form.

Equal Opportunity and Application Forms

Employers should carefully review their application forms to ensure they comply with equal employment laws. Questions concerning race, religion, age, sex, or national origin aren't necessarily illegal under federal laws, but are illegal under some state laws. But if the applicant shows that the questions screen out a disproportionate number of protected group applicants, the employer will have to prove that the potentially discriminatory items are related to success on the job and not unfairly discriminatory. One survey of 41 Internet-based applications found that over 97% contained at least one inadvisable question. Questions regarding the applicant's age and driver's license information led the list.[120]

Figure 3-9 presents the FBI application. Note that in signing the application, good practice dictates that the applicant certifies several things. For example, that falsified statements may be cause for dismissal; that investigation of credit, employment, and driving records is authorized; that drug screening tests may be required; and that employment is for no definite period of time.

MANDATORY DISPUTE RESOLUTION   Although the EEOC is generally opposed, more employers are requiring applicants to sign mandatory alternative dispute resolution forms as part of the application process. These generally require applicants to agree to arbitrate certain legal disputes related to their application for employment or employment with the company. Courts, federal agencies, and even arbitrators are concerned that binding arbitration strips away too many employees' rights (*voluntary* arbitration is not under attack).[121]

After You Receive the Application

After you receive the application, screening the applicants begins, and we turn to selection and screening in Chapter 4. Here you'll review the applicant's résumé and application, as well as any other information you've gleaned during the screening process.

COURTESY   Some employers develop expensive recruiting programs and then drop the ball by treating applicants discourteously. A Monster.com survey illustrates this. What interviewer behaviors most annoyed job seekers? Seventy percent of job seekers listed, "Acting as if there is no time to talk to me." About half listed "turning interview into cross-examination" and "showing up late."[122]

FEDERAL BUREAU OF INVESTIGATION

**Preliminary Application for
Special Agent Position
(Please Type or Print in Black Ink)**

Date: _____

FIELD OFFICE USE ONLY
Right Thumb Print

Div: _____   Program: _____

I. PERSONAL HISTORY

Name in Full   (Last, First, Middle)

List College Degree(s) Already Received or Pursuing, Major, School, and Month/Year:

Marital Status: ☐ Single ☐ Engaged ☐ Married ☐ Separated ☐ Legally Separated ☐ Widowed ☐ Divorced

Birth Date (Month, Day, Year)
Birth Place:

Social Security Number: (Optional)

Do you understand FBI employment requires availability for assignment anywhere in the U.S.?

Current Address

Home Phone _____

| Street | Apt. No. | Area Code | Number |

Work Phone _____

| City | State | Zip Code | Area Code | Number |

Are you: CPA ☐ Yes ☐ No   Licensed Driver ☐ Yes ☐ No   U. S. Citizen ☐ Yes ☐ No

Have you served on active duty in the U. S. Military? ☐ Yes ☐ No If yes, indicate branch of service and dates (month/year) of active duty. Include military school attendance (month/year):

How did you learn or become interested in FBI employment as a Special Agent?

Have you previously applied for FBI employment? ☐ Yes ☐ No
If yes, location and date:

Do you have a foreign language background? ☐ Yes ☐ No   List proficiency for each language on reverse side.

Have you ever been arrested for any crime (include major traffic violations such as Driving Under the Influence or While Intoxicated, etc.)?
☐ Yes ☐ No If so, list all such matters on a continuation sheet, even if not formally charged, or no court appearance or found not guilty, or matter settled by payment of fine or forfeiture of collateral. Include date, place, charge, disposition, details, and police agency on reverse side.

II. EMPLOYMENT HISTORY

Identify your most recent three years FULL-TIME work experience, after high school (excluding summer, part-time and temporary employment).

From Month/Year	To Month/Year	Title of Position and Description of Work	# of hrs. Per week	Name/Location of Employer

III. PERSONAL DECLARATIONS

Persons with a disability who require an accommodation to complete the application process are required to notify the FBI of their need for the accommodation.

Have you used marijuana during the last three years or more than 15 times? ☐ Yes ☐ No

Have you used any illegal drug(s) or combination of illegal drugs, other than marijuana, more than 5 times or during the last 10 years? ☐ Yes ☐ No

All information provided by applicants concerning their drug history will be subject to verification by a preemployment polygraph examination.

Do you understand all prospective FBI employees will be required to submit to an urinalysis for drug abuse prior to employment? ☐ Yes ☐ No

Please do not write below this line.

I am aware that willfully withholding information or making false statements on this application constitutes a violation of Section 1001. Title 18, U.S. Code and if appointed, will be the basis for dismissal from the Federal Bureau of Investigation. I agree to these conditions and I hereby certify that all statements made by me on this application are true and complete, to the best of my knowledge.

Signature of applicant as usually written (**Do Not Use Nickname**)

FIGURE 3-9 Employment Application.

REVIEW

Summary

1. Employers today often view all the staff–train–reward activities as part of a single integrated *talent management* process. We defined talent management as the *goal-oriented* and *integrated* process of *planning, recruiting, developing, managing, and compensating* employees. When a manager takes a talent management perspective, he or she should keep in mind that the talent management tasks are parts of a single interrelated talent management process, make sure talent management decisions such as staffing and pay are goal-directed, consistently use the same "profile" for formulating recruitment plans for a job as you do for making selection, training, appraisal, and payment decisions for it, actively segment and manage employees, and integrate/coordinate all the talent management functions.

2. Developing an organization structure results in jobs that have to be staffed. Job analysis is the procedure through which you find out (1) what the job entails and (2) what kinds of people should be hired for the job. It involves six steps: (1) Determine the use of the job analysis information, (2) collect background information, (3) select the positions to be analyzed, (4) collect job analysis data, (5) review information with participants, and (6) develop a job description and job specification.

3. A good policy is to ask: Will the new employee understand the job if he or she reads the job description?

4. The job specification supplements the job description to answer the question: What human traits and experience are necessary to do this job well? It tells what kind of person to recruit and for what qualities that person should be tested. Job specifications are based on the educated guesses of managers or on statistical analysis.

5. Increasingly, firms don't want employees to feel limited by a specific set of responsibilities such as those listed in a job description. As a result, more employers are deemphasizing detailed job descriptions, often substituting summaries of the competencies or skills required for the position.

6. Developing personnel plans requires three forecasts: one for personnel requirements, one for the supply of outside candidates, and one for the supply of inside candidates. To predict the need for personnel, first project the demand for the product or service. Next relate personnel needs to these estimates.

7. Once personnel needs are projected, the next step is to build a pool of qualified applicants. We discussed several sources of candidates, including internal sources, the Web, advertising, employment agencies, executive recruiters, college recruiting, and referrals and walk-ins.

8. Once you have a pool of applicants, the work of selecting the best can begin. We turn to employee selection in the Chapter 4.

Key Terms

talent management *59*
job analysis *60*
job description *60*
job specification *60*
workforce planning *67*
trend analysis *69*

ratio analysis *69*
scatter plot *69*
qualifications inventory *71*
personnel replacement
   chart *71*

predictive workforce
   monitoring *73*
job posting *75*
application form *86*

Discussion Questions

1. What items are typically included in a job description? What items are not shown?
2. What is job analysis? How can you make use of the information it provides?
3. We discussed several methods for collecting job analysis data. Compare these methods, explain what each is useful for, and list the pros and cons of each.
4. Explain how you would conduct a job analysis.
5. Compare five sources of job candidates.
6. What types of information can an application form provide?

Individual and Group Activities

1. Bring to class several classified and display ads from the Sunday help wanted ads. Analyze the effectiveness of these ads.
2. Working individually or in groups, develop a 5-year forecast of occupational market conditions for an occupation such as accountant or nurse.
3. Working individually or in groups, visit the local office of your state employment agency. Come back to class prepared to discuss the following questions: What types of jobs seem to be available through this agency, predominantly? To what extent do you think this agency would be a good source of professional and/or managerial applicants? What sorts of paperwork are applicants to the state agency required to complete before their applications are processed? What other services does the office provide?
4. Working individually or in groups, interview a manager between the ages of 25 and 35 at a local business who manages employees age 40 or older. Ask the manager to describe three or four of his or her most challenging experiences managing older employees.
5. Working individually or in groups, review help wanted ads placed over the past few Sundays by local employment agencies. Do some employment agencies seem to specialize in some types of jobs? If you were an HR manager, which local agencies would you turn to first, based on their help wanted ad history, for these jobs: engineers, secretaries, accountants, and factory workers?
6. Working individually or in groups, obtain copies of job descriptions for clerical positions at the college or university you attend or the firm where you work. How would you improve the descriptions?

APPLICATION EXERCISES

CASE INCIDENT

Finding People Who Are Passionate about What They Do

Trilogy Enterprises Inc. provides software solutions to giant global firms for improving sales and performance. It prides itself on its unique and unorthodox culture.

There is no dress code and employees make their own hours, often very long. They tend to socialize together (the average age is 26), both in the office's well-stocked kitchen and on company-sponsored events and trips to places like local dance clubs and retreats in Hawaii. An in-house jargon has developed, and the shared history of the firm has taken on the status of legend. Responsibility is heavy and comes early, with a "just do it now" attitude that dispenses with long apprenticeships. New recruits are given a few weeks of intensive training, known as Trilogy University and described by participants as "more like boot camp than business school." Information is delivered as if with "a fire hose," and new employees are expected to commit their expertise and vitality to everything they do. Jeff Daniel, director of college recruiting, admits the intense and unconventional firm is not for everybody. "But it's definitely an environment where people who are passionate about what they do can thrive."

The firm employs about 700 such passionate people. Trilogy's managers know the rapid growth they seek depends on having a staff of the best people they can find, quickly trained and given broad responsibility and freedom as soon as possible. CEO Joe Liemandt says, "At a software company, people are everything. You can't build the next great software company, which is what we're trying to do here, unless you're totally committed to that. Of course, the leaders at every company say, 'People are everything.' But they don't act on it."

Trilogy makes finding the right people (it calls them "great people") a company-wide mission. Recruiters actively pursue the freshest people in the job market, scouring college career fairs and computer science departments for talented overachievers with ambition and entrepreneurial instincts. Top managers conduct the first rounds of interviews, letting prospects know they will be pushed to achieve but will be well rewarded. Employees take top recruits and their significant others out on the town when they come to Austin for the 3-day preliminary visit. A typical day might begin with grueling interviews but end with mountain biking or laser tag. Executives have been known to fly out to meet and woo hot prospects.

One year, Trilogy reviewed 15,000 résumés, conducted 4,000 on-campus interviews, flew 850 prospects in for interviews, and hired 262 college graduates, who account for over a third of its current employees. The cost per hire was $13,000; Jeff Daniel believes it was worth every penny.

QUESTIONS

1. Identify some of the established recruiting techniques that underlie Trilogy's unconventional approach to attracting talent.
2. What particular elements of Trilogy's culture most likely appeal to the kind of employees it seeks? How does it convey those elements to job prospects?
3. Would Trilogy be an appealing employer for you? Why or why not?
4. What suggestions would you make to Trilogy for improving its recruiting processes?

Sources: Chuck Salter, "Insanity, Inc.," *Fast Company* (January 1999): 101–108; and www.trilogy.com/careers.php, accessed May 18, 2010.

CONTINUING CASE

Carter Cleaning Company

Getting Better Applicants

If you were to ask Jennifer and her father what the main problem was in running their firm, their answer would be quick and short: hiring good people. Originally begun as a string of coin-operated laundromats requiring virtually no skilled help, the chain grew to six stores, each heavily dependent on skilled managers, cleaner/spotters, and pressers. Employees generally have no more than a high school education (often less), and the market for them is very competitive. Over a typical weekend, literally dozens of want ads for experienced pressers or cleaner/spotters can be found in area newspapers. All these people usually are paid around $15 per hour, and they change jobs frequently. Jennifer and her father thus face the continuing task of recruiting and hiring qualified workers out of a pool of individuals they feel are almost nomadic in their propensity to move from area to area and job to job. Turnover in their stores (as in the stores of many of their competitors) often approaches 400%. "Don't talk to me about human resources planning and trend analysis," says Jennifer. "We're fighting an economic war and I'm happy just to be able to round up enough live applicants to be able to keep my trenches fully manned."

In light of this problem, Jennifer's father asked her to answer the following questions, and she would like to know what you would do:

QUESTIONS

1. First, how would you recommend we go about reducing the turnover in our stores?
2. Provide a detailed list of recommendations concerning how we should go about increasing our pool of acceptable job applicants so we no longer face the need to hire almost anyone who walks in the door. (Your recommendations regarding the latter should include completely worded online and hard-copy advertisements and recommendations regarding any other recruiting strategies you would suggest we use.)

EXPERIENTIAL EXERCISE

The Nursing Shortage

As of March 2012, the U.S. economy was improving in some respects, but unemployment was still high, and employers were still holding back on their hiring. However, while many people were unemployed, that was not the case with nurses. Virtually every hospital was aggressively recruiting nurses. Many were turning to foreign-trained nurses, for example, by recruiting nurses in the Philippines. Experts expected nurses to be in very short supply for years to come.

Purpose: The purpose of this exercise is to give you experience creating a recruitment program.

Required Understanding: You should be thoroughly familiar with the contents of this chapter, and with the nurse recruitment program of a hospital such as Lenox Hill Hospital in New York (see www.lenoxhillhospital.org/nursing/index.jsp, accessed March 4, 2012).

How to Set Up the Exercise/Instructions: If so desired, divide the class into teams. The groups should work separately and should not converse with each other. Each group should address the following tasks:

1. Based on information available on the hospital's website, create a hard-copy ad for the hospital to place in the Sunday edition of the *New York Times*. Which (geographic) editions of the *Times* would you use and why?
2. Analyze and critique the hospital's current online nurses' ad. How would you improve on it?
3. Prepare in outline form a complete nurses' recruiting program for this hospital, including all recruiting sources your group would use.

APPENDIX

Enrichment Topics in Job Analysis

ADDITIONAL JOB ANALYSIS METHODS

Job Analysis Record Sheet

You may encounter several other job analysis methods. Thus the U.S. Civil Service Commission has a standardized procedure for comparing and classifying jobs. Information is compiled on a *job analysis record sheet*. Identifying information (such as job title) and a brief summary of the job are listed first. Next list the job's tasks in order of importance. Then, for each task, specify such things as the knowledge required (for example, the principles the worker must be acquainted with to do his or her job), skills required (for example, the skills needed to operate machines), and abilities required (for example, mathematical, reasoning or interpersonal abilities).

Position Analysis Questionnaire

The position analysis questionnaire (PAQ) is a very structured job analysis questionnaire. The PAQ is filled in by a job analyst, who should be acquainted with the job to be analyzed. The PAQ contains 194 items, each of which (such as "written materials") represents a basic element that may play a role in the job. The job analyst decides whether the employee uses each of those 194 elements, and to what extent. Thus Figure A3-1 lists a few of the items a worker might use as visual sources of job information, such as Written Materials, and Pictorial Materials. So, for instance, "Written materials" here might receive a rating of 5, indicating that written materials (such as books, reports, office notes) play a very substantial role in this job.

The PAQ's advantage is that it provides a quantitative score for any job by enabling the analyst to add up the scores assigned for all the job's items. The PAQ thereby lets you assign a single quantitative score or value to each job. You can therefore use the PAQ results to compare jobs relative to one another; you can then use this information to assign pay levels for each job.

U.S. Department of Labor Procedure

The U.S. Department of Labor (DOL) procedure also aims to provide a standardized method *for quantitatively comparing different jobs.* The heart of this analysis is a rating of each job in terms of *data, people,* and *things.* As illustrated in Table A3-1, a set of basic activities called *worker functions* describes what a worker can do with respect to data, people, and things. With respect to *data*, for instance, the basic functions include synthesizing, coordinating, and copying. Note also that each worker function has been assigned an importance level. Thus "coordinating" is 1, and "copying" is 5. If you were analyzing the job of a receptionist/clerk, for example, you might label the job 5, 6, 7, which would represent copying data, speaking/signaling people, and handling things.

A PRACTICAL JOB ANALYSIS METHOD

Without their own job analysts or (in many cases) HR managers, many small-business owners and managers face two hurdles when doing job analyses and job descriptions. First, they often need a more streamlined approach than those provided by questionnaires like the one shown in Figure A3-2. Second, there is always the reasonable fear that in writing their job descriptions, they will overlook duties that subordinates should be assigned. What they need is a source listing positions they might encounter, including a listing of the duties normally assigned to these positions.

A. Information Input

A1. Visual Sources of Job Information

Using the response scale at the left, rate each of the following items on the basis of the extent to which it is used by the worker as a source of information in performing the job.

Extent of Use

0 Does not apply
1 Nominal/very infrequent
2 Occasional
3 Moderate
4 Considerable
5 Very substantial

1. Written materials
E.g., books, reports, office notes, articles, job instructions, or signs

2. Quantitative materials
Materials that deal with quantities or amounts, e.g., graphs, accounts, specifications, or tables of numbers

3. Pictorial materials
Pictures or picture-like materials used as sources of information, e.g., drawings, blueprints, diagrams, maps, tracings, photographic films, x-ray films, or TV pictures

4. Patterns or related devices
E.g., templates, stencils, or patterns used as sources of information when observed during use (Do not include materials described in item 3.)

5. Visual displays
E.g., dials, gauges, signal lights, radarscopes, speedometers, or clocks

6. Measuring devices
E.g., rules, calipers, tire pressure gauges, scales, thickness gauges, pipettes, thermometers, or protractors used to obtain visual information about physical measurements (Do not include devices described in item 5.)

7. Mechanical devices
E.g., tools, equipment, or machinery that are sources of information when observed during use or operation

FIGURE A3-1 Portion of a Completed Page from the Position Analysis Questionnaire.   *Source:* Reprinted by permission of PAQ Services, Inc.

TABLE A3-1	Basic U.S. Department of Labor (DOL) Procedure Worker Functions	
Data	**People**	**Things**
0 Synthesizing	0 Mentoring	0 Setting up
1 Coordinating	1 Negotiating	1 Precision working
2 Analyzing	2 Instructing	2 Operating/controlling
3 Compiling	3 Supervising	3 Driving/operating
4 Computing	4 Diverting	4 Manipulating
5 Copying	5 Persuading	5 Tending
6 Comparing	6 Speaking/signaling	6 Feeding/offbearing
	7 Serving	7 Handling
	8 Taking instructions/helping	

Note: Determine employee's job "score" on data, people, and things by observing his or her job and determining, for each of the three categories, which of the basic functions best reflects the person's job. "0" is high; "6," "8," and "7" are lows in each column.

Job Analysis Information Sheet

Job Title_____ Date _____

Job Code_____ Dept. _____

Superior's Title _____

Hours worked _____ AM to _____ PM

Job Analyst's Name _____

    1. **What is the job's overall purpose?**

    _____

    2. **If the incumbent supervises others,** list them by job title; if there is more than one employee with the same title, put the number in parentheses following.

    _____

    _____

    3. **Check those activities** that are part of the incumbent's supervisory duties.

        ☐ Training

        ☐ Performance appraisal

        ☐ Inspecting work

        ☐ Budgeting

        ☐ Coaching and/or counseling

        ☐ Others (please specify) _____

    4. **Describe the type and extent of supervision** received by the incumbent.

    _____

    5. **JOB DUTIES:** Describe briefly WHAT the incumbent does and, if possible, HOW he/she does it. Include duties in the following categories:

        a. daily duties (those performed on a regular basis every day or almost every day)

        _____

        b. periodic duties (those performed weekly, monthly, quarterly, or at other regular intervals)

        _____

        c. duties performed at irregular intervals

        _____

    6. Is the incumbent performing duties he/she considers unnecessary? If so, describe.

    _____

    7. Is the incumbent performing duties not presently included in the job description? If so, describe.

    _____

    8. **EDUCATION:** Check the box that indicates the educational requirements for the job (*not* the educational background of the incumbent).

        ☐ No formal education required   ☐ Eighth grade education

        ☐ High school diploma (or equivalent)   ☐ 2-year college degree (or equivalent)

        ☐ 4-year college degree (or equivalent)   ☐ graduate work or advanced degree (specify:)

        ☐ professional license (specify:)

FIGURE A3-2 Job Analysis Questionnaire for Developing Job Descriptions. *Use a questionnaire like this to interview job incumbents, or have them fill it out.* Source: Reprinted with permission of the publisher, Business and Legal Resources Inc. Copyright 2012 Business and Legal Resources, Inc.

(continued)

9. **EXPERIENCE**: Check the amount of experience needed to perform the job.

☐ None   ☐ Less than one month

☐ One to six months   ☐ Six months to one year

☐ One to three years   ☐ Three to five years

☐ Five to ten years   ☐ More than ten years

10. **LOCATION:** Check location of job and, if necessary or appropriate, describe briefly.

☐ Outdoor   ☐ Indoor

☐ Underground   ☐ Pit

☐ Scaffold   ☐ Other (specify)

11. **ENVIRONMENTAL CONDITIONS:** Check any objectionable conditions found on the job and note afterward how frequently each is encountered (rarely, occasionally, constantly, etc.)

☐ Dirt   ☐ Dust

☐ Heat   ☐ Cold

☐ Noise   ☐ Fumes

☐ Odors   ☐ Wetness/humidity

☐ Vibration   ☐ Sudden temperature changes

☐ Darkness or poor lighting   ☐ Other (specify)

12. **HEALTH AND SAFETY**: Check any undesirable health and safety conditions under which the incumbent must perform and note how often they are encountered.

☐ Elevated workplace   ☐ Mechanical hazards

☐ Explosives   ☐ Electrical hazards

☐ Fire hazards   ☐ Radiation

☐ Other (specify)

13. **MACHINES, TOOLS, EQUIPMENT, AND WORK AIDS**: Describe briefly what machines, tools, equipment, or work aids the incumbent works with on a regular basis:

_____

_____

14. Have concrete work standards been established (errors allowed, time taken for a particular task, etc.)? If so, what are they?

_____

15. Are there any personal attributes (special aptitudes, physical characteristics, personality traits, etc.) required by the job?

_____

16. Are there any exceptional problems the incumbent might be expected to encounter in performing the job under normal conditions? If so, describe.

_____

17. Describe the successful completion and/or end results of the job.

_____

18. What is the seriousness of error on this job? Who or what is affected by errors the incumbent makes?

_____

19. To what job would a successful incumbent expect to be promoted?

[*Note*: This form is obviously slanted toward a manufacturing environment. But it can be adapted quite easily to fit a number of different types of jobs.]

FIGURE A3-2 Continued

Help is at hand: The small-business owner has at least two options. Websites like www.jobdescription.com provide customizable descriptions by title and industry. The Department of Labor's O*NET is second alternative. We focus here on using O*NET for creating job descriptions.

Step 1. Decide on a Plan

Start by developing at least the outline of a business plan. What do you expect your sales revenue to be next year and in the next few years? What products do you intend to emphasize? What areas or departments in your company do you think will have to be expanded, reduced, or consolidated, given where you plan to go with your firm over the next few years? What kinds of new positions do you think you'll need to accomplish your goals?

Step 2. Develop an Organization Chart

Next, develop a company organization chart. Show who reports to each of the managers and supervisors in the firm. Start by drawing up the organization chart as it is now. Then, produce a chart showing how you'd like your chart to look in the immediate future (say, in 2 months) and perhaps other charts showing how you'd like your organization to evolve over the next 2 or 3 years.

You can use several tools here. For example, Microsoft (MS) Word includes an organization charting function: On the Insert menu, click Picture, then Organization Chart. Software packages such as OrgPublisher from TimeVision of Irving, Texas, are another option.

Step 3. Use a Job Analysis/Description Questionnaire

Next, use a job analysis questionnaire to determine what each job entails. You can use one of the more comprehensive questionnaires (see Figure A3-2); however, the job description questionnaire in Figure A3-3 is a simpler and often satisfactory alternative. Fill in the required information, and then ask the supervisors and/or employees to list the job's duties (on the bottom of the page), breaking them into daily duties, periodic duties, and duties performed at irregular intervals. You can distribute a sample of one of these duties (Figure A3-4) to facilitate the process.

Step 4. Obtain Lists of Job Duties from O*NET.

The list of job duties you uncovered in the previous step may or may not be complete. We'll therefore use O*NET to compile a more comprehensive list. (Refer to Figure A3-5 for a visual example as you read along.) Start by going to www.onetonline.org (top). Click on Find Occupations. Assume you want to create job descriptions for retail salespeople. Type in Retail Sales for the Key Word. This brings you to the Quick Search Result at www.onetonline.org/find/result?s=retail+sales&g=Go (middle). Clicking on Retail Salespersons—snapshots—produces the job summary and specific occupational duties for retail salespersons at www.onetonline.org/link/summary/41-2031.00 (bottom). For a small company or department, you might want to combine the duties of the retail salesperson with those of first-line supervisors/managers of retail salespeople.

Step 5. Compile the Job's Specification from O*NET

Next, return to the Snapshot for Retail Salesperson (bottom). Instead of choosing occupation-specific information, choose, for example, Worker Experiences, Occupational Requirements, and Worker Characteristics. You can use this information to develop a job specification for the job.

Step 6. Complete Your Job Description

Finally, using Figure A3-3, write a job summary for the job. Then use the information obtained in steps 4 and 5 to create a complete listing of the tasks, duties, and human requirements of each of job you must fill.

**Background Data
for Job Description**

Job Title _____   Department _____

Job Number _____   Written By _____

Today's Date _____   Applicable Codes _____

   I. **Applicable Job Titles from O*NET:**

  II. **Job Summary:**
     (List the more important or regularly performed tasks)

 III. **Reports To:**

 IV. **Supervises:** _____

  V. **Job Duties:** _____
     (Briefly describe, for each duty, what *employee does and, if possible,* how
     *employee does it. Show in parentheses at end of each duty the approximate
     percentage of time devoted to duty.)*

     A. Daily Duties:

     B. Periodic Duties:
       (Indicate whether weekly, monthly, quarterly, etc.)

     C. Duties Performed at Irregular Intervals:

FIGURE A3-3 Job Description Questionnaire.   *Source:* Gary Dessler, PhD.

Example of Job Title: Customer Service Clerk

Example of Job Summary: Answers inquiries and gives directions to customers, authorizes cashing of customers' checks, records and returns lost charge cards, sorts and reviews new credit applications, works at customer-service desk in department store.

Example of One Job Duty: Authorizes cashing of checks: authorizes cashing of personal or payroll checks (up to a specified amount) by customers desiring to make payment by check. Requests identification, such as driver's license, from customers and examines check to verify date, amount, signature, and endorsement. Initials check and sends customer to cashier.

FIGURE A3-4 Background Data for Examples.

FIGURE A3-5 Shown in These Three Screen Captures, O*NET Easily Allows the User to Develop Job Descriptions.   *Source:* From O*NET Online, created for the U.S. Department of Labor.

Four

Testing and Selecting Employees

When you finish studying this chapter you should be able to:

- Define *basic testing concepts, including validity and reliability.*
- Discuss *at least four basic types of personnel tests.*
- Explain *the pros and cons of background investigations and preemployment information services.*
- Explain *the factors that can undermine an interview's usefulness and the techniques for eliminating them.*

OVERVIEW

Everything about the candidate looked great, except that after they hired him, they discovered he didn't really have that college degree. Recruiting is futile unless the manager has the tools to select the right employees. The main purpose of this chapter is to explain how to use the basic employee selection tools. The topics we cover include The Basics of Testing and Selecting Employees, Using Tests at Work, Interviewing Prospective Employees, and Using Other Selection Techniques.

THE BASICS OF TESTING AND SELECTING EMPLOYEES

With a pool of applicants, your next step is to select the best person for the job. This usually means using the screening tools in this chapter, including tests, background checks, and interviews.

Why Careful Selection Is Important

Selecting the right employees is important for several reasons. First, your own performance always depends on your subordinates. Employees with the right skills and attributes will do a better job for you and the company. Employees without these skills or who are obstructionist won't perform effectively, and your own performance and the firm's will suffer.

Second, you want to screen out undesirables. By some estimates, almost 25% of employees say they've had knowledge of illicit drug use among coworkers.[1] The time to screen out undesirables is before they are in the door.

Third, screening is important because of costs. Hiring and training even a clerk can cost $5,000 or more in fees and supervisory time. The total cost of hiring a manager could easily be 10 times as high, including search fees.

LEGAL IMPLICATIONS AND NEGLIGENT HIRING   Finally, selection is important because of the legal implications of incompetent hiring. For one thing, EEO legislation requires that you avoid unfairly discriminating.[2]

Furthermore, courts will find employers liable when employees with criminal records or other problems use their access to customers' homes or similar opportunities to commit crimes. Hiring workers with such backgrounds without proper safeguards is *negligent hiring*. For example, lawyers sued Walmart, alleging that several employees with criminal convictions had assaulted young customers. Walmart then instituted a program of criminal background checks.[3] Employers "must make a systematic effort to gain relevant information about the applicant, verify documentation, follow up on missing records or gaps in employment, and keep a detailed log of all attempts to obtain information."[4]

The main aim of employee selection is to achieve person-job fit. **Person-job fit** means matching (1) the knowledge, skills, abilities (KSAs), and competencies that are needed for performing the job (as determined by job analysis) with (2) the prospective employee's knowledge, skills, abilities, and competencies.

Reliability

Effective screening is therefore important and depends, to a large degree, on the basic testing concepts of validity and reliability. **Reliability** refers to the test's consistency. It is "the consistency of scores obtained by the same person when retested with the identical tests or with an equivalent form of a test."[5] Test reliability is essential: If a person scored 90 on an intelligence test on Monday and 130 when retested on Tuesday, you probably wouldn't trust the test.

There are several ways to estimate a test's consistency or reliability. You could administer the same test to the same people at two different points in time, comparing their test scores at Time 2 and Time 1; this would be a *retest estimate*. Or you could administer a test and then administer an equivalent test later; this would be an *equivalent-form estimate.* The Scholastic Aptitude Test is an example.

A test's internal consistency is another reliability measure. For example, assume you have 10 items on a test of vocational interests. These items are each supposed to measure the person's interest in working outdoors. You administer the test and then statistically analyze the degree to which responses to these items vary together. This would provide a measure of the internal reliability of the test; experts call this an *internal comparison estimate.* Internal consistency is one reason you often find apparently repetitive questions on tests.

Validity

Any test is a sample of a person's behavior, but some tests more clearly reflect the behavior being sampled. A typing test, for instance, clearly corresponds to an on-the-job behavior—typing. At the other extreme, there may be no apparent relationship between the test and the behavior. For example, in the Rorschach test illustrated in Figure 4-1, the person is asked to explain how he or she interprets the blurred picture. Here, it is harder to "prove" that the tests are measuring what they are purported to measure—that they are *valid.*

Test validity answers the question, does this test measure what it's supposed to measure? Stated differently, "Validity refers to the confidence one has in the meaning attached to the scores."[6] With respect to employee selection tests, the term *validity* often refers to evidence that the test is job related; in other words, that performance on the test

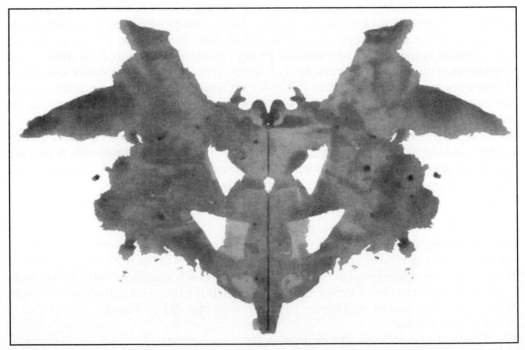

FIGURE 4-1 A Slide from the Rorschach Test.   *Source:* http://en.wikipedia.org/wiki/File:Rorschach1. jpg, accessed July 27, 2009.

is a *valid predictor* of subsequent performance on the job. A selection test must be valid because, without proof of its validity, there is no logical or legally permissible reason to continue using it.

In employment testing, there are two main ways to demonstrate a test's validity: **criterion validity** and **content validity.** Demonstrating criterion validity means demonstrating that those who do well on the test also do well on the job, and that those who do poorly on the test do poorly on the job. In psychological measurement, a *predictor* is the measurement (in this case, the test score) that you are trying to relate to a *criterion*, such as performance on the job. The term *criterion validity* comes from that terminology.

The employer demonstrates the *content validity* of a test by showing that the test constitutes a fair sample of the content of a job. For example, if the content of a typing test is a representative sample of the typist's job, then the test is probably content valid. *Construct validity* means demonstrating that (a) a selection procedure measures a construct (something believed to be an underlying human trait or characteristic, such as honesty) and (b) the construct is important for successful job performance.

How to Validate a Test

What makes a test such as the Graduate Record Examination (GRE) useful for college admissions directors?

The answer is usually that people's scores on the test have been shown to be predictive of how people perform. Thus, students who score high on the GRE usually do better in graduate school.

Strictly speaking, an employer should be sure that scores on the test are related in a predictable way to performance on the job before using that test to screen employees. You generally do this by ensuring that test scores are a good predictor of some criterion such as job performance. In other words, you should demonstrate the test's *criterion validity.* At best, invalid tests (tests not related to employee performance) are a waste of time. At worst, they may be discriminatory (if they screen out larger proportions of minority candidates). Tests you buy "off the shelf" should include information on their validity. Test publishers will generally supply information on the validity of their testing products."[7] An employer can also easily purchase an online report on a test's validity from The Buros Institute of Mental Measurements, at http://buros.unl.edu/buros/jsp/lists.jsp. But ideally, employers should revalidate the tests for the job(s) at hand. This validation process (see Figure 4-2) usually requires an industrial psychologist.

Validity Generalization

However, many employers won't find it cost-effective to conduct validity studies. These employers must identify tests and other screening tools that have been shown to be valid in other settings (companies), and then bring them in-house in the hopes that they'll be valid there, too.[8] **Validity generalization** "refers to the degree to which evidence of a measure's validity obtained in one situation can be generalized to another situation without further study."[9]

Under the Uniform Guidelines, validation of selection procedures is desirable, but the guidelines don't require users to produce evidence of validity unless adverse impact is shown to exist. "If there is no adverse impact, there is no validation requirement under the Guidelines."[10]

Step 1: Analyze the Job. First, analyze the job and write job descriptions and job specifications. Specify the human traits and skills you believe are required for adequate job performance. For example, must an applicant be aggressive? (Employers like Google and Bon-Ton Stores now use "data-mining" techniques to sift through huge amounts of employee data to find patterns and identify the traits that correlate most closely with performance and tenure). These traits become your predictors. They are the human traits and skills you believe predict success on the job.

In this first step, you must also define what you mean by "success on the job" because it is this success for which you want predictors. The standards of success are called *criteria*. You could focus on production-related criteria (quantity, quality, and so on), personnel data (absenteeism, length of service, and so on), or judgments (of worker performance by persons such as supervisors). For an assembler's job, predictors for which to test applicants might include manual dexterity and patience. Criteria that you would hope to predict with your test might then include quantity produced per hour and number of rejects produced per hour.

Step 2: Choose the Tests. Next, choose tests that you think measure the attributes (predictors) important for job success. This choice is usually based on experience, previous research, and best guesses, and you usually won't start off with just one test. Instead, you choose several tests, combining them into a test battery aimed at measuring a variety of possible predictors, such as aggressiveness, extroversion, and numeric ability.

Step 3: Administer Tests. Administer the selected test(s) to employees. Predictive validation is the most dependable way to validate a test. Here the test is administered to applicants before they are hired. Then these applicants are hired using only existing selection techniques, not the results of the new test you are developing. After they have been on the job for some time, you measure their performance and compare it to their performance on the earlier test. You can then determine whether their performance on the test could have been used to predict their subsequent job performance.

Step 4: Relate Test Scores and Criteria. Next, determine whether there is a significant relationship between scores (the predictor) and performance (the criterion). The usual way to do this is to determine the statistical relationship between scores on the test and performance through correlation analysis, which shows the degree of statistical relationship.

Step 5: Cross-Validate and Revalidate. Before putting the test into use, you may want to confirm it by cross-validating, by again performing steps 3 and 4 on a new sample of employees. At a minimum, an expert should validate the test periodically.

FIGURE 4-2 How to Validate a Test.

Bias

Bias—systematic distortion—is a potential problem in employment testing and selection. For example, there may be bias in how the test measures some trait. Thus "if test scores indicate that males perform better in verbal reasoning tasks than do females, when in fact (using other measures of verbal reasoning) they both perform equally well, the test provides a biased measure of verbal reasoning."[11] Most employers know they shouldn't use biased tests in the selection process.[12] Employers should ensure that their tests aren't producing biased decisions.[13]

Ethical and Legal Questions in Testing

EQUAL EMPLOYMENT OPPORTUNITY ASPECTS OF TESTING   We've seen that various federal and state laws bar discrimination on the basis of race, color, age, religion, sex, disability, and national origin. With respect to testing, these laws boil down to two things: (1) You must be able to prove that your tests are related to success or failure on the job, and (2) you must prove that your tests don't unfairly discriminate against either minority or nonminority subgroups. Once the plaintiff shows that one of your selection procedures has an adverse impact on his or her protected class, you must demonstrate the validity and selection fairness of the allegedly discriminatory test or item. *Adverse impact* means there is a significant measurable discrepancy between rates of rejection of members of the protected groups and others. For example, a federal court ruled that Dial Corp. discriminated against female job applicants at a meatpacking facility by requiring employees to take a preemployment strength test. The test had an adverse impact on women and there appeared to be no compelling need for strength on the job.[14]

You can't avoid EEO laws by not using tests. EEO laws apply to all screening or selection devices. In other words, the same burden of proving job relatedness falls on interviews and other techniques (such as performance appraisals) that fall on tests.

INDIVIDUAL RIGHTS OF TEST TAKERS AND TEST SECURITY   Test takers have various privacy and information rights. Under the American Psychological Association's standard for educational and psychological tests (which guide professional psychologists but are not legally enforceable), they have the right to the confidentiality of the test results and the right to informed consent regarding the use of these results. They have the right to expect that only people qualified to interpret the scores will have access to them or that sufficient information will accompany the scores to ensure their appropriate interpretation. They have the right to expect that no person taking the test should have prior information concerning the questions or answers.

USING TESTS AS SUPPLEMENTS   Do not use tests as your only selection technique; instead, use them to supplement other techniques such as interviews and background checks. Tests are fallible. Even in the best cases, the test score usually accounts for only about 25% of the variation in the measure of performance. In addition, tests are often better at revealing which candidates will fail than which will succeed.

Utility Analysis

Answering the question, "Does it pay to use the test?" requires **utility analysis.** "Using dollar and cents terms, [utility analysis] shows the degree to which use of a selection measure improves the quality of individuals selected over what would have happened if the measure had not been used."[15] The accompanying HR as a Profit Center feature provides an illustrative example.

HR AS A PROFIT CENTER

Reducing Turnover at KeyBank

Financial services firm KeyBank calculated it cost about $10,000 to select and onboard a new employee, but it was losing 13% of new tellers and call center employees in the first 90 days.[16] That turnover number dropped to 4% after KeyBank implemented a virtual "job tryout" assessment screening tool. "We calculated a $1.7 million cost savings in teller turnover in one year, simply by making better hiring decisions, reducing training costs, and increasing quality of hires."

USING TESTS AT WORK

Tests can be effective. For example, researchers administered an aggression questionnaire to high school hockey players prior to the season. Preseason aggressiveness as measured by the questionnaire predicted the amount of minutes they subsequently spent in the penalty box.[17]

Tests are also widely used by employers. For example, about 41% of companies the American Management Association surveyed tested applicants for basic skills (defined as the ability to read instructions, write reports, and perform common workplace arithmetic tasks).[18] Many people use the free online test illustrated in Figure 4-3 from www.mynextmove.org/explore/ip to assess their career interests and to help find suitable careers.

Types of Tests Used at Work

Employers use tests to measure a wide range of candidate attributes, including cognitive (mental) abilities, physical abilities, personality and interests, and achievement. Many firms have applicants take online or offline computerized tests—sometimes online, and sometimes by phone using the keypad—to prescreen applicants prior to in-depth interviews.[19] Employers don't just use tests for lower-level workers. For example, Barclays Capital gave recent graduates aptitude tests instead of first-round interviews.[20] Employers also don't use tests just to find good employees, but also to screen out bad ones. By one account, about 30% of all employees say they've stolen from their employers; about 41% are managers.[21] In retail, employers apprehended about 1 out of every 28 workers for stealing.[22]

EXAMPLE   Outback Steakhouse (which now has 45,000 employees) has used preemployment testing since 1991, just 2 years after the company started. Outback is looking for employees who are social, meticulous, sympathetic, and adaptable. It uses a special personality assessment test as part of its selection process. Applicants take the test, and the company then compares the candidate's results to the ideal Outback Steakhouse employee profile. Those who score low on certain traits (like compassion) don't move on.

FIGURE 4-3 Sample Free Online Career Interests Test.   *Source:* My Next Move is created for the U.S. Department of Labor, Employment & Training Administration, by the National Center for O*NET Development. www.mynextmove.org/explore/ip, accessed February 16, 2012.

Two managers interview those who do move on. They ask "behavioral" questions, such as *What would you do if a customer asked for a side dish we don't have on the menu?*[23]

The basic types of tests follow.

TESTS OF COGNITIVE ABILITIES Employers often want to assess cognitive or mental abilities. For example, you may be interested in determining whether a supervisory candidate has the intelligence to do the paperwork required of the job or a bookkeeper candidate has numeric aptitude.

Intelligence tests, such as IQ tests, are tests of general intellectual abilities. They measure a basket of abilities, including memory, vocabulary, verbal fluency, and numeric ability. Psychologists often measure intelligence with individually administered tests such as the Stanford-Binet or the Wechsler test. Employers use other IQ tests such as the Wonderlic to provide quick measures of IQ for both individuals and groups of people. In a study of firefighter trainees' performance over 23 years, researchers found that a measure of general intellectual ability and a physical ability assessment was highly predictive of firefighter trainee performance.[24]

There are also measures of specific mental abilities. Tests in this category are often called *aptitude tests* because they aim to measure the applicant's aptitudes for the job. For example, the Test of Mechanical Comprehension illustrated in Figure 4-4 tests the applicant's understanding of basic mechanical principles. It may therefore reflect a person's aptitude for jobs—such as engineer—that require mechanical comprehension.

TESTS OF MOTOR AND PHYSICAL ABILITIES There are many motor or physical abilities you might want to measure, such as finger dexterity, strength, manual dexterity, and reaction time (for instance, for police candidates). Thus applicants for the U.S. Marines must pass its Initial Strength Test (2 pull ups, 35 sit-ups, and a 1.5-mile run).[25] The Stromberg Dexterity Test measures the speed and accuracy of simple judgment as well as the speed of finger, hand, and arm movements.

MEASURING PERSONALITY A person's mental and physical abilities alone seldom explain his or her job performance. As one consultant put it, most people are hired based on qualifications, but most are fired for nonperformance. And *nonperformance* (or *performance*) "is usually the result of personal characteristics, such as attitude,

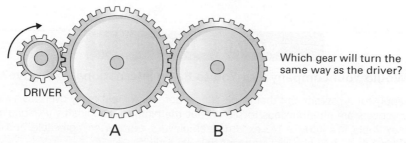

FIGURE 4-4 Sample Mechanical Comprehension Test Question.

motivation, and especially, temperament."[26] Employers use personality and interests inventories for measuring and predicting such intangibles. (Similarly, online dating services like eHarmony.com have prospective members take online personality tests, and reject those whom its software judges are unmatchable.) Employers such as Acxiom Corp. use tests like the Birkman Method® (www.birkman.com/) personality assessment to help new employees better understand the tasks at which they're best.[27]

Personality tests measure basic aspects of an applicant's personality, such as introversion, stability, and motivation. Many of these tests are projective, meaning that the person taking the test must interpret or react to an ambiguous stimulus such as an inkblot or clouded picture. Because the pictures are ambiguous, the person supposedly projects into the picture his or her own attitudes about life. For example, what do you see in Figure 4-1 (page 102)?

Personality tests—particularly the projective type—are the most difficult to evaluate and use. An expert must analyze the test taker's interpretations and reactions and infer from them the latter's personality. The usefulness of such tests then assumes that you find a relationship between a measurable personality trait (such as extroversion) and success on the job. Because they are personal in nature, employers should always use personality tests with caution, particularly where the focus is on aberrant behavior. Rejected candidates may (validly) claim that the results are false or that they violate the Americans with Disabilities Act (ADA).

PERSONALITY TEST EFFECTIVENESS   Historically, most experts assumed that personality tests help companies hire workers that are more effective. Industrial psychologists often study the "big five" personality dimensions: extroversion, emotional stability, agreeableness, conscientiousness, and openness to experience.[28] One study focused on how these five dimensions predicted performance (for instance, in terms of training proficiency) for professionals, police officers, managers, sales workers, and skilled/semiskilled workers. Conscientiousness showed a consistent relationship with all job performance criteria for all the occupations. Extroversion was a valid predictor of performance for managers and sales employees—two occupations involving the most social interaction. Openness to experience and extroversion predicted training proficiency for all occupations.[29] (See also the accompanying Global Issues in HR feature.)

Recently, though, a panel of distinguished industrial psychologists raised the question of whether *self-report* personality tests (which applicants fill out themselves) predict performance at all.[30] The bottom line is, make sure that any personality tests you use actually do predict performance of the job in question—that they are valid.[31]

GLOBAL ISSUES IN HR

Would Your Company Pick You to Be an International Executive?

You may apply for an assignment that involves time abroad. A great many overseas assignments fail, so employers are often anxious to screen out the high-risk candidates. *Personality* is one factor. For example, in a study of 143 expatriate employees, extroverted, agreeable, and emotionally stable individuals were less likely to want to leave early.[32]

INTEREST INVENTORIES *Interest inventories* compare one's interests with those of people in various occupations. Thus, if a person takes the Strong-Campbell Interest Inventory, he or she receives a report comparing his or her interests to those of people already in occupations such as accounting, engineering, management, and medical technology.

ACHIEVEMENT TESTS An *achievement test* is, basically, a measure of what a person has learned. Most of the tests you take in school are achievement tests. They measure your knowledge in areas such as economics, marketing, or management. In addition to job knowledge, achievement tests can measure applicants' abilities; a typing test is one example.[33]

COMPUTERIZED TESTING Computerized tests are increasingly replacing paper-and-pencil and manual tests. For example, one auto repair chain, City Garage, knew it couldn't implement its growth strategy without changing how it tested and hired employees.[34] Their old hiring process consisted of a paper-and-pencil application and one interview, immediately followed by a hire/don't hire decision. However, local shop managers didn't have time to evaluate every applicant, so "if they had been shorthanded too long, we would hire pretty much anybody who had experience," said City's training director. Complicating the problem was that City Garage competitively differentiates itself by letting customers interact directly with technicians. Therefore, finding mechanics that react positively to customer inquiries is essential.

City Garage's solution was to purchase the Personality Profile Analysis (PPA) online test from Dallas-based Thomas International USA. Now, after a quick application and background check, likely candidates take the 10-minute, 24-question PPA. City Garage staff then enter the answers into the PPA software system and receive test results in less than 2 minutes. These show whether the applicant is high or low in four personality characteristics. It also produces follow-up questions about potential problem areas. For example, applicants might be asked how they've handled possible weaknesses such as lack of patience. If candidates answer those questions satisfactorily, they're asked back for all-day interviews, after which hiring decisions are made.

WEB-BASED TESTING Employers also use the Web to test and screen applicants. For example, the financial firm Capital One's online system eliminates the previous time-consuming paper-and-pencil test process.[35] Applicants for call center jobs complete an online application and online math and biodata tests. They also take an online role-playing call simulation. Applicants (playing the role of operators) answer multiple-choice questions online regarding how they would respond to seven different customer situations.

As another example, with PreVisor's (www.shl.com/us/) personality test questions, the test adapts the next question to his or her previous answers. This improves test validity and may reduce cheating.[36] Service firms like Unicru score online preemployment tests. Applicant tracking systems often include online prescreening tests.[37] Most of the tests we describe in this chapter are available computerized. The site www.iphonetypingtest.com even offers an online iPhone typing test.[38]

Work Samples and Simulations

With work sample-type tests like the following, examinees respond to situations representative of the jobs for which they're applying.

WORK SAMPLING The **work sampling technique** tries to predict job performance by requiring job candidates to perform one or more actual samples of the job's tasks. (Thus for an auto mechanic's test, one task might include using a digital engine meter.) The basic procedure is to select a sample of several tasks crucial to performing the job and then to test applicants on them.[39] An observer monitors and assesses performance.

Realistic tests like work sampling measure actual job tasks, so it's harder to fake answers.[40] Work sampling also does not delve into the applicant's personality, so there's less chance of applicants viewing it as unfair.

MANAGEMENT ASSESSMENT CENTERS In a **management assessment center,** management candidates come together, take tests, and make decisions in simulated but realistic situations, and observers score them on their performance.[41] The time spent at the assessment center is usually 2 or 3 days. It involves 10 to 12 management candidates performing realistic management tasks (such as making presentations) under the observation of expert assessors. The Cheesecake Factory created its Professional Assessment and Development Center to help select promotable managers. Candidates spend 2 days of exercises, simulations, and classroom learning to see if they have the skills for key management positions.[42]

Sample exercises include:

- *The in-basket.* Here the candidate confronts an accumulation of reports, memos, notes of incoming phone calls, letters, and other materials. The candidate takes appropriate action on each of these materials.
- *The leaderless group discussion.* A leaderless group receives a discussion question and must arrive at a group decision. The raters evaluate each group member's interpersonal skills, acceptance by the group, leadership ability, and influence.
- *Individual presentations.* Raters evaluate a participant's communication skills and persuasiveness by having the person make an oral presentation on an assigned topic.

Employers use assessment centers for selection, promotion, and development. Supervisor recommendations usually play a big role in choosing center participants. Line managers usually act as assessors and typically arrive at their ratings through consensus.[43] Centers are expensive to set up, but at least one study (of 40 police candidates) found they are well worth the cost.[44]

SITUATIONAL JUDGMENT TESTS Situational judgment tests require candidates to answer questions that are representative of situations actually found on the job. As an example, You are facing a project deadline and are concerned that you may not complete the project by the time it is due. It is very important to your supervisor that you complete a project by the deadline. You can't get anyone to help you with the work. You would:[45]

A. Ask for an extension of the deadline.
B. Let the supervisor know that you may not meet the deadline.
C. Work as many hours as it takes to get the job done by the deadline.
D. Explore different ways to do the work so it can be completed by the deadline.
E. Do the most critical parts of the project by the deadline and complete the remaining parts after the deadline.
F. Tell your supervisor that the deadline is unreasonable.

G. Give your supervisor an update and express your concern about your ability to complete the project by the deadline.

H. Quit your job.

Studies suggest that situational judgment tests are effective and widely used.[46]

INTERVIEWING PROSPECTIVE EMPLOYEES

Although not all companies use tests or assessment centers, it is very unusual for a manager not to interview a prospective employee; interviewing skills are thus indispensable. An **interview** is a procedure designed to solicit information from a person's oral responses to oral inquiries. A *selection interview* is "a selection procedure designed to predict future job performance on the basis of applicants' oral responses to oral inquiries."[47]

Types of Selection Interviews

As you probably know from your own experience, there are several types of selection interviews.

STRUCTURE   First, most interviews vary in the degree to which the interviewer structures or standardizes the interview process.[48] Thus the interview may be *nonstructured* or *structured*. In the former, you ask questions as they come to mind, and there is generally no format to follow. In a structured or directive interview, questions and perhaps even acceptable responses are specified in advance, and the responses may be rated for appropriateness of content (see Figure 4-5). In practice, many or most interviews include some mix of standardized and nonstructured questions and/or procedures.[49]

TYPE OF QUESTIONS   Second, the interviewer can use various types of questions. In *situational interviews,* questions focus on the candidate's ability to project what his or her behavior *would be* in a given situation. For example, you might ask a candidate for a supervisor position how he or she would respond to a subordinate coming to work late three days in a row. A *behavioral interview* is another type of interview. Here you ask interviewees how they behaved in the past in some situation. When Citizens Banking Corporation found that 31 of the 50 people in its call center quit in 1 year, the center's head switched to behavioral interviews. Many of those who left did so because they didn't enjoy fielding questions from irate clients. So she no longer tries to predict how candidates will act based on asking them if they want to work with angry clients. Instead, she asks behavioral questions like, "Tell me about a time you were speaking with an irate person and how you turned the situation around." She says this makes it harder to fool the interviewer; only four people left her center in the following year.[50] More employers today are using behavioral interviews.[51]

HOW ADMINISTERED   Third, we can also classify interviews based on how we administer them. For example, most interviews are *one-on-one:* Two people meet alone, and one interviews the other by seeking oral responses to oral inquiries. Most selection processes are also sequential. In a *sequential interview,* several people interview the applicant in sequence before making a hiring decision. In a *panel interview* the candidate is interviewed simultaneously by a group (or panel) of interviewers, rather than sequentially.

Competency: Interpersonal Skills

Definition of Interpersonal Skills Competency:
Shows understanding, courtesy, tact, empathy, concern; develops and maintains relationships; may deal with people who are difficult, hostile, distressed; relates well to people from varied backgrounds and situations; is sensitive to individual differences.

Interview Lead-in Questions:
Describe a situation in which you had to deal with people who were upset about a problem. What specific actions did you take? What was the outcome or result?

Benchmark Level	Level Definition	Level Examples
5 (High)	Establishes and maintains ongoing working relationships with management, other employees, internal or external stakeholders, or customers. Remains courteous when discussing information or eliciting highly sensitive or controversial information from people who are reluctant to give it. Effectively handles situations involving a high degree of tension or discomfort involving people who are demonstrating a high degree of hostility or distress.	Presents controversial findings tactfully to irate organization senior management officials regarding shortcomings of a newly installed computer system, software programs, and associated equipment.
4		Mediates disputes concerning system design/architecture, the nature and capacity of data management systems, system resources allocations, or other equally controversial/sensitive matters.
3	Cooperates and works well with management, other employees, or customers, on short-term assignments. Remains courteous when discussing information or eliciting moderately sensitive or controversial information from people who are hesitant to give it. Effectively handles situations involving a moderate degree of tension or discomfort involving people who are demonstrating a moderate degree of hostility or distress.	Courteously and tactfully delivers effective instruction to frustrated customers. Provides technical advice to customers and the public on various types of IT such as communication or security systems, data management procedures or analysis.
2		Familiarizes new employees with administrative procedures and office systems.
1 (Low)	Cooperates and works well with management, other employees, or customers during brief interactions. Remains courteous when discussing information or eliciting non-sensitive or non-controversial information from people who are willing to give it. Effectively handles situations involving little or no tension, discomfort, hostility, or distress.	Responds courteously to customers' general inquiries. Greets and assists visitors attending a meeting within own organization.

FIGURE 4-5 Structured Interview Rating Scale. *Source:* www.state.gov/documents/organization/107843.pdf, and United States Office of Personnel Management. Structured Interviews: Interview Guide and Evaluation Materials for Structured Interviews.

Managers conduct some interviews by *phone*. Somewhat counterintuitively, such interviews can actually be more accurate than face-to-face ones, possibly because both parties focus more on substantive answers, rather than on things like handshake firmness or smiles.[52] In a typical study, interviewers tended to evaluate applicants more favorably in telephone versus face-to-face interviews, particularly where the interviewees were less physically attractive. The interviewers came to about the same conclusions regarding the interviewees whether the interview was face-to-face or by videoconference. Applicants themselves preferred face-to-face interviews.[53]

For better or worse, some employers are using a speed dating approach to interviewing applicants. One employer sent e-mails to all applicants for an advertised position. Over the next few hours, applicants first mingled with employees, and then (in a so-called speed dating area) had one-on-one contacts with employees for a few minutes. Based on this, the recruiting team chose 68 candidates for follow-up interviews.[54]

COMPUTERIZED INTERVIEWS   A *computerized selection interview* is one in which a job candidate's oral and/or computerized replies are obtained in response to computerized (often online) oral, visual, or written questions and/or situations.

THE BAIN & COMPANY CASE INTERVIEW   Bain & Company uses case interviews as part of its candidate selection process. By having job candidates explain how they would address the case client's problems, the case interview combines behavioral and situational questioning to provide a realistic assessment of the candidate's consulting skills.

How Useful Are Interviews?

Although virtually all employers use interviews, the evidence regarding their validity is mixed. Much of the early research gave selection interviews low marks for reliability and validity.[55] However, today studies confirm that the "validity of the interview is greater than previously believed."[56] The key is how you administer it. Specifically:

- With respect to predicting job performance, *situational interviews* yield a higher mean (average) validity than do behavioral interviews.
- *Structured interviews* are more valid than unstructured interviews for predicting job performance. They are more valid partly because they are more reliable—for example, the same interviewer administers the interview more consistently from candidate to candidate.[57]
- Whether structured or unstructured, *individual interviews* tend to be more valid than are panel interviews, in which multiple interviewers provide ratings in one setting.[58]

In summary, structured situational interviews (in which you ask the candidates what they would do in a particular situation) conducted one-on-one seem to be the most useful for predicting job performance. But in practice, effective interviewing also depends on avoiding common interviewing mistakes, a subject to which we now turn.

How to Avoid Common Interviewing Mistakes

Several common interviewing mistakes can undermine an interview's usefulness.

SNAP JUDGMENTS   Perhaps the most consistent finding is that interviewers tend to jump to conclusions—make snap judgments—about candidates during the first few minutes of the interview. This often occurs even before the interview begins, based on test scores or résumé data.[59] One psychologist interviewed the CEOs of 80 top companies. She concluded that to make a good impression you "don't even get time to open your mouth."[60] Instead, the interviewer will size up things like your posture, handshake, smile, and whether you have "a captivating aura." And after that, it will be difficult (if not impossible) for the interviewee to overcome that first impression during the interview.

For interviewees, this underscores why it's important to start right with the interviewer. For interviewers, the findings underscore why it's important to keep an open mind until the interview is over.

NEGATIVE EMPHASIS   Jumping to conclusions is especially troublesome, given the fact that interviewers also tend to be more influenced by unfavorable than favorable information. Furthermore, their impressions are much more likely to change from favorable to unfavorable than from unfavorable to favorable. Often, in fact, interviews are mostly searches for negative information.

What are the implications? As an interviewer, remember to keep an open mind and work against being preoccupied with negative impressions. As an interviewee, remember, "You only have one chance to make a good first impression."

NOT KNOWING THE JOB   Interviewers who don't know what the job entails and what sort of candidate is best suited for it usually make decisions based on incorrect stereotypes about what makes a good applicant. They then erroneously match interviewees against these incorrect stereotypes. Interviewers should therefore know as much as possible about the position for which they're interviewing and about its required skills.[61]

PRESSURE TO HIRE   Being under pressure to hire undermines an interview's usefulness. In one study, several managers thought they were behind in their recruiting quota. A second group thought they were ahead of their quota. Those behind evaluated the same recruits more highly than did those ahead.[62]

CANDIDATE ORDER (CONTRAST) ERROR   Candidate order (or contrast) error means that the order in which you see applicants affects how you rate them. In one study, researchers asked managers to evaluate a candidate who was "just average" after first evaluating several "unfavorable" candidates. The managers evaluated the average candidate more favorably than he might otherwise have been, because in contrast to the unfavorable candidates the average one looked better than he actually was.[63]

INFLUENCE OF NONVERBAL BEHAVIOR   It's not just what the candidate says but how he or she looks and behaves that determines the interview rating. For example, studies show that interviewers rate applicants who demonstrate more eye contact, head moving, smiling, and similar nonverbal behaviors higher.[64] In another study, vocal cues (such as the interviewee's pitch, speech rates, and pauses) and visual cues (such as physical attractiveness and smile) correlated with the evaluator's judgments of whether the interviewees could be trusted.[65] In one study of 99 graduating college seniors, the interviewee's apparent level of extroversion influenced whether he or she received job offers.[66]

Extroverted applicants seem particularly prone to self-promotion, and self-promotion strongly affects the interviewer's perceptions of candidate job fit.[67]

ATTRACTIVENESS[68]   In general, studies of attractiveness find that individuals ascribe more favorable traits and life outcomes to attractive people.[69] In another study, men were perceived to be more suitable for hire and more likely to advance to the next executive level than were equally qualified women, and more attractive candidates, especially men, were preferred over less attractive ones.[70] These stereotypes are changing. However, women still account for only about 16% of corporate officers at Fortune 500 companies.[71]

In general, candidates evidencing various attributes and disabilities (such as child-care demands, HIV-positive status, and being wheelchair-bound) have less chance of obtaining a positive decision, even when they performed very well in the structured interview.[72] Even with structured interviews, "… nonverbal cues cause interviewers to make attributions about candidates."[73]

RESEARCH INSIGHT   Researchers gave 100 working MBA students (34% female) copies of a job description summary for assistant vice president. The students also got a "promotion applicant information form" to evaluate for each fictitious "applicant." The forms included fictitious information on marital status. Some "applicants" were working mothers.[74] The student evaluators viewed the mothers as less competent and were less likely to recommend them for the job. "These data are consistent with mounting evidence that women suffer disadvantages in the workplace when they are mothers."[75]

RACE   Race also plays a role. One study examined racial differences in ratings when the interviewees appeared before three interview panels: panels in which the racial composition was primarily black, racially balanced, and primarily white.[76] On the primarily black panels, black and white raters judged black and white candidates similarly. On the other hand, in the primarily white and the balanced panels, white interviewers rated white candidates higher, and black interviewers rated black candidates higher.

INGRATIATION   Interviewees boost their chances for job offers through self-promotion and ingratiation. *Ingratiation* involves, for example, agreeing with the recruiter's opinions. *Self-promotion* means promoting one's own skills and abilities to create the impression of competence.[77]

IMPLICATIONS   Evidence like this suggests two implications. With respect to nonverbal behavior (such as eye contact), it seems apparent that otherwise inferior candidates who "act right" in interviews are often appraised more highly than are more competent applicants who lack nonverbal skills. Therefore focus on the content of what the person is saying.

Similarly, because physical attributes are generally irrelevant to job performance, interviewers should guard against letting them influence their ratings.

APPLICANT DISABILITY AND THE EMPLOYMENT INTERVIEW   Researchers studied what disabled people who use assistive technology (such as voice recognition software) expect and prefer from interviewers.[78]

The basic finding was that interviewers tend to avoid addressing the disability, and make their decisions without the facts. What the disabled people prefer is an open discussion, one that allows the employer to reach a knowledgeable conclusion. Among the questions disabled persons said they would like interviewers to ask were these:

- Is there a setting or special equipment that will facilitate the interview process for you?
- Is there a technology that you currently use or have used in previous jobs that assists the way you work?

Guidelines for Conducting an Interview

The evidence suggests a number of sensible guidelines for managers.

PLAN THE INTERVIEW   Begin by reviewing the candidate's application and résumé, and note any areas that are vague or that may indicate strengths or weaknesses. Review the job specification to start the interview with a clear picture of the traits of an ideal candidate.

STRUCTURE THE INTERVIEW   Take steps to structure or standardize the interview. There are several ways to do this:[79]

1. Study the job description and *base questions on actual job duties*.[80]
2. Use *job knowledge, situational or behavioral questions*, and *objective criteria* to evaluate the interviewee's responses. Questions that ask for opinions and attitudes, goals and aspirations, and self-descriptions encourage self-promotion and allow candidates to avoid revealing weaknesses. Examples of structured questions include:
   - Situational questions like "Suppose you were giving a sales presentation and a difficult technical question arose that you could not answer. What would you do?"
   - Past behavior questions like "Can you provide an example of a specific instance where you developed a sales presentation that was highly effective?"
   - Background questions like "What work experiences, training, or other qualifications do you have for working in a teamwork environment?"
   - Job knowledge questions like "What factors should you consider when developing a TV advertising campaign?"
3. *Train interviewers* to avoid irrelevant or potentially discriminatory questions.[81]
4. Use the *same questions* with all candidates. This can improve consistency and reduce bias by giving all the candidates the same opportunity.
5. Use *rating scales* to rate answers. For each question, have in mind a range of sample ideal answers and a quantitative score for each. Then rate each candidate's answers against this scale.
6. Use *multiple interviewers*. Doing so can reduce bias by diminishing the importance of one interviewer's idiosyncratic opinions and by bringing in more points of view.[82]
7. If possible, use a *structured interview form*. Interviews based on structured guides (as in Figure 4-5) usually result in superior interviews.[83] At the very least, list your questions before the interview.
8. *Take brief notes* during the interview. Doing so may help to keep an open mind rather than making a snap judgment based on inadequate early information.[84]

The interview should take place in a private room where telephone calls are not accepted and you can minimize interruptions.

1. How did you choose this line of work?
2. What did you enjoy most about your last job?
3. What did you like least about your last job?
4. What has been your greatest frustration or disappointment on your present job? Why?
5. What are some of the pluses and minuses of your last job?
6. What were the circumstances surrounding your leaving your last job?
7. Did you give notice?
8. Why should we be hiring you?
9. What do you expect from this employer?
10. What are three things you will not do in your next job?
11. What would your last supervisor say your three weaknesses are?
12. What are your major strengths?
13. How can your supervisor best help you obtain your goals?
14. How did your supervisor rate your job performance?
15. In what ways would you change your last supervisor?
16. What are your career goals during the next 1–3 years? 5–10 years?
17. How will working for this company help you reach those goals?
18. What did you do the last time you received instructions with which you disagreed?
19. What are some of the things about which you and your supervisor disagreed? What did you do?
20. Which do you prefer, working alone or working with groups?
21. What motivated you to do better at your last job?
22. Do you consider your progress on that job representative of your ability? Why?
23. Do you have any questions about the duties of the job for which you have applied?
24. Can you perform the essential functions of the job for which you have applied?

FIGURE 4-6 Suggested Supplementary Questions for Interviewing Applicants. *Source:* "Suggested Supplementary Questions for Interviewing Candidates." Reprinted with permission of the publisher, Business and Legal Resources Inc. Copyright 2012 Business & Legal Resources, Inc.

ESTABLISH RAPPORT The point is to find out about the applicant. To do this, start by putting the person at ease, perhaps with a question about the weather.

ASK QUESTIONS Try to follow a structured interview guide or the questions you wrote out ahead of time. You'll find a menu of additional questions to choose from in Figure 4-6.

One way to get answers that are more candid is to state you're going to check references. Ask, "If I were to ask your boss, what's your best guess as to what he or she would say are your strengths, weaker points, and overall performance?"[85]

The accompanying HR in Practice feature summarizes some do's and don'ts for asking questions.

WHAT *NOT* TO ASK As a rule, avoid questions based on age, race, gender, national origin, handicap, or other prohibited criteria. Can you pick out the inappropriate questions in the following list?[86]

- What kinds of things do you look for in a job?
- What types of interests or hobbies are you involved in?
- Do you have any handicaps?
- What university subjects do you like the most?
- What qualities should a successful manager possess?

HR IN PRACTICE

Do's and Don'ts of Asking Interview Questions

- **Don't** ask questions that can be answered yes or no.
- **Don't** put words in the applicant's mouth or telegraph the desired answer, for instance, by nodding.
- **Don't** interrogate the applicant, or be patronizing, sarcastic, or inattentive.
- **Don't** monopolize the interview or let the applicant dominate the interview so you can't ask all your questions.
- **Do** ask open-ended questions.
- **Do** listen to the candidate.
- **Do** draw out the applicant's opinions and feelings by repeating the person's last comment as a question (e.g., "You didn't like your last job?").
- **Do** ask for examples.[87] For instance, if the candidate lists specific strengths, follow up with, "What are specific examples that demonstrate each of your strengths?"

- Do you have any plans for marriage and children?
- What do you think you have to offer a company like ours?
- What is your date of birth?
- What is the nature of your previous work experience?
- What kinds of things do you look for in a job?
- Have you ever been arrested for a crime?
- What do you consider your greatest strengths?

CLOSE THE INTERVIEW   Toward the close of the interview, leave time to answer any questions the candidate may have and, if appropriate, to advocate your firm to the candidate.

Try to end all interviews on a positive note. Tell the applicant whether there is an interest and, if so, what the next step will be. Similarly, make rejections diplomatically (for instance, "Although your background is impressive, there are other candidates whose experiences are closer to our requirements"). As one recruiter says, "An interview experience should leave a lasting, positive impression of the company, whether the candidate receives and accepts an offer or not."[88]

REVIEW THE INTERVIEW   After the candidate leaves, review your interview notes, and complete any structured interview guide.

Talent Management: Profiles and Employee Interviews

Talent management is the goal-oriented and integrated process of planning for, recruiting, selecting, developing, and compensating employees. To ensure an integrated, goal-oriented effort, talent management dictates using the same set (profile) of competencies, traits, knowledge, and experience for recruiting employees as for selecting, training, appraising, and paying them.

Table 4-1 illustrates how to do this for an interview. It summarizes competency, knowledge, trait, and experience elements for a chemical engineer, along with sample

TABLE 4-1	Asking Profile-Oriented Interview Questions	
Profile Component	**Example**	**Sample Interview Question**
Competency	Able to use computer drafting software	Tell me about a time you used CAD Pro computerized design software.
Knowledge	How extreme heat affects hydrochloric acid (HCL)	Suppose you have an application where HCL is heated to 400 degrees Fahrenheit at 2 atmospheres of pressure; what happens to the HCL?
Trait	Willing to travel abroad at least 4 months per year visiting facilities	Suppose you had a big affair that you had to attend next week and our company informed you that you had to leave for a job abroad immediately, and stay 3 weeks. How would you handle that?
Experience	Designed pollution filter for acid-cleaning facility	Tell me about a time when you designed a pollution filter device for an acid-cleaning facility. How did it work? What particular problems did you encounter? How did you address them?

interview questions. Selecting engineers based on this profile would help to ensure that you focus your questions on the things that someone must be proficient at to do this job successfully. The same profile should ideally guide how to recruit candidates for this position, and on what basis to train, appraise, and pay them.

USING OTHER SELECTION TECHNIQUES

Background Investigations and Reference Checks

About 82% of HR managers report checking applicants' backgrounds; 80% do criminal convictions searches, and 35% do credit history reports.[89]

There are two key reasons for checking backgrounds. One is to verify the facts provided by the applicant (for example, a survey found that 23% of 7,000 executive résumés contained exaggerated or false information).[90] The other reason is to uncover damaging background information such as criminal records. In Chicago, for instance, a pharmaceutical firm hired gang members in mail delivery and computer repair. The gang members were stealing almost a million dollars a year in computer parts and using the mail department to ship them to a nearby computer store they owned.[91]

WHAT TO VERIFY   The most commonly verified background areas are generally legal eligibility for employment (to comply with immigration laws), dates of prior employment, military service (including discharge status), education, and identification (including date of birth and address). Other items should include county criminal records (current residence, last residence), motor vehicle record, credit, licensing verification, Social Security number, and reference checks.[92] With diploma mills proliferating, you should check academic backgrounds.[93] Most employers at least try to verify an applicant's current position, salary, and employment dates with his or her current employer by phone (assuming that the candidate cleared doing so).[94] Others call the applicant's current and previous supervisors to try to discover more about the person's motivation, technical competence, and ability to work with others. Some employers check executive candidates' lawsuit records, with the candidate's prior approval.[95]

The position determines how deeply you search. Thus, a credit and education check is more important for an accountant than a groundskeeper. Also periodically check, say, the credit ratings of current employees with easy access to company assets.

CHECKING SOCIAL NETWORKING SITES   One employer went to Facebook.com and found that a top candidate described his interests as smoking marijuana and shooting people. The student may have been kidding but did not get the offer.[96] After conducting such online reviews, recruiters found that 31% of applicants lied about their qualifications and 19% posted information about their drinking or drug use, according to Careerbuilder .com.[97] However, while Googling is probably safe enough, checking social networking sites raises legal issues. For example, while the Fair Credit Reporting Act refers more to getting official reports, it's still probably best to get the candidate's prior approval for social networking searches.[98] And do not use a pretext or fabricate an identity.[99]

USING PREEMPLOYMENT INFORMATION SERVICES   Online databases make it easy to check candidates' background information. Numerous employment-screening services access dozens of databases, by county, to compile background information for employers quickly.

The employer should ensure the screening service doesn't take any actions that conflict with Equal Employment Opportunity (EEO) laws. For example, under the ADA, employers should avoid preemployment inquiries into the existence or severity of a disability. In choosing a preemployment screening service, ensure it requires an applicant-signed release authorizing the background check, complies with relevant laws such as the Fair Credit Reporting Act, and uses only legal data sources. Major employment screening providers include ADP (www.ADP.com) and HireRight/USIS commercial services (www.hireright.com).[100] A basic criminal check might cost $25; a comprehensive background check costs about $200.[101]

REFERENCE CHECK EFFECTIVENESS   Handled correctly, background checks are an inexpensive and straightforward way to verify facts (such as current and previous job titles). However, reference checking has its limits. One is legal. Most importantly, it's not always easy for references to prove that the bad reference they gave was warranted.[102] In one case, a man was awarded $56,000 after being turned down for a job because, among other things, a former employer called him a "character."

It is not just lawsuits. Many supervisors give incompetents good reviews just to get rid of them. The bottom line is that you must ask the right questions and be vigilant for evasiveness.

MAKING REFERENCE CHECKS MORE PRODUCTIVE   You can do several things to make your reference checking more productive.

First, use a structured form as in Figure 4-7. This helps ensure that you don't miss important questions.

Second, use the references offered by the applicant as merely a source for other references. For example, ask each reference, "Could you please give me the name of

(Verify that the applicant has provided permission before conducting reference checks.)

Candidate
Name _____

Reference
Name _____

Company
Name _____

Dates of Employment
From: _____ To: _____

Position(s)
Held _____

Salary
History _____

Reason for
Leaving _____

Explain the reason for your call and verify the above information with the supervisor
(including the reason for leaving)
_____
_____

1. Please describe the type of work for which the candidate was responsible.
_____
_____

2. How would you describe the applicant's relationships with coworkers, subordinates
(if applicable), and with superiors?
_____
_____

3. Did the candidate have a positive or negative work attitude? Please elaborate.
_____
_____

4. How would you describe the quantity and quality of output generated by the former
employee?
_____
_____

5. What were his/her strengths on the job?
_____
_____

6. What were his/her weaknesses on the job?
_____
_____

7. What is your overall assessment of the candidate?
_____
_____

8. Would you recommend him/her for this position? Why or why not?
_____
_____

9. Would this individual be eligible for rehire? Why or why not?
_____
_____

Other comments?
_____
_____

FIGURE 4-7 Reference Checking Form. *Source:* "Reference Checking Form, 2004," SHRM Online: Sample HR Forms. Copyright 2004 by SHRM. Reprinted with permission.

another person who might be familiar with the applicant's performance?" In that way, you begin getting more objective references. Perhaps contact two superiors, two peers, and two subordinates from each previous job.

Third, also ask open-ended questions, such as "How much direction does the applicant need in his or her work?" to get the references to talk more about the candidate.

Fourth, companies fielding requests for references should ensure that only authorized managers give them. There are companies [such as Allison & Taylor Reference Checking Inc. (www.allisontaylor.com/)] that, for a fee, will call former employers on behalf of former employees who believe they're getting bad references. One supervisor, describing a former city employee, reportedly "said he was incompetent and said that he almost brought the city down on its knees."[103]

Finally, always get at least two forms of identification and obtain a job application. Always compare the application to the résumé (people are less creative on their application forms, where they must certify the information).[104]

More employers are automating their reference-checking process. Instead of the employer calling the references, the recruiter sends an e-mail link to each candidate. The candidate then uses this link to contact five or more of his or her references, asking them to fill out a tailored online questionnaire. Special vendors then compile this information and create analytical reports for the employer.[105]

Honesty Testing

POLYGRAPH TESTS   The *polygraph* (or *"lie detector"*) machine measures physiological changes such as perspiration. The assumption is that such changes reflect changes in the emotional stress that accompanies lying. The usual procedure is to attach the applicant or current employee to the machine with painless electronic probes. The polygraph expert then asks several true neutral questions (such as "Is your name Jane Smith?"). After ascertaining the person's reactions to neutral questions, questions such as "Have you ever taken anything without paying for it?" are asked. In theory, the expert can determine whether the applicant is lying.

HR IN PRACTICE

How to Detect Dishonesty

- **Ask blunt questions.** You can ask very direct questions. For example, you can probably ask, "Have you ever stolen anything from an employer?" and "Is any information on your application misrepresented?"[106]
- **Ask for a credit check.** Include a clause in your application form that gives you the right to certain background checks on the applicant, including credit checks and motor vehicle reports.
- **Check all references.**
- **Consider using a test.** Consider honesty tests and psychological tests as part of your honesty screening.
- **Test for drugs.** Devise and institute a drug-testing program.
- **Conduct searches.** Establish a search-and-seizure policy. This should state that all lockers, desks, and similar property remain the property of the company and may be inspected routinely.
- **Use caution.** Some states, including Massachusetts and Rhode Island, limit the use of honesty tests. Therefore, protect your candidates and employees' privacy rights and adhere to the law.

Doubts about the polygraph's accuracy culminated in the Employee Polygraph Protection Act of 1988. With few exceptions, it prohibits most employers from conducting polygraph exams of all applicants and most employees. Even for ongoing investigations of theft, the employer's right to use polygraphs is limited.[107]

HONESTY TESTS   The virtual elimination of the polygraph as a screening device triggered a burgeoning market for other honesty testing devices. Paper-and-pencil or computerized honesty tests are psychological tests designed to predict job applicants' proneness to dishonesty. Most of these tests measure attitudes regarding things such as tolerance of others who steal and admission of theft-related activities.

Studies tend to support honesty tests' validity. One study focused on 111 employees hired by a major retail convenience store chain.[108] "Shrinkage" was estimated at 3% of sales, and internal theft was believed to account for much of this. The researchers found that scores on an honesty test successfully predicted theft, as measured by termination for theft.

In practice, detecting dishonest candidates involves not only tests but also a comprehensive procedure including reference checking and interviews. One expert suggests following the steps in the preceding HR in Practice feature.

Graphology

Graphology (handwriting analysis) assumes that the writer's basic personality traits will be expressed in his or her handwriting. Handwriting analysis thus has some resemblance to projective personality tests.

Although some writers estimate that more than 1,000 U.S. companies use handwriting analysis, the validity of handwriting analysis is questionable. One reviewer says, "There is essentially no evidence of a direct link between handwriting analysis and various measures of job performance."[109]

"Human Lie Detectors"

While perhaps no more valid than graphology, some employers are using so-called "human lie detectors."[110] One Wall Street firm uses a psychologist and former FBI agent. He sits in on interviews and watches for signs of candidate deceptiveness. Signs include pupils changing size (which often corresponds to emotions, such as fear), irregular breathing (may flag nervousness), micro-expressions (quick transitory facial expressions that may portray emotions such as fear), crossing legs (liars typically try to distance themselves from an untruth), and quick verbal responses (possibly reflecting scripted statements).

Physical Exams

Physical examinations are often the next step in the selection process, and there are several reasons for requiring them. Such exams can confirm that the applicant qualifies for the physical requirements of the position and can unearth any medical limitations to take into account in placing the applicant. Under the ADA, a person with a disability can't be rejected for the job if he or she is otherwise qualified and if the person could perform the essential job functions with reasonable accommodation. A physical exam is permissible during the period between the job offer and the commencement of work, if one is standard practice for all applicants for that job category.[111]

Drug Screening

Most employers conduct drug tests. Employers may use urine testing to test for illicit drugs, breath alcohol tests to determine the amount of alcohol in the blood, blood tests to measure alcohol or drug in the blood at the time of the test, hair analyses to reveal drug history, saliva tests for substances such as marijuana and cocaine, and skin patches to determine drug use.[112] The most common practice is to test new applicants just before formally hiring them. Many firms also test current employees when there is reason to believe an employee has been using drugs, such as after a work accident or when there are behavioral symptoms like high absenteeism. Some firms administer drug tests on a random or periodic basis, whereas others do so only when transferring or promoting an employee.[113]

PROBLEMS   Although roadside alcohol breathalyzers correlate closely with impairment levels, urine and blood tests for drugs only indicate whether drug residues are present.[114] They cannot measure impairment, habituation, or addiction.[115] Furthermore, "there is a swarm of products that promise to help employees beat drug tests."[116]

Drug testing therefore raises several issues. Some argue that drug testing violates citizens' rights to privacy and due process and are intrusive. Others argue that workplace drug testing might identify one's use of drugs during leisure hours but have little relevance to the job itself.[117]

One study concluded that other than alcohol, there is no clear evidence that drugs diminish safety or job performance.[118] Another study concluded that preemployment drug testing seemed to have little or no effect on workplace accidents. However, a combination of preemployment and random ongoing testing was associated with a significant reduction in workplace accidents.[119]

LEGAL ISSUES   Several federal laws apply. Under the ADA, courts might well view a former drug user (one who no longer uses illegal drugs and successfully completed or is participating in a rehabilitation program) as a qualified applicant with a disability.[120] U.S. Department of Transportation regulations require firms with more than 50 eligible employees in transportation industries to conduct alcohol testing on workers with sensitive or safety-related jobs. These include mass-transit workers, air traffic controllers, and school-bus drivers.[121]

Particularly with safety-sensitive jobs, courts often side with employers. In one case, a U.S. Court of Appeals ruled that Exxon acted properly in firing a truck driver who failed a drug test. In this case, the employee drove a tractor-trailer carrying 12,000 gallons of flammable motor fuel and tested positive for cocaine. Exxon discharged him.[122]

Realistic Job Previews

A dose of realism makes a good screening tool. For example, Walmart found that many new associates quit within 3 months. After Walmart began explicitly explaining and asking about work schedules and work preferences, turnover improved.[123] In general, applicants who receive realistic job previews are more likely to turn down job offers but more likely to have lower turnover.[124]

Tapping Friends and Acquaintances

Testing and interviewing aside, don't ignore tapping the opinions of people you trust who have direct personal knowledge of the candidate. It may be an exaggeration, but as a CEO of Continental Airlines said, "the best possible interview is minuscule in value compared to somebody who's got even a couple of months of work experience with [the candidate]"[125]

Complying with the Immigration Law

Under the Immigration Reform and Control Act of 1986, prospective employees must prove that they are eligible for employment in the United States.

HOW TO COMPLY There are two basic ways to show eligibility for employment. One is to show a document such as a U.S. passport or alien registration card with a photograph that proves both identity and employment eligibility.[126] The other is to show a document that proves the person's identity, along with a separate document showing the person's employment eligibility, such as a work permit. More employers are using the federal government's voluntary electronic employment verification program, E-Verify.[127] Federal contractors must use it.[128]

Employers can protect themselves against fraudulent documents in several ways. Systematic background checks should include employment verification, criminal record checks, drug screens, and reference checks. You can verify Social Security cards by calling the Social Security Administration. Employers can avoid accusations of discrimination by verifying the documents of all applicants, not just those they think are suspicious.[129] Employers may not use the I-9 Employment Eligibility Verification form required to document eligibility to discriminate based on race or country of national origin as long as that person can prove his or her identity and employment eligibility.[130]

Making the Selection Decision

Once you've collected all your selection information, the question arises, how do you combine it all and make a selection decision? If you're only using one predictor (such as one test score) then the decision is straightforward. For example, hire the applicant with the highest score.

In practice, it's not so simple. For one thing, you'll probably not make your decision based on a single predictor (in this case, one test score). You'll also want to factor in the person's references, his or her interview and application information (such as school attended), and perhaps the results of other tests. Furthermore, you'll probably have more than one candidate.[131] Will you just choose the one with the highest Wonderlic score? Probably not. So again, you'll need some way to weigh all the sources of information you have about each candidate and to make a choice.

There are three basic approaches. You could use, first, a clinical (or "intuitive," or "judgmental") approach. Here you intuitively weigh all the evidence from the various sources about the candidate and make your decision. Second, you could take a statistical (or "mechanical") approach. In its purest sense, the mechanical approach involves quantifying all the information you collect about the candidate (including, for example, subjective information from references). You then combine all this quantified information to get an answer, perhaps using a formula that predicts the candidate's likely job success. And third, you could take a hybrid approach, one that fine-tunes the mechanical results you obtained from your formula with judgment. Strictly speaking, the mechanical/statistical approach is usually the most defensible. However, the traditional judgemental approach is still usually better than nothing.[132]

REVIEW

Summary

1. Test validity answers the question: What does this test measure? Criterion validity means demonstrating that those who do well on the test do well on the job. Content validity is demonstrated by showing that the test constitutes a fair sample of the content of the job.

2. As used by psychologists, the term *reliability* always means "consistency." One way to measure reliability is to administer the same (or equivalent) tests to the same people at two different points in time. Or you could focus on internal consistency, comparing the responses to roughly equivalent items on the same test.

3. There are many types of personnel tests in use, including intelligence tests, tests of physical skills, tests of achievement, aptitude tests, interest inventories, and personality tests.

4. Under equal opportunity legislation, an employer may have to prove that his or her tests are predictive of success or failure on the job. This usually requires a predictive validation study, although other means of validation are often acceptable.

5. Management assessment centers are screening devices that expose applicants to a series of real-life exercises. Examples of such real-life exercises include a simulated business game, an in-basket exercise, and group discussions.

6. Several factors and problems can undermine the usefulness of an interview: making premature decisions, letting unfavorable information predominate, not knowing the requirements of the job, being under pressure to hire, not allowing for the candidate order effect, and nonverbal behavior.

7. The steps in the interview include plan, establish rapport, structure, ask questions, close the interview, and review the data.

8. Other screening tools include reference checks, background checks, physical exams, and realistic previews.

9. Managers can use a job's competencies profile to formulate job-related situational, behavioral, and knowledge questions.

10. Once you've selected and hired your new employees, they must be trained. We turn to training in Chapter 5.

Key Terms

person-job fit *101*
reliability *101*
test validity *102*
criterion validity *103*

content validity *103*
validity generalization *103*
utility analysis *105*
work sampling technique *110*

management assessment center *110*
interview *111*

Discussion Questions

1. Explain what is meant by *reliability* and *validity*. What is the difference between them? In what respects are they similar?
2. Write a short essay discussing some of the ethical and legal considerations in testing.
3. Give some examples of how interest inventories could be used to improve employee selection. In doing so, suggest several examples of occupational interests that you believe might predict success in various occupations, including college professor, accountant, and computer programmer.
4. Why is it important to conduct preemployment background investigations? How would you go about doing so?
5. For what sorts of jobs do you think computerized interviews are most appropriate? Why?
6. Give a short presentation titled "How to Be Effective as an Interviewer."
7. Briefly discuss and give examples of at least five common interviewing mistakes. What recommendations would you give for avoiding these interviewing mistakes?

Individual and Group Activities

1. Working individually or in groups, develop a list of specific selection techniques that you would suggest your dean use to hire the next HR professor at your school. Explain why you chose each selection technique.
2. Working individually or in groups, access the publisher of a standardized test such as the Scholastic Assessment Test and obtain from it information regarding the test's validity and reliability. Present a short report in class discussing what the test is supposed to measure and the degree to which you think the test does what it is supposed to do, based on the reported validity and reliability scores.

APPLICATION EXERCISES

CASE INCIDENT

The Tough Screener

Everyone who knows Mack Rosen knows he is tough when it comes to screening applicants for jobs in his firm. His company, located in the northeast, provides financial planning advice to wealthy clients, sells insurance, and sets up pension plans for individuals and businesses. His firm's clients range from professionals such as doctors and lawyers to business owners, who are sophisticated in financial matters and very busy people. They expect accurate advice provided in a clear and expeditious manner.

Rosen is always described as somewhat autocratic. The need to be very selective in whom he hires has led him to be extraordinarily careful about how he screens applicants. Some of his methods are probably beyond reproach. For example, he requires every applicant to provide a list of names and phone numbers of at least five people he or she worked with at each previous employer to use as references.

On the other hand, given legislation including the Civil Rights Act of 1991 and the ADA, some of his other "tough" screening methods could be problematic. For example, Rosen requires that all applicants take a purported honesty test, which he found in the catalog of an office supply store.

(continued)

He also believes it's extremely important to check every viable applicant's credit history and workers' compensation history. Unknown to his applicants, he runs a credit check on each of them, and retains the services of a firm that checks workers' compensation and driving violation histories.

QUESTIONS

1. What specific legal problems do you think Rosen might run into because of his firm's screening methods? How would you suggest he eliminate these problems?

2. Given what you know about Rosen's business, write a two-page proposal describing an employee testing and selection program that you would recommend. Say a few words about the sorts of tests, if any, you would recommend and the application form questions you would ask, as well as other methods, including drug screening and reference checking.

CONTINUING CASE

Carter Cleaning Company

Honesty Testing at Carter Cleaning Company

Jennifer Carter, of the Carter Cleaning Centers, and her father have what the latter describes as an easy but hard job when it comes to screening job applicants. It is easy because for two important jobs—the people who actually do the pressing and those who do the cleaning/spotting—the applicants are easily screened with about 20 minutes of on-the-job testing. As with typists, Jennifer points out, "Applicants either know how to press clothes fast enough or how to use cleaning chemicals and machines, or they don't, and we find out very quickly by just trying them out on the job." On the other hand, applicant screening for the stores can also be frustratingly hard because of the nature of some of the other qualities that Jennifer would like to screen for. Two of the most critical problems facing her company are employee turnover and employee honesty. Jennifer and her father sorely need to implement practices that will reduce the rate of employee turnover. If there is a way to do this through employee testing and screening techniques, Jennifer would like to know about it because of the management time and money that are now being wasted by the never-ending need to recruit and hire new employees. Of even greater concern to Jennifer and her father is the need to institute new practices to screen out those employees who may be predisposed to steal from the company.

Employee theft is an enormous problem for the Carter Cleaning Centers, and one that is not limited to employees who handle the cash. For example, the cleaner/spotter and/or the presser often open the store themselves, without a manager present, to get the day's work started, and it is not unusual to have one or more of these people steal supplies or "run a route." Running a route means that an employee canvasses his or her neighborhood to pick up people's clothes for cleaning and then secretly cleans and presses them in the Carter store, using the company's supplies, gas, and power. It would also not be unusual for an unsupervised person (or his or her supervisor, for that matter) to accept a 1-hour rush order for cleaning or laundering, quickly clean and press the item, and return it to the customer for payment without making out a proper ticket for the item posting the sale. The money, of course, goes into the worker's pocket instead of into the cash register.

The more serious problem concerns the store manager and the counter workers who actually handle the cash. According to Jack Carter, "You would not believe the creativity employees use to get around the management controls we set up to cut down on employee theft." As one extreme example of this felonious creativity, Jack tells the following story: "To cut down on the amount of money my employees were stealing, I had a small sign printed and placed in front of all our cash registers. The sign said: YOUR ENTIRE ORDER FREE IF WE DON'T GIVE YOU A CASH REGISTER RECEIPT WHEN YOU PAY. CALL 552–0235. It was my intention with this sign to force all our cash-handling employees to give receipts so the cash register would record them for my accountants. After all, if all the cash that comes in is recorded in the cash register, then we should have a much better handle on stealing in our stores. Well, one of our managers found a diabolical way around this. I came into the store one night and noticed that the cash register this particular manager was using just didn't look right, although the sign was placed in front of it. It turned out that every afternoon at about 5:00 P.M. when the other employees left, this character would pull his own cash register out of a box that he hid underneath our supplies. Customers coming in would notice the sign and, of course, the fact that he was meticulous in ringing up every sale. But unknown

to them and us, for about 5 months the sales that came in for about an hour every day went into his cash register, not mine. It took us that long to figure out where our cash for that store was going."

The following are the questions Jennifer would like you to answer.

QUESTIONS

1. What would be the advantages and disadvantages to the company of routinely administering honesty tests to all its employees?
2. Specifically, what other screening techniques could the company use to screen out theft-prone and turnover-prone employees, and how exactly could these be used?
3. How should the company terminate employees caught stealing, and what kind of procedure should be set up for handling reference calls about these employees when they go to other companies looking for jobs?

EXPERIENTIAL EXERCISE

The Most Important Person You'll Ever Hire

Purpose: The purpose of this exercise is to give you practice using some of the interview techniques you learned from this chapter.

Required Understanding: You should be familiar with the information presented in this chapter, and read this: For parents, children are precious. It's therefore interesting that parents who hire "nannies" to take care of their children usually do little more than ask several interview questions and conduct what is often, at best, a perfunctory reference check. Given the often questionable validity of interviews, and the (often) relative inexperience of the father or mother doing the interviewing, it's not surprising that many of these arrangements end in disappointment. You know from this chapter that it is difficult to conduct a valid interview unless you know exactly what you're looking

for and, preferably, structure the interview. Most parents simply aren't trained to do this.

How to Set Up the Exercise/Instructions:

1. If so desired, divide the class into teams. Two students should be the interviewees; the others will serve as panel interviewers. The interviewees will develop an interviewer assessment form, and the panel interviewers will develop a structured situational interview for a "nanny."
2. Instructions for the interviewees: The interviewees should leave the room for about 20 minutes. While out of the room, the interviewees should develop an "interviewer assessment form" based on the information presented in this chapter regarding factors that can undermine the usefulness of an interview. During the panel interview, the interviewees should assess the interviewers by using the interviewer assessment form. After the panel interviewers have conducted the interview, the interviewees should leave

(continued)

the room to discuss their notes. Did the interviewers exhibit any of the problems that can undermine the usefulness of an interview? If so, which ones? What suggestions would you (the interviewees) make to the interviewers on how to improve the usefulness of the interview?

3. Instructions for the interviewers: While the interviewees are out of the room, the panel interviewers should develop a short structured situational interview form (see for instance Figure 4-5 and Table 4-1) for a "nanny." The panel interview team will interview two candidates for the position. During the panel interview, each interviewer should take notes on a copy of the structured situational interview form. After the panel interview, the panel interviewers should discuss their notes. What were your first impressions of each interviewee? Were your impressions similar? Which candidate would you all select for the position and why?

Five

Training and Developing Employees

When you finish studying this chapter you should be able to:

- Explain *each of the steps in the ADDIE training process.*
- Discuss *at least two techniques used for assessing training needs.*
- Explain *the pros and cons of at least five training techniques.*
- Explain *what management development is and why it is important.*
- Describe *the main management development techniques.*

OVERVIEW

After the recession hit, Macy's focused on cutting costs, and its sales associates' customer service suffered. Management now must put in place a comprehensive training plan. The main purpose of this chapter is to explain how to plan, develop, and implement training programs. The topics we cover include Orienting Employees, The Training Process, Implementation: Training Techniques, Management Development and Training, Managing Organizational Change and Development, and Evaluating the Training Effort.

ORIENTING EMPLOYEES

After screening and selecting new employees, management turns to orienting and training them. **Employee orientation** (often called "onboarding" today) involves more than what most people realize.[1] It should of course provide new employees with the basic background information they need to perform their jobs, such as company rules. But orientation should also help to socialize the employee into the employer's way of doing things. *Socialization* is the ongoing process of instilling in employees the attitudes, standards, values, and patterns of behavior that the organization expects.[2] Appreciating the company's culture and values distinguishes today's *onboarding* from traditional orientation.[3] For example, the Mayo Clinic's "heritage and culture" program emphasizes core Mayo Clinic values such as teamwork, personal responsibility, and mutual respect.[4]

Types of Programs

Orientation programs range from brief introductions to lengthy programs. In either, new employees usually receive printed or Web-based handbooks covering things like working hours, performance reviews, and vacations, as well as a facilities tour. Other information might cover employee benefits, personnel policies, the employee's daily routine, company organization and operations, and safety regulations.[5] (Courts may find that your employee handbook represents a contract. Make it clear that statements of company policies, benefits, and regulations do not constitute the terms and conditions of an employment contract.) In firms like Macy's, the onboarding may include videos, lectures by company officers, and exercises covering matters like company history, vision, and values.

Purposes

A successful orientation should make the new employee should feel welcome. He or she should understand the organization in a broad sense (its past, present, culture, and vision of the future). The employee should be clear about what the firm expects in terms of policies, procedures, and work and behavior, and also start becoming socialized into the firm's ways of doing things.[6]

Technology

Technology improves orientation. For example, some firms provide new managers with preloaded personal digital assistants. These contain information such as key contact information, and even images of employees the new manager needs to know.[7] Some firms provide all new employees with URLs or disks containing discussions of corporate culture, videos of corporate facilities, and welcoming addresses from top managers. ION Geophysical uses an online onboarding portal called RedCarpet. New hires view things like photos and profiles of members of their work teams.[8]

The HR specialist usually starts the orientation, explaining matters like working hours and vacations. The employee's new supervisor continues the orientation by explaining the exact nature of the job, introducing the person to his or her new colleagues, and familiarizing the new employee with the workplace and the job.

THE TRAINING PROCESS

Training refers to the methods employers use to give new or present employees the skills they need to perform their jobs.

The best training departments measure their own performance in terms of how much impact they have on the company's performance.[9] Training has an impressive record of influencing organizational effectiveness, scoring higher than appraisal and just below goal setting in its effect on productivity.[10]

Aligning Strategy and Training

The employer's strategic plans should ultimately govern its training goals.[11] In essence, the task is to identify the employee behaviors the firm will require to execute its strategy, and from that deduce what competencies employees will need. Then, put in place training goals and programs to instill these competencies. As one trainer said, "We sit down with management and help them identify strategic goals and objectives and the skills and knowledge needed to achieve them."[12]

STRATEGY AND HR   As an example, having navigated its way through the recession, Macy's top management turned to a new strategy in 2011. As its CEO said, "We are [now] talking about a cultural shift . . . becoming more of a growth company."[13] To produce the improved customer service that Macy's new growth strategy depended on, Macy's installed a new training program. Rather than just watching a 90-minute video as they previously did, sales associates now attend 3½-hour training sessions. Macy's management believes the resulting improvement in service will be the biggest factor in achieving Macy's growth goals.[14]

Training and Performance

One survey found that "establishing a linkage between learning and organizational performance" was the number-one pressing issue facing training professionals.[15] Some training experts use the phrase "workplace learning and performance" instead of "training" to underscore training's dual aims of employee learning and organizational performance.[16] Training has an impressive record of influencing performance.[17] Companies recently spent on average $1,103 per employee for training per year and offered each about 28 hours of training.[18]

The ADDIE Five-Step Training Process

The employer should use a rational training process. The gold standard here is still the basic analysis–design–develop–implement–evaluate (**ADDIE**) **training process** model that training experts have used for years.[19] As an example, one training vendor describes its training process as follows:

- *Analyze* the training need.
- *Design* the overall training program.
- *Develop* the course (actually assembling/creating the training materials).
- *Implement* training, by actually training the targeted employee group using methods such as on-the-job or online training.
- *Evaluate* the course's effectiveness.[20]

We'll look at each step next.

Analyzing the Training Needs

Analyzing employees' training needs usually involves either *task analysis*—breaking the jobs into subtasks and teaching each to the new employee—or *performance analysis*—determining the nature of the performance problem.

Employers use task analysis to determine *new* employees' training needs. With inexperienced personnel, your aim is to provide the skills and knowledge required for effective performance. **Task analysis** is a detailed study of the job to determine what specific skills—such as soldering (in the case of an assembly worker) or interviewing (in the case of a supervisor)—is required. The job description and job specification list the job's specific duties and skills and are the basic reference points for determining the training required. Figure 5-1 summarizes other methods for uncovering a job's training needs.

For *current* employees, requests for training often start with line managers expressing concerns, such as "we're getting too many complaints from clients."[21] The first step here is therefore to determine what training, if any, is required. Some call this the "skills gapping" process. Ideally, employers determine the skills each job requires and the skills of the job's current or prospective employees. The employer then designs a training program to eliminate the skills gap.[22]

The problem here is that training may not be the solution. **Performance analysis** means verifying that there is a performance deficiency and determining whether that deficiency should be rectified through training or through some other means (such as transferring the employee or changing the compensation plan). Analytical tools here include:

- Supervisor, peer, self-, and 360-degree performance reviews
- Job-related performance data (such as productivity, absenteeism, accidents, waste, late deliveries, product quality, and customer complaints)
- Observation by supervisors or other specialists
- Interviews with the employee or his or her supervisor
- Tests of things like job knowledge, skills, and attendance
- Attitude surveys
- Assessment centers[23]

Performance analysis usually starts with appraising the employee's performance. For example,

"Other plants our size average no more than two serious accidents per month; we're averaging five."

For current employees, distinguishing between "can't do" and "won't do" problems is the heart of performance analysis. First, determine whether it's a "can't do" problem and, if so, its cause. For example, perhaps the employees don't know what to do or what your standards are, or there are obstacles such as inadequate supplies. Perhaps job aids are needed, such as color-coded wires that show assemblers what wire goes where; or poor screening results in people who haven't the skills to do the job; or training is inadequate. Or, it might be a "won't do" problem. Here, employees *could* do a good job if they wanted to. If this is the case, the manager may have to change the reward system, perhaps by implementing an incentive plan.

Tools for Uncovering Training Needs	Training Need Information
1. Job Descriptions	Outlines the job's typical duties and responsibilities but is not meant to be all-inclusive. Helps define performance discrepancies.
2. Job Specifications or Task Analysis	List specified tasks required for each job. More specific than job descriptions. Specifications may extend to judgments of knowledge and skills required of job incumbents.
3. Performance Standards	Objectives of the job, and standards by which they are judged.
4. Performing the Job	Most effective way of identifying a job's specific training needs, but has serious limitations in higher-level jobs because of longer gaps between performance and resulting outcomes.
5. Observe Job-Work Sampling	Same as 4 above.

6. Review Literature Concerning the Job
   a. Research in other industries
   b. Professional journals
   c. Documents
   d. Government sources
   e. Ph.D. theses
	Possibly useful, but far removed from the job within any specific organization or specific performance requirements.

7. Ask Questions About the Job
   a. Of the job holder
   b. Of the supervisor
   c. Of higher management
	Inputs from several viewpoints can often reveal training needs or training desires.

8. Training Committees or Conferences	Same as 7 above.

9. Analysis of Operating Problems
   a. Downtime reports
   b. Waste
   c. Repairs
   d. Late deliveries
   e. Quality control
	Indications of problems that interfere with job performance.

FIGURE 5-1 Tools for Uncovering a Job's Training Needs. *Source:* Blanchard, P. Nick; Thacker, James W, *Effective Training: Systems, Strategies and Practices,* © 1999. Printed and Electronically reproduced by permission of Pearson Education, Inc., Upper Saddle River, New Jersey.

TALENT MANAGEMENT: USING PROFILES AND COMPETENCY MODELS   Talent management involves using the same set or list of competencies for recruiting employees as for selecting, training, appraising, and paying them. The **competency model** consolidates, usually in one diagram, a precise summary of the competencies (the knowledge, skills, and behaviors) someone would need to do the job well. As an example, the competency rating form in chapter 4 (Figure 4-5, page 112) summarizes what to look for in someone with good (or bad) interpersonal competency skills.[24] At Sharp Electronics, training managers interview executives to identify Sharp's new strategic objectives, and to infer what employee competencies those objectives will require. Trainers also interview the job's top performers to identify competencies (such as "focuses on the customer") the latter believe are important.[25]

The employer would use the resulting profile (list of competencies) to formulate training objectives. Thus to develop a trainee's "test administration competency," one might use the training objective "By completion of the HR manager training program, the trainee will be fully skilled at using the five tools our firm uses to test applicants."

Designing the Training Program

Armed with the needs analysis results, the manager next designs the overall training program. *Design* means planning the overall training program including training objectives, delivery methods, and program evaluation. Sub-steps here include setting performance objectives, creating a detailed training outline (all training program steps from start to finish), choosing a program delivery format (such as lectures or Web), and verifying the overall program design with management. The design should include your learning objectives as well as how you plan to set a training environment that motivates your trainees to learn. It is also at the design stage that the manager reviews possible training program content (including workbooks, exercises, and activities), and estimates a budget for the training program.[26]

SETTING LEARNING OBJECTIVES   The learning objectives should address rectifying the performance deficiencies that you identified with needs analysis. Thus, if the sales team's sales are 40% too low, the objectives should focus on ensuring they get the knowledge, skills, and attitudes they need to boost sales. At the same time, the learning objectives must be practical. One constraint is financial. The employer will want to see and approve a training budget for the program.

CREATING A MOTIVATIONAL LEARNING ENVIRONMENT   Learning requires both ability and motivation, and the training program's learning environment should foster both. In terms of *ability*, the learner–trainee needs (among other things) the required reading, writing, and mathematics skills, and the educational level, intelligence, and knowledge base. Second, the learner must be motivated to learn the material. Many books have been written about how to motivate employees, but several specific observations are pertinent here.[27] The accompanying HR in Practice feature presents useful guidelines.

HR IN PRACTICE

How to Create a Motivational Learning Environment

Make the Learning Meaningful

Learners are always more motivated to learn something that has meaning for them. Therefore:

1. At the start of training, provide a bird's-eye view of the material that you are going to present.[28]
2. Use a variety of familiar examples.
3. Organize the information so you can present it logically, and in meaningful units.
4. Use terms and concepts that are already familiar to trainees.
5. Use as many visual aids as possible.
6. Create a perceived training need in trainees' minds.[29] For example, "before the training, managers need to sit down and talk with the trainees about why they are enrolled in the class, what they are expected to learn, and how they can use it on the job."[30]

Make Skills Transfer Easy

Make it easy to *transfer* new skills and behaviors from the training site to the job site:

1. Maximize the similarity between the training situation and the work situation.
2. Provide adequate practice.
3. Label or identify each feature of the machine and/or step in the process.
4. Direct the trainees' attention to important aspects of the job. For example, if you're training a customer service rep to handle calls, explain the different types of calls he or she will encounter.[31]
5. Provide "heads-up" information. For example, supervisors often face stressful conditions. You can reduce the negative impact of such events by letting supervisory trainees know they might occur.[32]
6. Trainees learn best at their own pace. If possible, let them pace themselves.

Reinforce the Learning

Make sure the learner gets plenty of feedback. In particular:

1. Trainees learn best when the trainers immediately reinforce correct responses, perhaps with a quick "well done."
2. The learning curve goes down late in the day. Therefore "full day training is not as effective as half the day or three-fourths of the day."[33]

In sum, one training expert suggests asking these questions prior to designing and implementing the training event:[34]

- What organizational need will the requested training address?
- What issues are driving the training request?
- Is training the solution?
- How will trainees' performance improve due to training?
- What can the organization expect as a return on its investment?

Developing the Program or Course

Program development means actually assembling/creating the program's training materials. It means choosing the actual content the program will present, as well as creating/obtaining the specific instructional methods (lectures, cases, Web-based, etc.)

you will use. Training equipment and materials include (for example) iPads, workbooks, lectures, PowerPoint slides, Web- and computer-based activities, course activities, trainer resources (manuals, for instance), and support materials.

Some employers create their own training content, but there's also a vast selection of online and offline content from which to choose. You'll find turnkey, off-the-shelf programs on virtually any topic—from occupational safety to sexual harassment to Web design—from tens of thousands of online and offline providers. (See, for example, the American Society for Training and Development's Infoline at www.astd.org, www.trainerswarehouse.com, and www.gneil.com, among thousands of such suppliers.)[35] Turnkey training packages may typically include trainer's guide, self-study book, video, and other content.

Once you design, approve, and develop the program, management can implement it. *Implement* means actually provide the training, using one or more of the instructional options (such as lectures) that we discuss next.

IMPLEMENTATION: TRAINING TECHNIQUES

After analyzing the training needs, and designing and developing the training program, the manager turns to implementing the program. We look at popular training techniques next.

On-the-Job Training

The most familiar **on-the-job training** (OJT) technique is the coaching or understudy method. Here an experienced worker or supervisor trains the employee, on the job. Job rotation, in which an employee (usually a management trainee) moves from job to job at planned intervals, is another on-the-job technique. Special assignments similarly give lower-level executives firsthand experience in working on actual problems. The Men's Wearhouse, with stores nationwide, uses on-the-job training. It has few full-time trainers. Instead, it has a formal process of "cascading" responsibility for training: Every manager is formally accountable for the development of his or her direct subordinates.[36]

Many firms use "peer training" for OJT. Here, for instance, expert employees answer calls at selected times during the day or participate in in-house "radio programs" to answer their peers' call-in questions about technical aspects of doing their jobs.[37]

Informal Learning

Surveys estimate that as much as 80% of what employees learn on the job they learn through informal means, including collaboration with their colleagues.[38]

Although managers don't arrange informal learning, they can help to ensure that it occurs. For example, Siemens Power Transmission and Distribution, in North Carolina, places tools in cafeterias to capitalize on work-related discussions. Even installing whiteboards and keeping them stocked with markers can facilitate informal learning. Sun Microsystems implemented an informal online learning tool called Sun Learning exchange. This is now a platform containing more than 5,000 informal learning items addressing topics ranging from sales to technical support.[39]

Apprenticeship Training

Apprenticeship training is a structured process by which individuals become skilled workers through a combination of classroom instruction and on-the-job training, usually under the tutelage of a master craftsperson.[40] When steelmaker Dofasco discovered that many of its employees would be retiring during the next 5 to 10 years, it revived its apprenticeship-training program. Applicants are prescreened; new recruits then spend about 32 months learning various jobs under the tutelage of experienced craftspersons.[41]

The U.S. Department of Labor's National Apprenticeship System promotes apprenticeship programs. Over 460,000 apprentices participate in 28,000 programs, and registered programs can receive federal and state contracts and other assistance.[42] Figure 5-2 lists popular recent apprenticeships.

Behavior Modeling

Behavior modeling involves showing trainees the right (or model) way of doing something, letting each person practice the right way to do it, and providing feedback regarding performance. The basic behavior modeling procedure is as follows:

1. *Modeling.* First, trainees watch DVDs showing model persons behaving effectively in a problem situation.
2. *Role playing.* Next, the trainees are given roles to play in a simulated situation.
3. *Social reinforcement.* The trainer provides praise and constructive feedback based on how the trainee performs in the role play.
4. *Transfer of training.* Finally, trainees are encouraged to apply their new skills when they are back on their jobs.

Vestibule Training

Vestibule training is a technique in which trainees learn on the actual or simulated equipment they will use on the job but receive their training off the job. Such training is necessary when on-the-job training is too costly or dangerous. Putting new assembly-line workers right to work could slow production, for instance. Vestibule training may

---

The U.S. Department of Labor's Registered Apprenticeship program offers access to 1,000 career areas, including the following top occupations:

- Able seaman
- Carpenter
- Chef
- Child care development specialist
- Construction craft laborer
- Dental assistant
- Electrician
- Elevator constructor
- Fire medic
- Law enforcement agent
- Over-the-road truck driver
- Pipefitter

FIGURE 5-2 Some Popular Apprenticeships.   *Source:* From United States Department of Labor.

just take place in a separate room with the equipment the trainees will actually use on the job (thus "vestibule" training). However, it often involves the use of equipment simulators, as in pilot training. As an example, UPS uses a realistic learning lab for a 46-hour, 5-day training program for drivers.[43]

Audiovisual and Traditional Distance Learning Techniques

Audiovisual tools, including DVDs, films, closed-circuit TV, and audiodiscs, are widely used. Ford uses videos in its dealer training sessions to simulate sample reactions to customer complaints, for example. Firms, of course, also use various distance-learning methods for training. Distance learning includes traditional correspondence courses, as well as videoconferencing and Internet-based classes.[44] For example, the Macy's Satellite Network teletraining (television-based training) program supports training the firm's employees around the country.

VIDEOCONFERENCE DISTANCE LEARNING   Videoconferencing is popular for training geographically dispersed employees, and involves delivering programs via compressed audio and video signals over cable broadband lines, the Internet, or satellite. Vendors offer videoconference products such as Webex (www.cisco.com/en/US/products/ps10352/index.html) and TelePresence. Employers typically use videoconferencing technology with other technology. For example, Cisco's Unified Video Conferencing (CUVC) product line combines Cisco group collaboration and decision-making software with videoconferencing, video telephony, and realistic "TelePresence" capabilities.[45]

INTERACTIVE LEARNING   Employers are also moving from textbook and classroom-based learning to interactive learning. For example, Cheesecake Factory employees use VideoCafé, a YouTube-type platform, to let employees "upload and share video snippets on job-related topics, including customer greetings and food preparation."[46] The company is also emphasizing interactive games, including a simulation that shows employees how to build the "perfect hamburger."

Computer-Based Training

In **computer-based training (CBT)**, the trainee uses a computer-based system to increase his or her knowledge or skills interactively. This often involves computerized simulations and multimedia.[47] For example, in one training program, recruitment trainees start with a computer screen that shows the "applicant's" employment application, as well as information about the job. The trainee then begins a simulated interview by typing in questions, which are answered by a videotaped model acting as the applicant and whose responses to a multitude of questions have been programmed into the computer. At the end of the session, the computer tells the trainee where he or she went wrong and offers further instructional material.

SIMULATED LEARNING   One survey asked training professionals what experiences qualified as "simulated learning." The percentages choosing each experience were:

- Virtual reality-type games, 19%
- Step-by-step animated guide, 8%
- Scenarios with questions and decision trees overlaying animation, 19%
- Online role play with photos and videos, 14%

- Software training including screenshots with interactive requests for responses, 35%
- Other, 6%[48]

Employers increasingly rely on computerized simulations to inject more realism into their training programs. For example, Orlando-based Environmental Tectonics Corporation created an Advanced Disaster Management simulation for emergency medical response trainees. One simulated scenario involves a passenger plane crashing into a runway. So realistic that it's "unsettling," trainees including firefighters respond to the simulated crash's sights and sounds via pointing devices and radios.[49]

Other employers capitalize on "Web 2.0". *Web 2.0 learning* utilizes online technologies such as social networks (for example Facebook, twitter, and LinkedIn), virtual worlds (such as Second Life), and systems that blend synchronous and asynchronous delivery with blogs, chat rooms, Internet researchers, bookmark sharing, and tools such as 3-D simulations. For example, British Petroleum (BP) uses it to train new gas station employees. The aim is to show new gas station employees how to use the safety features of gasoline storage tanks. BP built three-dimensional renderings of the tank systems in Second Life. Trainees could use these to "see underground" and observe the effects of the safety devices.[50]

Internet-Based Training

Trainers of course employ Internet-based learning to deliver programs. Delta Air Lines customer service personnel receive much of their annual required FAA training via the Internet. Prior to this, employees had to travel to one of five training centers, keeping them away from their jobs for at least the day.[51] The Italian eyewear company Luxottica (whose brands include LensCrafters, Pearl Vision, and Sunglass Hut) provides standardized training to its 38,000 employees worldwide via instant access online to information such as new products and regulations.[52]

LEARNING PORTALS Companies increasingly set up and deliver employee training through internal intranet portals. They often contract with *applications service providers* such as SkillSoft (www.skillsoft.com) or, for health and safety training, PureSafety (www.puresafety.com), to deliver online training courses to the firms' employees.

LEARNING MANAGEMENT SYSTEMS Online learning management systems (LMSs) help employers to identify training needs, and to schedule, deliver, and assess and manage the online training itself. For example, General Motors uses an LMS to help its dealers in Africa and the Middle East deliver training programs. The Internet-based LMS includes a course catalog, supervisor-approved self-enrollment, facilities and training schedule management, and assessment systems (including pre- and post-course tests).[53]

In practice, many employers opt for "blended learning." Here the trainees use several delivery methods (such as manuals, in-class lectures, self-guided e-learning programs, and Web-based seminars, or "webinars") to learn the material.[54]

Mobile Learning

Mobile learning (or "on-demand learning") means delivering learning content on demand via mobile devices like cell phones, iPads, and iPhones, wherever and whenever the learner wants to access it.[55] For example, using dominKnow's (www.dominknow.com/)

iPod touch and iPhone-optimized Touch Learning Center Portal, trainees can log in and take full online courses.[56]

Capital One Bank purchased 3,000 iPods for trainees who had enrolled in one of the instructor-led courses at its Capital One University.[57] The training department then had an Internet audio book provider create an audio learning site within Capital One's firewall. Employees used it to download the instructor-requested books and other materials to their iPods.[58] IBM uses mobile learning to deliver just-in-time information (for instance, about new product features) to its sales force. To increase accessibility, IBM's training department often breaks up, say, an hour program into 10-minute pieces.[59] J.P. Morgan encourages employees to use instant messaging (IM) as a quick learning device. Employers also use IM to supplement classroom training, for instance, by using IM for online office hours and for group chats. One training manager sends short personal development ideas each day for others to access via his Twitter account.[60]

THE VIRTUAL CLASSROOM   A **virtual classroom** uses special collaboration software to enable multiple remote learners, using their PCs, laptops, or iPads to participate in live audio and visual discussions, communicate via written text, and learn via content such as PowerPoint slides.

The virtual classroom combines the best of Web-based learning offered by systems like Blackboard and WebCT with live video and audio. WizIQ is one example (www.wiziq.com/Virtual_Classroom.aspx). It enables learners to communicate with clear two-way audio, build communities with user profiles and live video, collaborate with chat and shared whiteboards, and learn with shared applications such as PowerPoint slides.

Training for Special Purposes

Training today does more than just prepare employees to perform their jobs. Training for special purposes—dealing with diversity, for instance—is required too. A sampling of special-purpose training programs follows.

LITERACY TRAINING TECHNIQUES   Functional illiteracy—the inability to do basic reading, writing, and arithmetic—is a serious problem at work.[61] One study called the American workforce "ill-prepared."[62]

Employers take various approaches to teaching basic skills. For example, at one Borg-Warner plant, managers chose employee participants and placed them in three classes of 15 students each based on math and reading test scores. There were two trainers from a local training company. Each session was to run a maximum of 200 hours. However, employees could leave when they reached a predetermined skill level.[63] Classes were 5 days per week, 2 hours per day, with classes scheduled so that one hour was during the employee's personal time and the second was on company time.

Other employers turn to private firms like Education Management Corporation or local teachers to design and provide the required education.[64] Another simple approach is to have supervisors teach basic skills. For example, if an employee needs to use a manual to find out how to change a part, teach that person how to use an index to locate the relevant section.

MANAGING THE NEW WORKFORCE: DIVERSITY TRAINING   *Diversity training* aims to improve cross-cultural sensitivity with the goal of fostering more harmonious working relationships among a firm's employees. It includes improving interpersonal skills, understanding and valuing cultural differences, socializing employees into the corporate culture, indoctrinating new workers into the U.S. work ethic, improving English proficiency and basic math skills, and improving bilingual skills for English-speaking employees.[65] IBM has online diversity programs regarding inclusive leadership and sexual harassment. Training materials include interactive learning modules. These enable trainees to practice what they've learned, testimonials from IBM executives, and self-assessment tools.[66]

Most employers opt for an off-the-shelf diversity training program such as *Just Be F.A.I.R.: A practical approach to diversity and the workplace*, from VisionPoint productions. The package includes streaming video, a facilitator's discussion guide, participant materials and workbook, a DVD with print materials, PowerPoint slides, and two videos (the purchase price for the entire program is about $1,000). It includes vignettes illustrating such things as the importance of communicating and the potential pitfalls of stereotyping people.[67]

TEAM TRAINING   Teamwork doesn't always comes naturally. Companies therefore devote many hours to training new employees to listen to each other and to cooperate. A team-building program at a Baltimore Coca-Cola plant illustrates what team training typically involves.[68] In this case, the plant suffered from high turnover and absenteeism. The new plant manager decided to re-organize around teams and to use team training to support the new organization. Team training here focused on technical, interpersonal, and team management issues. In terms of *technical training*, for instance, management encouraged team employees to learn each other's jobs, with the aim of encouraging flexible team assignments. **Cross training** means training employees to do different tasks or jobs than their own; doing so facilitates flexibility and job rotation, as when you expect team members to occasionally share jobs.

PROVIDING EMPLOYEES WITH LIFELONG LEARNING   **Lifelong learning** means providing employees with continuing learning experiences over their tenure with the firm, with the aims of ensuring they have the opportunity to learn the skills they need to do their jobs and to expand their horizons. With more emphasis today on employee empowerment and decision making, programs like these might range from training in English as a second language to computer literacy to college work.[69]

The accompanying Global Issues in HR feature discusses some special training needs abroad.

GLOBAL ISSUES IN HR

Supervisory Training Abroad

Sometimes, supervisory training programs address special issues when implemented abroad. For example, Gap Inc. signed an agreement with a World Bank affiliate to provide supervisory training for line managers in the Cambodian garment factories of Gap's suppliers.[70] The firm's goal was to improve labor relations of their vendors abroad. Gap's supervisory training program therefore covers matters such as how to handle worker complaints, human resource management, personal productivity, and conflict resolution.

MANAGEMENT DEVELOPMENT AND TRAINING

Management development is any attempt to improve managerial performance by imparting knowledge, changing attitudes, or increasing skills. The ultimate aim of such development programs is to enhance the organization's future performance. For this reason, the overall management development process ideally consists of assessing the company's needs (for instance, to fill future executive openings, appraising the managers' performance, and then developing the managers themselves).[71]

The program should make sense in terms of the company's strategy and goals. Caterpillar Inc. created Caterpillar University to oversee its training and development programs. The university has a board of directors comprised of company executives. They set the university's policies and oversee "the alignment of the corporation's learning needs with the enterprise's business strategy."[72]

There is a trend toward supplementing traditional development methods (such as lectures and case discussions) with realistic methods like action learning, where trainees solve actual company problems.[73] The most popular development methods include classroom-based learning, executive coaching, action learning, 360-degree feedback, experiential learning, off-site retreats (where managers meet with colleagues for learning), mentoring, and job rotation.[74] We look at some of these.

Managerial On-the-Job Training

On-the-job training isn't just for workers. It's also a popular manager development method. Important variants include **job rotation**, the **coaching/understudy method**, and **action learning**. *Job rotation* means moving management trainees from department to department to broaden their understanding of all parts of the business. The trainee—often a recent college grad—may spend several months in each department; this helps the trainee to not only broaden his or her experience but also discover the jobs he or she prefers. The trainee thus learns each department's business by actually doing it. With the *coaching/understudy* method, the new manager receives ongoing advice, often from the person he or she is to replace.

Action Learning

Action learning means letting managers work full time on real projects, analyzing and solving problems, usually in departments other than their own. The trainees meet periodically within a four- or five-person project group to discuss their findings. The groups then present their recommendations to the president and executive staff and the head of the division they've been studying.

The Case Study Method

The **case study method** presents a trainee with a written description of an organizational problem. The person analyzes the case, diagnoses the problem, and presents his or her findings and solutions in a discussion with other trainees.[75]

The case study method aims, first, to give trainees realistic experience in identifying and analyzing complex problems in an environment wherein their discussion leader can subtly guide their progress. Through the class discussion, trainees also learn that there are usually many ways to approach and solve organizational problems. They also learn that their own needs and values often influence the solutions they suggest.

Management Games

Computerized **management games** enable trainees to learn by making realistic decisions in simulated situations. One game, *Interpret*, aims to improve team communication and the planning and implementation of a strategy.[76]

Improvisation is a recent variant. For example, trainers working for Nike used an improvisational game called "word ball." Here trainees pass a make-believe ball to one another, each time calling out one word. (Thus, the first person might pass the ball and call out "cat." Then the second catches and then passes on the make-believe ball and calls out "furry," and so on.) The aim was to get the Nike engineers "to instantly react without thinking,...to be unafraid to look foolish."[77]

Outside Programs and Seminars

Many vendors offer management development seminars and conferences. The American Management Association (AMA), for instance, provides thousands of courses in general management, human resources, and sales and marketing. Courses cover topics such as how to sharpen business writing skills, strategic planning, and assertiveness training.[78] Other vendors include AMR International, Inc., the Conference Board, and many universities.[79] The Society for Human Resource Management offers numerous courses for HR professionals.

University-Related Programs

Colleges and universities provide several types of management development activities. Many offer certificates, courses, and programs in areas such as business, management, and health care administration. Managers can take these as matriculated or nonmatriculated students to fill skills gaps.

JOINT PROGRAMS Some employers offer their employees in-house degree programs in cooperation with colleges and universities. Many also offer a variety of in-house lectures and seminars by university staff. University-based executive education is becoming more realistic, relying more on action learning, business simulations, and experiential learning.[80]

EXAMPLE For example, when Hasbro Inc. needed to improve the creativity skills of its top executives, it turned to the Amos Tuck business school at Dartmouth University. It wanted "a custom approach...built from the ground up to suit Hasbro's specific needs."[81]

Hasbro and Tuck's program directors designed a special version of Tuck's 1-week Global Leadership Development Program, with four elements. First, when participants first arrive, they receive sealed envelopes containing their "360-degree" performance assessment reports, carefully secured for confidentiality. Second, managers receive group and individual coaching from special "executive coaches." The aim here is to help Hasbro executives identify blind spots that may be hampering their performance and to develop plans to address them. Third, they participate in MBA-type courses, based on their and Hasbro's needs. Finally, the executives work in action-learning teams, under the guidance of Hasbro's in-house coaches.

In-House Development Centers

Many firms have **in-house development centers** or "universities." These usually combine classroom learning (lectures and seminars, for instance) with other techniques such as assessment centers and online learning to help develop employees and other managers. For example, at General Electric's (GE) Leadership Institute, courses range from entry-level programs in manufacturing and sales to a business course for English majors. General Electric is known for its ability to develop executive talent. Its current mix of executive development programs illustrates what is available:[82]

Leadership Programs: These multiyear training programs rotate about 3,000 employees per year through various functions with the aim of enabling people to run a large GE business by age 30.

Session C: This is GE's intense multi-level performance appraisal process. The CEO personally reviews GE's top 625 officers every year.

Crotonville: This is GE's corporate training campus in New York; it offers a mix of conventional classroom learning and team-based training and cultural trips.

Boca Raton: At this annual meeting, GE's top 625 officers network, share their best ideas, and get to understand the company's strategy for the coming year.

The Next Big Thing: Whether it's productivity and quality improvement through "six Sigma" or "innovation," GE focuses its employees on central themes or initiatives.

Monthly Dinners: Jeffrey Immelt, GE's CEO, meets periodically at dinners and breakfasts with selected executives individually to learn more about them and to "strengthen his connections with his top team."[83]

LEARNING PORTALS   Employers increasingly offer virtual—rather than bricks-and-mortar—corporate university services. For example, Cerner, a health care information technology company, offers its employees a portal called "Cerner KnowledgeWorks." This provides employees with three categories of knowledge: (1) Dynamic knowledge "is real-time content that flows back and forth, such as e-mails, instant messages, or conference calls"; (2) moderated content "includes best practices, such as case studies or wikis that capture information about situations where we did well and how we did it"; and (3) codified content "is more formal documentation of official company practices, and includes installation guides, help files, and formal training or courses."[84]

EXECUTIVE COACHES   Many firms use executive coaches to develop their top managers' effectiveness. An *executive coach* is an outside consultant who questions the executive's boss, peers, subordinates, and (sometimes) family in order to identify the executive's strengths and weaknesses and to counsel the executive so he or she can capitalize on those strengths and reduce weaknesses.[85] Coaches come from a variety of backgrounds including teaching, counseling, and the mental health professions.[86]

Executive coaching can be effective. Participants in one study were more likely to set more effective, specific goals for their subordinates and to have received improved ratings from subordinates and supervisors.[87] Experts recommend using formal assessments prior to coaching to uncover strengths and weaknesses and provide more focus for the coaching.[88]

Talent Management and Mission-Critical Employees: Differential Development Assignments

In today's competitive environment, the traditional HR practice of allocating pay raises, development opportunities, and other scarce resources more-or-less across the board or based mostly on performance is no longer viable. Talent management–oriented employers often focus more of their development resources on their "mission-critical employees"—those deemed critical to the companies' future growth. For example, a telecommunications firm previously spread pay and development money evenly over its 8,000 employees. When the recent recession came, company leaders began segmenting their talent into four groups: business impact, high performers, high potentials, and critical skills. Then they shifted their dollars away from low performers and those not making an impact. "While the company lost some low performers, the high performers and high potentials felt like they finally received recognition."[89]

MANAGING ORGANIZATIONAL CHANGE AND DEVELOPMENT

Today, intense international competition means companies have to change fast, perhaps changing their strategies to enter new businesses, or their organization charts, or their employees' attitudes and skills.

What to Change

The first question is, "What should we change?" A few years ago, Nokia was the world-wide leader in smartphones. Then, Apple introduced its iPhone. Within a year, Nokia's market share plummeted. By 2010, Nokia's board appointed a new CEO with Silicon Valley experience, Stephen Elop.[90] He knew Nokia's market share was down, and that Nokia's R&D was behind the times. He had to jumpstart Nokia.

Faced with situations like these, managers like Stephen Elop can change one or more of five aspects of their companies—their *strategy, culture, structure, technologies,* or the *attitudes and skills* of the employees.

STRATEGIC CHANGE Organizational turnarounds often start with a change in the firm's strategy, mission, and vision—with *strategic change*. For example, Elop partnered with Microsoft with the aim of introducing a new Microsoft-based smartphone within a year.

OTHER CHANGES Nokia's new CEO instituted other organizational changes. In terms of *structure,* Nokia split responsibility for its smartphones and handsets into two new units. He replaced managers in Nokia's mobile phones unit. In *technology,* Elop reduced the Symbian operating system's central role in its smartphones, replacing it with Microsoft's mobile operating system. With its *culture,* Elop had his new management team change the firm's culture, for instance by impressing on Nokia's employees the need to eradicate bureaucratic decision making and to execute on Nokia's new strategy. He put in place new training programs to provide the new required *skills.*

Major organizational changes like these are never easy, but perhaps the hardest part of leading a change is overcoming the resistance to it. Employees may resist the change, perhaps because they're accustomed to the usual way of doing things or because of perceived threats to their influence.[91]

Lewin's Process for Overcoming Resistance

Psychologist Kurt Lewin formulated a model of change to summarize what he believed was the basic process for implementing a change with minimal resistance. To Lewin, all behavior in organizations was a product of two forces: those striving to maintain the status quo and those pushing for change. Implementing change meant either reducing the forces for the status quo or building up the forces for change. Lewin's process consisted of three steps:

1. *Unfreezing* means reducing the forces that are striving to maintain the status quo, usually by presenting a provocative problem or event to get people to recognize the need for change.
2. *Moving* means developing new behaviors, values, and attitudes, either by reorganizing the company or by using other management development techniques (such as team building).
3. *Refreezing* means building in the reinforcement (such as new incentive plans) to make sure the organization does not slide back into its former ways of doing things.

Of course, actually choosing the right methods that will help you accomplish each of those three steps and then applying them is the tricky part. You'll find a 10-step process for leading organizational change in the HR in Practice feature.[92]

Organizational Development

There are many ways to reduce the resistance associated with organizational change. Among the suggestions are that managers impose rewards or sanctions to guide employee behaviors, explain why the change is needed, negotiate with employees, give inspirational speeches, or ask employees to help design the change.[93] Organizational development (OD) taps into the latter. **Organizational development** is a change process through which employees diagnose and formulate the change that's required and implement it, often with the assistance of trained consultants.

Action research is the foundation of most OD programs or interventions. It means gathering data about the organization and its operations and attitudes, with an eye toward solving a particular problem (for example, conflict between the sales and production departments); feeding back these data to the employees involved; and then having them team-plan solutions to the problems.

Specific examples of OD efforts (or "interventions") include survey feedback, sensitivity training, and team building. **Survey feedback** uses questionnaires to survey employees' attitudes and to provide feedback. The aim here is usually to crystallize for managers that there is a problem to address. They then use the results to discuss and solve the problem.

Sensitivity training aims to increase participants' insights into their behavior and the behavior of others by encouraging an open expression of feelings in the trainer-guided "T-group laboratory" (the "T" is for training). Sensitivity training seeks to accomplish its aim of increasing interpersonal sensitivity by requiring frank, candid discussions of each other in the small off-site T-group, specifically discussions of participants' personal feelings, attitudes, and behavior. As a result, it is a controversial method surrounded by debate and is used much less today than in the past.

Finally, **team building** refers to OD techniques aimed at improving the effectiveness of teams at work. The typical team-building program begins with the consultant

HR IN PRACTICE

A 10-Step Process for Leading Organizational Change

1. *Establish a sense of urgency.* For instance, create a crisis by exposing managers to major weaknesses relative to competitors.
2. *Mobilize commitment to change through joint diagnosis of business problems.* Next, create one or more task forces to diagnose the business problems. Such teams can produce a shared understanding of what changes can and must be made, and thereby mobilize the commitment of those who must actually implement the changes.
3. *Create a guiding coalition.* No leader can accomplish any significant change alone. That's why most leaders create a guiding coalition of influential people who can be missionaries and implementers of change.
4. *Develop a shared vision.* Create a general statement of the organization's intended direction that evokes emotions in organization members.
5. *Communicate the vision.* Use multiple forums, repetition, and leading by example.
6. *Remove barriers to the change.* For example, Sony's CEO removed his former studio executives and installed a new team when he set about fixing Sony's movie business. Former AlliedSignal CEO Lawrence Bossidy put all of his 80,000 employees through quality training within 2 years.
7. *Generate short-term wins.* Maintain employees' motivation by ensuring that they have short-term goals to achieve as part of the change plan, from which they receive positive feedback.
8. *Consolidate gains and produce more change.* As changes occur, the leader has to guard against renewed complacency. To do this, the leader and guiding coalition can use the increased credibility that comes from short-term wins to change all the systems, structures, and policies that don't fit well with the company's new vision.
9. *Anchor the new ways of doing things in the company's culture.* For example, if you want to emphasize more openness, camaraderie, and customer service, you as a leader must get the organization's employees to share those values. Do this by issuing a core value statement, by "walking the talk," and by using signs, symbols, rewards, and ceremonies to reinforce the values you want your employees to share.
10. *Monitor progress and adjust the vision as required.* For example, use regular surveys to monitor customer and employee attitudes.

interviewing each of the group members prior to the group meeting. He or she asks what their problems are, how they think the group functions, and what obstacles are in the way of the group performing better.[94] The consultant usually categorizes the interview or attitude survey data into themes and presents the themes to the group at the beginning of the meeting. For example, "Not enough time to get my job done," or "I can't get any cooperation." The group then ranks the themes by importance. The most important ones form the agenda for the meeting. The group examines and discusses the issues, examines the underlying causes of the problem, and begins work on a solution to the problems.

WEB-BASED TOOLS There are many Web-based tools you can use to facilitate organizational development programs. For example, there are Web-based surveys, including ones at surveymonkey.com, zoomerang.com, and brainbench.com. The manager will also find OD-related self-assessment tools at websites such as CPP.com.[95]

Building Learning Organizations

Employers use training and development to develop what some call learning organizations. A **learning organization** "is an organization skilled at creating, acquiring, and transferring knowledge, and at modifying its behavior to reflect new knowledge and insights."[96] Xerox, for instance, trains employees to analyze and display data on special simple statistical charts and to plan the actions they will take to solve the problem using special planning charts.

EVALUATING THE TRAINING EFFORT

There are two basic issues to address when evaluating a training program. The first is whether to use controlled experimentation or (on the other hand) to only assess the changes in those you've trained. The second is what training effect to measure.

Controlled experimentation is the best method to use in evaluating a training program. A controlled experiment uses both a training group and a control group (the latter receives no training). Data (for instance, on production quantity) are obtained both before and after the training effort in the group exposed to training and before and after a corresponding work period in the control group. In this way it is possible to determine the extent to which any change in performance in the training group resulted from the training itself rather than from some organization-wide change such as a raise in pay; we assume that the latter would have equally affected employees in both groups. This controlled approach is feasible.[97] In terms of current practice, however, few firms use it. Most simply measure trainees' reactions to the program; some also measure the trainees' job performance before and after training.

Training Effects to Measure

Employers can measure four basic categories of training outcomes:

1. *Reaction.* First, evaluate trainees' reactions to the program. Did they like the program?
2. *Learning.* Second, test the trainees to determine whether they learned the principles, skills, and facts they were supposed to learn.
3. *Behavior.* Next, ask whether the trainees' behavior on the job changed because of the training program. For example, are employees in the store's complaint department more courteous toward disgruntled customers than previously?
4. *Results.* Finally, but probably most importantly, ask: What results were achieved in terms of the training objectives previously set? For example, did the number of customer complaints drop? Did the reject rate improve?

EVALUATION IN PRACTICE   Employers increasingly demand quantified training evaluations, of reactions, learning, behavior, results, or some combination of these.[98] In one survey, most responding employers said they set formal response-rate goals (in terms of number of trainees responding) for end-of-training class evaluations. In general, the actual response rate depended on the method the employer used. The response rate of trainees was about 82% with paper-and-pencil end-of-class evaluation surveys, 59%

with online surveys, and 53% with e-mail surveys. About 90% of firms collecting end-of-class evaluation data use paper-and-pencil surveys.[99] McDonald's asks trainees to evaluate classes and tests them on what they've learned. McDonald's also speaks with the employees' supervisors about how the trainees did before and after the training, to assess whether the trainees changed their behavior.[100]

Computerization facilitates evaluation. For example, Bovis Lend Lease offers its 625 employees numerous courses in construction and other subjects. The firm uses special learning management software to monitor which employees are taking which courses and the extent to which employees are improving their skills.[101]

REVIEW

Summary

1. The ADDIE training process consists of five program development steps: needs analysis, instructional design, implementation, and evaluation.

2. Vestibule training, or simulated training, combines the advantages of on- and off-the-job training.

3. On-the-job training might take the form of the coaching/understudy method, job rotation, or special assignments and committees. Other training methods include audiovisual techniques, lectures, computer-aided instruction, apprenticeship training, simulated training, DVD/CD-ROM- and Internet-based training, learning portals, and special-purpose training.

4. Management development aims at preparing employees for future managerial jobs with the organization and at improving organizational effectiveness.

5. On-the-job experience is the most popular form of management development.

6. Managerial on-the-job training methods include job rotation, coaching, and action learning. Case studies, management games, outside seminars, university-related programs, behavior modeling, and in-house development centers are other methods.

7. Overcoming employee resistance is a crucial aspect of implementing organizational change.

8. Organizational development is an approach to instituting change in which employees themselves play a major role in the change process by providing data, by obtaining feedback on problems, and by team-planning solutions. There are several OD methods, including sensitivity training, team development, and survey feedback.

Key Terms

employee orientation *132*
training *133*
ADDIE training process *133*
task analysis *134*
performance analysis *134*
competency model *136*

on-the-job training
  (OJT) *138*
behavior modeling *139*
vestibule training *139*
computer-based training
  (CBT) *140*

virtual classroom *142*
cross training *143*
lifelong learning *143*
management
  development *144*
job rotation *144*

coaching/understudy
method *144*
action learning *144*
case study method *144*
management games *145*
improvisation *145*

in-house development
centers *146*
organizational
development (OD) *148*
survey
feedback *148*

sensitivity training *148*
team building *148*
learning
organization *150*
controlled
experimentation *150*

Discussion Questions

1. Explain how you would go about developing a training program for teaching this course.
2. What do you think are some of the main drawbacks of relying on informal on-the-job training for helping new employees become competent on their jobs?
3. Experts argue that one reason for implementing special diversity training programs is the need to avoid lost business "due to

cultural insensitivity." What sort of cultural insensitivity do you think this refers to, and how might that translate into lost business? What sort of training program would you recommend to avoid such cultural insensitivity?
4. Assume you have a professor who you believe is underperforming. How would you determine if training is the solution?

Individual and Group Activities

1. You're the supervisor of a group of employees whose task is to assemble disk drives that go into computers. You find that quality is not what it should be and that many of your group's devices come back for rework; your boss says, "You'd better start doing a better job of training your workers."
   a. What are some of the "staffing" factors that could be causing this problem?
   b. Explain how you would go about assessing whether it is in fact a training problem.
2. Pick out some task with which you are familiar—mowing the lawn, making a salad, or studying for a test—and develop a training program for it.
3. Working individually or in groups, develop a short training program on the subject "Guidelines for Giving a More Effective Lecture."
4. Find a provider of management development seminars. Obtain copies of its recent listings of seminar offerings. At what levels of

managers are the offerings aimed? What seem to be the most popular types of development programs?
5. Working individually or in groups, develop several specific examples to illustrate how a professor teaching human resource management could use at least four of the training techniques described in this chapter in teaching his or her HR course.
6. Working individually or in groups, develop an orientation program for high school graduates entering a university.
7. A well-thought-out orientation program is especially important for employees (such as recent graduates) who have had little or no work experience. Explain why you agree or disagree with this statement.
8. John Santos is an undergraduate business student majoring in accounting. He just failed Accounting 101. Explain how you would use performance analysis to identify what, if any, are Santos's training needs.

APPLICATION EXERCISES

CASE INCIDENT

Reinventing the Wheel at Apex Door Company

Jim Delaney, president of Apex Door Company, has a problem. No matter how often he tells his employees how to do their jobs, they invariably "decide to do things their way," as he puts it, and arguments ensue between Delaney, the employee, and the employee's supervisor. One example is in the door-design department. The designers are expected to work with the architects to design doors that meet the specifications. Although it's not "rocket science," as Delaney puts it, the designers often make mistakes—such as designing in too much steel—a problem that can cost Apex tens of thousands of wasted dollars, especially considering the number of doors in, say, a 30-story office tower.

The order-processing department is another example. Although Jim has a specific, detailed way he wants each order written up, most of the order clerks don't understand how to use the multipage order form, and they improvise when it comes to a question such as whether to classify a customer as "industrial" or "commercial."

The current training process is as follows. None of the jobs have training manuals per se, although several have somewhat out-of-date job descriptions. The training for new employees is all on the job: Usually, the person leaving the company trains the new person during the 1- or 2-week overlap period, but if there's no overlap, the new person is trained as well as possible by other employees who have occasionally filled in on the job in the past. The training is basically the same for jobs throughout the company.

QUESTIONS

1. What do you think of Apex's training process? How might it help to explain why employees "do things their way"?
2. What role do job descriptions play in training?
3. Explain in detail what you would do to improve the training process at Apex. Make sure to provide specific suggestions.

CONTINUING CASE

Carter Cleaning Company

The New Training Program

The Carter Cleaning Centers currently have no formal orientation or training policies or procedures, and Jennifer believes this is one reason why the standards to which she and her father would like employees to adhere are generally not followed.

The Carters would prefer that certain practices and procedures be used in dealing with the customers at the front counters. For example, all customers should be greeted with what Jack refers to as a "big hello." Garments they drop off should immediately be inspected for any damage or unusual stains so these can be brought to the customer's attention, lest the customer later return to pick up the garment and erroneously blame the store. The garments are then supposed to be immediately placed together in a nylon sack to separate them from other customers' garments. The ticket also has to be carefully written up, with the customer's name and telephone number and the date precisely and clearly noted on all copies. The counter person is also supposed to take the opportunity to try to sell the customer additional services such as waterproofing, or

(continued)

simply notify the customer that "Now that people are doing their spring cleaning, we're having a special on drapery cleaning all this month." Finally, as the customer leaves, the counter person is supposed to make a courteous comment like "Have a nice day" or "Drive safely." Each of the other jobs in the stores—pressing, cleaning/spotting, and so forth—similarly contain certain steps, procedures, and most importantly, standards the Carters would prefer to see upheld.

The company has had problems, Jennifer feels, because of a lack of adequate employee training and orientation. For example, two new employees became very upset last month when they discovered that they were not paid at the end of the week, on Friday, but instead were paid (as are all Carter employees) on the following Tuesday. The Carters use the extra two days in part to give them time to obtain everyone's hours and compute their pay. The other reason they do it, according to Jack, is that "frankly, when we stay a few days behind in paying employees it helps to ensure that they at least give us a few days' notice before quitting on us. While we are certainly obligated to pay them anything they earn, we find that psychologically they seem to be less likely to just walk out on us Friday evening and not show up Monday morning if they still haven't gotten their pay from the previous week. This way they at least give us a few days' notice so we can find a replacement."

There are other matters that could be covered during orientation and training, says Jennifer.

These include company policy regarding paid holidays, lateness and absences, health benefits (there are none, other than workers' compensation), substance abuse, and eating or smoking on the job (both forbidden), and general matters like the maintenance of a clean and safe work area, personal appearance and cleanliness, time sheets, personal telephone calls, and personal e-mail.

Jennifer believes that implementing orientation and training programs would help to ensure that employees know how to do their jobs the right way. And she and her father further believe that it is only when employees understand the right way to do their jobs that there is any hope their jobs will be accomplished the way the Carters want them to be accomplished. She wants your advice.

QUESTIONS

1. Specifically, what should the Carters cover in their new employee orientation program and how should they convey this information?
2. In the HR management course Jennifer took, the book suggested using a job instruction sheet to identify tasks performed by an employee. Should the Carter Cleaning Centers use a form like this for the counter person's job? If so, what should the form look like, say, for a counter person?
3. Which specific training techniques should Jennifer use to train her pressers, her cleaner/spotters, her managers, and her counter people? Why should these training techniques be used?

EXPERIENTIAL EXERCISE

Flying the Friendlier Skies

Purpose: The purpose of this exercise is to give you practice in developing a training program for the job of airline reservation clerk for a major airline.

Required Understanding: You should be fully acquainted with the material in this chapter and should read the following description of an airline reservation clerk's duties:

Description: Customers contact our airlines reservation clerks to obtain flight schedules, prices, and itineraries. The reservation clerks look up the requested information on our airline's online flight schedule system, which is updated continuously. The reservation clerk must deal courteously and expeditiously with the customer and be able to find alternative flight arrangements quickly in order to provide the customer with the itinerary that fits his or her needs. Alternative flights and prices must be found quickly, so that the customer is not kept waiting and so that our reservations operations group maintains its efficiency standards. It is often necessary to look under various routings, since there may be a dozen or more alternative routes between the customer's starting point and destination.

You may assume that we just hired 30 new clerks, and that you must create a 3-day training program.

How to Set Up the Exercise/Instructions: If so desired, divide the class into teams. Airline reservation clerks obviously need numerous skills to perform their jobs. This major airline has asked you to develop quickly the outline of a training program for its new reservation clerks. You may want to start by listing the job's main duties. In any case, please produce the requested training program outline, making sure to be very specific about what you want to teach the new clerks and what methods and aids you suggest using to train them.

VIDEO CASE

RECRUITING AT HAUTELOOK

Synopsis

The online fashion retailer Hautelook is growing quickly and needs to recruit new employees. The video discusses the company's methods for recruiting job applicants and for finding the best potential employees from among applicants. Hautelook prefers to promote internal job candidates, but also to hire applicants who are most familiar with the company—ideally, previous customers

DISCUSSION QUESTIONS

1. Explain the importance of employee referrals to Hautelook's recruiting.

2. Based on the chapter, what other recruiting tools would you suggest a company like this use, and why?
3. How would you suggest it deal with the problem of receiving too many résumé applications?
4. Given that it loves to promote internally, what other steps would you suggest it take to facilitate this?
5. From what the company says, is it really necessary for it to use employment agencies? Why?

VIDEO CASE

EMPLOYEE TESTING AND SELECTION AT PATAGONIA

Synopsis

Patagonia strives to select employees whose values are in sync with its values. The interviewing process is multifaceted, and candidates take part in group interviews. These interviews follow a conversational style, in an attempt to reveal as much about a potential employee's interests, passions, and personality as possible. It is important that those hired by Patagonia not only have an interest in outdoor activities and the products

(continued)

the company produces, but also are passionate about preserving the environment, which is the mission of Patagonia.

DISCUSSION QUESTIONS

1. If you had to create a talent management-type job profile for the average employee at Patagonia, what would the profile look like, in terms of its specific contents?
2. What traits does Patagonia look for in its future employees during the interview process?
3. In what respects does Patagonia's employee selection process reflect a talent management approach to selection?
4. What is the employee turnover rate at Patagonia? Is this higher or lower than the industry average? What reason can you give for why Patagonia's turnover rate is as you described?
5. Describe the interview process used by Patagonia. How is this process similar to others in the industry? How does the process used by Patagonia differ?

VIDEO CASE

TRAINING AT WILSON LEARNING

Synopsis

Maxene Raices is a senior manager at Wilson Learning, a company that specializes in developing training programs. She describes the best practices that make training most effective. She explains how training sessions have to be planned carefully with an outcome in mind, and have to consist of more than just lecturing. Good training programs help employees do their jobs, and ideally produce measurable results. Managers can use technology to make training even more effective, giving opportunities for people spread over various locations to attend training sessions.

DISCUSSION QUESTIONS

1. How does Wilson Learning's "know, show, do" approach in the video fit with the training process that Chapter 5 described?
2. Explain what specific training tools and processes discussed in Chapter 5 would you use to implement a "know, show, do" training approach?
3. What you think of the experimental design Wilson used to assess the call center training program? How would you suggest the company improve it?
4. Discuss four types of technology Wilson could use to deliver training, based on the chapter.
5. What are two reasons that Maxene gives for thinking it is important for different learning styles to be recognized?
6. How does identifying the intended outcomes of a training shape the training itself?

Six

Performance Management, Appraisals, and Careers

When you finish studying this chapter you should be able to:

- Explain *the purpose of performance appraisal.*
- Answer *the question, Who should do the appraising?*
- Discuss *the pros and cons of at least eight performance appraisal methods.*
- Explain *how to conduct an appraisal feedback interview.*
- Define *career management and discuss career assessment tools.*
- List *the elements in performance management.*

OVERVIEW

Four months after taking over as supervisor, Ralph had to give his first performance appraisal, and his employee just kept saying, "that's not fair," before walking out in tears. The main purpose of this chapter is to explain how to prepare for and administer effective performance appraisals. The topics we cover include Basic Concepts in Performance Appraisal and Management, Basic Appraisal Methods, Some Practical Suggestions for More Effective Appraisals, Coaching and Career Management, Performance Management, and Talent Management Practices for Strategic Employee Appraisals.

BASIC CONCEPTS IN PERFORMANCE APPRAISAL AND MANAGEMENT

Performance appraisal means evaluating an employee's current and/or past performance relative to his or her performance standards. You may equate appraisal forms like that in Figure 6-1 with performance appraisals, but appraisal involves more. Appraising performance also assumes that performance standards have been set, and that the employee gets feedback to help eliminate performance deficiencies or to continue to perform above par. In this chapter, we also address a modern approach to appraisal called *performance management.* This is the *continuous* process of identifying, measuring, and developing the performance of individuals and teams and *aligning* their performance with the organization's *goals.*

Why Appraise Performance?

Few things managers do are fraught with more peril than appraising subordinates' performance. Employees are overly optimistic about what their ratings will be. And, they know that their raises, careers, and peace of mind may hinge on how you rate them. As if that's not enough, few appraisal processes are as fair and above-board as employers think they are. Hundreds of obvious and not-so-obvious problems (such as bias, and the tendency for managers to rate everyone "average") undermine the process. However, the perils notwithstanding, performance appraisal is a crucial part of what managers do.[1]

Instructions: Thoughtful evaluations help the faculty member better understand and improve his or her teaching practices. For each of the following 8 items, please assign a score, giving your highest score of <u>7</u> for Outstanding, a score of <u>4</u> for Average, your lowest score of <u>1</u> for Needs Improvement, and an <u>NA</u> if the question is not applicable:

Evaluation Items:

_____ (1) The instructor was prepared for his/her lectures.

_____ (2) The course was consistent with the course objectives.

_____ (3) The instructor was fair in how he/she graded me.

_____ (4) The instructor carefully planned and organized this course.

_____ (5) The instructor was available during his/her posted office hours.

_____ (6) The instructor responded to online inquiries in a timely manner.

_____ (7) In terms of knowledge and/or experience, the instructor was competent to teach this course.

_____ (8) Overall how would you rate this course?

FIGURE 6-1 Sample Faculty Evaluation Survey.

There are several reasons to appraise subordinates' performance. First, appraisals help managers identify problems that may diminish performance. They also help managers make *promotion and salary* raise decisions.[5] Appraisals let the boss and subordinate *develop a plan* for correcting deficiencies. And appraisals facilitate *career planning*, by providing an opportunity to review the employee's career plans in light of his or her exhibited strengths and weaknesses.

The Importance of Continuous Feedback

For accomplishing several of these aims, traditional annual or semiannual appraisal reviews make sense. For example, promotions and raises tend to be periodic decisions. However, aligning the employee's efforts with the job's standards should be continuous. With a performance problem, there is no substitute for nudging your employee's performance right back into line. Similarly, reinforcement for a job well done best comes at once.

Performance Management

Many employers therefore offer feedback continuously. For example, at Toyota Motor's Lexington, Kentucky, Camry plant, the supervisors don't sit with individual employees to fill out forms and appraise them. Instead, teams of employees monitor their own results, even posting individual daily performance metrics. In frequent meetings, they continuously align those results with the work team's standards and with the plant's overall quality and productivity needs. Team members who need coaching and training receive it, and procedures that need changing are changed. This is *performance management* in action.

PERFORMANCE MANAGEMENT DEFINED   Performance management means different things to different people. Some use "performance management" as synonymous with "performance appraisal." Others say performance appraisal represents just the "appraisal" step of a three-step goal-setting/appraisal/feedback performance management cycle. In this book, we assume that **performance management** is a special goal-oriented and continuous way to appraise and manage employees' performance. It is the " *continuous* process of identifying, measuring, and developing the performance of individuals and teams and *aligning* their performance with the organization's *goals*."[6]

The difference between performance management and performance appraisal is more than a matter of degree; it's a matter of substance. Many employers have what they call performance management processes, but in fact still use traditional performance appraisal. They don't emphasize continuous feedback and measuring goal-oriented behavior the way performance management does.[7] We'll address performance management more fully later in this chapter.

The Appraisal Cycle

Stripped to its essentials, performance appraisal always involves the three-step **performance appraisal process**: (1) setting work standards, (2) assessing the employee's actual performance relative to those standards (this usually involves using a rating form), and (3) providing feedback to the employee with the aim of helping him or her to eliminate performance deficiencies or to continue to perform above par.

HR AS A PROFIT CENTER

Setting Performance Goals at Ball Corporation

Ball Corporation supplies metal packaging to customers such as food and paint manufacturers.[2] The management team at one Ball plant concluded that it could improve plant performance by instituting a better process for setting goals and for ensuring that the plant's employees' behaviors were in synch with these goals.[3] The new program included training plant leaders to set and communicate daily performance goals. Management tracked daily goal attainment by distributing team scorecards to work teams to fill out. Plant employees received special coaching and training to ensure they had the skills to achieve the goals.

According to management, within 12 months the plant raised production by 84 million cans, improved customer complaints by 50 percent, and yielded a return-on-investment of more than $3 million.[4]

Setting Effective Goals and Work Standards

Employees should always know ahead of time how and on what basis you're going to appraise them.[8] Gurus like to say that effective goals are "SMART." They are *specific*, and clearly state the desired results. They are *measurable*. They are *attainable*. They are *relevant*, and clearly derive from what the manager and company want to achieve (such as improved sales). And, they are *timely*, and reflect deadlines. Research provides useful insights into setting motivational goals. It suggests four things:

1. *Assign specific goals.* Employees who receive specific goals usually perform better than those who do not. The HR as a Profit Center feature illustrates this.
2. *Assign measurable goals.* Put goals in quantitative terms (such as "an average daily output of 300 units") and always include target dates or deadlines.
3. *Assign challenging but doable goals.* Goals should be challenging, but not unrealistic.
4. *Encourage participation.* Should you just tell your employees what their goals are, or should you let them participate in setting their goals? The evidence suggests that participatively set goals do *not* consistently result in higher performance. It is only when the participatively set goals are more difficult (are set higher) than the assigned ones that the participatively set goals produce higher performance. It does tend to be easier to set higher standards when your employees can participate in the process, so to that extent participation can facilitate performance.[9]

Who Should Do the Appraising?

Appraisals by the immediate supervisor are still the heart of most appraisals. The supervisor should be—and usually is—in the best position to observe and evaluate his or her subordinate's performance.

Yet relying just on supervisors' ratings isn't advisable. For example, an employee's supervisor may not understand how customers and colleagues who depend on the employee rate the person's performance.

PEER APPRAISALS   With more firms using self-managing teams, appraisal of an employee by his or her peers—**peer appraisal**—is more popular. At one firm, for example, an employee due for an annual appraisal chooses an appraisal chairperson. The latter then selects one supervisor and three peers to evaluate the employee's work.

One study found that peer appraisals had "an immediate positive impact on [improving] perception of open communication, task motivation, social loafing, group viability, cohesion, and satisfaction."[10] Peer appraisals are also good for predicting who will succeed in management.

RATING COMMITTEES Some companies use rating committees.[11] A rating committee is usually composed of the employee's immediate supervisor and three or four other supervisors.

Using multiple raters can help cancel out problems such as individual raters' bias. They also help to ensure that the appraisal reflects the different facets of an employee's performance observed by different appraisers.[12]

SELF-RATINGS The basic problem with self-ratings is that employees usually rate themselves higher than supervisors do.[13] One study found that, when asked to rate their own job performances, 40% of employees in jobs of all types placed themselves in the top 10%, and virtually all remaining employees rated themselves at least in the top 50%.[14] In another study, a person's self-ratings actually correlated negatively with the person's subsequent assessment center performance.[15]

APPRAISAL BY SUBORDINATES Some firms let subordinates rate their supervisors' performance, a process some call **upward feedback**.[16] Such feedback can help top managers understand their subordinates' management styles, identify potential people problems, and take corrective action with individual managers, as required.

Anonymity affects usefulness. Managers who get feedback from subordinates who identify themselves view the upward feedback more positively than do managers who get anonymous feedback. However, subordinates who must identify themselves tend to give inflated ratings.[17]

Research supports the usefulness of upward feedback. One study focused on 252 managers during five annual administrations of an upward feedback program. Managers who were initially "rated poor or moderate showed significant improvements in [their] upward feedback ratings over the five-year period." Furthermore, managers who met with their subordinates to discuss their upward feedback improved more than the managers who did not.[18]

360-DEGREE FEEDBACK With 360-degree feedback, the employer collects performance information from the employee's supervisors, subordinates, peers, and internal or external customers.[19] The usual process is to have the raters complete online appraisal surveys.[20] Computerized systems then compile all this feedback into individualized reports that go to the employee. The person then meets with his or her supervisor to develop a self-improvement plan.

Results are mixed. Participants seem to prefer this approach, but one study concluded that multisource feedback led to "generally small" improvements on subsequent ratings. Such 360-degree appraisals are also more helpful when they're for developmental rather than pay or promotion decisions.[21]

There are several ways to make such appraisals more useful.

- Anchor the 360-degree appraisal items (Excellent, Good, and so on) with behavioral descriptors (such as "effectively deals with conflicts").[22]
- Use a Web-based or a PC-based 360 system such as EchoSpan 360 Appraisal (www.echospan.com).[23]

Even if you do not opt for a 360-degree approach, it still makes sense to have more than one supervisor who is familiar with the employee's work review the appraisal.[24] Multiple raters often do see different facets of an employee's performance.[25]

BASIC APPRAISAL METHODS

The manager usually conducts the appraisal using one or more of the methods described in this section.

Graphic Rating Scale Method

A **graphic rating scale** lists a number of traits and a range of performance for each. As in Figure 6-2, it lists traits (such as knowledge) and a range of performance values (in this case from below expectations to role model) for each trait. The supervisor rates each subordinate by circling or checking the score that best describes the subordinate's performance for each trait and then totals the scores for all traits.

Alternation Ranking Method

Ranking employees from best to worst on a trait or traits is another popular method. Because it is usually easier to distinguish between the worst and best employees than to rank them, an **alternation ranking method** is useful. With this method a form like that in Figure 6-3 (page 165) is used to indicate the employee who is highest on the trait being measured and also the one who is the lowest, alternating between highest and lowest until you've addressed all employees to be rated.

Paired Comparison Method

With the **paired comparison method,** every subordinate to be rated is paired with and compared to every other subordinate on each trait.

For example, suppose there are five employees to be rated. With this method, a chart such as that in Figure 6-4 (page 165) shows all possible pairs of employees for each trait. Then for each trait, the supervisor indicates (with a plus or minus) who is the better employee of the pair. Next, the number of times an employee is rated better is added up. In Figure 6-4, employee Maria ranked highest (has the most plus marks) for "quality of work," and Art ranked highest for "creativity."

Forced Distribution Method

With the **forced distribution method,** the manager places predetermined percentages of subordinates in performance categories, as when professors "grade on a curve." About a fourth of Fortune 500 companies including Microsoft, Conoco, and Intel use forced distribution. GE popularized forced ranking, but now tells managers not to adhere to its famous 20/70/10 split.[26]

While widely used, some balk at forced distribution appraisals. The biggest complaints: 44% said it damages morale, and 47% said it creates interdepartmental inequities, since "high-performing teams must cut 10% of their workers while low-performing teams are still allowed to retain 90% of theirs."[27] Some writers call them "Rank and Yank" appraisals.[28]

Sample Performance Rating Form

Employee's Name _____   Level: Entry-level employee

Manager's Name _____

Key Work Responsibilities   Results/Goals to be Achieved
1._____   1._____

2._____   2._____

3._____   3._____

4._____   4._____

Behavioral Assessment of Competencies

Communication

1	2	3	4	5
Below Expectations		**Meets Expectations**		**Role Model**
Even with guidance, fails to prepare straightforward communications, including forms, paperwork, and records, in a timely and accurate manner; products require minimal corrections.		With guidance, prepares straightforward communications, including forms, paperwork, and records, in a timely and accurate manner; products require minimal corrections.		Independently prepares communications, such as forms, paperwork, and records, in a timely, clear, and accurate manner; products require few, if any, corrections.
Even with guidance, fails to adapt style and materials to communicate straightforward information.		With guidance, adapts style and materials to communicate straightforward information.		Independently adapts style and materials to communicate information.

Organizational Know-How

1	2	3	4	5
Below Expectations		**Meets Expectations**		**Role Model**
<performance standards appear here>		<performance standards appear here>		<performance standards appear here>

Personal Effectiveness

1	2	3	4	5
Below Expectations		**Meets Expectations**		**Role Model**
<performance standards appear here>		<performance standards appear here>		<performance standards appear here>

Teamwork

1	2	3	4	5
Below Expectations		**Meets Expectations**		**Role Model**
<performance standards appear here>		<performance standards appear here>		<performance standards appear here>

Achieving Business Results

1	2	3	4	5
Below Expectations		**Meets Expectations**		**Role Model**
<performance standards appear here>		<performance standards appear here>		<performance standards appear here>

FIGURE 6-2 Sample Graphic Rating Form with Behavioral Examples.   *Source: Performance Management: A Roadmap for Developing, Implementing, and Evaluating Performance Management Systems* by Elaine D. Pulakos. © 2000 SHRM, pp. 16–17. Reprinted with permission.

(continued)

Results Assessment

Accomplishment 1: _____

1	2	3	4	5
Low Impact		**Moderate Impact**		**High Impact**
The efficiency or effectiveness of operations remained the same or improved only minimally. The quality of products remained the same or improved only minimally.		The efficiency or effectiveness of operations improved quite a lot. The quality of products improved quite a lot.		The efficiency or effectiveness of operations improved tremendously. The quality of products improved tremendously.

Accomplishment 2: _____

1	2	3	4	5
Low Impact		**Moderate Impact**		**High Impact**
The efficiency or effectiveness of operations remained the same or improved only minimally. The quality of products remained the same or improved only minimally.		The efficiency or effectiveness of operations improved quite a lot. The quality of products improved quite a lot.		The efficiency or effectiveness of operations improved tremendously. The quality of products improved tremendously.

Narrative

_____

_____

_____

_____

_____

Areas to be Developed	Actions	Completion Date

Manager's Signature _____ Date _____

Employee's Signature _____ Date _____

The above employee signature indicates receipt of, but not necessarily concurrence with, the evaluation herein.

FIGURE 6-2 Continued

ALTERNATION RANKING SCALE

For the Trait: _____

For the trait you are measuring, list all the employees you want to rank. Put the highest-ranking employee's name on line 1. Put the lowest-ranking employee's name on line 20. Then list the next highest ranking on line 2, the next lowest ranking on line 19, and so on. Continue until all names are on the scale.

Highest-ranking employee

1. _____   11. _____

2. _____   12. _____

3. _____   13. _____

4. _____   14. _____

5. _____   15. _____

6. _____   16. _____

7. _____   17. _____

8. _____   18. _____

9. _____   19. _____

10. _____   20. _____

Lowest-ranking employee

FIGURE 6-3 Alternation Ranking Method.

FOR THE TRAIT "QUALITY OF WORK"					
Employee rated:					
As Compared to:	A Art	B Maria	C Chuck	D Diane	E José
A Art		+	+	−	−
B Maria	−		−	−	−
C Chuck	−	+		+	−
D Diane	+	+	−		+
E José	+	+	+	−	

Maria Ranks Highest Here

FOR THE TRAIT "CREATIVITY"					
Employee rated:					
As Compared to:	A Art	B Maria	C Chuck	D Diane	E José
A Art		−	−	−	−
B Maria	+		−	+	+
C Chuck	+	+		−	+
D Diane	+	−	+		−
E José	+	−	−	+	

Art Ranks Highest Here

FIGURE 6-4 Paired Comparison Method. *Note:* + means "better than," − means "worse than." For each chart, add up the number of +'s in each column to get the highest-ranked employee.

As most students know, if you're in the bottom 5% or 10% with a forced distribution system you get an "F", no questions asked. Given this, employers should be doubly careful to protect forced rankings from managerial abuse.[29] Appoint a review committee to review any employee's low ranking. Train raters to be objective.

Critical Incident Method

The **critical incident method** entails keeping a record of uncommonly good or undesirable examples of an employee's work-related behavior and reviewing it with the employee periodically.

Employers often use critical incidents to supplement a rating or ranking method. Doing so provides concrete examples of what subordinates can do to eliminate performance deficiencies and opportunities for mid-year corrections.

Behaviorally Anchored Rating Scales

A behaviorally anchored rating scale (BARS) anchors a quantified rating scale with narrative examples of good and poor performance. Job experts typically go through a formal process to develop and choose what those examples are.

To illustrate, Figure 6-5 shows a BARS for one performance dimension for a car salesperson—the dimension "automobile salesmanship skills." Note how behavioral examples anchor each performance level.

Appraisal Forms in Practice

Effective appraisal forms typically merge several approaches. For example, Figure 6-2 (pages 163–164) merges a graphic rating scale with narrative examples. This form also illustrates an important fact regarding appraisals. Even if the company does not use a formal behaviorally anchored rating scale approach, anchoring the scale with illustrative examples, as here, usually improves the appraisal scale's reliability and validity.

The Management by Objectives Method

The **management by objectives (MBO)** method requires the manager to set measurable goals with each employee and then periodically discuss the latter's progress toward these goals. The term *MBO* usually refers to an organization-wide goal setting and appraisal program that consists of six steps:

1. *Set the organization's goals.* Establish an organization-wide plan for next year and set goals.
2. *Set departmental goals.* Department heads and their superiors jointly set goals for their departments.
3. *Discuss departmental goals.* Department heads discuss the department's goals with all subordinates in the department and ask them to develop their own individual goals. In other words, how can each employee contribute to the department attaining its goals?
4. *Define expected results (set individual goals).* Department heads and their subordinates set short-term performance targets.

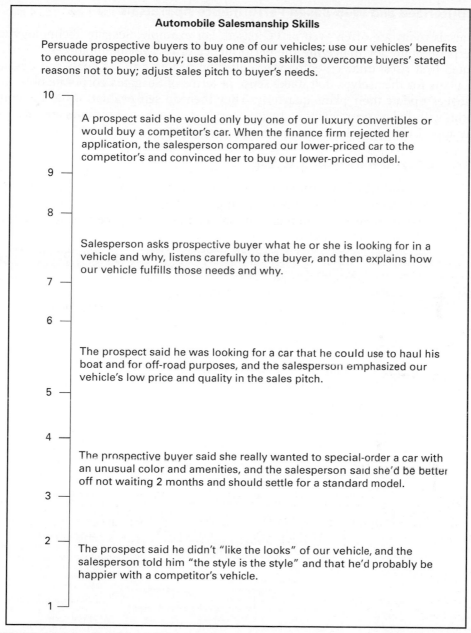

FIGURE 6-5 Behaviorally Anchored Rating Scale.

5. *Conduct performance reviews and measure the results.* Department heads compare the actual performance of each employee with expected results.
6. *Provide feedback.* Department heads hold periodic performance review meetings with subordinates to discuss and evaluate the subordinates' progress in achieving expected results.

Computerized and Web-Based Performance Appraisals

Appraisals today are often Web or PC based. For example, Seagate Technology uses "Enterprise Suite" for managing the performance of its 39,000 employees.[30] Early in Seagate's first fiscal quarter, employees enter the system and set goals and development plans for themselves that make sense in terms of Seagate's corporate objectives. Employees update their plans quarterly. They then do self-evaluations at the end of the year, with follow-up reviews by their supervisors. Figure 6-6 outlines another good online appraisal tool, in this case from PerformancePro.

Electronic Performance Monitoring

Electronic performance monitoring (EPM) systems use computer technology to allow managers access to their employees' computers and telephones. They thus allow "managers to determine at any moment throughout the day the pace at which employees

FIGURE 6-6 Online Performance Appraisal Tool.   *Source:* HRNonline.com. Copyright HRN. Reprinted with permission.

Factor Info

Available Factors: Communication
Weight: 20%

◄ Back   Next ►   ⊟ Details

Definition:
The ability to effectively converse and listen to others concerning company matters. The use of proper written and grammatical skills, and the meaningful application of computer technology [e-mail, Internet, etc.].

Evaluation

Compare   Enter/Review Comments

Last 4.5   Current 4

5 - High Performer
Communication skills are superior. Listening and interpersonal communication skills strengthen others. Effectively uses all available communication technology. Written

4 - Valued Performer
Communication skills are excellent. Listening and interpersonal skills are above average. Effectively uses most available communication technology. Written

3 - Contributor
Communication and listening skills are good. Effectively uses some available communication technology. Written documents convey information appropriately.

2 - Needs Improvement
Communication skills are lacking in some areas. Verbal communication skills of listening and speaking impede job performance. More effective use of communication

1 - Unacceptable
Communication skills are inadequate for the job. Immediate improvement is necessary in one or more key areas [listening, speaking, writing, using communication

Comments: Comment Coaching

Annette is a clear and concise communicator. She uses the appropriate method, and tone in her communication that is required by the situation. She presents facts and recommends alternatives effectively.

Rating an employee is fast and easy. Simply glide the slider to the appropriate rating level and add in optional appraiser comments.

E-Signature

Date Completed	Employee	Item	Status
4/3/2007	Henry L Smith	Appraisal	Unsigned

Routing In-Box

Items Routed to You

Date Routed	Routed By	Item	Status
4/3/2007	Smith, Henry	Record of Oral Warning FORM: Murray, Annette	

Routing Out-Box

Items Routed by You

Status Date	Status	Routed To	Item
4/3/2007	Approved	Granger, Francis	Employee Commendation FORM: Smith, Henry L

Employee Notes

Date	Title	View/Edit	Delete
3/15/2007	Schedule staff Q2 goal status meetings by 5/1		
2/13/2007	Quarterly report completed		
			Add Note

From the Performance Pro employee home screen, clearly monitor routed or sent documents and performance notes. Also receive notification of documents requiring electronic signature.

We are committed to building long term client relationships based upon total customer satisfaction. Read what some of our nearly 600 Performance Pro customers are saying about their experience and the benefits they have realized since implementing Performance Pro in their organization.

FIGURE 6-6 Continued

are working, their degree of accuracy, log-in and log-off times, and even the amount of time spent on bathroom breaks."[31]

Research indicates that EPM can improve productivity in certain circumstances. For example, for less complex jobs, high-skilled and monitored subjects keyed in more data entries than did high-skilled unmonitored participants.[32] However, in this same study, low-skilled but monitored participants did more poorly than did low-skilled, unmonitored participants. Empirical studies also link EPM with increased stress.[33]

PRACTICAL SUGGESTIONS FOR MORE EFFECTIVE APPRAISALS

As we said earlier, few supervisory tasks are fraught with more peril than appraising performance.[34] Managers therefore need to know the typical problems and how to deal with them.[35]

Ensure Fairness

Probably your first challenge is to make sure the subordinate views the appraisal as fair. Studies confirm that, in practice, some managers ignore accuracy in performance appraisals.[36] The employees' standards should be clear, employees should understand the basis on which you're going to appraise them, and the supervisor-employee inter-relationship is hopefully open and trusting.[37] Figure 6-7 summarizes some best practices for administering fair performance appraisals.

Deal with Common Appraisal Problems[38]

Several problems undermine appraisals and graphic rating scales in particular. Fortunately, there are ways to avoid or deal with these problems.

UNCLEAR STANDARDS   The unclear standards appraisal problem means the appraisal scale is too open to interpretation. As in Figure 6-8, the rating scale may seem objective but different supervisors would probably describe "good" performance differently. The same is true of traits such as "quality of work." The best way to rectify this problem is to include descriptive phrases that define each trait and degree of merit.[39]

- Base the performance review on duties and standards from a job analysis.
- Base the performance review on objective performance data.
- Make it clear ahead of time what your performance expectations are.
- Use a standardized performance review procedure for all employees.
- Make sure the reviewers have frequent opportunities to observe the employee's performance.
- Either use multiple raters or have the rater's supervisor review the appraisal results.
- Include an appeals mechanism.
- Document the appraisal results.
- Discuss the appraisal results with the employee.
- Let the employee provide input regarding the assessment.
- Indicate what the employee needs to do to improve.

FIGURE 6-7 Selected Best Practices for Fair Performance Appraisals.   *Source:* See, for example, Manuel London, Edward Mone, and John C. Scott, "The Contributions of Psychological Research to HRM: Performance Management and Assessment—Methods for Improved Rater Accuracy and Employee Goal Setting," *Human Resource Management* 43, no. 4 (Winter 2004): 319–336.

	Excellent	Good	Fair	Poor
Quality of work				
Quantity of work				
Creativity				
Integrity				

FIGURE 6-8 A Graphic Rating Scale with Unclear Standards.   *Note:* For example, what exactly is meant by "good," "quantity of work," and so forth?

HALO EFFECT   The **halo effect** means that the rating of a subordinate on one trait (such as "gets along with others") influences the way you rate the person on other traits (such as "quantity of work"). Thus a manager might rate an unfriendly employee unsatisfactory for all traits rather than just for the trait "gets along with others." Being aware of this problem is a major step toward avoiding it.

CENTRAL TENDENCY   The **central tendency** problem refers to a tendency to rate all employees about average. For example, if the rating scale ranges from 1 to 7, a supervisor may tend to rate most of his or her employees between 3 and 5. Ranking employees instead of using a graphic rating scale can eliminate this problem.

LENIENCY OR STRICTNESS   Conversely, some supervisors tend to rate all their subordinates consistently high or low, a problem known as strictness/leniency. As with central tendency, supervisors who do this restrict the range of their appraisals (the appraisals can't range from high to low), and therefore bestow appraisals that don't validly describe their subordinates' actual performance. Again, one solution is to insist on ranking subordinates; doing so forces the supervisor to distinguish between high and low performers. One study focused on how personality influenced the evaluations that students gave their peers. Raters who scored higher on "conscientiousness" tended to give their peers lower ratings; those scoring higher on "agreeableness" gave higher ratings.[40]

BIAS[41]   Studies suggest rater bias often has a big effect on performance ratings.[42]

For example, studies found that raters tend to demean women's performance, particularly when they excel at what seems like male-typical tasks. The researchers found, "it is only women, not men, for whom a unique propensity toward dislike is created by success in a nontraditional work situation."[43]

The bottom line is that the appraisal often says more about the appraiser than about the appraisee.[44] This is a powerful reason for having the supervisor's boss review the rating or for using multiple raters.

Table 6-1 compares and summarizes the pros and cons of popular rating methods.

Understand the Legal Aspects of Performance Appraisal

Performance appraisals have legal implications, because they affect raises, promotions, training opportunities, and other HR actions. You will find recommendations in the following accompanying HR in Practice feature for ensuring an appraisal's legal defensibility.

TABLE 6-1	Important Similarities and Differences, and Advantages and Disadvantages, of Appraisal Tools		
Tool	**Similarities/Differences**	**Advantages**	**Disadvantages**
Graphic rating scale	These are both absolute scales aimed at measuring an employee's *absolute* performance based on objective criteria as listed on the scales.	Simple to use; provides a quantitative rating for each employee.	Standards may be unclear; halo effect, central tendency, leniency, bias can also be problems.
BARS		Provides behavioral "anchors." BARS is very accurate.	Difficult to develop.
Alternation ranking	These are both methods for judging the *relative* performance of employees relative to each other but still based on objective criteria.	Simple to use (but not as simple as graphic rating scales); avoids central tendency and other problems of rating scales.	Can cause disagreements among employees and may be unfair if all employees *are*, in fact, excellent.
Forced distribution method		Ends up with a predetermined number of people in each group.	Appraisal results depend on the adequacy of your original choice of cutoff points.
Critical incident method	These are both more subjective narrative methods for appraising performance, generally based, however, on the employee's absolute performance.	Helps specify what is "right" and "wrong" about the employee's performance; forces supervisor to evaluate subordinates on an ongoing basis.	Difficult to rate or rank employees relative to one another.
MBO		Tied to jointly agreed-upon performance objectives.	Time consuming.

Conduct the Appraisal Feedback Interview Effectively

An appraisal usually culminates in an **appraisal interview,** in which the supervisor and subordinate review the appraisal and make plans to remedy deficiencies and reinforce strengths. Few people like to receive—or give—negative feedback.[45] Adequate preparation and effective implementation are therefore essential.

HR IN PRACTICE

Making Sure Your Appraisals Are Legally Defensible

Steps to take to ensure your appraisals are legally defensible include:

1. Conduct a job analysis to establish performance criteria and standards.
2. Communicate performance standards to employees and to those rating them, in writing.
3. With graphic rating scales, avoid undefined generic trait names (such as "loyalty").
4. Use subjective narratives as only one component of the appraisal.
5. Train supervisors to use the rating instrument.
6. Allow appraisers substantial daily contact with the employees they're evaluating.
7. Remember that using a single overall rating of performance is usually not acceptable to the courts.[46]
8. Never let one appraiser have absolute authority to determine a personnel action.
9. Give employees the opportunity to review and make comments, and have a formal appeals process.
10. Document everything: "Without exception, courts condemn informal performance evaluation practices that eschew documentation."[47]

PREPARING FOR THE APPRAISAL INTERVIEW   Adequate preparation involves three steps. First, give the subordinate enough notice to review his or her work, and to compile questions and comments. Next, study his or her job description, compare the employee's performance to his or her standards, and review the files of the person's previous appraisals. Finally, find a mutually agreeable time for the interview and leave enough time—perhaps one-half-hour for lower-level personnel such as clerical workers and maintenance staff and an hour or so for management employees.

CONDUCTING THE INTERVIEW   Keep several things in mind when actually conducting appraisal interviews.

- First, conduct the interview in a *private area* without interruptions.
- Second, *talk in terms of objective work data*, using examples such as absences, quality records, inspection reports, and tardiness.
- Third, *get agreement* before the subordinate leaves on how things will improve and by when. An action plan showing steps and expected results is advisable. If a formal written warning is required, it should make it clear that the employee was aware of the standard, specify any violation of the standard, and show that the employee had an opportunity to correct his or her behavior.
- Fourth, ensure that the process is *fair*. Let the person express his or her opinions.[48]
- Fifth, know how to *deal with defensiveness*. For example, when a person is accused of poor performance, the first reaction is usually denial. By denying the fault, the employee avoids having to question his or her own competence. Such defensiveness is normal. Do not attack the person's defenses (for instance, "You know the real reason you're using that excuse is that you can't bear to be blamed for anything").

COACHING AND CAREER MANAGEMENT

After appraising performance, the manager typically faces several tasks. The employee may require coaching, career advice, and mentoring. And, the manager may want to review the employee's performance in the context of the company's overall talent management needs. The purpose of this section is to help you be more effective at coaching and mentoring employees and at supporting career planning and talent management needs.

Improving Your Coaching Skills

Great supervisors tend to be great coaches because they bring out the best in their employees. Coaching and the closely related *mentoring* are thus key supervisory skills. **Coaching** means educating, instructing, and training subordinates. *Mentoring* means advising, counseling, and guiding. Coaching focuses on teaching shorter-term job-related skills, mentoring on helping employees navigate longer-term career hazards. Supervisors have coached and mentored employees from the dawn of management. But with more managers leading self-managing teams, supporting, coaching, and mentoring are fast replacing giving orders for getting things done.

The Basic Coaching Process

We can best think of coaching in terms of a four-step process: preparation, planning, active coaching, and follow-up.[49]

PREPARING TO COACH   *Preparation* means understanding the problem, the employee, and the employee's skills. Preparation is partly an observational process. You'll watch the employee to see what he or she is doing and observe the workflow and how coworkers interact with the employee. In addition to observation, you may review the appraisal as well as other objective data on things like productivity, absenteeism, and tardiness (as we explained in more detail in Chapter 5, regarding training needs analysis).

PLANNING   Developing a plan requires reaching consensus on the problem and on what to change. The manager then sets out a change plan in the following form: *Steps to Take, Measures of Success,* and *Date to Complete.*

ACTIVE COACHING   With agreement on a plan, you can start the actual "educating, instructing, and training"—namely, coaching. Your toolkit will include what you learned about on-the-job training in Chapter 5 (such as to motivate learners). However, interpersonal communications skills are the heart of effective coaching. As one writer says, "[a]n effective coach offers ideas and advice in such a way that the subordinate can hear them, respond to them, and appreciate their value."[50]

FOLLOW-UP   Bad habits sometimes reemerge. Re-observe the person's progress periodically.

Career Management Methods

Once you've appraised their performance, it's often necessary to address subordinates' career-related issues. **Career management** is the process of enabling employees to better understand and develop their career skills and interests and to use these skills and interests both within the company and even after they leave the firm. *Career development* is the ongoing series of activities (such as internships and workshops) that contribute to a person's career exploration, establishment, success, and fulfillment. *Career planning* is the deliberate process through which someone becomes aware of his or her personal skills, interests, knowledge, motivations, and other characteristics; acquires information about career opportunities and choices; identifies career-related goals; and establishes action plans to attain specific goals. The employee, the manager, and the employer all have roles in guiding the employee's career.

The Employee's Role in Career Management

Although the employer and manager have roles in guiding employees' careers, no employee should ever abandon this task to others. For the employee, career planning means matching individual strengths and weaknesses with occupational opportunities and threats. In other words, the person wants to pursue occupations, jobs, and a career that capitalize on his or her interests, aptitudes, values, and skills. He or she also wants to choose occupations, jobs, and a career that make sense in terms of the projected future demand and prospects for various occupations. The consequences of a bad choice (or of no choice) are too severe to leave to others. There is a wealth of sources to turn to.

As an example, career-counseling expert John Holland says that personality (including values, motives, and needs) is one career choice determinant. For example, a person with what Holland calls a strong social orientation might be attracted to careers that entail interpersonal rather than intellectual or physical activities and to occupations such as social work. Holland found six such personality types or orientations. Individuals can use his Self-Directed Search (SDS) test (available online at www.self-directed-search .com) to assess their occupational orientations and preferred occupations.

O*Net (see the screen grab below) offers a comprehensive online career assessment and planning system. Other examples are at Workday.com, and in the following exercises.

EXERCISE   One useful exercise for identifying occupational skills is to head a page "The School or Occupational Tasks I Was Best At." Then write a short essay describing the tasks. Provide as much detail as you can about your duties and responsibilities, and what

Source: From O*NET Online, created for the U.S. Department of Labor (www.onetonline.org).

you found enjoyable about each task. Next, do the same thing for two other tasks you've had. Now scrutinize the three essays. Underline the skills that you mentioned the most often. For example, did you especially enjoy the hours you spent doing research for your boss when you worked one summer as an intern?[51]

EXERCISE   On a page, answer the question: "If you could have any kind of job, what would it be?" Invent your own job if need be, and don't worry about what you can do—just what you want to do.[52]

Mentoring

Having a mentor—a senior person who can be a sounding board for your career questions and concerns—can enhance career satisfaction and success.[53] Suggestions for using a mentor include:

- Choose an appropriate mentor. For objectivity, someone other than your boss may be best.
- Make it easier for a potential mentor to agree to your request by clarifying what you expect in terms of time and advice.
- Have an agenda. Bring an agenda to your first mentoring meeting that lays out key issues and topics for discussion.
- Respect the mentor's time. Be selective about the work-related issues that you bring to the table.

The Employer's and Manager's Roles in Career Management

The employer's career development roles depend on how long the employee has been with the firm.

Before hiring, *realistic job interviews* can help prospective employees gauge more accurately whether the job is indeed for them.

Especially for recent college graduates, the first job can be crucial for building confidence and a more realistic picture of strengths and weaknesses: Providing *challenging first jobs* and having an experienced mentor who can help the person learn the ropes are important. Some refer to this as preventing "reality shock." This occurs when a new employee's high expectations confront the reality of a boring, unchallenging job.

After the person has been on the job for a while, an employer can take steps to contribute in a positive way to the employee's career. *Career-oriented appraisals*—in which the manager is trained not just to appraise the employee but also to match the person's strengths and weaknesses with a feasible career path and required development work—is one important step. Similarly, providing periodic *job rotation* can help the person develop a more realistic picture of what he or she is good at. Other employer career development initiatives may also include, for example:[54]

1. *Provide each employee with an individual career development budget.* He or she can use this budget for learning about career options and personal development.[55]
2. *Offer on-site or online career centers.* These might include an on- or offline library of career development materials, career workshops, and individual career coaches for career guidance.

3. *Encourage role reversal.* Have employees temporarily work in different positions to develop a better appreciation of their occupational strengths and weaknesses.

4. *Provide career coaches.* The coaches help individual employees identify their development needs and obtain the training, professional development, and networking opportunities that they need.[56]

5. *Provide career-planning workshops.* A career-planning workshop is a "planned learning event in which participants are expected to be actively involved, completing career planning exercises and inventories and participating in career skills practice sessions."[57]

6. *Computerized on- and offline programs are available for improving the organizational career-planning process.* For example, employees can use Self-Directed Search (www.self-directed-search.com) to identify career preferences.

Gender Issues in Career Development

Women face different challenges as they advance through their careers. In one study, promoted women had to receive higher performance ratings than promoted men to get promoted, "suggesting that women were held to stricter standards for promotion."[58] Women also report greater barriers (such as being excluded from informal networks) than do men, and more difficulty getting developmental assignments. Because developmental experiences like these are so important, "organizations that are interested in helping female managers advance should focus on breaking down barriers that interfere with women's access to developmental experiences."[59]

MINORITY WOMEN   In these matters, minority women seem particularly at risk. Women of color hold only a small percentage of professional and managerial private-sector positions.[60]

Adding to the problem is the fact that some corporate career development programs may be inconsistent with the women's needs. For example, such programs may assume that career paths are continuous; yet the need to stop working for a time due to family issues punctuates the career paths of many women (and often men).[61] One study concluded that fast-track development programs, individual career counseling, and career-planning workshops were less available to women than to men.[62] Many refer to this combination of subtle and not-so-subtle barriers to women's career progress as the *glass ceiling*.

Managing Employees' Promotions and Transfers

Promotions are one of the more significant career decisions to result from the performance appraisal. In developing promotion policies, employers need to address several issues.

One issue concerns seniority versus competence. Competence is normally the basis for promotions, although in many organizations civil service or union requirements still give an edge to seniority.

Furthermore, if competence is to be the basis for promotion, how should we measure it? Defining past performance is usually straightforward. Managers use performance appraisals for this. However, sizing up how even a high-performing employee *will do* in a new job is not so easy. Innumerable great salespeople turn out to be awful managers, for instance. Many employers therefore use formal selection devices like tests and assessment centers to supplement the performance appraisals.

With more companies downsizing and flattening their organizations, "promotions" today often mean lateral moves or transfers. Here the promotional aspect is not so much a higher-level job or more pay, but the opportunity to assume new same-level responsibilities (such as a salesperson moving into HR) or increased decision-making responsibilities within the same job.

A *transfer* is a move from one job to another, usually with no salary or grade change. Employees may seek transfers not just for advancement but also for noncareer reasons, such as better hours, location of work, and so on.

Retirement

For most employees, years of appraisals and career development end with retirement. Retirement planning is now a significant issue for employers. With many older employees moving into the traditional 60-plus retirement age, employers will face a labor shortage. Many have wisely chosen to fill their staffing needs in part with current or soon-to-be retirees.

Therefore, "retirement planning" no longer means just helping current employees slip into retirement.[63] It should also enable the employer to retain, in some capacity, the skills and brainpower of those who would normally leave the firm. Fortuitously, 78% of employees in one survey said they expect to continue working in some capacity after normal retirement age (64% said they want to do so part time).[64]

Not surprisingly, studies show that employees who are more committed and loyal to the employer are more likely to stay beyond their normal retirement age.[65] Beyond that, specific suggestions for retaining retirees include:

- **Create a culture that honors experience.** For example, the CVS pharmacy chain works through the National Council on Aging, city agencies, and community organizations to find such employees. As one dedicated older worker said, "I'm too young to retire. [CVS] is willing to hire older people. They don't look at your age but your experience."[66]
- **Modify selection procedures.** For example, one British bank stopped using psychometric tests, replacing them with role-playing exercises to gauge how candidates deal with customers.
- **Offer flexible work.** One of the simplest ways is to offer flexible hours and telecommuting.[67]
- **Phased retirement.** Phased retirement programs combine reduced work hours, job change, and reduced responsibilities to extend the employee's participation in the company.

Employers should conduct the necessary numerical analyses for dealing with the impact of retirements. This assessment should include a demographic analysis of the company's employees and a determination of the average retirement age for the company's employees, and of how many are expected to retire, and when. The employer can then take fact-based steps to address the "retirement problem."[68]

PERFORMANCE MANAGEMENT

Earlier in this chapter, we said that performance management is the continuous process of identifying, measuring, and developing the performance of individuals and teams and aligning their performance with the organization's goals.[69] We look at performance management more closely in this final section.

Performance Management vs. Performance Appraisal

The distinction between performance management and performance appraisal "is the contrast between a year-end event—the completion of the appraisal form—and a process that starts the year with performance planning and is integral to the way people are managed throughout the year."[70] Three main things distinguish performance management from performance appraisal.

1. First, performance management never means just meeting with a subordinate once or twice a year to "review your performance." It means *continuous, daily, or weekly* interactions and feedback to ensure continuous improvement.[71]
2. Second, performance management is always *goal-directed*. The ongoing performance reviews always involve comparing the employee's or team's performance against goals that specifically stem from and link to the company's strategic goals.
3. Third, performance management means continuously re-evaluating and (if need be) *modifying how the employee and team get their work done*. Depending on the issue, this may mean additional training, changing work procedures, or instituting new incentive plans, for instance.

More precisely, we can summarize performance management's six basic elements as follows:[72]

- *Direction sharing* means communicating the company's goals throughout the company and then translating these into doable departmental, team, and individual goals.
- *Goal alignment* means having a method that enables managers and employees to see the link between the employees' goals and those of their department and company.
- *Ongoing performance monitoring* usually includes using computerized systems that measure and then e-mail progress and exception reports based on the person's progress toward meeting his or her performance goals.
- *Ongoing feedback* includes both face-to-face and computerized feedback regarding progress toward goals.
- *Coaching and developmental support* should be an integral part of the feedback process.
- *Recognition and rewards* provide the consequences needed to keep the employee's goal-directed performance on track.

Using Information Technology to Support Performance Management

Performance management needn't be high-tech. For example, in many facilities, work teams simply meet, often daily, to review their performance and to get their efforts aligned with their performance standards and goals.

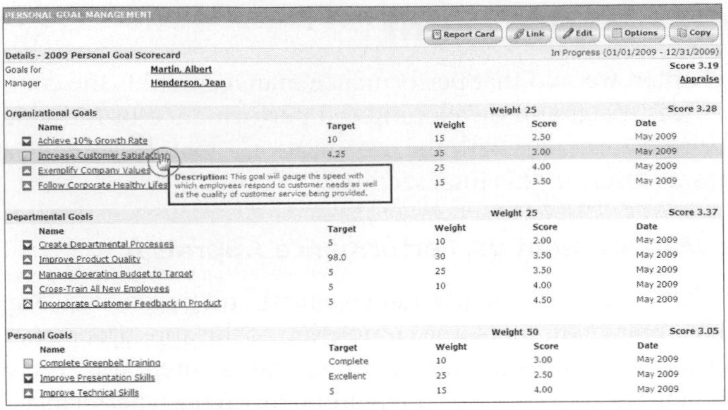

FIGURE 6-9 Summary of Performance Management Process Report.

However, information technology enables management to automate performance management. We can sum up this IT-supported performance management process as follows:

- *Assign financial and nonfinancial goals* to each team's activities along the strategy map chain of activities leading from the team's activities up to the company's overall strategic goals. (For example, an airline might measure aircraft turnaround time in terms of "improve turnaround time from an average of 30 minutes per plane to 26 minutes per plane this year.")
- *Inform all employees* of their goals.
- *Special performance management software* then shows a real-time overview of each team's performance relative to its goals, enabling the team to take corrective action before things swing out of control. Figure 6-9 presents an example of an employee's online performance management report.

Improving Productivity Through HRIS

Performance management, particularly for larger companies, usually requires Web-based performance management systems. For example, as we noted earlier, Seagate Technology uses "Enterprise Suite" for managing the performance of its 39,000 employees.[73] Employees update their plans quarterly and then do self-evaluations at the end of the year, with follow-up reviews by their supervisors.

A Web-based system like this helps each employee see where his or her goals fit in the overall framework of what the company is trying to accomplish. Specifically, it enables individual employees to set their goals based on a "cascading goals" system: With Enterprise Suite, they can easily see the company's goals, their unit's goals, and their supervisor's goals. This makes it easier for employees to set goals that make sense in terms of Seagate's goals. And, of course, a system like this makes it easier for Seagate's widely disbursed employees to fill in and update their goals, plans, and appraisals whenever and wherever they need to.

TALENT MANAGEMENT PRACTICES FOR STRATEGIC EMPLOYEE APPRAISALS

Appraising and Actively Managing Employees

Employers tend to allocate pay and development opportunities across the board or based on performance ratings (or both). In contrast, talent management requires *actively managing* decisions like these. Figure 6-10 illustrates one way to do this. Accenture uses a 4 × 4 Strategic Role Assessment matrix to plot employees by *Performance* (exceptional, high, medium, low) and *Value to the Organization* (mission-critical, core, necessary, nonessential). As an example, consider a chemical engineering company that designs pollution control equipment. Here, assume we may classify the firm's senior engineers as "mission-critical"; engineer-trainees as "core"; sales, accounting, and HR employees as "necessary"; and outsource-able employees like those in maintenance as "nonessential." The employer would then tie pay, development, dismissal, and other personnel decisions, not just to the employee's performance, but to each employee's place in the matrix.

Segmenting and Actively Managing Employees in Practice

Several examples illustrate how employers actually execute this active management approach.

- Compass Group PLC identifies top performers. Then Compass assesses them for promotability, promotability time-frame, and leadership potential. Top employees then get special coaching and feedback, as well as development opportunities. Compass monitors their progress.
- GE prioritizes jobs and focuses on what it calls its employee "game changers."[74]
- Tesco PLC segments employees according to personal and professional goals to better communicate and motivate its employees.[75]

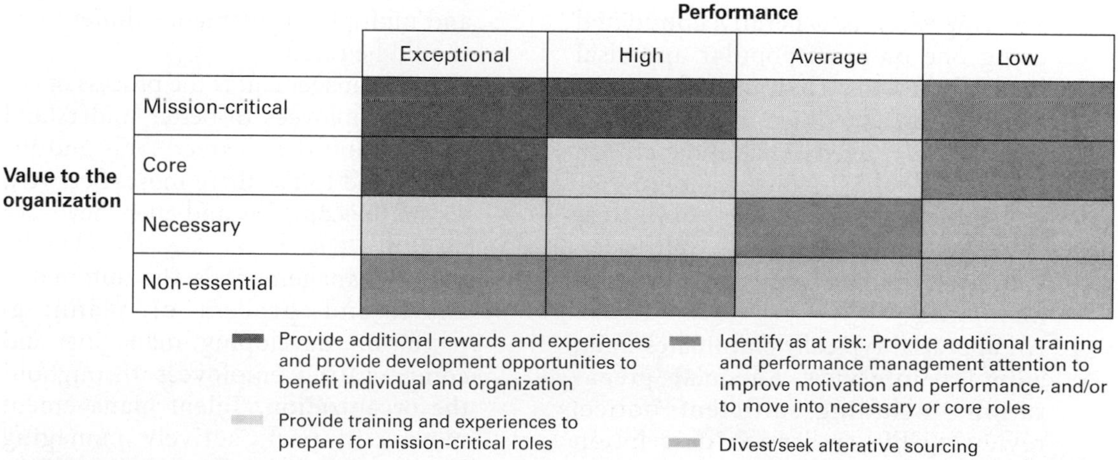

FIGURE 6-10 Accenture's Strategic Role Assessment Matrix. *Source:* This information originally appeared in "The New Talent Equation" from the June 2009 issue of *Outlook*, an Accenture publication. © 2009 Accenture. All rights reserved. Chart reprinted by permission.

- McKinsey & Co. recommends limiting the high potential group in whom the company invests heavily to no more than 10 to 20% of managerial and professional staff.[76]
- Unilever includes 15% of employees per management level in its high potential list each year, and expects these people to move to the next management level within five years.[77]
- Shell China appoints "career stewards" to meet regularly with "emerging leaders." They assess their level of engagement, help them set realistic career expectations, and make sure they're getting the right development opportunities.[78]

REVIEW

Summary

1. Performance appraisal means evaluating an employee's current or past performance relative to his or her performance standards. Performance management is the continuous process through which companies ensure that employees are working toward organizational goals.

2. Managers appraise their subordinates' performance to obtain data on which promotion and salary raise decisions can be made, to develop plans for correcting performance deficiencies, and for career planning. Supervisory ratings are still the heart of most appraisal processes.

3. The appraisal is generally conducted using one or more popular appraisal methods or tools. These include graphic rating scales, alternation ranking, paired comparison, forced distribution, critical incidents, behaviorally anchored rating scales, management by objectives (MBO), computerized or Web-based appraisals, and electronic performance monitoring.

4. An appraisal typically culminates in an appraisal interview. Adequate preparation, including sufficient notice, reviewing his or her job description and past performance, choosing the right place for the interview, and leaving enough time are essential. In conducting the interview, the aim is to reinforce satisfactory performance or to diagnose and improve unsatisfactory performance. Employee defensiveness is normal and needs to be dealt with.

5. The appraisal process can be improved, for instance by eliminating common problems such as unfairness, unclear standards, halo effect, central tendency, leniency or strictness, and bias.

6. Care should also be taken to ensure that the performance appraisal is legally defensible. For example, base appraisal criteria on documented job analyses. Employees should receive performance standards in writing,w and multiple performance dimensions should be rated.

7. Career management is the process of enabling employees to better understand and develop their career skills and interests, and to use these most effectively, within the company and after they leave the firm.

8. Talent management is the automated end-to-end process of planning, recruiting, developing, managing, and compensating employees throughout the organization. Talent management means, in part, actively managing how the employer allocates rewards to employees, based not just on performance but on the employees at you to the company as well.

Key Terms

performance appraisal *158*
performance
    management *159*
performance appraisal
    process *159*
peer appraisal *160*
upward feedback *161*
graphic rating scale *162*

alternation ranking
    method *162*
paired comparison
    method *162*
forced distribution
    method *162*
critical incident
    method *166*

management
    by objectives (MBO) *166*
halo effect *171*
central tendency *171*
appraisal
    interview *172*
coaching *174*
career management *174*

Discussion Questions

1. Discuss the pros and cons of at least four performance appraisal tools.
2. Explain how you would use the alternation ranking method, the paired comparison method, and the forced distribution method.
3. Explain the problems to be avoided in appraising performance.
4. Discuss the pros and cons of using various potential raters to appraise an employee's performance.
5. Explain how to conduct an appraisal interview.

Individual and Group Activities

1. Working individually or in groups, develop a graphic rating scale for the following jobs: secretary, professor, directory assistance operator.
2. Working individually or in groups, describe the advantages and disadvantages of using the forced distribution appraisal method for college professors.
3. Working individually or in groups, develop, over the period of a week, a set of critical incidents covering the classroom performance of one of your instructors.
4. Working individually or in groups, evaluate the rating scale in Figure 6-1. Discuss ways to improve it.

APPLICATION EXERCISES

CASE INCIDENT

Appraising the Secretaries at Sweetwater U

Rob Winchester, newly appointed vice president for administrative affairs at Sweetwater State University, faced a tough problem shortly after his university career began. Three weeks after he came on board in September, Sweetwater's president, Rob's boss, told Rob that one of his first tasks was to improve the appraisal system used to evaluate secretarial and clerical performance at Sweetwater U. The main difficulty was that the performance appraisal was tied to salary increases given at the end of the year. Therefore, most administrators were less than accurate when they used the graphic rating forms that were the basis of the clerical staff evaluation. Each administrator simply rated his or her clerk or secretary as "excellent." This cleared the way for all support staff to receive a maximum pay increase every year.

(*continued*)

But the current university budget did not include enough money to fund another "maximum" annual increase for everyone. Furthermore, Sweetwater's president felt that the custom of providing invalid performance feedback to each secretary was not productive, so he had asked the new vice president to revise the system. In October, Rob sent a memo to all administrators telling them that in the future no more than half the secretaries reporting to any particular administrator could be appraised as "excellent." This move, in effect, forced each supervisor to begin ranking his or her secretaries for quality of performance. The vice president's memo met widespread resistance immediately—from administrators, who were afraid that many of their secretaries would leave for lucrative jobs; and from secretaries, who felt that the new system was unfair. A handful of secretaries had begun quietly picketing outside the president's home on the university campus. The picketing, caustic remarks by disgruntled administrators, and rumors of an impending slowdown by the secretaries (there were about 250 on campus) made Rob Winchester wonder whether he had made the right decision by setting up forced ranking. He knew, however, that there were a few performance appraisal experts in the School of Business, so he set up an appointment with them to discuss the matter.

He met with them the next morning. He explained the situation as he had found it: The present appraisal system had been set up when the university first opened 10 years earlier. A committee of secretaries had developed it. Under that system, Sweetwater's administrators filled out forms similar to the one in Figure 6-8. This once-a-year appraisal (in March) had run into problems almost immediately, since it was apparent from the start that administrators varied widely in their interpretations of job standards, as well as in how conscientiously they filled out the forms and supervised their

secretaries. Moreover, at the end of the first year it became obvious to everyone that each secretary's salary increase was tied directly to the March appraisal. For example, those rated "excellent" received the maximum increases, those rated "good" received smaller increases, and those given neither rating received only across-the-board cost-of-living increases. Since universities in general—and Sweetwater in particular—have paid secretaries somewhat lower salaries than those in private industry, some secretaries left in a huff that first year. From that time on, most administrators simply rated all secretaries excellent in order to reduce staff turnover, thus ensuring each a maximum increase. In the process, they also avoided the hard feelings aroused by the significant performance differences otherwise highlighted by administrators.

Two Sweetwater experts agreed to consider the problem, and in 2 weeks they came back to the vice president with the following recommendations. First, the form used to rate the secretaries was grossly insufficient. It was unclear what "excellent" or "quality of work" meant, for example. They recommended instead a form like that in Figure 6-2. In addition, they recommended that the vice president rescind his earlier memo and no longer attempt to force university administrators to rate at least half their secretaries as less than excellent. The two consultants pointed out that this was, in fact, an unfair procedure since it was quite possible that any particular administrator might have staffers who were all excellent—or conceivably, although less likely, all below standard. The experts said that the way to get all the administrators to take the appraisal process more seriously was to stop tying it to salary increases. In other words, they recommended that every administrator fill out a form like that in Figure 6-2 for each secretary at least once a year and then use this form as the basis of a counseling session.

Salary increases would be made on some basis other than the performance appraisal, so that administrators would no longer hesitate to fill out the rating forms honestly.

Rob thanked the two experts and went back to his office to ponder their recommendations. Some of the recommendations (such as substituting the new rating form for the old) seemed to make sense. Nevertheless, he still had serious doubts as to the efficacy of any graphic rating form, particularly if he were to decide in favor of his original forced ranking approach. The experts' second recommendation—to stop tying the appraisals to automatic salary increases—made sense but raised a practical problem: If salary increases were not to be based on performance appraisals, on what were they to be based? He began wondering whether the experts' recommendations weren't simply based on ivory-tower theorizing.

QUESTIONS

1. Do you think that the experts' recommendations will be sufficient to get most of the administrators to fill out the rating forms properly? Why? Why not? What additional actions (if any) do you think will be necessary?
2. Do you think that Vice President Winchester would be better off dropping graphic rating forms, substituting instead one of the other techniques discussed in this chapter, such as a ranking method? Why?
3. What performance appraisal system would you develop for the secretaries if you were Rob Winchester? Defend your answer.

CASE INCIDENT

Back with a Vengeance

Conducting an effective appraisal is always important. However, an appraisal can have life-and-death implications when you're dealing with unstable employees, particularly those who must be dismissed. An employee of a U.S. Postal Service station was terminated. The employee came back and shot and killed several managers who had been instrumental in the former employee's dismissal. It turned out this person had a history as a troublemaker and that many clues regarding his unstable nature over many years had been ignored.

QUESTIONS

1. Could a company with an effective appraisal process have missed so many signals of instability over several years? Why? Why not?
2. What safeguards would you build into your appraisal process to avoid missing such potentially tragic signs of instability and danger?
3. What would you do if confronted during an appraisal interview by someone who began making threats regarding the use of firearms?

CONTINUING CASE

Carter Cleaning Company

The Performance Appraisal

After spending several weeks on the job, Jennifer was surprised to discover that her father had not formally evaluated any employee's performance for all the years that he had owned the business. Jack's position was that he had "a hundred higher-priority things to attend to," such as boosting sales and lowering costs, and, in any case, many employees didn't stick around long enough to be appraisable anyway. Furthermore, contended Jack, manual workers such as those doing the pressing and the cleaning did periodically get positive feedback in terms of praise from Jack for a job well done, or criticism, also from Jack, if things did not look right during one of his swings through the stores. Similarly, Jack was

(continued)

never shy about telling his managers about store problems so that they, too, got some feedback on where they stood.

This informal feedback notwithstanding, Jennifer believes that a more formal appraisal approach is required. She believes that there are criteria such as quality, quantity, attendance, and punctuality that should be evaluated periodically even if a worker is paid on piece rate. Furthermore, she feels quite strongly that the managers need to have a list of quality standards for matters such as store cleanliness, efficiency, safety, and adherence to budget on which they know they are to be formally evaluated. She would like your opinion and advice.

QUESTIONS

1. Is Jennifer right about the need to evaluate the workers formally? The managers? Why or why not?
2. Develop a performance appraisal method for the workers and managers in each store.

EXPERIENTIAL EXERCISE

Appraising an Instructor

Purpose: The purpose of this exercise is to give you practice in developing and using a performance appraisal form.

Required Understanding: You are going to develop a performance appraisal form for an instructor and should therefore be thoroughly familiar with the discussion of performance appraisals in this chapter.

How to Set Up the Exercise/Instructions: If so desired, divide the class into teams.

1. First, based on what you now know about performance appraisals, do you think Figure 6-1 is an effective scale for appraising instructors? Why or why not?
2. Next, you or your group should develop its own tool for appraising the performance of an instructor. Decide which of the appraisal tools (graphic rating scales, alternation ranking, and so on) you are going to use, and then design the instrument itself.
3. Next, put (or have a spokesperson from each group put his or her group's) your appraisal tool on the board. How similar are the tools? Do they all measure about the same factors? Which factor appears most often? Which do you think is the most effective tool on the board? Can you think of any way of combining the best points of several of the tools into a new performance appraisal tool?

Seven

Compensating Employees

When you finish studying this chapter you should be able to:

- Discuss *four basic factors determining pay rates.*
- Explain *each of the steps in establishing market-competitive pay rates.*
- Compare *and* contrast *piecework and team or group incentive plans.*
- List *and* describe *each of the basic benefits most employers might be expected to offer.*

OVERVIEW

Rosa was thrilled with her 5% raise, until she discovered that Jean received 2% more. "We're doing the same job and I'm as good as her," Rosa said. Now their manager has to decide what to do. The main purpose of this chapter is to explain how to create and implement an equitable pay plan. The main topics we cover include What Determines How Much You Pay, How to Create a Market-Competitive Pay Plan, Incentive Plans, Employee Benefits, and Current Compensation Trends.

WHAT DETERMINES HOW MUCH YOU PAY?

Employee compensation refers to all forms of pay or rewards going to employees and arising from their employment. It has two main components: *direct financial payments* (in the form of wages, salaries, incentives, commissions, and bonuses) and *indirect payments* (in the form of financial benefits like employer-paid insurance and vacations). *Total rewards* encompass traditional pay, incentives, and benefits, but also things such as employee recognition programs and more challenging jobs.

Four basic factors determine what people are paid: legal, union, policy, and equity factors.

Legal: Important Compensation Laws

Numerous laws stipulate what employers can or must pay in terms of minimum wages, overtime rates, and benefits.[1]

1938 FAIR LABOR STANDARDS ACT   The **Fair Labor Standards Act (FLSA),** passed in 1938 and since amended many times, contains minimum wage, maximum hours, overtime pay, equal pay, recordkeeping, and child labor provisions covering most U.S. workers—virtually anyone engaged in producing or selling goods for interstate and foreign commerce.

One well-known provision governs overtime pay. It states that employers must pay overtime at a rate of at least one and a half times normal pay for any hours worked over 40 in a workweek.

The act also sets a minimum wage, which sets a floor for employees covered by the act (and usually bumps up wages for most workers when Congress raises the minimum). The minimum wage was $7.25 per hour in 2012.[2] (Several states and about 80 municipalities have their own, higher, minimum wages.)[3] The act's child labor provisions prohibit employing those between 16 and 18 years of age in hazardous occupations, and restricts employment of those under 16.[4]

EXEMPT/NONEXEMPT   Employers do not have to pay all employees overtime pay. Specific jobs are *exempt* from the act or certain provisions of the act, and particularly from the act's overtime provisions. People in these jobs are "exempt employees." A person's exemption depends on his or her responsibilities, duties, and salary. Bona fide executive, administrative (like office managers), and professional employees (like architects) are generally exempt from the act's minimum wage and overtime requirements.[5] A white-collar worker earning more than $100,000 and performing any one exempt administrative, executive, or professional duty is automatically ineligible for overtime pay. Other employees can generally earn up to $23,660 per year and still automatically get overtime pay (so most employees earning less than $455 per week are nonexempt and earn overtime). Figure 7-1 presents a procedure for deciding if a job is exempt.

If an employee is exempt from the FLSA's minimum wage provisions, then he or she is also exempt from its overtime pay provisions. However, certain employees are always exempt from overtime pay provisions. They include, among others, agricultural employees, live-in household employees, taxicab drivers, and outside sales employees.[6]

A study of low-wage workers in Chicago, New York, and Los Angeles found that about one-fourth were paid below the minimum wage, 76% also had unpaid or underpaid overtime, and 56% didn't receive pay stubs as required by law.[7]

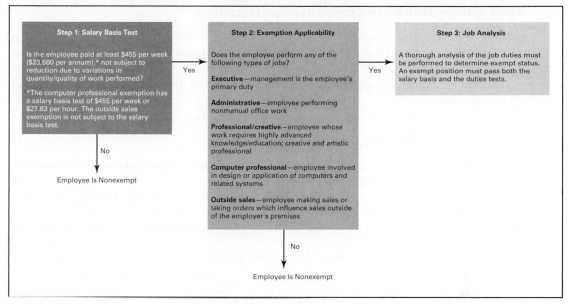

FIGURE 7-1 Who Is Exempt?

Even giant firms make errors. Walmart recently agreed to pay up to $640 million to settle 63 wage and hour suits alleging infractions such as failing to pay overtime.[8] Other firms assert that some individuals are not employees but "independent contractors," more like consultants not covered by the Act. For example, FedEx argues that its roughly 15,000 delivery truck owner-operators act as independent contractors.[9]

Whether the person is an employee or an *independent contractor* depends on numerous factors such as the amount of control the employer exercises over the person's duties and schedule.[10]

1963 EQUAL PAY ACT The **Equal Pay Act,** an amendment to the Fair Labor Standards Act, states that employees of one sex may not be paid wages at a rate lower than that paid to employees of the opposite sex for roughly equivalent work.[11] Specifically, if the work requires equal skills, effort, and responsibility and is performed under similar working conditions, employees of both sexes must receive equal pay unless the differences in pay are based on a seniority system, a merit system, the quantity or quality of production, or any factor other than sex.[12]

1964 CIVIL RIGHTS ACT Title VII of the **Civil Rights Act** makes it unlawful for an employer to discriminate against any individual with respect to hiring, compensation, terms, conditions, or privileges of employment because of race, color, religion, sex, or national origin.

OTHER DISCRIMINATION LAWS Various other discrimination laws influence compensation decisions. As a few examples, the Age Discrimination in Employment Act prohibits age discrimination against employees who are 40 years of age and older. The Americans with Disabilities Act similarly prohibits discrimination against qualified persons with disabilities in all aspects of employment, including compensation.

How Unions Influence Compensation Decisions

For unionized companies, union negotiations of course influence pay plan design. Historically, the wage rate has been the main issue in collective bargaining. Other pay-related issues include time off with pay, income security (for those in industries with periodic layoffs), cost-of-living adjustments, and various benefits such as health care.[13]

Compensation Policies

An employer's strategy and compensation policies significantly affect the wages and benefits it pays. For example, a hospital might have a policy of paying nurses 10% above the prevailing market wage. Other important policies include the basis for salary increases, foreign pay differentials, and overtime pay policy. Locality also plays a role. For example, the average base pay for an office supervisor ranges from $47,210 in Florida to $57,970 in New York.[14]

Distinguishing between high and low performers is another important pay policy. For example, for many years Payless ShoeSource hardly distinguished in pay among high and low performers. After seeing its market share drop, management's turnaround strategy included revising its compensation policies to differentiate more between top performers and others.[15]

STRATEGY AND HR   Employers should ask, What skills and performance does achieving our strategic goals require, and do our compensation policies make sense in terms of producing the skills and performance?[16]

For example, supermarket chain Wegmans Foods pays above-average wages and provides all employees with free health coverage. Management says, "If we take care of our employees, they will take care of our customers."[17] Wegmans' competitive strategy is to compete with other grocery chains based on productivity and service. Its compensation strategy supports that strategy, and it seems to be working. Its larger stores each average about $950,000 a week in sales, compared to the national average of about $361,564 for grocery stores. And Wegmans' employee retention figures are well above national averages. The point is that the compensation plan should produce an *aligned reward strategy*. The aim is to create a total reward package, including wages, incentives, benefits, and other rewards that produces the employee behaviors the firm needs to support and achieve its competitive strategy.[18]

Equity and Its Impact on Pay Rates

Maintaining equity is a key factor in determining pay rates.[19] Externally, pay must compare favorably with rates in other companies, or an employer will find it hard to attract and retain qualified employees. Pay must also be equitable internally: Each employee should view his or her pay as equitable given other employees' pay in the organization.[20]

To head off discussions that might prompt feelings of internal inequity, some firms maintain strict secrecy over pay rates, with mixed results. But for external equity, online pay sites like Salary.com make it easy for employees to see what they could earn elsewhere.[21]

HOW TO CREATE A MARKET-COMPETITIVE PAY PLAN

In practice, setting pay rates while ensuring external and internal equity (in other words, creating a market-competitive pay plan) usually entails six steps:

1. Determine the worth of each job in your organization through *job evaluation* (to help ensure internal equity).
2. Group similar jobs into *pay grades*.
3. Price each pay grade with a *wage curve*.
4. Conduct a *salary survey* of what other employers are paying comparable jobs.
5. Compare and adjust *current* and *market* wage rates for jobs or grades.
6. Develop *rate ranges*.

We explain each of these steps in this section, starting with salary surveys.

Step 1: Determine the Worth of Each Job: Job Evaluation

The job evaluation helps the employer build a pay plan that is internally equitable.

PURPOSE OF JOB EVALUATION   **Job evaluation** is a formal and systematic comparison of jobs to determine the worth of one job relative to another. The basic job evaluation procedure is to compare the "content" of jobs in relation to one another, for example, in terms of each job's effort, responsibility, and skills. Suppose you use job evaluation to determine the relative worth of the jobs in your firm, and also know what others are paying for these jobs (based on a salary survey of what others are paying). Then you are on your way to being able to price all jobs so their pay is equitable both internally and externally.

COMPENSABLE FACTORS   There are two basic approaches to comparing the worth of several jobs to each other. First, you might decide that one job is simply more important than another is and not dig any deeper into why.

As an alternative, you could compare the jobs by determining how much of certain basic factors each job has. Compensation managers call these basic factors **compensable factors.** They are the factors that determine how the jobs compare to each other. For example, the Equal Pay Act focuses on four compensable factors: skills, effort, responsibility, and working conditions. The federal government sets pay for its own jobs based on each job's level of skill, effort, responsibility, and working conditions. Walmart has a wage structure based on each job's knowledge, problem-solving skills, and accountability requirements.

JOB EVALUATION METHODS   The simplest job evaluation method ranks each job relative to all other jobs, usually based on some overall compensable factor such as job difficulty. There are several steps in this *job ranking* method, as the accompanying HR in Practice feature summarizes. *Job classification* is another simple, widely used job evaluation method. Here the manager categorizes jobs into groups based on their similarity in terms of compensable factors such as skill and responsibility categories. The groups are called *classes* if they contain similar jobs (such as "Bookkeeper II") or *grades* if they contain jobs that are similar in difficulty but are otherwise different. Thus, in the federal government's pay grade system, a press secretary and a fire chief might both be graded GS-10 (GS stands for

---

HR IN PRACTICE

Steps in Ranking Method of Job Evaluation

1. *Obtain job information.* Job analysis is the first step in the **ranking method**. Ranking involves ordering jobs from high to low, usually based on some overall measure such as job difficulty. You'll usually use the job description for each job to decide each job's rank, typically based on the whole job rather than separate compensable factors.
2. *Select raters and jobs to be rated.* The usual procedure is to rank jobs by department or in clusters (such as factory workers and clerical workers). This eliminates the need for having to compare directly, say, factory jobs and clerical jobs.
3. *Select compensable factors.* In the ranking method, it is common to use just one factor (such as job difficulty) and to rank jobs based on the whole job.
4. *Rank jobs.* Next, rank the jobs. Give each rater a set of index cards, each of which contains a brief description of a job. Then have them rank them from lowest to highest. Jobs in a small health facility (Table 7-1) rank from cleaner to office manager. The corresponding pay scales are shown on the right.
5. *Combine ratings.* Usually several raters rank the jobs independently. Then the rating committee (or employer) can average the rankings. Online programs, as at www.hr-guide .com/data/G909.htm, can help rank your positions.

General Schedule). The *point method* is a quantitative job evaluation technique. It involves identifying several compensable factors, each having several degrees. Then decide how many degrees each job contains, and based on that, the total number of points for each job.

Step 2: Group Similar Jobs into Pay Grades

Once a job evaluation method has been used to determine the relative worth of each job, the evaluation committee can start assigning pay rates to each job. However, it will first probably group jobs into pay grades. A *pay grade* comprises jobs of approximately equal difficulty or importance as determined by job evaluation. If the point method were used, the pay grade would consist of jobs falling within a range of points. If the ranking

TABLE 7-1   Job Ranking by Jackson Hospital

Ranking Order	Annual Pay Scale
1. Office manager	$48,000
2. Chief nurse	47,500
3. Bookkeeper	39,000
4. Nurse	37,500
5. Cook	36,000
6. Nurse's aide	33,500
7. Cleaner	30,500

Note: After ranking, it becomes possible to slot additional jobs between those already ranked and to assign each an appropriate wage rate.

plan were used, the grade would consist of all jobs that fall within two or three ranks. If the classification system were used, then the jobs are already categorized into classes or grades (such as Accountant I, II, III and so on). Ten to 16 grades per job cluster (such as factory jobs, clerical jobs, etc.) are common.

Step 3: Price Each Pay Grade: Wage Curves

The next step is to assign average pay rates to each of the pay grades. (Of course, if you choose not to slot jobs into pay grades, you'll have to assign an individual pay rate to each individual job.) Assigning pay rates to each pay grade (or to each job) is usually accomplished with the help of a **wage curve.** This shows the average pay rates currently being paid for jobs in each pay grade, relative to the points or rankings assigned to each job or grade by the job evaluation.

Figure 7-2 illustrates a wage curve. The purpose of a wage curve is to show the relationship between (1) the value of each grade (in this case based on points) as determined by one of the job evaluation methods and (2) the current average pay rates for the grades. Basically, you create a wage curve as you would any graph: in this case, by showing current (or "internal") pay rates on the "Y" vertical axis and job value or difficulty on the "X" horizontal axis, and then plotting the corresponding points based on what you are paying now on average, for jobs in each grade. The wage curve or line then shows the wages or salary rates for the jobs in each pay grade.

Step 4: Conduct the Salary Survey

So far, the employer has a wage curve that shows the average pay rate for each pay grade relative to the average value to the company of the jobs in that pay grade (for instance as measured by each job's points). The question is, are these pay rates competitive with what other employers are paying?

Salary (or compensation) surveys—formal or informal surveys of what other employers are paying for similar jobs—therefore play a central role in pricing jobs.

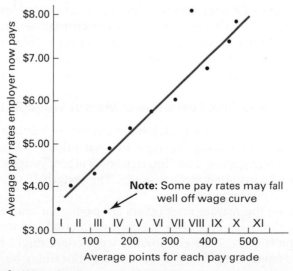

FIGURE 7-2 Example of a Wage Curve.

TABLE 7-2 Some Pay Data Websites

Sponsor	Internet Address	What It Provides	Downside
Salary.com	http://salary .com	Salary by job and zip code, plus job and description, for hundreds of jobs	Adapts national averages by applying local cost-of-living differences
U.S. Office of Personnel Management	www.opm.gov/ oca/09Tables/ index.asp	Salaries and wages for U.S. government jobs, by location	Limited to U.S. government jobs
Job Smart	http://jobstar .org/tools/salary/ index.php	Profession-specific salary surveys	Necessary to review numerous salary surveys for each profession
cnnmoney.com	http://money .cnn.com	Input your current salary and city to get comparable salary in destination city	Based on national averages adapted to cost-of-living differences

Employers use salary surveys in three ways. First, they use them to price *benchmark jobs.* These anchor the employer's pay scale. The manager slots other jobs around them, based on their relative worth to the firm, (rather then evaluating every one of the jobs using job evaluation). Second, employers usually price 20% or more of their positions directly in the marketplace (rather than relative to the firm's benchmark jobs), based on a formal or informal survey of what comparable firms are paying for comparable jobs. Finally, surveys also collect data on benefits such as insurance, sick leave, and vacations.[22]

Table 7-2 summarizes some popular salary websites. In addition, the U.S. Department of Labor's Bureau of Labor Statistics' (BLS) *National Compensation Survey (NCS)* provides comprehensive reports of occupational earnings, compensation cost trends, and benefits (www.bls.gov/bls/wages.htm). Detailed occupational earnings are available from this survey for over 800 occupations in the United States, regions, states, and many metropolitan areas (http://stats.bls.gov/oes/current/oes_nat.htm</URL).

Armed with this salary information, the employer can create a second wage curve. This "external" or "market" wage curve shows what the pay rates are in the marketplace for jobs comparable to the employer's jobs.

Step 5: Compare and Adjust Current and Market Wage Rates for Jobs

The employer wants its pay rates for each job to be equitable not just internally (relative to each other) but also externally (relative to what others are paying). To do this we compare the two wage curves. The "internal" or "current" wage curve plots what we are now paying for jobs grouped in each grade. The "external" wage curve plots what others are paying for these same jobs.

How different are the market rates others are paying for our jobs and our current rates? To determine this, we merge both the current/internal and market/external wage curves on one graph (Figure 7-3). The market wage curve might be higher than our current wage curve (suggesting that our current pay rates may be low). Or it may be

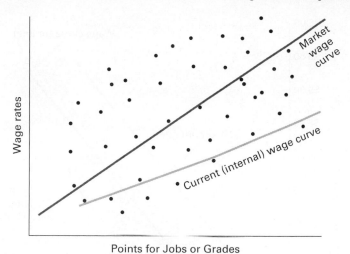

FIGURE 7-3 Merging Market and Internal Wage Curves.

below our current wage curve (suggesting that our current wage rates might be high). Or perhaps market wage rates are higher for some of our jobs, and lower for others.[23]

Based on comparing the current/internal wage curve and market/external wage curve in Figure 7-3, we must decide whether to adjust the current pay rates for our jobs, and if so how. This calls for a management policy decision. (For example, we might decide to move our current internal wage curve up, and thereby give everyone a raise.) In any case, the wage curve we end up with (the middle line in Figure 7-4) should now be equitable internally (in terms of the point value of each job) and equitable externally (in terms of what other firms are paying.)[24]

Step 6: Develop Rate Ranges

Finally, most employers do not just pay one rate for all jobs in a particular pay grade. Instead, they develop rate ranges for each grade. So, there might be 10 levels or steps within each grade, and 10 corresponding pay rates within each pay grade (see for instance Figure 7-4). The employer may then fine-tune pay rates for each job to account for any unique circumstances.

Pricing Managerial and Professional Jobs

For managerial and professional jobs, job evaluation provides only a partial answer to the question of pay. Managerial and professional jobs tend to emphasize nonquantifiable factors like judgment and problem solving more than do production and clerical jobs. There is also more of a tendency to pay managers and professionals based on their performance, on what competitors are paying, or on what they can do, rather than on intrinsic job demands such as working conditions. One study concluded that three main factors—*job complexity* (span of control, the number of divisions over which the executive has direct responsibility, and management level), the employer's *ability to pay* (total profit and rate of return), and the executive's *human capital* (educational level, field of study, work experience)—accounted for most of executive compensation

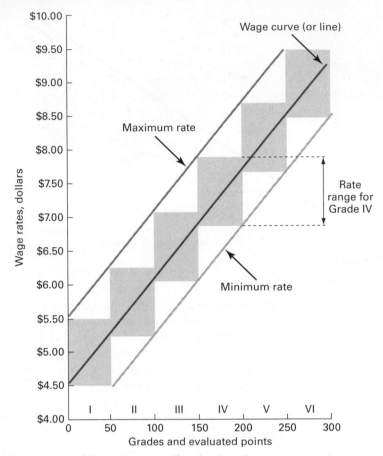

FIGURE 7-4 Wage Curve and Wage Structure, Showing Rate Ranges.

variance.[25] In another study labor market factors such as competitors' pay levels and whether the CEO was likely to be "raided" by other firms were as or more important than firm size and annual performance in determining CEO pay.[26]

PAY PACKAGE ELEMENTS   Top executives' pay plans generally consist of base salary, short-term incentives, long-term incentives, and executive benefits and perks.[27] *Base salary* includes the obvious fixed compensation paid regularly as well as, often, guaranteed bonuses such as "10% of pay at the end of the fourth fiscal quarter, regardless of whether the company makes a profit." *Short-term incentives* are usually paid in cash or stock for achieving short-term goals, such as year-to-year increases in sales revenue. Incentives equal 31% or more of a typical executive's base pay.[28] *Long-term incentives* include such things as stock options. These generally give the executive the right to purchase stock at a specific price for a specific period. They aim to encourage the executive to take actions that will drive up the price of the company's stock. Finally, special *executive benefits and perks* might include supplemental executive retirement plans, and health insurance without a deductible or coinsurance.

Employers are shifting from long-term incentives to short-term performance and incentives.[29] Most firms have **annual bonus** plans for motivating managers' short-term performance. Such short-term incentives can easily produce plus or minus adjustments of 25% or more to total pay. More employers are offering executives as well as employees below the executive level single annual incentive plans "in which both executives and other employees participate."[30] This reflects the fact that more employees—not just top managers—are now responsible for (and thus rewarded bonuses for) measurable contributions.

STRATEGY AND EXECUTIVE PAY   As with any pay plans, those for managers and professionals should make sense strategically. To accomplish this:

- Identify the company's strategic direction, and translate this into specific business goals.
- List the skills and competencies your professional employees should have and the behaviors they should exhibit to accomplish these goals.
- Evaluate the extent to which the existing pay plan produces these skills, competencies, and behaviors. (For example, ask, Does it motivate executives to achieve their goals?)[31]
- If not, design and implement a new pay plan.[32]

Pay for Professionals

In compensating professionals, employers should first ensure that each employee is actually a "professional" under the law.[33] In addition to earning at least $455 per week, the person's main duty must "be the performance of work requiring advanced knowledge" and "the advanced knowledge must be customarily acquired by a prolonged course of specialized intellectual instruction."[34]

Firms rarely rely on just job evaluation for professional jobs. Factors like creativity are hard to measure and market pay pressures change quickly. Google recently raised its employees' salaries by 10% when faced with defections by even their highest paid professionals to Facebook.[35]

INCENTIVE PLANS

Many—perhaps most—employees don't just earn a salary or hourly wage. They also earn some type of incentive. This section addresses some popular **incentive plans.** *Individual incentive programs* give performance-based pay to individual employees. *Team-based incentives* of course aim to incentivize work teams. *Variable pay* refers to group pay plans that tie payments to productivity or to some other measure of the firm's profitability.[36] **Productivity** "is the ratio of outputs (goods and services) divided by the inputs (resources such as labor and capital)."[37]

Traditionally, all incentive plans are "pay-for-performance" plans. They pay all employees based on the employee's performance. Roughly 70% of employees feel that their firms' incentive plans are ineffective, so designing the plan right is paramount.[38]

Piecework Plans

Piecework is the oldest incentive plan and still the most common. The person is paid a "piece rate" for each unit he or she produces. Thus, if Tom gets $0.40 apiece for finding addresses on the Web, he would make $40 for finding 100 a day.

Team or Group Incentive Plans

Companies often want to pay groups (rather than individuals) on an incentive basis, such as when they want to encourage teamwork. Most firms pay all team members the same incentive, based on the team's overall performance. However, a group incentive plan's main drawback is that each worker's rewards don't necessarily reflect his or her own efforts. So if the person decides to relax and let others carry the load, the group plan may be less effective than an individual plan.[39] Therefore, some plans endeavor to pay team members somewhat different amounts, based on their individual efforts.

Incentives for Managers and Executives

Managers play a central role in influencing divisional and corporate profitability, and most firms therefore put considerable thought into how to reward them.[40]

As noted, most managers get short-term bonuses and long-term incentives in addition to salary.[41] For firms offering short-term incentive plans, virtually all— 96%—provide those incentives in cash. For those offering long-term incentive plans, about 48% offer stock options. These aim to motivate and reward management for long-term corporate growth in shareholder value. The size of the bonus (in terms of percentage of salary) is usually greater for top-level executives.

While many employers focus on singular criteria (such as bottom-line profitability) in awarding top executive incentive pay, using multiple, strategy-based criteria is best. The latter include financial performance, number of strategic goals met, performance assessment by the board, employee productivity measures, customer satisfaction surveys, and employee morale surveys. The bottom line is that the top executive's pay package should direct his or her attention toward accomplishing the company's strategic goals.[42]

STOCK OPTIONS   A **stock option** is the right to purchase a specific number of shares of company stock at a specific price during a specific period. The executive hopes to profit by buying the shares in the future but at today's price.[43]

The chronic problem is that managers sometimes get stock options for even lackluster performance, but there are other issues. Executives sometimes manipulate the dates they receive their options to maximize returns. Options may also encourage perilous risks in pursuit of profits.[44]

One solution is tying rewards more explicitly to performance goals. Thus, more firms grant shares such as *performance-contingent restricted stock*; the executive receives his or her shares only once meeting the preset performance targets.[45] With *restricted stock plans*, the firm usually awards rights to the shares without cost to the executive but the employee is restricted from acquiring the shares for, say, 5 years.[46] With *indexed options*, if the company's stock does no better than some market index, the manager's options are worthless. With *premium priced options*, the exercise price is higher than the stock's closing price on the date of the grant, so the executive can't profit from the options until the stock makes significant gains.[47] Under *phantom stock plans*, executives receive not shares but "units" that are similar to but not stock. Then at some future time, they receive value (usually in cash) equal to the appreciation of their "phantom" stock.

SARBANES-OXLEY   The Sarbanes-Oxley Act of 2002 affects how employers formulate executive incentive programs. It makes executives and board members personally liable for violating their fiduciary responsibilities to their shareholders. The act also requires that CEOs and CFOs of a public company repay any bonuses, incentives, or equity-based compensation received from the company during the 12-month period following the issuance of a financial statement that the company must restate due to material noncompliance with a financial reporting requirement as a result of misconduct.[48]

Incentives for Salespeople

Most companies pay their salespeople a combination of salary and commissions, usually with a sizable salary component. Typical is a 70% base salary/30% incentive mix.[49] Commission plan alternatives include quota bonuses (for meeting particular quotas), straight commissions, management by objectives programs (pay is based on achieving specific goals), and ranking programs (these reward high achievers but pay little or no bonuses to the lowest performing salespeople).[50]

Setting effective sales quotas is an art.[51] Questions to ask include, Does the sales force know how their quotas are set? Are quotas stable through the performance period?[52] One expert suggests the following as a rule of thumb as to whether the sales incentive plan is effective: 75% or more of the sales force achieving quota or better; 10% of the sales force achieving higher performance level (than previously); 5% to 10% of the sales force achieving below-quota performance and receiving development coaching.[53] However, with the recent recession, employers are factoring in more growth-oriented goals, and reviewing their sales pay plans more often.[54]

AN EXAMPLE: AUTO DEALERS Commission rates vary by industry, but a look at how auto dealers set their salesperson's commission rates provides some insights. Compensation for car salespeople ranges from a high of 100% commission to a small base salary with commission accounting for most compensation. Dealers generally base commissions on the net profit on the car delivered to the buyer. This encourages salespeople to hold firm on the retail price and to push "after-sale products" like floor mats. And, for helping to sell slow-moving vehicles, the salesperson may get a "spiff"—an extra incentive.[55] Yet faced with the difficulty of attracting and keeping salespeople, a Buick-GMC dealership in Lincolnton, North Carolina, offers straight salary as an option to salespeople who sell an average of at least eight vehicles a month (plus a small "retention bonus" per car sold).[56]

Nontangible and Recognition-Based Awards

An employee's total rewards include not just benefits, but less-tangible awards as well, such as recognition.

Studies show that recognition has a positive impact on performance, either alone or in conjunction with financial rewards.[57] It's therefore not surprising that in one survey, 78% of CEOs and 58% of HR vice presidents said their firms were using performance recognition programs.[58] One survey of 235 managers found that the most-used rewards to motivate employees (down from most used to least) included:[59]

- Employee recognition
- Gift certificates
- Cash rewards
- Merchandise incentives

- Training programs
- Work/life benefits
- Individual travel
- Sweepstakes

Many employers are bulking up their recognition programs. For example, Baudville, a workplace recognition vendor, recently unveiled an e-card service called ePraise. Employers use this to remind employees of how much they're appreciated.

ONLINE AWARD PROGRAMS The downside to recognition programs is that they're expensive to administer. Many firms therefore use online incentive firms to expedite the whole process. Intuit outsourced its employee recognition, years of service, patent, and wellness awards programs to Globoforce several years ago.[60] Other incentive/recognition sites include sales-driver.com and kudoz.com.

Merit Pay as an Incentive

Merit pay, or a **merit raise,** is any salary increase awarded to an employee based on his or her individual performance. Unlike a bonus, it usually becomes part of the employee's base salary, whereas a bonus is a one-time payment. Although the term *merit pay* can apply to the incentive raises given to any employee, the term is more often used with professional, office, and clerical employees.

Merit pay has advocates and detractors. Advocates argue that rewards tied directly to performance can motivate performance. Detractors say it can undermine teamwork, and that, since the merit pay typically depends on the performance appraisal, unfair appraisals lead employees to perceive pay as unfair, too. One must therefore differentiate between top and mediocre performers.[61]

Profit-Sharing Plans

In a **profit-sharing plan,** most employees receive a share of the company's annual profits. Research on the effectiveness of such plans is sketchy. One study concludes that there is "ample" evidence that profit-sharing plans boost productivity, but that their effect on profits is insignificant, once you factor in their costs.[62] Cash plans are the most popular. Here, the employees receive, say, 15% to 20% of profits as profit shares at regular intervals.

Employee Stock Ownership Plan

Employee stock ownership plans (ESOPs) are company-wide plans in which a corporation transfers shares of its own stock—or cash to purchase such stock—to a trust established to purchase shares of that stock for employees. The firm generally makes these contributions annually in proportion to total employee compensation, with a limit of 15% of compensation. The trust holds the stock in individual employee accounts. It then distributes it to employees upon retirement (or other separation), assuming the person has worked long enough to earn ownership of the stock. (Traditional stock options, as discussed elsewhere in this chapter, go directly each year to the employees individually.[63])

The corporation receives a tax deduction equal to the fair market value of the shares that it transfers. It can also claim an income tax deduction for dividends paid on stock the ESOP owns. Employees are not taxed until they receive a distribution from the trust, usually at retirement when they usually have a reduced tax rate. And the **Employee Retirement Income Security Act (ERISA)** allows a firm to borrow against employee stock held in trust. The employer can then repay the loan in pretax rather than in after-tax dollars, another ESOP tax incentive. ESOPs may also encourage employees to develop a sense of commitment to the firm.[64]

BROAD-BASED STOCK OPTIONS For many years, some employers awarded stock options directly to all or most employees ("broad-based stock options") as part of the employers' profit-sharing incentive plans. Recently, a number of large companies including Microsoft and Charles Schwab announced they were discontinuing this. With companies now having to show the options as an expense when awarded, they apparently feel awarding stock instead of stock options is a more direct way to link pay to performance.[65]

Gainsharing Plans

There are many **gainsharing plans,** the aim of which is to encourage improved employee productivity by sharing resulting financial gains with employees. The oldest is the **Scanlon plan,** an incentive plan developed many years ago by Joseph Scanlon, a union official.[66] Other popular gainsharing plans include the Rucker and Improshare plans. The U.S. Department of Health and Human Services approved certain hospital gainsharing plans, wherein the hospital pays physicians a share of any cost savings attributable in part to the physicians' efforts.

Earnings-at-Risk Pay Plans

In an *earnings-at-risk* pay plan, employees agree to put some portion of their normal pay (say, 6%) at risk (forego it) if they don't meet their goals, in return for possibly obtaining a much larger bonus (say, 12%) if they exceed their goals. Suppose in one department the employees' base pay will be 94% of their counterparts' in a not-at-risk department. If the former department then achieves its goals, the employees get their full pay; if it exceeds its goals, they receive a 12% bonus.

Incentives at Nucor Corporation

Nucor Corp. is the largest steel producer in the United States; it also has the highest productivity, highest wages, and lowest labor cost per ton in the American steel industry.[67]

Nucor employees can earn bonuses of 100% or more of base salary. All participate in one of four performance-based incentive plans. With the *production incentive plan,* plant operating and maintenance employees and supervisors get weekly bonuses based on their workgroup's productivity. The *department manager incentive* pays department managers annual incentive bonuses based mostly on the ratio of net income to dollars of assets employed for their division. With the *professional and clerical bonus plan,* employees who are not in one of the two previous plans get bonuses based on their division's net income return on assets. Finally, under the *senior officers' incentive plan,* Nucor senior managers (whose base salaries are lower than those in comparable firms) get bonuses based on Nucor's annual overall percentage of net income to stockholder's equity.[68]

Improving Productivity Through HRIS

Incentives are becoming more complicated. For one thing, as we've seen, more employees—not just salespeople—now get incentives. Furthermore, the range of behaviors for which employers pay incentives is now quite broad, from better service to cutting costs to answering more calls per hour.[69]

Tracking performance of dozens or hundreds of measures like these and then computing individual employees' incentives is time consuming. Several companies such as Incentive Systems Inc. therefore provide Enterprise Incentive Management (EIM) systems. As one expert says, "EIM software automates the planning, calculation, modeling, and management of incentive compensation plans, enabling companies to align their employees with corporate strategy and goals."[70]

Employers also increasingly use the Web to support their sales and other incentive programs. For example, SalesDriver, in Maynard, Massachusetts, runs Web-based sales performance–based incentive programs. Using the SalesDriver template, the sales manager can select from a catalog of 1,500 reward items, and award these to sales and marketing reps for meeting quotas for things like lead generation and total sales.[71]

Job Design

Job design—reorganizing jobs to give workers more autonomy and responsibility—can be part of an employer's total rewards program. Thus a study by Harvard Business School researchers concluded that job design is a primary driver of employee engagement. A study by Towers Watson concluded that challenging work ranked as the seventh most important driver for attracting employees.[72]

Designing Effective Incentive Programs

Roughly 70% of employees feel that their firms' incentive plans are ineffective. We look at how to improve their effectiveness.[73]

THE FIVE BUILDING BLOCKS OF EFFECTIVE INCENTIVE PLANS

1. **Ask: Does it make sense to use incentives here?**[74] It makes more sense to use an incentive plan when:

   - Motivation (not ability) is the problem.
   - There is a clear relationship between employee effort and quantity or quality of output.
   - The employees can control the quantity or quality of the work.

2. **Link the incentive with your strategy.**[75] For example, one incentive program at Sun Microsystems (now part of Oracle) supported Sun's customer satisfaction goals. Employees received incentives based on improvements in activities like on-time delivery and customer returns.[76]

3. **Make sure the program is motivational.** Professor Victor Vroom would say there should be a clear link between *effort and performance*, and between *performance and reward*, and that the reward must be *attractive* to the employee. Employees must therefore have the skills and training to do the job. Employers should support the incentive plan with performance feedback, as in the form of daily results on graphs.

4. **Set complete standards.** For example, don't just pay for quantity if quality is an issue, too.
5. **Be scientific.** Don't waste money on incentives that may not be contributing to performance. *Gather evidence* and analyze the effects of the incentive plan over time, to ascertain whether it is indeed influencing the measures (such as employee turnover, and so on) that you intended to improve through your plan.[77]

EMPLOYEE BENEFITS

We can define **benefits** as indirect monetary and nonmonetary payments an employee receives for continuing to work for the company (rather than direct payments, as for wages). Benefits include things like time off with pay, health insurance, and child care.

Most full-time employees in the United States receive benefits. Virtually all employers—99%—offer some health insurance coverage.[78] In one survey, 78% of employees cited health care benefits as most crucial to retaining them; 75% cited compensation. But the survey found that only 34% are satisfied with their health care benefits.[79]

Health care benefit costs are rising. They rose 8% in 2011 and an estimated 8.5% in 2012, making total 2012 health benefit costs per employee well over $9,500.[80] Virtually all employers offer some health insurance coverage.[81] Employee benefits account for between 33%–40% of wages and salaries (or about 28% of total payrolls). Legally required benefits (like unemployment insurance) are the most expensive benefits costs, followed by health insurance.

We will classify benefits as pay for time not worked, insurance benefits, retirement benefits, and employee services benefits.

Pay for Time Not Worked

Supplemental pay benefits, or pay for time not worked (such as vacations), are one of an employer's most expensive benefits because of all the time off that employees receive. Common time-off-with-pay benefits include holidays, vacations, sick leave, maternity leave, and unemployment insurance payments.

UNEMPLOYMENT INSURANCE All states have unemployment insurance or compensation acts. These provide for weekly benefits if a person is unable to work through no fault of his or her own. Unemployment tax rates are rising in many states. For example, prior to the recent recession, Maryland's unemployment insurance tax rate was 0.3% (of the employer's payroll) or lower. It now averages 2.2% to 13.5% per employee, depending upon the employer's claim history.[82] An employer's unemployment tax reflects its experience with personnel terminations.

Strictly speaking, only employees dismissed through no fault of their own are eligible for unemployment. But in practice, many managers are lackadaisical about protecting their employers against unwarranted claims. Therefore, employers spend thousands of dollars more per year on unemployment taxes than would be necessary if they protected themselves—for instance, by keeping careful records of absences.[83]

VACATIONS AND HOLIDAYS About 90% of full-time workers and 40% of part timers get paid holidays, an average of 8 paid holidays off.[84] On average, American workers get about 9 days of vacation leave after 1 year's employment, about 14 days after 5 years, and 17 after 10 years.[85] Common U.S. paid holidays include New Year's Day, Memorial Day, Independence Day, Labor Day, Thanksgiving Day, and Christmas Day.[86]

SICK LEAVE   Sick leave provides pay to employees when they are out of work because of illness. Most sick leave policies grant full pay for a specified number of permissible sick days, usually up to about 12 per year. The sick days often accumulate at the rate of about 1 day per month of service.

The problem is that many employees (in the eyes of some employers) take advantage of sick leave by using it whether they are sick or not.[87] Tactics employers utilize to reduce this problem include:

- Using *pooled paid leave* (or paid time off, or "PTO") plans. These plans—which lump together sick leave, vacation, and holidays into a single leave pool—have grown in popularity.
- Buying back unused sick leave at the end of the year (although this can encourage sick employees to come to work despite illness).
- Holding lotteries in which only employees with perfect attendance can participate to win a cash prize.
- Aggressively investigating all unplanned absences, for instance, by calling the absent employees at their homes. (See the accompanying HR as a Profit Center feature.)

FMLA   Sick leave policy depends to some extent on the Family and Medical Leave Act of 1993 (FMLA). Among its provisions, the law stipulates that:

1. Private employers of 50 or more employees must provide eligible employees up to 12 weeks of unpaid leave for their own serious illness, the birth or adoption of a child, or the care of a seriously ill child, spouse, or parent.
2. Employers may require employees to take any unused paid sick leave or annual leave as part of the 12-week leave.

HR AS A PROFIT CENTER

Cutting Absences at the Driver and Vehicle Licensing Agency

When she came in as a director of the United Kingdom's Driver and Vehicle Licensing Agency, Judith Whitaker saw that steps were needed to address the agency's sickness absence rate.[88] The rate had peaked at 14 days out per employee in 2005, at a cost of about $20 million per year (£10.3 million).

The new director organized a human resource management initiative to address the problem.[89] The agency set a goal of reducing absences by 30% by 2010. Agency directors received absence-reduction goals, and their progress was tracked. The agency introduced new policies and procedures dealing with special leave, rehabilitation support, and keeping in touch with absentees. They introduced new policies to make it easier for employees to swap work shifts, and introduced a guaranteed leave day policy. By 2010, the average annual sickness absence rate was down to 7.5 days per employee. Improved attendance contributed to about a 7% productivity increase in 2009–2010. That translates into cost savings of about $48 million dollars (£24.4 million).

3. Employees taking leave are entitled to receive health benefits while they are on unpaid leave under the same terms as when they were on the job.
4. Employers must guarantee most employees the right to return to their previous or equivalent position with no loss of benefits at the end of the leave.[90]

SEVERANCE PAY   Many employers provide **severance pay**—a onetime separation payment—when terminating an employee. Others provide "bridge" severance pay by keeping employees (especially managers) on the payroll for several months. About half of employers surveyed give white-collar and exempt employees one week of severance pay per year of service, and about one-third do the same for blue-collar workers. Severance pay is common as part of a reduction in workforce, less common when dismissing someone for poor performance or cause.[91] We discuss severance more fully in Chapter 8 in the context of dismissals.

The Worker Adjustment and Retraining ("plant closing") Act of 1989 requires covered employers to give employees 60 days' written notice of plant closures or mass layoffs (but not to necessarily award severance pay).

Insurance Benefits

Employers also provide a range of insurance benefits.

WORKERS' COMPENSATION   **Workers' compensation** laws aim to provide sure, prompt income and medical benefits to work-related employee accident victims or their dependents, regardless of fault. Every state has its own workers' compensation law, with some offering their own insurance programs. However, most require that employers purchase workers' compensation insurance through private state-approved insurance companies.

Workers' compensation benefits can be either monetary or medical. In the event of a worker's death or disablement, the person or his or her beneficiary receives a cash benefit based on prior earnings. Most states set a time limit—such as 500 weeks—for which an employee can receive benefits. In addition to these cash benefits, employers must furnish medical, surgical, and hospital services needed by the employee. For an injury or illness to be covered by workers' compensation, the employee need only prove that it arose while he or she was on the job. It does not matter that the employee may have been at fault.

Supervisors should be aware of typical red flags of fraudulent claims, including vague accident details, minor accidents resulting in major injuries, and lack of witnesses.[92] Getting the employee back to work fast is essential to controlling costs.[93]

Hospitalization, Medical, and Disability Insurance

Health care benefits top employees' desired benefits.[94] Most employers therefore offer their employees some type of hospitalization, medical, and disability insurance (see Table 7-3). Many offer membership in a health maintenance organization (HMO). The HMO consists of medical specialists operating out of a health care center. Preferred provider organizations (PPOs) let employees select participating physicians who agree to provide price discounts and submit to certain utilization controls, such as on the number of diagnostic tests.[95] Employers are shifting from higher-cost HMOs to PPOs.[96]

TABLE 7-3	Percentage of Employers Offering Some Popular Health Benefits—Change Over Time	
	Yes (%) 2005	Yes (%) 2011
Prescription drug program coverage	97	96
Dental insurance	95	94
Mail order prescription program	90	91
PPO (preferred provider organization)	87	84
Chiropractic coverage	56	83
Mental health insurance	72	82
Vision insurance	80	76
Employee assistance program	73	75
Medical/Flexible spending account	80	73
HMO (health maintenance organization)	53	33

Source: SHRM Employer Benefits Survey Report. Copyright 2011 by SHRM. Reprinted with permission.

THE PREGNANCY DISCRIMINATION ACT   The Pregnancy Discrimination Act (PDA) aims to prohibit sex discrimination based on "pregnancy, childbirth, or related medical conditions."

The act requires employers to treat women affected by pregnancy, childbirth, or related medical conditions the same as any employee not able to work, with respect to all benefits, including sick leave and health and medical insurance. For example, if an employer provides up to 26 weeks of temporary disability income to employees for all illnesses, it also must provide up to 26 weeks for pregnancy and childbirth.

COBRA REQUIREMENTS   The ominously titled COBRA—Consolidated Omnibus Budget Reconciliation Act—requires most private employers to make available to terminated or retired employees and their families continued health benefits for a period of time, generally 18 months. A former employee who chooses to continue these benefits during this period must pay for them, plus a small administrative fee.[97]

You do not want a separated employee to be injured and come back and claim she didn't know she could have continued her COBRA insurance. Therefore, new employees should receive and acknowledge an explanation of COBRA rights. And all employees separated from the company should sign a form acknowledging that they received and understand their COBRA rights.[98]

HEALTH-CARE INSURANCE COST CONTROL   With health care costs rising, containing those costs is a huge employer concern. Since 2004, health care premiums have risen about 78% while inflation rose only 17%.[99] Employers are therefore endeavoring to rein in health care costs. Many retain *cost-containment specialists* to help reduce health care costs. Most negotiate aggressively with their health care insurance providers.[100] Most cost control efforts start by instituting methods for measuring and tracking health care costs.[101]

For many employers, *deductibles and copays* are the low-hanging fruit in health care cost control. For example, 22% of employers imposed deductibles of at least $1,000 in 2011, up from 8% in 2008.[102] Other cost control strategies include:[103]

- **Online Administration** Savings come from automating health care plan administration, for instance, requiring online enrollment by employees.[104]
- **Outsourcing** For example, 84% of firms in one survey said they were outsourcing employee assistance and counseling, and 53% were outsourcing health care benefits administration.[105]
- **Wellness Programs** Medical experts believe that controlling health risks can reduce illnesses and health care costs.[106] Many employers therefore offer some preventive services. *Clinical prevention* programs include things like mammograms and routine checkups.[107] Top wellness programs include obesity management, stress management, senior health improvement, and tobacco cessation programs.[108] Incentives can boost participation in wellness programs.[109]
- **Claims Audits** The industry standard for percentage of claims dollars paid in error is 1%; in two recent years the *actual* percentage of claims dollars paid in error were about 3.4%. Setting standards for errors, and then aggressively auditing the claims paid, may be the most direct way to reduce employer health care expenses.[110] Ensure that dependents enrolled are eligible for coverage.[111]
- **Medical Tourism** Here employers encourage employees to have some non-urgent medical procedures done overseas. Hospitals abroad may charge half what a U.S. hospital would for shoulder surgery, for instance. The key question is quality of care.[112]
- **Technology** Experts hope that health information technology funding will help employers reduce health care benefit costs by automating their paper-based systems.[113]
- **Mini Plans** New limited-benefit health care insurance mini plans have annual caps of about $2,000 to $10,000 per year, with correspondingly lower premiums.[114]

PROTECTION AND AFFORDABLE CARE ACT OF 2010   Signed into law by President Obama in 2010, employers face several requirements under the new Patient Protection and Affordable Care Act, unless Congress changes the law. For example, employers must begin reporting the value of health care benefits on employees' W-2 statements; contributions to health care flexible spending arrangements will be limited to $2,500 as of January 1, 2013; and in 2018 a 40% excise tax on high-cost health insurance plans goes into effect.[115] Individual and group health plans that already provide dependent coverage must expand eligibility up to age 26.[116] The Act also encourages employers with 50 or more employees to offer health insurance or pay a "shared responsibility payment" if the government has to subsidize an employee's health care.

Employers in one recent survey expected this Act to raise their annual health care expenses by 2% to 5%.[117] The excise tax on high-cost plans was the employers' main cost concern. Other potential cost-raisers include the expanded coverage for older children, and the rule that employers must offer coverage to employees working less than 30 hours per week.[118]

Separately, the *Genetic Information Nondiscrimination Act* of 2008 (GINA) prohibits certain genetically related employer actions. For example, if a health plan administrator learns that a member's father passed away from cancer and makes a note, doing so could conceivably be held as violations of the act.[119]

Long-Term Care

Today, there are many types of long-term care—care to support older persons in their old age—for which employers provide insurance benefits. For example, adult day-care facilities offer social and recreational activities. Assisted-living facilities (ALFs) offer shared housing and supervision. Home care is care received at home from a nurse, an aide, or another specialist.

Retirement Benefits

SOCIAL SECURITY   There are actually three types of Social Security benefits. First are the familiar *retirement benefits*, which provide an income if an employee insured under the Social Security Act retires at age 62 or thereafter.[120] Second, survivor's or *death benefits* provide monthly payments to dependents regardless of the employee's age at death, again assuming the employee was insured under the Social Security Act. Finally, *disability payments* provide monthly payments to an employee and his or her dependents if the employee becomes disabled for work and meets specified work requirements.

"Full retirement age"—the usual age for receiving your full Social Security benefit—used to be 65. However, it rose gradually and is now 67 for those born in 1960 or later. A tax on the employee's wages funds Social Security (technically, "Federal Old Age and Survivor's Insurance"). As of 2012, the maximum amount of earnings subject to Social Security tax was $110,000; the employer pays 7.65% and the employee 7.65%.[121]

PENSION PLANS   Pensions provide income to individuals in their retirement, and just over half of full-time workers participate in some type of pension plan at work.

We can classify pension plans in three ways: contributory versus noncontributory plans; qualified versus nonqualified plans; and defined contribution versus defined benefit plans.[122] The employee contributes to the contributory pension plan while the employer makes all contributions to the noncontributory pension plan. Employers derive tax benefits for contributing to qualified pension plans (they are "qualified" for preferred tax treatment by the IRS); nonqualified pension plans get less favorable tax treatment.

With **defined benefit plans,** the employee knows ahead of time the pension benefits he or she will receive. There is usually a formula that ties the person's pension to (1) a percentage of (2) the person's preretirement pay (for instance, to an average of his or her last 5 years of employment), multiplied by (3) the number of years he or she worked for the company. Due to tax law changes and other reasons, defined benefit plans now represent a minority of pension benefit plans.[123]

Defined contribution plans specify ("define") what contribution the employee and employer will make to the employee's retirement or savings fund. With a *defined benefit* plan, the employee can compute what his or her retirement benefits will be upon retirement. With a *defined contribution* plan, the person only knows for sure what he or she is contributing to the pension plan; the actual pension will depend on the amounts contributed to the fund *and* on the success of the retirement fund's investment earnings. Defined contribution plans are popular among employers because of their relative ease of administration, favorable tax treatment, and other factors. **Portability**—making it easier for employees who leave the firm prior to retirement to take their accumulated pension funds with them—is also easier with defined contribution plans.

401(K) PLANS   The 401(k) plan is one defined contribution plan. Under the 401(k) plan (based on Section 401(k) of the Internal Revenue Code), employees have the employer place a portion of their compensation, which would otherwise be paid in cash, into a company profit-sharing or stock bonus plan, or into investments (such as mutual funds) the employee selects. This results in a pretax reduction in salary, so the employee isn't taxed on those set-aside dollars until after he or she retires (or removes the money from the pension fund). Some employers also match a portion of what the employee contributes to the 401(k) plan.

The employer has a fiduciary responsibility to its employees, and must monitor the pension fund and its administration.[124] Under the Pension Protection Act of 2006, employers who sponsor plans that facilitate both *automatic enrollment* and allocation to *default investments* (such as age-appropriate "lifestyle funds") reduce their compliance burdens.[125]

CASH BALANCE PENSION PLANS   One problem with defined benefits plans is that to get your maximum pension, you generally must stay with your employer until you retire— the formula, recall, takes the number of years you work into consideration. With defined contribution plans, your pension is more portable—you can leave with it at any time, perhaps rolling it over into your next employer's pension plan. Without delving into the details, *cash balance* plans are a hybrid; they have a defined benefit plan's more predictable benefits, but they have the portability advantages of defined contribution plans.[126]

ERISA   The Employee Retirement Income Security Act (ERISA) aims to protect the pensions of workers and to stimulate pension plan growth. Before ERISA, pension plans often failed to deliver expected benefits to employees, due to various reasons, such as business failure and inadequate funding.

VESTING   Under ERISA, pension rights must be **vested**—guaranteed to the employee— under one of two minimum vesting schedules (employers can allow funds to vest faster if they wish). With *cliff vesting*, the period for acquiring a nonforfeitable right in employer matching contributions (if any) is 3 years. With the second option (*graded vesting*) pension plan participants must receive nonforfeitable rights to the matching contributions as follows: 20% after 2 years, and then 20% for each succeeding year, with a 100% nonforfeitable right by the end of 6 years.

The Pension Benefits Guarantee Corporation (PBGC) was established under ERISA to ensure that pensions meet their obligations should a plan fail. However, the PBGC guarantees only defined benefit, not defined contribution plans. Furthermore, it will only pay a pension of up to about $56,000 per year for someone 65 years of age with a plan terminating in 2012.[127] High-income workers may still receive reduced pensions if their plan fails.

Employee Services and Family-Friendly/Work-Life Benefits

Although an employer's time off, insurance, and retirement benefits account for the main part of its benefits costs, many employers also provide various services. These include personal services (such as legal and personal counseling), job-related services (such as subsidized child care), educational subsidies, and executive perquisites ("perks" such as company cars and planes for executives).

For example, **Employee Assistance Programs (EAPs)** provide counseling and advisory services, such as personal legal and financial services, child- and elder-care referrals, adoption assistance, and mental health counseling.[128] More than 60% of larger firms offer them. Most employers contract for the necessary services with vendors such as CIGNA Behavioral Health.[129]

Some employers offer employees full or partial *college tuition* reimbursement. These may help employers attract applicants, retain employees who might otherwise leave, and provide promotable employees with the educations they need to move up. However, that same enhanced mobility makes it easier for employees to leave. Two researchers found that the U.S. Navy's tuition assistance program decreased the probability of staying in the Navy.[130]

FAMILY-FRIENDLY BENEFITS   Companies today also offer *"family-friendly"* (or "work-life") benefits. For example, software giant SAS Institute offers preschool child-care centers, a gym, a full-time eldercare consultant, 3 weeks' paid vacation, a flexible ("flextime") work schedule, and a standard 35-hour workweek.[131]

More employers, such as Canadian financial services company CIBC, are also offering *emergency child-care benefits*, for instance, for when a young child's regular babysitter is a no-show.[132] Similarly, with the average age rising, employers increasingly offer *adult-care support*, including counseling and adult day-care centers.[133] Some employers enrich their *parental leave plans* to make it more attractive for mothers to return from maternity leave, for instance, offering meaningful jobs with reduced travel and hours.[134]

WHY WORK-LIFE BENEFITS?   For the employer, programs like these produce advantages, not just costs. For example, sick family members and health problems such as depression account for much of the sick leave employees take. Employers can reduce such absences with eldercare referrals, and personal counseling.[135] Work-life benefits may improve a firm's bottom line in some less-obvious ways. One study found that when employees experienced work–family conflict, they were more likely to exhibit hostility at work.[136]

WORKPLACE FLEXIBILITY   As anyone who has flown next to someone tapping away on their laptop knows, employees are increasingly conducting business from nontraditional settings.[137] **Workplace flexibility** means arming employees with the information technology tools they need to get their jobs done wherever they are. For example, Capital One Financial Corp. has its Future of Work program. Some Capital One employees received mobile technology tools such as wireless access laptops. The program seems to have led to about a 41% increase in overall workplace satisfaction, and a 53% increase in those who say their workplace enhances group productivity.[138]

Flexible Benefits

Employees tend to differ in what benefits they want and need. Flexible benefits plans are thus popular.

Flexible benefits plans (also called cafeteria plans) enable employees to spend their benefits allowances on a choice of benefits options. The idea is to let the employee design his or her own benefit package, subject to two constraints. First, the employer must limit total cost for each person's package. Second, each benefit plan must include certain nonoptional items, including, for example, Social Security and unemployment insurance.

Benefits and Employee Leasing

Employee leasing firms (also known in various versions as *professional employer organizations*, or *human resource outsourcers*) arrange to have the employer's employees transferred to the employee leasing firm's payroll. The leasing firm becomes the legal employer and handles the employer's employee-related paperwork. This usually includes recruiting, hiring, paying tax liabilities (such as Social Security payments), and performance appraisals (with the onsite supervisor's input). However, it is with respect to benefits management that employee leasing is often most advantageous.

Getting insurance is often the biggest personnel problem smaller employers face. This is where employee leasing comes in. The leasing firm is the legal employer of the client company's employees. Therefore, those employees are absorbed into a much larger insurable group (along with other clients' former employees). The employee leasing company can therefore often offer benefits smaller companies can't obtain at such a low cost.

Employee leasing is sometimes too good to be true. Some apparently successful employee leasing firms have gone out of business, in which case the original employer has to hire back all its employees and find new insurance. And when the employer views employees (such as highly trained engineers) strategic to its success, it may be reluctant to hand over hiring and training to others.

Benefits Websites

To reduce the costs of administering benefits, many employers enable employees to manage much of their own benefits changes (dependents, 401(k), and so on) themselves, via the employer's (or an outside vendor's) website.

Employers are adding new services to their benefits websites. For example, click on USAA website's "today, I'm feeling…" menu. Here employees can respond to a list of words (such as "stressed"), and from there see suggestions for dealing with (in this case) stress.[139]

CURRENT COMPENSATION TRENDS

How employers pay employees is evolving.[140] This section looks at important trends including competency-based pay, actively managing compensation, broadbanding, board oversight of executive pay, and total rewards.[141]

Competency- and Skill-Based Pay

Some question whether job evaluation's tendency to slot jobs into narrow cubbyholes ("Machinist I," "Machinist II," and so on) might not actually be counterproductive in today's high-performance work systems. Systems like these depend on flexible, multiskilled job assignments, and on teamwork. There's thus no place here for employees who say, "That's not my job."

Competency-based pay (and broadbanding, explained later) aims to avoid that problem.[142] With competency- or skill-based pay, you pay the employee for the skills and knowledge he or she is capable of using rather than for the responsibilities of the job currently held.[143] *Competencies* are demonstrable personal characteristics such as knowledge, skills, and behaviors.

Why pay employees based on the skill levels they achieve, rather than based on the jobs they're assigned to? With more companies organizing around project teams, you want employees to be able to rotate among jobs. Doing so requires more skills.

ELEMENTS   Competency or skill-based pay programs generally contain five elements. The employer *defines* specific required skills and chooses a *method* for tying the person's pay to his or her skill competencies. A *training* system lets employees seek and acquire skills. There is a formal competency *testing* system. And, the work is *designed* so that employees can easily move among jobs of varying skill levels.

In practice, competency-based pay usually comes down to pay for knowledge or skill-based pay.[144] As an example, review Chapter 3's Figure 3-4 (on page 67). For this job, BP lists the minimum level for each skill (such as Technical Expertise, and Problem Solving) someone holding this job must attain. As an employee achieves each level of each skill, he or she would assumedly receive a bump in pay.

Broadbanding

Most firms end up with pay plans that slot jobs into classes or grades, each with its own vertical pay rate range. For example, the U.S. government's pay plan consists of 18 main grades (GS-1 to GS-18), each with its own pay range. For an employee whose job falls in one of these grades, the pay range for that grade dictates his or her minimum and maximum salary.

The question is, how wide should the salary grades be, in terms of the number of job evaluation points they include? There is a downside to narrow grades. For instance, if you want someone whose job is in grade 2 to learn about a job that happens to be in grade 3, the employee might object without a corresponding raise to grade 3 pay. Traditional grade pay plans thus may tend to encourage inflexibility.

One solution is broader pay grades. Broadbanding means collapsing salary grades and ranges into just a few wide ranges, or bands, each of which contains a relatively wide range of jobs and salary levels (see Figure 7-5). It combines the company's previous six pay grades into two broadbands. The pay rate range of each broadband is relatively large, since it ranges from the minimum pay of the lowest grade the firm merged into the broadband up to the maximum pay of the highest merged grade. For the jobs that fall in each broadband, there is therefore a much wider range of pay rates. You can move employees from job to job within the broadband more easily, without worrying about the employees moving outside the relatively narrow rate range associated with a traditional narrow pay grade. Broadbanding therefore facilitates flexibility. The accompanying Global Issues in HR feature explains some issues in paying expatriate employees.

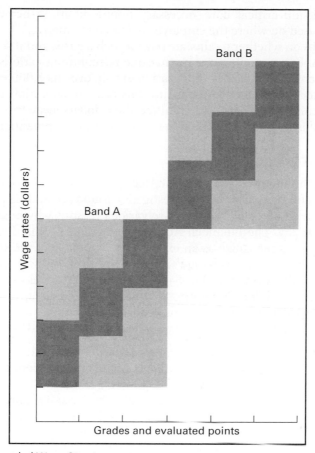

FIGURE 7-5 Broadbanded Wage Structure.

Actively Managing Pay Allocations and Talent Management

As we saw in previous chapters, employers are actively allocating resources to employees they deem "mission-critical." Recall, for instance, that Accenture uses a 4 × 4 matrix to plot employees by Performance (exceptional, high, medium, low), and Value to the

GLOBAL ISSUES IN HR

Compensating Expatriate Employees

Most North American companies use what experts call the *balance sheet method* to compute the expatriate manager's pay. The aim here is to make the person's compensation consistent with what it would have been if he or she had stayed home. The person's base salary reflects the salaries in his or her home country. Then, the employer adds supplements to cover things like housing costs, tax differences, and other living expenses (such as private schools for the person's children).[145]

Organization (mission-critical, core, necessary, nonessential). It then allocates pay and other resources based on where the employee places in the matrix.[146]

The decisions on whether to allocate pay on such a basis, and if so how, are important policy issues. For example, we saw that one telecommunications firm previously spread development money and compensation evenly over its 8,000 employees. When the recession came, it segmented them into business impact, high performers, high potentials, and critical skills. Then they shifted their dollars away from low performers and those not making an impact to high performers and high potentials.[147]

Board Oversight of Executive Pay

Several years ago, the antivirus company McAfee apparently pushed out its president and saw its CEO leave after "a stock options investigation found accounting problems that will require financial restatements."[148] There are various reasons why boards are clamping down on executive pay. The Financial Accounting Standards Board now requires that most public companies recognize as an expense the fair value of the stock options they grant.[149] The Securities and Exchange Commission (SEC) now requires filing more compensation-related information. The Sarbanes-Oxley Act makes executives personally liable, under certain conditions, for corporate financial oversight lapses.[150] The net result is that lawyers specializing in executive pay suggest that boards of directors need to be fastidious about setting executive pay today. Questions they should ask include:

- Is our compensation committee being appropriately advised?
- Do our procedures demonstrate diligence and independence? (This demands careful deliberations and records.)
- Is our committee appropriately communicating its decisions? How will shareholders react?[151]

Total Rewards

As noted earlier, *total rewards* encompass the traditional compensation components, but also things such as recognition, redesigned more challenging jobs, telecommuting programs, health and well-being programs, and training and career development. Some employers distribute annual total rewards statements to employees, to help them appreciate the full range of rewards that they are receiving.

REVIEW

Summary

1. Establishing pay rates involves six steps: evaluate jobs, conduct salary survey, compare current and external pay rates, develop pay grades, use wage curves, and develop pay ranges.

2. Job evaluation aims to determine the relative worth of a job. It compares jobs to one another based on their content, usually defined in terms of compensable factors such as skills, effort, responsibility, and working conditions.

3. Most managers group similar jobs into wage or pay grades for pay purposes. These grades are composed of jobs of

approximately equal difficulty or importance as determined by job evaluation.

4. For executive, managerial, and professional personnel, factors like performance and creativity take precedence over static factors such as working conditions. Market rates, performance, and incentives and benefits thus play a much greater role than does job evaluation here.

5. Piecework is the oldest type of incentive plan; a worker is paid a piece rate for each unit he or she produces.

6. Profit sharing and the Scanlon plan are examples of organization-wide incentive plans. Here just about all employees can share in part of the company's profits.

7. Supplemental pay benefits provide pay for time not worked. They include unemployment insurance, vacation and holiday pay, and severance pay.

8. Insurance benefits are another type of employee benefit. Workers' compensation,

for example, aims to ensure prompt income and medical benefits to work accident victims or their dependents, regardless of fault. Most employers also provide group life insurance and group hospitalization, accident, and disability insurance.

9. Social Security covers not only retirement benefits but also survivors and disability benefits. One of the critical issues in pension planning is vesting the money that employer and employee have placed in the latter's pension fund, which cannot be forfeited for any reason. ERISA ensures that pension rights become vested and protected after a reasonable amount of time.

10. Broadbanding means collapsing salary grades and ranges into just a few wide levels or bands, each of which then contains a relatively wide range of jobs and salary levels.

Key Terms

employee compensation *188*
Fair Labor Standards
  Act (FLSA) *188*
Equal Pay Act *189*
Civil Rights Act *189*
job evaluation *191*
compensable factors *191*
ranking method *192*
wage curve *193*
salary (or compensation)
  surveys *193*
annual bonus *197*
incentive plan *197*

productivity *197*
piecework *197*
stock option *198*
merit pay (merit raise) *200*
profit-sharing plan *200*
employee stock ownership
  plan (ESOP) *200*
Employee Retirement
  Income Security
  Act (ERISA) *201*
gainsharing plan *201*
Scanlon plan *201*
benefits *203*

severance pay *205*
workers' compensation *205*
defined benefit
  plan *208*
defined contribution
  plan *208*
portability *208*
vested *209*
Employee Assistance
  Program (EAP) *210*
workplace flexibility *210*
flexible benefits
  plan *210*

Discussion Questions

1. What is the difference between exempt and nonexempt jobs?

2. What are examples of compensable factors?

3. What is merit pay? Do you think it's a good idea to award employees merit raises? Why or why not?

Individual and Group Activities

1. Working individually or in groups, conduct salary surveys for an entry-level accountant and an entry-level chemical engineer. What sources did you use, and what conclusions did you reach? If you were the HR manager for a local engineering firm, what would you recommend that you pay for each job?

2. Working individually or in groups, develop compensation policies for the teller position at a local bank. Assume that there are four tellers: two were hired in May and the other two were hired in December. The compensation policies should address the following: appraisals, raises, holidays, vacation pay, overtime pay, method of pay, garnishments, and time cards.

3. Working individually or in groups, access relevant websites to determine what equitable pay ranges are for the jobs of chemical engineer, marketing manager, and HR manager, all with a bachelor's degree and 5 years of experience. Do so for the following cities: New York; San Francisco; Miami; and Washington, D.C. For each position in each city, what are the pay ranges and the average pay? Does geographical location affect the salaries of the different positions? How?

4. Working individually or in groups, use published (Internet or other) wage surveys to determine local area earnings for the following positions: file clerk I, accounting clerk II, and secretary V. How do the published figures compare with comparable jobs listed in your Sunday newspaper? What do you think accounts for any discrepancy?

5. Working individually or in groups, use the ranking method to evaluate the relative worth of the jobs listed in question 4.

6. Working individually or in groups, develop an incentive plan for the following positions: chemical engineer, plant manager, and used-car salesperson. What factors did you have to consider in reaching your conclusions?

7. A state university system in the Southeast instituted a Teacher Incentive Program for its faculty. Faculty committees within each of the university's colleges were told to award $5,000 raises (not bonuses) to about 40% of their faculty members based on how good a job they did teaching undergraduates and how many they taught per year. What are the potential advantages and pitfalls of such an incentive program? How well do you think it was accepted by the faculty? Do you think it had the desired effect?

8. Working individually or in groups, research and compile a list of the perks available to the following individuals: the head of your local airport, the president of your college or university, and the president of a large company in your area. Do they all have certain perks in common? What do you think accounts for any differences?

9. You are the HR consultant to a small business with about 40 employees. Currently, the business offers 5 days of vacation, five paid holidays, and legally mandated benefits such as unemployment insurance payments. Develop a list of other benefits you believe the firm should offer, along with your reasons for suggesting them.

APPLICATION EXERCISES

CASE INCIDENT

Salary Inequities at Acme Manufacturing

Joe Black was trying to figure out what to do about a salary problem he had in his plant. Black recently took over as president of Acme Manufacturing.

The founder, Bill George, had been president for 35 years. The company was family owned and located in a small eastern Arkansas town. It had approximately 250 employees and was the largest employer in the community. Black was a member of the family that owned Acme, but he had never worked for the company prior to becoming president. He had an MBA and a law degree, plus 15 years of management experience with a large manufacturing organization, where he was senior vice president for human resources when he moved to Acme.

A short time after joining Acme, Black started to notice that there was considerable inequity in the pay structure for salaried employees. A discussion with the human resources director led him to believe that salaried employees' pay was very much a matter of individual bargaining with the past president. Hourly paid factory employees were not part of the problem because they were unionized with wages set by collective bargaining. An examination of the salaried payroll showed that there were 25 employees, ranging in pay from that of the president to that of the receptionist. A closer examination showed that 14 of the salaried employees were female. Three of these were frontline factory supervisors and one was the HR director. The other 10 were nonmanagement.

This examination also showed that the human resources director seemed underpaid, and that the three female supervisors were paid somewhat less than were any of the male supervisors. However, there were no similar supervisory jobs with both male and female job incumbents. When asked, the HR director said she thought the female supervisors may have been paid at a lower rate mainly because they were women, and perhaps Bill George did not think that women needed as much money because they had working husbands. However, she added that they may have been paid less because they supervised less-skilled employees than did male supervisors. Black was not sure that this was true.

The company from which Black had moved had a job evaluation system. Although he was thoroughly familiar and capable with this compensation tool, Black did not have time to do a job evaluation at Acme. Therefore, he decided to hire a compensation consultant from a nearby university to help him. Together they decided that all 25 salaried jobs should be in the job evaluation cluster, that they should use a ranking method, and that the job descriptions recently completed by the HR director were current and usable.

The job evaluation showed that there was no evidence of serious inequities or discrimination in the nonmanagement jobs. However, the HR director and the three female supervisors were underpaid relative to comparable male salaried employees.

Black was not sure what to do. He knew that if the underpaid female supervisors took the case to the local EEOC office, the company could be found guilty of sex discrimination and then have to pay back wages. He was afraid that if he gave these women an immediate salary increase large enough to bring them up to where they should be, the male supervisors would be upset, and the female supervisors might also want back pay. The HR director told Black that the female supervisors had never complained about pay differences, and they probably did not know the law to any extent.

The HR director agreed to take a sizable salary increase with no back pay, solving this part of the problem. Black believed he had four choices relative to the female supervisors:

1. To do nothing
2. To gradually increase the female supervisors' salaries
3. To increase their salaries immediately
4. To call the three supervisors into his office, discuss the situation with them, and jointly decide what to do

QUESTIONS

1. What would you do if you were Black? Why?
2. How do you think the company got into this situation in the first place?
3. Why would you suggest Black pursue the alternative you suggested?

Source: "Salary Inequities at Acme Manufacturing," by James C. Hodgetts. Reprinted by permission of the James C. Hodgetts estate.

CONTINUING CASE
Carter Cleaning Company

The Incentive Plan

The question of whether to pay Carter Cleaning Center employees an hourly wage or an incentive of some kind has always intrigued Jack Carter.

His basic policy has been to pay employees an hourly wage, except that his managers do receive an end-of-year bonus depending, as Jack puts it, "on whether their stores do well or not that year."

However, he is considering using an incentive plan in one store. Jack knows that a presser should press about 25 "tops" (jackets, dresses, blouses) per hour. Most of his pressers do not attain this ideal standard, though. In one instance, a presser named Walt was paid $8 per hour, and Jack noticed that regardless of the amount of work he had to do, Walt always ended up going home at about 3:00 p.m., so he earned about $300 at the end of the week. If it was a holiday week, for instance, and there were a lot of clothes to press, he might average 22 to 23 tops per hour (someone else did pants) and so he'd earn perhaps $300 and still finish up each day in time to leave by 3:00 p.m. so he could pick up his children at school. But when things were very slow in the store, his productivity would drop to perhaps 12 to 15 pieces an hour, so that at the end of the week he'd end up earning perhaps $280, and in fact not go home much earlier than he did when it was busy.

Jack spoke with Walt several times, and while Walt always promised to try to do better, it gradually became apparent to Jack that Walt was simply going to earn his $300 per week no matter what. Though Walt never told him so directly, it dawned on Jack that Walt had a family to support and was not about to earn less than his "target" wage, regardless of how busy or slow the store was. The problem was that the longer Walt kept pressing each day, the

longer the steam boilers and compressors had to be kept on to power his machines, and the fuel charges alone ran close to $6 per hour. Jack clearly needed some way short of firing Walt to solve the problem, since the fuel bills were eating up his profits.

His solution was to tell Walt that, instead of an hourly $8 wage, he would henceforth pay him $0.33 per item pressed. That way, said Jack to himself, if Walt presses 25 items per hour at $0.33 he will in effect get a small raise. He'll get more items pressed per hour and will therefore be able to shut the machines down earlier.

On the whole, the experiment worked well. Walt generally presses 25 to 35 pieces per hour now. He gets to leave earlier, and with the small increase in pay, he generally earns his target wage. Two problems have arisen, though. The quality of Walt's work has dipped a bit, plus his manager has to spend a minute or two each hour counting the number of pieces Walt pressed that hour. Otherwise, Jack is fairly pleased with the results of his incentive plan, and he's wondering whether to extend it to other employees and other stores. He wants your opinion.

QUESTIONS

1. Should this plan be extended to pressers in the other stores?
2. Should other employees (cleaner/spotters, counter people) be put on a similar plan? Why? Why not? If so, how, exactly?
3. Is there another incentive plan you think would work better for the pressers? Describe it.
4. A store manager's job is to keep total wages to no more than 30% of sales and to maintain the fuel bill and the supply bill at about 9% of sales each. Managers can also directly affect sales by ensuring courteous customer service and by ensuring that the work is done properly. What suggestions would you make to Jennifer and her father for an incentive plan for store managers or counter people?

EXPERIENTIAL EXERCISE

Ranking the College's Administrators' jobs

Purpose: The purpose of this exercise is to give you experience in performing a job evaluation using the ranking method.

Required Understanding: You should be thoroughly familiar with the ranking method of job evaluation and obtain job descriptions for your college's dean, department chairperson, and your professor.

How to Set Up the Exercise/Instructions:
If so desired, divide the class into teams. The aim is to perform a job evaluation of the positions of dean, department chairperson, and professor using the ranking method.

1. Perform a job evaluation by ranking the jobs. You may use one or more compensable factors.
2. If time permits, you or a spokesperson from each group can put his or her group's rankings on the board. Did the groups end up with about the same results? How did they differ? Why do you think they differed?

VIDEO CASE

COMPENSATION (FOCUS POINTE)

Synopsis

In this video, two HR staff members, Cheryl and Gina, must determine if an employee, Angelo, is worthy of a pay raise. The company, Focus Pointe, provides market research services. One of these services involves recruiting consumer, medical, and other respondents for the market research industry. It's important to get good, qualified respondents. To distinguish itself from its competitors, Focus Pointe uses a special "triple screening" process to ensure that the respondents it recruits meet its clients' specifications. In this case, Angelo seems to be recruiting inadequate respondents. The two HR staff members are trying to determine if giving Angelo a raise would solve the problem.

As Angelo says in the video, he'd like to be better compensated. Cheryl and Gina point out to him that his pay is falling because his recruits often don't qualify. They ask him what he would like—an increase in salary or an increase in the amount per recruit that he is paid. He responds that he'd like both. They tell them they will go along with his request but that they must see higher levels of recruit qualifications within 3 months. As the panel's human resource managers (including Paul, from BMG) point out in assessing this video, they don't necessarily agree with giving someone who is underperforming a raise. As Paul says, "They should have just told him to improve first."

DISCUSSION QUESTIONS

1. Do you think Angelo is underperforming as a result of motivation or something else, such as the need for improved training? How would you find out?
2. Is it a good idea to give someone who is underperforming a raise? Does it send the wrong signal, insofar as it seems to suggest that poor performance leads to rewards?
3. Do you think the idea of paying recruiters like Angelo per recruit might actually backfire, and if so how?

VIDEO CASE

PERFORMANCE MANAGEMENT CALIFORNIA HEALTH FOUNDATION

Synopsis

Kim Galvin, the Human Resources Director of the California Health Foundation, explains the nature of the company's performance management system. The employee appraisal system is open-ended and includes just a few general categories, covering the employee's past performance with respect to objectives set at the previous year's appraisal, and future goals in the company.

DISCUSSION QUESTIONS

1. Specifically what type of appraisal tool does the company seem to be using, based on what you read in Chapter 6? How would you modify it?

2. What do you think of the idea of getting anonymous third-party feedback on the employee? Why?

3. Why does Kim Galvin think that, besides the Human Resources Director, only an employee and his or her manager should review the employee's performance review? What (if any) is the drawback of not having the supervisor's own manager review the appraisal? Would you require some type of review, and why?

4. Suppose, as Kim Galvin says, you have an employee who is very well liked but not meeting the job expectations. What would you do?

5. How does the California Health Foundation handle employees who may be a candidate for future promotion?

6. What does Kim Galvin look for when reviewing employee appraisals?

VIDEO CASE

JOIE DE VIVRE HOSPITALITY: PAY FOR PERFORMANCE AND FINANCIAL INCENTIVES

Synopsis

Chip Conley is the founder of Joie de Vivre Hospitality (JDV), a collection of boutique hotels, restaurants, and spas in California. Conley aims to foster employee motivation using Maslow's Hierarchy of Needs and has written books and lectured on the subject. Joie de Vivre pays average wages, but experiences low turnover due to the nature of the relationships it has formed with each employee.

DISCUSSION QUESTIONS

1. Chip Conley, founder of Joie de Vivre Hospitality, believes that most companies

frame their financial incentives in the wrong way. Explain what he means. What does JDV do differently?

2. Why does JDV offer free hotel stays to all employees as part of its incentive plan?

3. According to the video, what separates a world-class organization is its ability to care for its employees in good times and in bad. How did JDV accomplish this during the dot-com crash and post-9/11 industry recession?

4. Of the compensation, benefits, and incentives practices we discussed in Chapter 7, which would you recommend JDV implement, and why?

Eight

Managing Employee Ethics, Engagement, Retention, and Fair Treatment

When you finish studying this chapter you should be able to:

- Explain *what is meant by ethics.*
- Discuss *important factors that shape ethical behavior at work.*
- Exercise *fair disciplinary practices.*
- Discuss *at least four important factors in managing dismissals effectively.*
- Describe *a comprehensive approach to retaining employees.*
- Explain *why employee engagement is important, and how to foster engagement.*

OVERVIEW

The small firm's CEO paid higher than average salaries but couldn't keep good employees. "Perhaps you should stop screaming at them," advised his wife. The main purpose of this chapter is to explain how to manage employee ethics, engagement, retention, and fair treatment at work. The topics we cover include Ethics and Fair Treatment at Work, Managing Employee Discipline and Privacy, Managing Dismissals, Managing Voluntary Employee Turnover and Retention, and Employee Engagement.

ETHICS AND FAIR TREATMENT AT WORK

People make ethical choices at work every day. Should I come in today, or call in sick and get my paper done? Should I take ink cartridges from work, or buy my own home supplies? Our biggest supplier just offered me a paid vacation—should I take it? My boss says she wants this order out by morning, and that she doesn't care if the pressure could trigger accidents tonight at the plant—what should I do?

Why Ethics?

Most everyone reading this book rightfully views himself or herself as an ethical person, so we should start by asking, "Why include ethics in a human resource management book?" For two reasons. First, "ethics" is not theoretical. Instead, it oils the wheels that make businesses work. Managers who promise raises but don't deliver; salespeople who say, "The order's coming" when it's not; production managers who take suppliers' kickbacks—all corrode the trust on which business transactions depend, and eventually undermine the businesses (and the managers). Thus, after Pfizer Inc. allegedly suppressed unfavorable studies about one of its drugs, plaintiffs were suing for billions.[1]

Second, managers' personnel decisions (including those in this chapter, namely discipline, dismissal, retention, and withdrawal) almost always hold ethical consequences.[2] One survey found that 6 of the 10 most serious ethical work issues, such as workplace safety and employee theft, were human resource management–related.[3]

The Meaning of Ethics

Ethics refers to "the principles of conduct governing an individual or a group"—in other words, to the standards people use to decide what their conduct should be.[4] Ethical decisions always require making normative judgments.[5] A *normative judgment* implies that "something is good or bad, right or wrong, better or worse."[6] Ethical decisions are also always rooted in *morality*, which is society's accepted standard of behavior.[7] Morality addresses matters of serious consequence, such as murder, lying, and slander. Many people believe that moral judgments are never situational. They say that something morally wrong in one situation would also be wrong in another situation. One cannot legalize immoral acts by passing laws that make them "legal."[8]

Ethics and the Law

Laws therefore aren't the best guide about what is ethical, because something may be legal but not right, and something may be right but not legal. Firing a 38-year-old employee with 20 years' tenure without notice may be unethical, but still legal, for instance. Sometimes behavior is both illegal and unethical. For example, a meat processor faced a federal indictment charging it with smuggling illegal immigrants from Mexico to cut costs.[9] One vice president for business practices put it this way: "*Ethics* means making decisions that represent what you stand for, not just what the laws are."[10]

The law may not be a foolproof guide to what's ethical, but some managers use it as if it is. "Is it profitable?" tends to be the first screen managers use to make decisions. "Is it legal?" may come next, because breaking laws often triggers consequences. The question, "is it ethical?" may then arise just as an afterthought, if at all.

What Shapes Ethical Behavior at Work?

Several experts reviewed the research concerning things that influence ethical behavior in organizations. Here's what they found:[11]

- Ethical behavior starts with *moral awareness*. In other words, does the person even recognize that a moral issue exists in the situation?
- *Managers* can do a lot to influence employee ethics by carefully cultivating the right norms, leadership, reward systems, and culture.
- Ethics slide when people undergo "*moral disengagement*." For example, you're more likely to harm others when you view them as "outsiders."
- The most powerful morality comes from *within*. In effect, when the moral person asks, "Why be moral?" the answer is that failure to act morally makes the person feel deeply uncomfortable.[12]
- Beware the seductive power of an *unmet goal*. Unmet goals pursued blindly can contribute to unethical behavior.[13]
- Offering *rewards* for ethical behavior can backfire. Doing so may actually undermine the intrinsic value of ethical behavior. Conversely, don't promote someone who got a big sale through devious means.[14]
- Employers should have strong *ethics codes* laying out what is and is not acceptable. Employees who observe unethical behavior expect you to discipline the perpetrators.
- The degree to which employees *openly talk about ethics* is a good predictor of ethical conduct.
- People tend to alter their *moral compasses* when they join organizations. They tend to equate "what's best for this organization (or team, or department)" with "what's the right thing to do?"

Ethics, Fair Treatment, and Justice

Companies that employees view as "fair and just" also tend to score higher on ethics. One study concluded that, "to the extent that survey respondents believed that employees were treated fairly...[they] reported less unethical behavior in their organizations."[15] In practice, fair treatment reflects concrete actions such as "employees are trusted," "employees are treated with respect," and "employees are treated fairly" (see Figure 8-1).[16]

Fairness, Bullying, and Victimization

Some supervisors are workplace bullies, yelling at or threatening subordinates. Employers should always prohibit such behavior. Many firms have anti-harassment policies. (For example, at one state agency, "It is the policy of the department that all employees, customers, contractors, and visitors to the work site are entitled to a positive, respectful, and productive work environment.")[17] Employees of abusive supervisors are more likely to quit their jobs, and to report lower job and life satisfaction and higher stress.[18] Mistreatment makes it more likely the employee will also show higher levels of "work withdrawal" (show up for work, but not do his or her best).[19] Such employees also exhibit more workplace deviance, for instance, theft and sabotage.[20]

What is your organization like most of the time? Circle YES if the item describes your organization, NO if it does not describe your organization, and ? if you cannot decide.

IN THIS ORGANIZATION . . .

	Yes	?	No
1. Employees are praised for good work	Yes	?	No
2. Supervisors yell at employees (R)	Yes	?	No
3. Supervisors play favorites (R)	Yes	?	No
4. Employees are trusted	Yes	?	No
5. Employees' complaints are dealt with effectively	Yes	?	No
6. Employees are treated like children (R)	Yes	?	No
7. Employees are treated with respect	Yes	?	No
8. Employees' questions and problems are responded to quickly	Yes	?	No
9. Employees are lied to (R)	Yes	?	No
10. Employees' suggestions are ignored (R)	Yes	?	No
11. Supervisors swear at employees (R)	Yes	?	No
12. Employees' hard work is appreciated	Yes	?	No
13. Supervisors threaten to fire or lay off employees (R)	Yes	?	No
14. Employees are treated fairly	Yes	?	No
15. Coworkers help each other out	Yes	?	No
16. Coworkers argue with each other (R)	Yes	?	No
17. Coworkers put each other down (R)	Yes	?	No
18. Coworkers treat each other with respect	Yes	?	No

FIGURE 8-1 Perceptions of Fair Interpersonal Treatment Scale.

Note: R = the item is reverse scored.

Source: Michelle A. Donovan et al., "The Perceptions of Their Interpersonal Treatment Scale: Development and Validation of a Measure of Interpersonal Treatment in the Workplace," *Journal of Applied Psychology* 83, no. 5 (1998): 692. Copyright © 1997 by Michelle A. Donovan, Fritz Drasgow, and Liberty J. Munson at the University of Illinois at Urbana-Champaign. All rights reserved. Reprinted with permission.

Bullying—singling out someone to harass and mistreat them—is an increasingly serious problem. The U.S. government (www.stopbullying.gov/#) says that most would agree that bullying involves three things:

- **Imbalance of Power:** People who bully use their power to control or harm and the people being bullied may have a hard time defending themselves.
- **Intent to Cause Harm:** Actions done by accident are not bullying; the person bullying has a goal to cause harm.
- **Repetition:** Incidents of bullying happen to the same person repeatedly by the same person or group.

It also says that bullying can take many forms, such as:

- **Verbal:** name-calling, teasing
- **Social:** spreading rumors, leaving people out on purpose, breaking up friendships
- **Physical:** hitting, punching, shoving
- **Cyber bullying:** using the Internet, mobile phones, or other digital technologies to harm others

The person to blame for any bullying is the perpetrator. Employers must have systems in place, similar to those we discuss later in this chapter, to ensure that the company can identify unfair treatment and deal with it. This includes monitoring employees' use of social media websites.[21]

However, numerous studies show that some people's traits, and how they behave, make them more likely targets of bullying.[22] These include submissive victims (who seem more cautious, quiet, and sensitive), provocative victims (who display aggressive behavior), and victims low in self-determination (who seem to leave it to others to make decisions for them and to determine the course of their careers).

RESEARCH INSIGHT   A study illustrates the interpersonal dynamics. Research suggests that people with higher intellectual capability often suffer bullying in school, for instance, in the form of derogatory names such as "geek" and "nerd." In one study, the researchers found that it wasn't just whether the person was very smart that determined whether he or she became a victim, but how the person behaved.[23] People with high cognitive ability who behaved more independently were more likely to be victimized by bullying. Team players were less likely to be victimized.

Why Treat Employees Fairly?

There are many reasons that managers should be fair. The *golden rule* is one obvious reason: As management guru Peter Drucker has said, "[t]hey're not employees, they're people," and the manager should treat people with dignity and respect.

What may not be so obvious is that fairness also has *organizational implications*. For example, perceptions of fairness relate to enhanced employee commitment, and enhanced satisfaction with the organization, jobs, and leaders.[24]

EXAMPLE   A study provides an illustration. College instructors completed surveys regarding the extent to which they saw their colleges as treating them with *procedural* and *distributive justice*. The former refers to fair processes, while the latter refers to fair outcomes. The *procedural* justice questions included, for example, "In general, the department/college's procedures allow for requests for clarification or for additional information about a decision." The *distributive* justice questions included, "I am fairly rewarded considering the responsibilities I have." These instructors also completed organizational commitment questionnaires. These included questions such as "I am proud to tell others that I am part of this department/college." Their students then completed surveys containing items such as "the instructor put a lot of effort into planning this course."

The results were telling. Instructors who perceived high distributive and procedural justice reported higher organizational commitment. Furthermore, their students had more positive reactions to their instructors, and reported higher levels of instructor effort, pro-social behaviors, and fairness.[25]

RIGHTS AND FAIRNESS   An increasingly *litigious workforce* is a third reason to be fair. Few societies rely solely on managers' sense of fairness to ensure that they do what's right by their employees. They also pass laws. Laws like Title VII give employees (or prospective employees, and, sometimes, past employees) various *rights*. Managers therefore need to institute disciplinary and discharge procedures that will survive scrutiny by arbitrators and the courts.[26] Figure 8-2 lists some other legislated areas under which workers have rights.[27]

Aside from legislation, employees also have certain rights under common law.[28] For example, an employee may have the right to sue an employer whose supervisor published embarrassing private and personal information about the employee.[29]

- Leave of absence and vacation rights
- Injuries and illnesses rights
- Noncompete agreement rights
- Employees' rights on employer policies
- Discipline rights
- Rights on personnel files
- Employee pension rights
- Employee benefits rights
- References rights
- Rights on criminal records
- Employee distress rights
- Defamation rights
- Employees' rights on fraud
- Rights on assault and battery
- Employee negligence rights
- Right on political activity
- Union/group activity rights
- Whistle-blower rights
- Workers' compensation rights

FIGURE 8-2 Some Areas under Which Workers Have Legal Rights.

MANAGING EMPLOYEE DISCIPLINE AND PRIVACY

Disciplining employees is one task that should follow ethical guidelines. The purpose of **discipline** is to encourage employees to behave sensibly at work (where *sensible* means adhering to rules and regulations). Rules and regulations are basically the company's laws. Discipline is called for when someone violates one of these rules or regulations.[30] A fair and just discipline process has three pillars: rules and regulations, a system of progressive penalties, and an appeals process.

The Three Pillars

RULES   A set of clear rules and regulations is the first pillar. These rules address issues such as theft, destruction of company property, drinking on the job, and insubordination. Examples of rules include:

> **Poor performance is not acceptable.** Each employee is expected to perform his or her work properly and efficiently and to meet established standards of quality.
>
> **Alcohol and drugs do not mix with work.** The use of either during working hours and reporting for work under the influence are both prohibited.
>
> **Gambling in any form is forbidden.**

The purpose of these rules is to inform employees ahead of time what is and is not acceptable behavior. Employees must be told, preferably in writing, what isn't permitted. This usually occurs during the employee's orientation. The employee handbook usually contains the rules and regulations.

PENALTIES   A system of progressive penalties is a second pillar of effective discipline. Penalties may range from oral warnings to written warnings to suspension from the job to discharge. The severity of the penalty is usually a function of the type of offense and the number of times the offense occurred. For example, most companies issue warnings for the first unexcused lateness. However, for a fourth offense, discharge is the usual disciplinary action.

APPEALS PROCESS   Finally, an appeals process should be part of the disciplinary process; this helps to ensure that supervisors mete out discipline fairly and equitably.

Consider FedEx's **guaranteed fair treatment** multistep program. In *step 1, management review,* the complainant submits a written complaint to a member of management (manager, senior manager, or managing director). Then the manager, senior manager, and managing director of the employee's group review the information and make a decision to uphold, modify, or overturn management's action.

If not satisfied, then in *step 2, officer complaint,* the complainant submits a written appeal to the vice president or senior vice president of the division within 7 calendar days of the step 1 decision.

Finally, in *step 3, executive appeals review,* the complainant may submit a written complaint within 7 calendar days of the step 2 decision to the employee relations department. The appeals board—the CEO, the COO, the chief HR officer, and three senior vice presidents—then reviews all relevant information and makes a decision to uphold, overturn, or initiate a board of review or to take other appropriate action.

Some supervisory behavior is difficult or impossible to overcome. For example, the employer can sometimes mitigate the effects of unfair disciplinary procedures by establishing disciplinary procedures that contain appeals processes. However, behaviors that attack the employee's personal and/or social identity are difficult to remedy. The accompanying HR in Practice feature summarizes fair discipline guidelines.[31]

HR IN PRACTICE

Fair Discipline Guidelines

- Make sure the evidence supports the charge.
- Make sure the employee's due process rights are protected.
- Warn the employee of the disciplinary consequences.
- The rule that was allegedly violated should be "reasonably related" to the efficient and safe operation of the work environment.
- Fairly and adequately investigate the matter before administering discipline.
- The investigation should produce substantial evidence of misconduct.
- Apply all rules, orders, or penalties evenhandedly.
- The penalty should be reasonably related to the misconduct and to the employee's past work.
- Maintain the employee's right to counsel.
- Don't rob a subordinate of his or her dignity.
- Remember that the burden of proof is on you.
- Get the facts. Don't base a decision on hearsay or on your general impression.
- Don't act while angry.
- In general, do not attempt to deal with an employee's "bad attitude." Focus on improving the specific behaviors creating the workplace problem.

Non-Punitive Discipline

Traditional discipline has two potential flaws. It often leaves a residue of ill will. And, it may gain short-term compliance, but not ongoing cooperation.

Discipline without punishment (or non-punitive discipline) aims to avoid these disciplinary problems. It does this by gaining the employees' acceptance of your rules and by reducing the punitive nature of the discipline itself. Typical steps include:

1. *Issue an oral reminder.* Here, your goal is to get the employee to agree to solve the disciplinary problem.
2. *Should another incident arise within 6 weeks, issue the employee a formal written reminder, and place a copy in the personnel file.* In addition, privately hold a second discussion with the employee, again without any threats.
3. *Give a paid 1-day "decision-making leave."* If another incident occurs after the written warning in the next 6 weeks or so, the employee is told to take a 1-day leave with pay to stay home and consider whether the job is right for him or her and whether he or she wants to abide by the company's rules.
4. *If no further incidents occur in the next year or so, the 1-day paid suspension is purged from the person's file.* If the behavior reoccurs, dismissal (see later discussion) is required.[32]

The process would not apply to exceptional circumstances. Criminal behavior or in-plant fighting might be grounds for immediate dismissal for instance. And if several incidents occurred at very close intervals, the supervisor might skip step 2—the written warning.

Electronic Employee Privacy

A New Jersey court recently found an employer liable when one of its employees used his company computer at work to distribute child pornography. (Someone had previously alerted the employer to the suspicious activity, and the employer had not taken action.[33])

Managing and monitoring company e-mail is an urgent problem.[34] About one-third of U.S. companies recently investigated suspected leaks, via e-mail, of confidential or proprietary information. One hospital found that, to facilitate working at home, many medical staff were e-mailing patients' confidential health care records to themselves, in violation of federal privacy statutes.

EXTENT   It's therefore not surprising that in one recent survey, over half of employers said they were monitoring their employees' incoming and outgoing e-mail; 27% monitor internal e-mail as well.[35] One survey found that 41% of employers with more than 20,000 employees have someone reading employee e-mails.[36] Ninety-six percent block access to adult websites, and 61% to game sites.[37] Employers ranging from UPS to the City of Oakland, California, use GPS units to monitor their truckers' and street sweepers' whereabouts.[38] And, many more employers, like Bronx Lebanon Hospital in New York, use biometric scanners, for instance, to ensure that the employee that clocks in is really who he or she says they are.[39] Some employers check employees' personal blogs or Facebook sites, to see if they're publicizing work-related matters.[40] Such monitoring raises privacy issues.[41]

LEGAL ISSUES   Electronic eavesdropping is legal—up to a point. For example, federal law and most state laws allow employers to monitor their employees' phone calls "in the ordinary course of business," says one legal expert. However, they must stop listening once they see the conversation is not business related.[42] E-mail service may be intercepted under federal law when it is to protect the property rights of the provider.[43] However, one recent U.S. Court of Appeals case suggests employers may have fewer rights to monitor e-mail than previously assumed.[44]

More employers are therefore issuing e-mail and online usage policies, and having employees sign e-mail and telephone monitoring acknowledgment statements.[45] One reason for explicit policy statements is the risk that employers may be liable for illegal acts committed by their employees via e-mail or blogging.[46] For example, messages sent by supervisors that contain sexual innuendo could cause problems for an employer who hasn't taken steps to prohibit such e-mail misuse. An attorney should review the e-mail policy. At a minimum, it must make it clear that employees should have no expectation of privacy in their e-mail and Internet usage, and that all messages sent and received on the employer's e-mail system are company property and not confidential.[47]

Videotaping in the workplace calls for more legal caution. In one case, one U.S. Court of Appeals ruled that an employer's continuous video surveillance of employees in an office setting did not constitute an unconstitutional invasion of privacy.[48] Yet a Boston employer had to pay over $200,000 to five workers it secretly videotaped in an employee locker room, after they sued in state court.[49]

MANAGING DISMISSALS

Because dismissal is the strongest disciplinary step, the manager should ensure that the dismissal is fair, ethical, warranted, and just. On those occasions that require immediate dismissal, the manager still needs to ensure that the action is humane.

The best way to "handle" a dismissal is to avoid it in the first place. Many dismissals start with bad hiring decisions. Using good selection practices including tests, reference and background checks, drug testing, and clearly defined jobs can reduce the need for dismissals.[50]

Termination at Will

For more than 100 years, the prevailing rule in the United States has been that without an employment contract, either the employer or the employee can **terminate at will** the employment relationship. In other words, the employee could resign for any reason, at will, and the employer could similarly dismiss an employee for any reason, at will.

TERMINATION AT WILL EXCEPTIONS   However, three main protections against wrongful discharge have eroded the termination-at-will doctrine. The three are statutory exceptions, common law exceptions, and public policy exceptions.

First, in terms of *statutory exceptions*, federal and state equal employment and workplace laws prohibit specific types of dismissals. For example, Title VII of the Civil Rights Act of 1964 prohibits discharging employees based on race, color, religion, sex, or national origin.[51]

Second, numerous *common law exceptions* exist. For example, a court may decide that an employee handbook promising termination only "for just cause" may create an exception to the at-will rule.[52]

Finally, under the *public policy exception*, courts have held a discharge to be wrongful when it was against an explicit, well-established public policy (for instance, the employer fired the employee for refusing to break the law).

Grounds for Dismissal

There are four bases for dismissal: unsatisfactory performance, misconduct, lack of qualifications for the job, and changed requirements (or elimination) of the job. We can define *unsatisfactory performance* as a persistent failure to perform assigned duties or to meet prescribed standards on the job.[53] Specific reasons include excessive absenteeism; tardiness; a persistent failure to meet normal job requirements; or an adverse attitude toward the company, supervisor, or fellow employees. *Misconduct* is deliberate and willful violation of the employer's rules and may include stealing, rowdy behavior, and insubordination. *Lack of qualifications for the job* is an employee's inability to do the assigned work, although he or she is diligent. Because this employee may be trying, it is reasonable to try to salvage him or her—perhaps by assigning the employee to another job. *Changed requirements of the job* involve an employee's incapability of doing the work assigned, after the nature of the job has changed. Similarly, you may have to dismiss an employee when his or her job is eliminated. Again, the employee may be industrious, so it is reasonable to retrain or transfer this person, if possible.

Insubordination, a form of misconduct, is sometimes the grounds for dismissal. Managers should deem some acts as insubordinate whenever they occur. These include, for instance, direct disregard of the boss's authority, and disobedience of, or refusal to obey, the boss's orders—particularly in front of others.

Dismissing employees is never easy, but at least the employer can try to ensure that the employee views the process as fair and just. One study found that "individuals who reported that they were given full explanations of why and how termination decisions were made were more likely to (1) perceive their layoff as fair, (2) endorse the terminating organization, and (3) indicate that they did not wish to take the past employer to court."[54]

Avoiding Wrongful Discharge Suits

In what it referred to as "fear of the firing," one magazine described several examples of how some employers were reluctant to terminate disruptive employees for fear of lawsuits. In practice, plaintiffs only win a tiny fraction of such suits. However, the cost of defending the suits is still huge.[55]

Wrongful discharge occurs when an employee's dismissal does not comply with the law or with the contractual arrangement stated or implied by the firm via its employment application, employee manuals, or other promises. (In a *constructive discharge* claim, the plaintiff argues that he or she quit, but had no choice because the employer made the situation so intolerable at work.[56])

PROCEDURAL STEPS   Avoiding wrongful discharge suits requires a two-step process. First is to *lay the groundwork* that will help avoid such suits. Steps here include[57]

- Have applicants sign the employment application. It should contain a statement that employment is for no fixed term and that the employer can terminate at any time.
- Review your employee manual and delete statements that could prejudice your defense, such as, "employees can be terminated only for just cause."
- Have written rules listing infractions that may require discipline and discharge.
- If a rule is broken, get the worker's side of the story in front of witnesses, and preferably get it signed.
- Be sure that employees get a written appraisal at least annually. If necessary, give the person a warning and an opportunity to improve.
- Keep confidential records of all actions such as employee appraisals, warnings or notices, and so on.
- Consider his or her legal rights. For example, ask: Is the employee covered by any type of written agreement, including a collective bargaining agreement?

FAIRNESS SAFEGUARDS   Second, use practices (as discussed in this chapter, such as appeals processes) that help ensure that your *actions are fair*.[58] People who are fired and who walk away feeling that they've been embarrassed or treated unfairly financially are more likely to seek retribution in the courts. To some extent, employers can use severance pay to blunt a dismissal's sting.

SEVERANCE PAY   The reason for the dismissal affects whether the employee gets severance pay. About 95% of employees dismissed due to downsizings got severance pay, while only about a third of employers offer severance when terminating for poor performance. It is uncommon to pay when employees quit. The average maximum severance is 39 weeks for executives and about 30 weeks for other downsized employees.[59] About half of employers surveyed give white-collar and exempt employees one week of severance pay per year of service, and about one-third do the same for blue-collar workers.[60] As the economy worsened in 2008–2009 and layoffs rose, more employers were reducing what they awarded for severance pay, for instance, awarding lump-sum payments rather than payments tied to years with the company.[61]

Severance payments are humanitarian and good public relations. In addition, most managers expect employees to give them notice so it's appropriate (and in some states mandatory) to provide at least one pay period's severance pay. Doing so can also reduce the possibility of litigation.

When designing the severance plan:

- List the situations for which the firm will pay severance, such as layoffs resulting from reorganizations. Indicate that management will determine action regarding other situations and reserves the right to end or alter the policy.
- Require signing of a waiver/general release prior to paying any severance, absolving the employer from employment-related liability.
- Remember that the employer must make any severance payments equitably.[62]

Personal Supervisory Liability

Courts sometimes hold managers personally liable for their supervisory actions such as dismissals, particularly with respect to actions covered by the Fair Labor Standards Act and the Family and Medical Leave Act.[63] The Fair Labor Standards Act defines *employer* to include "any person acting directly or indirectly in the interest of an employer in relation to any employee," and this can mean the individual supervisor.

STEPS TO TAKE   The manager can take several steps to avoid personal liability becoming an issue. *Follow company policies and procedures.* An employee may initiate a claim against a supervisor who he or she alleges did not follow company policies and procedures. Administer the discipline in a manner that does not add to the *emotional hardship* on the employee (as would making him or her publicly collect belongings and leave the office). Let the employee present "their side of the story." *Do not act in anger.* Doing so personalizes the situation and undermines the appearance of objectivity. Finally, *ask the HR department* for advice on how to handle difficult disciplinary situations.

If humanitarianism and wrongful discharge suits aren't enough to encourage you to be fair in dismissing, consider this. Managers run double their usual risk of suffering a heart attack during the week after they fire an employee.[64] During one 5-year period, physicians interviewed 791 working people who had just undergone heart attacks to find out what might have triggered them. The researchers concluded that the stress associated with firing someone doubled the usual risk of a heart attack for the person doing the firing in the week following the dismissal.

The Termination Interview

Dismissing an employee is one of the most difficult tasks you can face at work.[65] The dismissed employee, even if warned many times in the past, may still react with disbelief or even violence. Guidelines for the **termination interview** itself are as follows:

1. *Plan the interview carefully.* According to experts at Hay Associates, this includes:
   - Make sure the employee keeps the appointment time.
   - Allow 10 minutes as sufficient time for the interview.
   - Use a neutral site, not your own office.
   - Have employee agreements and a release announcement (internal and external) prepared in advance.
   - Be available at a time after the interview in case questions or problems arise.
   - Have phone numbers ready for medical or security emergencies.
2. *Get to the point.* As soon as the employee enters your office, give the person a moment to get comfortable and then inform him or her of your decision.
3. *Describe the situation.* Briefly, in three or four sentences, explain why the person is being let go. For instance, "Production in your area is down 4%, and we are continuing to have quality problems. We have to make a change."[66] Describe the situation rather than personalizing it. Emphasize that the decision is final.
4. *Listen.* Continue the interview until the person appears to be talking freely and reasonably calmly.
5. *Review the severance package.* Describe severance payments, benefits, access to office support people, and the way references will be handled. However, do not make or imply any promises or benefits beyond those already in the support package.
6. *Identify the next step.* The terminated employee may be disoriented and unsure what to do next. Explain where the employee should go upon leaving the interview.

OUTPLACEMENT COUNSELING With **outplacement counseling,** the employer arranges to provide terminated employees with career planning and job search skills. Outplacement firms such as Right Management, usually provide the actual outplacement services. Managers who are let go typically have office space and secretarial services they can use at local offices of such firms, in addition to the counseling services. The outplacement counseling is part of the terminated employee's support or severance package.

EXIT INTERVIEWS Many employers conduct final **exit interviews** with employees who are leaving the firm. The HR department usually conducts them. The aim is to elicit information that might give the employer a better insight into what is right—or wrong—about the company. Exit interview questions to ask include, Why did you join the company? Was the job presented correctly? And, Why did you decide to leave?[67]

The assumption is that because the employee is leaving, he or she will be candid, but based on one older survey this is doubtful. The researchers found that at the time of separation, 38% of those leaving blamed salary and benefits, and only 4% blamed supervision. Followed up 18 months later, 24% blamed supervision and only 12% blamed salary and benefits.[68]

Layoffs and the Plant Closing Law

Non-disciplinary separations may arise from either employer or employee actions. For the *employer*, reduced sales or profits or recession or the desire for more productivity may require layoffs.[69] *Employees* may leave, for instance to retire or to seek better jobs.

A **layoff,** in which the employer sends workers home for a time for lack of work, is usually not a permanent dismissal (although it may turn out to be). Rather it's a temporary one, which the employer expects will be short term. However, some employers use the term *layoff* as a euphemism for discharge or termination. In the recession years of 2008 and 2009 combined, employers carried out about 51,000 mass layoffs, idling over 5 million workers in total.[70] The Worker Adjustment and Retraining Notification Act (WARN Act, or the plant closing law) requires employers of 100 or more employees to give 60 days' notice before closing a facility or starting a layoff of 50 or more people.[71]

Layoffs are often subject to additional constraints abroad, as the accompanying Global Issues in HR feature illustrates.

THE LAYOFF PROCESS A study illustrates one firm's layoff process. In this company, senior management first met to make strategic decisions about the size and timing of the layoffs. These managers also debated the relative importance of the skill sets they thought the firm needed going forward. Frontline supervisors assessed their subordinates, rating their nonunion employees either A, B, or C (union employees were laid off based on seniority). The supervisors then informed each subordinate about his or her A, B, or C rating and told them that those with C grades were likely to be laid off.[72]

Interestingly, the preparatory focus probably shouldn't be on the layoffs, but on the employer's appraisal systems. One expert says that in preparing for large-scale layoffs, management needs to make sure appraisals are up to date, and identify top performers.[73] The essential point about layoffs is to prepare in advance by making sure you have an effective performance appraisal system. If you don't, then when the time comes to lay off employees, you may find yourself with no rational basis on which to decide who stays or leaves.[74]

GLOBAL ISSUES IN HR

Employment Contracts

Businesses expanding abroad soon discover that hiring, disciplining, and discharging employees in Europe require much more stringent communication than they do in the United States. For example, the European Union (EU) has a directive (law) that requires employers to provide employees with very explicit contracts of employment, usually within 2 months of their starting work.

How employers must comply with this law varies by country. In the United Kingdom, the employee must receive a written contract specifying, among other things, name of employer, grievance procedure, job title, rate of pay, disciplinary rules, hours of work, and vacation and sick-leave policies. In Germany, the contracts need not be in writing (although they customarily are) and include details like wages, vacations, maternity/paternity rights, equal pay, invention rights, and sickness pay. The contract need not be in writing in Italy, but usually is. Items covered include start date, probationary period, working hours, and a noncompete clause. In France, the contract must be in writing, and specify information such as place of work, type of job, notice period, dates of payment, and work hours.

LAYOFF'S EFFECTS   Layoffs "tend to result in deleterious psychological and physical health outcomes for employees who lose their jobs," as well as for the survivors, who face uncertainty and discomfort.[75] Alternatives to layoffs therefore make particular sense for high performance work system–type firms that depend on employee expertise.[76] For example, cut costs without reducing the workforce, perhaps through pay cuts; introduce a hiring freeze; provide candid communications about the need for the downsizing; give employees an opportunity to express their opinions about the downsizing; and be fair and compassionate in implementing the downsizing.[77] Some reduce layoffs by cutting work hours and mandating short vacations.[78]

Adjusting to Downsizings and Mergers

Yet **downsizing**—reducing, usually dramatically, the number of people employed by a firm—is on the rise.[79] Downsizings (some call them "productivity transformation programs")[80] require careful consideration of several matters. First, make sure you let go *the right people*; this requires having an effective appraisal system in place. Second, comply *with all applicable laws*, including WARN. Third, ensure that the employer executes the dismissals in a manner that is *just and fair*. Fourth, consider *security*, for instance, with respect to retrieving keys and ensuring that those leaving don't take any prohibited items with them.

Finally, take steps to reduce the remaining *employees' uncertainty* and to address their concerns. This typically involves a post-downsizing announcement and meetings where senior managers deal with questions from the remaining employees. Make no assertions about "no more layoffs" unless they are true.

MANAGING VOLUNTARY EMPLOYEEE TURNOVER AND RETENTION

Involuntary turnover prompted by dismissals and layoffs is one reason why employees leave their firms. Many other employees of course leave voluntarily.

Managing voluntary turnover is important. *Voluntary turnover*—the rate at which employees voluntarily leave their firms—varies markedly among industries.

HR AS A PROFIT CENTER: THE COST OF TURNOVER

A research team analyzed the tangible and intangible costs of turnover in a call center with 31 agents and 4 supervisors.[81] Tangible costs associated with an agent's leaving included things like the costs of recruiting, screening, interviewing, and testing applicants, and the cost of wages while the new agent was oriented and trained. Intangible costs included the cost of lost productivity for the new agent (who is less productive at first than his or her predecessor), the cost of rework for errors the new agent makes, and the supervisory cost for coaching the new agent. For this call center, the researchers' mathematical model estimated the cost of an agent leaving at about $21,551. This call center averaged 18.6 vacancies per year (about a 60% turnover rate). Therefore, the researchers estimated the total annual cost of agent turnover here at $400,853. Taking steps to cut this turnover rate in, say, half could save this firm about $200,000 per year.

For example, turnover in the accommodation and food services industry is chronically high, with over half the industry's employees voluntarily leaving each year. In contrast, voluntary annual turnover in the educational services industry is about 12%.[82]

Again, such figures only reflect employees who leave voluntarily, for instance, for better jobs or for retirement. They don't include dismissals and layoffs.[83] Combining voluntary and involuntary turnover produces some astounding statistics. For example, the total turnover in many food service organizations is around 100% per year. The average restaurant may need to replace just about all its employees every year.

Turnover (whether voluntary or involuntary) is expensive.[84] The accompanying HR as a Profit Center feature provides an illustrative example.

Managing Voluntary Turnover

Given the costs of losing good employees, managing voluntary turnover is an important human resource management task. *Managing voluntary turnover* requires identifying its causes and then addressing them.

Unfortunately, identifying why employees voluntarily leave is easier said than done. People who are dissatisfied with their jobs are more likely to leave, but the sources of dissatisfaction are numerous and varied. Figure 8-3 provides an example.[85] The consultants collected survey data from 262 U.S. organizations having a minimum of 1,000 employees. In this survey, the five top reasons high commitment/top-performing employees gave for leaving (ranked from high to low) were pay, promotional opportunities, work/life balance, career development, and health care benefits. In contrast, *employers* ranked the top five reasons employees left as promotion, career development, pay, relationship with supervisor, and work/life balance. Other reasons employees voluntarily leave include unfairness, not having their voices heard, and a lack of recognition.[86] (Simply asking, "All things considered, how satisfied are you with your job?" can be as effective as using surveys for soliciting employees' attitudes toward various facets of the job, such as supervision and pay.[87]) Practical considerations affect turnover. For example, high unemployment reduces voluntary turnover, and some locales have fewer job opportunities (and thus turnover) than do others.

Of course, turnover isn't necessarily bad. For example, losing low-performing employees isn't as problematical as losing high-performing ones. Some firms, such as the restaurant chain Applebee's, even incentivize their managers differentially, with higher incentives for reducing turnover among top-performing employees.[88]

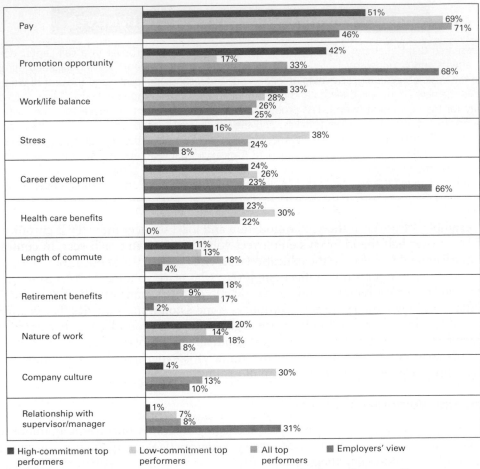

Pay 51% 69% 71% 46%

Promotion opportunity 42% 17% 33% 68%

Work/life balance 33% 28% 26% 25%

Stress 16% 38% 24% 8%

Career development 24% 26% 23% 66%

Health care benefits 23% 30% 22% 0%

Length of commute 11% 13% 18% 4%

Retirement benefits 18% 9% 17% 2%

Nature of work 20% 14% 18% 8%

Company culture 4% 30% 13% 10%

Relationship with supervisor/manager 1% 7% 8% 31%

■ High-commitment top performers   ■ Low-commitment top performers   ■ All top performers   ■ Employers' view

* Percentage reporting element as one of the top three reasons top-performing employees consider leaving an organization

FIGURE 8-3 Reasons Top-Performing Employees Leave Their Jobs.   *Source:* www.worldatwork.org/waw/adimLink?id=17180, accessed April 3, 2011.

Retention Strategies

In any case, given the variety of things prompting employees to leave, what can one do to reduce voluntary turnover? There is no silver bullet. Retaining employees is a multi-faceted talent management issue. For example, employees who aren't interested in their jobs, or who sense that they're not suited for their jobs, or who feel undercompensated, are more likely to leave. Employers can only address such issues by instituting effective and comprehensive talent management (recruitment, selection, training, appraisal, and compensation) practices. Put another way, turnovers (both voluntary and involuntary) often start with poor selection decisions, compounded by inadequate training, insensitive appraisals, and inequitable pay. Therefore trying to formulate a "retention strategy" without considering all one's HR practices is futile.

Identifying the issues is an important first retention strategy. As we saw earlier, exit interviews, conducted effectively, provide useful insights into potential turnover problem areas. Many employers routinely administer attitude surveys to monitor employees' feelings about matters such as supervision and pay. Open door policies and anonymous "hotlines" help management identify and remedy morale problems before they get out of hand. Sometimes, analyzing the situation leads to simple solutions. For example, Walmart discovered it could significantly reduce voluntary turnover by providing aggressively realistic previews about the job's demands and work hours.

A Comprehensive Approach to Retaining Employees

Assuming pay is already competitive, experts from the consulting company Development Dimensions International (DDI) and from the employment firm Robert Half International suggest building comprehensive retention programs around the following steps.

SELECTION   "Retention starts up front, in the selection and hiring of the right employees."[89] Selection refers not just to the worker but to choosing the right supervisors as well. For example, FedEx conducts periodic employee attitude surveys. The supervisor then meets to review the results with his or her employees, to address any problems the surveys raise.

PROFESSIONAL GROWTH   Inadequate career and professional development prospects prompt many employees to leave. Conversely, a well-conceived training and career development program can provide a strong incentive for staying with the company. As one expert says, "professionals who feel their company cares about their development and progress are much more likely to stay."[90]

PROVIDE CAREER DIRECTION   Periodically discuss with employees their career preferences and prospects at your firm, and help them lay out potential career plans. Furthermore, "don't wait until performance reviews to remind top employees how valuable they are to your company."[91]

MEANINGFUL WORK AND OWNERSHIP   People can't do their jobs if they don't know what to do or what their goals are. Therefore, an important part of retaining employees is making it clear what your expectations are regarding their performance and what their responsibilities are.

RECOGNITION AND REWARDS   We've seen that in addition to pay and benefits, employees need and appreciate recognition for a job well done.

CULTURE AND ENVIRONMENT   For example, companies that are very tense and "political" may prompt employees to leave, while companies that make them feel comfortable encourage them to stay.

PROMOTE WORK/LIFE BALANCE   In one survey conducted by Robert Half and careerbuilder.com, workers identified "flexible work arrangements" and "telecommuting" as the two top benefits that would convince them to choose one job or another.

ACKNOWLEDGE ACHIEVEMENTS   When employees feel underappreciated, they're more likely to leave. Surveys suggest that frequent recognition of accomplishments is an effective nonmonetary reward.

Managing Involuntary Turnover

We discussed involuntary turnover and dismissal earlier in this chapter, but several points are pertinent here. Dismissals and layoffs are inevitable. Even under the best conditions, the employer will have to let some employers go when jobs are restructured, or when competitive pressures necessitate reductions in force. However, dismissals due to poor performance are sometimes avoidable. As with voluntary turnover, performance-based dismissals may stem from breakdowns in the employer's talent management system. Therefore, as with voluntary turnover, reviewing and improving one's recruitment, selection, training, appraisal, and compensation/incentive plans can reduce dismissals by addressing the reasons for poor performance.

Talent Management and Employee Retention

All employees are important, but talent management–oriented employers put special emphasis on developing and retaining mission-critical employees. For example, we saw that Accenture ties pay, development, dismissal, and other personnel decisions to each employee's position in the firm's matrix. Compass Group identifies top performers, and then assesses them for promotability and leadership potential. Shell China appoints career stewards to meet regularly with "emerging leaders." Novartis China assesses the attitudes of its most mission-critical employees. In sum, taking a talent management approach to retaining employees requires focusing augmented efforts on the firm's most important employees.

Job Withdrawal

Unfortunately, voluntary turnover is just one way that employees withdraw. Withdrawal in general means separating oneself from one's current situation—it's a means of escape for someone who is dissatisfied or fearful. At work, **job withdrawal** has been defined as "actions intended to place physical or psychological distance between employees and their work environments."[92]

Poor attendance and voluntary turnover are two job withdrawal examples. Other types of job withdrawal can be less obvious if no less problematical. Some withdrawal examples include "taking undeserved work breaks, spending time in idle conversation and neglecting aspects of the job one is obligated to perform."[93] Other employees stop "showing up" mentally ("psychological withdrawal"), perhaps daydreaming at their desks while productivity suffers.[94] The employee is there, but mentally absent. In fact, the *job withdrawal process* is often incremental, for instance, evolving from daydreaming to absences to quitting: "[W]hen an employee perceives that temporary withdrawal will not resolve his/her problems, then the employee is apt to choose a more permanent form of withdrawal (i.e., turnover, assuming that alternative work opportunities are available)."[95]

DEALING WITH JOB WITHDRAWAL   Studies confirm the high costs of job withdrawal behavior, so understanding withdrawal's causes is important.[96] Because many people have experienced the desire to withdraw—to "get away" from—some situation, it's perhaps not difficult to empathize with those who feel they must escape. The simplest way to think about it is in terms of pain versus pleasure. People tend to move toward situations that make them feel good, and away from those that make them feel bad. More technically, "negative emotional states make people aware that their current situation is problematic, and this awareness motivates them to take action."[97] People are repelled by situations that produce unpleasant, uncomfortable emotions, and are attracted to those that produce pleasant, comfortable ones.[98] The point is that the more negative and less positive the person's mood about a situation, the more likely he or she will try to avoid or withdraw from the situation.[99]

The manager can therefore usefully think of withdrawal-reducing strategies in terms of reducing the job's negative effects, and/or of raising its positive effects. Because potential negatives and positives are virtually limitless, addressing withdrawal problems again requires a comprehensive human resource management approach. Illustrative potential negatives include, for instance, boring jobs, poor supervision, low pay, bullying, lack of career prospects, and poor working conditions. Potential positives include job enrichment, supportive supervision, equitable pay/family-friendly benefits, disciplinary/appeals processes, career development opportunities, and safe and healthy working conditions.[100] Interviews, surveys, and observation can help identify issues to address.

EMPLOYEE ENGAGEMENT

Poor attendance, voluntary turnover, and psychological withdrawal often also reflect diminished employee engagement. **Engagement** refers to being psychologically involved in, connected to, and committed to getting one's jobs done.

Why Engagement Is Important

Employee engagement is important because many employee behaviors, including turnover and withdrawal, reflect the degree to which employees are "engaged." As an example, surveys by the Gallup organization found that business units with the highest levels of employee engagement had an 83% chance of performing above the company median while those with the lowest employee engagement had only a 17% chance of performing better than the company median.[101] A survey by consultants Watson Wyatt Worldwide concluded that companies with highly engaged employees have 26% higher revenue per employee.[102] The director of recruiting at the nonprofit organization Fair Trade USA believes boosting engagement helps to explain the firm's subsequent 10% drop in turnover. A recent *Harvard Business Review* article notes that when it comes to customer service, satisfied employees aren't enough. Instead, "Employees should be engaged by providing them with reasons and methods to satisfy customers and then rewarded for appropriate behavior."[103] Yet studies conclude that only about 21% of the global workforce is engaged, and almost 40% is disengaged.[104]

Actions That Foster Engagement

A survey by consultants Towers Perrin illustrates the managerial actions that can foster employee engagement. Figure 8-4 summarizes these findings.[105] These suggest that engagement supporting actions include making sure employees (1) understand how their departments contribute to the company's success, (2) see how their own efforts contribute to achieving the company's goals, and (3) get a sense of accomplishment from working at the firm.

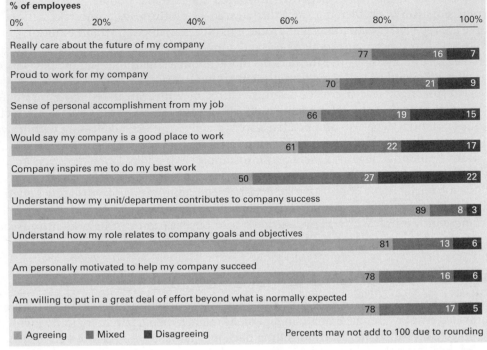

% of employees

	0%	20%	40%	60%	80%	100%

Really care about the future of my company — 77 | 16 | 7

Proud to work for my company — 70 | 21 | 9

Sense of personal accomplishment from my job — 66 | 19 | 15

Would say my company is a good place to work — 61 | 22 | 17

Company inspires me to do my best work — 50 | 27 | 22

Understand how my unit/department contributes to company success — 89 | 8 | 3

Understand how my role relates to company goals and objectives — 81 | 13 | 6

Am personally motivated to help my company succeed — 78 | 16 | 6

Am willing to put in a great deal of effort beyond what is normally expected — 78 | 17 | 5

■ Agreeing   ■ Mixed   ■ Disagreeing   Percents may not add to 100 due to rounding

FIGURE 8-4 Factors That Contribute to Engagement.   *Source:* © Towers Watson. Reprinted with Permission. towerswatson.com.

Monitoring Employee Engagement

Monitoring employee engagement needn't be complicated. With about 180,000 employees worldwide, the consulting firm Accenture uses a three part "shorthand" engagement assessment method it calls "say, stay, and strive." First, it assesses the employee's pride in being with the organization in terms of how positively he or she speaks about the company and recommends it to others. Second, it looks at who stays with a company. Finally, it looks at "strive," for instance, "do employees take an active role in the overall success of the organization by moving beyond just doing tasks to going above and beyond?"[106]

REVIEW

Summary

1. Ethics refers to the principles of conduct governing an individual or a group and specifically to the standards you use to decide what your conduct should be.

2. Ethical decisions always involve normative judgments, and ethical decisions always involve morality, which we defined as society's accepted standards of behavior.

3. A fair and just discipline process is based on rules and regulations, a system of progressive penalties, and an appeals process. A number of guidelines are important, including that discipline should be in line with the way management usually responds to similar incidents; that management must adequately investigate the matter before administering discipline; and that managers should not rob a subordinate of his or her dignity.

4. The basic aim of discipline without punishment is to gain an employee's acceptance of the rules by reducing the punitive nature of the discipline itself. The employee is given a paid day off to consider his or her infraction before more punitive disciplinary steps are taken.

5. Among the reasons for dismissal are unsatisfactory performance, misconduct, lack of qualifications, changed job requirements, and insubordination. In dismissing one or more employees, however, remember that exceptions in many states have weakened the termination at will policy. Furthermore, take care to avoid wrongful discharge suits.

6. Dismissing an employee is always difficult, and the termination interview should be handled properly. Specifically, plan the interview carefully and then get to the point. Then discuss the severance package and identify the next step.

7. Non-disciplinary separations such as layoffs and retirement occur all the time. The plant closing law (the Worker Adjustment and Retraining Notification Act) outlines requirements to follow with regard to official notice before operations with 50 or more people are to be closed down.

8. Managing voluntary turnover requires identifying its causes and then addressing them. A comprehensive approach to retaining employees should be multifaceted, and include improved selection, a well-thought-out training and career development program, and provide employees with meaningful work and recognition and rewards.

9. Employee engagement is important. Numerous employee outcomes including turnover and performance reflect the degree to which employees are engaged.

Key Terms

ethics *222*
bullying *224*
discipline *226*
guaranteed fair treatment *227*
terminate at will *229*

insubordination *230*
wrongful discharge *230*
termination interview *232*
outplacement
  counseling *233*

exit interview *233*
layoff *233*
downsizing *234*
job withdrawal *238*
engagement *239*

Discussion Questions

1. Provide three examples of behaviors that would probably be unethical but legal, and three that would probably be illegal but ethical.
2. List 10 things your college or university does to encourage ethical behavior by students and/or faculty.
3. You need to select a nanny for your or a relative's child, and want someone ethical. Based on what you read in this chapter, what would you do to help ensure you ended up hiring someone ethical?
4. Explain how you would ensure fairness in disciplining, discussing particularly the prerequisites to disciplining, disciplining guidelines, and the discipline without punishment approach.
5. Why is it important to manage dismissals properly?

6. Why is it advisable for an employee retention effort to be comprehensive? What actions would you undertake to improve employee retention?

7. Explain why employee engagement is important, and how to foster such engagement. What exactly would you as a supervisor do to increase your employees' engagement?

Individual and Group Activities

1. Working individually or in groups, interview managers or administrators at your college in order to identify the employee discipline process. Do they think it is effective? What do the employees (or faculty members) think of the programs in use?

2. Working individually or in groups, obtain copies of the student handbook for your college or employer and determine to what extent there is a formal process through which students or employees can air grievances. Based on your contacts with other students, has it been an effective grievance process? Why or why not?

3. Working individually or in groups, determine the nature of the academic discipline process in your college. Do you think it is effective? Based on what you read in this chapter, would you recommend any modifications?

4. What techniques would you use as alternatives to traditional discipline? What do such alternatives have to do with "organizational justice"? Why do you think alternatives like these are important, given industry's current need for highly committed employees?

5. Many rightfully offer IBM as an example of an employer that works hard to improve employee retention and engagement. Browse through the employment pages of IBM's website (such as www-03.ibm.com/employment/build_your_career.html). In this chapter, we discussed actions employers can take to improve employee retention and engagement. From the information on IBM's Web pages, what is IBM doing to support retention and engagement?

APPLICATION EXERCISES

CASE INCIDENT

Enron, Ethics, and Organizational Culture

For many people, a company called Enron Corp. still ranks as one of history's classic examples of ethics run amok. During the 1990s and early 2000s, Enron was in the business of wholesaling natural gas and electricity. Rather than actually owning the gas or electric, Enron made its money as the intermediary (wholesaler) between suppliers and customers. Without getting into all the details, the nature of Enron's business, and the fact that Enron didn't actually own the assets, meant that its accounting procedures were unusual. For example, the profit statements and balance sheets listing the firm's assets and liabilities were unusually difficult to understand.

It turned out that the lack of accounting transparency enabled the company's managers to make Enron's financial performance look much better than it actually was. Outside experts began questioning Enron's financial statements in 2001. In fairly short order, Enron's house of cards collapsed, and courts convicted several of its top executives of things like manipulating Enron's reported assets and profitability. Many investors (including former Enron employees) lost all or most of their investments in Enron.

It's probably always easier to understand ethical breakdowns like this in retrospect, rather than to predict they are going to happen. However, in Enron's case the breakdown is perhaps more perplexing than usual. As one writer said, "Enron had all the elements usually found in comprehensive ethics and compliance programs: a code of ethics, a reporting system, as well as a training video on vision and values led by [the company's top executives]."[107]

Experts subsequently put forth many explanations for how a company that was apparently so ethical on its face could actually have been making so many bad ethical decisions without other managers (and the board of directors) noticing. The explanations ranged from a "deliberate concealment of information by officers" to more psychological explanations (such as employees not wanting to contradict their bosses) and the "surprising role of irrationality in decision-making."

But perhaps the most persuasive explanation of how an apparently ethical company could go so wrong concerns organizational culture. The reasoning here is that it's not the rules but what employees feel they should do that determines ethical behavior. For example, to paraphrase the executive director of the Ethics Officer Association, employers can't write enough regulations to control what employees do; they must develop the sort of ethical culture that encourages employees to do the right thing.[108]

How can one tell or measure when a company has an "ethical culture"? Key attributes of a healthy ethical culture include:

- Employees feel a sense of responsibility and accountability for their actions and for the actions of others.[109]
- Employees freely raise issues and concerns without fear of retaliation.
- Managers model the behaviors they demand of others.
- Managers communicate the importance of integrity when making difficult decisions.

QUESTIONS

1. Based on what you read in this chapter, summarize in one page or less how you would explain Enron's ethical meltdown.
2. It is said that when one securities analyst tried to confront Enron's CEO about the firm's unusual accounting statements, the CEO publicly used vulgar language to describe the analyst, and that Enron employees subsequently thought doing so was humorous. If true, what does that say about Enron's ethical culture?
3. This case and chapter both had something to say about how organizational culture influences ethical behavior. What role do you think culture played at Enron? Give five specific examples of things Enron's CEO could have done to create a healthy ethical culture.

CONTINUING CASE

Carter Cleaning Company

Guaranteeing Fair Treatment

Being in the laundry and cleaning business, the Carters have always felt strongly about not allowing employees to smoke, eat, or drink in their stores. Jennifer was therefore surprised to walk into a store and find two employees eating lunch at the front counter. There was a large

pizza in its box, and the two of them were sipping colas and eating slices of pizza and submarine sandwiches off paper plates. Not only did it look messy, there were grease and soda spills on the counter and the store smelled from onions and pepperoni, even with the 4-foot-wide exhaust fan pulling air out through the roof. In addition to being a turnoff to customers, the mess on the counter increased the possibility that a customer's order might actually become soiled in the store.

(continued)

Although this was a serious matter, neither Jennifer nor her father felt that what the counter people were doing was grounds for immediate dismissal, partly because the store manager had apparently condoned their actions. The problem was, they didn't know what to do. It seemed to them that the matter called for more than just a warning but less than dismissal. Here is what she would like to know.

QUESTIONS

1. What would you do if you were me, and why?
2. Should a disciplinary system be established at Carter Cleaning Centers?
3. If so, what should it cover? How would you suggest it deal with a situation such as the one with the errant counter people?
4. How would you deal with the store manager?

EXPERIENTIAL EXERCISE

To Discipline or Not?

Purpose: The purpose of this exercise is to provide you with some experience in analyzing and handling an actual disciplinary action.

Required Understanding: Students should be thoroughly familiar with the following case, titled "Botched Batch." However, *do not read the "Award" or "Discussion" sections until after the groups have completed their deliberations.*

How to Set Up the Exercise/Instructions: If so desired, divide the class into teams. Take the arbitrator's point of view and assume that you are to analyze the case and make the arbitrator's decision. Review the Botched Batch case again at this point, but please do not read the award and discussion sections.

Answer the following questions:

1. What would your decision be if you were the arbitrator? Why?
2. Do you think that following their experience in this arbitration the parties will be more or less inclined to settle disputes by themselves without resorting to arbitration?

Botched Batch

Facts: A computer department employee made an entry error that botched an entire run of computer reports. Efforts to rectify the situation produced a second set of improperly run reports. As a result of the series of errors, the employer incurred extra costs of $2,400, plus a weekend of overtime work by other computer department staffers. Management suspended the employee for 3 days for negligence, and also revoked a promotion for which the employee had previously been approved.

Protesting the discipline, the employee stressed that she had attempted to correct her error in the early stages of the run by notifying the manager of computer operations of her mistake. Maintaining that the resulting string of errors could have been avoided if the manager had followed up on her report and stopped the initial run, the employee argued that she had been treated unfairly because the manager had not been disciplined even though he compounded the problem, whereas she was severely punished. Moreover, citing her "impeccable" work record and management's acknowledgment that she had always been a "model employee," the employee insisted that the denial of her previously approved promotion was "unconscionable." *(Please do not read beyond this point until after you have answered the questions in the Experiential Exercise.)*

Award: The arbitrator upholds the 3-day suspension, but decides that the promotion should be restored.

Discussion: "There is no question," the arbitrator notes, that the employee's negligent act "set in motion the train of events that resulted in running two complete sets of reports reflecting improper information." Stressing that the employer incurred substantial cost because of the error, the arbitrator cites "unchallenged" testimony that management had commonly issued 3-day suspensions for similar infractions in the past. Thus, the arbitrator decides, the employer acted with just cause in meting out an "evenhanded" punishment for the negligence.

Turning to the denial of the already approved promotion, the arbitrator says to view this action "in the same light as a demotion for disciplinary reasons." In such cases, the arbitrator notes, management's decision normally is based on a pattern of unsatisfactory behavior, an employee's inability to perform, or similar grounds. Observing that management had never before reversed a promotion as part of a disciplinary action, the arbitrator says that by tacking on the denial of the promotion in this case, the employer substantially varied its disciplinary policy from its past practice. Because this action on management's part was not "evenhanded," the arbitrator rules, the promotion should be restored.[110]

Nine

Managing Labor Relations and Collective Bargaining

When you finish studying this chapter, you should be able to:

- Discuss *the major federal labor relations laws.*
- Describe *the process of a union drive and election.*
- Discuss *the main steps in the collective bargaining process.*
- List *the traits of an effective grievance process.*

OVERVIEW

The U.S. Department of Labor accused several Starbucks store supervisors of breaking the law by questioning their baristas about their union inclinations. Starbucks denied the allegation, but it still caused trouble for the company. The main purpose of this chapter is to explain how to respond to and manage union efforts at work. The topics we cover include The Labor Movement, Unions and the Law, The Union Drive and Election, The Collective Bargaining Process, and What's Next for Unions.

THE LABOR MOVEMENT

About 14.7 million U.S. workers belong to unions—about 12% of the men and women working in this country.[1] Many are blue-collar workers. But doctors, psychologists, graduate teaching assistants, and even fashion models are joining unions.[2] About 40% of America's 20 million federal, state, and municipal public employees belong to unions.[3] And in some industries—including transportation and public utilities, where over 26% of employees are union members—it's hard to get a job without joining a union.[4]

Why Study Unions?

While only about 12% of employees belong to unions, *union relations* is still an important topic for supervisors and for human resource managers. For one thing, union membership is twice as high in many states (such as New York) and for certain occupations (such as public employees and factory workers). So in many organizations, union relations is a big part of managing and includes, for instance, gathering information for negotiations, helping to lead the employer's negotiating team, overseeing the union agreement's implementation, and handling union–management grievances. Furthermore, *working* with unions is just part of the union relations job; "the other part involves *preventing* unions from entering the company," says one writer, for instance, by minimizing pressures to unionize by ensuring fair disciplinary processes and equitable pay.[5] Furthermore, union relations may "soar" if Congress passes and the president signs the Employee Free Choice Act (EFCA). Among other things, this would make it easier for unions to unionize employers.

Why Do Workers Organize?

Workers generally don't unionize just to get more pay, although the pay issue is important. For example, median weekly wages for union workers are around $781, while that for nonunion workers is $612.[6] More often, the urge to unionize reflects the workers' belief that they can only protect themselves from managerial mistreatment through unity.[7]

RESEARCH FINDINGS For example, studies suggest that two things—employer unfairness and the availability of a union that the employees believed had clout—explain why employees unionize.

In one study of an Australia-based banking firm, researchers found that employer unfairness played a big role in unionizing: "Individuals who believe that the company rules or policies were administered unfairly or to their detriment were more likely to turn to unions as a source of assistance."[8] One labor relations lawyer put it this way: "The one major thing unions offer is making you a 'for cause' instead of an 'at will' employee, which guarantees a hearing and arbitration if you're fired."[9]

But unfairness itself was not enough to prompt a union vote; the union needed clout. Employees were more likely to unionize where they "perceived that the union was effective in the area of wages and benefits and protection against unfair dismissals."[10]

What Do Unions Want?

We can generalize by saying that unions have two sets of aims, one for *union security* and one for *improved wages, hours, working conditions, and benefits* for their members.

UNION SECURITY   First and probably foremost, unions seek to establish security for themselves. They fight hard for the right to represent a firm's workers and to be the *exclusive* bargaining agent for all employees in the unit. (As such, they negotiate contracts for all employees, including nonunion members.) Five types of union security are possible:

1. *Closed shop.*[11] The company can hire only union members. Outlawed in 1947, this still exists in some industries (such as printing).
2. *Union shop.* The company can hire nonunion people, but they must join the union after a prescribed period and pay dues.
3. *Agency shop.* Employees who do not belong to the union still must pay union dues on the assumption that the union's efforts benefit *all* the workers.
4. *Preferential shop.* Union members get preference in hiring, but the employer can still hire nonunion members.
5. *Maintenance of membership agreement.* Employees do not have to belong to the union. However, union members employed by the firm must maintain membership in the union for the contract period.

Not all states give unions the right to require union membership as a condition of employment. **Right to work** "is a term used to describe state statutory or constitutional provisions banning the requirement of union membership as a condition of employment."[12] Labor relations law permits states to forbid the negotiation of compulsory union membership provisions. Right-to-work laws don't outlaw unions. They do outlaw (within those states) any form of union security. This understandably inhibits union formation in those states. Several years ago, Oklahoma became the 22nd state to pass right-to-work legislation. Some believe that this helps explain why Oklahoma's union membership dropped dramatically in the next 3 years.[13] Recently there were 23 right-to-work states.[14]

IMPROVED WAGES, HOURS, WORKING CONDITIONS, AND BENEFITS FOR MEMBERS   Once their security is assured, unions fight to improve their members' wages, hours, and working conditions. The typical labor agreement also gives the union a role in other HR activities, including recruiting, selecting, compensating, promoting, training, and discharging employees.

The AFL-CIO and the SEIU

Employees join local unions, which in turn belong to national or international union federations such as the AFL-CIO and SEIU. The American Federation of Labor and Congress of Industrial Organizations (AFL-CIO) is a voluntary federation of about 56 national and international labor unions in the United States. The Service Employees International Union (SEIU) is a fast-growing federation of more than 2.2 million members. It includes the largest health care union, with more than 1.1 million members in the field, including nurses, LPNs, and doctors, and the second largest public employees union, with more than 1 million local and state government workers.[15]

STRATEGY AND HR   It's not easy competing with Walmart's low prices, but Costco has found a way. How? In part with "strong labor relations, low employee turnover and liberal benefits."[16] For example, Costco pays about 90% of the health care insurance costs of its employees, and its union relations are relatively benign.[17] Costco's strategy is built on fending off Walmart's low labor costs by paying more and getting better productivity and service from its employees. And, in fact, Costco's sales per employee are about $500,000 a year versus $340,000 at Sam's Clubs.[18] So having a labor relations strategy that supports Costco's overall strategic aims works for Costco.

UNIONS AND THE LAW

Until about 1930, there were no special labor laws. Employers didn't have to engage in collective bargaining with employees and were virtually unrestrained in their behavior toward unions: The use of spies, blacklists, and the firing of agitators was widespread. "Yellow dog" contracts, whereby management could require nonunion membership as a condition for employment, were widely enforced. Most union weapons—even strikes—were illegal.

This one-sided situation lasted in the United States from the Revolution to the Great Depression (around 1930). Since then, in response to changing public attitudes, values, and economic conditions, labor law has gone through three stages, from "strong encouragement" of unions, to "modified encouragement coupled with regulation," to "detailed regulation of internal union affairs."[19]

Period of Strong Encouragement: The Norris-LaGuardia Act (1932) and the National Labor Relations Act (1935)

The **Norris-LaGuardia Act** set the stage for an era in which government encouraged union activity. The act guaranteed to each employee the right to bargain collectively "free from interference, restraint, or coercion." It declared yellow dog contracts unenforceable. It limited the courts' abilities to issue injunctions for activities such as peaceful picketing.[20]

Yet this act did little to restrain employers, so Congress passed the National Labor Relations Act (or **Wagner Act**) in 1935. The Wagner Act added teeth to the Norris-LaGuardia Act by banning certain unfair labor practices, providing for secret-ballot elections and majority rule for determining whether a firm's employees were to unionize, and creating the **National Labor Relations Board (NLRB),** the agency which oversees and enforces these two provisions.[21]

UNFAIR EMPLOYER LABOR PRACTICES The Wagner Act deemed as "statutory wrongs" (but not crimes) five unfair employer labor practices:

1. It is unfair for employers to "interfere with, restrain, or coerce employees" in exercising their legal right of self-organization.
2. It is an unfair practice for company representatives to dominate or interfere with either the formation or the administration of labor unions. Among other management actions found to be unfair under practices 1 and 2 are bribing employees, using company spy systems, and moving a business to avoid unionization.
3. Employers are prohibited from discriminating in any way against employees for their legal union activities.
4. Employers are forbidden to discharge or discriminate against employees simply because the latter file unfair practice charges against the company.
5. Finally, it is an unfair labor practice for employers to refuse to bargain collectively with their employees' duly chosen representatives.

The union files the unfair labor practice charge (see Figure 9-1) with the NLRB. The board investigates the charge and determines whether to take action. Possible actions include dismissal of the complaint, request for an injunction against the employer, and an order that the employer cease and desist.

FORM EXEMPT UNDER 44 U.S.C 3512

INTERNET FORM NLRB-501 (2-08)	UNITED STATES OF AMERICA NATIONAL LABOR RELATIONS BOARD CHARGE AGAINST EMPLOYER	DO NOT WRITE IN THIS SPACE

	Case	Date Filed

INSTRUCTIONS:
File an original with NLRB Regional Director for the region in which the alleged unfair labor practice occurred or is occurring.

1. EMPLOYER AGAINST WHOM CHARGE IS BROUGHT

a. Name of Employer		b. Tel. No.
		c. Cell No.
		f. Fax No.
d. Address (Street, city, state, and ZIP code)	e. Employer Representative	g. e-Mail
		h. Number of workers employed
i. Type of Establishment (factory, mine, wholesaler, etc.)	j. Identify principal product or service	

k. The above-named employer has engaged in and is engaging in unfair labor practices with in the meaning of section 8(a), subsections(1)

and (list subsections) _____ of the National Labor Relations Act, and these unfair

labor practices are practices affecting commerce with in the meaning of the Act, or these unfair labor practices are unfair practices affecting commerce with in the meaning of the Act and the Postal Reorganization Act.

2. Basis of the Charge (set forth a clear and concise statement of the facts constituting the alleged unfair labor practices)

3. Full name of party filing charge (if labor organization, give full name, including local name and number)

4a. Address (Street and number, city, state, and ZIP code)	4b. Tel. No.
	4c. Cell No.
	4d. Fax No.
	4e. e-Mail

5. Full name of national or international labor organization of which it is an affiliate or constituent unit (to be filled in when charge is filed by a labor organization)

| 6. DECLARATION
I declare that I have read the above charge and that the statements are true to the best of my knowledge and belief.	Tel. No.
By _____ _____
(signature of representative or person making charge) (Print/typename and title or office, if any)	Office, if any, Cell No.
	Fax No.
Address_____ (date)	e-Mail

WILLFUL FALSE STATEMENTS ON THIS CHARGE CAN BE PUNISHED BY FINE AND IMPRISONMENT (U.S. CODE, TITLE 18, SECTION 1001)

PRIVACY ACT STATEMENT

Solicitation of the information on this form is authorized by the National Labor Relations Act (NLRA), 29 U.S.C. § 151 *et seq*. The principal use of the information is to assist the National Labor Relations Board (NLRB) in processing unfair labor practice and related proceedings or litigation.The routine uses for the information are fully set forth in the Federal Register, 71 Fed. Reg. 74942-43 (Dec.13,2006). The NLRB will further explain these uses upon request. Disclosure of this information to the NLRB is voluntary; however, failure to supply the information will cause the NLRB to decline to invoke its processes.

FIGURE 9-1 NLRB Form 501: Filing an Unfair Labor Practice Charge.

FROM 1935 TO 1947   Union membership increased quickly after passage of the Wagner Act in 1935. Other factors such as an improving economy and aggressive union leadership contributed to this as well. But by the mid-1940s, largely because of a series of massive postwar strikes, public policy began to shift against what many viewed as union excesses.

PERIOD OF MODIFIED ENCOURAGEMENT COUPLED WITH REGULATION: THE TAFT-HARTLEY ACT (1947)   The **Taft-Hartley** (or Labor Management Relations) **Act** reflected the less enthusiastic attitudes toward unions. It amended the Wagner Act in four ways: by prohibiting unfair *union* labor practices, by enumerating the rights of union members, by enumerating the rights of employers, and by allowing the president of the United States to bar national emergency strikes temporarily.

UNFAIR UNION LABOR PRACTICES   First, the Taft-Hartley Act enumerated certain prohibited union labor practices:

1. Unions were banned from restraining or coercing employees from exercising their guaranteed bargaining rights.
2. It is an unfair labor practice for a union to cause an employer to discriminate in any way against an employee in order to encourage or discourage his or her membership in a union.
3. It is an unfair labor practice for a union to refuse to bargain in good faith with the employer about wages, hours, and other employment conditions.

RIGHTS OF EMPLOYEES   The Taft-Hartley Act also protected the rights of employees against their unions. For example, new *right-to-work laws* sprang up in 19 states (mainly in the South and Southwest), outlawing labor contracts that made union membership a condition for keeping one's job.

In general, the National Labor Relations Act does not restrain unions from unfair labor practices to the extent that it does employers. Unions may not restrain or coerce employees. However, "violent or otherwise threatening behavior or clearly coercive or intimidating union activities are necessary before the NLRB will find an unfair labor practice."[22] In one typical case, *Pattern Makers* v. *National Labor Relations Board,* the U.S. Supreme Court found the union guilty of an unfair labor practice when it tried to fine some members for resigning from the union and returning to work during a strike.[23]

RIGHTS OF EMPLOYERS   The Taft-Hartley Act also gave employers certain rights. For example, it gave them full freedom to express their views concerning union organization. Thus, a manager can tell his or her employees that in his or her opinion unions are worthless, dangerous to the economy, and immoral. A manager can even hint, generally speaking, that unionization and subsequent high-wage demands might result in the permanent closing of the plant (but not in its relocation). Employers can set forth the union's record concerning violence and corruption, if appropriate, and can play on the racial prejudices of workers by describing the union's philosophy toward integration. But there can be no threat of reprisal or force or promise of benefit.[24]

The employer also cannot meet with employees on company time within 24 hours of an election or suggest to employees that they vote against the union while they are at home or in the employer's office. But he or she can do so while in their work area or where they normally gather.

NATIONAL EMERGENCY STRIKES   The Taft-Hartley Act also allows the U.S. president to intervene in **national emergency strikes,** which are strikes (for example, on the part of steel firm employees) that might imperil national health and safety. The president may appoint a board of inquiry and, based on its report, apply for an injunction restraining the strike for 60 days, which can be extended for another 20 days.

PERIOD OF DETAILED REGULATION OF INTERNAL UNION AFFAIRS: THE LANDRUM-GRIFFIN ACT (1959)   In the 1950s, Senate investigations revealed unsavory practices by some unions, and the result was the **Landrum-Griffin Act** (officially, the Labor Management Reporting and Disclosure Act). Its aim was to protect union members from possible wrongdoing on the part of their unions.

The Landrum-Griffin Act contains a bill of rights for union members. Among other things, this provides for certain rights in the nomination of candidates for union office. It also affirms a member's right to sue his or her union. And it ensures that no member can be fined or suspended without due process (such as a fair hearing).

The act also laid out rules regarding union elections. For example, national and international unions must elect officers at least once every 5 years, using a secret-ballot mechanism.

The Senate investigators also discovered flagrant examples of employer wrongdoing. The Landrum-Griffin Act therefore also greatly expanded the list of unlawful employer actions. For example, companies can no longer pay their own employees to entice them not to join the union.

THE UNION DRIVE AND ELECTION

It is through the union drive and election that a union tries to be recognized to represent employees. This process has five basic steps: initial contact, authorization cards, hearing, campaign, and the election.

Step 1: Initial Contact

During the initial contact stage, the union determines the employees' interest in organizing and establishes an organizing committee.

The initiative for the first contact between the employees and the union may come from the employees, from a union already representing other employees of the firm, or from a union representing workers elsewhere. Sometimes, a union effort starts with a disgruntled employee's contacting the local union to learn how to organize his or her place of work. Sometimes, though, the campaign starts when a union decides it wants to expand to representing other employees in the firm, or when the company looks easy to organize, or when it already represents competitors' employees. (Thus the Teamsters Union—already in place at UPS—began organizing FedEx.) In any case, there is an initial contact between a union representative and a few employees.

THE UNION REP   When an employer becomes a target, a union official usually assigns a representative to assess employee interest. The representative visits the firm to determine whether enough employees are interested to make a campaign worthwhile. He or she also identifies employees who would make good leaders in the organizing campaign and calls them together to create an organizing committee. The objective is to "educate the committee about the benefits of forming a union, the law and procedures involved in forming a local union, and the issues management is likely to raise during a campaign."[25]

CONTACT GUIDELINES   The union must follow certain guidelines when it starts contacting employees. The law allows union organizers to solicit employees for membership as long as it doesn't endanger the performance or safety of the employees. Therefore, much of the contact takes place off the job, perhaps at home or at places near work. Organizers can also safely contact employees on company grounds during off hours (such as lunch or break time). Under some conditions, union representatives may solicit employees at their workstations, but this is rare. In practice, there will be much informal organizing and debate at the workplace. In any case, this initial contact stage may be deceptively quiet. In some instances the first inkling management has of a union campaign is the distribution or posting of a handbill soliciting union membership.

LABOR RELATIONS CONSULTANTS   Labor relations consultants are increasingly influencing the unionization process, with both management and unions using outside advisors. The use by management of consultants (who unions often refer to as *union busters*) has grown considerably. One study found management consultants involved in 75% of the elections they surveyed.[26]

One expert says an employer's main goal shouldn't be to win representation elections but to avoid them altogether. He says doing so means taking fast action when the first signs of union activity appear. His advice in a nutshell: Don't just ignore the union's efforts while it spreads pro-union rumors, such as "If we had a union, we wouldn't have to work so much overtime." Retain an attorney and react at once.[27]

UNION SALTING   **Union salting** refers to a union-organizing tactic by which undercover union organizers who are employed full time by a union are hired by unwitting employers. The National Labor Relations Board defines "salting" as "placing of union members on nonunion job sites for the purpose of organizing."[28] A U.S. Supreme Court decision, *NLRB* v. *Town and Country Electric,* held the tactic to be legal.

THE WEB   The Web is a potent union contact tool. Unions can mass e-mail announcements to collective bargaining unit members, and use mass e-mail to reach supporters and government officials for their corporate campaigns. For example, the group trying to organize Starbucks workers (the Starbucks Workers Union) has their own website (www.starbucksunion.org). It includes notes like, "Starbucks managers monitored Internet chat rooms and eavesdropped on party conversations in a covert campaign to identify employees agitating for union representation."[29]

Step 2: Authorization Cards

For the union to petition the NLRB for the right to hold an election, it must show that a sizable number of employees may be interested in being organized. The next step is thus for union organizers to try to get the employees to sign **authorization cards** (see Figure 9-2). Before they can petition an election, 30% of the eligible employees in an appropriate bargaining unit must sign.

SAMPLES UNIONS of AMERICA
Authorization for Representation

I hereby authorize Local 409 of the SAMPLES union to be my exclusive representative for the purposes of collective bargaining with my employer. I understand that my signature on this card may be used to obtain certification of Local 409 as our exclusive bargaining representative without an election.

This card will verify that I have applied for union membership and that effective _____I hereby authorize you to deduct each pay period from my earnings an amount equal to the regular current rate of monthly union dues and initiation fee.

Employer _____   Worksite _____

Date: _____ Name: _____

Street Address: _____ City:_____ Zip Code:_____

Home Phone: _____Cell Phone: _____ Home E-mail:_____

Department: _____

Job Title/Classification _____

Signature _____

You must print and mail in this authorization card for it to be recognized. Only original cards are valid and should be submitted. Mail to:

SAMPLES Unions of America, Local 409

301 Samples Way

Miami, FL 33101

FIGURE 9-2 Illustrative Authorization Card.

Here union and management promote their positions. The union claims it can improve working conditions, raise wages, increase benefits, and generally get the workers better deals. Management need not be silent; it can attack the union on ethical and moral grounds and cite the cost of union membership, for example. Management can also explain its record, express facts and opinions, and explain to its employees the law applicable to organizing campaigns and the meaning of the duty to bargain in good faith (if the union should win the election). However, neither side can threaten, bribe, or coerce employees. Further, an employer may not make promises of benefit to employees or make unilateral changes in terms and conditions of employment that were not planned to be implemented prior to the onset of union-organizing activity. Managers also should not look through signed authorization cards, lest the NLRB view them as spying on those who signed. During this stage, the union can picket the company (subject to several constraints).[30]

Step 3: The Hearing

After the authorization cards are collected, three things can occur. The employer may choose not to contest *union recognition*, in which case no hearing is needed and a *consent election* is held immediately. The employer may choose not to contest the union's *right to an election* (and/or the scope of the bargaining unit, or which employees are eligible to vote in the election), in which case no hearing is needed and the parties can stipulate an election. Or the employer may contest the union's right to an election, in which case it can insist on a *hearing* to determine those issues. An employer's decision about whether to insist on a hearing is a strategic one based on the facts of each case, and on whether it feels it needs additional time to develop a campaign to try to persuade its employees not to elect a union.

Most companies contest the union's right to represent their employees, and thus decline to recognize the union voluntarily: They claim that a significant number of their employees do not really want the union. (For example, did 30% or more of the employees in an appropriate bargaining unit sign the authorization cards?) It is at this point that the U.S. Labor Department's NLRB gets involved. The NLRB is usually contacted by the union, which requests a hearing. Based on this, the NLRB sends a hearing officer to investigate. The examiner sends both management and the union a notice of representation hearing that states the time and place of the hearing.

The **bargaining unit** is one decision to come out of the hearing; it is the group of employees that the union will be authorized to represent and bargain for collectively.

Finally, if the results of the hearing are favorable for the union, the NLRB directs that an election be held. It issues a Decision and Direction of Election notice to that effect and has the employer post NLRB Form 666, Notice to Employees, announcing that an election may be held. The form also informs employees of their rights (to organize, for instance) and of examples of unfair employer conduct (such as threatening loss of jobs or promising raises to influence the vote).

Step 4: The Campaign

During the campaign that precedes the election, the union and employer appeal to employees for their votes. The union emphasizes that it will prevent unfairness, set up a grievance/seniority system, and will improve unsatisfactory wages. Union strength, they'll say, will give employees a voice in determining wages and working conditions. Management emphasizes that improvements such as those don't require unionization, and that wages are equal to or better than they would be with a union contract. Management also emphasizes the financial cost of union dues; the fact that the union is an "outsider"; and that if the union wins, a strike may follow.[31] It can even attack the union on ethical and moral grounds, while insisting that employees will not be as well off and may lose freedom. But neither side can threaten, bribe, or coerce employees.

THE SUPERVISOR'S ROLE IN THE CAMPAIGN   Supervisors are the first line of defense when it comes to the unionizing effort. They are often in the best position to sense evolving employee attitude problems, and to discover union activity. Unfortunately, they can also inadvertently hurt their employer's union-related efforts. For example, unfair labor practices could (1) cause the NLRB to hold a new election after your company has won a previous election, or (2) cause your company to forfeit the second election and go directly to contract negotiation. In one case, a plant superintendent reacted to a union's initial organizing attempt by prohibiting distribution of union literature in the plant's lunchroom. Since solicitation of off-duty workers in nonwork areas is generally legal, the company subsequently allowed the union to distribute literature. However, the NLRB still ruled that the initial act of prohibiting distribution of the literature was an unfair labor practice. The NLRB used the superintendent's action as one reason for invalidating an election that the company had won.[32]

Supervisors can use the acronym *TIPS* to remember what *not* to do during the organizing or pre-election campaigns:[33] *Do not* Threaten, Interrogate, make Promises to, or Spy on employees.

Use *FORE* for what you *can* do. *You may* give employees Facts (such as what signing the authorization card means), express your Opinion about unions, explain factually correct Rules (such as that the law permits replacing striking employees), and share your Experiences about unions. Figure 9-3 summarizes some other things supervisors should keep in mind.

USEFUL SUPERVISORY RULES REGARDING UNION LITERATURE AND SOLICITATION   What sorts of steps can supervisors take to restrict union organizing activity?[34]

1. Supervisors can always bar nonemployees from soliciting employees when the employee is on duty and not on a break.
2. Supervisors can usually stop employees from soliciting other employees for any purpose if one or both employees are on paid-duty time and not on a break.
3. Most employers (generally not including retail stores, shopping centers, and certain other employers) can bar nonemployees from the building's interiors and work areas as a right of private property owners.[35]
4. Supervisors can deny on- or off-duty employees access to interior or exterior areas only if they can show the rule is required for reasons of production, safety, or discipline.

Such restrictions are valid only if the supervisor and employer do not discriminate against the union. For example, if your employer lets employees collect money for baby gifts, or to sell things like Avon products or Tupperware, it may not be able lawfully to prohibit them from union soliciting during work time.

Managers and human resources professionals must be very careful during union activities at their companies:

- Watch what you say. Angry feelings of the moment may get you in trouble.
- Never threaten workers with what you will do or what will happen if a union comes in. Do not say, for example, that the business will move, that wages will go down or overtime will be eliminated, that there will be layoffs, and so on.
- Don't tell union sympathizers that they will suffer in any way for their support. Don't terminate or discipline workers for engaging in union activities.
- Don't interrogate workers about union sympathizers or organizers.
- Don't ask workers to remove union screensavers or campaign buttons if you allow these things for other organizations.
- Don't treat pro-union or anti-union workers any differently.
- Don't transfer workers on the basis of union affiliation or sympathies.
- Don't ask workers how they are going to vote or how others may vote.
- Don't ask employees about union meetings or any matters related to unions. You can listen, but don't ask for any details.
- Don't promise workers benefits, promotions, or anything else if they vote against the union.
- Avoid becoming involved—in any way—in the details of the union's election or campaign, and don't participate in any petition movement against the union.
- Don't give financial aid or any support to any unions.

Any one of these practices may result in a finding of "unfair labor practices," which may in turn result in recognition of a union without an election, as well as fines for your company.

FIGURE 9-3 Union Avoidance: What Not to Do.   *Source:* Reprinted with permission of the publisher, Business & Legal Resources Inc. Copyright 2012 Business & Legal Resources, Inc.

Step 5: The Election

Finally, the election can be held within 30 to 60 days after the NLRB issues its Decision and Direction of Election. The election is by secret ballot. The NLRB provides the ballots (see Figure 9-4), the voting booth and ballot box, and counts and certifies the results. Historically, the more workers that vote, the less likely is a union victory. This is probably because more workers who are not strong union supporters end up voting. The union is important, too: The Teamsters union is less likely than other unions to win a representation election.[36]

The union becomes the employees' representative if it wins the election, and winning means getting a majority of the votes cast, not a majority of the workers in the bargaining unit. (Also remember that if an employer commits an unfair labor practice, a "no union" election may be reversed. Supervisors must therefore be very careful not to commit such unfair practices.) In one recent year, the union win rate rose to 66.8%, higher than it had been for decades.[37]

Decertification Elections: When Employees Want to Oust Their Union

Winning an election and signing an agreement do not necessarily mean that the union is in the company to stay—quite the opposite. The same law that grants employees the right to unionize also gives them a legal way to terminate the union's right to represent them. The process is *decertification*. There are around 450 to 500 decertification elections each

---

UNITED STATES OF AMERICA

National Labor Relations Board

OFFICIAL SECRET BALLOT

FOR CERTAIN EMPLOYEES OF

_____

Do you wish to be represented for purposes of collective bargaining by —

_____

MARK AN "S" IN THE SQUARE OF YOUR CHOICE

YES	NO
☐	☐

DO NOT SIGN THIS BALLOT. Fold and drop in ballot box.
If you spoil this ballot return it to the Board Agent for a new one.

FIGURE 9-4 Sample NLRB Ballot.

year, of which unions usually win around 30%.[38] That's actually a more favorable rate for management than the rate for the original representation elections.

Decertification campaigns don't differ much from certification campaigns.[39] The union organizes membership meetings and house-to-house visits, mails literature to homes, and uses phone calls, NLRB appeals, and (sometimes) threats and harassment to win the election. Managers use meetings—including one-on-one meetings, small-group meetings, and meetings with entire units—as well as legal or labor expert assistance, letters, improved working conditions, and subtle or not-so-subtle threats in its attempts to win a decertification vote.

THE COLLECTIVE BARGAINING PROCESS

What Is Collective Bargaining?

When and if the union is recognized as a company's employees' representative, a day is set for meeting at the bargaining table. Representatives of management and the union meet to negotiate a labor contract that contains agreements on specific provisions covering wages, hours, and working conditions.

What exactly is **collective bargaining**? According to the National Labor Relations Act:

> For the purpose of (this act) to bargain collectively is the performance of the mutual obligation of the employer and the representative of the employees to meet at reasonable times and confer in good faith with respect to wages, hours, and terms and conditions of employment, or the negotiation of an agreement, or any question arising thereunder, and the execution of a written contract incorporating any agreement reached if requested by either party, but such obligation does not compel either party to agree to a proposal or require the making of a concession.

In plain language, this means that both management and labor are required by law to negotiate wages, hours, and terms and conditions of employment "in good faith."

What Is Good-Faith Bargaining?

Good-faith bargaining means that proposals are matched with counterproposals and that both parties make every reasonable effort to arrive at an agreement. Neither party is compelled to agree to a proposal.

WHEN IS BARGAINING NOT IN GOOD FAITH?   In assessing whether a party violated its good-faith obligations, the totality of each party's conduct is of prime importance.[40] Examples of a violation of the requirements for good-faith bargaining may include:

1. *Proposals and demands.* The NLRB considers the advancement of proposals as a positive factor in determining overall good faith.
2. *Withholding information.* The NLRB and courts expect management to furnish usable information on matters such as wages, hours, and other terms of employment that union negotiators request and legitimately require. Failing to do so may reflect bad-faith bargaining.[41]

3. *Dilatory tactics.* The law requires that the parties meet and "confer at reasonable times and intervals." It does not require management to meet at the time and place dictated just by the union. It may be that employers try to delay the meeting to "disrupt a union's bargaining momentum."[42] However, inordinately delaying the meeting or refusing to meet with the other party may reflect bad-faith bargaining.
4. *Unilateral changes in conditions.* This is viewed as a strong indication that the employer is not bargaining with the required intent of reaching an agreement.

The Negotiating Team

Both union and management send a negotiating team to the bargaining table, and both teams usually go into the bargaining sessions having done their research. Union representatives have sounded out union members on their desires and conferred with union representatives of related unions.

Similarly, management compiles pay and benefit data, including comparisons to local pay rates and rates paid for similar jobs in the industry. Management also carefully "costs" the current labor contract and determines the increased cost—total, per employee, and per hour—of the union's demands. It also tries to identify probable union demands and to size up which demands are more important to the union. It uses information from grievances, and feedback from supervisors, to determine ahead of time what the union's demands might be and thus prepare counteroffers and arguments.[43]

Bargaining Items

"Wages, hours, and conditions of employment" is too broad to be useful in negotiations, so labor law and court decisions have set out categories of items that are subject to bargaining: These are *mandatory, voluntary,* and *illegal items.*

Voluntary (or permissible) **bargaining items** are neither mandatory nor illegal; they become a part of negotiations only through the joint agreement of both management and union. Neither party can be compelled against its wishes to negotiate over voluntary items. An employee cannot hold up signing a contract because the other party refuses to bargain on a voluntary item.

Illegal bargaining items are forbidden by law. The clause agreeing to hire "union members exclusively" would be illegal in a right-to-work state, for example.

About 70 **mandatory bargaining items** exist, some of which are in Figure 9-5. They include wages, hours, rest periods, layoffs, transfers, benefits, and severance pay. Others are added as the law evolves. For instance, drug testing evolved into a mandatory item as a result of NLRB decisions.

Bargaining Stages[44]

Bargaining typically goes through several stages.[45] First, each side presents its demands. At this stage, both parties are usually quite far apart on some issues. Indeed, labor negotiators use the term *blue sky* to refer to demands (such as swimming pools and 17 paid holidays, including Valentine's Day) that some negotiators have brought to the table.

Second, there is a reduction of demands. At this stage, each side trades off some of its demands to gain others, a process called *trading points.* Third are the subcommittee studies: The parties form joint subcommittees or study groups to try to work out reasonable

Mandatory	Permissible	Illegal
Rates of pay	Indemnity bonds	Closed shop
Wages	Management rights as	Separation of employees
Hours of employment	to union affairs	based on race
Overtime pay	Pension benefits of	Discriminatory treatment
Shift differentials	retired employees	
Holidays	Scope of the bargaining unit	
Vacations	Including supervisors in the	
Severance pay	contract	
Pensions	Additional parties to the	
Insurance benefits	contract such as the	
Profit-sharing plans	international union	
Christmas bonuses	Use of union label	
Company housing, meals,	Settlement of unfair labor	
and discounts	charges	
Employee security	Prices in cafeteria	
Job performance	Continuance of past	
Union security	contract	
Management–union	Membership of bargaining	
relationship	team	
Drug testing of employees	Employment of strikebreaker	

FIGURE 9-5 Bargaining Items. *Source*: Carrell, Michael R.; Heavrin, J.D., Christina, *Labor Relations and Collective Bargaining: Cases, Practice, and Law*, 4th, C. 1995. Printed and Electronically reproduced by permission of Pearson Education Inc., Upper Saddle River, New Jersey.

HR IN PRACTICE

Negotiating Guidelines

1. *Set clear objectives* for every bargaining item.
2. *Do not hurry.*
3. When in doubt, *caucus* with your associates.
4. Be *well prepared* with firm data supporting your position.
5. Always strive to keep some *flexibility* in your position.
6. Don't just concern yourself with what the other party says and does; *find out why.*
7. Respect the importance of *face saving* for the other party.
8. Constantly be alert to the *real intentions* of the other party with respect not only to goals but also to priorities.
9. Be a good *listener.*
10. Build a reputation for *being fair but firm.*
11. Learn to *control your emotions;* don't panic.
12. Be sure as you make each bargaining move that you know its *relationship* to all other moves.
13. Measure each move against your *objectives.*
14. Pay close attention to the *wording* of every clause renegotiated; words and phrases are often sources of grievances.
15. Remember that collective bargaining negotiations are, by nature, part of a *compromise* process.
16. Consider the impact of present negotiations on those in *future years.*
17. Don't be so open and straightforward that you start making excessive concessions.[46]

alternatives. Fourth, the parties reach an informal settlement, and each group goes back to its sponsor. Union representatives check informally with their superiors and the union members; management representatives check with top management. Finally, when everything is in order, the parties fine-tune, proofread, and sign a formal agreement. The preceding HR in Practice feature summarizes negotiating guidelines.

Impasses, Mediation, and Strikes

IMPASSES   Signing the agreement assumes that there are no insurmountable disagreements. If there are, the parties may declare an impasse. For example, a few years ago, the National Hockey League informed the NLRB that it had reached an impasse in its negotiations with the National Hockey League Players Association. The parties must get past the impasse for the contract to be finalized and signed.

An impasse usually occurs because one party demands more than the other offers. Sometimes an impasse can be resolved through a third party, a disinterested person such as a mediator or arbitrator. If the impasse is not resolved in this way, the union may call a work stoppage, or *strike,* to pressure management.

THIRD-PARTY INVOLVEMENT   Three types of third-party interventions are used to overcome an impasse: mediation, fact-finding, and arbitration. With **mediation,** a neutral third party tries to assist the principals in reaching agreement. A mediator usually holds meetings with each party to determine where each stands regarding its position. He or she then uses this information to find common ground. For example, the union representing U.S. Airways pilots, which had been seeking a new contract since U.S. Air merged with America West Holdings Corp., applied for federal mediation.[47] The mediator is always a go-between. He or she communicates assessments of the likelihood of a strike, the settlement packages available, and the like. The mediator does not have the authority to insist on a position or make a concession.

In certain situations (as in a national emergency dispute in which the president of the United States determines that it would be a national emergency for, say, a transportation strike to occur), a fact-finder may be appointed. A **fact-finder** studies the issues and makes a public recommendation of what a reasonable settlement ought to be.

Arbitration is the most definitive type of third-party intervention because the arbitrator may have the power to decide and dictate settlement terms. Unlike mediation and fact-finding, arbitration can guarantee a solution to an impasse. With *binding arbitration,* both parties commit to accepting the arbitrator's award. With *nonbinding arbitration,* they do not. Arbitration may also be voluntary or compulsory (in other words, imposed by a government agency). In the United States, voluntary binding arbitration is the most prevalent. The parties use *interest arbitration* when labor agreements do not yet exist or when one or both parties are seeking to change the agreement. *Rights arbitration* really means "contract interpretation arbitration." It usually involves interpreting existing contract terms, for instance, when an employee files a grievance.

SOURCES OF THIRD-PARTY ASSISTANCE   Various public and professional agencies make arbitrators and mediators available. For example, the American Arbitration Association (AAA) represents and provides the services of thousands of arbitrators and mediators to employers and unions requesting their services. The U.S. Office of Arbitration Services, part of the U.S. Office of Mediation & Conciliation Service (www.fmcs.gov/internet/), maintains a roster of arbitrators qualified to hear and decide disputes.

STRIKES   A strike is a withdrawal of labor. There are four main types of strikes. An **economic strike** results from a failure to agree on the terms of a contract—from an impasse, in other words. **Unfair labor practice strikes** protest illegal conduct by the employer. A **wildcat strike** is an unauthorized strike occurring during the term of a contract. A **sympathy strike** occurs when one union strikes in support of the strike of another.

Strikes needn't be an inevitable result of the bargaining process. Instead, they are often avoidable, but occur because of mistakes made during the bargaining process. Mistakes include discrepancies between union leaders' and rank-and-file members' expectations, and misperceptions regarding each side's bargaining goals.[48]

The likelihood of and severity of a strike depends partly on the parties' willingness to **"take a strike."**[49] For instance, a few years ago baseball owners were willing to lose a season, because they had "consistently agreed that the players had been ruining the game by getting too much money and that only a hard line against such excesses" would stop that.[50]

Picketing is one of the first activities occurring during a strike. The purpose of picketing is to inform the public about the existence of the labor dispute and often to encourage others to refrain from doing business with the employer against whom the employees are striking.

DEALING WITH A STRIKE   Employers can make several responses when they become the object of a strike. One is to temporarily halt their operations. A second alternative is to contract out work during the duration of the strike in order to blunt the effects of the strike on the employer. A third alternative is for the employer to continue operations, perhaps using supervisors and other nonstriking workers. A fourth alternative is the hiring of replacements for the strikers. In an economic strike, such replacements can be deemed permanent and would not have to be let go to make room for strikers who decided to return to work. If the strike were an unfair labor practice strike, the strikers would be entitled to return to their jobs if the employer makes an unconditional offer for them to do so.

When the former Northwest Airlines began giving permanent jobs to 1,500 substitute workers it hired to replace striking mechanics, the strike by the Aircraft Mechanics Fraternal Association basically fell apart.[51]

OTHER RESPONSES   Management and labor both use other methods to try to break an impasse. The union, for example, may resort to a *corporate campaign*. This is an organized effort by the union that exerts pressure on the corporation by pressuring the company's other unions, shareholders, directors, customers, creditors, and government agencies, often directly. Thus, the union might picket the homes of members of the board of directors, and organize a **boycott**—a removal of patronage—of the company's banks.[52]

Unions continue to use corporate campaigns to good effect. Also called *advocacy* or *comprehensive campaigns,* they helped unions organize several health care firms, including Sutter Health in California.[53] The head of the United Auto Workers recently said the union planned a new campaign to organize foreign-owned car plants in the United States. The union then began picketing U.S. Hyundai, Daimler, Toyota, and Nissan dealerships.[54]

Inside games are union efforts to encourage employees to impede or to disrupt production. They might do this, for example, by slowing the work pace, refusing to work overtime, filing mass charges with governmental agencies, or refusing to do work without detailed instructions from supervisors.[55] In one inside game at Caterpillar's Aurora, Illinois, plant, United Auto Workers' grievances in the final stage before arbitration rose from 22 to 336. The effect, of course, was to clog the grievance procedure and tie up workers and management.[56]

LOCKOUTS   Employers can also try to break an impasse with lockouts. A **lockout** is a refusal by the employer to provide opportunities to work. The company (often literally) locks out employees and prohibits them from doing their jobs (and thus from being paid). In 2011, the National Football League (NFL) locked out football players when the two couldn't agree on a new contract.[57]

The NLRB generally does not view a lockout as an unfair labor practice. For example, if the employer's product is perishable (such as vegetables), then it might legitimately use lockout to neutralize the union's power. The NLRB views a lockout as an unfair labor practice only when the employer acts for a prohibited purpose. It is not a prohibited purpose to try to bring about a settlement of negotiations on terms favorable to the employer.[58]

INJUNCTIONS   During the impasse, both employers and unions can seek injunctive relief if they believe the other side is taking actions that could irreparably harm the other party. To obtain such relief, the NLRB must show the district court that an unfair labor practice (such as interfering with the union-organizing campaign), if left unremedied, will irreparably harm the other party's statutory rights. (For example, if the employer is unfairly interfering with the union's organization campaign, or if the union is retaliating against employees who are trying to gain access to the NLRB, the other side might press the NLRB for "10[j] injunctive relief.") Such relief is requested after the NLRB issues an unfair labor practices complaint. The *injunctive relief* is a court order compelling a party or parties either to resume or to desist from a certain action.[59]

The Contract Agreement

The contract agreement itself may be 20 or 30 pages long or longer. It may contain just general declarations of policy or a detailed specification of rules and procedures. However, the tendency today is toward the longer, more detailed contract. The main sections of a typical contract cover subjects such as:

1. Management rights
2. Union security and automatic payroll dues deduction
3. Grievance procedures
4. Arbitration of grievances
5. Disciplinary procedures
6. Compensation rates
7. Hours of work and overtime
8. Benefits such as vacation, holidays, and pension
9. Health and safety provisions
10. Employee security seniority provisions
11. Contract expiration date

Handling Grievances

Signing the labor agreement is not the end of the process, because questions will always arise about what various clauses really mean. The *grievance process* addresses these issues. It is the process or steps that the employer and union have agreed to follow to ascertain whether some action violated the agreement. The grievance process is not supposed to renegotiate contract points. Instead, the aim is to clarify what those points mean, in the context of addressing grievances regarding some employer action.

The potential for grievances and discontent is always present at work. Employees will use just about any issue involving wages, hours, or conditions of employment as the basis of a grievance. Discipline cases and seniority problems (including promotions, transfers, and layoffs) probably top the list. Others include grievances growing out of job evaluations and work assignments, overtime, vacations, and incentive plans. The Cleveland Browns' head coach fined one of his players $1,701 for not paying the hotel's bill for a $3 bottle of water. Some of the other players quickly filed grievance with the NFL.[60]

Sometimes the grievance process gets out of hand. For example, members of American Postal Workers Union, Local 482, filed 1,800 grievances at the Postal Service's Roanoke, Virginia, mail-processing facility (the usual rate is about 800 grievances per year). The employees apparently were responding to job changes, including transfers triggered by the Postal Service's automation efforts.[61]

Whatever the source of the grievances, many firms today (and virtually all unionized ones) do (or should) give employees some means through which to air and settle their grievances. Grievance procedures are invariably a part of the labor agreement. But, even in nonunion firms, such procedures can help ensure that labor–management peace prevails.

THE GRIEVANCE PROCEDURE   Grievance procedures are typically multistep processes. For example, step one might require the grievant to try to work out an agreement with his or her supervisor, perhaps with a union officer or colleague present. Appeals may then be taken successively to the supervisor's boss, then that person's boss, and perhaps finally to a special arbitrator.

CONTRACT ADMINISTRATION   In unionized companies, grievance handling is often called *contract administration,* because, since no labor contract can ever be so complete that it covers all contingencies, a process is required for "administering" the contract's clauses. For example, suppose the contract says you can discharge an employee only for "just cause." You discharge someone for speaking back to you in harsh terms. Was speaking back to you harshly "just cause"?

SUPERVISOR'S GUIDELINES FOR HANDLING GRIEVANCES   The best way for a supervisor to handle a grievance is to develop a work environment in which grievances don't arise in the first place. Hone your ability to avoid, recognize, diagnose, and correct the causes of potential employee dissatisfaction (such as unfair appraisals or poor communications) before they become grievances.

Given that many factors (including union pressure) prompt grievances, it would be naïve to think that grievances only arise due to supervisor unfairness. However, there's little doubt that the quality of the interpersonal relations among you and your subordinates will influence your team's grievance rate. You should be thoroughly familiar with our discussions of fairness in Chapter 8.

HR IN PRACTICE

How to Handle a Grievance[62]

DO:

- Investigate and handle every case as though it may eventually result in an arbitration hearing.
- Talk with the employee about his or her grievance.
- Require the union to identify specific contractual provisions allegedly violated.
- Comply with the contractual time limits for handling the grievance.
- Visit the work area of the grievance.
- Determine whether there were any witnesses.
- Examine the personnel record of the grievant.
- Treat the union representative as your equal.
- Hold your grievance discussion privately.
- Fully inform your own supervisor of grievance matters.

DON'T:

- Discuss the case with the union steward alone—the grievant should be there.
- Make arrangements with individual employees that are inconsistent with the labor agreement.
- Hold back the remedy if the company is wrong.
- Admit to the binding effect of a past practice.
- Relinquish to the union your rights as a manager.
- Settle grievances based on what is "fair." Instead, stick to the labor agreement.
- Bargain over items not covered by the contract.
- Treat as subject to arbitration claims demanding the discipline or discharge of managers.
- Give long written grievance answers.
- Trade a grievance settlement for a grievance withdrawal (or try to make up for a bad decision in one grievance by bending over backward in another).
- Deny grievances on the premise that your "hands have been tied by management."
- Agree to informal amendments in the contract.

The supervisor must steer a course between treating employees fairly and maintaining management's rights and prerogatives. One expert developed a list of supervisor do's and don'ts as useful guides in handling grievances.[63] The accompanying HR in Practice feature presents some critical do's and don'ts for handling a grievance.

WHAT'S NEXT FOR UNIONS?

Union membership as a percent of the workforce is about one-third of what it was 40 years ago. What happened?

Why the Union Decline?

Several factors contributed to the decline in union membership. Unions traditionally appealed mostly to blue-collar workers, and the proportion of blue-collar jobs has decreased as service-sector and white-collar service jobs increased. Globalization increases competition, and competition increases pressures on employers to cut costs and boost productivity. This in turn puts unions in a squeeze (as in the American auto industry, where workers recently had to accept salary reductions). Other factors pressuring employers and unions include the deregulation of trucking, airlines, and communications (which also made competition more intense), outdated equipment and factories, mismanagement, and government regulations supporting workers' rights (such as Title VII). The 2008 recession triggered budget cuts, prompting anti-union public policy attitudes, and the loss of about one million public-sector union jobs.

The effect of all this has been the permanent layoff of hundreds of thousands of union members, the permanent closing of company plants, the relocation of companies to nonunion settings (either in the United States or overseas), and mergers and acquisitions that have eliminated union jobs and affected collective bargaining agreements.

How Unions Are Changing

Unions are not sitting idly by.[64] For example, the union Change to Win says it will be very aggressive about trying to organize workers, will focus on organizing women and minority workers, will focus more on organizing temporary or contingent workers, and will target specific multinational companies for international campaigns.

The steps the union UNITE took against Cintas Corp. illustrate some of the new union tactics. UNITE didn't petition for an NLRB election. Instead, it filed a $100 million class action suit against the company. Then Cintas workers in California filed a lawsuit claiming that the company was violating a nearby municipality's "living wage" law. UNITE then joined forces with the Teamsters union, which in turn began targeting Cintas' delivery people.[65]

EMPLOYEE FREE CHOICE ACT   Unions are pushing Congress to pass the Employee Free Choice Act. Among other things, this would make it more difficult for employers to inhibit workers from trying to form a union. Unions are also pushing for a new means of obtaining union recognition. Instead of secret-ballot elections, unions are pushing for a "*card check*" system. Here the union would win recognition when a majority of workers signed authorization cards saying they want to unionize. Several large employers, including Cingular Wireless, agreed to the card check process.[66]

CLASS ACTION LAWSUITS   Unions are also using class action lawsuits to support employees in nonunionized companies to pressure employers. For example, unions recently used class action lawsuits to support workers' claims under the Fair Labor Standards Act and the Equal Pay Act.[67]

COORDINATION   Unions are becoming more proactive in terms of coordinating their efforts.[68] For example, UNITE used its "Voice at Work" campaign to coordinate 800 workers at one employer's distribution center with others at the employer's New York City headquarters and with local activists and international unions throughout Europe. This forced the employer's parent company, a French conglomerate, to cease resisting the union's organizing efforts.

GLOBAL CAMPAIGNS   Unions are also forcefully extending their reach overseas, as the accompanying Global Issues in HR feature explains.

COOPERATIVE ARRANGEMENTS   About half of all collective bargaining agreements encourage cooperative labor–management relationships. *Cooperative clauses* cover things like joint committees to review drug problems and safety issues.[69] The author of a recent

---

Unions Go Global

Any company that thinks it can avoid unions by sending manufacturing and jobs abroad is mistaken. Today, as we've seen, most businesses are "going global," and regional trade treaties like the North American Free Trade Agreement (NAFTA) are further boosting the business done by firms abroad. This fact is not lost on unions, some of which are already expanding their influence abroad.

The unions' new global campaigns reflect the belief, as the Service Employees International Union puts it, that "Huge global service sector companies routinely cross national borders and industry lines as they search for places where they can shift operations to exploit workers with the lowest possible pay and benefits." The Service Employees International Union, for instance, is therefore strengthening its alliances with unions in other nations, with the goal of uniting workers in particular multinational companies and industries, around the globe.[70]

For example, the former head of the SEIU recently worked with China's All China Federation of Trade Unions (ACFTU) to help the latter organize China's Walmart stores.[71] Similarly, U.S. unions are helping Mexican unions to organize, especially in U.S.-owned factories. Thus, the United Electrical Workers is subsidizing organizers at Mexican plants of the General Electric Company. And recently, the United Steelworkers merged with the largest labor union in Britain to create "Workers Uniting" to better help the new union deal with multinational employers.[72]

By helping workers in other countries unionize, unions help raise the wage and living standards of local workers. That may in turn discourage U.S. employers from offshoring jobs. Unions also help their own positions in the United States with the added leverage they get from having unions abroad that can help them fight their corporate campaigns back in the United States. And, the UAW is training activists about how to organize rallies and protests in support of union campaigns, and sending them abroad to help organize workers at car plants overseas.[73] So, any company that thinks it can avoid unionization by sending jobs abroad may be in for a surprise.

---

review of union research says that unions "that have a cooperative relationship with management can play an important role in overcoming barriers to the effective adoption of practices that have been linked to organizational competitiveness."[74] However, she concludes that employers who want to capitalize on that potential must change their way of thinking, avoiding adversarial labor relations and instead emphasizing a cooperative partnership with unions.

REVIEW

Summary

1. The labor movement is important. About 14.7 million U.S. workers belong to unions. In addition to improved wages and working conditions, unions seek security when organizing. In addition to a completely open shop, there are five possible arrangements, including the closed shop, the union shop, the agency shop, the preferential shop, and maintenance of membership.

2. The AFL-CIO is a national federation comprising about 56 national and international unions.

3. During the period of strong encouragement of unions, the Norris-LaGuardia Act and the NLRA were passed; these marked a shift in labor law from repression to strong encouragement of union activity. They did this by banning certain types of unfair labor practices, providing for secret-ballot elections, and creating the NLRB.

4. The Taft-Hartley Act reflected the period of modified encouragement coupled with regulation. It enumerated the rights of employees with respect to their unions, enumerated the rights of employers, and allowed the U.S. president to bar temporarily national emergency strikes. Among other things, it also enumerated certain union unfair labor practices. For example, it banned unions from restraining or coercing employees from exercising their bargaining rights. And employers were explicitly given the right to express their views concerning union organization.

5. The Landrum-Griffin Act reflected the period of detailed regulation of internal union affairs. It grew out of discoveries of wrongdoing on the part of both management and union leadership and contained a bill of rights for union members. (For example, it affirms a member's right to sue his or her union.)

6. There are five steps in a union drive and election: the initial contact, obtaining authorization cards, holding a hearing with the NLRB, the campaign, and the election itself. Remember that the union need only win a majority of the votes cast, *not* a majority of the workers in the bargaining unit.

7. Bargaining collectively in good faith is the next step if the union wins the election. Good faith means that both parties communicate and negotiate, and that proposals are matched with counterproposals. Some hints on bargaining include do not hurry, be prepared, find out why, and be a good listener.

8. An impasse occurs when the parties aren't able to move further toward settlement. Third-party involvement—namely, arbitration, fact-finding, or mediation—is one alternative. Sometimes, though, a strike occurs. Responding to the strike involves such steps as shutting the facility, contracting out work, or possibly replacing the workers. Boycotts and lockouts are two other anti-impasse weapons sometimes used by labor and management.

Key Terms

right to work *248*
Norris-LaGuardia Act *249*
Wagner Act *249*
National Labor Relations Board (NLRB) *249*
Taft-Hartley Act *251*
national emergency strikes *252*
Landrum-Griffin Act *252*
union salting *253*

authorization cards *253*
bargaining unit *255*
collective bargaining *258*
good-faith bargaining *258*
voluntary bargaining items *259*
illegal bargaining items *259*
mandatory bargaining items *259*
mediation *261*

fact-finder *261*
arbitration *261*
economic strike *262*
unfair labor practice strike *262*
wildcat strike *262*
sympathy strike *262*
"take a strike" *262*
boycott *262*
lockout *263*

Discussion Questions

1. Discuss the steps in an NLRB election.
2. Describe important tactics you would expect the union to use during the union drive and election.
3. Briefly explain why labor law has gone through a cycle of repression and encouragement.
4. What is good-faith bargaining? When is bargaining not in good faith?

5. Define *impasse, mediation,* and *strike,* and explain the techniques used to overcome an impasse.
6. Individually or in teams of five to six students, choose an organization (such as this university or a company in which one student works), and list the areas in which the union has had an impact.

Individual and Group Activities

1. You are the manager of a small manufacturing plant. The union contract covering most of your employees is about to expire. Working individually or in groups, discuss how to prepare for union contract negotiations.
2. Working individually or in groups, use Internet resources to find situations where company management and the union reached an impasse at some point during their negotiation process, but eventually resolved the impasse. Describe the issues on both sides that led to the impasse. How did they move past the impasse? What were the final outcomes?

3. Several years ago, 8,000 Amtrak workers agreed not to disrupt service by walking out, at least not until a court hearing was held. Amtrak had asked the courts for a temporary restraining order, and the Transport Workers Union of America was actually pleased to postpone its walkout. The workers were apparently not upset at Amtrak, but at Congress, for failing to provide enough funding for Amtrak. What, if anything, can an employer do when employees threaten to go on strike, not because of what the employer did, but what a third party—in this case, Congress—has done or not done? What laws would prevent the union from going on strike in this case?

APPLICATION EXERCISES

CASE INCIDENT

Negotiating with the Writers Guild of America

The talks between the Writers Guild of America (WGA) and the Alliance of Motion Picture & Television Producers (producers) began tense in 2007, and then got tenser. In their first meeting, the two sides got nothing done. As *Law & Order* producer Dick Wolf said, "Everyone in the room is concerned about this."[75]

The two sides were far apart on just about all the issues. However, the biggest issue was how to split revenue from new media, such as when

television shows move on to DVDs or the Internet. The producers said they wanted a profit-splitting system rather than the current residual system. Under the residual system, writers continue to receive "residuals," or income from shows they write, every time they're shown (such as when the Jerry Seinfeld show appears in reruns, years after they shot the last original show). Writers Guild executives did their homework. They argued, for instance, that their projections showed producers'

(continued)

revenues from advertising and subscription fees jumped by about 40% between 2002 and 2006.[76]

The situation grew tenser. After the first few meetings, one producers' representative said, "we will see after the dogfight whose position will win out. The open question there, of course, is whether each of us takes several lumps at the table, reaches an agreement then licks their wounds later—none the worse for wear—or whether we inflict more lasting damage through work stoppages that benefit no one before we come to an agreement."[77] Even after meeting six times, it seemed that, "the parties' only apparent area of agreement is that no real bargaining has yet to occur."[78]

In October 2007, the Writers Guild asked its members for strike authorization; the producers claimed that the guild was just trying to delay negotiations until the current contract expired (at the end of October). As the president of the television producers association said, "We have had six across the table sessions and there was only silence and stonewalling from the WGA leadership.... The WGA leadership apparently has no intention to bargain in good faith."[79] As evidence, the producers claimed that the WGA negotiating committee left one meeting after less than an hour at the bargaining table.

Both sides knew timing in these negotiations was crucial. During the fall and spring, television series production is in full swing. So a strike now by the writers would have a bigger impact than waiting until, say, the summer to strike.

Perhaps not surprisingly, by January 2008, some movement was discernible. In a separate set of negotiations, the Directors Guild of America reached an agreement with the producers that addressed many of the issues that the writers were focusing on, such as how to divide the new media income.[80] In February 2008, the WGA and producers finally reached agreement. The new contract was "the direct result of renewed negotiations between the two sides, which culminated Friday with a marathon session including top WGA officials and the heads of the Walt Disney Co. and News Corp."[81]

QUESTIONS

1. The producers said the WGA was not bargaining in good faith. What did they mean by that, and do you think the evidence is sufficient to support the claim?
2. The WGA did eventually strike. What tactics could the producers have used to fight back once the strike began? What tactics do you think the WGA used?
3. This was a conflict between professional and creative people (the WGA) and TV and movie producers. Do you think the conflict was therefore different in any way than are the conflicts between, say, the auto workers or Teamsters unions against auto and trucking companies? Why?
4. What role (with examples, please) did negotiating skills seem to play in the WGA–producers negotiations?

CONTINUING CASE

Carter Cleaning Company

The Grievance

On visiting one of Carter Cleaning Company's stores, Jennifer was surprised to be taken aside by a long-term Carter employee, who met her as she was parking her car. "Murray (the store manager) told me I was suspended for 2 days without pay because I came in late last Thursday," said George. "I'm really upset, but around here the store manager's word seems to be law, and it sometimes seems like the only way anyone can file a grievance is by meeting you or your father like this in the parking lot." Jennifer was very disturbed by this revelation and promised the employee she would look into it and discuss the situation with her father. In the car heading back to headquarters, she began mulling over what Carter Cleaning Company's alternatives might be. She wants your advice on the following.

QUESTIONS

1. Do you think it is important for Carter Cleaning Company to have a formal grievance process? Why or why not?

2. Based on what you know about the Carter Cleaning Company, outline the steps for what you think would be the ideal grievance process for this company.

3. In addition to the grievance process, can you think of anything else that Carter Cleaning Company might do to make sure grievances and gripes like this one are expressed and are heard by top management?

EXPERIENTIAL EXERCISE

The Union-Organizing Campaign at Pierce U

Purpose: The purpose of this exercise is to give you practice in dealing with some of the elements of a union-organizing campaign.[82]

Required Understanding: You should be familiar with the material covered in this chapter, as well as the following incident, "An Organizing Question on Campus."

INCIDENT: An Organizing Question on Campus: Art Tipton is HR director of Pierce University, a private university located in a large urban city. Ruth Zimmer, a supervisor in the maintenance and housekeeping services division of the university, has just come into Tipton's office to discuss her situation. Zimmer's division is responsible for maintaining and cleaning physical facilities of the university. Zimmer is one of the department supervisors who supervise employees who maintain and clean on-campus dormitories.

In the next several minutes, Zimmer proceeds to express her concerns about a union-organizing campaign that has begun among her employees. According to Zimmer, a representative of the Service Workers Union has met with several of her employees, urging them to sign union authorization cards. She has observed several of her employees "cornering" other employees to talk to them about joining the union and to urge

them to sign union authorization (or representation) cards. Zimmer even observed this during working hours as employees were going about their normal duties in the dormitories. Zimmer reports that a number of her employees have come to her asking for her opinions about the union. They told her that several other supervisors in the department had told their employees not to sign any union authorization cards and not to talk about the union at any time while they were on campus. Zimmer also reports that one of her fellow supervisors told his employees that anyone caught talking about the union or signing a union authorization card would be disciplined and perhaps dismissed.

Zimmer says that her employees are very dissatisfied with their wages and with the conditions that they have endured from students, supervisors, and other staff people. She says that several employees told her that they had signed union cards because they believed that the only way university administration would pay attention to their concerns was if the employees had a union. Zimmer says that she made a list of employees whom she felt had joined or were interested in the union, and she could share these with Tipton if he wanted. Zimmer closed her presentation with the comment that she and other department supervisors need to know what they should do in order to stomp out the threat of unionization in their department.

How to Set Up the Exercise/Instructions: If so desired, divide the class into groups. Assume that

(continued)

you are labor relations consultants the university retained to identify the problems and issues involved and to advise Tipton on the university's rights and what to do next. Each group will spend about 45 minutes discussing the issues. Then, outline those issues, as well as an action plan for Tipton. What should he do next?

If time permits, list on the board the issues involved and the group's recommendations. What should Tipton do?

Ten

Protecting Safety and Health

When you finish studying this chapter, you should be able to:

- Discuss *OSHA—What it is and how it operates.*
- Describe *the supervisor's role in safety.*
- Explain *in detail three basic causes of accidents.*
- Explain *how to prevent accidents at work.*
- Discuss *major health problems at work and how employers remedy them.*

OVERVIEW

It was a frightening way to die. The worker "suffocated when the tumbling dirt and debris rose to his chest, creating pressure so great that he could not breathe, even though his head remained uncovered."[1] The main purpose of this chapter is to explain how to prevent accidents at work. The main topics we cover include Employee Safety and Health: An Introduction, What Causes Accidents, How to Prevent Accidents, and Workplace Health Hazards: Problems and Remedies.

EMPLOYEE SAFETY AND HEALTH: AN INTRODUCTION

Why Employee Safety and Health Are Important

Safety and accident prevention concern managers for several reasons, one of which is the staggering number of workplace accidents. The accident rate is falling but in one recent year 4,551 U.S. workers died in workplace incidents.[2] Workplace accidents in the United States cause over 3.8 million occupational injuries and illnesses per year—roughly 3.6 cases per 100 equivalent full-time workers.[3] More than 80% of the workers in one survey ranked workplace safety as more important than minimum wages, sick days, and maternity leave.[4]

Dangerous workplaces aren't limited to manufacturing plants. For example, in restaurants, slips and falls account for about a third of worker injury cases. Employers could eliminate most of these falls by requiring slip-resistant shoes.[5]

A Manager's Briefing on Occupational Law

Congress passed the **Occupational Safety and Health Act** in 1970 "to assure so far as possible every working man and woman in the nation safe and healthful working conditions and to preserve our human resources."[6] The main employers not covered by the act are self-employed persons, farms in which only immediate members of the employer's family work, and certain workplaces covered by other federal agencies or statutes. The act covers federal agencies, but usually not state and local governments in their role as employers.

The act created the **Occupational Safety and Health Administration (OSHA)** within the Department of Labor. OSHA's basic purpose is to administer the act and to set and enforce the safety and health standards that apply to almost all workers in the United States. OSHA has inspectors working out of branch offices throughout the United States.

OSHA STANDARDS   OSHA operates under the "general duty clause" that each employer "shall furnish to each of his [or her] employees employment and a place of employment which are free from recognized hazards that are causing or are likely to cause death or serious physical harm to his [or her] employees."

To carry out this basic mission, OSHA is responsible for promulgating legally enforceable standards. The standards are very complete and cover just about every conceivable hazard, in detail (see Figure 10-1).

OSHA RECORD-KEEPING PROCEDURES   Under OSHA's regulations, employers with 11 or more employees must maintain a record of, and report, occupational injuries and occupational illnesses. An *occupational illness* is any abnormal condition or disorder

---

> Guardrails not less than 2″ × 4″ or the equivalent and not less than 36″ or more than 42″ high, with a midrail, when required, of a 1″ × 4″ lumber or equivalent, and toeboards, shall be installed at all open sides on all scaffolds more than 10 feet above the ground or floor. Toeboards shall be a minimum of 4″ in height. Wire mesh shall be installed in accordance with paragraph [a] (17) of this section.

FIGURE 10-1 OSHA Standards Example.   *Source:* From United States Department of Labor, OSHA (www.osha.gov/pls/oshaweb/owadisp.show_document?p_id=9720&p_table=STANDARDS, accessed May 25, 2012).

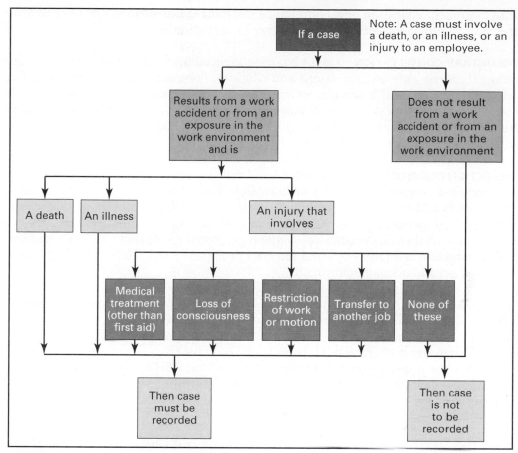

FIGURE 10-2 What Accidents Must Be Reported under the Occupational Safety and Health Act?

caused by exposure to environmental factors associated with employment. This includes acute and chronic illnesses caused by inhalation, absorption, ingestion, or direct contact with toxic substances or harmful agents.

As summarized in Figure 10-2, employers must report all occupational illnesses.[7] They must also report occupational injuries that result in medical treatment (other than first aid), loss of consciousness, restriction of work (1 or more lost workdays), restriction of motion, or transfer to another job.[8]

If an on-the-job accident results in the death of an employee or in the hospitalization of five or more employees, all employers, regardless of size, must report the accident to the nearest OSHA office. OSHA's latest record-keeping rules allow the employer to conclude that the event was not job related (and needn't be reported) if the facts so warrant—such as if a worker breaks his leg on his car's bumper when parked on the company lot.

INSPECTIONS AND CITATIONS   OSHA enforces its standards through inspections and (if necessary) citations. The inspection is usually unannounced. OSHA may not conduct inspections without a search warrant or the employer's consent.[9] With a limited number of inspectors, OSHA recently has focused on "fair and effective enforcement," combined with outreach, education and compliance assistance, and various OSHA–employer cooperative programs (such as its "Voluntary Protection Programs").[10]

VOLUNTARY CONSULTATION   OSHA has tried to encourage cooperative safety programs rather than rely only on inspections and citations. For example, OSHA provides free on-site safety and health services for small businesses, using state government safety experts. As the owner of one small business who used this service said, "Our workers' compensation costs have decreased significantly, we have had no accidents, and there is an awareness that we take safety seriously."[11]

INSPECTION PRIORITIES   However, OSHA still makes extensive use of inspections, taking a "worst-first" approach. Priorities include, from highest to lowest, imminent dangers, catastrophes and fatal accidents, employee complaints, high-hazard industries inspections, and follow-up inspections.[12] In one recent year, OSHA conducted over 39,000 inspections. Of these, complaints or accidents prompted 9,176; about 21,500 were high-hazard targeted; and follow-ups and referrals prompted 8,415. Those with high injury rates may get additional monitoring.[13]

THE INSPECTION   OSHA inspectors look for violations of all types, but some potential problem areas seem to grab more of their attention. Figure 10-3 summarizes the most frequent OSHA standards violation areas. Employers may and should restrict admittance until the manager in charge/OSHA coordinator is on site.[14]

    After the inspector submits the report to the local OSHA office, the area director determines what citations, if any, to issue. The **citations** inform the employer and employees of the regulations and standards violated and of the time set for rectifying the problem.

PENALTIES   OSHA can also impose penalties.[15] In general, OSHA calculates these based on the gravity of the violation and usually takes into consideration such factors as the size of the business, the firm's compliance history, and the employer's good faith efforts. Penalties generally range from $5,000 to up to $70,000 for willful or repeat serious violations, but can be higher. Many employers settle with OSHA before litigation in

---

Scaffolding, general requirements, construction
Fall protection, construction
Hazard communication standard, general industry
Respiratory protection, general industry
Control of hazardous energy (lockout/tagout)
Electrical, wiring methods, components and equipment
Powered industrial trucks, general industry
Ladders, construction
Electrical systems design, general requirements
Machines, general requirements

FIGURE 10-3 Most Frequently Cited OSHA Standards.   *Source:* www.osha.gov/dcsp/compliance_assistance/frequent_standards.html accessed May 28, 2012.

pre-citation settlements.[16] The citation and agreed-on penalties are issued simultaneously, after the employers initiate negotiation settlements with OSHA.[17]

Inspectors and their superiors don't look just at specific hazards but also for evidence of a comprehensive safety approach. For example, factors contributing to a firm's OSHA liability include lack of a systematic safety approach, not following up on employee safety complaints, and failure to inspect the workplace regularly.[18]

While some employers understandably view OSHA inspections with some trepidation, the inspection checklist in Figure 10-4 can help the manager reduce problems ahead of time.[19]

RESPONSIBILITIES AND RIGHTS OF EMPLOYERS AND EMPLOYEES Both employers and employees have responsibilities and rights under the Occupational Safety and Health Act. For example, employers are responsible for providing "a workplace free from recognized hazards," for being familiar with OSHA standards, and for ensuring that workplace conditions conform with applicable standards.

Employees also have rights and responsibilities, but OSHA can't cite them for violations of their responsibilities. They are responsible, for example, for complying with all applicable OSHA standards, for following all employer safety and health rules and regulations, and for reporting hazardous conditions to the supervisor. Employees have a right to demand safety and health on the job without fear of punishment. Employers may not punish or discriminate against workers who complain to OSHA about safety and health hazards. But the Occupational Safety and Health Review Commission (which reviews OSHA decisions) says employers must make "a diligent effort to discourage, by discipline if necessary, violations of safety rules by employees."[20] Although employees have a responsibility to comply with OSHA standards, they often resist; the employer usually remains liable for any penalties.[21]

WHAT CAUSES ACCIDENTS?

Following an accident in which four workers lost their lives, management at the Golden Eagle refinery east of San Francisco Bay shut down the facility for 4 months, retrained all employees in safety methods, and created six new safety management positions.[22]

Accidents occur for three main reasons: chance occurrences, unsafe working conditions, and unsafe acts by employees. Chance occurrences (such as getting hit by a car) contribute to accidents but are more or less beyond management's control; we will therefore focus on unsafe conditions and unsafe acts.

Unsafe Conditions

Unsafe conditions are one main cause of accidents. These include:

- Improperly guarded equipment
- Defective equipment
- Unsafe storage, such as overloading
- Improper illumination, such as insufficient light
- Improper ventilation, such as insufficient air change[23]

FORM **CD-574**
(2/03)

U.S. Department of Commerce
Office Safety Inspection Checklist for
Supervisors and Program Managers

Name:	Division:
Location:	Date:
Signature:	

This checklist is intended as a guide to assist supervisors and program managers in conducting safety and health inspections of their work areas. It includes questions relating to general office safety, ergonomics, fire prevention, and electrical safety. Questions which receive a "NO" answer require corrective action. If you have questions or need assistance with resolving any problems, please contact your safety office. More information on office safety is available through the Department of Commerce Safety Office website at **http://ohrm.doc.gov/safetyprogram/safety.htm**

Work Environment

Yes	No	N/A	
O	O	O	Are all work areas clean, sanitary, and orderly?
O	O	O	Is there adequate lighting?
O	O	O	Is the noise level within an acceptable range?
O	O	O	Is ventilation adequate?

Walking/Working Surfaces

Yes	No	N/A	
O	O	O	Are aisles and passages free of stored material that may present trip hazards?
O	O	O	Are tile floors in places like kitchens and bathrooms free of water and slippery substances?
O	O	O	Are carpet and throw rugs free of tears or trip hazards?
O	O	O	Are hand rails provided on all fixed stairways?
O	O	O	Are treads provided with anti-slip surfaces?
O	O	O	Are step ladders provided for reaching overhead storage areas and are materials stored safely?
O	O	O	Are file drawers kept closed when not in use?
O	O	O	Are passenger and freight elevators inspected annually and are the inspection certificates available for review on-site?
O	O	O	Are pits and floor openings covered or otherwise guarded?
O	O	O	Are standard guardrails provided wherever aisle or walkway surfaces are elevated more than 48 inches above any adjacent floor or the ground?
O	O	O	Is furniture free of any unsafe defects?
O	O	O	Are heating and air conditioning vents clear of obstructions?

Ergonomics

Yes	No	N/A	
O	O	O	Are employees advised of proper lifting techniques?
O	O	O	Are workstations configured to prevent common ergonomic problems? (Chair height allows employees' feet to rest flat on the ground with thighs parallel to the floor, top of computer screen is at or slightly below eye level, keyboard is at elbow height. Additional information on proper configuration of workstations is available through the Commerce Safety website at http://ohrm.doc.gov/safetyprogram/safety.htm)
O	O	O	Are mechanical aids and equipment, such as; lifting devices, carts, or dollies provided where needed?
O	O	O	Are employees surveyed annually on their ergonomic concerns?

Emergency Information (Postings)

Yes	No	N/A	
O	O	O	Are established emergency phone numbers posted where they can be readily found in case of an emergency?
O	O	O	Are employees trained on emergency procedures?
O	O	O	Are fire evacuation procedures/diagrams posted?
O	O	O	Is emergency information posted in every area where you store hazardous waste?
O	O	O	Is established facility emergency information posted near a telephone?
O	O	O	Are the OSHA poster and other required posters displayed conspicuously?
O	O	O	Are adequate first aid supplies available and properly maintained?
O	O	O	Are an adequate number of first aid trained personnel available to respond to injuries and illnesses until medical assistance arrives?
O	O	O	Is a copy of the facility fire prevention and emergency action plan available on site?
O	O	O	Are safety hazard warning signs/caution signs provided to warn employees of pertinent hazards?

FIGURE 10-4 Manager's Safety Checklist.   *Source:* From U.S. Department of Commerce (http://ocio.os.doc.gov).

FORM **CD-574**
(2/03)

Fire Prevention

Yes	No	N/A	
O	O	O	Are flammable liquids, such as gasoline, kept in approved safety cans and stored in flammable cabinets?
O	O	O	Are portable fire extinguishers distributed properly (less than 75 feet travel distance for combustibles and 50 feet for flammables)?
O	O	O	Are employees trained on the use of portable fire extinguishers?
O	O	O	Are portable fire extinguishers visually inspected monthly and serviced annually?
O	O	O	Are areas around portable fire extinguishers free of obstructions and properly labeled?
O	O	O	Is heat-producing equipment used in a well ventilated area?
O	O	O	Are fire alarm pull stations clearly marked and unobstructed?
O	O	O	Are proper clearances maintained below sprinkler heads (i.e., 18" clear)?

Emergency Exits

Yes	No	N/A	
O	O	O	Are doors, passageways or stairways that are neither exits nor access to exits and which could be mistaken for exits, appropriately marked "NOT AN EXIT," "TO BASEMENT," "STOREROOM," etc.?
O	O	O	Are a sufficient number of exits provided?
O	O	O	Are exits kept free of obstructions or locking devices which could impede immediate escape?
O	O	O	Are exits properly marked and illuminated?
O	O	O	Are the directions to exits, when not immediately apparent, marked with visible signs?
O	O	O	Can emergency exit doors be opened from the direction of exit travel without the use of a key or other significant effort when the building is occupied?

Electrical Systems

(Please have your facility maintenance person or electrician accompany you during this part of the inspection)

Yes	No	N/A	
O	O	O	Are all cord and cable connections intact and secure?
O	O	O	Are electrical outlets free of overloads?
O	O	O	Is fixed wiring used instead of flexible/extension cords?
O	O	O	Is the area around electrical panels and breakers free of obstructions?
O	O	O	Are high-voltage electrical service rooms kept locked?
O	O	O	Are electrical cords routed such that they are free of sharp objects and clearly visible?
O	O	O	Are all electrical cords grounded?
O	O	O	Are electrical cords in good condition (free of splices, frays, etc.)?
O	O	O	Are electrical appliances approved (Underwriters Laboratory, Inc. (UL), etc)?
O	O	O	Are electric fans provided with guards of not over one-half inch, preventing finger exposures?
O	O	O	Are space heaters UL listed and equipped with shutoffs that activate if the heater tips over?
O	O	O	Are space heaters located away from combustibles and properly ventilated?
O	O	O	In your electrical rooms are all electrical raceways and enclosures securely fastened in place?
O	O	O	Are clamps or other securing means provided on flexible cords or cables at plugs, receptacles, tools, equipment, etc., and is the cord jacket securely held in place?

Material Storage

Yes	No	N/A	
O	O	O	Are storage racks and shelves capable of supporting the intended load and materials stored safely?
O	O	O	Are storage racks secured from falling?
O	O	O	Are office equipment stored in a stable manner, not capable of falling?

FIGURE 10-4 Continued

The basic remedy here is to eliminate or minimize the unsafe conditions. OSHA standards address the mechanical and physical working conditions that cause accidents. The manager can use a checklist of unsafe conditions for spotting problems as in Figure 10-4; another checklist is in the following HR in Practice feature. The *EHS Today* website for environment, health, and safety officers (http://ehstoday.com/) is a good source for safety and health information.

HR IN PRACTICE

Checklist of Accident-Causing Conditions

I. General Housekeeping

Adequate and wide aisles—no materials protruding into aisles

Parts and tools stored safely after use—not left in hazardous positions that could cause them to fall

Even and solid flooring—no defective floors or ramps that could cause falling or tripping accidents

Waste and trash cans—safely located and not overfilled

Material piled in safe manner—not too high or too close to sprinkler heads

All work areas clean and dry

All exit doors and aisles clean of obstructions

Aisles kept clear and properly marked; no air lines or electric cords across aisles

II. Material-Handling Equipment and Conveyances

On all conveyances, electric or hand, check to see that the following items are all in sound working condition:

Brakes—properly adjusted

Not too much play in steering wheel

Warning device—in place and working

Wheels—securely in place; properly inflated

Fuel and oil—enough and right kind

No loose parts

Cables, hooks, or chains—not worn or otherwise defective

Suspended chains or hooks

Safety loaded

Properly stored

III. Ladders, Scaffold, Benches, Stairways, etc.

The following items of major interest to be checked:

Safety feet on straight ladders

Guardrails or handrails

Treads, not slippery

No splintered, cracked, or rickety stairs

Ladders properly stored

Extension ladder ropes in good condition

Toeboards

IV. Power Tools (Stationary)

Point of operation guarded

Guards in proper adjustment

Gears, belts, shafting, counterweights guarded

Foot pedals guarded

Brushes provided for cleaning machines

Adequate lighting

Properly grounded

Tool or material rests properly adjusted

Adequate work space around machines

Control switch easily accessible

Safety glasses worn

Gloves worn by persons handling rough or sharp materials

No gloves or loose clothing worn by persons operating machines

V. Hand Tools and Miscellaneous

In good condition—not cracked, worn, or otherwise defective

Properly stored

Correct for job

Goggles, respirators, and other personal protective equipment worn where necessary

VI. Spray Painting

Explosion-proof electrical equipment

Proper storage of paints and thinners in approved metal cabinets

Fire extinguishers adequate and suitable; readily accessible

Minimum storage in work area

VII. Fire Extinguishers

Properly serviced and tagged

Readily accessible

Adequate and suitable for operations involved

Source: Courtesy of the Insurance Services Office, Inc., from "A Safety Committee Man's Guide" (1977): 1–64. Includes copyrighted material of ISO Properties, Inc. with its permission.

Although accidents can occur anywhere, there are high-danger zones. About one-third of industrial accidents occur around forklift trucks, wheelbarrows, and other handling and lifting areas. The most serious accidents usually occur near metal and woodworking machines and saws, or around gears, pulleys, and flywheels.

OTHER WORKING CONDITION–RELATED CAUSES OF ACCIDENTS   Some working condition–related causes of accidents involve the psychology or "safety climate" of the workplace. One early study focused on the official hearings of fatal accidents suffered by British oil workers in the North Sea.[24] It found that some of the less obvious working conditions that set the stage for accidents included a strong pressure to complete the work quickly, and employees who were under stress. Another study involved 1,127 nurses working in 42 large hospitals in the United States. The researchers measured safety climate using items such as "job duties on this unit often prevent nurses from acting as safely as they would like." Here "the results revealed that safety climate predicted medication errors, nurse back injuries, urinary tract infections, [and] patient satisfaction."[25] Accidents also occur more frequently in plants with a high seasonal layoff rate, hostility among employees, garnished wages, and blighted living conditions. Temporary stress factors such as high workplace temperature and a congested workplace also relate to accident rates.

Similarly, accident rates usually don't increase noticeably during the first 5 or 6 hours of the workday, but after 6 hours, the accident rate accelerates. This is due partly to fatigue and partly to the fact that accidents occur more often during night shifts.

Unsafe Acts

In practice, you can't eliminate accidents just by reducing unsafe conditions. People cause accidents, and there's no surefire way to eliminate **unsafe acts** such as:

- Throwing materials
- Operating or working at unsafe speeds—either too fast or too slow
- Lifting improperly[26]

There is no one explanation for why an employee behaves unsafely. Sometimes (as noted earlier) working conditions such as stress may set the stage. Sometimes, employers don't provide employees with the correct safe procedures, and employees then simply develop their own (often bad) work habits. However, the employee's attitudes, personality, or skills often explain the bad behavior.

What Traits Characterize "Accident-Prone" People?

It may seem intuitively obvious that some people are simply accident prone, but the research isn't clear. On closer inspection it turns out some "accident repeaters" were just unlucky, or may have been more meticulous about reporting their accidents.[27] However, people who are impulsive, sensation seeking, extremely extroverted, and less conscientious (in terms of being less fastidious and dependable) are more likely to have accidents.[28]

Furthermore, the person who is accident prone on one job may not be so on a different job. Driving is one example. Personality traits that correlate with filing vehicular insurance claims include *entitlement* ("bad drivers think there's no reason they should not speed or run lights"), *impatience* ("drivers with high claim frequency were 'always in a hurry'"), and *aggressiveness* ("always the first to want to move when the red light turns green").[29]

HOW TO PREVENT ACCIDENTS

The thing to remember about accidents is that it's not always the employee's fault. Certainly, screening out or firing impulsive employees may reduce unsafe behaviors. However, so will mopping up oil spills and placing guardrails around machines.[30] In practice, accident causes tend to be multifaceted, so the manager has to take a multifaceted approach to preventing them.[31] In this section we will address about 15 accident-prevention methods.

Reduce Unsafe Conditions

Reducing unsafe conditions is an employer's first line of safety defense. For example, *lockout/tagout* is a procedure to disable equipment to avoid an unexpected release of electrical or other energy. It includes affixing a lockout/tagout tag to, say, a power saw, to show it's disabled.[32] For machinery, employees can also use emergency stop devices, such as oversized buttons, to instantly cut power.[33]

Next, management can provide personal protective equipment (PPE). For example, Prevent Blindness America estimates that each year more than 700,000 Americans injure their eyes at work, and that employers could avoid 90% of these injuries with safety eyewear.[34]

Getting employees to wear personal protective equipment is difficult.[35] In addition to providing reliable protection, protective gear should fit properly; be easy to care for and maintain; be flexible and lightweight; provide comfort and reduce heat stress; have rugged construction; be relatively easy to put on and take off; and be easy to clean, dispose of, and recycle.[36]

However, reducing unsafe conditions should always come first. Then use administrative controls (such as job rotation to reduce long-term exposure to the hazard). Only then turn to personal protective equipment.[37]

MANAGING THE NEW WORKFORCE: PROTECTING VULNERABLE WORKERS   Employers should pay special attention to vulnerable workers. Among others, these may include young, immigrant, older or women workers.[38]

For example, hand injuries account for about one million emergency department visits annually by U.S. workers.[39] However, while about half of all workers are women, most machinery and PPE (like gloves) are designed for men.[40] As the CEO of one safety engineering company said, "For decades, women essentially were ignored when it came to designing eye and face protection."[41] The solution is to make sure the equipment and machines women use are appropriate for their size.[42]

Similarly, older workers can do manufacturing jobs very effectively.[43] However, there are potential physical changes associated with aging, including loss of strength, loss of muscular flexibility, and reduced reaction time.[44] This means that employers should make special provisions, such as designing jobs to reduce heavy lifting.[45] The fatality rate for older workers is about three times that of younger workers.[46]

JOB HAZARD ANALYSIS   Recently, a Yale University science student, working late in a lab, was injured critically when her hair became caught in a spinning lathe. **Job hazard analysis** involves a systematic approach to identifying and eliminating such hazards before they occur. According to OSHA, job hazard analysis "focuses on the relationship between the worker, the task, the tools, and the work environment," and ends by reducing the potential risks to acceptable levels.[47]

Performing a job hazard analysis at the Yale science lab might involve looking at the situation and asking these questions:

- **What can go wrong?** A student's hair or clothing could come into contact with the lathe, a rotating object that "catches" it and pulls it into the machine.
- **What are the consequences?** The student could receive a severe injury as his or her body part or hair is caught up in and drawn to the spinning lathe.
- **How could it happen?** The accident could happen as a result of the student leaning too close to the lathe while working at the bench, or walking too close to the lathe, or bending to reach for an article that fell close to the lathe.
- **What are other contributing factors?** Speed is one contributing factor. The problem would occur so quickly that the student would be unable to take evasive action once the lathe ensnarled the hair.

The job hazard analysis should provide the basis for creating countermeasures. For example, given the speed with which such an accident would occur here, it's unlikely that training by itself would suffice. Instead, the lathe area should be ensconced in its own protective casing, and changes made to ensure that the lathe can't spin unless the student takes action via a foot pedal to keep the lathe power on.

OPERATIONAL SAFETY REVIEWS   After the Fukushima nuclear power plant in northern Japan exploded in 2011, many wondered if the International Atomic Energy Agency (IAEA) had conducted the necessary operational safety reviews. **Operational safety reviews** (or safety operations reviews) are conducted by agencies to ascertain whether units under their jurisdiction are complying with applicable safety laws and rules.[48]

Reducing Unsafe Acts

While guardrails and personal protective equipment are indispensable, human misbehavior will short-circuit the best safety efforts. Misbehavior needn't be intentional. For example, distractions—whether from texting or glancing back to check on a child—contribute to at least half of all car accidents. At work, not noticing moving or stationary objects or that a floor is wet are frequent accident causers.[49] Furthermore (and ironically), "making a job safer with machine guards or PPE lowers people's risk perceptions and thus can lead to an increase in at-risk behavior."[50]

Unfortunately, just telling workers to "pay attention" is usually not enough. Instead, it requires a process. First, identify and try to eliminate potential risks, such as slippery floors. Next, reduce potential distractions, such as noise, heat, and stress. (Thus, President Obama signed an executive order prohibiting most federal employees from text messaging while driving on official business.[51]) Then, carefully screen and train employees, as we explain next.

Use Screening to Reduce Unsafe Acts

Accidents are similar to other types of poor performance, and psychologists have had success in screening out people who might be accident prone for specific jobs. The basic technique is to identify the human trait (such as visual skill) that might relate to accidents on the specific job. Thus, screening prospective delivery drivers for impatience and aggressiveness might be sensible.[52]

Use Posters

Safety posters can also help reduce unsafe acts. In one older study, their use apparently increased safe behavior by more than 20%.[53] However, posters should be combined with other techniques like screening and training to reduce unsafe conditions and acts.

Provide Safety Training

Safety training reduces unsafe acts, especially for new employees. You should instruct employees in safe practices and procedures, warn them of potential hazards, and work on developing a safety-conscious attitude. Delta Air Lines encourages supervisors to use personal anecdotes to motivate employees to wear hearing protection. For example, "a lot of the old-timers have terrible stories and terrible hearing, because whatever they did in their past jobs … they didn't wear hearing protection."[54]

Employers use the Web to support their safety training programs.[55] For example, PureSafety (www.puresafety.com) enables firms to create their own training websites, complete with a "message from the safety director." Once an employer installs the PureSafety website on its intranet, it can populate the site with courses from companies that supply safety courses via PureSafety.com.[56] OSHA, the National Institute for Occupational Safety and Health (NIOSH), and numerous private vendors also provide online safety training solutions.[57]

OSHA's standards require more than training. Employees must demonstrate that they actually learned what to do. (For example, OSHA's respiratory standard requires that each employee demonstrate how to inspect, put on, and remove respirator seals.[58]

OSHA has two booklets, "Training Requirements under OSHA" and "Teaching Safety and Health in the Workplace.")

However, note that the main aim of safety training is not to meet OSHA training standards. It is to impart the knowledge and skills required to reduce accidents.[59] The most effective safety training uses behavioral modeling, simulation, and hands-on training.[60]

Use Incentives and Positive Reinforcement

Some firms award incentives (such as bonuses) for meeting safety goals. However, OSHA has argued that such plans don't actually cut down on injuries or illnesses but only on injury and illness *reporting*. One option is to emphasize nontraditional reinforcement, for instance, by providing recognition awards for attending safety meetings, or for identifying hazards.[61]

Safety incentives needn't be complicated. One employer uses a suggestion box. Employees make suggestions for improvements regarding unsafe acts or conditions, the best of which result in gift certificates for their authors.[62] At the Golden Eagle refinery in California, employees earn "WINGS" points for engaging in one or more of 28 safety activities, such as taking emergency response training. Employees can earn up to $20 per month per person by accumulating points.[63]

THREE CAVEATS With respect to safety incentives, keep three things in mind. First, such programs are *not substitutes for* but just parts of comprehensive safety programs.[64]

Second, make sure that your incentives program doesn't simply produce *false accident reporting*, by encouraging workers to underreport their accidents to obtain rewards.[65]

Third, such programs can have *unforeseen consequences*. Their basic aim is to produce safe habits through reinforcement. But habitual behavior takes place without thinking, and when it comes to safety, it's usually better to have employees thinking about what they're doing.[66]

Emphasize Top-Management Commitment[67]

Safety programs require a strong and observable management commitment to safety. For example:

> One of the best examples I know of in setting the highest possible priority for safety takes place at a DuPont Plant in Germany. Each morning at the DuPont Polyester and Nylon Plant, the director and his assistants meet at 8:45 to review the past 24 hours. The first matter they discuss is not production, but safety. Only after they have examined reports of accidents and near misses and satisfied themselves that corrective action has been taken do they move on to look at output, quality, and cost matters.[68]

Similarly, Weyerhaeuser discharged the plant manager and safety manager at its West Virginia facility, allegedly because they failed to report 38 injuries and illnesses.[69]

The Supervisor's Role in Safety

After inspecting a work site where workers were installing pipes in a trench, an OSHA inspector cited an employer for violating the rule requiring employers to have a "stairway, ladder, ramp, or other safe means of egress" in deep trenches.[70] Workers needed a quick way out. As in most such cases, while the employer had the primary responsibility for safety, the local supervisor was responsible for day-to-day inspections. Here, the supervisor did not properly do his inspection. The trench collapsed, and several employees were severely injured. The point is that for a supervisor, "a daily [safety] walk-through of your workplace—whether you are working in outdoor construction, indoor manufacturing, or any place that poses safety challenges—is an essential part of your work."[71]

Foster a Culture of Safety

When it comes to creating a safety-oriented workplace, what supervisors do is usually more important than what they say.[72] For example, a strong pressure to complete the work as quickly as possible, employees who are under stress, and supervisors who never mention safety are some of the psychological signals that will trump pleas to "work safely." Important characteristics of a culture of safety include:

1. An *obvious management commitment* to safety, for instance, as exemplified by rewarding safe behavior, and beginning each workday with safety reviews;
2. *Safety communications* are frequent, and visible;
3. A *shared vision* that all accidents are preventable, for instance, as exemplified by frequent reference to safety in team meetings;
4. *Assignment of critical safety functions* (such as using checklists to identify potential hazards) to specific individuals or teams; and,
5. A *continuous process of identifying* and correcting workplace hazards.[73]

Similarly, a recent study suggests that creating a supportive environment improves safety. "Organizations can develop a supportive environment by training supervisors to be better leaders, emphasizing the importance of teamwork and social support, and establishing the value of safety."[74]

Establish a Safety Policy

The firm's safety policy should emphasize that the firm will do everything practical to reduce accidents and injuries, and that accident and injury prevention is paramount.

Set Specific Loss Control Goals

Analyze the number of accidents and safety incidents, and then set specific safety goals to achieve, for example, in terms of "lost-time injuries per number of full-time employees."

Conduct Safety and Health Inspections Regularly

Inspection is important. Safety-conscious employers routinely inspect their premises for possible safety and health problems, using checklists as in the HR in Practice feature (pp. 280–281). Similarly, they investigate all accidents and "near misses," and have a system for letting employees notify management about hazardous conditions. *Safety audits* measure injury and illness statistics, workers' compensation costs, and vehicle accident statistics.[75] Typical *safety committee* activities include evaluating safety

- Reduce unsafe conditions.
- Reduce unsafe acts.
- Use posters and other propaganda.
- Provide safety training.
- Perform a job hazard analysis.
- Conduct operational safety reviews.
- Foster a culture of safety.
- Use positive reinforcement.
- Emphasize top-management commitment.
- Emphasize safety.
- Establish a safety policy.
- Set specific loss control goals.
- Conduct safety and health inspections regularly.
- Conduct safety awareness programs.

FIGURE 10-5 Steps to Take to Reduce Workplace Accidents.

adequacy, monitoring safety audit findings, and suggesting strategies for improving safety performance. Safety metrics might include, for instance, percent conformance to safety critical behaviors and processes, level of exposure present in the workplace as measured through valid samples, and rate of adverse outcomes, such as injury rates.[76]

SAFETY AWARENESS PROGRAMS   A **safety awareness program** means that trained supervisors orient new workers regarding common safety hazards and simple prevention methods. For example, the Roadway Safety Awareness Program covers trucker safety issues such as stopping distances required at various speeds.

The trend is away from making safety something "employees are supposed to do," to making safety part of how each person lives. To paraphrase one safety director, "we made the transition to the belief that safety is each employee's moral obligation."[77]

Figure 10-5 summarizes these and other safety steps.

STRATEGY AND HR   Several years ago, a BP rig in the Gulf of Mexico exploded, with tragic consequences. To many critics of BP's safety practices, the Deepwater Horizon disaster in the Gulf rightly or wrongly reflected the fact that BP's corporate strategy emphasized cost cutting and profitability at the expense of safety. For example, 5 years earlier, a report by the Chemical Safety Board blamed a huge blast at BP's Texas City, Texas, oil refinery on cost cutting, and on a safety strategy that left in place "unsafe and antiquated equipment." To the Board and to some others who studied BP's safety practices, Deepwater was another example of how safety must start at the top, and how top management's strategy (in this case allegedly focused on cost-cutting) can trump even earnest efforts to improve employee safety behaviors.[78]

WORKPLACE HEALTH HAZARDS: PROBLEMS AND REMEDIES

Most workplace hazards aren't obvious like unguarded equipment or slippery floors. Many are unseen hazards (like chemicals) that the company produces as part of its production processes. Other problems, like drug abuse, the employees may create for themselves. In either case, these hazards are often more dangerous to workers' health and safety than are obvious hazards like slippery floors. Typical workplace exposure hazards include chemicals and other hazardous materials such as asbestos, as well as alcohol abuse, stressful jobs, ergonomic hazards (such as uncomfortable equipment), infectious diseases, smoking, and biohazards (such as mold and anthrax).[79]

Chemicals and Industrial Hygiene

For example, OSHA standards list exposure limits for about 600 chemicals. Hazardous substances like these require air sampling and other precautionary measures.

Managing such exposure hazards comes under the area of *industrial hygiene* and involves recognition, evaluation, and control. First, the facility's health and safety officers must *recognize* possible exposure hazards. This typically involves activities like facility walk-around surveys.

Having identified a possible hazard, the *evaluation* phase involves determining how severe the hazard is. This requires measuring the exposure and comparing it to some benchmark.[80]

Finally, the hazard *control* phase involves eliminating or reducing the hazard. Personal protective gear (such as face masks) is generally the last option. Before relying on these, the employer must install engineering controls (such as ventilation) and administrative controls (including training); doing so is mandatory under OSHA.

ASBESTOS EXPOSURE AT WORK   OSHA standards regarding asbestos are representative of what employers can expect here. The standards require that companies monitor the air whenever an employer expects the level of asbestos to rise to half the allowable limit (0.1 fibers per cubic centimeter). Engineering controls—walls, special filters, and so forth—are required to maintain an asbestos level that complies with OSHA standards. Only if additional efforts are required to achieve compliance can respirators be used.

Air Quality

One of the downsides of opting for environmentally "green "office buildings is that emissions from printers and other chemical pollutants can dramatically reduce air quality.[81] One solution is to institute continuous monitoring systems.

Alcoholism and Substance Abuse

About two-thirds of people with alcohol disorders work full time.[82] One study concluded that about 15% of the U.S. workforce "has either been hung over at work, been drinking shortly before showing up for work, or been drinking or impaired while on the job at least once during the previous year."[83] Some estimate that almost 13 million workers use drugs illicitly.[84] Employee alcoholism may cost U.S. employers $226 billion per year.[85] Recognizing the alcoholic on the job isn't easy. Early symptoms such as tardiness are difficult to classify.[86]

TOOLS   The most widely used self-reporting screening instruments for alcoholism are the 4-item CAGE and the 25-item MAST.[87] The former asks questions such as: Have you ever (1) attempted to Cut back on alcohol, (2) been Annoyed by comments about your drinking, (3) felt Guilty about drinking, or (4) had an Eye-opener first thing in the morning to steady your nerves.

TABLE 10-1	Observable Behavior Patterns Indicating Possible Alcohol-Related Problems	
Alcoholism Stage	**Some Possible Signs of Alcoholism Problems**	**Some Possible Alcoholism Performance Issues**
Early	Arrives at work late Untrue statements Leaves work early	Reduced job efficiency Misses deadlines
Middle	Frequent absences, especially Mondays Colleagues mentioning erratic behavior Mood swings Anxiety Late returning from lunch Frequent multi-day absences	Accidents Warnings from boss Noticeably reduced performance
Advanced	Personal neglect Unsteady gait Violent outbursts Blackouts and frequent forgetfulness Possible drinking on job	Frequent falls, accidents Strong disciplinary actions Basically incompetent performance

Sources: Based on Gopal Patel and John Adkins Jr., "The Employer's Role in Alcoholism Assistance," *Personnel Journal* 62, no. 7 (July 1983): 570; Mary-Anne Enoch and David Goldman, "Problem Drinking and Alcoholism: Diagnosis and Treatment," *American Family Physician* (February 1, 2002), www.aafp.org/afp/20020201/441.html, accessed July 20, 2008; and Ken Pidd et al., "Alcohol and Work: Patterns of Use, Workplace Culture, and Safety," www.nisu.flinders.edu.au/pubs/reports/2006/injcat82.pdf, accessed July 20, 2008.

Table 10-1 shows observable behavior patterns that indicate alcohol-related problems. As you can see, alcohol problems range from tardiness in the earliest stages of alcohol abuse to prolonged absences in its later stages.[88] Whether the alcohol abuse reflects a "disability" under the ADA depends on several things including whether the person is alcohol dependant.[89] In general, employers can hold alcohol-dependent employees to the same performance standards as they hold nonalcoholics. Many employers offer employee assistance programs (EAPs) to provide counseling.

Dealing with Substance Abuse

Ideally, a drug-free workplace program includes five components: a drug-free workplace policy, supervisor training, employee education, employee assistance, and drug testing. The policy should state, at a minimum, "The use, possession, transfer, or sale of illegal drugs by employees is prohibited." It should lay out the rationale for the policy, and the consequences for violating it. Supervisors should be trained to monitor employees' performance and to be alert for drug-related performance problems.

For many employers, dealing with substance abuse involves drug testing. In fact, many states require mandatory random drug testing of high-hazard workers. For example, New Jersey now requires random drug testing of electrical workers.[90]

Preemployment drug testing discourages drug users from both applying for and working for employers who test.[91] Some applicants or employees may try to evade the test, for instance, by purchasing "clean" specimens to use. Several states have laws making drug-test fraud a crime. An oral fluid test is more reliable.[92]

Unfortunately, drug testing may not reduce workplace accidents. One study, conducted in three hotels, concluded that preemployment drug testing seemed to have little or no effect on workplace accidents. However, a combination of preemployment and random ongoing testing was associated with a significant reduction in workplace accidents.[93]

Increasingly, by the way, it's not intoxicated drivers but "intexicated" ones that are causing the problem. Studies suggest that smartphone activity probably contributes to over 636,000 motor vehicle crashes per year. Many businesses are therefore banning cell phone use and texting activities among their drivers.[94]

The Problems of Job Stress and Burnout

Problems such as alcoholism sometimes stem from stress.[95] One survey found that one-fourth of all employees surveyed viewed their jobs as the number-one stressor in their lives.[96] Yet only 5% of surveyed U.S. employers say they're addressing workplace stress.[97]

Various external factors can trigger stress. These include work schedule, pace of work, job security, route to and from work, workplace noise, and the number and nature of customers.[98] In part due to reduced headcount and more people with second jobs, employee fatigue is a growing problem.[99] Many employers are therefore taking steps to reduce employee fatigue, such as banning mandatory overtime.

However, no two people react the same way to stressors because personal factors also influence stress. For example, people who are **workaholics** and who feel driven to always meet deadlines normally put themselves under more stress than do others.

CONSEQUENCES   Job stress has serious consequences. The human consequences of job stress may include anxiety, depression, anger, cardiovascular disease, headaches, and heart attacks.[100] Organizational consequences include diminished performance, and increased absenteeism, turnover, and grievances.[101] In one study, high-stress workers' health care costs were 46% higher than were those of their less-stressed coworkers.[102] Yet not all stress is dysfunctional. Some people, for example, find that they are more productive as a deadline approaches.

REDUCING YOUR OWN JOB STRESS   One can do several things to alleviate stress.[103] Finding a more suitable job, getting more sleep and eating better, getting counseling, and planning each day's activities are sensible responses.[104] Various experts suggest the following to reduce job stress:[105]

Build pleasant, cooperative relationships with as many of your colleagues as you can.

Work to resolve conflicts with other people.

Find time every day for detachment and relaxation.

Get away from your office from time to time for a change of scene and a change of mind.

Write down the problems that concern you, and what you're going to do about each.

Participate in something you don't find stressful, such as sports, social events or hobbies.

Create realistic goals and deadlines for yourself, and set regular progress reviews.

Prepare a list of tasks and rank them in order of priority. Throughout the day, review your list and work on tasks in priority order.

Ask for help from a parent, friend, counselor, doctor, or pastor. Talk with them about the stress you feel and problems you face.

Take care of yourself:

- Eat a healthy, well-balanced diet
- Exercise on a regular basis
- Get plenty of sleep
- Give yourself a break if you feel stressed out

Meditation is another possibility. Choose a quiet place with soft light and sit comfortably. Then focus your thoughts (for instance, by counting breaths, or by visualizing a calming location such as a beach). When your mind wanders, bring it back to focusing on your breathing, or the beach.[106] Several years ago, World Bank employees were apparently experiencing high stress levels. Trainers from a Buddhist meditation instruction group ran meditation classes at the bank. Employees generally felt the classes were useful in reducing stress.[107]

WHAT THE EMPLOYER CAN DO   The employer can help reduce job stress. One British firm follows a three-tiered approach to managing workplace stress.[108] First is *primary prevention*, which focuses on ensuring that things like job designs and workflows are correct. Second involves *intervention*, including individual employee assessment, attitude surveys to find sources of stress at work, and supervisory intervention. Third is *rehabilitation* through employee assistance programs and counseling.[109]

Some employers use "resilience training." As one example, "participants consider previous stressful situations in their lives that they have overcome and identify factors that made the situations manageable."[110]

BURNOUT   **Burnout** is a phenomenon closely associated with job stress. Experts define *burnout* as the total depletion of physical and mental resources caused by excessive striving to reach an unrealistic work-related goal. Burnout builds gradually, manifesting itself in symptoms such as irritability, discouragement, entrapment, and resentment.[111] Employers can head off burnout, for instance, by monitoring employees in potentially high-pressure jobs such as sales managers.[112]

What can a burnout candidate do? In his book *How to Beat the High Cost of Success*, Dr. Herbert Freudenberger suggests:

- *Break your patterns.* The more well rounded your life is, the better protected you are against burnout.
- *Get away from it all periodically.* Schedule occasional periods during which you get away from your usual routine.
- *Reassess your goals in terms of their intrinsic worth.* Are the goals you've set for yourself attainable? Are they really worth the sacrifice?
- *Think about your work.* Could you do as good a job without being so intense?
- *Forget about your job once you go home.* In one study, researchers measured psychological detachment from work during nonwork time with items such as "during after-work hours, I forget about work."[113] Lack of detachment from work during nonwork time predicted higher emotional exhaustion one year later.

DEPRESSION   Stress and burnout aren't the only psychological problems at work.[114] For example, employers need to work harder to ensure that depressed employees utilize support services. One survey found that while about two-thirds of large firms offered employee assistance programs covering depression, only about 14% of employees with depression said they used one.[115] Training managers to recognize signs of depression—persistent sad moods, sleeping too little, reduced appetite, difficulty in concentrating, and loss of interest in activities once enjoyed, for instance—and then making assistance more readily available can help. Depression is a disease. It does no more good to tell a depressed person to "snap out of it" than it would to tell someone with a heart condition to stop acting tired. Women (and men) should have access to domestic crisis hotlines, such as www.ndvh.org, and to the employer's employee assistance programs.

Infectious Diseases

With many employees traveling to and from international destinations, monitoring and controlling infectious diseases is an important safety issue.

Employers can take steps to prevent the entry or spread of infectious diseases:[116]

1. Closely monitor Centers for Disease Control and Prevention (CDC) travel alerts. Access this information at www.cdc.gov.
2. Provide daily medical screenings for employees returning from infected areas.
3. Deny access for 10 days to employees or visitors who have had contact with suspected infected individuals.
4. Tell employees to stay home if they have a fever or respiratory system symptoms.
5. Clean work areas and surfaces regularly. Make sanitizers easily available.
6. Stagger breaks. Offer several lunch periods to reduce overcrowding.

Special situations prompt special requirements. For example, in 2009 the CDC advised employers that health care workers working with H1N1 flu patients should use special respirators to reduce virus inhalation risks.[117]

Workplace Smoking

To some extent, the problem of workplace smoking is becoming moot. For example, many states including Delaware, Connecticut, California, and New York bar smoking in most workplaces.[118] Yet smoking continues to be a problem for employees and employers. Costs derive from higher health and fire insurance, as well as increased absenteeism and reduced productivity (which occurs, for instance, when a smoker takes a 10-minute cigarette break).[119]

WHAT YOU CAN AND CANNOT DO   In general, you can probably deny a job to a smoker as long as you don't use smoking as a surrogate for other discrimination.[120] A "no-smokers-hired" policy does not, according to one expert, violate the Americans with Disabilities Act (since smoking is not considered a disability), and in general "employers' adoption of a no-smokers-hired policy is not illegal under federal law." Most employers these days ban indoor smoking, often designating outdoor areas where smoking is permitted. Many states and municipalities ban indoor smoking in public areas (see http://www.lungusa2.org/slati/ for a list). WEYCO Inc. gave employees 15 months'

HR AS A PROFIT CENTER

Wellness Pays

The payback for wellness programs isn't theoretical. For example, over the past 20 or so years, the percentage of employees at Johnson & Johnson who smoke has dropped by more than two-thirds, in part thanks to J&J's comprehensive wellness effort. It's been reported that the company's leaders estimate that such wellness programs have saved the company about $250 million on health care costs from 2002 to 2008, a return of about $2.71 for every dollar spent on the wellness programs.[121]

---

warning and offered smoking cessation assistance. Then it began firing or forcing out all its workers who smoked, including those who did so just in their homes.[122]

WELLNESS PROGRAMS   We discussed wellness programs in Chapter 7 (Compensating Employees), but for many employers, wellness is part of their safety and health initiatives. Wegmans Food Markets Inc., for instance, encourages its employees to eat 5 cups of fruit and vegetables and walk 10,000 steps each day.[123] The accompanying HR as a Profit Center feature illustrates one program's advantages.

Computer Monitor Health Problems and How to Avoid Them

Even with flat-panel screens, there's still a risk of monitor-related health problems at work. Problems include short-term eye burning, itching, and tearing, as well as eyestrain. Backaches and neck aches also often occur because employees try to compensate for glare by maneuvering into awkward body positions. There may also be a tendency to suffer from carpal tunnel syndrome, caused by repetitive use of the hands at uncomfortable angles.[124] OSHA has no specific standards for computer workstations.[125]

   NIOSH provides general recommendations regarding computer monitors. These include:[126]

1. *Give employees rest breaks.* NIOSH recommends a 15-minute rest break after 2 hours of continuous work.
2. *Design the maximum flexibility into the workstation so that it can be adapted to the individual operator.* For example, use movable keyboards and adjustable chairs.
3. *Reduce glare with devices such as shades over windows, antiglare screen filters, and recessed or indirect lighting.*
4. *Give workers a complete preplacement vision exam to ensure properly corrected vision.*

   Other suggestions include:

5. The height of the table or chair should allow positioning of wrists at the same level as the elbow.
6. The wrists should be able to rest lightly on a pad for support.
7. The feet should be flat on the floor, or on a footrest.

Dealing with Violence at Work

A disgruntled long-term employee walked into Chrysler's Ohio Jeep assembly plant and fatally shot one worker, after reportedly being involved in an argument with a supervisor.[127]

Violence against employees is a big problem at work. As at the Jeep plant, a coworker or personal associate commits roughly one of seven workplace homicides (although robbery was the main motive for workplace homicide).[128] One report called bullying the "silent epidemic" of the workplace, "where abusive behavior, threats, and intimidation often go unreported."[129] And, workplace violence can also manifest itself in sabotaging the firm's property, software, or information databases.[130]

Most workplace violence is predictable and avoidable. *Risk Management Magazine* estimates that about 86% of past workplace violence incidents were anticipated by coworkers, who had brought them to management's attention prior to the incidents actually occurring. Yet, in most cases, management did little or nothing.[131] Steps to take include:

ADOPT A WORKPLACE VIOLENCE POLICY   Start with adopting a workplace violence policy that outlines unacceptable employee behavior and a zero-tolerance policy toward workplace violence.[132]

HEIGHTEN SECURITY MEASURES   Heightened security measures are an employer's next line of defense against workplace violence. According to OSHA, these measures include:[133]

- Improve external lighting.
- Use drop safes and post signs noting that only a limited amount of cash is on hand.
- Install silent alarms and surveillance cameras; increase the number of staff on duty.
- Issue a weapons policy that states, for instance, that regardless of their legality, firearms or other dangerous or deadly weapons cannot be brought onto the facility, either openly or concealed.[134]

IMPROVE EMPLOYEE SCREENING   With about 30% of workplace attacks committed by coworkers, screening out potentially explosive applicants is the employer's next line of defense.

Personal and situational factors both influence workplace aggression. In general, individuals scoring higher on "trait anger" (the predisposition to respond to situations with hostility) are more likely to exhibit workplace aggression. In terms of the situation, interpersonal injustice and poor leadership predict aggression against supervisors.[135]

STEPS TO TAKE   Screening is important. Obtain a detailed employment application and solicit an applicant's employment history, educational background, and references. Ask questions like, "What frustrates you?" and "Who was your worst supervisor and why?" Certain background circumstances, such as the following, may provide red flags:[136]

- An unexplained gap in employment
- Incomplete or false information on the résumé or application
- A negative, unfavorable, or false reference
- Prior insubordinate or violent behavior on the job

- A criminal history involving harassing or violent behavior
- A prior termination for cause with a suspicious (or no) explanation
- History of drug or alcohol abuse
- Strong indications of instability in the individual's work or personal life as indicated, for example, by frequent job changes or geographic moves
- Lost licenses or accreditations

USE WORKPLACE VIOLENCE TRAINING   Supervisors can be trained to identify the clues that typify potentially violent employees. Common clues include:[137]

- An act of violence on or off the job
- Erratic behavior evidencing a loss of perception or awareness of actions
- Overly confrontational or antisocial behavior
- Sexually aggressive behavior
- Isolationist or loner tendencies
- Insubordinate behavior with a threat of violence[138]
- Tendency to overreact to criticism
- Exaggerated interest in war, guns, violence, mass murders, catastrophes, and so on
- Commission of a serious breach of security
- Possession of weapons, guns, knives, or like items in the workplace
- Violation of privacy rights of others, such as searching desks or stalking
- Chronic complaining and the raising of frequent, unreasonable grievances
- A retributory or get-even attitude

The U.S. Postal Service took steps to reduce workplace threats and assaults. The steps include more background checks, drug testing, a 90-day probationary period for new hires, more stringent security (including a hotline that allows employees to report threatening situations), a zero-tolerance policy for reporting and recording potentially violent incidents, and training managers to create a healthier workplace culture.[139]

The accompanying HR in Practice feature presents suggestions for dismissing high-risk employees.

VIOLENCE TOWARD WOMEN AT WORK   While men have more fatal occupational injuries than do women, the proportion of women who are victims of assault is much higher. The Gender-Motivated Violence Act, part of the Violence against Women Act passed by Congress in 1994 (and expanded in 2006), imposes significant liabilities on employers whose women employees become violence victims.[140]

Of all females murdered at work, more than three-fourths are victims of random criminal violence carried out by an assailant unknown to the victim, as during a robbery. Coworkers, family members, or previous friends or acquaintances carry out the remaining criminal acts.[141] Tangible security improvements including better lighting, cash-drop boxes, and similar steps are especially pertinent in reducing such violent acts against women.

Terrorism

The employer can take several steps to protect its employees and physical assets from terrorist attack. Steps to take include the following: *institute policies* to check mail carefully; identify ahead of time a lean *crisis organization* that can run the company on

---

HR IN PRACTICE

Firing a High-Risk Employee

When firing a high-risk employee:

- Plan all aspects of the meeting, including its time, location, the people to be present, and agenda.
- Involve security enforcement personnel.
- Advise the employee that he or she is no longer permitted onto the employer's property.
- Conduct the meeting in a room with a door leading to the outside of the building.
- Keep the termination brief and to the point.
- Make sure he or she returns all company-owned property at the meeting.
- Don't let the person return to his or her workstation.
- Offer as generous a severance package as possible, and protect the employee's dignity by not publicizing the event.[142]

---

an interim basis; identify in advance under what conditions you will *close the company* down, what the shutdown process will be, and who can order it; institute a process to put the *crisis management team* together; prepare *evacuation plans* and make sure exits are well marked and unblocked; designate an employee who will *communicate with families* and off-site employees; identify an off-site location near your facility to use as a *staging area* for evacuated personnel; and designate in advance several employees who will do *headcounts* at the evacuation staging area.[143] Employers also use text messaging to communicate hazardous conditions quickly.[144]

Enterprise Risk Management

Identifying security and other corporate risks falls within the domain of *enterprise risk management,* which means identifying risks, and planning to and actually mitigating these risks. Thus, as part of its risk management, Walmart asks questions such as, "What are the risks? And what are we going to do about these risks?"[145] Eliminating crime and enhancing facility security are two important issues here.

SETTING UP A BASIC SECURITY PROGRAM   In simplest terms, instituting a basic security program[146] requires analyzing the current level of risk and then installing mechanical, natural, and organizational security systems.

Security programs often start with an analysis of the facility's current level of risk, preferably with security experts. For example, what is the neighborhood like? Is your facility close to major highways or railroad tracks (where, for instance, toxic fumes from the trains could present a problem)?

Having assessed the potential current level of risk, the employer then turns to assessing and improving three basic sources of facility security: natural security, mechanical security, and organizational security.[147]

Natural security means taking advantage of the facility's natural or architectural features to minimize security problems. For example, do stacks of boxes in front of your windows prevent police from observing what's happening? Are there unlit spots in your parking lot?

GLOBAL ISSUES IN HR

Crime and Punishment Abroad

Language difficulties, cultural misunderstandings, and lack of normal support systems can combine to make an accident or illness abroad a disaster. In one hospital abroad, for instance, the doctor would not perform a heart surgery until receiving $40,000 in cash. Legally, employers have a duty of care for protecting international assignees and their dependents and international business travelers.[148]

As a result, many multinationals brief their business travelers and expatriates about what to expect and how to react when confronted with a health or safety problem abroad. Many employers contract with international security firms. For example, International SOS has over 1,300 medical professionals staffing its regional centers and clinics.[149]

One security expert says that employers need a way to track global employees, as well as methods for assessing overseas risks, and a response plan should a crisis occur.[150]

Mechanical security is the utilization of security systems such as locks, intrusion alarms, access control systems, and surveillance systems that will reduce the need for continuous human surveillance.[151] Here, technological advances are making it easier for employers. Thus, for access security, biometric scanners that read thumb or palm prints or retina or vocal patterns make it easier to enforce plant security.

Finally, *organizational security* means using good management to improve security. For example, it means making sure that security staff have clearly defined duties, especially in situations such as fire, elevator entrapment, or suspicious packages.[152]

The accompanying Global Issues in HR feature provides a global perspective on safety abroad.

REVIEW

Summary

1. The area of safety and accident prevention is of concern because of the staggering number of deaths and accidents occurring at work.

2. The purpose of the Occupational Safety and Health Act is to ensure every working person a safe and healthful workplace. OSHA standards are complete and detailed, and are enforced through a system of workplace inspections. OSHA inspectors can issue citations and recommend penalties.

3. There are three basic causes of accidents: chance occurrences, unsafe conditions, and unsafe acts on the part of employees. In addition, three other work-related factors—the job itself, the work schedule, and the psychological climate—contribute to accidents.

4. Unsafe acts on the part of employees are a main cause of accidents.

5. Experts differ on whether there are accident-prone people who have accidents regardless of the job. The consensus seems to be that the person who is accident prone in one job may not be on a different job. For example, vision

is related to accident frequency for drivers, but not for other workers, such as accountants.

6. There are several approaches to preventing accidents. One is to reduce unsafe conditions. The other is to reduce unsafe acts—for example, through selection and placement, training, positive reinforcement, propaganda, and top-management commitment.

7. Alcoholism, drug addiction, stress, and emotional illness are four important health problems among employees. Alcoholism is a particularly serious problem that can drastically lower the effectiveness of your organization. Techniques including disciplining, discharge, in-house counseling, and referrals to an outside agency help deal with these problems.

8. Stress and burnout are other potential health problems at work. An employee can reduce job stress, for instance, by getting away from work for a while each day.

9. Violence against employees is an enormous problem at work. Steps that can reduce workplace violence include improved security arrangements, better employee screening, and violence-reduction training.

10. Basic facility security relies on natural security, mechanical security, and organizational security.

Key Terms

Occupational Safety
  and Health Act *274*
Occupational Safety and
  Health Administration
  (OSHA) *274*
citations *276*

unsafe conditions *277*
unsafe acts *281*
job hazard analysis *283*
operational safety
  reviews *283*

safety awareness
  program *287*
workaholic *290*
burnout *291*

Discussion Questions

1. How would you go about providing a safer workplace for your employees?
2. Discuss how you would go about minimizing the occurrence of unsafe acts on the part of your employees.
3. Discuss the basic facts about the Occupational Safety and Health Act—its purpose, standards, inspection, and rights and responsibilities.
4. Explain the supervisor's role in safety.
5. Explain what causes unsafe acts.
6. Based on what you read here, is there such a thing as an accident-prone person?
7. Describe at least five techniques for reducing accidents.
8. Explain how an employee could reduce stress at work.

Individual and Group Activities

1. Working individually or in groups, answer the question, "Is there such a thing as an accident-prone person?" Develop your answer using examples of actual people you know who seemed to be accident prone on some endeavor.

2. Working individually or in groups, compile a list of the factors at work or in school that create dysfunctional stress for you. What methods do you use for dealing with the stress?

3. An issue of the journal *EHS Today* presented information about what happens when OSHA refers criminal complaints about willful violations of its standards to the U.S. Department of Justice (DOJ). Between 1982 and 2002, OSHA referred 119 fatal cases allegedly involving willful violations of OSHA to the DOJ for criminal prosecution. The DOJ declined to pursue 57% of them, and some were dropped for other reasons. Of the remaining 51 cases, the DOJ settled 63% with pretrial settlements involving no prison time. So, counting acquittals, of the 119 cases OSHA referred to the DOJ, only 9 resulted in prison time for at least one of the defendants. "The Department of Justice is a disgrace," charged the founder of an organization for family members of workers killed on the job.

One possible explanation for this low conviction rate is that the crime in cases like these is generally a misdemeanor, not a felony, and the DOJ generally tries to focus its attention on felony cases. Given this information, what implications do you think this has for how employers and their managers should manage their safety programs, and why do you take that position?

4. A few years ago, a 315-foot-tall, 2-million-pound crane collapsed on a construction site in East Toledo, Ohio, killing four ironworkers. Do you think catastrophic failures like this are avoidable? If so, what steps would you suggest the general contractor to take to avoid a disaster like this?

5. Individually or in groups of three or four students, spend 15 minutes walking around the building in which your class is held or where you are now, listing possible natural, mechanical, and organizational security measures you'd suggest to the building's owner.

APPLICATION EXERCISES

CASE INCIDENT

The New Safety and Health Program

At first glance, a dot-com company is one of the last places you'd expect to find potential safety and health hazards—or so the owners of the training website LearnInMotion.com thought. There's no danger of moving machinery, no high-pressure lines, no cutting or heavy lifting, and certainly no forklift trucks. However, there are safety and health problems.

In terms of accident-causing conditions, for instance, the one thing dot-com companies have are cables and wires. There are cables connecting the computers to screens and to the servers, and in many cases separate cables running from some computers to separate printers. There are 10 telephones in this particular office, all on 15-foot phone lines that always seem to

be snaking around chairs and tables. There is, in fact, an astonishing amount of cable considering this is an office with fewer so-called wireless connections and with fewer than 10 employees. When the installation specialists wired the office (for electricity, high-speed cable, phone lines, burglar alarms, and computers), they estimated they used well over 5 miles of cables of one sort or another. Most of these are hidden in the walls or ceilings, but many of them snake their way from desk to desk, and under and over doorways. Several employees have tried to reduce the nuisance of having to trip over wires whenever they get up by putting their plastic chair pads over the wires closest to them. However, that still leaves many wires unprotected. In other

(continued)

cases, they brought in their own packing tape and tried to tape down the wires in those spaces where they're particularly troublesome, such as across doorways.

The cables and wires are only one of the more obvious potential accident-causing conditions. The firm's programmer, before leaving the firm, had tried to repair the main server while the unit was still electrically alive. To this day, they're not sure exactly where he stuck the screwdriver, but the result was that he was "blown across the room," as one manager put it. He was all right, but it was still a scare. And while they haven't received any claims yet, every employee spends hours at his or her computer, so carpal tunnel syndrome is a risk, as are a variety of other problems such as eyestrain and strained backs.

One recent accident particularly scared the owners. The firm uses independent contractors to deliver the firm's book- and DVD-based courses in New York and two other cities. A delivery person was riding his bike east at the intersection of Second Avenue and East 64th Street in New York when he was struck by a car going south on Second Avenue. Luckily he was not hurt, but the bike's front wheel was wrecked, and the narrow escape got the firm's two owners, Mel and Linda thinking about their lack of a safety program.

It's not just the physical conditions that concern the two owners. They also have concerns about potential health problems such as job stress and burnout. Although the business may be (relatively) safe with respect to physical conditions, it is also relatively stressful in terms of the demands it makes in hours and deadlines. It is not at all unusual for employees to get to work by 7:30 or 8 o'clock in the morning and to work through until 11 or 12 o'clock at night, at least 5 and sometimes 6 or 7 days per week.

The bottom line is that both Linda and Mel feel quite strongly that they need to do something about implementing a health and safety plan. Now they want you, their management consultants, to help them do it. Here's what they want you to do for them.

QUESTIONS

1. Based upon your knowledge of health and safety matters and your actual observations of operations that are similar to theirs, make a list of the potential hazardous conditions employees and others face at LearnInMotion.com. What should they do to reduce the potential severity of the top five hazards?
2. Would it be advisable for them to set up a procedure for screening out stress-prone or accident-prone individuals? Why or why not? If so, how should they screen them?
3. Write a short position paper on the subject, "What should we do to get all our employees to behave more safely at work?"
4. Based on what you know and on what other dot-coms are doing, write a short position paper on the subject, "What can we do to reduce the potential problems of stress and burnout in our company?"

CONTINUING CASE

Carter Cleaning Company

The New Safety Program

Employees' safety and health are very important matters in the laundry and cleaning business. Each facility is a small production plant in which machines, powered by high pressure steam and compressed air, work at high temperatures washing, cleaning, and pressing garments, often under very hot, slippery conditions. Chemical vapors are produced continually, and caustic chemicals are used in the cleaning process. High-temperature stills are almost continually "cooking down" cleaning solvents in order to remove impurities so that the solvents can be reused. If a mistake is made in this process—like injecting too much steam into the still— a boilover occurs, in which boiling chemical solvent erupts out of the still and over the floor, and on anyone who happens to be standing in its way.

As a result of these hazards and the fact that chemically hazardous waste is continually produced in these stores, several government agencies (including OSHA and the Environmental Protection Agency) have instituted strict guidelines regarding the management of these plants. For example, posters have to be placed in each store notifying employees of their right to be told what hazardous chemicals they are dealing with and what the proper method for handling each chemical is. Special waste-management firms must be used to pick up and properly dispose of the hazardous waste.

A chronic problem the Carters (and most other laundry owners) have is the unwillingness on the part of the cleaning/spotting workers to wear safety goggles. Not all the chemicals they use require safety goggles, but some—like the hydrofluoric acid used to remove rust stains from garments—are very dangerous. The latter is kept in special plastic containers, since it dissolves glass. The problem is that wearing safety goggles can be troublesome. They are somewhat uncomfortable, and they become smudged easily and thus cut down on visibility. As a result, Jack has always found it almost impossible to get these employees to wear their goggles.

QUESTIONS

1. How should the firm go about identifying hazardous conditions that should be rectified? Use checklists such as those in the HR in Practice feature (page 280) and Figure 10-4 to list at least 10 possible dry-cleaning store hazardous conditions.
2. Would it be advisable for the firm to set up a procedure for screening out accident-prone individuals? How should they do so?
3. How would you suggest the Carters get all employees to behave more safely at work? Also, how would you advise them to get those who should be wearing goggles to do so?

EXPERIENTIAL EXERCISE

Checking for Unsafe Conditions

Purpose: The purpose of this exercise is to give you practice in identifying unsafe conditions.

Required Understanding: You should be familiar with material covered in this chapter, particularly that on unsafe conditions and the checklist in the HR in Practice feature (pages 280–281), and Figure 10-4.

How to Set Up the Exercise/Instructions: If so desired divide the class into groups.

Assume that you are part of a safety committee retained by your school to identify and report on any possible unsafe conditions in and around the school building.

Spend about 45 minutes in and around the building you are now in for the purpose of identifying and listing possible unsafe conditions. (*Hint:* Make use of the HR in Practice checklist.)

Return to the class in about 45 minutes, and on the board list the unsafe conditions you think you have identified. How many were there? Do you think these also violate OSHA standards? How would you go about checking?

VIDEO CASE

UNION-MANAGEMENT RELATIONS (UPS)

Synopsis

The former human resources head for UPS describes what it's like (for both an employer and an employee) to work with a labor union. The roles and functions of labor unions are discussed, and the advantages and disadvantages that can accrue to both employees and management are explained. The future of unions, and other arrangements that fulfill some of the same roles that they do, are also discussed.

DISCUSSION QUESTIONS

1. From what you know about UPS, what do you think would make the union believe that the company was ripe for being organized?
2. Do you agree that unions "stifle creativity"? Why or why not?
3. Do you agree that employees who excel in nonunion environments earn more than they would in unionized companies? Why?
4. What other " replacements " for unions have helped reduce union membership, according to the chapter?

VIDEO CASE

SAFETY (CALIFORNIA HEALTH FOUNDATION)

Synopsis

Company initiatives to promote safety and emergency preparedness are discussed. These include proactive measures to encourage employee health and to prevent injuries, especially ergonomic ones. Different methods of preventing injuries are discussed, including employee health programs that reimburse employees for gym memberships, smoking cessation, weight loss, and other programs. When the company helps foster better employee health, they are more likely to perform well and remain free of injuries.

DISCUSSION QUESTIONS

1. What are some ways of lowering stress that the California Health Foundation emphasizes?
2. How are the employees at the California Health Foundation involved in ensuring an adequate response to an emergency?
3. Why are proactive measures the most appropriate for addressing ergonomic injuries?
4. Based on what you've seen to this point, how comprehensive would you say that the company's safety program is? What suggestions would you make for additional steps it should take?
5. What are the other economic side effects of accidents?
6. Do you agree that "safety in the office is a matter of attitude"? Why or why not?
7. What other steps would you suggest the company take to boost safety, for instance, what would you have supervisors do to improve the company's safety and accident record?

Module A

Practical HR Tools, Guidelines, and Systems for Managers

This module contains practical human resource management tools for first-line supervisors, managers, and small business owners. Its aim is to supplement Chapters 1–10 by providing additional HR tools, guidelines and systems managers can use for common tasks like recruiting and interviewing candidates and communicating with your employees.

RECRUITMENT

Even department managers in Fortune 500 companies who have open positions to fill may find that recruiting good candidates isn't easy. For example, you may find that your local HR office will do little recruiting, other than, perhaps, placing an ad on the company website or on an online job board or in the local paper. On the other hand, your firm almost surely will not let you place your own help wanted ads. What to do? There are good options. Use word of mouth to "advertise" your open position within and outside your company. Make sure everyone in your company who may conceivably know of a candidate knows that the position is open, and what it entails. And, be aggressive about letting your friends and colleagues in other firms know you are recruiting, and to watch for possible candidates.

On the other hand, those managing small businesses may well have to do their own recruiting, without an HR department's aid. According to *Inc.* magazine, it is especially important here to be highly focused in how you spend your recruiting dollars. For example, use job boards that target your particular industry or city to minimize irrelevant applicants.[1] Thus, Jobing.com maintains 41 city-specific job sites in 19 states. Beyond.com hosts more than 15,000 industry-specific communities. To reduce the interviewing burden, consider using online tests like those we discussed in this book to test skills such as proficiency at QuickBooks or even ability to sell over the phone. Vendors such as PreVisor and Kenexa offer several inexpensive online testing packages.[2]

NuView, which costs about $6 to $15 per month per user, can ask applicants online questions and bump out those who lack, for instance, the required education.[3] And, here, too, tap friends and employees for recommendations, and use social networking sites such as LinkedIn and Facebook to find candidates who may not even be actively seeking new positions.[4]

EMPLOYEE SELECTION

Managers' Guidelines for Safe EEOC Preemployment Inquiries[5]

For most supervisors, knowing what to ask job applicants—or not to ask—is the big issue when it comes to equal employment law. State and federal equal opportunity laws do *not* clearly forbid employers from making preemployment inquiries that relate to race, color, sex, national origin, religion, or age. (Employers *are* explicitly prohibited from making preemployment inquiries about disability.) However, equal employment officials may use such inquiries as evidence of an employer's intent to discriminate, so they are definitely potential problem questions.

This doesn't just apply to obvious questions ("How old are you?") but to more subtle inquiries. For example, you should generally avoid making inquiries about organizations, clubs, societies, and lodges of which an applicant may be a member.

Similarly, do not ask for a photograph of an applicant. If needed for identification purposes, a photograph may be obtained after an offer of employment is made and accepted.

We discussed employment interviewing in Chapter 4 (Testing and Selecting Employees). Here we focus on what managers can and cannot do regarding preemployment inquiries.

PREEMPLOYMENT INQUIRIES AND RACE   In general, *do not request information that discloses or tends to disclose an applicant's race ("Are you Chinese?" or "Where were your parents from?" for instance)* unless there is a legitimate business need for such information. For example, if an employer legitimately needs information about its applicants' race for affirmative action reporting purposes, it may obtain the information by using a mechanism such as application blank "tear-off" sheets; these go to HR, rather than to the hiring manager.

PREEMPLOYMENT INQUIRIES AND HEIGHT AND WEIGHT   Height and weight requirements tend to limit disproportionately the employment opportunities of some protected groups (women tend to weigh less than men do, for instance). Unless the employer can demonstrate how the need is related to the job, such requirements may be illegal under federal law as well as many state and locality laws. Therefore, unless job-related, *avoid inquiries about height and weight*.

PREEMPLOYMENT INQUIRIES AND CREDIT RATING OR ECONOMIC STATUS   *Inquiries into an applicant's current or past assets, liabilities, or credit rating, including bankruptcy or garnishment, refusal or cancellation of bonding, car ownership, rental or ownership of a house, length of residence at an address, charge accounts, furniture ownership, or bank accounts generally should be avoided* because they tend to impact more adversely on minorities and females. Exceptions exist if the employer can show that such information is essential to the particular job in question (perhaps in hiring a comptroller, for instance).

PREEMPLOYMENT INQUIRIES AND RELIGIOUS AFFILIATION OR BELIEFS The EEOC generally views *questions about an applicant's religious affiliation or beliefs* [unless the religion is a bona fide occupational qualification (BFOQ)], as problematic under federal law.

PREEMPLOYMENT INQUIRIES AND CITIZENSHIP *Do not ask whether a job applicant is a U.S. citizen before making an offer of employment.* The Immigration Reform and Control Act of 1986 (IRCA) prohibits employers from hiring only U.S. citizens or lawful permanent residents unless required to do so by law, regulation, or government contract. It also prohibits employers from preferring to hire temporary visa holders or undocumented workers over qualified U.S. citizens or other protected individuals, such as refugees or individuals granted asylum.

PREEMPLOYMENT INQUIRIES AND MARITAL STATUS OR NUMBER OF CHILDREN Interviewers frequently use questions about *marital status and number and ages of children* to discriminate against women. Even if asked of both men and women, the EEOC may view such questions as evidence of intent to discriminate against, for example, women with children. The EEOC may regard these preemployment inquiries as evidence of intent to discriminate when asked in the preemployment context:

- *Whether applicant is pregnant.*
- *Marital status of applicant or whether applicant plans to marry.*
- *Number and age of children or future child-bearing plans.*
- *Child care arrangements.*
- *Employment status of spouse.*
- *Name of spouse.*

PREEMPLOYMENT INQUIRIES AND GENDER Similarly, it is usually best to avoid questions about *an applicant's sex* (unless it is a bona fide occupational qualification (BFOQ) and is essential to a particular position or occupation). Similarly avoid potentially problematic questions like those regarding *medical history of pregnancy, future child-bearing plans, number and/or ages of children or dependents, provisions for child care, abortions, birth control, ability to reproduce, and name or address of spouse or children.*

PREEMPLOYMENT INQUIRIES AND ARREST AND CONVICTION No federal law clearly prohibits an employer from asking about *arrest and conviction records.* However, using such records as the sole measure to prevent someone from being hired could limit employment opportunities for some protected groups and so should not be used in this way.

PREEMPLOYMENT INQUIRIES AND SECURITY/BACKGROUND CHECKS FOR CERTAIN RELIGIOUS OR ETHNIC GROUPS If the employer requires all other applicants to undergo background checks before being offered a position, the employer may require members of particular religious or ethnic groups to undergo the same preemployment investigations. However, the employer *may not subject only particular religious or ethnic groups, such as Muslims or Arabs, to heightened security checks.* Some employers, such as defense contractors, may require a security clearance for certain jobs pursuant to a federal statute or Executive Order.

PREEMPLOYMENT INQUIRIES AND DISABILITY *Employers are explicitly prohibited from making preemployment inquiries about disability.* Under the law, employers generally cannot ask disability-related questions or require medical examinations until after an applicant has been given a conditional job offer. Employers may ask if the applicant will need an accommodation to perform a specific job duty. If the answer is yes, the employer may then ask what the accommodation would be. *The employer may not ask any questions about the nature or severity of the disability.*

PREEMPLOYMENT INQUIRIES AND MEDICAL QUESTIONS AND EXAMINATIONS An employer also *may not ask a job applicant to answer medical questions or take a medical exam before making a job offer.*

A Simple Interviewing Process

The supervisor, pressed for time, may use the following practical, streamlined employment interview process:[6]

PREPARING FOR THE INTERVIEW   Focus your interview on obtaining information on four things—the candidate's knowledge and experience, motivation, intellectual capacity, and personality. Start by determining the job's requirements in each of these areas, by asking yourself questions such as:

- *Knowledge and experience:* What must the candidate know to perform the job? What experience is necessary to perform the job?
- *Motivation:* What should the person like doing to enjoy this job? Is there anything the person should not dislike? Are there any essential goals or aspirations the person should have?
- *Intellectual capacity:* Are there any specific intellectual aptitudes required (mathematical, mechanical, and so on)? How complex are the problems the person must solve? What must a person be able to demonstrate he or she can do intellectually?
- *Personality factor:* What are the critical personality qualities needed for success on the job (ability to withstand boredom, decisiveness, stability, and so on)? How must the job incumbent handle stress, pressure, and criticism? What kind of interpersonal behavior is required in the job?

SPECIFIC FACTORS TO PROBE IN THE INTERVIEW   Next, ask a combination of situational ("What would you do . . .") questions plus open-ended questions to probe the candidate's suitability for the job. For example:

- *Knowledge and experience factor:* Here, probe with situational questions such as "How would you organize such a sales effort?" or "How would you design that kind of website?"
- *Motivation factor:* Probe such areas as the person's likes and dislikes (for each thing done, what he or she liked or disliked about it), aspirations (including the validity of each goal in terms of the person's reasoning about why he or she chose it), and energy level, perhaps by asking what he or she does on, say, a "typical Tuesday."
- *Intellectual factor:* Here, ask questions that judge such things as complexity of tasks the person has performed, grades in school, test results (including scholastic aptitude tests, and so on), and how the person organizes his or her thoughts and communicates.

- *Personality factor:* Here, probe by looking for self-defeating behaviors (aggressiveness, compulsive fidgeting, and so on) and by exploring the person's past interpersonal relationships. Ask questions about the person's past interactions (working in a group at school, working with fraternity brothers or sorority sisters, leading the work team on the last job, and so on). Also, try to judge the person's behavior in the interview itself—Is the candidate personable? Shy? Outgoing?

CONDUCTING THE INTERVIEW Devise and use a plan to guide the interview. According to interviewing expert John Drake, significant areas to touch on include the candidate's:

- College experiences
- Work experiences—summer, part-time
- Work experience—full-time (one by one)
- Goals and ambitions
- Reactions to the job you are interviewing for
- Self-assessments (by the candidate of his or her strengths and weaknesses)
- Military experiences
- Present outside activities[7]

FOLLOW YOUR PLAN Perhaps start with an open-ended question for each topic, such as "Could you tell me about what you did when you were in college?" At each stage of your interview (college, work experiences on each job, and so forth) keep in mind that you want to ask questions that shed light on the candidate's knowledge and experience, motivation, intelligence, and personality. Follow up by asking questions like "Could you elaborate on that, please?"

MATCH THE CANDIDATE TO THE JOB By following your interview plan, you should now be able to draw conclusions about the person's knowledge and experience, motivation, intellectual capacity, and personality, and to summarize the candidate's strengths and limits. Next, compare your conclusions to the list of knowledge/experience, motivation, intellectual, and personality requirements you developed in the first, preparing for the interview step. This should provide a rational basis for matching the candidate to the job—one based on an analysis of the traits and aptitudes the job actually requires.

Work-Sampling Tests

What should you do if you are trying to hire, say, a marketing manager, and want a simple way to screen your job applicants? Devising a *work-sampling test* is one solution. A work-sampling test means having the candidates perform actual samples of the job in question. Such tests have face validity (clearly measure actual job duties) and are easy to devise. Break down the job's main duties into component tasks. Then have the candidate complete a sample task. For example, for a marketing manager position, ask the candidate to spend 30 minutes designing an ad for a hypothetical product.

EMPLOYMENT TRAINING

Four-Step Training Process

A simple but effective four-step training process follows.

Step 1:   Write a Job Description   A detailed job description is the heart of a training program. List the tasks of each job, along with a summary of the steps in each task.

Step 2:   Develop a Task Analysis Record Form   You can use an abbreviated *Task Analysis Record Form* (Table M-1) containing four columns to guide the required coaching.

- In the first column, list *specific tasks*, such as "start motor."
- In the second column, list *performance standards* (in terms of quantity, quality, accuracy, and so on).
- In the third column, list *trainable skills* required—things the employee must know or do to perform the task. Include skills (such as "Keep both hands on the wheel") that you want to emphasize in training.
- In the fourth column, list *aptitudes required*. These are the human aptitudes (such as "ability to understand written instructions") the employee must have to be trainable, and for which he or she should be screened.

Step 3:   Develop a Job Instruction Sheet   Next, perhaps develop a Job Instruction Sheet for the job. As in Table M-2, a Job Instruction Sheet shows the steps in each task as well as key points the worker should be aware of for each.

Step 4:   Prepare Training Program for the Job   At a minimum, the job's training manual should include the job description, Task Analysis Record Form, and Job Instruction Sheet, all compiled in a training manual. Perhaps also include a brief overview/introduction to the job, and a graphical and/or written explanation of how the job fits with other jobs in the plant or office. Then, have a supervisor or experienced person explain each step in the job to the trainee.

Informal Training Methods

Training expert Stephen Covey says employers can do many things to provide job-related training without actually establishing expensive formal training programs. His suggestions include:[8]

- Offer to cover the tuition for special classes.
- Identify online training opportunities.
- Provide a library of DVDs and CDs for systematic, disciplined learning during commute times.
- Encourage the sharing of best practices among associates.
- When possible, send people to special seminars and association meetings for learning and networking.
- Create a learning ethic by having everyone teach each other what they are learning.

TABLE M-1	Sample Summary Task Analysis Record Form for the Main Task "Operate Paper Cutter"		

Task List	Performance Standards	Trainable Skills Required	Aptitudes Required
1. Operate paper cutter			
1.1 Start motor	Start by push-button on first try	To start machine without accidentally attempting re-start while machine is running	Ability to understand written and spoken instructions
1.2 Set cutting distance	Maximum +/– tolerance of 0.007 inches	Read gauge	Able to read tolerances on numerical scale
1.3 Place paper on cutting table	Must be completely even to prevent uneven edges	Lift paper correctly	At least average manual dexterity
1.4 Push paper up to paper cutter blade		Must be even with blade	At least average manual dexterity
1.5 Grasp safety release with left hand	100% of the time, for safety	Must keep both hands on releases to prevent hand contact with cutting blade	Ability to understand written and spoken warnings

Note: This shows the first five steps (steps 1.1 to 1.5) in one of the tasks (operate paper cutter) for which a printing factory owner would train the person doing the cutting of the paper before placing the paper on the printing presses.

Online and Packaged Training Programs

The manager or small business owner can also tap hundreds of suppliers of prepackaged training solutions. These solutions range from self-study programs from the American Management Association (www.amanet.org) and SHRM (www.shrm.org), to specialized programs. For example, the employer might arrange with PureSafety to have its employees take occupational safety courses from www.puresafety.com.

SkillSoft is another example (http://skillsoft.com/catalog/default.asp). Its courses include software development, business strategy and operations, professional effectiveness, and desktop computer skills. As an example, the course "interviewing effectively" targets managers, team leaders, and human resource professionals. About 2 1/2 hours long, it shows trainees how to use behavioral questioning to interview candidates.[9]

The buyer's guide from the American Society of Training and Development (www.astd.org/) is a good place to start to find a vendor (check under Resources).

TABLE M-2	Sample Job Instruction Sheet for the Task "Operate Paper Cutter"
Steps in Task	**Key Points to Keep in Mind**
1. Start motor	None
2. Set cutting distance	Carefully read scale—to prevent wrong-sized cut
3. Place paper on cutting table	Make sure paper is even—to prevent uneven cut
4. Push paper up to cutter	Make sure paper is tight—to prevent uneven cut
5. Grasp safety release with left hand	Do not release left hand—to prevent hand from being caught in cutter
6. Grasp cutter release with right hand	Do not release right hand—to prevent hand from being caught in cutter
7. Simultaneously pull cutter and safety releases	Keep both hands on corresponding releases—avoid hands being on cutting table
8. Wait for cutter to retract	Keep both hands on releases—to avoid having hands on cutting table
9. Retract paper	Make sure cutter is retracted; keep both hands away from releases
10. Shut off motor	None

THE SBA   The federal government's Small Business Administration (www.SBA.gov/) provides a virtual campus that offers online courses, workshops, publications, and learning tools aimed toward supporting entrepreneurs.[10] For example, the small business owner can follow the link under "Counseling & Training" to "Writing a Business Plan," "Managing Employees: Employee Handbooks," and "Foreign Workers, Immigration, and Employee Eligibility."

NAM   The National Association of Manufacturers (NAM) is the largest industrial trade organization in the United States. It represents about 14,000 member manufacturers, including 10,000 small and midsized companies.

NAM's Virtual University (www.namvu.com) helps employees maintain and upgrade their work skills and continue their professional development. It offers almost 650 courses.[11] There are no long-term contracts to sign. Employers simply pay about $10–$30 per course taken by each employee. The catalog includes OSHA, quality, and technical training as well as courses in areas like business and finance, personal development, and customer service.

EMPLOYMENT APPRAISAL

Managers have easy access to hard-copy and computerized appraisal and compensation services. For example, find both appraisal forms and appraisal software at HR suppliers such as G Neil (www.gneil.com/products/performanceappraisal/default.aspx).

BENEFITS AND REWARDS

The Family and Work Institute surveyed the benefits practices of about 1,000 small and large companies.[12] The gist of what they found is that small business owners, by personally interacting with all employees each day, did a better job of "…understanding when work/life issues emerge."[13] Here are some examples of informal "benefits" managers can use to address such issues:[14]

- *Extra time off*—For example, Friday afternoons off in the summer.
- *Compressed workweeks*—For example, compressed summer workweeks.
- *Bonuses at critical times*—Small business owners and astute managers are more likely to know what's happening with their employees' lives. Use this knowledge to provide special bonuses, for instance, if an employee has a new baby.
- *Flexibility*—For example "if an employee is having a personal problem, help him or her create a work schedule that allows the person to solve problems without feeling like they're going to be in trouble."[15]
- *Sensitivity to employees' strengths and weaknesses*—The managers should be attuned to his or her employees' strengths, weaknesses, and aspirations. For example, ask them which jobs they feel most comfortable doing, and give them an opportunity to train for and move into the jobs they desire.
- *Help them better themselves*—For example, offer to pay employees to take a class to help them develop their job skills.
- *Make them feel like owners*—For example, let them work directly with clients, get them client feedback, share company performance data with them, and let them share in the company's financial success.
- *Make sure they have what they need to do their jobs*—For instance, the necessary training, procedures, computers, and so on.
- *Constantly recognize a job well done*—Capitalize on your day-to-day interactions with employees to "never miss an opportunity to give your employees the recognition they deserve."[16]

Recognition

Studies show that recognition can often be as powerful as financial rewards. Any managers in small or large firms can use these. The personal nature of small business interactions makes it particularly easy to provide such recognition. A short list would include:[17]

- Challenging work assignments
- Freedom to choose own work activity
- Having fun built into work
- More of preferred task
- Role as boss's stand-in when he or she is away
- Role in presentations to top management
- Job rotation
- Encouragement of learning and continuous improvement
- Being provided with ample encouragement
- Being allowed to set own goals
- Compliments

- Expression of appreciation in front of others
- Note of thanks
- Employee-of-the-month award
- Special commendation
- Bigger desk
- Bigger office or cubicle

Simple Retirement Benefits

Access to retirement benefits is more prevalent in large firms than small ones. About 75% of large firms offer them, while about 35% of small ones do.[18]

The easiest way for small businesses to provide retirement benefits is through a *SIMPLE IRA plan.* With the *SIMPLE* (for *Savings Incentive Match Plan for Employees*) *IRA,* employers must (and employees may) make contributions to traditional employee IRAs. These plans are for employers or small businesses with 100 or fewer employees and no other retirement plan.

SIMPLE IRAs are inexpensive and (of course) simple. The owner contacts an eligible financial institution and fills out several IRS forms. The IRS needs to have previously approved the financial institution. However, banks, mutual funds, and insurance companies that issue annuity contracts are generally eligible.[19] The plan has very low administrative costs. Employer contributions are tax-deductible.[20] A typical employer contribution might match employee contributions dollar for dollar up to 3% of pay. The financial institution usually handles the IRS paperwork and reporting.

How to Improve Interpersonal Communication

Tasks that require interpersonal communication—communication between two people—fill a manager's day. The manager disciplines an employee for breaking a rule, shows a new employee how to improve her performance, or tries to convince an employee to work harder.

The problem is that a host of problems can intervene between what you meant to say to someone and what that person actually hears. There is noise, for instance, in the form of ambiguous muddled messages, cultural misunderstandings, or just plain not listening. There's the influence of non-verbal aspects of the interchange (such as when your apparent anger belies the feigned gentleness of your words). And there are psychological factors to consider, as when the subordinate's nervousness renders him or her incapable of understanding what you're trying to convey.

And yet, you need to be able to get around these potential barriers. Guidelines for doing so include the following.

Make Yourself Clear—If you garble the initial message, then you're starting off at less than zero, as far as making yourself understood is concerned.

The fact is, most people are a little lazy when it comes to communicating their ideas. They do not take the time to conscientiously translate what they're thinking into words. Ambiguous, unclear communiqués, therefore, usually reflect sloppy thinking. Or, to restate this, fuzzy words reflect fuzzy thinking. Make sure you say what you mean. For example, if you mean immediately, say "immediately"; don't leave the timing open-ended or say something like, "as soon as you can."

Be Consistent—Much of what the other person "hears" reflects not just your words but your tone, expression, and eye contact. Therefore, endeavor to be consistent. Make sure your tone, expression, and words send a consistent meaning. In terms of body language, come across as open and receptive. Maintain eye contact, smile, keep hands away from your face and mouth, and use open-handed gestures.[21]

Consider the Distractions—You'll rarely have the luxury of communicating with someone under perfect (distraction-less) conditions. There will almost certainly be interruptions, background noise, trucks driving by, and numerous other distractions. In delivering a particularly important and personal message (a performance assessment or dismissal notice, for instance), try to factor in the potential distractions (for instance, by speaking louder, or by not shouting across the room).

Confirm "Message Received"—Airport flight controllers know that many sources of noise—static, cockpit noise, a pilot's preoccupation, language barriers—can undermine a message. Both pilot and controller are therefore trained to confirm and reconfirm each message. You should do the same.

Don't Attack the Person's Defenses—There will be many times when communicating requires that you point out a subordinate's deficiencies. This just comes with the supervisor's territory. Yet doing so raises the particular risk that you'll run full speed into the other person's defenses. No one likes being criticized. The normal reaction is to mount a defense (as in, "I didn't understand what you meant").

The important thing here is, don't attack the other person's defenses. For example, don't try to "explain a person to himself or herself" by saying things like, "You know the reason you're saying that is that you can't bear being be blamed for anything." Words to avoid include *blame, catastrophe, demand, destroyed, idiotic*, and *misguided*. Phrases to avoid include "better shape up," "don't come to me about it," "don't want to hear it," "figure it out for yourself," "you don't understand," and "you'd better."[22]

Be an Active Listener—Because of peoples' perceptions, emotions, and defenses, what one person says is often much different from what the other person hears. Behavioral scientist Carl Rogers says the way to get around this is with active listening. Active listening means taking steps to listen, not just to what the speaker says, but to understand and respond to the feelings behind the words.[23] Active listeners try to understand the person from his or her point of view and to convey the message that they do understand. Guidelines here include these:

- **Listen for total meaning.** For example, if the salesperson says, "We can't sell that much this year," the supervisor's typical knee-jerk response might be "Sure you can." An active listener would instead strive to understand the underlying feelings (such as the pressure the salesperson is under): "I know how you feel, so let's see what we can work out."
- **Reflect feelings.** Show the person that his or her message is getting through. For example, say something like, "They're pushing you pretty hard, aren't they?"

- **Note all cues.** Remember that not all communication is verbal. Facial expressions and gestures reveal feelings, too.
- **Give the person your full attention.** Turn off the cell phone, ignore the computer screen, don't look at your watch.
- **Show that you are listening with an open mind.** Don't rush to interrupt the person, or to finish his or her sentences. Avoid conversation-stoppers such as "You've got to be kidding," or rolling your eyes.

MANAGING HR SYSTEMS, PROCEDURES, AND PAPERWORK

Consider the paperwork required to run a five-person retail shop. Just to start with, recruiting and hiring an employee might require a help wanted advertising listing, an employment application, an interviewing checklist, various verifications—of education and immigration status, for instance—and a telephone reference checklist. You then might need an employment agreement, confidentiality and noncompetition agreements, and an employer indemnity agreement. To process that new employee you might need a background verification, a new employee checklist, and forms for withholding tax and to obtain new employee data. And to keep track of the employee once on board, you'd need—just to start—a personnel data sheet, daily and weekly time records, an hourly employee's weekly time sheet, and an expense report. Then come all the performance appraisal forms, a disciplinary notice, an employee orientation record, separation notice, and employment reference response.

Basic Components of Manual HR Systems

Very small employers (say, with 10 employees or less) will probably start with a manual human resource management system. From a practical point of view, this generally means obtaining and organizing a set of standardized personnel forms covering each important aspect of the HR—recruitment, selection, training, appraisal, compensation, safety, as well as some means for organizing all this information for each of your employees.

BASIC FORMS   The number of forms needed for even a small firm is large, as the illustrative list in Table M-3 shows.[24] One simple way to obtain the basic forms for a manual HR system is to start with one of the books, CDs, or forms compilers that provide HR forms, such as HRdirect, at www.hrdirect.com. The forms you want can then be adapted from these sources for your particular situation. Office supply stores (such as Office Depot and Office Max) also sell packages of personnel forms. For example, Office Depot sells packages of individual personnel forms as well as a "Human Resource Kit" containing 10 copies of forms such as Application, Employment Interview, Reference Check, Employee Record, and Performance Evaluation.[25] Also available is a package of Employee Record Folders. Some employers still use such folders to maintain files on each employee; on the outside of the pocket is a place for recording information such as name, start date, company benefits, and so on.

OTHER SOURCES   Several direct-mail catalog companies similarly offer HR materials. For example, as noted earlier, HRdirect (www.hrdirect.com) offers packages of personnel forms. These include, for instance, Short- and Long-Form Employee Applications, Applicant Interviews, Employee Performance Reviews, and Absentee Calendars and Reports. There

TABLE M-3	Some Important Employment Forms	
New Employee Forms	**Current Employee Forms**	**Employee Separation Forms**
Application	Employee Status	Retirement Checklist
New Employee Checklist	Change Request	Termination Checklist
Employment Interview	Employee Record	COBRA Acknowledgment
Reference Check	Performance Evaluation	Unemployment Claim
Telephone Reference Report	Warning Notice	Employee Exit Interview
Employee Manual Acknowledgment	Vacation Request	
Employment Agreement	Probation Notice	
Employment Application Disclaimer	Job Description	
Employee Secrecy Agreement	Probationary Evaluation	
	Absence Report	
	Disciplinary Notice	
	Grievance Form	
	Expense Report	
	401(k) Choices Acknowledgment	
	Injury Report	

are also various legal compliance forms, including standardized Harassment Policy and FMLA Notice forms, as well as posters (for instance, covering legally required postings for matters such as the Americans with Disabilities Act) available.

The G. Neil Company, of Sunrise, Florida (www.gneil.com), is another direct-mail personnel materials source. In addition to a complete line of personnel forms, documents, and posters, it also carries manual systems for matters like attendance history, job analyses, and for tracking vacation requests and safety records. It has a complete HR "start-up" kit containing 25 copies of each of the basic components of a manual HR system. These include, for instance, Long Form Application for Employment, Attendance History, Payroll/Status Change Notice, Absence Report, and Vacation Request & Approval, all organized in a file box.

Automating Individual HR Tasks

As the business grows, it becomes unwieldy to rely on manual HR systems. It is therefore at this point that most small- to medium-sized firms begin computerizing individual human resource management tasks such as attendance monitoring and appraisal.

PACKAGED SYSTEMS There are many resources available. For example, at the website for the International Association for Human Resource Information Management (www.ihrim.org) you'll find, within the Buyers Guide tab, a categorical list of HR software vendors.[26] These firms provide software solutions for virtually all personnel tasks, ranging from benefits management to compensation, compliance, employee relations, outsourcing, payroll, and time and attendance systems.

The G. Neil Company sells software packages for monitoring attendance, employee record keeping, writing employee handbooks, and conducting computerized employee appraisals. HRdirect offers software for tasks such as writing employee policy manuals, writing performance reviews, creating job descriptions, and tracking attendance and hours worked for each employee. *People Manager*® (see for example, www.hallogram.com/peoplemanager/) maintains employee records (including name, address, marital status, number of dependents, emergency contact and phone numbers, hire date, and job history). It also enables management to produce 30 standard reports on matters such as attendance, benefits, and ethnic information quickly.

Then, as the company grows, the owner may decide to transition to an integrated human resource management system; we discuss this next.

HUMAN RESOURCE INFORMATION SYSTEMS (HRIS)   Companies need information systems to get their work done. For example, the sales team needs some way to tell accounting to bill a customer, and to tell production to fill the order. The term *human resource information system (HRIS)* refers to the interrelated people, data, technology, and organizational procedures a company uses to collect, process, store, integrate, and disseminate its human resource information.

INTEGRATING THE HR SYSTEM   Because an HRIS's software components (record keeping, payroll, appraisal, and so forth) are integrated (made to communicate with each other), they enable the employer to reengineer and integrate its HR functions. The system PeopleSoft (now part of Oracle Corporation) installed in its own offices provides an illustration. For example, it electronically routes salary increases, transfers, and other e-forms through the organization to the proper managers for approval. If anyone forgets to process a document, a smart agent issues reminders until the task is completed.

HRIS VENDORS   Many firms today offer HRIS packages. The website for the International Association for Human Resource Information Management (www.ihrim.org/), for instance, lists Automatic Data Processing, Inc., Business Information Technology, Inc., Human Resource Microsystems, Lawson Software, Oracle Corporation, SAP America, Inc., and about 25 other firms as HRIS vendors.

HR AND INTRANETS   Employers are increasingly creating intranet-based HR information systems. For example, LG&E Energy Corporation uses its intranet for benefits communication. Employees can access the benefits home page and (among other things) review the company's 401(k) plan investment options, get answers to frequently asked questions about the company's medical and dental plans, and report changes in family status. Other uses for human resource intranets include, for instance, to: automate job postings and applicant tracking; set up training registration; provide electronic pay stubs; publish an electronic employee handbook; and let employees update their personal profiles and accounts, such as 401(k)s.

APPENDIX

Comprehensive Cases

BANDAG AUTOMOTIVE*

Jim Bandag took over his family's auto supply business in 2005, after helping his father, who founded the business, run it for about 10 years. Based in Illinois, Bandag employs about 300 people, and distributes auto supplies (replacement mufflers, bulbs, engine parts, and so on) through two divisions, one that supplies service stations and repair shops, and a second that sells retail auto supplies through five "Bandag Automotive" auto supply stores.

Jim's father, and now Jim, have always endeavored to keep Bandag's organization chart as simple as possible. The company has a full-time controller, managers for each of the five stores, a manager that oversees the distribution division, and Jim Bandag's executive assistant. Jim (along with his father, working part-time) handles marketing and sales.

Jim's executive assistant administers the firm's day-to-day human resource management tasks, but the company outsources most HR activities to others, including an employment agency that does its recruiting and screening, a benefits firm that administers its 401(k) plan, and a payroll service that handles its paychecks. Bandag's human resource management systems consist almost entirely of standardized HR forms purchased from an HR supplies company. These include forms such as application and performance appraisal forms, as well as an "honesty" test Bandag uses to screen the staff that works in the five stores. The company performs informal salary surveys to see what other companies in the area are paying for similar positions, and use these results for awarding annual merit increases (which in fact are more accurately cost-of-living adjustments).

Jim's father took a fairly paternal approach to the business. He often walked around speaking with his employees, finding out what their problems were, and even helping them out with an occasional loan—for instance, when he discovered that one of their children was sick, or for part of a new home down payment. Jim, on the other hand, tends to be more abrupt, and does not enjoy the same warm relationship with the employees as did his father. Jim is not unfair or dictatorial. He's just very focused on improving Bandag's financial performance, and so all his decisions, including his HR-related decisions, generally come down to cutting costs. For example, his knee-jerk reaction is usually to offer fewer days off rather than more, fewer benefits rather than more, and to be less flexible when an employee needs, for instance, a few extra days off because a child is sick.

It's therefore perhaps not surprising that over the past few years Bandag's sales and profits have increased markedly, but that the firm has found itself increasingly enmeshed in HR/equal employment–type issues. Indeed, Jim now finds himself spending a day or two a week addressing HR problems. For example, Henry Jaques, an employee at

*© Gary Dessler, Ph.D.

one of the stores, came to Jim's executive assistant and told her he was "irate" about his recent firing and was probably going to sue. Henry's store manager stated on his last performance appraisal that Henry did the technical aspects of his job well, but that he had "serious problems interacting with his coworkers." He was continually arguing with them, and complaining to the store manager about working conditions. The store manager had told Jim that he had to fire Henry because he was making "the whole place poisonous," and that (although he felt sorry because he'd heard rumors that Henry suffered from some mental illness) he felt he had to go. Jim approved the dismissal.

Gavin was another problem. Gavin had worked for Bandag for 10 years, the last two as manager of one of the company's five stores. Right after Jim Bandag took over, Gavin told him he had to take a Family and Medical Leave Act medical leave to have hip surgery, and Jim approved the leave. When Gavin returned from leave, Jim told him that his position had been eliminated. Bandag had decided to close his store and open a new, larger store across from a shopping center about a mile away, and had appointed a new manager in Gavin's absence. However, the company did give Gavin a (nonmanagerial) position in the new store as a counter salesperson, at the same salary and with the same benefits as he had before. Even so, "This job is not similar to my old one," Gavin insisted. "It doesn't have nearly as much prestige." His contention is that the FMLA requires that the company bring him back in the same or equivalent position, and that this means a supervisory position, similar to what he had before he went on leave. Jim said no, and they seem to be heading toward litigation.

In another sign of the times at Bandag, the company's controller, Miriam, who had been with the company for about 6 years, went on pregnancy leave for 12 weeks in 2011 (also under the FMLA), and then received an additional 3 weeks' leave under Bandag's extended illness days program. Four weeks after she came back, she asked Jim Bandag if she could arrange to work fewer hours per week, and spend about a day per week working out of her home. He refused, and about 2 months later fired her. Jim Bandag said, "I'm sorry, it's not anything to do with your pregnancy-related requests, but we've got ample reasons to discharge you—your monthly budgets have been several days late, and we've got proof you may have forged documents." She replied, "I don't care what you say your reasons are, you're really firing me because of my pregnancy, and that's illegal."

Jim felt he was on safe ground as far as defending the company for these actions, although he didn't look forward to spending the time and money that he knew it would take to fight each. However, what he learned over lunch from a colleague undermined his confidence about another case that Jim had been sure would be a "slam dunk" for his company. Jim was explaining to his friend that one of Bandag's truck maintenance service people had applied for a job driving one of Bandag's distribution department trucks, and that Jim had turned him down because the worker was deaf. Jim (whose wife has occasionally said of him, "No one has ever accused Jim of being politically correct") was mentioning to his friend the apparent absurdity of a deaf person asking to be a truck delivery person. His friend, who happens to work for UPS, pointed out that the U.S. Court of Appeals for the Ninth Circuit had recently decided that UPS had violated the Americans with Disabilities Act by refusing to consider deaf workers for jobs driving the company's smaller vehicles.

Although Jim's father is semi-retired, the sudden uptick in the frequency of such EEO-type issues troubled him, particularly after so many years of labor peace. However, he's not sure what to do about it. Having handed over the reins of the company to his son, he was loath to inject himself back into the company's operational decision making. On the other hand, he was afraid that in the short run these issues were going to drain a great deal of Jim's time and resources, and that in the long run they might be a sign of things to come, with problems like these eventually overwhelming Bandag Auto. He comes to you, who he knows consults in human resource management, and asks you the following questions.

Questions

1. Given Bandag Auto's size, and anything else you know about it, should we reorganize the human resource management function, and if so why and how?
2. What, if anything, would you do to change and/or improve upon the current HR systems, forms, and practices that we now use?
3. Do you think that the employee that Jim fired for creating what the manager called a poisonous relationship has a legitimate claim against us, and if so why and what should we do about it?
4. Is it true that we really had to put Gavin back into an equivalent position, or was it adequate to just bring him back into a job at the same salary, bonuses, and benefits as he had before his leave?
5. Miriam, the controller, is basically claiming that the company is retaliating against her for being pregnant, and that the fact that we raised performance issues was just a smokescreen. Do you think the EEOC and/or courts would agree with her, and, in any case, what should we do now?
6. An employee who is deaf has asked us to be one of our delivery people and we turned him down. He's now threatening to sue. What should we do, and why?
7. In the previous 10 years, we've had only one equal employment complaint, and now in the last few years we've had four or five. What should I do about it? Why?

Source: Based generally on actual facts, but Bandag is a fictitious company. Bandag source notes: "The Problem Employee: Discipline or Accommodation?" *Monday Business Briefing*, March 8, 2005; "Employee Says Change in Duties After Leave Violates FMLA," *BNA Bulletin to Management*, January 16, 2007, p. 24; "Manager Fired Days After Announcing Pregnancy," *BNA Bulletin to Management*, January 2, 2007, p. 8; "Ninth Circuit Rules UPS Violated ADA by Barring Deaf Workers from Driving Jobs," *BNA Bulletin to Management*, October 17, 2006, p. 329.

ANGELO'S PIZZA[*]

Angelo Camero was brought up in the Bronx, New York, and basically always wanted to be in the pizza store business. As a youngster, he would sometimes spend hours at the local pizza store, watching the owner knead the pizza dough, flatten it into a large circular crust, fling it up, and then spread on tomato sauce in larger and larger loops. After graduating from college as a marketing major, he made a beeline back to the Bronx, where he opened his first Angelo's Pizza store, emphasizing its clean, bright interior; its crisp green, red, and white sign; and his all-natural, fresh ingredients. Within 5 years, Angelo's store was a success, and he had opened three other stores and was considering franchising his concept.

Eager as he was to expand, his 4 years in business school had taught him the difference between being an entrepreneur and being a manager. As an entrepreneur/small-business owner, he knew he had the distinct advantage of being able to personally run the whole operation himself. With just one store and a handful of employees, he

[*]© Gary Dessler, Ph.D.

could make every decision and watch the cash register, check in the new supplies, oversee the takeout, and personally supervise the service.

When he expanded to three stores, things started getting challenging. He hired managers for the two new stores (both of whom had worked for him at his first store for several years) and gave them only minimal "how to run a store"–type training, on the assumption that, having worked with him for several years, they already knew pretty much everything they needed to know about running a store. However, he was already experiencing human resource management problems, and he knew there was no way he could expand the number of stores he owned, or (certainly) contemplate franchising his idea, unless he had a system in place that he could clone in each new store to provide the manager (or the franchisee) with the necessary management knowledge and expertise to run their stores. Angelo had no training program in place for teaching his store managers how to run their stores. He simply (erroneously, as it turned out) assumed that by working with him they would learn how to do things on the job. Since Angelo really had no system in place, the new managers were, in a way, starting off below zero when it came to how to manage a store.

There were several issues that particularly concern Angelo. Finding and hiring good employees was number one. He'd read the new National Small Business Poll from the National Federation of Independent Business Education Foundation. It found that 71% of small-business owners believed that finding qualified employees was "hard." Furthermore, "the search for qualified employees will grow more difficult as demographic and education factors" continue to make it more difficult to find employees. Similarly, reading *The Kiplinger Letter* one day, he noticed that just about every type of business couldn't find enough good employees to hire. Small firms were particularly in jeopardy; the *Letter* said: Giant firms can outsource many (particularly entry-level) jobs abroad, and larger companies can also afford to pay better benefits and to train their employees. Small firms rarely have the resources or the economies of scale to allow outsourcing or to install the big training programs that would enable them to take untrained new employees and turned them into skilled ones.

Although finding enough employees was his biggest problem, finding enough honest ones scared him even more. Angelo recalled from one of his business school courses that companies in the United States are losing a total of well over $400 billion a year in employee theft. As a rough approximation, that works out to about $9 per employee per day and about $12,000 lost annually for a typical company. Furthermore, it was small companies like Angelo's that were particularly in the crosshairs, because companies with fewer than 100 employees are particularly prone to employee theft. Why are small firms particularly vulnerable? Perhaps they lack experience dealing with the problem. More importantly: Small firms are more likely to have a single person doing several jobs, such as ordering supplies and paying the delivery person. This undercuts the checks and balances managers often strive for to control theft. Furthermore, the risk of stealing goes up dramatically when the business is largely based on cash. In a pizza store, many people come in and buy just one or two slices and a cola for lunch, and almost all pay with cash, not credit cards.

And, Angelo was not just worried about someone stealing cash. They can steal your whole business idea, something he learned from painful experience. He had been planning to open a store in what he thought would be a particularly good location, and was thinking of having one of his current employees manage the store. Instead, it turned out that this employee was, in a manner of speaking, stealing Angelo's brain—what Angelo knew about customers, suppliers, where to buy pizza dough, where to buy tomato sauce, how much everything should cost, how to furnish the store, where to buy ovens, store layout—everything. This employee soon quit and opened up his own pizza store, not far from where Angelo had planned to open his new store.

That he was having trouble hiring good employees, there was no doubt. The restaurant business is particularly brutal when it comes to turnover. Many restaurants turn over their employees at a rate of 200% to 300% per year—so every year, each position might have a series of two to three employees filling it. As Angelo said, "I was losing two to three employees a month." As he said, "We're a high-volume store, and while we should have [to fill all the hours in a week] about six employees per store, we were down to only three or four, so my managers and I were really under the gun."

The problem was bad at the hourly employee level: "We were churning a lot at the hourly level," said Angelo. "Applicants would come in, my managers or I would hire them and not spend much time training them, and the good ones would leave in frustration after a few weeks, while often it was the bad ones who'd stay behind." But in the last 2 years, Angelo's three company-owned stores also went through a total of three store managers—"They were just blowing through the door," as Angelo put it, in part because, without good employees, their workday was brutal. As a rule, when a small-business owner or manager can't find enough employees (or an employee doesn't show up for work), about 80% of the time the owner or manager does the job himself or herself. So, these managers often ended up working 7 days a week, 10 to 12 hours a day, and many just burned out in the end. One night, working three jobs himself with customers leaving in anger, Angelo decided he'd never just hire someone because he was desperate again, but would start doing his hiring more rationally.

Angelo knew he should have a more formal screening process. As he said, "If there's been a lesson learned, it's much better to spend time up front screening out candidates that don't fit than to hire them and have to put up with their ineffectiveness." He also knew that he could identify many of the traits that his employees needed. For example, he knew that not everyone has the temperament to be a waiter (he has a small pizza/Italian restaurant in the back of his main store). As Angelo said, "I've seen personalities that were off the charts in assertiveness or overly introverted, traits that obviously don't make a good fit for a waiter a waitress."

As a local business, Angelo recruits by placing help wanted ads in two local newspapers, and he's been "shocked" at some of the responses and experiences he's had in response to the ads. Many of the applicants left voicemail messages (Angelo or the other workers in the store were too busy to answer), and some applicants Angelo "just axed" on the assumption that people without good telephone manners wouldn't have very good manners in the store, either. He also quickly learned that he had to throw out a very wide net, even if only hiring one or two people. Many people, as noted, he eliminated from consideration because of the messages they left, and about half the people he scheduled to come in for interviews didn't show up. He'd taken courses in human resource management, so (as he said) "I should know better," but he hired people based almost exclusively on a single interview (he occasionally made a feeble attempt to check references). In total, his HR approach was obviously not working. It wasn't producing enough good recruits, and the people he did hire were often problematical.

What was he looking for? Service-oriented courteous people, for one. For example, he'd hired one employee who used profanity several times, including once in front of a customer. On that employee's third day, Angelo had to tell her, "I think Angelo's isn't the right place for you," and he fired her. As Angelo said, "I felt bad, but also knew that everything I have is on the line for this business, so I wasn't going to let anyone run this business down." Angelo wants reliable people (who'll show up on time), honest people, and people who are flexible about switching jobs and hours as required.

Angelo's Pizza business has only the most rudimentary human resource management system. Angelo bought several application forms at a local Office Depot, and rarely uses other forms of any sort. He uses his personal accountant for reviewing the company's books, and Angelo himself computes each employee's paycheck at the end of the week and writes the checks. Training is entirely on-the-job. Angelo personally trained each of his employees. For those employees who go on to be store managers, he assumes that they are training their own employees the way that Angelo trained them (for better or worse, as it turns out). Angelo pays "a bit above" prevailing wage rates (judging by other help wanted ads), but probably not enough to make a significant difference in the quality of employees that he attracts. If you asked Angelo what his reputation is as an employer, Angelo, being a candid and forthright person, would probably tell you that he is a supportive but hard-nosed employer who treats people fairly, but whose business reputation may suffer from disorganization stemming from inadequate organization and training. He approaches you to ask you several questions.

Questions

1. My strategy is to (hopefully) expand the number of stores and eventually franchise, while focusing on serving only high-quality fresh ingredients. What are three specific human resource management implications of my strategy (including specific policies and practices)?
2. Identify and briefly discuss five specific human resource management errors that I'm currently making.
3. Develop a structured interview form that we can use for hiring (1) store managers, (2) wait staff, and (3) counter people/pizza makers.
4. Based on what you know about Angelo's, and what you know from having visited pizza restaurants, write a one-page outline showing specifically how you think Angelo's should go about selecting employees.

Source: Based generally on actual facts, but Angelo's Pizza is a fictitious company. Angelo's Pizza source notes: Dino Berta, "People Problems: Keep Hiring from Becoming a Crying Game," *Nation's Business News* 36, no. 20 (May 20, 2002), pp. 72–74; Ellen Lyon, "Hiring, Personnel Problems Can Challenge Entrepreneurs," *Patriot-News*, October 12, 2004; Rose Robin Pedone, "Businesses' $400 Billion Theft Problem," *Long Island Business News* 27 (July 6, 1998), pp. 1B–2B; "Survey Shows Small-Business Problems with Hiring, Internet," *Providence Business News* 16 (September 10, 2001), pp. 1B; "Finding Good Workers Is Posing a Big Problem as Hiring Picks Up," *The Kiplinger Letter* 81 (February 13, 2004).

GOOGLE[*]

Fortune magazine named Google the best of the 100 best companies to work for, and there is little doubt why. Among the benefits it offers are free shuttles equipped with Wi-Fi to pick up and drop off employees from San Francisco Bay area locations, unlimited sick days, annual all-expense-paid ski trips, free gourmet meals, five on-site free doctors, $2,000 bonuses for referring a new hire, free flu shots, a giant lap pool, on-site oil changes, on-site car washes, volleyball courts, TGIF parties, free on-site washers and dryers (with

---

[*]© Gary Dessler, Ph.D.

free detergent), Ping-Pong and foosball tables, and free famous people lectures. For many people, it's the gourmet meals and snacks that make Google stand out. For example, human resources director Stacey Sullivan loves the Irish oatmeal with fresh berries at the company's Plymouth Rock Cafe, near Google's "people operations" group. "I sometimes dream about it," she says. Engineer Jan Fitzpatrick loves the raw bar at Google's Tapis restaurant, down the road on the Google campus. Then, of course, there are the stock options—each new employee gets about 1,200 options to buy Google shares (recently worth about $480 per share). In fact, dozens of early Google employees ("Googlers") are already multimillionaires thanks to Google stock. The recession that began around 2008 did prompt Google and other firms to cut back on some of these benefits (cafeteria hours are shorter today, for instance), but Google still pretty much leads the benefits pack.

For their part, Googlers share certain traits. They tend to be brilliant, team oriented (teamwork is the norm, especially for big projects), and driven. *Fortune* describes them as people who "almost universally" see themselves as the most interesting people on the planet, and who are happy-go-lucky on the outside, but type A—highly intense and goal directed—on the inside. They're also super-hardworking (which makes sense, since it's not unusual for engineers to be in the hallways at 3 A.M. debating some new mathematical solution to a Google search problem). They're so team oriented that when working on projects, it's not unusual for a Google team to give up its larger, more spacious offices and to crowd into a small conference room, where they can "get things done." Historically, Googlers generally graduate with great grades from the best universities, including Stanford, Harvard, and MIT. For many years, Google wouldn't even consider hiring someone with less than a 3.7 average—while also probing deeply into the why behind any B grades. Google also doesn't hire lone wolves, but wants people who work together and people who also have diverse interests (narrow interests or skills are a turnoff at Google). Google also wants people with growth potential. The company is expanding so fast that it needs to hire people who are capable of being promoted five or six times—it's only, the company says, by hiring such overqualified people that it can be sure that the employees will be able to keep up as Google and their own departments expand.

The starting salaries are highly competitive. Experienced engineers start at about $130,000 a year (plus about 1,200 shares of stock options, as noted), and new MBAs can expect between $80,000 and $120,000 per year (with smaller option grants). Most recently, Google had about 10,000 staff members, up from its beginnings with just three employees in a rented garage.

Of course, in a company that's grown from three employees to 10,000 and from zero value to hundreds of billions of dollars, it may be quibbling to talk about "problems," but there's no doubt that such rapid growth does confront Google's management, and particularly its "people operations" group, with some big challenges. Let's look at these.

For one, Google, as noted earlier, is a 24-hour operation, and with engineers and others frequently pulling all-nighters to complete their projects, the company needs to provide a package of services and financial benefits that supports that kind of lifestyle, and that helps its employees maintain an acceptable work–life balance.

As another challenge, Google's enormous financial success is a two-edged sword. Although Google usually wins the recruitment race when it comes to competing for new employees against competitors like Microsoft or Yahoo!, Google does need some way to stem a rising tide of retirements. Most Googlers are still in their twenties and thirties, but many have become so wealthy from their Google stock options that they can afford to retire. One 27-year-old engineer received a million-dollar founder's award for her work on the program for searching desktop computers, and wouldn't think of leaving "except to start her own company." Similarly a former engineering vice president retired (with his Google stock profits) to pursue his love of astronomy. The engineer who dreamed up Gmail recently retired (at the age of 30).

Another challenge is that the work not only involves long hours but can also be very tense. Google is a very numbers-oriented environment. For example, consider a typical weekly Google user interface design meeting. Marisa Meyer, the company's vice president of search products and user experience, runs the meeting, where her employees work out the look and feel of Google's products. Seated around a conference table are about a dozen Googlers, tapping on laptops. During the 2-hour meeting, Meyer needs to evaluate various design proposals, ranging from minor tweaks to a new product's entire layout. She's previously given each presentation an allotted amount of time, and a large digital clock on the wall ticks off the seconds. The presenters must quickly present their ideas, but also handle questions such as "what do users do if the tab is moved from the side of the page to the top?" Furthermore, it's all about the numbers—no one at Google would ever say, for instance, "the tab looks better in red"—you need to prove your point. Presenters must come armed with usability experiment results, showing, for instance, that a certain percent preferred red or some other color. While the presenters are answering these questions as quickly as possible, the digital clock is ticking, and when it hits the allotted time, the presentation must end, and the next team steps up to present. It is a tough and tense environment, and Googlers must have done their homework.

Growth can also undermine the "outlaw band that's changing the world" culture that fostered the services that made Google famous. Even cofounder Sergi Brin agrees that Google risks becoming less "zany" as it grows. To paraphrase one of its top managers, the hard part of any business is keeping that original innovative, small-business feel even as the company grows.

Creating the right culture is especially challenging now that Google is truly global. For example, Google works hard to provide the same financial and service benefits every place it does business around the world, but it can't exactly match its benefits in every country because of international laws and international taxation issues. Offering the same benefits everywhere is more important than it might initially appear. All those benefits make life easier for Google staff, and help them achieve a work–life balance. Achieving the right work–life balance is the centerpiece of Google's culture, but this also becomes more challenging as the company grows. On the one hand, Google does expect all of its employees to work super hard; on the other hand, it realizes that it needs to help them maintain some sort of balance. As one manager says, Google acknowledges "that we work hard but that work is not everything."

Recruitment is another challenge. While Google certainly doesn't lack applicants, attracting the right applicants is crucial if Google is to continue to grow successfully. Working at Google requires a special set of traits, and screening employees is easier if it recruits the right people to begin with. For instance, Google needs to attract people who are super-bright, love to work, have fun, can handle the stress, and who also have outside interests and flexibility.

As the company grows internationally, it also faces the considerable challenge of recruiting and building staff overseas. For example, Google now is introducing a new vertical market–based structure across Europe, to attract more business advertisers to its search engine. (By vertical market–based structure, Google means focusing on key vertical industry sectors such as travel, retail, automotive, and technology.) To build these industry groupings abroad from scratch, Google promoted its former head of its U.S. financial services group to be the vertical markets director for Europe; he moved there recently. Google is thus looking for heads for each of its vertical industry groups for all of its key European territories. Each of these vertical market heads will have to educate their market sectors (retailing, travel, and so on) so Google can attract new advertisers. Google already has offices across Europe, and its London office had tripled in size to 100 staff in just 2 years.

However, probably the biggest challenge Google faces is gearing up its employee selection system, now that the company must hire thousands of people per year. When Google started in business, job candidates typically suffered through a dozen or more in-person interviews, and the standards were so high that even applicants with years of great work experience often got turned down if they had just average college grades. But recently, even Google's cofounders have acknowledged to security analysts that setting such an extraordinarily high bar for hiring was holding back Google's expansion. For Google's first few years, one of the company's cofounder's interviewed nearly every job candidate before he or she was hired, and even today one of them still reviews the qualifications of everyone before he or she gets a final offer.

The experience of one candidate illustrates what Google is up against. A 24-year-old was interviewed for a corporate communications job at Google. Google first made contact with the candidate in May, and then, after two phone interviews, invited him to headquarters. There he had separate interviews with about six people and was treated to lunch in a Google cafeteria. They also had him turn in several "homework" assignments, including a personal statement and a marketing plan. In August, Google invited the candidate back for a second round, which it said would involve another four or five interviews. In the meantime, he decided he'd rather work at a start-up, and accepted another job at a new Web-based instant messaging provider.

Google's new head of human resources, a former GE executive, says that Google is trying to strike the right balance between letting Google and the candidate get to know each other while also moving quickly. To that end, Google recently administered a survey to all Google's current employees in an effort to identify the traits that correlate with success at Google. In the survey, employees responded to questions relating to about 300 variables, including their performance on standardized tests, how old they were when they first used a computer, and how many foreign languages they speak. The Google survey team then went back and compared the answers against the 30 or 40 job performance factors they keep for each employee. They thereby identified clusters of traits that Google might better focus on during the hiring process. Google is also moving from the free-form interviews it used in the past to a more structured process.

Questions

1. What do you think of the idea of Google correlating personal traits from the employees' answers on the survey to their performance, and then using that as the basis for screening job candidates? In other words, is it or is it not a good idea? Please explain your answer.
2. The benefits that Google pays obviously represent an enormous expense. Based on what you know about Google and on what you read in this book, how would you defend all these benefits if you're making a presentation to the security analysts who were analyzing Google's performance?

3. If you wanted to hire the brightest people around, how would you go about recruiting and selecting them?

4. To support its growth and expansion strategy, Google wants (among other traits) people who are super-bright and who work hard, often round-the-clock, and who are flexible and maintain a decent work–life balance. List five specific HR policies or practices that you think Google has implemented or should implement to support its strategy, and explain your answer.

5. What sorts of factors do you think Google will have to take into consideration as it tries transferring its culture and reward systems and way of doing business to its operations abroad?

6. Given the sorts of values and culture Google cherishes, briefly describe four specific activities you suggest they pursue during new-employee orientation.

Source: Source notes for Google: "Google Brings Vertical Structure to Europe," *New Media Age*, August 4, 2005, p. 2; Debbie Lovewell, "Employer Profile—Google: Searching for Talent," *Employee Benefits*, October 10, 2005, p. 66; "Google Looking for Gourmet Chefs," *Internet Week*, August 4, 2005; Douglas Merrill, "Google's 'Googley' Culture Kept Alive by Tech," *eWeek*, April 11, 2006; Robert Hof, "Google Gives Employees Another Option," *BusinessWeek Online*, December 13, 2005; Kevin Delaney, "Google Adjusts Hiring Process as Needs Grow," *The Wall Street Journal*, October 23, 2006, pp. B1, B8; Adam Lishinsky, "Search and Enjoy," *Fortune*, January 22, 2007, pp. 70–82; www.nypost.com/seven/10302008/business/frugal_google_cuts_perks_136011.htm, accessed July 12, 2009; Adam Bryant, "The Quest to Build a Better Boss," *New York Times*, March 13, 2011, p. 1, 7.

MUFFLER MAGIC*

Muffler Magic is a fast-growing chain of 25 automobile service centers in Nevada. Originally started 20 years ago as a muffler repair shop by Ronald Brown, the chain expanded rapidly to new locations, and as it did so Muffler Magic also expanded the services it provided, from muffler replacement to oil changes, brake jobs, and engine repair. Today, one can bring an automobile to a Muffler Magic shop for basically any type of service, from tires to mufflers to engine repair.

Auto service is a tough business. The shop owner is basically dependent upon the quality of the service people he or she hires and retains, and the most qualified mechanics find it easy to pick up and leave for a job paying a bit more at a competitor down the road. It's also a business in which productivity is very important. The single largest expense is usually the cost of labor. Auto service dealers generally don't just make up the prices that they charge customers for various repairs; instead, they charge based on standardized industry rates for jobs like changing spark plugs or repairing a leaky radiator. Therefore, if someone brings a car in for a new alternator and the standard number of hours for changing the alternator is an hour, but it takes the mechanic 2 hours, the service center's owner may end up making less profit on the transaction.

Quality is a persistent problem as well. For example, "rework" has recently been a problem at Muffler Magic. A customer recently brought her car to a Muffler Magic to have the car's brake pads replaced, which the service center did for her. Unfortunately, when she left she drove only about two blocks before she discovered that she had no brake power at all. It was simply fortuitous that she was going so slowly she was able to stop her car by slowly rolling up against a parking bumper. It subsequently turned out that the mechanic who replaced the brake pads had failed to properly tighten a fitting on the

*© Gary Dessler, Ph.D.

hydraulic brake tubes and the brake fluid had run out, leaving the car with no braking power. In a similar problem the month before that, a (different) mechanic replaced a fan belt, but forgot to refill the radiator with fluid; that customer's car overheated before he got four blocks away, and Muffler Magic had to replace the whole engine. Of course problems like these not only diminish the profitability of the company's profits, but, repeated many times over, have the potential for ruining Muffler Magic's word-of-mouth reputation.

Organizationally, Muffler Magic employs about 300 people, and Ron runs his company with eight managers, including himself as president, a controller, a purchasing director, a marketing director, and the human resource manager. He also has three regional managers to whom the eight or nine service center managers in each area of Nevada report. Over the past 2 years, as the company has opened new service centers, company-wide profits have diminished rather than increased. In part, these diminishing profits probably reflect the fact that Ron Brown has found it increasingly difficult to manage his growing operation ("Your reach is exceeding your grasp" is how Ron's wife puts it).

The company has only the most basic HR systems in place. It uses an application form that the human resource manager modified from one that he downloaded from the Web, and the standard employee status change request forms, sign-on forms, I-9 forms, and so on that it purchased from a human resource management supply house. Training is entirely on-the-job. Muffler Magic expects the experienced technicians that it hires to come to the job fully trained; to that end, the service center managers generally ask candidates for these jobs basic behavioral questions that hopefully provide a window into these applicants' skills. However, most of the other technicians hired to do jobs like rotating tires, fixing brake pads, and replacing mufflers are untrained and inexperienced. They are to be trained by either the service center manager or by more experienced technicians, on-the-job.

Ron Brown faces several HR-type problems. One, as he says, is that he faces the "tyranny of the immediate" when it comes to hiring employees. Although it's fine to say that he should be carefully screening each employee and checking their references and work ethic, from a practical point of view, with 25 centers to run, the centers' managers usually just hire anyone who seems to be breathing, as long as they can answer some basic interview questions about auto repair, such as, "What do you think the problem is if a 2001 Camry is overheating, and what would you do about it?"

Employee safety is also a problem. An automobile service center may not be the most dangerous type of workplace, but it is potentially dangerous. Employees are dealing with sharp tools, greasy floors, greasy tools, extremely hot temperatures (for instance, on mufflers and engines), and fast-moving engine parts including fan blades. There are some basic things that a service manager can do to ensure more safety, such as insisting that all oil spills be cleaned up immediately. However, from a practical point of view, there are a few ways to get around many of the problems—such as when the technician must check out an engine while it is running.

With Muffler Magic's profits going down instead of up, Brown's human resource manager has taken the position that the main problem is financial. As he says, "You get what you pay for" when it comes to employees, and if you compensate technicians better than your competitors do, then you get better technicians, ones who do their jobs better and stay longer with the company—and then profits will rise. So, the HR manager scheduled a meeting between himself, Ron Brown, and a professor of business who teaches compensation management at a local university. The HR manager has asked this professor to spend about a week looking at each of the service centers, analyzing the situation, and coming up with a compensation plan that will address Muffler Magic's quality and productivity problems. At this meeting, the professor makes three basic recommendations for changing the company's compensation policies.

Number one, she says that she has found that Muffler Magic suffers from what she calls "presenteeism"—in other words, employees drag themselves into work even when they're sick, because the company does not pay them if they are out; the company offers no sick days. In just a few days the professor couldn't properly quantify how much Muffler Magic is losing to presenteeism. However, from what she could see at each shop, there are typically one or two technicians working with various maladies like the cold or flu, and it seemed to her that each of these people was probably really only working about half of the time (although they were getting paid for the whole day). So, for 25 service centers per week, Muffler Magic could well be losing 125 or 130 personnel days per week of work. The professor suggests that Muffler Magic start allowing everyone to take 3 paid sick days per year, a reasonable suggestion. However, as Ron Brown points out, "Right now, we're only losing about half a day's pay for each employee who comes in and who works unproductively; with your suggestion, won't we lose the whole day?" The professor says she'll ponder that one.

Second, the professor recommends putting the technicians on a skill-for-pay plan. Basically, she suggests the following. Give each technician a letter grade (A through E) based upon that technician's particular skill level and abilities. An "A" technician is a team leader and needs to show that he or she has excellent diagnostic troubleshooting skills, and the ability to supervise and direct other technicians. At the other extreme, an "E" technician would typically be a new apprentice with little technical training. The other technicians fall in between those two levels, based on their individual skills and abilities.

In the professor's system, the "A" technician or team leader would assign and supervise all work done within his or her area but generally not do any mechanical repairs himself or herself. The team leader does the diagnostic troubleshooting, supervises and trains the other technicians, and test drives the car before it goes back to the customer. Under this plan, every technician receives a guaranteed hourly wage within a certain range, for instance:

A tech = $25–$30 an hour
B tech = $20–$25 an hour
C tech = $15–$20 an hour
D tech = $10–$15 an hour
E tech = $8–$10 an hour

Third, to directly address the productivity issue, the professor recommends that each service manager calculate each technician-team's productivity at the end of each day and at the end of each week. She suggests posting the running productivity total conspicuously for daily viewing. Then, the technicians as a group get weekly cash bonuses based upon their productivity. To calculate productivity, the professor recommends dividing the total labor hours billed by the total labor hours paid to technicians, in other words, total labor hours billed *divided by* total hours paid to technicians.

Having done some homework, the professor says that the national average for labor productivity is currently about 60%, and that only the best-run service centers achieve 85% or greater. By her rough calculations, Muffler Magic was attaining about industry average (about 60%—in other words, they were billing for only about 60 hours for each 100 hours that they actually had to pay technicians to do the jobs). (Of course, this was not entirely the technicians' fault. Technicians get time off for breaks and for lunch, and if a particular service center simply didn't have enough business on a particular day or during a particular week, then several technicians may well sit around idly waiting for the next car to come in.) The professor recommends setting a labor efficiency goal of 80% and posting each team's daily productivity results in the workplace to provide them with additional feedback. She recommends that if at the end of a week the team is able to boost its productivity ratio from the current 60% to 80%, then that team would get an additional 10% weekly pay bonus. After that, for every 5% boost of increased productivity above 80%, technicians would receive an additional 5% weekly bonus. So, if a technician's normal weekly pay is $400, that employee would receive an extra $40 at the end of the week when his team moves from 60% productivity to 80% productivity.

After the meeting, Ron Brown thanked the professor for her recommendations and told her he would think about it and get back to her. After the meeting, on the drive home, Ron was pondering what to do. He had to decide whether to institute the professor's sick leave policy, and whether to implement the professor's incentive and compensation plan. Before implementing anything, however, he wanted to make sure he understood the context in which he was making his decision. For example, did Muffler Magic really have an incentive pay problem, or were the problems more broad? Furthermore, how, if at all, would the professor's incentive plan impact the quality of the work that the teams were doing? And should the company really start paying for sick days? Ron Brown had a lot to think about.

Questions

1. Write a one-page summary outline listing three or four recommendations you would make with respect to each HR function (recruiting, selection, training, and so on) that you think Ron Brown should be addressing with his HR manager.
2. Develop a 10 question structured interview form Ron Brown's service center managers can use to interview experienced technicians.
3. If you were Ron Brown, would you implement the professor's recommendation addressing the presenteeism problem—in other words, start paying for sick days? Why or why not?
4. If you were advising Ron Brown, would you recommend that he implement the professor's skill-based pay and incentive pay plan as is? Why? Would you implement it with modifications? If you would modify it, please be specific about what you think those modifications should be, and why.

Source: Based generally on actual facts, but Muffler Magic is a fictitious company. This case is based largely on information in Drew Paras, "The Pay Factor: Technicians' Salaries Can Be the Largest Expense in a Server Shop, as Well as the Biggest Headache. Here's How One Shop Owner Tackled the Problem," *Motor Age*, November 2003, pp. 76–79; see also Jennifer Pellet, "Health Care Crisis," *Chief Executive*, June 2004, pp. 56–61; "Firms Press to Quantify, Control Presenteeism," *Employee Benefits*, December 1, 2002.

BP TEXAS CITY[*]

When BP's Horizon oil rig exploded in the Gulf of Mexico in 2010, it triggered tragic reminders for experts in the safety community. In March 2005, an explosion and fire at British Petroleum's (BP) Texas City, Texas, refinery killed 15 people

[*]© Gary Dessler, Ph.D.

and injured 500 people in the worst U.S. industrial accident in more than 10 years. The disaster triggered three investigations: one internal investigation by BP, one by the U.S. Chemical Safety Board, and an independent investigation chaired by former U.S. Secretary of State James Baker and an 11-member panel that was organized at BP's request.

To put the results of these three investigations into context, it's useful to understand that under its current management, BP had pursued, for the past 10 or so years before the Texas City explosion, a strategy emphasizing cost-cutting and profitability. The basic conclusion of the investigations was that cost-cutting helped compromise safety at the Texas City refinery. It's useful to consider each investigation's findings.

The Chemical Safety Board's (CSB) investigation, according to Carol Merritt, the board's chairwoman, showed that "BP's global management was aware of problems with maintenance, spending, and infrastructure well before March 2005." Apparently, faced with numerous earlier accidents, BP did make some safety improvements. However, it focused primarily on emphasizing personal employee safety behaviors and procedural compliance, and on thereby reducing safety accident rates. The problem (according to the CSB) was that "catastrophic safety risks remained." For example, according to the CSB, "unsafe and antiquated equipment designs were left in place, and unacceptable deficiencies in preventive maintenance were tolerated." Basically, the CSB found that BP's budget cuts led to a progressive deterioration of safety at the Texas City refinery. Said Ms. Merritt, "In an aging facility like Texas City, it is not responsible to cut budgets related to safety and maintenance without thoroughly examining the impact on the risk of a catastrophic accident."

Looking at specifics, the CSB said that a 2004 internal audit of 35 BP business units, including Texas City (BP's largest refinery), found significant safety gaps they all had in common, including for instance, a lack of leadership competence, and "systemic underlying issues" such as a widespread tolerance of noncompliance with basic safety rules and poor monitoring of safety management systems and processes. Ironically, the CSB found that BP's accident prevention effort at Texas City had achieved a 70% reduction in worker injuries in the year before the explosion. Unfortunately, this simply meant that individual employees were having fewer accidents. The larger, more fundamental problem was that the potentially explosive situation inherent in the depreciating machinery remained.

The CSB found that the Texas City explosion followed a pattern of years of major accidents at the facility. In fact, there had apparently been an average of one employee death every 16 months at the plant for the last 30 years. The CSB found that the equipment directly involved in the most recent explosion was an obsolete design already phased out in most refineries and chemical plants, and that key pieces of its instrumentation were not working. There had also been previous instances where flammable vapors were released from the same unit in the 10 years prior to the explosion. In 2003, an external audit had referred to the Texas City refinery's infrastructure and assets as "poor" and found what it referred to as a "checkbook mentality," one in which budgets were not sufficient to manage all the risks. In particular, the CSB found that BP had implemented a 25% cut on fixed costs between 1998 and 2000 and that this adversely impacted maintenance expenditures and net expenditures, and refinery infrastructure. Going on, the CSB found that in 2004, there were three major accidents at the refinery that killed three workers.

BP's own internal report concluded that the problems at Texas City were not of recent origin, and instead were years in the making. It said BP was taking steps to address them. Its investigation found "no evidence of anyone consciously or intentionally taking actions or making decisions that put others at risk." Said BP's report, "The underlying reasons for the behaviors and actions displayed during the incident are complex, and the team has spent much time trying to understand them—it is evident that they were many years in the making and will require concerted and committed actions to address." BP's report concluded that there were five underlying causes for the massive explosion:

- A working environment had eroded to one characterized by resistance to change, and a lack of trust.
- Safety, performance, and risk reduction priorities had not been set and consistently reinforced by management.
- Changes in the "complex organization" led to a lack of clear accountabilities and poor communication.
- A poor level of hazard awareness and understanding of safety resulted in workers accepting levels of risk that were considerably higher than at comparable installations.
- Adequate early warning systems for problems were lacking, and there were no independent means of understanding the deteriorating standards at the plant.

The report from the BP-initiated but independent 11-person panel chaired by former U.S. Secretary of State James Baker contained specific conclusions and recommendations. The Baker panel looked at BP's corporate safety oversight, the corporate safety culture, and the process safety management systems at BP at the Texas City plant as well at BP's other refineries.

Basically, the Baker panel concluded that BP had not provided effective safety process leadership and had not established safety as a core value at the five refineries it looked at (including Texas City).

Like the CSB, the Baker panel found that BP had emphasized personal safety in recent years and had in fact improved personal safety performance, but had not emphasized the overall safety process, thereby mistakenly interpreting "improving personal injury rates as an indication of acceptable process safety performance at its U.S. refineries." In fact, the Baker panel went on, by focusing on these somewhat misleading improving personal injury rates, BP created a false sense of confidence that it was properly addressing process safety risks. It also found that the safety culture at Texas City did not have the positive, trusting, open environment that a proper safety culture required. The Baker panel's other findings included the following.

- BP did not always ensure that adequate resources were effectively allocated to support or sustain a high level of process safety performance.
- BP's refinery personnel are "overloaded" by corporate initiatives.
- Operators and maintenance personnel work high rates of overtime.
- BP tended to have a short-term focus and its decentralized management system and entrepreneurial culture delegated substantial discretion to refinery plant managers "without clearly defining process safety expectations, responsibilities, or accountabilities."
- There was no common, unifying process safety culture among the five refineries.

- The company's corporate safety management system did not make sure there was timely compliance with internal process safety standards and programs.
- BP's executive management either did not receive refinery-specific information that showed that process safety deficiencies existed at some of the plants, or did not effectively respond to any information it did receive.[1]

The Baker panel made several safety recommendations for BP, including the following.

1. The company's corporate management must provide leadership on process safety.
2. The company should establish a process safety management system that identifies, reduces, and manages the process safety risks of the refineries.
3. The company should make sure its employees have an appropriate level of process safety knowledge and expertise.
4. The company should involve "relevant stakeholders" in developing a positive, trusting, and open process safety culture at each refinery.
5. BP should clearly define expectations and strengthen accountability for process safety performance.
6. BP should better coordinate its process safety support for the refining line organization.
7. BP should develop an integrated set of leading and lagging performance indicators for effectively monitoring process safety performance.
8. BP should establish and implement an effective system to audit process safety performance.
9. The company's board should monitor the implementation of the panel's recommendations and the ongoing process safety performance of the refineries.
10. BP should transform into a recognized industry leader in process safety management.

In making its recommendations, the panel singled out the company's chief executive at the time, Lord Browne, by saying, "In hindsight, the panel believes if Browne had demonstrated comparable leadership on and commitment to process safety [as he did for responding to climate change] that would have resulted in a higher level of safety at refineries."

Overall, the Baker panel found that BP's top management had not provided "effective leadership" on safety. It found that the failings went to the very top of the organization, to the company's chief executive, and to several of his top lieutenants. The Baker panel emphasized the importance of top management commitment, saying, for instance, that "it is imperative that BP leadership set the process safety tone at the top of the organization and establish appropriate expectations regarding process safety performance." It also said BP "has not provided effective leadership in making certain its management and U.S. refining workforce understand what is expected of them regarding process safety performance."

Lord Browne, the chief executive, stepped down about a year after the explosion. About the same time, some BP shareholders were calling for the company's executives and board directors to have their bonuses more closely tied to the company's safety

---

[1]These findings and the following suggestions based on "BP Safety Report Finds Company's Process Safety Culture Ineffective," *Global Refining & Fuels Report*, January 17, 2007.

and environmental performance in the wake of Texas City. In October 2009, OSHA announced it was filing the largest fine in its history for this accident, for $87 million, against BP. One year later, BP's Horizon oil rig in the Gulf of Mexico exploded, taking 11 lives.

Questions

1. The textbook defines ethics as "the principles of conduct governing an individual or a group," and specifically as the standards one uses to decide what their conduct should be. To what extent do you believe that what happened at BP is as much a breakdown in the company's ethical systems as it is in its safety systems, and how would you defend your conclusion?

2. Are the Occupational Safety and Health Administration's standards, policies, and rules aimed at addressing problems like the ones that apparently existed at the Texas City plant? If so, how would you explain the fact that problems like these could have continued for so many years?

3. Since there were apparently at least three deaths in the year prior to the major explosion, and an average of about one employee death per 16 months for the previous 10 years, how would you account for the fact that mandatory OSHA inspections missed these glaring sources of potential catastrophic events?

4. The textbook lists numerous suggestions for "how to prevent accidents." Based on what you know about the Texas City explosion, what do you say Texas City tells you about the most important three steps an employer can take to prevent accidents?

5. Based on what you learned in Chapter 10 (Safety), would you make any additional recommendations to BP over and above those recommendations made by the Baker panel and the CSB? If so, what would those recommendations be?

6. Explain specifically how strategic human resource management at BP seems to have supported the company's broader strategic aims. What does this say about the advisability of always linking human resource strategy to a company's strategic aims?

Source: Source notes for BP Texas City: Sheila McNulty, "BP Knew of Safety Problems, Says Report," *The Financial Times*, October 31, 2006, p. 1; "CBS: Documents Show BP Was Aware of Texas City Safety Problems," *World Refining & Fuels Today*, October 30, 2006; "BP Safety Report Finds Company's Process Safety Culture Ineffective," *Global Refining & Fuels Report*, January 17, 2007; "BP Safety Record Under Attack," *Europe Intelligence Wire*, January 17, 2007; Mark Hofmann, "BP Slammed for Poor Leadership on Safety, Oil Firm Agrees to Act on Review Panel's Recommendations," *Business Intelligence*, January 22, 2007, p. 3; "Call for Bonuses to Include Link with Safety Performance," *The Guardian*, January 18, 2007, p. 24; www.bp.com/genericarticle.do?categoryId=9005029&contentId=7015905, accessed July 12, 2009; Steven Greenhouse, "BP Faces Record Fine For '05 Blast," *The New York Times*, October 30, 2009, pp. 1, 6; Kyle W. Morrison, "Blame to Go Around," *Safety & Health* 183, no. 3 (March 2011) p. 40.

GLOSSARY

action learning. A training technique by which management trainees are allowed to work full time analyzing and solving problems in other departments.

adverse impact. The overall impact of employer practices that result in significantly higher percentages of members of minorities and other protected groups being rejected for employment, placement, or promotion.

affirmative action. Steps that are taken for the purpose of eliminating the present effects of past discrimination.

Age Discrimination in Employment Act (ADEA) of 1967. The act prohibiting age discrimination and specifically protecting individuals over 40 years old.

Albemarle Paper Company v. *Moody.* Supreme Court case in which it was ruled that the validity of job tests must be documented and that employee performance standards must be job related.

alternation ranking method. An appraisal process in which the employee who is highest on a trait being measured and also the one who is lowest is identified, alternating between highest and lowest until all employees to be rated have been addressed.

alternative dispute resolution (ADR) program. Grievance program that requires employees to pursue mediation prior to pressing a claim.

Americans with Disabilities Act (ADA). The act requiring employers to make reasonable accommodations for disabled employees; it prohibits discrimination against disabled persons.

annual bonus plans. Plans that are designed to motivate short-term performance of managers and which are tied to company profitability.

application form. The form that provides information on an applicant's education, prior work record, and skills.

appraisal interview. The culmination of an appraisal, in which the supervisor and subordinate review the appraisal and make plans to remedy deficiencies and reinforce strengths.

arbitration. The most definitive type of third-party intervention, in which the arbitrator often has the power to determine and dictate the settlement terms.

authority. The right to make decisions, direct others' work, and give orders.

authorization cards. In order to petition for a union election, the union must show that at least 30% of employees may be interested in being unionized. Employees indicate this interest by signing authorization cards.

bargaining unit. The group of employees the union will be authorized to represent.

behavior modeling. A training technique in which trainees are first shown good management techniques and are then asked to play roles in a simulated situation, and are then given feedback and praise by their supervisor.

benefits. Indirect financial payments given to employees. They may include health and life insurance, vacation, pension, education plans, and discounts on company products, for instance.

bona fide occupational qualification (BFOQ). Requirement that an employee be of a certain religion, sex, or national origin where that is reasonably necessary to the organization's normal operation. Specified by the 1964 Civil Rights Act.

boycott. The combined refusal by employees and other interested parties to buy or use the employer's products.

bullying. Singling out someone to harass and mistreat them.

burnout. The total depletion of physical and mental resources caused by excessive striving to reach an unrealistic work-related goal.

business necessity. Justification for an otherwise discriminatory employment practice, provided there is an overriding legitimate business purpose.

career management. A process for enabling the employees to better understand and develop their career skills and interests, and to use the skills and interests most effectively both within the company and, if necessary, after they leave the firm.

case study method. A development method in which the manager is presented with a written description of an organizational problem to diagnose and solve.

central tendency. The tendency to rate all employees about average.

citations. Summons informing employers and employees of the regulations and standards that have been violated in the workplace.

Civil Rights Act of 1991 (CRA 1991). This act places burden of proof back on employers and permits compensatory and punitive damages.

coaching. Educating, instructing, and training subordinates.

coaching/understudy method. A training technique in which an experienced worker or supervisor trains the employee on the job.

collective bargaining. The process through which representatives of management and the union meet to negotiate a labor agreement.

competency model. A graphic model that consolidates, usually in one diagram, a precise overview of the competencies (the knowledge, skills, and behaviors) someone would need to do a job well.

competitive advantage. The basis for differentiation over competitors and thus for hoping to claim certain customers.

competitive strategy. A strategy that identifies how to build and strengthen the business's long-term competitive position in the marketplace.

computer-based training (CBT). A training method where employees use a computer-based system to interactively increase their knowledge or skills.

content validity. A test that is *content valid* is one in which the test contains a fair sample of the tasks and skills actually needed for the job in question.

controlled experimentation. Formal methods for testing the effectiveness of a training program, preferably with before-and-after tests and a control group that is not exposed to training.

corporate-level strategy. A strategy that identifies the sorts of businesses that will comprise the company and the ways in which these businesses relate to each other.

criterion validity. A type of validity based on showing that scores on the test (*predictors*) are related to job performance (*criterion*).

critical incident method. Keeping a record of uncommonly good or undesirable examples of an employee's work-related behavior and reviewing it with the employee at predetermined times.

cross training. Training employees to do different tasks or jobs than their own; doing so facilitates flexibility and job rotation.

defined benefit plan. A plan that contains a formula for specifying retirement benefits.

defined contribution plan. A plan in which the employer's contribution to employees' retirement or savings funds is specified.

digital dashboard. Presents the manager with desktop graphs and charts, so he or she gets a picture of where the company has been and where it's going, in terms of each activity in the strategy map.

discipline. A procedure that corrects or punishes a subordinate for violating a rule or procedure.

discrimination. Taking specific actions toward or against the person based on the person's group.

dismissal. Involuntary termination of an employee's employment with the firm.

disparate impact. An unintentional disparity between the proportion of a protected group applying for a position and the proportion getting the job.

disparate treatment. An intentional disparity between the proportion of a protected group and the proportion getting the job.

diversity. Having a workforce comprised of two or more groups of employees with various racial, ethnic, gender, cultural, national origin, handicap, age, and religious backgrounds.

downsizing. Refers to the process of reducing, usually dramatically, the number of people employed by the firm.

economic strike. Strike that results from a failure to agree on the terms of a contract.

Employee Assistance Program (EAP). A formal employer program for providing employees with counseling and/or treatment programs for problems such as alcoholism, gambling, or stress.

employee compensation. Refers to all forms of pay or rewards going to employees and arising from their employment.

employee orientation. A procedure for providing new employees with basic background information about the firm.

Employee Retirement Income Security Act (ERISA). Act signed into law by President Ford in 1974 to require that pension rights be vested and protected by a government agency, the Pension Benefits Guarantee Corporation.

employee stock ownership plan (ESOP). With an ESOP, a corporation contributes shares of its own stock to a trust to purchase company stock for employees.

The trust distributes the stock to employees upon retirement or separation from service.

engagement. The commitment and dedication of a firm's employees.

Equal Employment Opportunity Commission (EEOC). The commission, created by Title VII, empowered to investigate job discrimination complaints and sue on behalf of complainants.

Equal Pay Act of 1963. An amendment to the Fair Labor Standards Act designed to require equal pay for women doing the same work as men.

ethics. The study of standards of conduct and moral judgment; also the standards of right conduct.

ethnocentrism. The tendency to view members of other social groups less favorably than one's own.

exit interview. Interview conducted by the employer immediately prior to the employee leaving the firm with the aim of better understanding what the employee thinks about the company.

fact-finder. In labor relations, a neutral party who studies the issues in a dispute and makes a public recommendation for a reasonable settlement.

Fair Labor Standards Act. Act passed by Congress in 1936 to provide for minimum wages, maximum hours, overtime pay, and child labor protection. The law has been amended many times and covers most employees.

federal agency guidelines. Guidelines issued by federal agencies explaining recommended employer equal employment federal legislation procedures in detail.

flexible benefits plan. Individualized plans allowed by employers to accommodate employee preferences for benefits.

forced distribution method. An appraisal method by which the manager places predetermined percentages of subordinate in performance categories.

functional strategy. A strategy that identifies the basic courses of action that each department will pursue in order to help the business attain its competitive goals.

gain-sharing plan. An incentive plan that engages employees in a common effort to achieve productivity objectives and share the gains.

gender harassment. A form of hostile environment harassment that appears to be motivated by hostility toward individuals who violate gender ideals.

gender-role stereotypes. The tendency to associate women with certain (frequently nonmanagerial) jobs.

good-faith bargaining. A term that means both parties are communicating and negotiating and that proposals are being matched with counterproposals, with both parties making every reasonable effort to arrive at agreements. It does not mean that either party is compelled to agree to a proposal.

graphic rating scale. A scale that lists a number of traits and a range of performance for each. The employee is then rated by identifying the score that best describes his or her level of performance for each trait.

Griggs v. *Duke Power Company.* Supreme Court case in which the plaintiff argued that his employer's requirement that coal handlers be high school graduates was unfairly discriminatory. In finding for the plaintiff, the Court ruled that discrimination need not be overt to be illegal, that employment practices must be related to job performance, and that the burden of proof is on the employer to show that hiring standards are job related.

guaranteed fair treatment. Employer programs aimed at ensuring that all employees are treated fairly, generally by providing formalized, well-documented, and highly publicized vehicles through which employees can appeal any eligible issues.

halo effect. A common appraisal problem in which the rating of a subordinate on one trait influences the way the person is rated on other traits.

HR Scorecard. Process for measuring the HR function's effectiveness and efficiency in producing employee behaviors needed to achieve the company's strategic goals.

human resource management. The policies and practices one needs to carry out the "people" or human resource aspects of a management position, including recruiting, screening, training, rewarding, and appraising.

illegal bargaining items. Items in collective bargaining that are forbidden by law; for example, the clause agreeing to hire "union members exclusively" would be illegal in a right-to-work state.

improvisation. A form of management training in which the trainees learn skills such as openness and creativity by playing games that require that they improvise answers and solutions.

incentive plan. A compensation plan that ties pay to performance.

in-house development centers. A company-based facility for exposing current or prospective managers to exercises to develop improved management skills.

insubordination. Willful disregard or disobedience of the boss's authority or legitimate orders.

interview. A procedure designed to solicit information from a person's oral responses to oral inquiries.

job analysis. The procedure for determining the duties and skill requirements of a job and the kind of person who should be hired for it.

job description. A list of a job's duties, responsibilities, reporting relationships, working conditions, and supervisory responsibilities—one product of a job analysis.

job hazard analysis. A systematic approach to identifying and eliminating workplace hazards before they occur.

job posting. Posting notices of job openings on company bulletin boards as a recruiting method.

job rotation. A management training technique that involves moving a trainee from department to department to broaden his or her experience and identify strengths and weaknesses.

job specification. A list of a job's "human requirements," that is, the requisite education, skills, personality, and so on—a product of a job analysis.

job withdrawal. Actions intended to place physical or psychological distance between employees and negative work environments.

Landrum-Griffin Act. A law aimed at protecting union members from possible wrongdoing on the part of their unions.

layoff. A situation in which employees are told there is no work for them but that management intends to recall them when work is again available.

learning organization. An organization "skilled at creating, acquiring, and transferring knowledge and at modifying its behavior to reflect new knowledge and insights."

lifelong learning. Providing employees with continuing learning experiences over their tenure with the firm, with the aim of ensuring they have the opportunity to obtain the knowledge and skills they need to do their jobs effectively.

line authority. Authority that gives managers the right to issue orders to other managers or employees.

line manager. A manager who is authorized to direct the work of subordinates and responsible for accomplishing the organization's goals.

lockout. A refusal by the employer to provide opportunities to work.

management assessment center. A facility in which management candidates are asked to make decisions and to take managerial actions in hypothetical situations and are scored on their performance.

management by objectives (MBO). A performance management method through which the manager sets organizationally relevant goals with each employee and then periodically discusses progress toward these goals, in an organization-wide effort.

management development. Any attempt to improve current or future management performance by imparting knowledge, changing attitudes, or increasing skills.

management games. A development technique in which teams of managers compete by making usually computerized decisions regarding realistic but simulated situations.

mandatory bargaining items. Items in collective bargaining that a party must bargain over if they are introduced by the other party—for example, pay.

mediation. Labor relations intervention in which a neutral third party tries to assist the principals in reaching agreement.

merit pay (merit raise). Any salary increase awarded to an employee based on his or her individual performance.

national emergency strikes. Strikes that might "imperil the national health and safety."

National Labor Relations Board (NLRB). The agency created by the Wagner Act to investigate unfair labor practice charges and to provide for secret-ballot elections and majority rule in determining whether or not a firm's employees want a union.

Norris-LaGuardia Act. This law marked the beginning of the era of strong encouragement of unions and guaranteed to each employee the right to bargain collectively "free from interference, restraint, or coercion."

Occupational Safety and Health Act. The law passed by Congress in 1970 "to assure so far as possible every working man and woman in the nation safe and healthful working conditions and to preserve our human resources."

Occupational Safety and Health Administration (OSHA). The agency created within the Department of Labor to set safety and health standards for almost all workers in the United States.

Office of Federal Contract Compliance Programs (OFCCP). The office responsible for implementing executive orders and ensuring compliance of federal contractors.

on-the-job training (OJT). Training a person to learn a job while working at it.

operational safety reviews. Reviews conducted by agencies to ascertain whether units under their jurisdiction are complying with all the applicable safety laws, regulations, orders, and rules.

organizational development (OD). A development method aimed at changing the attitudes, values, and beliefs of employees so that employees can improve the organization.

outplacement counseling. A systematic process by which a terminated person is trained and counseled in the techniques of self-appraisal and securing a new position.

paired comparison method. An appraisal method in which every subordinate to be rated is paired with and compared to every other subordinate on each trait.

peer appraisal. Appraisal of an employee by his or her peers.

performance analysis. Verifying that there is a performance deficiency and determining whether that deficiency should be rectified through training or through some other means (such as transferring the employee).

performance appraisal. Evaluating an employee's current and/or past performance relative to his or her performance standards.

performance appraisal process. A three-step process involving: (1) setting work standards, (2) assessing the employee's actual performance relative to those standards (this usually involves some rating form), and (3) providing feedback to the employee with the aim of helping him or her to eliminate performance deficiencies or to continue to perform above par.

performance management. The continuous process through which companies ensure that employees are working toward organizational goals. It includes practices through which the manager defines the employee's goals and work, develops the employee's skills and capabilities, evaluates the person's goal-directed behavior, and then rewards him or her in a fashion consistent with the company's and the person's needs.

person-job fit. The goal of matching (1) the knowledge, skills, abilities (KSAs), and competencies that are central to performing the job (as determined by job analysis) with (2) the prospective employee's knowledge, skills, abilities and competencies.

personnel replacement charts. Company records showing present performance and promotability of inside candidates for the firm's most important positions.

piecework. A system of incentive pay tying pay to the number of items processed by each individual worker.

portability. Making it easier for employees who leave the firm prior to retirement to take their accumulated pension funds with them.

predictive workforce monitoring. Paying continuous attention to and frequently adapting to workforce planning needs.

Pregnancy Discrimination Act (PDA). An amendment to Title VII of the Civil Rights Act that prohibits sex discrimination based on "pregnancy, childbirth, or related medical conditions."

productivity. The ratio of outputs (goods and services) divided by the inputs (resources such as labor and capital).

profit-sharing plan. A plan whereby most employees share in the company's profits.

protected class. Persons such as older workers and women protected by equal opportunity laws including Title VII.

qualifications inventories. Manual or computerized records listing employees' education, career and development interests, languages, special skills, and so on, to be used in identifying inside candidates for promotion.

ratio analysis. A forecasting technique that involves analyzing and extrapolating the ratio of a dependent variable, such as salespersons required, with an independent variable, such as sales.

reliability. The characteristic that refers to the consistency of scores obtained by the same person when retested with the identical or equivalent tests.

right to work. A term used to describe state statutory or constitutional provisions banning the requirement of union membership as a condition of employment.

safety awareness program. Program that enables trained supervisors to orient new workers arriving at a jobsite regarding common safety hazards and simple prevention methods.

salary (or compensation) surveys. Surveys aimed at determining prevailing pay rates. Provide specific wage rates for specific jobs.

Scanlon plan. An incentive plan developed in 1937 by Joseph Scanlon and designed to encourage cooperation, involvement, and sharing of benefits.

scatter plot. A graphical method used to help identify the relationship between two quantitative variables.

sensitivity training. A method for increasing employees' insights into their own behavior through candid discussions in groups led by special trainers.

severance pay. A onetime payment that employers provide when terminating an employee.

sexual harassment. Harassment on the basis of sex that has the purpose or effect of substantially interfering with a person's work performance or creating an intimidating, hostile, or offensive work environment.

staff authority. Authority that gives a manager the right to advise other managers or employees.

staff manager. A manager who assists and advises line managers.

standard deviation rule. In selection, the standard deviation rule holds that as a rule of thumb, the difference between the numbers of minority candidates we *would have expected* to hire and whom *we actually hired* should be less than two standard deviations.

stereotyping. A process in which someone ascribes specific behavioral traits to individuals based on their apparent membership in a group.

stock option. The right to purchase a stated number of shares of company stock at a set price at some time in the future.

strategy. The company's plan for how it will match its internal strengths and weaknesses with external opportunities and threats in order to maintain a competitive advantage.

strategic human resource management. Linking HRM policies and practices with strategic goals and objectives in order to improve business performance.

strategic management. The process of identifying and executing the organization's mission by matching its capabilities with the demands of its environment.

strategic plan. The company's plan for how it will match its internal strengths and weaknesses with external opportunities and threats in order to maintain a competitive advantage.

strategy map. A graphical tool that summarizes the chain of activities that contribute to a company's success.

survey feedback. A method that involves surveying employees' attitudes and providing feedback to facilitate problems being solved by the managers and employees.

sympathy strike. A strike that takes place when one union strikes in support of another's strike.

Taft-Hartley Act. A law prohibiting union unfair labor practices and enumerating the rights of employees as union members. It also enumerates the rights of employers.

"Take a strike." Degree to which parties in a labor dispute are willing to tolerate employees going on strike.

talent management. The goal-oriented and integrated process of planning, recruiting, developing, managing, and compensating employees throughout the organization.

task analysis. A detailed study of a job to identify the skills required so that an appropriate training program may be instituted.

team building. Improving the effectiveness of teams through the use of consultants and team-building meetings and experiences.

terminate at will. The idea, based in law, that the employment relationship can be terminated at will by either the employer or the employee for any reason.

termination interview. The interview in which an employee is informed of the fact that he or she has been dismissed.

test validity. The degree to which a test, interview, and so on measures what it purports to measure or fulfills the function it was designed to fill.

Title VII of the 1964 Civil Rights Act. The section of the Act that says an employer cannot discriminate on the basis of race, color, religion, sex, or national origin with respect to employment.

tokenism. Occurs when a company appoints a small group of women or minorities to high-profile positions, rather than more aggressively seeking full representation for that group.

training. The process of teaching new employees the basic skills they need to perform their jobs.

trend analysis. Study of a firm's past employment needs over a period of years to predict future needs.

unfair labor practice strike. Strike to protest illegal conduct by the employer.

union salting. A union organizing tactic by which workers who are employed by a union as undercover union organizers are hired by unwitting employers.

unsafe acts. Behaviors that potentially cause accidents.

unsafe conditions. The mechanical and physical conditions that cause accidents.

upward feedback. Having subordinates evaluate their supervisors' performance.

utility analysis. The degree to which use of a selection measure improves the quality of individuals selected over what would have happened if the measure had not been used.

utilization analysis. The process of comparing the percentage of minority employees in a job (or jobs) at the company with the number of similarly trained minority employees available in the relevant labor market.

validity generalization. The degree to which evidence of a measure's validity obtained in one situation can be generalized to another situation without further study.

vested. Point at which accumulated pension rights are guaranteed to the employee.

vestibule training. A technique in which trainees learn on the actual or simulated equipment they will use on the job but receive their training off the job.

virtual classroom. Special collaboration software used to enable multiple remote learners, using their PCs or laptops, to participate in live audio and visual discussions, communicate via written text, and learn via content such as PowerPoint slides.

Vocational Rehabilitation Act of 1973. The act requiring certain federal contractors to take affirmative action for disabled persons.

voluntary bargaining items. Items in collective bargaining for which bargaining is neither illegal nor mandatory—neither party can be compelled to negotiate over those items.

Wagner Act. A law that banned certain types of unfair labor practices and provided for secret-ballot elections and majority rule for determining whether or not a firm's employees want to unionize.

wildcat strike. An unauthorized strike occurring during the term of a contract.

workaholic. A person who feels driven to always be on time and meet deadlines.

workers' compensation. Provides income and medical benefits to work-related accident victims or their dependents regardless of fault.

workforce analysis. Employers use *workforce analysis* to obtain and to analyze the data regarding the firm's use of protected versus nonprotected employees in various job classifications.

workforce planning. The process of deciding what positions the firm will have to fill, and how to fill them.

workplace flexibility. Arming employees with the information technology tools they need to get their jobs done wherever they are.

work sampling technique. Tries to predict candidates' job performance by requiring job candidates to perform one or more actual samples of the job's tasks.

wrongful discharge. An employee dismissal that does not comply with the law or does not comply with the contractual arrangement stated or implied by the firm via its employment application forms, employee manuals, or other promises.

ENDNOTES

Chapter 1

1. Quoted in Fred K. Foulkes, "The Expanding Role of the Personnel Function," *Harvard Business Review* (March/April 1975): 71–84. See also www.bls.gov/oco/ocos021.htm, accessed October 3, 2011.

2. Steve Bates, "No Experience Necessary? Many Companies Are Putting Non-HR Executives in Charge of HR with Mixed Results," *HR Magazine* 46, no. 11 (November 2001): 34–41. See also Fay Hansen, "Top of the Class," *Workforce Management* (June 23, 2008): 1, 25–30.

3. "A Profile of Human Resource Executives," *BNA Bulletin to Management* (June 21, 2001): S5.

4. These data come from "Small Business: A Report of the President" (1998), www.SBA.gov/ADV/stats; see also "Statistics of US Businesses and Non-Employer Status," www.SBA.gov/ADV oh/research/data.html, accessed March 9, 2006.

5. "Human Resource Activities, Budgets & Staffs, 1999–2000," *BNA Bulletin to Management* 51, no. 25 (June 29, 2000): S1–S6. In fact, one study found that delegating somewhat more of the HR activities to line managers "had a positive effect on HR managers' perceptions of their units' reputation among line managers." Carol Kulik and Elissa Perry, "When Less Is More: The Effect of Devolution on HR as a Strategic Role and Construed Image," *Human Resource Management* 47, no. 3 (Fall 2008): 541–558.

6. Some employers, like Google, are adding "chief sustainability officers" within human resource management, responsible for fostering the company's environmental sustainability efforts. Nancy Woodward, "New Breed of Human Resource Leader," *HR Magazine* (June 2008): 53–57.

7. See Dave Ulrich, "The New HR Organization," *Workforce Management* (December 10, 2007): 40–44; and Dave Ulrich, "The 21st-Century HR Organization," *Human Resource Management* 47, no. 4 (Winter 2008): 829–850. Some writers distinguish among three basic human resource management subfields: micro HRM (which covers the HR subfunctions such as recruitment and selection), strategic HRM, and international HRM. Mark Lengnick Hall et al., "Strategic Human Resource Management: The Evolution of the Field," *Human Resource Management Review* 19 (2009): 64–85.

8. Robert Grossman, "Saving Shared Services," *HR Magazine* (September 2010): 26–31.

9. Robert Grossman, "IBM's HR Takes a Risk," *HR Management* (April 2007): 54–59.

10. "Immigrants in the Workforce," *BNA Bulletin to Management Datagraph* (August 15, 1996): 260–261. See also Shari Caudron et al., "80 People, Events and Trends that Shaped HR," *Workforce* (January 2002): 26–56.

11. See, for example, "HR 2018: Top Predictions," *Workforce Management* 87, no. 20 (December 15, 2008): 20–21.

12. For discussions of some other important trends, see, for example, "Workplace Trends: An Overview of the Findings of the Latest SHRM Workplace Forecast," *Society for Human Resource Management, Workplace Visions* 3 (2008): 1–8; and Ed Frauenheim, "Future View," *Workforce Management* (December 15, 2008): 18–23.

13. www.census.gov/foreign-trade/statistics/historical/gands.pdf, accessed March 3, 2012.

14. "Human Resources Wharton," www.knowledge.wharton.upe.edu, accessed January 8, 2006.

15. See, for example, Anthea Zacharatos et al., "High-Performance Work Systems and Occupational Safety," *Journal of Applied Psychology* 90, no. 1 (2005): 77–93.

16. http://facebookrecruiting.net/, accessed May 8, 2011.

17. Ibid.

18. Timothy Appel, "Better Off a Blue-Collar," *Wall Street Journal* (July 1, 2003): B-1. See also "A Third Industrial Revolution," The Economist (April 21, 2012): 1–20.

19. "Workforce Readiness and the New Essential Skills," *Society for Human Resource Management, Workplace Visions* 2 (2008): 5.

20. See "Charting the Projections: 2004–2014," *Occupational Outlook Quarterly* (Winter 2005–2006).

21. Richard Crawford, *In the Era of Human Capital* (New York: Harper Business, 1991), p. 26. See also, Russell Crook, et al., "Does Human Capital Matter? A Meta-Analysis of the Relationship Between Human Capital and Firm Performance," *Journal of Applied Psychology* 96, no. 3 (2011): 443–456.

22. Frank Levy and Kyoung-Hee Yu, "Offshoring Radiology Services to India," Industrial Performance Center, Massachusetts Institute of Technology, September 2006, web.mit.edu/ipc/publications/pdf/06-005.pdf, accessed February 15, 2012.

23. Michael Schroeder, "States Fight Exodus of Jobs," *Wall Street Journal* (June 3, 2003): 84. See also Roger J. Moncarz, Michael G. Wolf, and Benjamin Wright, "Service-Providing Occupations, Offshoring, and the Labor Market," *Monthly Labor Review* (December 2008): 71–86. Some employers are bringing jobs, particularly higher-tech manufacturing jobs, back to the United States. See for example, www.usatoday

.com/money/economy/2010-08-06-manufacturing04_CV_N.htm, accessed May 8, 2011.

24. "Charting the Projections: 2004–2014," *Occupational Outlook Quarterly* (Winter 2005–2006): 48–50; and www.bls.gov/emp/emplabor01.pdf, accessed October 20, 2008.

25. "Percent Growth in Labor Force by Race, Projected 2008–18," *Occupational Outlook Quarterly* (Winter 2009–2010): 35, and "Percent Growth in Labor Force by Ethnic Origin, Projected 2008–2018," *Occupational Outlook Quarterly* (Winter 2009–2010): 36.

26. Tony Carnevale, "The Coming Labor and Skills Shortage," *Training & Development* (January 2005): 39.

27. Bruce Tulgan, quoted in Stephanie Armour, "Generation Y: They've Arrived at Work with a New Attitude," *USA Today,* www.usatoday.com/money/workplace/2005-11-06-gen-y_x.htm, accessed May 10, 2010.

28. Nadira Hira, "You Raised Them, Now Manage Them," *Fortune* (May 28, 2007): 38–46; Katheryn Tyler, "The Tethered Generation," *HR Magazine* (May 2007): 41–46; Jeffrey Zaslow, "The Most Praised Generation Goes to Work," *Wall Street Journal* (April 20, 2007): W1, W7.

29. Stephanie Armour, "Generation Y: They've Arrived at Work with a New Attitude," *USA Today,* www.usatoday.com/money/workplace/2005-11-06-gen-y_x.htm, accessed May 10, 2010.

30. "Talent Management Leads in Top HR Concerns," *Compensation & Benefits Review* (May/June 2007): 12.

31. Jennifer Schramm, "Exploring the Future of Work: Workplace Visions," *Society for Human Resource Management* 2 (2005): 6; Rainer Strack, Jens Baier, and Anders Fahlander, "Managing Demographic Risk," *Harvard Business Review* (February 2008): 119–128.

32. Adrienne Fox, "At Work in 2020," *HR Magazine* (January 2010): 18–23.

33. Rita Zeidner, "Does the United States Need Foreign Workers?" *HR Magazine* (June 2009): 42–44.

34. www.census.gov/foreign-trade/statistics/historical/gands.pdf, accessed March 3, 2012.

35. www.bls.gov/opub/ted/2006/may/wk2/art01.htm, accessed April 18, 2009.

36. Sydney Robertson and Vic Dayal, "When Less Is More: Managing Human Resources with Reduced Staff," *Compensation & Benefits Review (*March/April 2009): 21–26.

37. "Immigrants in the Workplace," *BNA Bulletin to Management Datagraph* (March 15, 1996): 260–261. See also Tanuja Agarwala, "Human Resource Management: The Emerging Trends," *Indian Journal of Industrial Relations* (January 2002): 315–331. See also Edward Lawler III, "Celebrating 50 Years: HR: Time for a Reset?" *Human Resource Management* 50, no. 2 (March–April 2011): 171–173.

38. "Human Capital Critical to Success," *Management Review* (November 1998): 9. See also "HR 2018: Top Predictions," *Workforce Management* 87, no. 20 (December 15 2008): 20–21.

39. Ben Nagler, "Recasting Employees into Teams," *Workforce* (January 1998): 101–106.

40. A recent survey found that HR managers referred to "strategic/critical thinking skills" as the top "most important factor in attaining next HR job." See "Career Development for HR Professionals," *Society for Human Resource Management Research Quarterly* (Second Quarter 2008): 3.

41. John Boudreau and Peter Ramstad, *Beyond HR: The New Science of Human Capital* (Boston: Harvard Business School Publishing Corporation, 2007): 9.

42. For example, see Sandra Fisher et al., "Human Resource Issues in Outsourcing: Integrating Research and Practice," *Human Resource Management* 47, no. 3 (Fall 2008): 501–523; and "Sizing Up the HR Outsourcing Market," *HR Magazine* (November 2008): 78.

43. Susan Ladika, "Socially Evolved," *Workforce Management* (September 2010): 18–22.

44. Studies suggest that IT usage does support human resource managers' strategic planning. See Victor Haines III and Genevieve LaFleur, "Information Technology Usage and Human Resource Roles and Effectiveness," *Human Resource Management* 47, no. 3 (Fall 2008): 525–540. See also R. Zeidner, "The Tech Effect on Human Resources," *HR Magazine* (2009 HR Trendbook supp): 49–50, 52.

45. Paul Loftus, "Tackle Talent Management to Achieve High Performance," *Plant Engineering* 61, no. 6 (June 15, 2007): 29.

46. "Survey: Talent Management a Top Concern," *CIO Insight* (January 2, 2007).

47. www.talentmanagement101.com, accessed December 10, 2007.

48. Dean Smith, "Engagement Matters," *T+D* 63, no. 10 (October 14, 2009).

49. Quoted in op. cit.

50. Robert Grossman, "IBM's HR Takes a Risk," *HR Management* (April 2007): 54–59. See also Robert Grossman, "Close the Gap Between Research and Practice," *HR Magazine* (November 2009): 31–37.

51. Chris Brewster et al., "What Determines the Size of the HR Function? A Cross National Analysis," *Human Resource Management* 45, no. 1 (Spring 2006): 3–21.

52. Contact the Society for Human Resource Management, 703.535.6366.

53. Susan Wells, "From HR to the Top," *HR Magazine* (June 2003): 49. See also "HR Will Have More Opportunities to Demonstrate Value in 2002," *BNA Bulletin to Management* (January 17, 2012): 22.

54. Chad van Iddekinge et al., "Effects of Selection and Training on Unit Level Performance over Time: A Latent Growth Modeling Approach," *Journal of Applied Psychology* 94, no. 4 (2009): 829–843.

55. "Super Human Resources Practices Result in Better Overall Performance, Report Says," *BNA Bulletin*

to Management (August 26, 2004): 273–274. See also Wendy Boswell, "Aligning Employees with the Organization's Strategic Objectives: Out of Line of Sight, Out of Mind," *International Journal of Human Resource Management* 17, no. 9 (September 2006): 1014–1041. Another study suggests that it's not always necessary to implement the full range of high-performance HR practices to achieve improved results. Even implementing smaller "bundles" of HR related practices (such as empowerment, motivation, and improving skills) can improve business outcomes if the activities themselves are synergistic. Mahesh Subramony, "A Meta-Analytic Investigation of the Relationship between HRM Bundles and Firm Performance," *Human Resource Management* 48, no. 5 (September–October 2009): 745–758.

56. As one expert puts it, "A great deal of what passes as 'best practice' in HRM most likely is not. In some cases, there is simply no evidence that validates what are thought to be best practices, while in other cases there is evidence to suggest that what are thought to be best practices are inferior practices." Edward Lawler III, "Why HR Practices Are not Evidence-Based," *Academy of Management Journal* 50, no. 5 (2007): 1033.

57. See, for example, www.personneltoday.com/blogs/hcglobal-human-capital-management/2009/02/theres-no-such-thing-as-eviden.html, accessed April 18, 2009.

58. Ibid.

59. The evidence-based movement began in medicine. In 1996, in an editorial published by the *British Medical Journal,* David Sackett, M.D., defined "evidence-based medicine" as "use of the best-available evidence in making decisions about patient care," and urged his colleagues to adopt its tenets. "Evidence-Based Training(tm): Turning Research Into Results for Pharmaceutical Sales Training," An AXIOM White Paper (c) 2006 AXIOM Professional Health Learning LLC. All rights reserved.

60. Chris Brewster et al., "What Determines the Size of the HR Function? A Cross National Analysis," *Human Resource Management* 45, no. 1 (Spring 2006): 3–21. See also "SHRM Survey Report, 2006 Strategic HR Management," *Society for Human Resource Management,* pp. 18–19.

61. Bill Roberts, "How to Put Analytics on Your Side," *HR Magazine* (October 2009): 43–46.

62. Kevin Wooten, "Ethical Dilemmas in Human Resource Management," *Human Resource Management Review* 11 (2001): 161.

63. Except as noted, most of this section is based on Richard Vosburgh, "The Evolution of HR: Developing HR as an Internal Consulting Organization," *Human Resource Planning* 30, no. 3 (September 2007): 11–24.

64. See, for example, "Employers Seek HR Executives with Global Experience, SOX Knowledge, Business Sense," *BNA Bulletin to Management* (September 19, 2006): 297–298; and Robert Rodriguez, "HR's New Breed," *HR Magazine* (January 2006): 67–71.

65. Susan Wells, "From HR to the Top," *HR Magazine* (June 2003): 49. SHRM's 2008 Managing Your HR Career Survey Report concluded that HR professionals need several key skills "to get to the top," including interpersonal communication, drive/ambition, reputation in the organization, and strategic/critical thinking skills. Kathy Gurchiek, "Survey: 'Key' Skills Advance HR Career," *HR Magazine* (April 2008): 38. See also Adrienne Fox, "Do Assignments Outside HR Pay Off?" *HR Magazine* (November 2011): 31–36.

66. www.elearning.shrm.org/newhrcompetency.aspx, accessed April 4, 2011.

67. The state of the HR profession, The RBL White Paper Series, The **RBL** Group (c) 2011, page 8.

68. www.elearning.shrm.org/newhrcompetency.aspx, accessed April 4, 2011.

69. SHRM no longer makes it possible for college graduates without HR experience to sit for one of the chairman certification exams. However it does provide a SHRM Assurance of learning assessment preparation guide book. This helps students study for a SHRM exam that aims to verify that the student has acquired the knowledge required to enter the human resource management profession at the entry level. See www.SHRM.org/assuranceoflearning/index.html, accessed April 4, 2011.

70. "Efforts to recruit and retain employees, the growing importance of employee training, and new legal standards are expected to increase employment of these workers." "The 2008–2018 Job Outlook in Brief," *Occupational Outlook Quarterly* 54, no. 1 (Spring 2010): 9.

71. For example, in 2009, the head of human resources and labor relations at Delta Air Lines earned about $5 million in total compensation, and the senior vice president for human resources at eBay earned over $4 million. Jessica Marquez, "As the Economy Goes," *Workforce Management* (August 17, 2009): 27–33.

72. Patrick Gunnigle and Sarah Moore, "Linking Business Strategy and Human Resource Management: Issues and Implications," *Personnel Review* 23, no. 1 (1994): 63–84; Gary Dessler, *Human Resource Management* (Upper Saddle River, NJ: Prentice Hall, 2008): 77–97.

73. Gunnigle and Moore, "Linking Business Strategy," 64.

74. Michael Porter, *Competitive Strategy* (New York: The Free Press, 1980): 14.

75. See, for example, Evan Offstein, Devi Gnyawali, and Anthony Cobb, "A Strategic Human Resource Perspective of Firm Competitive Behavior," *Human Resource Management Review* 15 (2005): 305–318.

76. "Automation Improves Retailer's Hiring Efficiency and Quality," *HR Focus* 82, no. 2 (February 2005): 3.

77. When focusing on HR activities, managers call this an "HR Scorecard." When applying the same process

broadly to all the company's activities, including, for example, sales, production, and finance, managers call it the "balanced scorecard process."

78. The idea for the HR Scorecard derives from a broader measurement tool managers call the "balanced score-card." This does for the company as a whole what the HR Scorecard does for HR, summarizing instead the impact of various functions including HRM, sales, production, and distribution. The "balanced" in balanced scorecard refers to a balance of goals—financial and nonfinancial.

Chapter 2

1. Kevin McGowan, "Court Approves $175 Million Settlement of Novartis Sales Reps and Sex Bias Claims," *BNA Bulletin to Management* (November 30, 2010): 377.

2. Betsy Morris, "How Corporate America Is Betraying Women," *Fortune* (January 10, 2005): 64–70.

3. Plaintiffs still bring equal employment claims under the Civil Rights Act of 1866. For example, in 2008, the U.S. Supreme Court held that the act prohibits retaliation against someone who complains of discrimination against others when contract rights (in this case an employment agreement) are at stake. Charles Louderback, "US Supreme Court Decisions Expand Employees' Ability to Bring Retaliation Claims," *Compensation & Benefits Review* (September/October 2008): 52.

4. Note that private employers are not bound by the U.S. Constitution.

5. Based on or quoted from Principles of Employment Discrimination Law (Washington, DC: International Association of Official Human Rights Agencies). See also Bruce Feldacker, *Labor Guide to Labor Law* (Upper Saddle River, NJ: Prentice Hall, 2000); "EEOC Attorneys Highlight How Employers Can Better Their Nondiscrimination Practices," *BNA Bulletin to Management* (July 20, 2008): 233. See also www.eeoc.gov. Employment discrimination law is a changing field, and the appropriateness of the rules, guidelines, and conclusions in this chapter and book may also be affected by factors unique to the employer's operation. They should be reviewed by the employer's attorney before implementation.

6. The Equal Employment Opportunity Act of 1972, Subcommittee on Labor or the Committee of Labor and Public Welfare, United States Senate, March 1972, p. 3. In general, it is not discrimination, but unfair discrimination against a person merely because of that person's race, age, sex, national origin, or religion that is forbidden by federal statutes. In the federal government's *Uniform Employee Selection Guidelines,* unfair discrimination is defined as follows: "Unfairness is demonstrated through a showing that members of a particular interest group perform better or poorer on the job than their scores on the selection procedure (test, etc.) would indicate through comparison with how members of the other groups performed." For a discussion of the meaning of fairness, see James Ledvinka, "The Statistical Definition of Fairness in the Federal Selection Guidelines and Its Implications for Minority Employment," *Personnel Psychology* 32 (August 1979): 551–562. In summary, it's not necessarily unfair for a selection device (such as a test) to discriminate—for example, between low performers and high performers. However, unfair discrimination—discrimination that is based solely on the person's race, age, sex, national origin, or religion—is illegal.

7. "The Employer Should Validate Hiring Tests to Withstand EEOC Scrutiny, Officials Advise," *BNA Bulletin to Management* (April 1, 2008): 107.

8. "Restructured, Beefed Up OFCCP May Shift Policy Emphasis, Attorney Says," *BNA Bulletin to Management* (August 18, 2009): 257.

9. Note that the U.S. Supreme Court (in *General Dynamics Land Systems Inc.* v. *Cline,* 2004) held that the ADEA does *not* protect younger workers from being treated worse than older ones. "High Court: ADEA Does Not Protect Younger Workers Treated Worse than Their Elders," *BNA Bulletin to Management* 55, no. 10 (March 4, 2004): 73–80. The U.S. Supreme Court also recently held that, unlike the 1964 Civil Rights Act Title VII, the Age Discrimination in Employment Act does not permit an employee to prove discrimination just by showing that age was a motivating factor. Instead, he or she might show that age was the determining factor in the personnel action. See "Justices, 5–4, Reject Burden Shifting," *BNA Bulletin to Management* (June 20, 2009): 199. See also www.eeoc.gov/laws/statutes/adea.cfm, accessed October 3, 2011.

10. Pregnancy claims to the EEOC rose about 39% in the early 2000s; plaintiff victories rose 66%. John Kohl, Milton Mayfield, and Jacqueline Mayfield, "Recent Trends in Pregnancy Discrimination Law," *Business Horizons* 48, no. 5 (September 2005): 442–429. See also www.eeoc.gov/eeoc/statistics/enforcement/pregnancy.cfm, accessed October 3, 2011.

11. www.eeoc.gov/eeoc/statistics/enforcement/pregnancy.cfm, accessed October 3, 2011.

12. Nancy Woodward, "Pregnancy Discrimination Grows," *HR Magazine* (July 2005): 79.

13. "Pregnancy Claims Rising; Consistent Procedures Paramount," BNA *Bulletin to Management* (November 23, 2010): 375.

14. Thomas Dhanens, "Implications of the New EEOC Guidelines," *Personnel* 56 (September/October): 32–39.

15. See, for example, www.uniformguidelines.com/uniformguidelines.html, accessed November 23, 2007.

16. *Griggs* v. *Duke Power Company,* 3FEP cases 175.

17. IOFEP cases 1181.

18. Bruce Feldacker, *Labor Guide to Labor Law* (Upper Saddle River, NJ: Prentice Hall, 2000), p. 513.

19. "The Eleventh Circuit Explains Disparate Impact, Disparate Treatment," *BNA Fair Employment Practices* (August 17, 2000): 102. See also Kenneth York, "Disparate Results in Adverse Impact Tests: The 4/5ths Rule and the Chi Square Test," *Public Personnel Management* 31, no. 2 (Summer 2002): 253–262; and "Burden of Proof Under the Employment Non-Discrimination Act," www.civilrights.org/lgbt/enda/burden-of-proof.html, accessed August 8, 2011.

20. Commerce Clearing House, "House and Senate Pass Civil Rights Compromise by Wide Margin," *Ideas and Trends in Personnel* (November 13, 1991): 182.

21. "Expansion of Employment Laws Abroad Impacts U.S. Employers," *BNA Bulletin to Management* (April 11, 2006): 119; Richard Posthuma, Mark Roehling, and Michael Campion, "Applying U.S. Employment Discrimination Laws to International Employers: Advice for Scientists and Practitioners," *Personnel Psychology* 59 (2006): 705–739.

22. Guidelines based on Richard Posthuma et al., "Applying U.S. Employment Discrimination Laws to International Employees: Advice for Scientists and Practitioners," *Personnel Psychology* 59 (2006): 710.

23. Larry Drake and Rachel Moskowitz, "Your Rights in the Workplace," *Occupational Outlook Quarterly* (Summer 1997): 19–20.

24. Richard Wiener et al., "The Fit and Implementation of Sexual Harassment Law to Workplace Evaluations," *Journal of Applied Psychology* 87, no. 4 (2002): 747–764.

25. www.eeoc.gov/eeoc/statistics/enforcement/sexual_harassment.cfm, accessed March 3, 2012.

26. Edward Felsenthal, "Justice's Ruling Further Defines Sexual Harassment," *Wall Street Journal* (March 5, 1998): B1, B5. Similarly, a series of compliments and "requests for a hug" were not sufficient to rise to the level of sexual harassment in one case involving a female supervisor and her female subordinate. ("Compliments, Request for Hug Were Not Harassment by Female Supervisor, Court Says," *BNA Human Resources Report* [November 20, 2003]: 1193.) The Federal Violence against Women Act of 1994 provides another avenue that women can use to seek relief for violent sexual harassment. It provides that a person "who commits a crime of violence motivated by gender and thus deprives another of her rights shall be liable to the party injured."

27. Hilary Gettman and Michele Gelfand, "When the Customer Shouldn't Be King: Antecedents and Consequences of Sexual Harassment by Clients and Customers," *Journal of Applied Psychology* 92, no. 3 (2007): 757–770.

28. For example, a server/bartender filed a sexual harassment claim against Chili's Bar & Grill. She claimed that her former boyfriend, also a restaurant employee, had harassed her. The court ruled that the restaurant's prompt response warranted ruling in favor of it. "Ex-Boyfriend Harassed, but Employer Acted Promptly," *BNA Bulletin to Management* (January 8, 2008): 14.

29. See Mindy D. Bergman et al., "The (Un)reasonableness of Reporting: Antecedents and Consequences of Reporting Sexual Harassment," *Journal of Applied Psychology* 87, no. 2 (2002): 230–242; see also www.eeoc.gov/policy/docs/harassment-facts.html, accessed October 2, 2011; and "Court Examines Workplace Flirtation," http://hr.blr.com/HR-news/Discrimination/Sexual-Harassment/Court-Examines-Workplace-Flirtation/, accessed October 2, 2011.

30. Chelsea Willness et al., "A Meta-Analysis of the Antecedents and Consequences of Workplace Sexual Harassment," *Personnel Psychology* 60, no. 60 (2007): 127–162.

31. Jennifer Berdahl and Celia Moore, "Workplace Harassment: Double Jeopardy for Minority Women," *Journal of Applied Psychology* 91, no. 2 (2006): 426–436.

32. Jennifer Berdahl and Karl Aquino, "Sexual Behavior at Work: Fun or Folly?" *Journal of Applied Psychology* 94, no. 1 (2009): 34–47.

33. Maria Rotundo et al., "A Meta-Analytic Review of Gender Differences in Perceptions of Sexual Harassment," *Journal of Applied Psychology* 86, no. 5 (2001): 914–922. See also Nathan Bowling and Terry Beehr, "Workplace Harassment from the Victim's Perspective: A Theoretical Model and Meta Analysis," *Journal of Applied Psychology* 91, no. 5 (2006): 998–1012.

34. Jennifer Berdahl, "The Sexual Harassment of Uppity Women," *Journal of Applied Psychology* 92, no. 2 (2007): 425–437.

35. Lilia Cortina and S. Arzu Wasti, "Profile to Coping: Response to Sexual Harassment across Persons, Organizations, and Cultures," *Journal of Applied Psychology* 90, no. 1 (2005): 182–192.

36. In fact, this apparently is common. Alleged harassers often say "yes, I did it, but…," and then explain they meant no harm. However, intent is usually not the issue to the court. The issues are whether the conduct was unwelcome and objectively offensive to a reasonable person. Jonathan Segal, "I Did It, But…: Employees May Be as Innocent as They Say, but Still Guilty of Harassment," *HR Magazine* (March 2008): 91.

37. See the discussion in "Examining Unwelcome Conduct in Sexual Harassment Claims," *BNA Fair Employment Practices* (October 19, 1995): 124. See also Molly Bowers et al., "Just Cause in the Arbitration of Sexual Harassment Cases," *Dispute Resolution Journal* 55, no. 4 (November 2000): 40–55.

38. Adapted from *Sexual Harassment Manual for Managers and Supervisors,* published in 1991, by CCH Incorporated, a Wolters-Kluwer Company; and www.eeoc.gov/policy/docs/harassment-facts.html, accessed October 2, 2011.

39. Bergman et al., "The (Un)reasonableness of Reporting," 237.

40. The quoted material goes on to say that "The employer still bears the burden of proving that the employee's failure was unreasonable. If the employee had a

justifiable fear of retaliation, his or her failure to utilize the complaint process may not be unreasonable," and is quoted from www.uiowa.edu/~eod/policies/sexual-harassment-guide/employer-liablity.htm, accessed October 3, 2011.

41. Elliot H. Shaller and Dean Rosen, "A Guide to the EEOC's Final Regulations on the Americans with Disabilities Act," *Employee Relations* 17, no. 3 (Winter 1991–1992): 405–420. See also Brenda Sunoo, "Accommodating Workers with Disabilities," *Workforce* 80, no. 2 (February 2001): 86–93.

42. Shaller and Rosen, "A Guide to the EEOC's Final Regulations," 408. Other, specific examples of disabilities include "epilepsy, diabetes, cancer, HIV infection, and bipolar disorder," www1.eeoc.gov//laws/regulations/adaaa_fact_sheet.cfm?renderforprint=1, accessed October 3, 2011.

43. Shaller and Rosen, op. cit., p. 409.

44. See, for example, Paul Starkman, "The ADA's 'Essential Job Function' Requirements: Just How Essential Does an Essential Job Function Have to Be?" *Employee Relations Law Journal* 26, no. 4 (Spring 2001): 43–102. For recent illustrative cases, see Tillinghast Licht, "Reasonable Accommodation and the ADA—Courts Draw the Line," http://library.findlaw.com/2004/Sep/19/133574.html, accessed September 6, 2011.

45. www.ada.gov/reg3a.html#Anchor-Appendix-52467, accessed January 23, 2009.

46. "Driver Fired After Seizure on Job Lacks ADA Claim," *BNA Bulletin to Management* (January 4, 2011): 6.

47. *Palmer* v. *Circuit Court of Cook County*, Illinois, c7#95–3659–6/26/97; reviewed in "No Accommodation for Violent Employee," *BNA Fair Employment Practices* (July 10, 1997): 79. This general rule may not apply under all circumstances. For example, a recent EEOC update suggests that employers may have to accommodate a disruptive employee who has a military-connected post-traumatic stress disorder. "EEOC Letter Addresses ADA Implications of PTSD, Medical Exams," *BNA Bulletin to Management* (June 3, 2008): 183.

48. "Odds Against Getting Even Longer in ADA Cases," *BNA Bulletin to Management* (August 20, 2000): 229.

49. "Supreme Court Says Manual Task Limitation Needs Both Daily Living, Workplace Impact," *BNA Fair Employment Practices* (January 17, 2002): 8.

50. Lawrence Postol, "ADAAA Will Result in Renewed Emphasis on Reasonable Accommodations," *Society for Human Resource Management Legal Report* (January 2009): 1–3. The EEOC's recent implementing rules add sitting, reaching, and interacting with others to the number of major life activities. "EEOC OKs Proposed Rule to Implement ADA Amendments Act," *BNA Bulletin to Management* (September 20, 2009): 303. "EEOC issued its final regulations for ADA Amendments Act," *Workforce Management* (June 2011): 12.

51. Mark Lengnick-Hall et al., "Overlooked and Underutilized: People with Disabilities Are an Untapped Human Resource," *Human Resource Management* 47, no. 2 (Summer 2008): 255–273.

52. Susan Wells, "Counting on Workers with Disabilities," *HR Magazine* (April 2008): 45. Similarly, Verizon Wireless has a formal program aimed at assisting current employees to better manage a transition from healthy to disabled. For example, it trains supervisors to identify potentially disability-related deterioration in their employees' performance and to speak with these employees to try to identify what the issues are. If it becomes necessary for an employee to take a disability leave, the program encourages the employee to remain in contact with Verizon's HR professionals and to work with them to set realistic return dates. J. Adam Shoemaker, "A Welcome Back for Workers with Disabilities," *HR Magazine* (October 2009): 30–32. See also Nicole LaPorte, "Hiring the Blind, While Making a Green Statement," *The New York Times* (March 25, 2012): b3.

53. www.eeoc.gov/press/2-25-09.html, accessed April 3, 2009.

54. Bill Leonard, "Bill to Ban Sexual Orientation Bias Introduced," *HR Magazine* 54, no. 8 (August 2009): 18. See also Ye Yang Zheng and Brenda White, "The Evaluation of a Diversity Program at an Academic Library," *Library Philosophy and Practice 2007,* http://unllib.unl.edu/LPP/yang.pdf, accessed October 2, 2011.

55. http://employment.findlaw.com/employment/employment-employee-discrimination-harassment/employment-employee-gay-lesbian-discrimination.html, accessed March 3, 2012.

56. www.leg.state.fl.us/Statutes/index.cfm?App_mode=Display_Statute&Search_String=&URL=Ch0448/SEC07.HTM&Title=%3E2009-%3ECh0448-%3ESection%2007# 0448.07, accessed April 5, 2010.

57. John Klinefelter and James Thompkins, "Adverse Impact in Employment Selection," *Public Personnel Management* (May/June 1976): 199–204. See also www.eeoc.gov/policy/docs/factemployment_procedures.html, accessed October 2, 2011.

58. John Moran, *Employment Law* (Upper Saddle River, NJ: Prentice Hall, 1997), p. 168. A study found that using the 4/5ths rule often resulted in false-positive ratings of adverse impact, and that incorporating tests of statistical significance could improve the accuracy of applying the 4/5ths rule. See Philip Roth, Philip Bobko, and Fred Switzer, "Modeling the Behavior of the 4/5ths Rule for Determining Adverse Impact: Reasons for Caution," *Journal of Applied Psychology* 91, no. 3 (2006): 507–522.

59. Protected groups are those protected from employment discrimination by law, including men and women on the basis of sex and any group with a common race, religion, color, or national origin; people over 40; and people with physical or mental handicaps.

60. As another example, sometimes courts use the *standard deviation rule* to confirm adverse impact. (The standard deviation is a statistical measure of variability. Suppose we measure the heights of every person in your management class. In simplest terms, the standard deviation helps to describe, among other things, how wide a range there is between the shortest and tallest students.) In selection, the standard deviation rule holds that as a rule of thumb, the difference between the numbers of minority candidates we *would have expected* to hire and whom *we actually hired* should be less than a number equal to "two standard deviations."

61. Don't be lulled into thinking that such cases are ancient history. For example, a U.S. Appeals Court recently upheld a $3.4 million jury verdict against Dial Corp. Dial allegedly rejected 52 women for entry-level jobs at a meat processing plant because they failed strength tests, although strength was not a job requirement. "Eighth Circuit OKs $3.4 Million EEOC Verdict Relating to Pre-Hire Strength Testing Rules," *BNA Bulletin to Management* (November 28, 2006): 377.

62. As noted earlier, one study found that using the 4/5ths rule often resulted in false-positive ratings of adverse impact, and that incorporating tests of statistical significance could improve the accuracy of applying the 4/5ths rule. See Philip Roth, Philip Bobko, and Fred Switzer, "Modeling the Behavior of the 4/5ths Rule for Determining Adverse Impact: Reasons for Caution," op. cit.

63. The Fair Treatment for Experienced Pilots Act raised commercial pilots' mandatory retirement age from 60 to 65 in 2008. Allen Smith, "Congress Gives Older Pilots a Reprieve," *HR Magazine* (February 2008): 24.

64. www.foxnews.com/story/0,2933,517334,00.html, accessed January 7, 2010.

65. *U.S. v. Bethlehem Steel Company,* 3FEP cases 589.

66. *Spurlock v. United Airlines,* 5FEP cases 17.

67. www.eeoc.gov/laws/types/retaliation.cfm, accessed March 3, 2012. In one U.S. Supreme Court case, the employee complained to a government agency that her employer paid her less than male counterparts. Soon after the company heard about the complaint, it fired her fiancé, who also worked for the firm. Finding for the employee, the U.S. Supreme Court decision said, "a reasonable worker might be dissuaded from engaging in protected activity" if she knew that her fiancé would be fired; Adam Liptak, "Fiancé's Firing Is Ruled an Illegal Reaction to a Discrimination Claim," *The New York Times* (January 25, 2011): A16. As of 2010, retaliation charges were the most common charges filed with the EEOC. See "Retaliation Becomes Most Common Charge," *HR Magazine* (March 2011): 16.

68. In other words, with the exception of personnel policies calling for outright discrimination against the members of some protected group, it is not really the intrinsic nature of an employer's personnel policies or practices that the courts object to. Instead, it is the result of applying a policy or practice in a particular way or in a particular context that leads to an adverse impact on some protected group. James Ledvinka and Robert Gatewood, "EEO Issues with Preemployment Inquiries," *Personnel Administrator* 22, no. 2 (February 1997): 22–26.

69. Howard Anderson and Michael Levin-Epstein, *Primer of Equal Opportunity* (Washington, D.C.: The Bureau of National Affairs, 1982): 28.

70. "Many Well-Intentioned HR Policies Hold Legal Headaches, Consultant Says," *BNA Bulletin to Management* (February 17, 2000): 47.

71. Jenessa Shapiro et al., "Expectations of Obese Trainees: How Stigmatized Trainee Characteristics Influence Training Effectiveness," *Journal of Applied Psychology* 92, no. 1 (2007): 239–249. See also Svetlana Shkolnikova, "Weight Discrimination Could Be as Common as Racial Bias," www. usatoday.com/news/health/weightloss/2008-05-20-overweight-bias_N .htm, accessed January 21, 2009.

72. T. A. Judge and D. M. Cable, "When It Comes to Pay, Do the Thin Win? The Effect of Weight on Pay for Men and Women," *Journal of Applied Psychology* (January 2011).

73. Rita Pyrillis, "Body of Work," *Workforce Management* (November 7, 2010): 20–26.

74. "EEOC Weighs Guidance on Use of Criminal Records in Hiring," *BNA Bulletin to Management* (November 20, 2008): 383.

75. This is based on Anderson and Levin-Epstein, *Primer of Equal Opportunity,* 93–97.

76. "EEOC Issues New Enforcement Guidance on Discrimination in Employee Benefits," *BNA Fair Employment Practices* (October 12, 2000): 123.

77. Matthew Miklave, "Sorting Out a Claim of Bias," *Workforce* 80, no. 6 (June 2001): 102–103. Dress codes are a different matter. For example, the U.S. Court of Appeals for the Third Circuit recently upheld the city of Philadelphia's decision to refuse to relax its dress code to permit a female Muslim police officer to wear a headscarf while in uniform. "City Can Bar Muslim Police Woman from Wearing Scarf," *BNA Bulletin to Management* (April 20, 2009): 126.

78. Prudent employers often purchase employment practices liability insurance to insure against some or all of the expenses involved with defending against discrimination, sexual harassment, and wrongful termination type claims. Antone Melton-Meaux, "Maximizing Employment Practices Liability Insurance Coverage," *Compensation & Benefits Review* (May/June 2008): 55–59. Some employers obtain employment practices liability insurance to cover against possible discrimination and retaliation claims. "EPLI Now Established

Employer Litigation Strategy," *BNA Bulletin to Management* (November 29, 2011): 382.

79. 127 S.Ct. 2162 (2007), Lilly M. LEDBETTER, Petitioner, v. The GOODYEAR TIRE & RUBBER CO., INC. No. 05-1074. Supreme Court of United States.

80. http://eeoc/gov/eeoc/statistics/enforcement/charges.cfm, accessed May 20, 2010.

81. "Workplace Bias Against Muslims Increasingly a Concern for Employers," *BNA Bulletin to Management* (October 26, 2010): 337.

82. Timothy Bland, "Sealed Without a Kiss," *HR Magazine* (October 2000): 85–92. See also www.eeoc.gov/employees/mediation.cfm, accessed October 2, 2011.

83. "EEOC Has 18 Nationwide, 300 Local Accords with Employers to Mediate Job Bias Claims Charges," *BNA Human Resources Report* (October 13, 2003): H-081.

84. *Sources:* "Tips for Employers on Dealing with EEOC Investigations," *BNA Fair Employment Practices* (October 31, 1996): 130; "Conducting Effective Investigations of Employee Bias Complaints," *BNA Fair Employment Practices* (July 13, 1995): 81; Commerce Clearing House, *Ideas and Trends* (January 23, 1987): 14–15; http://eeoc.gov/employers/investigations.html, accessed October 4, 2009.

85. See, for example, "Diversity Is Used as Business Advantage by Three Fourths of Companies, Survey Says," *BNA Bulletin to Management* (November 7, 2006): 355. See also Claire Armstrong et al., "The Impact of Diversity and Equality Management on Firm Performance: Beyond High Performance Work Systems," *Human Resource Management* 49, no. 6 (November–December 2010): 977–998.

86. Brian O'Leary and Bart Weathington, "Beyond the Business Case for Diversity in Organizations," *Employee Responsibilities and Rights* 18, no. 4 (December 2006): 283–292.

87. See for example, Michael Carrell and Everett Mann, "Defining Work-Force Diversity in Public Sector Organizations," *Public Personnel Management* 24, no. 1 (Spring 1995): 99–111; Richard Koonce, "Redefining Diversity," *Training and Development Journal* (December 2001): 22–33; Kathryn Canas and Harris Sondak, *Opportunities and Challenges of Workplace Diversity* (Upper Saddle River, NJ; Pearson, 2008), pp 3–27. One writer lists race and ethnicity diversity, gender diversity, age diversity, disability diversity, sexual orientation diversity, and cultural and national origin diversity as examples. Lynn Shore et al., "Diversity in Organizations: Where Are We Now and Where Are We Going?" *Human Resource Management Review*, 19 (2009): 117–133.

88. Taylor Cox Jr., *Cultural Diversity in Organizations* (San Francisco: Berrett Kohler, 1993), p. 88. Also see Stefanie Johnson et al., "The Strong, Sensitive Type: Effects of Gender Stereotypes and Leadership Prototypes on the Evaluation of Male and Female

Leaders," *Organizational Behavior and Human Decision Processes* 106, no. 1 (May 2008): 39–60.

89. Cox, op. cit., p. 64.

90. Ibid., pp. 179–80.

91. J. H. Greenhaus and S. Parasuraman, "Job Performance Attributions and Career Advancement Prospects: An Examination of Gender and Race Affects," *Organizational Behavior and Human Decision Processes* 55 (July 1993): 273–298. Much research here focuses on how ethnocentrism prompts consumers to avoid certain products based on their country of origin. See, for example, T. S. Chan et al., "How Consumer Ethnocentrism and Animosity Impair the Economic Recovery of Emerging Markets," *Journal of Global Marketing* 23, no. 3 (July/August 2010): 208–225.

92. Madeleine Heilmann and Lewis Saruwatari, "When Beauty Is Beastly: The Effects of Appearance and Sex on Evaluation of Job Applicants for Managerial and Nonmanagerial Jobs," *Organizational Behavior and Human Performance* (June 1979): 360–372. See also Tracy McDonald and Milton Hakel, "Effects of Applicant Race, Sex, Suitability, and Answers on Interviewer's Questioning Strategy and Ratings," *Personnel Psychology* (Summer 1985): 321–334.

93. Patrick McKay et al., "A Tale of Two Climates: Diversity Climate from Subordinates and Managers Perspectives and Their Role in Store Unit Sales Performance," *Personnel Psychology* 62 (2009): 767–791. Another study found that racial discrimination was related negatively to employee commitment, but that organizational efforts to support diversity reduced such negative effects; Maria del Carmen Triana, Maria Fernandez Garcia, and Adrian Colella, "Managing Diversity: How Organizational Efforts to Support Diversity Moderate the Effects of Perceived Racial Discrimination on Affective Commitment," *Personnel Psychology* 63 (2010): 817–843.

94. David Thomas, "Diversity as Strategy," *Harvard Business Review* (September 2004): 98–104. See also J. T. Childs Jr., "Managing Global Diversity at IBM: A Global HR Topic that Has Arrived," *Human Resource Management* 44, no. 1 (Spring 2005): 73–77.

95. Ibid., p. 99.

96. As another example, leaders who facilitated high levels of power sharing within their groups helped to reduce the frequently observed positive relationship between increased diversity and increase turnover. But leaders who were inclusive of only a select few followers "may actually exacerbate the relationship between diversity and turnover" (p. 1422). Lisa Nishii and David Mayer, "Do Inclusive Leaders Help to Reduce Turnover in Diverse Groups? The Moderating Role of a Leader-Member Exchange in the Diversity to Turn Over Relationship," *Journal of Applied Psychology* 94, no. 6 (2009): 1412–1426.

97. Patricia Digh, "Creating a New Balance Sheet: The Need for Better Diversity Metrics," *Mosaics, Society for Human Resource Management* (September/October 1999): 1. For diversity management steps, see Taylor Cox Jr., *Cultural Diversity in Organizations: Theory, Research and Practice* (San Francisco: Berrett-Koehler, 1993), p. 236; see also Richard Bucher, *Diversity Consciousness: Opening Our Minds to People, Cultures, and Opportunities* (Upper Saddle River, NJ: Pearson Prentice Hall, 2004), pp. 109–137.

98. Faye Cocchiara et al., "A Gem for Increasing the Effectiveness of Diversity Training," Human *Resource Management* 49, no. 6 (November–December 2010): 1089–1106.

99. James Coil and Charles Rice, "Managing Work-Force Diversity in the 90s: The Impact of the Civil Rights Act of 1991," *Employee Relations Law Journal* 18, no. 4 (1991): 548.

100. Ibid., pp. 562–563.

101. http://newsfeedresearcher.com/data/articles_n17/tests-city-court.html, accessed April 24, 2009.

102. David Harrison et al., "Understanding Attitudes Toward Affirmative Action Programs in Employment: Summary and Meta-Analysis of 35 Years of Research," *Journal of Applied Psychology* 91, no. 5 (2006): 1031–1036.

Chapter 3

1. www.talentmanagement101.com, accessed December 10, 2007.

2. www.talentmanagement101.com, accessed December 10, 2007.

3. For a good discussion of job analysis, see James Clifford, "Job Analysis: Why Do It, and How Should It Be Done?" *Public Personnel Management* 23, no. 2 (Summer 1994): 321–340. See also "Job Analysis," www.paq.com/index.cfm?FuseAction=bulletins .job-analysis, accessed February 3, 2009.

4. One writer recently called job analysis, "the hub of virtually all human resource management activities necessary for the successful functioning organizations." See Parbudyal Singh, "Job Analysis for a Changing Workplace," *Human Resource Management Review* 18 (2008): 87.

5. Note that job analysis enables the manager to list what a job's duties and demands are now. Job analysis does *not* answer questions such as "Should this job even exist?" To answer such questions, it's necessary to conduct a workflow analysis. *Workflow analysis* is a detailed study of the flow of work from job to job in a work process.

6. See Parbudyal Singh, "Job Analysis for a Changing Workplace," op. cit.

7. See also T. A. Stetz et al., "New Tricks for an Old Dog: Visualizing Job Analysis Results," *Public Personnel Management* 38, no. 1 (Spring 2009): 91–100.

8. Erik Dirdorff and Mark Wilson, "A Meta Analysis of Job Analysis Reliability," *Journal of Applied Psychology* 88, no. 4 (2003): 635–646.

9. Darin Hartley, "Job Analysis at the Speed of Reality," *Training & Development* (September 2004): 20–22.

10. Arthur Martinez et al., "Job Title Inflation," *Human Resource Management Review* 18 (2008): 19–27.

11. Roni Reiter-Palmon et al., "Development of an O*Net Web Based Job Analysis and Its Implementation in the U.S. Navy: Lessons Learned," *Human Resource Management Review* 16 (2006): 294–309.

12. Ibid., p. 294.

13. Matthew Mariani, "Replaced with a Data-Base: O*NET Replaces the *Dictionary of Occupational Titles*," *Occupational Outlook Quarterly* (Spring 1999): 3–9.

14. See, for example, Christelle Lapolice et al., "Linking O*Net Descriptors to Occupational Literacy Requirements Using Job Component Validation," *Personnel Psychology* 61 (2008): 405–441. See also "OMB, Federal Agencies Set to Update Job Descriptions for All Workers in 2010," *BNA Bulletin to Management* (March 10, 2009): 73.

15. Gary Dessler, *Human Resource Management*, 9th ed. (Upper Saddle River, NJ: Prentice Hall, 2002), pp. 64–76.

16. Michael Esposito, "There's More to Writing Job Descriptions than Complying with the ADA," *Employee Relations Today* (Autumn 1992): 279.

17. Deborah Kearney, *Reasonable Accommodations: Job Descriptions in the Age of ADA, OSHA, and Workers Comp* (New York: Van Nostrand Reinhold, 1994), p. 9.

18. Steven Hunt, "Generic Work Behavior: An Investigation into the Dimensions of Entry-Level, Hourly Job Performance," *Personnel Psychology* 49 (1996): 51–83.

19. Jeffrey Shippmann et al., "The Practice of Competency Modeling," *Personnel Psychology* 53, no. 3 (2000): 703.

20. Richard S. Wellins et al., "Nine Best Practices for Effective Talent Management," DDI Development Dimensions International, Inc. www.ddiworld.com/DDIWorld/media/white-papers/ninebestpracticetalentmanagement_wp_ddi.pdf?ext=pdf, accessed August 20, 2011. For a discussion of competency modeling, see Michael A. Campion, Alexis A. Fink, Brian J. Ruggeberg, Linda Carr, Geneva M. Phillips, and Ronald B. Odman, "Doing Competencies Well: Best Practices in Competency Modeling," *Personnel Psychology* 64, no. 1 (2011), pp. 225–262.

21. Jeffrey Shippmann et al., "The Practice of Competency Modeling," *Personnel Psychology* 53, no. 3 (2000): 703.

22. Ibid. For a good comparison of competency modeling and job analysis, see Juan Sanchez and Edward Levine, "What Is (or Should Be) the Difference between Competency Modeling and Traditional Job Analysis?" *Human Resource Management Review* 19 (2009): 53–63. See also Michael Campion, et al., "Doing Competencies Well: Best Practices in Competency Modeling," *Personnel Psychology* 64 (2011): 225–262.

23. See, for example, Carol Spicer, "Building a Competency Model," *HR Magazine* (April 2009): 34–36.

24. Robert Grossman, "IBM'S HR Takes a Risk," *HR Magazine* (April 27, 2007): 57.

25. "More Companies Turn to Workforce Planning to Boost Productivity and Efficiency," The Conference Board, press release/news (August 7, 2006); Carolyn Hirschman, "Putting Forecasting in Focus," *HR Magazine* (March 2007): 44–49.

26. Jean Phillips and Stanley Gully, *Strategic Staffing* (Upper Saddle River, NJ: Pearson Education, 2012), pp. 116–181.

27. See, for example, Fay Hansen, "The Long View," *Workforce Management* (April 20, 2008): 1, 14.

28. Chaman Jain and Mark Covas, "Thinking about Tomorrow: Seven Tips for Making Forecasting More Effective," *Wall Street Journal* (July 7, 2008): R10.

29. Based on an idea in Elmer H. Burack and Robert D. Smith, *Personnel Management: A Human Resource Systems Approach* (St. Paul, MN: West, 1997), pp. 134–135. Note that employers also use a mathematical process known as Markov analysis (or "transition analysis") to forecast availability of internal job candidates. Markov analysis involves creating a matrix that shows the probabilities that employees in the chain of feeder positions for a key job (such as from junior engineer, to engineer, to senior engineer, to engineering supervisor, to director of engineering) will move from position to position and therefore be available to fill the key job.

30. See, for example, Fay Hansen, "The Long View," op. cit.

31. Bill Roberts, "Can They Keep Our Lights On?" *HR Magazine* (June 2010): 62–68.

32. For a recent discussion, see, for example, "Pitfalls Abound for Employers Lacking Electronic Information Retention Policies," *BNA Bulletin to Management* (January 1, 2008): 1–2.

33. "Traditional Security Insufficient to Halt File-Sharing Threat," *BNA Bulletin to Management* (January 29, 2008): 39.

34. See, for example, David Day, "Developing Leadership Talent," SHRM Foundation, www.shrm.org/about/foundation/research/Documents/Developing%20 Lead%20Talent-%20FINAL.pdf, accessed October 4, 2011.

35. This is a modification of a definition found in Peter Wallum, "A Broader View of Succession Planning," *Personnel Management* (September 1993): 45. See also Michelle Harrison et al., "Effective Succession Planning," *Training & Development* (October 2006): 22–23.

36. Ibid., pp. 43–44. See also "Succession Planning: A Never-Ending Process that Must Mesh with Talent Management," *HR Focus* 84, no. 5 (May 2007): 8.

37. See, for example, "HR's Insight into the Economy," *Society for Human Resource Management Workplace Visions* 4 (2008): 5. See also D. Mattioli, "Only the Employed Need Apply," *Wall Street Journal* (Eastern Edition) (June 30, 2009): D1.

38. Benjamin Wright, "Employment, Trends, and Training in Information Technology," *Occupational Outlook Quarterly* (Spring 2009): 34–36.

39. "Next Generation Talent Management," www.hewittassociates.com/_MetaBasicCMAssetCache_/Assets/Articles/next_generation.pdf, accessed November 9, 2010.

40. Ibid.

41. Ed Frauenheim, "Valero Energy," *Workforce Management* (March 13, 2006).

42. Jean Phillips and Stanley Gully, *Strategic Staffing* (Upper Saddle River, NJ: Pearson Education, 2012), pp. 116–181.

43. Tony Carnevale, "The Coming Labor and Skills Shortage," *Training & Development* (January 2005): 36–41. "Report Says More Companies Focus on Workforce Planning to Heighten Productivity," *Training & Development* (October 2006): 10–12.

44. Tom Porter, "Effective Techniques to Attract, Hire, and Retain 'Top Notch' Employees for Your Company," *San Diego Business Journal* 21, no. 13 (March 27, 2000): B36.

45. Greet van Hoye and Filip Lievens, "Tapping the Grapevine: A Closer Look at Word-of-Mouth as a Recruitment Source," *Journal of Applied Psychology* 94, no. 2 (2009): 341–352.

46. Jonathan Segal, "Land Executives, Not Lawsuits," *HR Magazine* (October 2006): 123–130.

47. Susan Ladika, "Unwelcome Changes," *HR Magazine* (February 2005): 83–90.

48. Arthur R. Pell, *Recruiting and Selecting Personnel* (New York: Regents, 1969), pp. 10–12.

49. Jonathan Segal, "Strings Attached," *HR Magazine* (February 2005): 119–123.

50. Thomas Stewart, "In Search of Elusive Tech Workers," *Fortune* (February 16, 1998): 171–172. See also www.outsourcing-center.com/2006-10-ge-looks-to-recruitment-process-outsourcer-to-find-meat-and-potatoes-candidates-as-well-as-the-purple-squirrel-article-37479.html, accessed October 5, 2011.

51. Kevin Carlson et al., "Recruitment Evaluation: The Case for Assessing the Quality of Applicants Attracted," *Personnel Psychology* 55 (2002): 461–490. For a recent survey of recruiting source effectiveness, see "The 2007 Recruiting Metrics and Performance Benchmark Report, 2nd ed.," Staffing.org, Inc., 2007.

52. Stewart, op. cit, p. 120.

53. See, for example, C. Fernandez-Araoz et al., "The Definitive Guide to Recruiting in Good Times and Bad," *Harvard Business Review*, 87, no. 5 (May 2009): 74–84.

54. J. De Avila, "Beyond Job Boards: Targeting the Source," *Wall Street Journal* (Eastern Edition) (July 2, 2009): D1, D5. See also Deborah Silver "Niche Sites Gain Monster—Sized Following," *Workforce Management* (March 2011): 10–11.

55. Furthermore, strictly speaking, employers are supposed to track applicants' race, sex, and ethnic group. But many Internet applicants don't aim at specific jobs. Are these "applicants" under EEOC rules? Probably not. The EEOC says that an "applicant" must apply for a specific advertised job, and follow the employer's standard application procedure. "EEOC Issues Much Delayed Definition of 'Applicant,'" *HR Magazine* (April 2004): 29; Valerie Hoffman and Greg Davis, "OFCCP's Internet Applicant Definition Requires Overhaul of Recruitment and Hiring Policies," *Legal Report, Society for Human Resource Management* (January/February 2006): 2.

56. "Help Wanted—And Found," *Fortune* (October 2, 2006): 40.

57. James Breaugh, "Employee Recruitment: Current Knowledge and Important Areas for Future Research," *Human Resource Management Review* 18 (2008): 114.

58. Ibid., p. 111.

59. H. Jack Walker et al., "Displaying Employee Testimonials on Recruitment Websites: Effects of Communication Media, Employee Race, and Jobseeker Race on Organizational Attraction and Information Credibility," *Journal of Applied Psychology* 94, no. 5 (2009): 1354–1364.

60. Martha Frase-Blunt, "Make a Good First Impression," *HR Magazine* (April 2004): 81–86. See also "Corporate Recruiting Websites Luring Workers, but Could Be Improved, Experts Say," *BNA Bulletin to Management* (March 14, 2006): 81–82.

61. Jennifer Berkshire, "Social Network Recruiting," *HR Magazine* (April 2005): 95–98. See also S. DeKay, "Are Business-Oriented Social Networking Websites Useful Resources for Locating Passive Jobseekers? Results of a Recent Study," *Business Communication Quarterly* 72, no. 1 (March 2009): 101–105. See also "Many Workers Use Social Networking Sites in Job Hunt, Edit Own Content, Survey Finds," *BNA Bulletin to Management* (May 10, 2011): 147.

62. James Breaugh, "Employee Recruitment: Current Knowledge and Important Areas for Future Research," *Human Resource Management Review* 18 (2008): 114.

63. Joe Light, "Recruiters Rethink Online Playbook," http://online.wsj.com/article/SB10001424052748704 307404576080492613858846.html, accessed May 17, 2011. See also, Aliah Wright "Your Social Media is Showing," *HR Magazine* (March 2012): 16.

64. "Innovative HR Programs Cultivate Successful Employees," *Nation's Restaurant News* 41, no. 50 (December 17, 2007): 74.

65. J. De Avila, "Beyond Job Boards: Targeting the Source," *Wall Street Journal* (Eastern Edition) (July 2, 2009): D1, D5.

66. Jennifer Arnold, "Twittering at Face Booking While They Were," *HR Magazine* (December 2009): 54.

67. "ResumePal: Recruiter's Friend?" *Workforce Management* (June 20, 2009): 28.

68. Jennifer Taylor Arnold, "Recruiting on the Run," *HR Magazine* (February 2010): 65–67.

69. Elizabeth Agnvall, "Job Fairs Go Virtual," *HR Magazine* (July 2007): 85.

70. Gary Stern, "Virtual Job Fairs Becoming More of a Reality," *Workforce Management* (February 2011): 11.

71. Jim Meade, "Where Did They Go?" *HR Magazine* (September 2000): 81–84.

72. Note that the U.S. Department of Labor's office of federal contract compliance programs recently announced it would review federal contractors' online application tracking systems to ensure they're providing equal opportunity to qualify prospective applicants with disabilities. "Feds Want a Look at Online Job Sites," *HR Magazine* (November 2008): 12.

73. "E-recruiting Software Providers," *Workforce Management* (June 22, 2009): 14.

74. "As Hiring Folgers, More Workers Are Temporary," *New York Times* (December 20, 2010): A1, A4.

75. Robert Bogner Jr. and Elizabeth Salasko, "Beware the Legal Risks of Hiring Temps," *Workforce* (October 2002): 50–57. See also Robert Grossman, "Strategic Temp-tations," *HR Magazine* (March 2012): 24–34.

76. Fay Hansen, "A Permanent Strategy for Temporary Hires," *Workforce Management* (February 26, 2007): 27.

77. Carolyn Hirschman, "Are Your Contractors Legal?" *HR Magazine* (March 2004): 59–63.

78. See, for example, Stephenie Overman, "Searching for the Top," *HR Magazine* (January 2008): 49.

79. Stephen Miller, "Collaboration Is Key to Effective Outsourcing," *HR Magazine* (December 2007): 58, 60–61.

80. See G. Anders, "Secrets of the Talent Scouts," *New York Times* (Late New York Edition) (March 15, 2009): 1, 7 (Sec 3).

81. "In Negotiating Game, Most Recruiters Hold Back, Knowing Few Candidates Hold Out for Better Offer," *BNA Bulletin to Management* (2000): 291.

82. "Recruiters Look to Be Big Man on Campus," *Workforce Management* (September 2010): 12.

83. See, for example, James Breaugh, "Employee Recruitment: Current Knowledge and Important Areas for Future Research," *Human Resource Management Review* 18 (2008): 111.

84. Hao Zhao Oh and Robert Liden, "Internship: A Recruitment and Selected Perspective," *Journal of Applied Psychology* 96, no. 1 (2011): 221–229.

85. Lisa Munniksma, "Career Matchmakers," *HR Magazine* (February 2005): 93–96.

86. Joel Mullich, "Finding the Schools that Yield the Best Job Applicant ROI," *Workforce Management* (March 2004): 67–68.

87. Greet Van Hoye and Filip Lievens, "Tapping the Grapevine: A Closer Look at Word-of-Mouth as a Recruitment Source," *Journal of Applied Psychology* 94, no. 2 (2009): 341–352.

88. See, for example, "Economics of Offshoring Shifting, as Some Reconsider Ventures," *BNA Bulletin to Management* (September 23, 2008): 311.

89. Breaugh, "Employee Recruitment," 109.

90. Recruitment source has a significant effect on reducing turnover. Studies suggest that individuals recruited through personal recruitment sources such as employee referral programs are less likely to terminate their employment early. As a researcher says: "On the basis of the findings of this study, organizations suffering from high levels of premature turnover will likely benefit most from implementing and institutionalizing referral in rehiring practices" (p. 1157). Ingo Weller et al., "Level and Time Effects of Recruitment Sources on Early Voluntary Turnover," *Journal of Applied Psychology* 94, no. 5 (2009): 1146–1162.

91. www.kaiserpermanentejobs.org/employee-referral-program.aspx, accessed August 20, 2011.

92. Michelle Martinez, "The Headhunter Within," *HR Magazine* (August 2001): 48–56.

93. Bill Roberts, "Manage Candidates Right from the Start," *HR Magazine* (October 2008): 73–76.

94. Michael Zottoli and John Wanous, "Recruitment Source Research: Current Status and Future Directions," *Human Resource Management Review* 10 (November 4, 2000): 353–382.

95. Jennifer Taylor Arnold, "Customers as Employees," *HR Magazine* (April 2007): 77–82.

96. Martha Frase-Blunt, "Call Centers Come Home," *HR Magazine* (January 2007): 85–90.

97. www1.eeoc.gov//eeoc/meetings/2-16-11/owens .cfm?renderforprint=1, accessed March 5, 2013.

98. Theresa Minton-Eversole, "Mission: Recruitment," *HR Magazine* (January 2009): 43–45.

99. Derek Avery and Patrick McKay, "Target Practice: An Organizational Impression Management Approach to Attracting Minority and Female Job Applicants," *Personnel Psychology* 59 (2006): 157–189.

100. Daniel Newman and Julia Lyon, "Recruitment Efforts to Reduce Adverse Impact: Targeted Recruiting for Personality, Cognitive Ability, and Diversity," *Journal of Applied Psychology* 94, no. 2 (2009): 298–317.

101. Phaedra Brotherton, "Tapping into an Older Workforce," *Mosaics, Society for Human Resource Management* (March/April 2000). See also Thomas Ng and Daniel Feldman, "The Relationship of Age to Ten Dimensions of Job Performance," *Journal of Applied Psychology* 93, no. 2 (2008): 392–423.

102. "Older Workers Valued but Hard to Find, Employers Say," *BNA Bulletin to Management* (April 30, 1998): 129–134.

103. Gary Adams and Barbara Rau, "Attracting Retirees to Apply: Desired Organizational Characteristics of Bridge Employment," *Journal of Organizational Behavior* 26, no. 6 (September 2005): 649–660.

104. Sue Shellenbarger, "Firms Try Harder, but Often Fail to Help Workers Cope with Elder Care Problems," *Wall Street Journal* (June 23, 1993): B1. See also Robert Grossman, "Keep Pace with Older Workers," *HR Magazine* (May 2008): 39–46.

105. Judith Casey and Marci Pitt-Catsouphes, "Employed Single Mothers: Balancing Job and Home Life," *Employee Assistance Quarterly* 9, no. 3/4 (1994): 37–53; www.catalyst.org/publication/252/working-parents, accessed October 3, 2011.

106. Casey and Catsouples, "Employed Single Mothers," p. 48.

107. Jessica Marquez, "Tailor Made Careers," *Workforce Management* (January 2010): 16–18.

108. Ibid. See also Caroline Straub, "Antecedents and Organizational Consequences of Family Supportive Supervisor Behavior: A Multilevel Conceptual Framework for Research," *Human Resource Management Review* 22 (2012): 15–26.

109. Allison Wellner, "Welcoming Back Mom," *HR Magazine* (June 2004): 77–78.

110. Scott Graham, "Hospitals Recruiting Overseas," *Baltimore Business Journal* (June 1, 2001): 1.

111. Jennifer Laabs, "Recruiting in the Global Village," *Workforce* (Spring 1998): 30–33.

112. Ibid. See also Helen Deresky, *International Management* (Upper Saddle River, NJ: Pearson Prentice Hall, 2008), pp. 354–355.

113. Herbert Greenberg, "A Hidden Source of Talent," *HR Magazine* (March 1997): 88–91.

114. "Welfare-to-Work: No Easy Chore," *BNA Bulletin to Management* (February 13, 1997): 56.

115. See "Recruiting Disabled More than Good Deed, Experts Say," *BNA Bulletin to Management* (February 27, 2007): 71; and "Employment Status of the Civilian Population by Sex, Age, and Disability Status, Not Seasonally Adjusted," www.bls.gov/news.release/empsit.t06.htm, accessed March 5, 2012.

116. Murray Barrick and Ryan Zimmerman, "Hiring for Retention and Performance," *Human Resource Management* 48, no. 2 (March/April 2009): 183–206.

117. James Breaugh, "The Use of Biodata for Employee Selection: Test Research and Future Directions," *Human Resource Management Review* 19 (2009): 219–231. Utilizing biodata items of course presumes that the employer can show that the items predict performance. Biodata items such as "graduated from college" may have an adverse impact on minorities but studies suggest that employers can avoid that problem through judicious choice of biodata items. (p. 229)

118. This paragraph is based on Jennifer L. Wood, James M. Schmidtke, and Diane L. Decker, "Lying on Job Applications: The Effects of Job Relevance, Commission, and Human Resource Management Experience," *Journal of Business Psychology* 22 (2007): 1–9.

119. Kenneth Sovereign, *Personnel Law* (Upper Saddle River, NJ: Pearson, 1999), p. 51.

120. J. Craig Wallace et al., "Applying for Jobs Online: Examining the Legality of Internet-Based Application Forms," *Public Personnel Management* 20, no. 4 (Winter 2000): 497–504.

121. *Ryan's Family Steakhouse Inc.* v. *Floss*, "Supreme Court Let Stand Decision Finding Prehire Arbitration Agreements Unenforceable," *BNA Bulletin to Management* (January 11, 2001): 11. See also, H. John Bernardin, et al., "Mandatory and Binding Arbitration: Effects on Employee Attitudes and Recruiting Results," *Human Resource Management* 50, no. 2 (March–April 2011): 175–200.

122. Scott Erker, "What Does Your Hiring Process Say about You?" *Training & Development* (May 2007): 67–70.

Chapter 4

1. See Rebecca Bennett and Sandra Robinson, "Development of a Measure of Workplace Deviance," *Journal of Applied Psychology* 85, no. 3 (2000): 349.

2. For an example, see C. Tuna et al., "Job-Test Ruling Cheers Employers," *Wall Street Journal* (July 1, 2009): B1–B2.

3. "Wal-Mart to Scrutinize Job Applicants," *CNN Money* (August 12, 2004), http://money.cnn.com/ 2004/08/12/ News/fortune500/walmart_jobs/index.htm, accessed August 8, 2005.

4. Fay Hansen, "Taking 'Reasonable' Action to Avoid Negligent Hiring Claims," *Workforce Management* (September 11, 2006): 31.

5. Anne Anastasi, *Psychological Patterns* (New York: Macmillan, 1968). See also Kevin Murphy and Charles David Shafer, *Psychological Testing* (Upper Saddle River, NJ: Prentice Hall, 2001), pp. 108–124.

6. Robert M. Guion, "Changing Views for Personnel Selection Research," *Personnel Psychology* 40, no. 2 (Summer 1987): 199–213. The Standards for Educational and Psychological Testing define validity as "the degree to which accumulated evidence and theories support specific interpretations of test scores entailed by proposed uses of a test." Deborah Whetzel and Michael McDaniel, "Situational Judgment Tests: An Overview of Current Research," *Human Resource Management Review* 19 (2009): 191.

7. www.siop.org/workplace/employment%20testing/ information_to_consider_when_cre.aspx, accessed March 22, 2009.

8. The Uniform Guidelines say, "Employers should ensure that tests and selection procedures are not adopted casually by managers who know little about these processes.... no test or selection procedure should be implemented without an understanding of its effectiveness and limitations for the organization, its appropriateness for a specific job, and whether it can be appropriately administered and scored."

9. Jean Phillips and Stanley Gully, *Strategic Staffing* (Upper Saddle River, NJ: Pearson Education, 2012), p. 220.

10. www.uniformguidelines.com/qandaprint.html, accessed March 6, 2012.

11. Ibid.

12. In employment testing, bias has a precise meaning. Specifically, "bias is said to exist when a test makes systematic errors in measurement or prediction." Kevin Murphy and Charles Davidshofer, *Psychological Testing: Principles and Applications* (Upper Saddle River, NJ: Prentice Hall, 2001), p. 303.

13. Herman Aguinis, Steven Culpepper, and Charles Pierce, "Revival of Test Bias Research in Preemployment Testing," *Journal of Applied Psychology* 95, no. 4 (2010): 648. See also Christopher Berry et al., "Racial/Ethnic Differences in the Criterion—Related Validity of Cognitive Ability Tests: A Qualitative and Quantitative Review," *Journal of Applied Psychology* 96, no. 5 (2011): 81–96.

14. "Hiring Based on Strength Test Discriminates against Women," *BNA Bulletin to Management* (February 22, 2005): 62.

15. Robert Gatewood and Hubert Feild, *Human Resource Selection* (Fort Worth, TX: The Dryden Press, 1994), p. 243.

16. This is based on Dave Zielinski, "Effective Assessments," *HR Magazine* (January 2011): 61–64.

17. Brad Bushman and Gary Wells, "Trait Aggressiveness and Hockey Penalties: Predicting Hot Tempers on the Ice," *Journal of Applied Psychology* 83, no. 6 (1998): 969–974.

18. "One-Third of Job Applicants Flunked Basic Literacy and Math Tests Last Year, American Management Association Survey Finds," American Management Association, www.amanet.org/press/amanews/ bjp2001.htm, accessed January 11, 2008.

19. Scott Hayes, "Kinko's Dials into Automated Applicants Screening," *Workforce* 78, no. 11 (November 1999): 71–73. Note that the U.S. Department of Labor recently reminded federal contractors that even if they use a third party to prepare an employment test, the contractors themselves are "ultimately responsible" for ensuring the tests' job relatedness and EEO compliance. "DOL Officials Discuss Contractors' Duties on Validating Tests," *BNA Bulletin to Management* (September 4, 2007): 287. Furthermore, the EEOC and federal contract compliance office are increasing their scrutiny of employers who rely on tests and screening. See "Litigation Increasing with Employer Reliance on Tests, Screening," *BNA Bulletin to Management* (April 8, 2008): 119.

20. For some other examples, see William Shepherd, "Increasing Profits by Assessing Employee Work Styles," *Employment Relations Today* 32, no. 1 (Spring 2005): 19–23; and Eric Krell, "Personality Counts," *HR Magazine* (November 2005): 47–52.

21. Kevin Hart, "Not Wanted: Thieves," *HR Magazine* (April 2008): 119.

22. Sarah Needleman, "Businesses Say Theft by Their Workers Is Up," *Wall Street Journal* (December 11, 2008): B8.

23. Sarah Gale, "Three Companies Cut Turnover with Tests," *Workforce* (April 2002): 66–69.

24. Norman Henderson, "Predicting Long-Term Firefighter Performance from Cognitive and Physical Ability Measures," *Personnel Psychology* 63 (2010): 999–1039.

25. www.military.com/military-fitness/marine-corps-fitness-requirements/marine-corps-fitness-test, accessed October 4, 2011.

26. William Wagner, "All Skill, No Finesse," *Workforce* (June 2000): 108–116. See also, for example, James Diefendorff and Kajal Mehta, "The Relations of Motivational Traits with Workplace Deviance," *Journal of Applied Psychology* 92, no. 4 (2007): 967–977.

27. Toddi Gutner, "Applicants' Personalities Put to the Test," *Wall Street Journal* (August 20, 2008): D4.

28. See, for example, Douglas Cellar et al., "Comparison of Factor Structures and Criterion-Related Validity Coefficients for Two Measures of Personality Based on the Five Factor Model," *Journal of Applied Psychology* 81, no. 6 (1996): 694–704; Lisa Penney and Emily Witt, "A Review of Personality and Performance: Identifying Boundaries, Contingencies, and Future Research Directions," *Human Resource Management Review* 20, no. 1 (2011): 297–310.

29. Murray Barrick and Michael Mount, "The Big Five Personality Dimensions and Job Performance: A Meta Analysis," *Personnel Psychology* 44, no. 1 (Spring 1991): 1–26. See also Robert Schneider, Leatta Hough, and Marvin Dunnette, "Broad-Sided by Broad Traits: How to Sink Science in Five Dimensions or Less," *Journal of Organizational Behavior* 17, no. 6 (November 1996): 639–655. See also Paula Caligiuri, "The Big Five Personality Characteristics as Predictors of Expatriate's Desire to Terminate the Assignment and Supervisor Rated Performance," *Personnel Psychology* 53 (2000): 67–68; Timothy Judge and Amir Erez, "Interaction and Intersection: The Constellation of Emotional Stability and Extroversion in Predicting Performance," *Personnel Psychology* 60 (2007): 573–596; and Ryan Zimmerman, "Understanding the Impact of Personality Traits on Individuals' Turnover Decisions: A Meta-Analytic Path Model," *Personnel Psychology* 60, no. 1 (2008): 309–348. A review of personality testing reached several conclusions. Employers are increasingly using personality tests. The weight of evidence is that personality measures (particularly the big five) contribute to predicting job performance. And employers can reduce personality test faking by warning applicants that faking may reduce the chances of being hired. Mitchell Rothstein and Richard Goffin, "The Use of Personality Measures in Personnel Selection: What Does Current Research Support?" *Human Resource Management Review* 16 (2006): 155–180.

30. Frederick Morgeson et al., "Reconsidering the Use of Personality Tests in Personnel Selection Contexts," *Personnel Psychology* 60 (2007): 683. See also, Edwin A. J. van Hoot and Marise Ph. Born, "Intentional Response Distortion on Personality Tests: Using Eye Tracking to Understand Response Processes when Thinking," *Journal of Applied Psychology* 97, no. 2 (2012).

31. See, for example, W. A. Scroggins et al., "Psychological Testing in Personnel Selection, Part III: The Resurgence of Personality Testing," *Public Personnel Management* 38, no. 1 (Spring 2009): 67–77. Part of the problem with self-report personality tests is that some applicants will see through to the aim of the test and provide answers they think the employer is looking for (they "fake" the test). The problem here, of course, is that less-worthy candidates may actually succeed in earning higher test scores than more-worthy candidates. In one study, researchers extensively studied this question. They concluded that one way to minimize the effects of faking was to compute "pass fail" cut points by having nonapplicants such as supervisors and existing employees take the test (rather than applicants). It remains a tricky problem, however. Christopher Berry and Paul Sackett, "Faking in Personnel Selection: Trade-Offs in Performance versus Fairness Resulting from Two Cut Score Strategies," *Personnel Psychology* 62 (2009): 835–863.

32. Paula Caliguri, "The Big Five Personality Characteristics as Predictors of Expatriates' Desire to Terminate the Assignment and Supervisor-Rated Performance," *Personnel Psychology* 53, no. 1 (Spring 2000): 67–88.

33. Kathryn Tyler, "Put Applicants' Skills to the Test," *HR Magazine* (January 2000): 75–79.

34. Gilbert Nicholson, "Automated Assessments," *Workforce*, (December 2000), 102–107.

35. Ibid. See also, Ed Frauenheim, "More Companies Go with Online Test to Fill in the Blanks," *Workforce Management* (May 2011): 12.

36. Ed Frauenheim, "Personality Tests Adapt to the Times," *Workforce Management* (February 2010): 4.

37. Requiring job seekers to complete prescreening questionnaires and screening selected applicants out on this basis carries legal and business consequences. See, for example, Lisa Harpe, "Designing an Effective Employment Prescreening Program," *Employment Relations Today* 32, no. 3 (Fall 2005): 41–43.

38. www.iphonetypingtest.com, accessed March 23, 2009.

39. Laurence Siegel and Irving Lane, *Personnel and Organizational Psychology* (Burr Ridge, IL: McGraw-Hill, 1982), pp. 182–183.

40. However, studies suggest that blacks may be somewhat less likely to do well on work sample tests than whites. See, for example, Philip Roth, Philip Bobko, and Lynn McFarland, "A Meta-Analysis of Work Sample Test Validity: Updating and Integrating Some Classic Literature," *Personnel Psychology* 58, no. 4 (Winter 2005): 1009–1037; and Philip Roth et al., "Work Sample Tests in Personnel Selection: A Meta-Analysis of Black-White Differences in Overall and

Exercise Scores," *Personnel Psychology* 60, no. 1 (2008): 637–662.

41. See, for example, George Thornton III and Alyssa Gibbons, "Validity of Assessment Centers for Personnel Selection," *Human Resource Management Review* 19 (2009): 169–187.

42. "Help Wanted—and Found," *Fortune* (October 2, 2006): 40.

43. Annette Spychalski, Miguel Quinones, Barbara Gaugler, and Katja Pohley, "A Survey of Assessment Center Practices in Organizations in the United States," *Personnel Management* 50, no. 10 (Spring 1997): 71–90. See also Winfred Arthur Jr. et al., "A Meta Analysis of the Criterion Related Validity of Assessment Center Data Dimensions," *Personnel Psychology* 56 (2003): 124–154.

44. Kobi Dayan et al., "Entry-Level Police Candidate Assessment Center: An Efficient Tool or a Hammer to Kill a Fly?" *Personnel Psychology* 55 (2002): 827–848. See also, for example, John Meriac et al., "Further Evidence for the Validity of Assessment Center Dimensions: A Meta-Analysis of the Incremental Criterion-Related Validity of Dimension Ratings," *Journal of Applied Psychology* 93, no. 5 (2008): 1042–1052.

45. Quoted from Deborah Whetzel and Michael McDaniel, "Situational Judgment Tests: An Overview of Current Research," *Human Resource Management Review* 19 (2009): 188–202.

46. Ibid.

47. Michael McDaniel et al., "The Validity of Employment Interviews: A Comprehensive Review and Meta-Analysis," *Journal of Applied Psychology* 79, no. 4 (1994): 599. See also Richard Posthuma et al., "Beyond Employment Interview Validity: A Comprehensive Narrative Review of Recent Research and Trends over Time," *Personnel Psychology* 55 (2002): 1–81. For an argument against holding selection interviews, see D. Heath et al., "Hold the Interview," *Fast Company* no. 136 (June 2009): 51–52.

48. Therese Macan, "The Employment Interview: A Review of Current Studies and Directions for Future Research," *Human Resource Management Review* 19 (2009): 203–218.

49. Ibid.

50. Bill Stoneman, "Matching Personalities with Jobs Made Easier with Behavioral Interviews," *American Banker* 165, no. 229 (November 30, 2000): 8a.

51. Aparna Nancheria, "Anticipated Growth in Behavioral Interviewing," *Training & Development* (April 2008): 20.

52. "Phone Interviews Might Be the Most Telling, Study Finds," *BNA Bulletin to Management* (September 1998): 273.

53. Susan Strauss et al., "The Effects of Videoconference, Telephone, and Face-to-Face Media on Interviewer and Applicant Judgments in Employment Interviews," *Journal of Management* 27, no. 3 (2001): 363–381.

If the employer records a video interview with the intention of sharing it with hiring managers who don't participate in the interview, it's advisable to first obtain the candidate's written permission. Matt Bolch, "Lights, Camera...Interview!" *HR Magazine* (March 2007): 99–102.

54. Emily Maltby, "To Find the Best Hires, Firms Become Creative," *Wall Street Journal* (November 17, 2009): B6.

55. See, for example, M. M. Harris, "Reconsidering the Employment Interview: A Review of Recent Literature and Suggestions for Future Research," *Personnel Psychology* 42 (1989): 691–726; Richard Posthuma et al., "Beyond Employment Interview Validity: A Comprehensive Narrative Review of Recent Research and Trends over Time," *Personnel Psychology* 55, no. 1 (Spring 2002): 1–81.

56. Timothy Judge et al., "The Employment Interview: A Review of Recent Research and Recommendations for Future Research," *Human Resource Management* 10, no. 4 (2000): 392. There is disagreement regarding the relative superiority of individual versus panel interviews. See, for example, Marlene Dixon et al., "The Panel Interview: A Review of Empirical Research and Guidelines for Practice," *Public Personnel Management* (Fall 2002): 397–428.

57. Frank Schmidt and Ryan Zimmerman, "A Counter-intuitive Hypothesis about Employment Interview Validity and Some Supporting Evidence," *Journal of Applied Psychology* 89, no. 3 (2004): 553–561. See also Julie McCarthy et al., "Are Highly Structured Job Interviews Resistant to Demographic Similarity Effects?" *Personnel Psychology* 63, no. 2 (Summer 2010): 325–359.

58. The validity discussion and these findings are based on McDaniel et al., "Validity of Employment Interviews," 607–610. See also Robert Dipboye et al., "The Validity of Unstructured Panel Interviews," *Journal of Business & Strategy* 16, no. 1 (Fall 2001): 35–49; Marlene Dixon et al., "The Panel Interview: A Review of Empirical Research and Guidance," *Public Personnel Management* 3, no. 3 (Fall 2002): 397–428; and Todd Maurer and Jerry Solamon, "The Science and Practice of a Structured Employment Interview Coaching Program," *Personnel Psychology* 59 (2006): 433–456.

59. McDaniel et al., "Validity of Employment Interviews," 608.

60. Anita Chaudhuri, "Beat the Clock: Applying for a Job? A New Study Shows that Interviewers Will Make up Their Minds about You Within a Minute," *The Guardian* (June 14, 2000): 2–6.

61. Don Langdale and Joseph Weitz, "Estimating the Influence of Job Information on Interviewer Agreement," *Journal of Applied Psychology* 57 (1973): 23–27.

62. R. E. Carlson, "Selection Interview Decisions: The Effects of Interviewer Experience, Relative Quota Situation, and Applicant Sample on Interview Decisions," *Personnel Psychology* 20 (1967): 259–280.

63. R. E. Carlson, "Effects of Applicant Sample on Ratings of Valid Information in an Employment Setting," *Journal of Applied Psychology* 54 (1970): 217–222.

64. See, for example, Scott Fleischmann, "The Messages of Body Language in Job Interviews," *Employee Relations* 18, no. 2 (Summer 1991): 161–176. See also James Westphal and Ithai Stern, "Flattery Will Get You Everywhere (Especially if You're a Male Caucasian): How Ingratiation, Board Room Behavior, and a Demographic Minority Status Affect Additional Board Appointments at U.S. Companies," *Academy of Management Journal* 50, no. 2 (2007): 267–288.

65. Tim DeGroot and Stephen Motowidlo, "Why Visual and Vocal Interview Cues Can Affect Interviewer's Judgments and Predicted Job Performance," *Journal of Applied Psychology* (December 1999): 968–984.

66. David Caldwell and Jerry Burger, "Personality Characteristics of Job Applicants and Success in Screening Interviews," *Personnel Psychology* 51 (1998): 119–136.

67. Amy Kristof-Brown et al., "Applicant Impression Management: Dispositional Influences and Consequences for Recruiter Perceptions of Fit and Similarity," *Journal of Management* 28, no. 1 (2002): 27–46. See also Lynn McFarland et al., "Impression Management Use and Effectiveness Across Assessment Methods," *Journal of Management* 29, no. 5 (2003): 641–661.

68. See, for example, Cynthia Marlowe, Sondra Schneider, and Carnot Nelson, "Gender and Attractiveness Biases in Hiring Decisions: Are More Experienced Managers Less Biased?" *Journal of Applied Psychology* 81, no. 1 (1996): 11–21. See also Shari Caudron, "Why Job Applicants Hate HR," *Workforce* (June 2002): 36.

69. Marlowe et al., "Gender and Attractiveness Biases in Hiring Decisions," 11.

70. Ibid., p. 18. See also Timothy Judge, Charlice Hurst, and Lauren Simon, "Does It Pay to Be Smart, Attractive, or Confident (or All Three)? Relationships among General Mental Ability, Physical Attractiveness, Core Self-Evaluations, and Income," *Journal of Applied Psychology* 94, no. 3 (2009): 742–755.

71. Emily Duehr and Joyce Bono, "Men, Women, and Managers: Are Stereotypes Finally Changing?" *Personnel Psychology* 59 (2006): 837.

72. N. S. Miceli et al., "Potential Discrimination in Structured Employment Interviews," *Employee Responsibilities and Rights* 13, no. 1 (March 2001): 15–38.

73. Timothy DeGroot and Janaki Gooty, "Can Nonverbal Cues Be Used to Make Meaningful Personality Attributions in Employment Interviews?" *Journal of Business Psychology* 24 (2009): 179.

74. Madeline Heilman and Tyler Okimoto, "Motherhood: A Potential Source of Bias in Employment Decisions," *Journal of Applied Psychology* 93, no. 1 (2008): 189–198.

75. Ibid., p. 196. See also, Michelle Ryan, et al., "Think Crisis—Think Female: The Glass Cliff and Contextual Variation in the Think Manager—Think Male

Stereotype," *Journal of Applied Psychology* 96, no. 3 (2011): 470–484.

76. Amelia J. Prewett-Livingston et al., "Effects of Race on Interview Ratings in a Situational Panel Interview," *Journal of Applied Psychology* 81, no. 2 (1996): 178–186. See also Richard White Jr., "Ask Me No Questions, Tell Me No Lies: Examining the Uses and Misuses of the Polygraph," *Public Personnel Management* 30, no. 4 (Winter 2001): 483–493.

77. Chad Higgins and Timothy Judge, "The Effect of Applicant Influence Tactics on Recruiter Perceptions of Fit and Hiring Recommendations: A Field Study," *Journal of Applied Psychology* 89, no. 4 (2004): 622–632.

78. Andrea Rodriguez and Fran Prezant, "Better Interviews for People with Disabilities," *Workforce,* accessed from www.workforce.com, November 14, 2003. See also, Juan Madera and Michele Hebl, "Discrimination against Facially Stigmatized Applicants in Interviews: An Eye Tracking and Face-to-Face Investigation," *Journal of applied Psychology* 97, no. 2, pp. 317–330.

79. Williamson et al., "Employment Interview on Trial," 901–902; Michael Campion, David Palmer, and James Campion, "A Review of Structure in the Selection Interview," *Personnel Psychology* 50 (1997): 655–702.

80. See Williamson et al., "Employment Interview on Trial," 901–902; and Randy Myers, "Interviewing Techniques: Tips From the Pros," *Journal of Accountancy* 202, no. 2 (August 2006): 53–55.

81. Todd Maurer and Jerry Solamon, "The Science and Practice of a Structured Employment Interview Coaching Program," *Personnel Psychology* 59 (2006): 433–456.

82. With respect to addressing age bias in interviews, "Laboratory studies may create too much artificiality," in Frederick P. Morgeson, Matthew H. Reider, Michael A. Campion, and Rebecca A. Bull, "Review of Research on Age Discrimination in the Employment Interview," *Journal of Business Psychology* 22 (2008): 223–232.

83. Carlson, "Selection Interview Decisions," 259–280.

84. Catherine Middendorf and Therese Macan, "Note Taking in the Employment Interview: Effects on Recall and Judgment," *Journal of Applied Psychology* 87, no. 2 (2002): 293–303.

85. "Looking to Hire the Very Best? Ask the Right Questions. Lots of Them," *Fortune* (June 21, 1999): 192–194.

86. Panel Kaul, "Interviewing Is Your Business," *Association Management* (November 1992): 29. See also Nancy Woodward, "Asking for Salary Histories," *HR Magazine* (February 2000): 109–112. Gathering information about specific interview dimensions such as social ability, responsibility, and independence (as is often done with structured interviews) can improve interview accuracy, at least for more complicated jobs. See also Andrea Poe, "Graduate Work: Behavioral

Interviewing Can Tell You if an Applicant Just Out of College Has Traits Needed for the Job," *HR Magazine* 48, no. 10 (October 2003): 95–96.

87. These are from Alan M. Saks and Julie M. McCarthy, "Effects of Discriminatory Interview Questions and Gender on Applicant Reactions," *Journal of Business and Psychology* 21, no. 2 (Winter 2006): 175–191.

88. These are quoted or adapted from www.careerfaqs .com.au/getthatjob_video_interview.asp, accessed March 2, 2009.

89. "Are Your Background Checks Balanced? Experts Identify Concerns over Verifications," *BNA Bulletin to Management* (May 13, 2004): 153.

90. Matthew Heller, "Special Report: Background Checking," *Workforce Management* (March 3, 2008): 35.

91. Based on Samuel Greengard, "Have Gangs Invaded Your Workplace?" *Personnel Journal* (February 1996): 47–57; Carroll Lachnit, "Protecting People and Profits with Background Checks," *Workforce* (February 2002): 52.

92. Lachnit, "Protecting People and Profits with Background Checks," 52. See also Robert Howie and Laurence Shapero, "Preemployment Criminal Background Checks: Why Employers Should Look Before They Leap," *Employee Relations Law Journal* (Summer 2002): 63–77.

93. Bill Leonard, "Fraud Factories," *HR Magazine* (September 2008): 54–58.

94. See, for example, A. M. Forsberg et al., "Perceived Fairness of a Background Information Form and a Job Knowledge Test," *Public Personnel Management* 38, no. 1 (Spring 2009): 33–46.

95. Matthew Heller, "Special Report: Background Checking," *Workforce Management* (March 3, 2008): 35–54.

96. Alan Finder, "When a Risqué Online Persona Undermines a Chance for a Job," *New York Times* (June 11, 2006): 1.

97. "Vetting Via Internet Is Free, Generally Legal, But Not Necessarily Smart Hiring Strategy," *BNA Bulletin to Management* (February 20, 2007): 57–58.

98. Rita Zeidner, "How Deep Can You Probe?" *HR Magazine* (October 1, 2007): 57–62.

99. "Web Searches on Applicants Are Potentially Perilous for Employers," *BNA Bulletin to Management* (October 14, 2008): 335.

100. "Employment Related Screening Providers," *Workforce Management* (February 16, 2009): 14.

101. Lachnit, "Protecting People, and Profits with Background Checks," 52.

102. For example, see Lawrence Dube Jr., "Employment References and the Law," *Personnel Journal* 65, no. 2 (February 1986): 87–91. See also Mickey Veich, "Uncover the Resume Ruse," *Security Management* (October 1994): 75–76; and Anjali Athavaley, "Job References You Can't Control," *Wall Street Journal* (September 27, 2007): B1.

103. "Undercover Callers Tipoff Job Seekers to Former Employers' Negative References," *BNA Bulletin to Management* (May 27, 1999): 161. See also Diane

Cadrain, "Job Detectives Dig Deep for Defamation," *HR Magazine* 49, no. 10 (October 2004): 34 ff.

104. Lachnit, "Protecting People and Profits with Background Checks," 52; Shari Caudron, "Who Are You Really Hiring?" *Workforce* (November 2002): 31.

105. Adrienne Fox, "Automated Reference Checking Puts Onus on Candidates," *HR Magazine* 66, no. 9 (2009, HR Trendbook supplement).

106. Polygraphs are still widely used in law enforcement and reportedly quite useful. See, for example, Laurie Cohen, "The Polygraph Paradox," *Wall Street Journal* (March 22, 2008): A1.

107. These are based on "Divining Integrity Through Interviews," *BNA Bulletin to Management* (June 4, 1987): 184; and Commerce Clearing House, Ideas and Trends (December 29, 1998): 222–223.

108. John Bernardin and Donna Cooke, "Validity of an Honesty Test in Predicting Theft among Convenience Store Employees," *Academy of Management Journal* 36, no. 5 (1993): 1097–1108; and Bill Roberts, "Your Cheating Heart," *HR Magazine* (June 2011): 55–57. Note that some suggest that by possibly signaling mental illness, integrity tests may conflict with the Americans with Disabilities Act, but one review concludes that such tests pose little legal risk to employers. Christopher Berry et al., "A Review of Recent Developments in Integrity Test Research," *Personnel Psychology* 60 (2007): 271–301.

109. Steven Thomas and Steve Vaught, "The Write Stuff: What the Evidence Says about Using Handwriting Analysis in Hiring," *Advanced Management Journal* 66, no. 4 (Autumn 2001): 31–35.

110. This is based on Kyle Stock, "Wary Investors Turn to Lie Pros," *Wall Street Journal* (December 29, 2010). C3.

111. Mick Haus, "Pre-Employment Physicals and the ADA," *Safety and Health* (February 1992): 64–65. See also Bridget A. Styers and Kenneth S. Shultz, "Perceived Reasonableness of Employment Testing Accommodations for Persons with Disabilities," *Public Personnel Management* 38, no. 3 (Fall 2009): 71–91.

112. Rita Zeidner, "Putting Drug Screening to the Test," *HR Magazine* (November 2010): 26.

113. Scott MacDonald, Samantha Wells, and Richard Fry, "The Limitations of Drug Screening in the Workplace," *International Labor Review* 132, no. 1 (1993): 98. Not all agree that drug testing is worthwhile. See Veronica I. Luzzi et al., "Analytic Performance of Immunoassays for Drugs of Abuse Below Established Cutoff Values," *Clinical Chemistry* 50 (2004): 717–722.

114. MacDonald et al., "The Limitations of Drug Screening."

115. Ibid.

116. Diane Cadrain, "Are Your Employees' Drug Tests Accurate?" *HR Magazine* (January 2003): 40–45.

117. MacDonald et al., "The Limitations of Drug Screening," 98.

118. Lewis Maltby, "Drug Testing: A Bad Investment," *Business Ethics* 15, no. 2 (March 2001): 7; Veronica I. Luzzi et al., "Analytic Performance of Immunoassays for Drugs of Abuse Below Established Cutoff Values," *Clinical Chemistry* 50 (2004): 717–722

119. Frank Lockwood et al., "Drug Testing Programs and Their Impact on Workplace Accidents: A Time Series Analysis," *Journal of Individual Employment Rights* 8, no. 4 (2000): 295–306; and Sally Roberts, "Random Drug Testing Can Help Reduce Accidents for Construction Companies; Drug Abuse Blamed for Heightened Risk in the Workplace," *Business Insurance* 40 (October 23, 2006), p. 6.

120. O'Neill, "Legal Issues Presented by Hair Follicle Testing," *Employee Relations Today*, Winter 1991–1992, pp. 411–415; for an example, see www.americanscreeningcorp.com/default.aspx, accessed October 8, 2011.

121. Richard Lisko, "A Manager's Guide to Drug Testing," *Security Management* 38, no. 8 (August 1994): 92.

122. *Exxon Corp.* v. *Esso Workers Union, Inc.*, CA1#96–2241, July 8, 1997; discussed in *BNA Bulletin to Management* (August 7, 1997): 249.

123. Coleman Peterson, "Employee Retention, the Secrets behind Wal-Mart's Successful Hiring Policies," *Human Resource Management* 44, no. 1 (Spring 2005): 85–88. See also Murray Barrick and Ryan Zimmerman, "Reducing Voluntary, Avoidable Turnover Through Selection," *Journal of Applied Psychology* 90, no. 1 (2005): 159–166.

124. James Breaugh, "Employee Recruitment: Current Knowledge and Important Areas for Future Research," *Human Resource Management Review* 18 (2008): 106–107. See also Michael Tucker, "Show and Tell," *HR Magazine* (January 2012): 51–52.

125. Lawrence Kellner, "Corner Office," *New York Times* (September 26, 2009), http://projects.nytimes.com/corner-office, accessed April 8, 2010.

126. For the form, see www.uscis.gov/files/form/i-9.pdf, accessed October 4, 2011.

127. "Conflicting State E-Verify Laws Troubling for Employers," *BNA Bulletin to Management* (November 4, 2008): 359. See also, Davis Zielinski, "Automating I-9 Verification," *HR Magazine* (May 2011): 57–65.

128. "President Bush Signs Executive Order: Federal Contractors Must Use E-Verify," *BNA Bulletin to Management* (June 17, 2008): 193. "DHS to Implement E-Verify Mandate, Will Strengthen Eligibility Verification, Secretary Says," *BNA Bulletin to Management* (July 14, 2009): 217.

129. Russell Gerbman, "License to Work," *HR Magazine* (June 2000): 151–160. The I-9 form clearly states that the employer may not discriminate. See www.uscis.gov/files/form/i-9.pdf, accessed October 4, 2011. See also, "Identity Theft Remains Top Challenge for E-Verify," *BNA Bulletin to Management* (April 19, 2011): 121.

130. "As E-Verify, No Match Rules, I-9 Evolve, Employers Need to Stay on Top of Issues," *BNA Bulletin to Management* (April 15, 2008): 121.

131. Actually, there may be other complications too. For example, you may want to decide which of several possible potential jobs is best for your candidate.

132. This is based on Robert Gatewood and Hubert Feild, *Human Resource Selection* (Fort Worth, TX: The Dryden Press, 1994), pp. 278–279.

Chapter 5

1. Marjorie Derven, "Management Onboarding," *Training & Development* (April 2008): 49–52.

2. For a good discussion of socialization, see, for example, George Chao et al., "Organizational Socialization: Its Content and Consequences," *Journal of Applied Psychology* 79, no. 5 (1994): 730–743; see also Talya Bauer et al., "Newcomer Adjustment during Organizational Socialization: A Meta-Analytic Review of Antecedents, Outcomes, and Methods," *Journal of Applied Psychology* 92, no. 3 (2007): 707–721.

3. Charlotte Garvey, "The Whirlwind of a New Job," *HR Magazine* (June 2001): 111. See also Talya Bauer et al., "Newcomer Adjustment during Organizational Socialization: A Meta-Analytic Review of Antecedents, Outcomes, and Methods," *Journal of Applied Psychology* 92, no. 3 (2007): 707–721.

4. Sheila Hicks et al., "Orientation Redesign," *Training & Development* (July 2006): 43–46.

5. John Kammeyer-Mueller and Connie Wanberg, "Unwrapping the Organizational Entry Process: Disentangling Multiple Antecedents and Their Pathways to Adjustments," *Journal of Applied Psychology* 88, no. 5 (2003): 779–794.

6. Sabrina Hicks, "Successful Orientation Programs," *Training & Development* (April 2000): 59. For people with disabilities, integration and socialization is highly influenced by the behavior of coworkers and supervisors, less so by organizational practices. Mukta Kulkarni and Mark Lengnick-Hall, "Socialization of People with Disabilities in the Workplace," *Human Resource Management* 60, no. 4 (July–August 2011): 521–540.

7. This section is based on Darin Hartley, "Technology Kicks Up Leadership Development," *Training & Development* (March 2004): 22–24.

8. Jennifer Taylor Arnold, "Ramping Up Onboarding," *HR Magazine* (May 2010): 75–78.

9. Jack Barry, "Transforming HRD into an Economic Value Add," *Training & Development* (September 2011) at www.astd.org/Publications/Magazines/TD/TD-Archive/2011/09/Transforming-HRD-Into-An-Economic-Value-Add, accessed May 1, 2012.

10. Winfred Alfred Jr. et al., "Effectiveness of Training in Organizations: A Meta Analysis of Design and

Evaluation Features," *Journal of Applied Psychology* 88, no. 2 (2003): 242.

11. Rita Smith, "Aligning Learning with Business Strategy," *Training & Development* (November 2008): 41–43.

12. Christine Ellis and Sarah Gale, "A Seat at the Table," *Training & Development* (March 2001): 90–96.

13. Rachel Dodes, "At Macy's, a Makeover on Service," *Wall Street Journal* (April 11, 2011): B10.

14. Ibid.

15. Nancy DeViney and Brenda Sugrue, "Learning Outsourcing: A Reality Check," *Training & Development* (December 2004): 41. See also "How Are Organizations Training Today?" *HR Focus* 86, no. 7 (July 2009): 52–53.

16. Brenda Sugrue et al., "What in the World Is WLP?" *Training & Development* (January 2005): 51–54.

17. "Companies Invested More in Training Despite Economic Setbacks, Survey Says," *BNA Bulletin to Management* (March 7, 2002): 73; "Employee Training Expenditures on the Rise," *American Salesman* 49, no. 1 (January 2004): 26–28.

18. "Companies Invested More in Training Despite Economic Setbacks, Survey Says," op. cit.; Andrew Paradise, "The 2008 ASTD State of the Industry Report Shows Sustained Support for Corporate Learning," *Training & Development* (November 2008): 45–51.

19. W. Clayton Allen, "Overview and Evolution of the ADDIE Training System," *Advances in Developing Human Resources* 8, no. 4 (November 2006): 430–441.

20. www.intulogy.com/process/, accessed April 20, 2011.

21. Jay Bahlis, "Blueprint for Planning Learning," *Training & Development* (March 2008): 64–67.

22. Marcia Jones, "Use Your Head when Identifying Skills Gaps," *Workforce* (March 2000): 118.

23. P. Nick Blanchard and James Thacker, *Effective Training: Systems, Strategies, and Practices* (Upper Saddle River, NJ: Prentice Hall, 1999), pp. 154–156. See also Brian Hoffman et al., "Exercises and Dimensions are the Currency of Assessment Centers," *Personnel Psychology* 60, no. 4 (2011): 351–395.

24. See, for example, Jennifer Salopek, "The Power of the Pyramid," *Training & Development* (May 2009): 70–73.

25. Richard Montier et al., "Competency Models Develop Top Performance," *Training & Development* (July 2006): 47–50. See also Jennifer Salopek, "The Power of the Pyramid," *Training & Development* (May 2009): 70–73.

26. Employers increasingly utilize learning content management systems (LCMS) to compile and author training content. See, for example, Bill Perry, "Customized Content at Your Fingertips," *Training & Development* (June 2009): 29–30.

27. Blanchard and Thacker, op. cit.

28. Ibid., p. 90.

29. Kenneth Wexley and Gary Latham, *Developing and Training Human Resources in Organizations* (Upper Saddle River, NJ: Prentice Hall, 2002), p. 305.

30. Kathryn Tyler, "Focus on Training," *HR Magazine* (May 2000): 94–102. See also, J. S. Goodman et al., "Feedback Specificity, Information Processing, and Transfer of Training," *Organizational Behavior and Human Decision Processes* 115, no. 2 (July 2011): 253–267.

31. Janice A. Cannon-Bowers et al., "Framework for Understanding Pre-Practice Conditions and Their Impact on Learning," *Personnel Psychology* 51 (1998): 291–320.

32. Ibid., p. 305.

33. Ibid. Also see Kendra Lee, "Reinforce Training," *Training* 48, no. 3 (May/June 2011): 24.

34. Elaine Biech, "Learning Eye to Eye: Aligning Training to Business Objectives," *Training & Development* (April 2009): 50–53.

35. Large training providers include Element k, Geo Learning, learn.com, Outsmart, Plateau, Saba, and Sumtotal Systems. "Training Providers," *Workforce Management* (January 2011): 8.

36. Donna Goldwaser, "Me a Trainer?" *Training* (April 2001): 60–66. See also http://employment.menswearhouse.com/ats/advantageSelector.action;jsessionid=C6EA171584 51F5A2902F7195B678CF6A?type=training, accessed June 1, 2011.

37. See for example, www.aps-online.net/consulting/structured_ojt.htm, accessed June 1, 2011; and Kathryn Tyler, "15 Ways to Train on the Job," *HR Magazine* 53 no. 9 (September 2008) pp. 105–108.

38. Robert Weintraub and Jennifer Martineau, "The Just in Time Imperative," *Training & Development* (June 2002): 52; and Andrew Paradise, "Informal Learning: Overlooked or Overhyped?" *Training & Development* (July 2008): 52–53.

39. Aparna Nancherla, "Knowledge Delivered in Any Other Form Is…Perhaps Sweeter," *Training & Development* (May 2009): 54–60.

40. Harley Frazis et al., "Results from the 1995 Survey of Employer-Provided Training," www.bls.gov/mlr/1998/06/art1full.pdf, accessed April 11, 2010.

41. Cindy Waxer, "Steelmaker Revives Apprentice Program to Address Graying Workforce, Forge Next Leaders," *Workforce Management* (January 30, 2006): 40.

42. Kermit Kaleba, "New Changes to Apprenticeship Program Could Be Forthcoming," *Training & Development* (February 2008): 14.

43. Paula Ketter, "What Can Training Do for Brown?" *Training & Development* (May 2008): 30–36.

44. Michael Blotzer, "Distance Learning," *Occupational Hazards* (March 2000): 53–54.

45. www.radvision.com/Support/cisco.htm, accessed June 1, 2011.

46. Garry Kranz, "More to Learn," *Workforce Management* (January 2011): 27.

47. See, for example, Kim Kleps, "Virtual Sales Training Scores a Hit," *Training & Development* (December 2006): 63–64.

48. Michael Laff, "Simulations: Slowly Proving Their Worth," *Training & Development* (June 2007): 30–34.

49. Jenni Jarventaus, "Virtual Threat, Real Sweat," *Training & Development* (May 2007): 72–78.

50. Pat Galagan, "Second That," *Training & Development* (February 2008): 34–37. Description of Web 2.0 paraphrased from Manuel London and MJ Hall, "Unlocking the Value of Web 2.0 Technologies for Training and Development: The Shift from Instructor—Controlled, Adaptive Learning to Learner—Driven, Generative Learning," *Human Resource Management* 50, no. 6 (November-December 2011): 761.

51. Ellen Zimmerman, "Better Training Is Just a Click Away," *Workforce Management* (January 2001): 36–42. Kevin Alansky, "Blackboard Pays Off for ADP," *T+D* 65, no. 6 (June 2011): 68–69.

52. Greg Wright, "Retailers Buy Into Relearning," *HR Magazine* (December 7, 2010): 87–90.

53. John Zonneveld, "GM Dealer Training Goes Global," *Training & Development* (December 2006): 47–51. See also "What's Next for the LMS?" *Training & Development* (September 2011): 16.

54. "The Next Generation of Corporate Learning," *Training & Development* (June 2004): 47; and Jennifer Hofmann and Nanatte Miner, "Real Blended Learning Stands Up," *Training & Development* (September 2008): 28–31. J. Hofmann, "Top 10 Challenges of Blended Learning," *Training* 48, no. 2 (March/April 2011): 12–13; and Lee Salz, "Use Webinars for Training and Revenue," *Training* 48, no. 2 (March/April 2011): 14.

55. Jennifer Taylor Arnold, "Learning on-the-Fly," *HR Magazine* (September 2007): 137. A new Microsoft Word add-on enables someone to convert instantly any Word document into multimedia content that one can play on a portable MP3 player. Paul Harris, "A New Era for Accessibility," *Training & Development* (April 2009): 58–61. See also M. Donahue, "Mobile Learning Is the Next Generation in Training," *Hotel Management* 226, no. 4 (April 4, 2011): 17.

56. www.dominknow.com/, accessed March 23, 2009.

57. Elizabeth Agnvall, "Just-In-Time Training," *HR Magazine* (May 2006): 67–78.

58. Ibid.

59. For a similar program, and Accenture, see Don Vanthournout and Dana Koch, "Training at Your Fingertips," *Training & Development* (September 2008): 52–57. For a discussion of blogs in training see Becky Livingston, "Harnessing Blogs for Learning," *T+D* 65, no. 5 (May 2011): 76–77.

60. Marcia Conner, "Twitter 101: Are You Reading?" *Training & Development* (August 2009): 24–26.

61. Paula Ketter, "The Hidden Disability," *Training & Development* (June 2006): 34–40.

62. Jeremy Smerd, "New Workers Sorely Lacking Literacy Skills," *Workforce Management* (December 10, 2008): 6.

63. Valerie Frazee, "Workers Learn to Walk so They Can Run," *Personnel Journal* (May 1996): 115–120. See also Kathryn Tyler, "I Say Potato, You Say Patata: As Workforce and Customer Diversity Grow, Employers Offer Foreign Language Training to Staff," *HR Magazine* 49, no. 1 (January 2004): 85–87.

64. Jennifer Salopek, "The Growth of Succession Management," *Training & Development* (June 2007): 22–24; and Kermit Kalleba, "Businesses Continue to Push for Lifelong Learning," *Training & Development* (June 2007): 14.

65. Matthew Reis, "Do-It-Yourself Diversity," *Training & Development* (March 2004): 80–81.

66. www.prismdiversity.com/resources/diversity_training.html, accessed June 1, 2011.

67. Jennifer Salopek, "Trends: Lost in Translation," *Training & Development* (December 2003): 15; www.visionpoint.com/training-solutions/title/just-be-fair-basic-diversity-training, accessed June 17, 2011.

68. Blanchard and Thacker, pp. 403–405.

69. Susan Ladika, "When Learning Lasts a Lifetime," *HR Magazine* (May 2008): 57.

70. "For Gap, Management Training Doesn't Stop at the Border," *BNA Bulletin to Management* (February 2005): 63.

71. See, for example, Jeff Kristick, "Filling the Leadership Pipeline," *Training & Development* (June 2009): 49–51.

72. Christopher Glynn, "Building a Learning Infrastructure," *Training & Development* (January 2008): 38–43.

73. Jack Zenger, Dave Ulrich, and Norm Smallwood, "The New Leadership Development," *Training & Development* (March 2000): 22–27. See also W. David Patton and Connie Pratt, "Assessing the Training Needs of High Potential Managers," *Public Personnel Management* 31, no. 4 (Winter 2002): 465–474; and Ann Locke and Arlene Tarantino, "Strategic Leadership Development," *Training & Development* (December 2006): 53–55.

74. Mike Czarnowsky, "Executive Development," *Training & Development* (September 2008): 44–45.

75. Wexley and Latham, *Developing and Training Human Resources in Organizations* (Upper Saddle River, NJ: Prentice Hall, 2002), p. 193.

76. http://teamcommunication.blogspot.com/, accessed June 17, 2011.

77. Jean Thilmany, "Acting Out," *HR Magazine* (January 2007): 95–100.

78. "AMA Seminars," October 2009–2010, the American Management Association, www.AMAseminars.org.

79. Thus for a list of Harvard programs, see, for example, their intensive two-day conferences in the 2008 brochure from their Center for Management Research, "Programs on Leadership for Senior Executives," www.execseminars.com, 2008.

80. Chris Musselwhite, "University Executive Education Gets Real," *Training & Development* (May 2006): 57.

81. Ann Pomeroy, "Head of the Class," *HR Magazine* (January 2005): 57.

82. This is based on Diane Brady, "Can GE Still Manage?" *Bloomberg Businessweek* (April 25, 2010): 29.

83. Ibid.

84. Russell Gerbman, "Corporate Universities 101," *HR Magazine*, February 2000, pp. 101–106; Holly Dolezalek, "University 2.0," *Training* 44, no. 8 (September 2007).

85. See, for example, Joyce Bono et al., "A Survey of Executive Coaching Practices," *Personnel Psychology* 62 (2009): 361–364.

86. Joseph Toto, "Untapped World of Peer Coaching," *Training & Development* (April 2006): 69–72.

87. James Smither et al., "Can Working with an Executive Coach Improve Multiscore Feedback Ratings over Time?" *Personnel Psychology* 56, no. 1 (Spring 2003): 23–44.

88. "As Corporate Coaching Goes Mainstream, Keyed Prerequisite Overlooked: Assessment," *BNA Bulletin to Management* (May 16, 2006): 153.

89. Quoted and abstracted from "Five Rules for Talent Management in the New Economy," www.towerswatson.com/assets/pdf/1988/Five_rules_talent-mgmt_5-20-10.pdf, accessed March 7, 2012.

90. Nokia examples based on www.engadget.com/2011/02/05/nokia-reportedly-planning-organizational-changes-mobile-phone/, and http://press.nokia.com/press-release/, accessed June 17, 2011.

91. For an example of a successful organizational change see, for example, Jordan Mora et al., "Recipe for Change," *Training & Development* (March 2008): 42–46. See also, Shaul Oreg and Yair Berson, "Leadership and Employees' Reactions to Change: the Role of Leader's Personal Attributes and Transformational Leadership Style," *Personnel Psychology* 64 (2011): 627–659.

92. The 10 steps are based on Michael Beer et al., "Why Change Programs Don't Produce Change," *Harvard Business Review* (November/December 1990): 158–166; and John Kotter, *Leading Change* (Boston: Harvard Business School Press, 1996). See also David Herold et al., "Beyond Change Management: A Multilevel Investigation of Contextual and Personal Influences on Employee's Commitment to Change," *Journal of Applied Psychology* 92, no. 4 (2007): 949; Remco Schimmel and Dennis Muntslag, "Learning Barriers: A Framework for the Examination of Structural Impediments to Organizational Change," *Human Resource Management* 48, no. 3 (May–June 2009): 399–416; and John Austin, "Mapping Out a Game Plan for Change," *HR Magazine* (April 2009): 39–42.

93. Stacie Furst and Daniel Cable, "Employee Resistance to Organizational Change: Managerial Influence Tactics and Leader Member Exchange," *Journal of Applied Psychology* 3, no. 2 (2008): 453.

94. Wendell French and Cecil Bell Jr., *Organization Development* (Upper Saddle River, NJ: Prentice Hall,

1999). See also P. Nick Blanchard and James Thacker, *Effective Training* (Upper Saddle River, NJ: Pearson, 2007), pp. 38–46.

95. Darin Hartley, "OD Wired," *Training & Development* (August 2004): 20–24.

96. David A. Garvin, "Building a Learning Organization," *Harvard Business Review* (July/August 1993): 80.

97. See, for example, Charlie Morrow, M. Quintin Jarrett, and Melvin Rupinski, "An Investigation of the Effect and Economic Utility of Corporate-Wide Training," *Personnel Psychology* 50 (1997): 91–119. See also Jack Phillips and Patti Phillips, "Moving from Evidence to Proof," *T+D* 65, no. 8 (August 2011): 34–39 for a discussion of a process for gathering training assessment data.

98. See, for example, Jack Phillips and Patti Phillips, "Measuring What Matters: How CEOS View Learning Success," *Training & Development* (August 2009): 45–49.

99. Jeffrey Berk, "Training Evaluations," *Training & Development* (September 2004): 39–45.

100. Tony Bingaman and Pat Galagan, "Training: They're Lovin' It," *Training & Development* (November 2006): 30.

101. Todd Raphel, "What Learning Management Reports Do for You," *Workforce* 80, no. 6 (June 2001): 56–58.

Chapter 6

1. For a good recent discussion of this, see, for example, Samuel Culbert, "Get Rid of the Performance Review!" *Wall Street Journal* (October 20, 2008): R4. Also see Jonathan Segal, "Performance Management Blunders," *HR Magazine* (November 2010): 75–77.

2. Experts debate the pros and cons of tying appraisals to pay decisions. One side argues that doing so distorts the appraisals. A recent study concludes the opposite. Based on an analysis of surveys from over 24,000 employees in more than 6,000 workplaces in Canada, the researchers concluded that (1) linking the employees' pay to their performance appraisals contributed to improved pay satisfaction; (2) even when appraisals are not directly linked to pay, they apparently contributed to pay satisfaction, "probably through mechanisms related to perceived organizational justice"; and (3) whether or not the employees received performance pay, "individuals who do not receive performance appraisals are significantly less satisfied with their pay." Mary Jo Ducharme et al., "Exploring the Links between Performance Appraisals and Pay Satisfaction," *Compensation & Benefits Review* (September/October 2005): 46–52. See also Robert Morgan, "Making the Most of Performance Management Systems," *Compensation & Benefits Review* (September/October 2006): 22–27.

3. www.ball.com/page.jsp?page=1, accessed June 1, 2011.

4. "Aligning People and Processes for Performance Improvement," *T+D* 65, no. 3 (March 2011).

5. Ibid.

6. Peter Glendinning, "Performance Management: Pariah or Messiah," *Public Personnel Management* 31, no. 2 (Summer 2002): 161–178. See also Herman Aguinis, *Performance Management* (Upper Saddle River, NJ: Pearson, 2007), p. 2; and Bill Roberts, "Performance Review Redux: Value—Driven HR," *HR Magazine* (March 2012): 48.

7. Herman Aguinis, *Performance Management* (Upper Saddle River, NJ: Pearson, 2007), pp. 3–4. See also Marie–Helene Budworth, "Performance Management: Where Do We Go From Here?" *Human Resource Management Review* 20, no. 1 (2011): 81–84.

8. See, for example, Doug Cederblom and Dan Pemerl, "From Performance Appraisal to Performance Management: One Agency's Experience," *Personnel Management* 31, no. 2 (Summer 2002): 131–140.

9. See, for example, Robert Renn, "Further Examination of the Measurement of Properties of Leifer & McGannon's 1996 Goal Acceptance and Goal Commitment Scales," *Journal of Occupational and Organizational Psychology* (March 1999): 107–114. One recent study found that, at least in China, a sense of cooperation improves the positive aspects of participative leadership. Yi Feng Chen and Dean Tjosvold, "Participative Leadership by American and Chinese Managers in China: The Role of Relationships," *Journal of Management Studies* 43, no. 8 (December 2006): 1727–1752.

10. Vanessa Druskat and Steven Wolf, "Effects and Timing of Developmental Peer Appraisals in Self-Managing Work-Groups," *Journal of Applied Psychology* 84, no. 1 (1999): 58–74. For a recent review, see Erich Dierdorff and Eric Surface, "Placing Peer Ratings in Context: Systematic Influences beyond Ratee Performance," *Personnel Psychology* 60, no. 1 (Spring 2007): 93–126.

11. See, for example, Brian Hoffman and David Woehr, "Disentangling the Meaning of Multisource Performance Rating Source and Dimension Factors," *Personnel Psychology* 62 (2009): 735–765.

12. As one study recently concluded, "Far from being a source of nonmeaningful error variance, the discrepancies among ratings from multiple perspectives can in fact capture meaningful variance in multilevel managerial performance." In Sue Oh and Christopher Berry, "The Five Factor Model of Personality and Managerial Performance: Validity Gains Through the Use of 360° Performance Ratings," *Journal of Applied Psychology* 94, no. 6 (2009): 1510.

13. Such findings may be culturally related. One study compared self and supervisor ratings in "other-oriented" cultures (as in Asia, where values tend to emphasize teams). It found that self and supervisor ratings were related. M. Audrey Korsgaard et al., "The Effect of Other Orientation on Self: Supervisor Rating Agreement," *Journal of Organizational Behavior* 25, no. 7 (November 2004): 873–891.

14. Forest Jourden and Chip Heath, "The Evaluation Gap in Performance Perceptions: Illusory Perceptions of Groups and Individuals," *Journal of Applied Psychology* 81, no. 4 (August 1996): 369–379. See also Sheri Ostroff, "Understanding Self-Other Agreement: A Look at Rater and Ratee Characteristics, Context, and Outcomes," *Personnel Psychology* 57, no. 2 (Summer 2004): 333–375.

15. Paul Atkins and Robert Wood, "Self versus Others Ratings as Predictors of Assessment Center Ratings: Validation Evidence for 360 Degree Feedback Programs," *Personnel Psychology* 55, no. 4 (Winter 2002): 871–904.

16. Manuel London and Arthur Wohlers, "Agreement between Subordinate and Self-Ratings in Upward Feedback," *Personnel Psychology* 44 (1991): 375–390; see also Todd Maurer et al., "Peer and Subordinate Performance Appraisal Measurement Equivalents," *Journal of Applied Psychology* 83, no. 5 (1998): 693–702; and Herman Aguinis, *Performance Management* (Upper Saddle River, NJ: Pearson, 2007), p. 130.

17. David Antonioni, "The Effects of Feedback Accountability on Upward Appraisal Ratings," *Personnel Psychology* 47 (1994): 349–355.

18. Alan Walker and James Smither, "A Five-Year Study of Upward Feedback: What Managers Do with Their Results Matters," *Personnel Psychology* 52 (1999): 393–423; and Austin F. R. Smith and Vincent J. Fortunato, "Factors Influencing Employee Intentions to Provide Honest Upward Feedback Ratings," *Journal of Business Psychology* 22 (2008): 191–207.

19. Kenneth Nowack, "360-Degree Feedback: The Whole Story," *Training & Development* (January 1993): 69; Matthew Budman, "The Rating Game," *Across the Board* 31, no. 2 (February 1994): 35–38. See also "360-Degree Feedback on the Rise Survey Finds," *BNA Bulletin to Management* (January 23, 1997): 31; and Leanne Atwater et al., "Multisource Feedback: Lessons Learned and Implications for Practice," *Human Resource Management* 46, no. 2 (Summer 2007): 285.

20. However, a small number of employers are beginning to use 360-degree feedback for performance appraisals, rather than just development. See, for example, Tracy Maylett, "360° Feedback Revisited: The Transition from Development to Appraisal," *Compensation & Benefits Review* (September/October 2009): 52–59.

21. Herman Aguinis, *Performance Management* (Upper Saddle River, NJ: Pearson, 2007), p. 179.

22. Christine Hagan et al., "Predicting Assessment Center Performance with 360 Degree, Top-Down, and Customer-Based Competency Assessments," *Human Resource Management* 45, no. 3 (Fall 2006): 357–90.

23. www.echospan.com/echositenew/solutions/360_Feedback/default.asp, accessed June 2010.

24. Jeffrey Facteau and S. Bartholomew Craig, "Performance Appraisal Ratings from Different Rating

Scores," *Journal of Applied Psychology* 86, no. 2 (2001): 215–227.

25. See also Kevin Murphy et al., "Raters Who Pursue Different Goals Give Different Ratings," *Journal of Applied Psychology* 89, no. 1 (2004): 158–164.

26. Steven Scullen et al., "Forced Distribution Rating Systems and the Improvement of Workforce Potential: A Baseline Simulation," *Personnel Psychology* 58 (2005): 1; Jena McGregor, "The Struggle to Measure Performance," *BusinessWeek* (January 9, 2006): 26; Leslie Kwoh, "Rank and Yank Retains Vocal Fans," *The Wall Street Journal* (January 31, 2012): B12.

27. "Survey Says Problems with Forced Ranking Include Lower Morale and Costly Turnover," *BNA Bulletin to Management* (September 16, 2004): 297.

28. Steve Bates, "Forced Ranking: Why Grading Employees on a Scale Relative to Each Other Forces a Hard Look at Finding Keepers, Losers May Become Weepers," *HR Magazine* 48, no. 6 (June 2003): 62.

29. "Straight Talk about Grading Employees on a Curve," *BNA Bulletin to Management* (November 1, 2001): 351.

30. Drew Robb, "Building a Better Workforce," *HR Magazine*, October 2004, pp. 87–94.

31. John Aiello and Kathryn Kolb, "Electronic Performance Monitoring and Social Context: Impact on Productivity and Stress," *Journal of Applied Psychology* 80, no. 3 (1995): 339. See also Stoney Alder and Maureen Ambrose, "Towards Understanding Fairness Judgments Associated with Computer Performance Monitoring: An Integration of the Feedback, Justice, and Monitoring Research," *Human Resource Management Review* 15, no. 1 (March 2005): 43–67.

32. Aiello and Kolb, "Electronic Performance Monitoring and Social Context."

33. See, for example, David T. Goomas, "Electronic Performance Self-monitoring and Engineered Labor Standards For 'Man-Up' Drivers in a Distribution Center," *Journal of Business and Psychology* 21, no. 4 (Summer 2007): 541–558.

34. See, for example, "Communicating Beyond the Ratings Can Be Difficult," *Workforce Management* (April 24, 2006): 35.

35. See, for example, A. Fox, "Curing What Ails Performance Reviews," *HR Magazine* 54, no. 1 (January 2009): 52–56; and Rita Pyrielis, "The Reviews Are In," *Workforce Management* (May 2011): 20–25.

36. M. Ronald Buckley et al., "Ethical Issues in Human Resources Systems," *Human Resource Management Review* 11 (2001): 11, 29. See also Ann Pomeroy, "The Ethics Squeeze," *HR Magazine* (March 2006): 48–55.

37. G. R Weaver and L. K. Treviño, "The Role of Human Resources in Ethics/Compliance Management: A Fairness Perspective," *Human Resource Management Review* 11 (2001): 113–134. Researchers conducted studies of 490 police officers undergoing standardized promotional exams. Among their conclusions

was that "Organizations should strive to ensure that candidates perceived justice both in the content of personnel assessments and in the way they are treated during the assessment process." Julie McCarthy et al., "Progression Through the Ranks: Assessing Employee Reactions to High Stakes Employment Testing," *Personnel Psychology* 62 (2009): 826. See also, Howard Risher, "Getting Performance Management on Track," *Compensation & Benefits Review* 43, no. 5 (2011): 273–281; and E. Pulakos and R. O'Leary, "Why is Performance Management Broken?" *Industrial and Organizational Psychology* 4 (2011): 146–164.

38. Richard Posthuma, "Twenty Best Practices for Just Employee Performance Reviews," *Compensation & Benefits Review* (January/February 2008): 47–54.

39. See, for example, Adrienne Fox, "Curing What Ails Performance Reviews," *HR Magazine* (January 2009): 52–55; and "How to...Improve Appraisals," *People Management* 15, no. 3 (January 29, 2009): 57.

40. H. John Bernardin et al., "Conscientiousness and Agreeableness as Predictors of Rating Leniency," *Journal of Applied Psychology* 85, no. 2 (2000): 232–234.

41. Clinton Wingrove, "Developing a New Blend of Process and Technology in the New Era of Performance Management," *Compensation & Benefits Review* (January/February 2003): 25–30.

42. Gary Gregures et al., "A Field Study of the Effects of Rating Purpose on the Quality of Multiscore Ratings," *Personnel Psychology* 56 (2003): 1–21.

43. Madeleine Heilman et al., "Penalties for Success: Reactions to Women Who Succeed at Male Gender Type Tasks," *Journal of Applied Psychology* 89, no. 3 (2004): 416–427. Another study found that successful female managers didn't usually suffer such a fate when those rating them saw them as supportive, caring, and sensitive to their needs. Madeleine Heilmann and Tyler Okimoto, "Why Are Women Penalized for Success at Male Tasks? The Implied Communality Deficit," *Journal of Applied Psychology* 92, no. 1 (2007): 81–92.

44. Wingrove, "Developing a New Blend of Process and Technology."

45. James Austin, Peter Villanova, and Hugh Hindman, "Legal Requirements and Technical Guidelines Involved in Implementing Performance Appraisal Systems," in Gerald Ferris and M. Ronald Buckley (eds.), *Human Resources Management,* 3rd ed. (Upper Saddle River, NJ: Prentice Hall, 1996), pp. 271–288.

46. Ibid., p. 282.

47. Donald Fedor and Charles Parsons, "What Is Effective Performance Feedback?" in Gerald Ferris and M. Ronald Buckley (eds.), *Human Resources Management,* 3rd ed. (Upper Saddle River, NJ: Prentice Hall, 1996), pp. 265–70. See also Herman Aguinis, *Performance Management* (Upper Saddle River, NJ: Pearson 2007), pp. 196–219.

48. Brian Cawley et al., "Participation in the Performance Appraisal Process and Employee Reactions: A Meta-Analytic Review of Field Investigations," *Journal of Applied Psychology* 83, no. 4 (1998): 615–633.

49. This is based on Richard Luecke, *Coaching and Mentoring* (Boston: Harvard Business School Press, 2004), pp. 8–9.

50. Source: Adapted from Paula J. Caprioni, *The Practical Coach: Management Skills for Everyday Life* (Upper Saddle River, NJ: Prentice Hall, 2001), p. 86.

51. Richard Bolles, *What Color Is Your Parachute?* (Berkeley, CA: Ten Speed Press, 2003), pp. 5–6.

52. This example is based on Richard Bolles, *The Three Boxes of Life* (Berkeley, CA: Ten Speed Press, 1976). See also Richard Bolles, *What Color Is Your Parachute?* Richard Bolles updates his famous *What Color Is Your Parachute* annually. It contains this and many other career exercises. The 2011 edition is published by Ten-Speed Press in Berkeley, California.

53. Michael Doody, "A Mentor Is a Key to Career Success," *Health-Care Financial Management* 57, no. 2 (February 2003): 92–94.

54. See also Yehuda Baruch, "Career Development in Organizations and Beyond: Balancing Traditional and Contemporary Viewpoints," *Human Resource Management Review* 16 (2006): 131.

55. Barbara Greene and Liana Knudsen, "Competitive Employers Make Career Development Programs a Priority," *San Antonio Business Journal* 15, no. 6 (July 20, 2001): 27.

56. Julekha Dash, "Coaching to Aid IT Careers, Retention," *Computerworld* (March 20, 2000): 52.

57. Fred Otte and Peggy Hutcheson, *Helping Employees Manage Careers* (Upper Saddle River, NJ: Prentice Hall, 1992), p. 143.

58. Karen Lyness and Madeline Heilman, "When Fit Is Fundamental: Performance Evaluations and Promotions of Upper-Level Female and Male Managers," *Journal of Applied Psychology* 91, no. 4 (2006): 775–777.

59. Karen Lyness and Donna Thompson, "Climbing the Corporate Ladder: Do Female and Male Executives Follow the Same Route?" *Journal of Applied Psychology* 85, no. 1 (2000): 86–101.

60. "Minority Women Surveyed on Career Growth Factors," *Community Banker* 9, no. 3 (March 2000): 44.

61. In Ellen Cook et al., "Career Development of Women of Color and White Women: Assumptions, Conceptualization, and Interventions from an Ecological Perspective," *Career Development Quarterly* 50, no. 4 (June 2002): 291–306.

62. Jan Selmer and Alicia Leung, "Are Corporate Career Development Activities Less Available to Female than to Male Expatriates?" *Journal of Business Ethics* (March 2003): 125–137.

63. See, for example, Matt Bolch, "Bidding Adieu," *HR Magazine* (June 2006): 123–127; and Claudia Deutsch, "A Longer Goodbye," *New York Times* (April 20, 2008): H1, H10.

64. "Employees Plan to Work Past Retirement, but Not Necessarily for Financial Reasons," *BNA Bulletin to Management* (February 19, 2004): 57–58. See also Mo Wang, "Profiling Retirees in the Retirement Transition and Adjustment Process: Examining the Longitudinal Change Patterns of Retirees' Psychological Well-Being," *Journal of Applied Psychology* 92, no. 2 (2007): 455–474.

65. Andrew Luchak et al., "When Do Committed Employees Retire? The Effects of Organizational Commitment on Retirement Plans under a Defined Benefit Pension Plan," *Human Resource Management* 47, no. 3 (Fall 2008): 581–599.

66. Ken Dychtwald et al., "It's Time to Retire Retirement," *Harvard Business Review* (March 2004): 52.

67. Ibid.

68. Luis Fleites and Lou Valentino, "The Case for Phased Retirement," *Compensation & Benefits Review* (March/April 2007): 42–46.

69. Peter Glendinning, "Performance Management: Pariah or Messiah," *Public Personnel Management* 31, no. 2 (Summer 2002): 161–178. See also Herman Aguinis, *Performance Management* (Upper Saddle River, NJ: Pearson, 2007), p. 2.

70. Howard Risher, "Getting Serious about Performance Management," *Compensation and Benefits Review* (November/December 2005): 19.

71. Clinton Wingrove, "Developing an Effective Blend of Process and Technology in the New Era of Performance Management," *Compensation and Benefits Review* (January/February 2003): 27.

72. These are quoted or paraphrased from Howard Risher, "Getting Serious about Performance Management," *Compensation and Benefits Review* (November/December 2005): 19.

73. Drew Robb, "Building a Better Workforce," *HR Magazine* (October 2004): 87–94.

74. Adapted or quoted from "Next Generation Talent Management," Hewitt.com, accessed June 2010.

75. Ibid.

76. Adapted or quoted from Gunter Stahl et al., "Global Talent Management: How Leading Multinationals Build and Sustain their Talent Pipelines," Faculty & Research Working Paper, INSEAD, 2007.

77. Ibid.

78. Ibid.

Chapter 7

1. Richard Henderson, *Compensation Management* (Reston, VA: Reston, 1980); Joseph Martocchio, *Strategic Compensation* (Upper Saddle River, NJ: Prentice Hall, 2004), pp. 44–60; and Stacey L. Kaplan, "Total Rewards in Action: Developing a Total Rewards Strategy," *Benefits & Compensation Digest* 42, no. 8 (August 2005).

2. www.dol.gov/dol/topic/wages, accessed March 11, 2012.

3. John Kilgour, "Wage and Hour Law in California," *Compensation & Benefits Review* 42, no. 1 (January/February 2010): 17.

4. The recently approved Genetic Information Nondiscrimination Act amended the Fair Labor Standards Act to increase penalties for the death or serious injury of employees under age 18. Allen Smith, "Penalties for Child Labor Violations Increase," *HR Magazine* (July 2008): 19.

5. For a description of exemption requirements, see Jeffrey Friedman, "The Fair Labor Standards Act Today: A Primer," *Compensation* (January/February 2002): 51–54.

6. Because the overtime and minimum wage rules several years ago, exactly how to apply these rules is still in a state of flux. If there's doubt about exemption eligibility, it's probably best to check with the local Department of Labor Wage and Hour office. See, for example, "Attorneys Say FLSA Draws a Fine Line between Exempt/Nonexempt Employees," *BNA Bulletin to Management* (July 5, 2005): 219; "DOL Releases Letters on Administrative Exemption, Overtime," *BNA Bulletin to Management* (October 18, 2005): 335. The U.S. Labor Department occasionally changes its positions. For example, in 2010 it concluded that mortgage loan officers are subject to the administrative exemption from federal overtime pay, although several years previously they had ruled the opposite. Tim Watson and Barry Miller, "Tightening a White Collar Exemption," *HR* Magazine (December 2010): 95; See also, "Agencies, 11 States Join Forces to Fight Misclassification; IRS Launches Program," *BNA Bulletin to Management* (September 27, 2011): 305.

7. "Study Finds Widespread Wage Theft," *Workforce Management* (November 16, 2009): 29. See also Matthew Heller, "Quicken Verdict Gives Employers Hope on Overtime," *Workforce Management* (May 2011): 6, and James Coleman, "App Provides Reminder to Ensure Recordkeeping is in Order," *BNA Bulletin to Management* (June 14, 2011): 191.

8. "Wal-Mart to Settle 63 Wage and Hour Suits, Paying Up to $640 Million to Resolve Claims," *BNA Bulletin to Management* (January 13, 2009): 11.

9. "Federal Court Mostly Rules for FedEx Ground in Driver Lawsuits Alleging Misclassification," *BNA Bulletin to Management* (December 21, 2010): 403; see also, Eric Krell, "Status Check," *HR Magazine* (November 2011): 63–66, and Matthew Simpson "Five Steps to Reduce the Risks of Miscalculation," *BNA Bulletin to Management* (February 21, 2012): 63.

10. Recently, several state legislatures have moved to tighten regulations regarding misclassifying workers as independent contractors, some going so far as adding criminal penalties for violations. "Misclassification Cases Draw More Attention, Attorneys Say," *BNA Bulletin to Management* (December 15, 2009): 399.

11. Recently, women earned about 24% less than men overall. The gender gap was actually largest between men and women with advanced degrees (31%) and narrowest for those with high school degrees and some college (27%). "Women's Wage Gap Ranges from 25% to 31%, Census Bureau Report Finds," *BNA Bulletin to Management* (February 17, 2009): 51.

12. In January 2009, Congress passed the Lilly Ledbetter Fair Pay Act. This overturns the U.S. Supreme Court's Ledbetter decision, and basically says that each new paycheck triggers a new potential discrimination claim. See "Ledbetter Law Raises Open Legal Issues, Practical Issues for Covert Employees," *BNA Bulletin to Management* (November 17, 2009): 361.

13. See, for example, Barry Hirsch and Edward Schumacher, "Unions, Wages, and Skills," *Journal of Human Resources* 33, no. 1 (Winter 1998): 115; and www.bls.gov/opub/cwc/cm20030124ar01p1 .htm, accessed October 9, 2011.

14. www.bls.gov/oes/current/oes431011.htm#st, accessed June 1, 2011.

15. Jessica Marquez, "Raising the Performance Bar," *Workforce Management* (April 24, 2006): 31–32.

16. See, for example, Jessica Marquez, "Retooling Pay: Premium on Productivity," *Workforce Management* 84, no. 12 (November 7, 2005): 1, 22–23, 25–26, 28, 30; www.scribd.com/doc/12824332/NUCOR-CORP-8K-Events-or-Changes-Between-Quarterly-Reports-20090224, accessed November 3, 2009; and www.nucor .com/careers, accessed November 3, 2009.

17. Elayne Robertson Demby, "Two Stores Refused to Join the Race to the Bottom for Benefits and Wages," *Workforce Management* (February 2004): 57.

18. See, for example, Robert Heneman, "Implementing Total Rewards of Strategies," SHRM Foundation, www. shrm.org/foundation, accessed March 2, 2009.

19. As one study recently put it, "Our research suggests that employees who perceived the organization as providing competitive pay are likely to hold positive work attitudes and conceivably engage in behaviors leading to high levels of labor productivity and customer satisfaction." Mahdesh Subramony et al., "The Relationship between Human Resource Investments and Organizational Performance: A Firm Level Examination of Equilibrium Theory," *Journal of Applied Psychology* 93, no. 4 (2008): 786.

20. Michael Harris et al., "Keeping Up with the Joneses: A Field Study of the Relationships among Upwards, Lateral, and the Downward Comparisons and a Level Satisfaction," *Journal of Applied Psychology* 93, no. 3 (2008): 665–673. Pay inequities manifest in unexpected ways. In one study, the researchers studied the impact of keeping pay rates secret, rather than publicizing them on individual employees' test performance. They found that individuals with lower levels of tolerance for inequity reacted particularly harshly to pay secrecy in terms of weaker individual test performance. Peter Bamberger and Elena Belogolovsky, "The Impact of

Pay Secrecy on Individual Test Performance," *Personnel Psychology* 60, no. 3 (2010): 965.

21. Millicent Nelson et al., "Pay Me More: What Companies Need to Know about Employee Pay Satisfaction," *Compensation & Benefits Review* (March/April 2008): 35–42.

22. See, for example, www.watsonwyatt.com/search/publications.asp?ArticleID=21432, accessed October 29, 2009.

23. John Kilgour, "Job Evaluation Revisited: The Point Factor Method," *Compensation & Benefits Review* (July/August 2008): 37–46.

24. Ibid.

25. Syed Tahir Hijazi, "Determinants of Executive Compensation and Its Impact on Organizational Performance," *Compensation & Benefits Review* (March/April 2007): 58–59. See also "Appraising and Rewarding Managerial Performance in Challenging Economic Times: Part 2," *Journal of Compensation & Benefits* 25, no. 4 (July/August 2009): 5–12.

26. Ingrid Fuller, "The Elephant in the Room: Labor Market Influences on CEO Compensation," *Personnel Psychology* 62 (2009): 659–695.

27. Mark Meltzer and Howard Goldsmith, "Executive Compensation for Growth Companies," *Compensation & Benefits Review* (November/December 1997): 41–50. See also Bruce Ellig, "Executive Pay: A Primer," *Compensation & Benefits Review* (January/February 2003): 44–50.

28. "Executive Pay," *Wall Street Journal* (April 11, 1996): R16, R17; Fay Hansen, "Current Trends in Compensation and Benefits," *Compensation & Benefits Review* 36, no. 2 (March/April 2004): 7–8; and "Study: CEO Compensation Not Tied to Company Performance," *BNA Bulletin to Management* (March 22, 2011): 92.

29. James Reda, "Executive Compensation: Balancing Risk, Performance and Pay," *Financial Executive*, 25, no. 9 (November 2009): 46–50.

30. Max Smith and Ben Stradley, "New Research Tracks the Evolution of Annual Incentive Plans," *Executive Compensation*, Towers Watson, 2010, www.Towerswatson.com, accessed August 28, 2011.

31. Patricia Zingheim and Jay Schuster, "Designing Pay and Rewards in Professional Services Companies," *Compensation & Benefits Review* (January/February 2007): 55–62.

32. A recent analysis of how companies arrive at executive compensation decisions revealed six potential problem areas. For example, the compensation consultant may feel obligated to formulate CEO incentives that favor the CEO. See Michel Magnan and Imen Tebourbi, "A Critical Analysis of Six Practices Underlying Executive Compensation Practices," *Compensation & Benefits Review* (May/June 2009): 42–54.

33. www.dol.gov/whd/regs/compliance/fairpay/fs17d_professional.pdf, accessed June 1, 2011.

34. Ibid.

35. Farhad Manjoo, "Engineers to the Valley: Pay Up," *Fast Company* 38, no.153 (March 2011).

36. Note that the employer needs to beware of instituting so many incentive plans (cash bonuses, stock options, recognition programs, and so on) tied to so many different behaviors that employees don't have a clear picture of the employer's priorities. Stephen Rubenfeld and Jennifer David, "Multiple Employee Incentive Plans: Too Much of a Good Thing?" *Compensation & Benefits Review* (March/April 2006): 35–43.

37. Jay Heizer and Barry Render, *Operations Management* (Upper Saddle River, NJ: Pearson, 2001), p. 15.

38. Peter Kurlander, "Building Incentive Compensation Management Systems: What Can Go Wrong?" *Compensation and Benefits Review* (July/August 2001): 52–56. Employers may be moving to emphasize merit increases and deemphasize performance pay. The average percentage of payroll employers spent on broad-based performance pay plans pay rose until 2005, and then fell for the past few years. "Companies Pull Back from Performance Pay," *Workforce Management* (October 23, 2006): 26. For one of many good discussions of why pay for performance tends to be ineffectual, see, for example, Fay Hansen, "Merit-Pay Payoff?" *Workforce Management* (November 3, 2008): 33–39.

39. See, for example, Kimberly Merriman, "On the Folly of Rewarding Team Performance, While Hoping for Teamwork," *Compensation & Benefits Review* (January/February 2009): 61–66.

40. See, for example, Bruce Ellig, "Executive Pay Financial Measurements," *Compensation & Benefits Review* (September/October 2008): 42–49.

41. Mark Meltzer and Howard Goldsmith, "Executive Compensation for Growth Companies," *Compensation and Benefits Review* (November/December 1997): 41–50; Barbara Kiviat, "Everyone into the Bonus Pool," *Time* (December 15, 2003): A5, and Richard Ericson, "Benchmarking for Executive Incentive Pay: The Importance of Performance Standards," *Compensation & Benefits Review* 43, no. 2, pp. 92–99.

42. George Yancey, "Aligning the CEOs Incentive Plan with Criteria that Drive Organizational Performance," *Compensation & Benefits Review* 42, no. 3 (2010): 190–196.

43. Benjamin Dunford et al., "Underwater Stock Options and Voluntary Executive Turnover: A Multidisciplinary Perspective Integrating Behavioral and Economic Theories," *Personnel Psychology* 61 (2008): 687–726.

44. Wm. Gerard Sanders and Donald Hambrick, "Swinging for the Fences: The Effects of CEO Stock Options on Company Risk-Taking and Performance," *Academy of Management Journal* 50, no. 5 (2007): 1055–1078.

45. www.mercer.com/pressrelease/details.jhtml/dynamic/idContent/1263210, accessed January 2, 2007.

46. www.nceo.org/main/article.php/id/43/, accessed June 1, 2011.

47. Louis Lavelle, "How to Halt the Options Express," *Business Week*, September 9, 2002.

48. "Impact of Sarbanes-Oxley on Executive Compensation," Thelen, Reid, and Priest, L.L.P., www.thelenreid.com, accessed December 11, 2003. See also Brent Longnecker and James Krueger, "The Next Wave of Compensation Disclosure," *Compensation & Benefits Review* (January/February 2007): 50–54.

49. See, for example, Leslie Stretch, "From Strategy to Profitability: How Sales Compensation Management Drives Business Performance," *Compensation & Benefits Review* (May/June 2008): 32–37; Pankaj Madhani, "Sales Employees Compensation: An Optimal Balance between Fixed and Variable Pay," *Compensation & Benefits Review* (July/August 2009): 44–51; and Pankaj Madhani, "Realigning Fixed and Variable Pay in Sales Organizations: An Organizational Lifestyle Approach," *Compensation & Benefits Review* 42, no. 6 (November 2010): 488–498.

50. Scott Ladd, "May a Sales Force Be with You," *HR Magazine* (September 2010): 105.

51. See, for example, C. Albrecht, "Moving to a Global Sales Incentive Compensation Plan," *Compensation and Benefits Review* 41, no. 4 (July/August 2009): 52, and Pankaj Madhani, "Reallocating Fixed and Variable Pay in Sales Organizations: A Sales Carryover Perspective," *Compensation & Benefits Review* 43, no. 6, pp. 346–360.

52. S. Scott Sands, "Ineffective Quotas: The Hidden Threat to Sales Compensation Plans," *Compensation & Benefits Review* (March/April 2000): 35–42. "Driving Profitable Sales Growth: 2006/2007 Report on Sales Effectiveness," www.watsonwyatt.com/research/resrender.asp?id=2006-US-0060&page=1, accessed May 20, 2007.

53. Peter Gundy, "Sales Compensation Programs: Built to Last," *Compensation & Benefits Review* (September/October 2002): 21–28.

54. Deloitte Varicent, 2010 Strategic Sales Compensation Survey, www.deloitte.com/assets/Dcom-UnitedStates/Local%20Assets/Documents/us_consulting_2010StrategicSalesCompensationSurvey_072910.pdf, accessed March 11, 2012, p. 6.

55. Peter Glendinning, "Kicking the Tires of Automotive Sales Compensation," *Compensation & Benefits Review* (September/October 2000): 47–53; and Michele Marchetti, "Why Sales Contests Don't Work," *Sales and Marketing Management* 156 (January 2004): 19.

56. Donna Harris, "Dealers Rethink How They Pay Salespeople," *Automotive News* (June 14, 2010).

57. See, for example, Suzanne Peterson and Fred Luthans, "The Impact of Financial and Nonfinancial Incentives on Business Unit Outcomes over Time," *Journal of Applied Psychology* 91, no. 1 (2006): 156–165, and Daniel Morrell, "Employee Perceptions and the Motivation of Non-Monetary Incentives," *Compensation & Benefits Review* 43, no. 5, pp. 318–323.

58. "Employee Recognition," WorldatWork (April 2008), www.worldatwork.org/waw/adimLink?id=25653, accessed November 3, 2009.

59. Charlotte Huff, "Recognition That Resonates," *Workforce Management* (September 11, 2006): 25–29. See also Scott Jeffrey and Victoria Schaffer, "The Motivational Properties of Tangible Incentives," *Compensation & Benefits Review* (May/June 2007): 44–50. Reward and recognition programs like these represent about 2.7% of the annual payroll for U.S. employers. Michelle Rafter, "Back in a Giving Mood," *Workforce Management* (September 14, 2009): 25.

60. Michelle V. Rafter, "Back in a Giving Mood," *Workforce Management* 88, no. 10 (September 14, 2009): 25–29.

61. "Base Pay Will Rise More Slowly in 2009," *Compensation & Benefits Review* (November/December 2008): 5.

62. Seongsu Kim, "Does Profit Sharing Increase Firms' Profits?" *Journal of Labor Research* (Spring 1998): 351–371. See also Jacqueline Coyle-Shapiro et al., "Using Profit-Sharing to Enhance Employee Attitudes: A Longitudinal Examination of the Effects on Trust and Commitment," *Human Resource Management* 41, no. 4 (Winter 2002): 423–449. One recent study, conducted in Spain, concluded that profit-sharing plans can enhance employees' commitment toward the organization. Alberto Bayo-Moriones and Martin Larraza-Kintana, "Profit Sharing Plans and Effective Commitment: Does the Context Matter?" *Human Resource Management* 48, no. 2 (March–April 2009): 207–226.

63. See, for example, S. Coomes, "Employee Stock Plans Can Save Taxes, Attract Talent," *Nation's Restaurant News* 42, no. 36 (September 15, 2008): 12.

64. See, for example, www.dol.gov/dol/topic/health-plans/erisa.htm, accessed October 2, 2011.

65. "Time Warner Stops Granting Stock Options to Most of Staff," *New York Times* (February 19, 2005).

66. Brian Moore and Timothy Ross, *The Scanlon Way to Improved Productivity: A Practical Guide* (New York: Wiley, 1978), p. 2. See also Alexander Gardner, "Goal Setting and Gainsharing: The Evidence of Effectiveness," *Compensation & Benefits Review* 43, no. 4, pp. 236–244.

67. Janet Wiscombe, "Can Pay for Performance Really Work?" *Workforce* (August 2001): 30.

68. Susan Marks, "Incentives That Really Reward and Motivate," *Workforce* (June 2001): 108–114. For other examples, see "Delivering Incentive Compensation Plans That Work," *Financial Executive* 25, no. 7 (September 2009): 52–54.

69. William Bulkeley, "Incentives System Fine-Tunes Pay/Bonus Plans," *Wall Street Journal* (August 16, 2001): B4.

70. Nina McIntyre, "Using EIM Technology to Successfully Motivate Employees," *Compensation & Benefits Review* (July/August 2001): 57–60; see also Jeremy Wuittner, "Plenty of Incentives to Use E.I.M. Software Systems," *American Banker* 168, no. 129 (July 8, 2003): 680.

71. Kathleen Cholewka, "Tech Tools," *Sales and Marketing Management* 153, no. 7 (July 2001): 24. See also Andrew Perlmutter, "Taking Motivation and Recognition Online," *Compensation & Benefits Review* (March–April 2002): 70–74.

72. Frank Giancola, "Examining the Job Itself as a Source of Employee Motivation," *Compensation & Benefits Review* 43, no. 1 (2011): 23–29.

73. Peter Kurlander, "Building Incentive Compensation Management Systems: What Can Go Wrong?" *Compensation & Benefits Review* (July/August 2001): 52–56. The average percentage of payroll employers spent on broad-based performance pay plans rose until 2005, and then has fallen for the past few years. "Companies Pull Back from Performance Pay," *Workforce Management* (October 23, 2006): 26. For one of many good discussions of why pay for performance tends to be ineffectual, see Fay Hansen, "Where's the Merit-Pay Payoff?" *Workforce Management* (November 3, 2008): 33–39.

74. Reed Taussig, "Managing Cash-Based Incentives," *Compensation & Benefits Review* (March/April 2002): 65–68. See also Nigel Nicholson, "How to Motivate Your Problem People," *Harvard Business Review* (January 2003): 57–65; and "Incentives, Motivation and Workplace Performance," Incentive Research Foundation, www.incentivescentral.org/employees/whitepapers, accessed May 19, 2007.

75. "Two Frameworks for a More ROI-Minded Rewards Plan," *Pay for Performance Report* (February 2003): 1, www.ioma.com/issues/PFP/2003_02/518132-1.html, accessed November 3, 2009; and Alan Robinson and Dean Schroeder, "Rewards That Really Work," *Security Management* (July 2004): 30–34. See also Patricia Zingheim and Jay Schuster, "What Are Key Pay Issues Right Now?" *Compensation & Benefits Review* (May/June 2007): 51–55.

76. See, for example, Jessica Marquez, "Retooling Pay: Premium on Productivity," *Workforce Management* 84, no. 12 (November 7, 2005): 1, 22–23, 25–26, 28, 30; www.scribd.com/doc/12824332/NUCOR-CORP-8K-Events-or-Changes-Between-Quarterly-Reports-20090224, accessed November 3, 2009; and www.nucor.com/careers, accessed November 3, 2009.

77. Theodore Weinberger, "Evaluating the Effectiveness of an Incentive Plan Design Within Company Constraints," *Compensation & Benefits Review* (November/December 2005): 27–33; Howard Risher, "Adding Merit to Pay for Performance," *Compensation & Benefits Review* (November/December 2008): 22–29.

78. "Survey Finds 99 Percent of Employers Providing Health-Care Benefits," *Compensation & Benefits Review* (September/October 2002): 11. See also National Compensation Survey: Employee Benefits in Private Industry in the United States March 2006, U.S. Department of Labor, U.S. Bureau of Labor Statistics, August 2006.

79. "Trouble Ahead? Dissatisfaction with Benefits, Compensation," *HR Trendbook* (2008): 16.

80. "Costs This Year Increased at Highest Rate Since 2004, Survey Reveals," *HR Focus* 88, no. 1 (January 10, 2011); "Employer Medical Costs Expected to Increase by 8.5 Percent in 2012, According to PwC," www.pwc.com/us/en/press-releases/2011/employer-medical-costs-expected-to-increase.jhtml, accessed September 14, 2011.

81. "Survey Finds 99 Percent of Employers Providing Health-Care Benefits," *Compensation & Benefits Review* (September/October 2002): 11. See also "National Compensation Survey: Employee Benefits in Private Industry in the United States, March 2006," U.S. Department of Labor, U.S. Bureau of Labor Statistics (August 2006).

82. "HR Plays a Major Role in Curbing Company Unemployment Insurance Costs, Analysts Say," *BNA Bulletin to Management* (August 3, 2010): 241–242.

83. See, for example, Laurie Nacht, "Make an Appealing Case: How to Prepare for and Present an Unemployment Insurance Appeal," *Society for Human Resource Management Legal Report* (March/April 2004): 1–8.

84. www.bls.gov/opub/perspectives/issue2.pdf, accessed June 1, 2011.

85. Ibid.

86. Ibid.

87. "Unscheduled Employee Absences Cost Companies More than Ever," *Compensation & Benefits Review* (March/April 2003): 19. Robert Grossman, "Gone But Not Forgotten," *HR Magazine* 56, no. 9 (September 2011): 34–46.

88. The Department of Labor updated its revised regulations for administering the Family and Medical Leave Act in November 2008. See "DOL Issues Long-Awaited Rules; Address a Serious Health Condition, Many Other Issues," *BNA Bulletin to Management* (November 18, 2008): 369. In 2008, Congress also amended the Family and Medical Leave Act to include, among other things, leave rights particularly for military families. See Sarah Martin, "FMLA Protection Recently Expanded to Military Families: Qualifying Exigency and Servicemember Family Leave," *Compensation & Benefits Review* (September/October 2009): 43–51.

89. Judith Whitaker, "How HR Made a Difference," *People Management* 27 (October 28, 2010).

90. Ibid.

91. Terry Baglieri, "Severance Pay," www.SHRM.org, accessed December 23, 2006.

92. "Workers Comp Claims Rise with Layoffs, but Employers Can Identify, Prevent Fraud," *BNA Bulletin to Management* (October 4, 2001): 313.

93. The involvement of an attorney and the duration of the claim both influence the workers' claim cost. "Workers' Comp Research Provides Insight into Curbing Health Care Costs," *EHS Today* (February 2010): 18.

94. "Healthcare Tops List of Value Benefits," *BNA Bulletin to Management* (April 24, 2007): 132.

95. As an example of the direction new federal health insurance may take post-2009, see A. Mathews, "Making Sense of the Debate on Health Care," *Wall Street Journal* (Eastern Edition) (September 30, 2009): D1, D5.

96. "Costs This Year Increased at Highest Rate Since 2004, Survey Reveals," *HR Focus* 88, no. 1 (January 2011): 10.

97. When unemployment began rising in 2008–2009, Congress passed, and President Obama signed on February 17, 2009, the American Recovery and Reinvestment Act of 2009. His new law had the immediate effect of making it easier for qualified employees who were involuntarily dismissed for any reason (other than gross misconduct) anytime after September 1, 2008 (the act was retroactive), to sign up for COBRA. It makes it easier to utilize COBRA because the new law requires that the employer pay 65% of the premium. (The employer then receives a credit for that full amount back from the U.S. government.) The former employee must pay the remaining 35%. See www.recovery.gov, accessed March 21, 2009.

98. Note that the American Recovery and Reinvestment Act of 2009 includes changes to several benefits-related programs including COBRA, the Mental Health Parity Act, and the Americans with Disabilities Act Amendments Act. Susan Relland, "Compliance Requirements and What More to Expect for Health and Welfare Plan for Sponsors in 2009," *Compensation & Benefits Review* (May/June 2009): 29–41.

99. "Health Coverage Premiums: Upward Bound," *HR Trendbook* (2008): 8. However, in 2009, employee costs rose only 6.4% compared with an average 15% since 2002, largely because of the employer cost containment efforts we'll discuss shortly. "Health Benefit Costs Expected to Rise 7%," *BNA Bulletin to Management* (October 20, 2009): 332.

100. "Hewitt Says Employer Measures to Control Increases in Health Care Costs Are Working," *BNA Bulletin to Management* (October 7, 2008): 323.

101. James Curcio, "Creating Standardized Metrics and Benchmarking for Health, Absence and Productivity Management Programs: The EMPAQ Initiative," *Compensation & Benefits Review* 42, no. 2 (2010): 109–126.

102. Jerry Geisel, "Employers Accelerate Health Care Cost-Shifting," *Business Insurance* 45, no. 21 (May 23, 2011: 3, 21.

103. "Hewitt Says Employer Measures to Control Increases in Health Care Costs Are Working," *BNA Bulletin to Management* (October 7, 2008): 323. A survey concluded that employer medical benefit costs will rise

104. 7% in 2010, equaling an annual average of $10,000 per employee for the first time. "Health Benefit Trends: Employer Medical Benefit Costs Will Rise 7% in 2010," *Compensation & Benefits Review* 42, no. 1 (January/February 2010): 9–10.

104. "As Workers Feel the Effect of Cost Hikes, Employers Turn to Health Remedies," *BNA Bulletin to Management* (April 18, 2002): 121.

105. "HR Outsourcing: Managing Costs and Maximizing Provider Relations," *BNA, Inc.* 21, no. 11 (Washington, DC: November 2003): 10. Benefits management ranks high on any list of HR activities that employers outsource. For example, in one survey, 94% outsource flexible spending accounts, 89% outsource defined contribution plans, 72% outsource defined benefit plans, and 68% outsource the auditing of dependents. Bill Roberts, "Outsourcing in Turbulent Times," *HR Magazine* (November 2009): 45.

106. Ron Finch, "Preventive Services: Improving the Bottom Line for Employers and Employees," *Compensation & Benefits Review* (March/April 2005): 18.

107. Ibid. See also Josh Cable, "The Road to Wellness," *Occupational Hazards* (April 2007): 23–27.

108. George DeVries, "The Top 10 Wellness Trends for 2008 and Beyond," *Compensation & Benefits Review* (July/August 2008): 60–63.

109. Susan Wells, "Getting Paid for Staying Well," *HR Magazine* (February 2010): 59.

110. Vanessa Fuhrmanns, "Oops! As Health Plans Become More Complicated, They're Also Subject to a Lot More Costly Mistakes," *Wall Street Journal* (January 24, 2005): R4.

111. "Dependent Eligibility Audits Can Help Rein in Health Care Costs, Analysts Say," *BNA Bulletin to Management* (September 9, 2008): 289.

112. Betty Liddick, "Going the Distance for Health Savings," *HR Magazine* (March 2007): 51–55. J. Wojcik, "Employers Consider Short-Haul Medical Tourism," *Business Insurance* 43, no. 29 (August 24 2009): 1, 20.

113. Jeremy Smerd, "Digitally Driven," *Workforce Management* (April 6, 2009): 23–26.

114. Martha Frase, "Minimalist Health Coverage," *HR Magazine* (June 2009): 107–112.

115. "Deadlines Vary for Implementing Provisions of Health Care Law," *BNA Bulletin to Management* (May 4, 2010): 143.

116. "Regulation Will Allow Young Adults Up to Age 26 to Retain Dependent Coverage," *BNA Bulletin to Management* (May 18, 2010): 153.

117. www.mercer.com/press-releases/1380755, accessed July 25, 2011.

118. Ibid.

119. Kevin Maroney, "Prognosis Negative? Gina's Interim Incentives Ruling a Concern for Wellness Programs," *Compensation & Benefits Review* 42, no. 2 (2010): 94–101.

120. www.socialsecurity.gov/pressoffice/factsheets/colafacts2012.htm, accessed March 11, 2012. Note that the U.S. Treasury has reportedly spent most of the trust fund on other government programs, so that changes (for instance, in terms of reducing benefits, making people wait longer for benefits, or making some people pay more for benefits) will be necessary. John Kilgour, "Social Security in the 21st Century," *Compensation & Benefits Review* 42, no. 6 (2010): 459–469.

121. In addition, tax rates under the Medicare program are 1.45 percent for employees and employers. http://ssa-custhelp.ssa.gov/app/answers/detail/a_id/240/~/2011-social-security-tax-rate-and-maximum-taxable-earnings, accessed June 1, 2011.

122. Martocchio, *Strategic Compensation,* pp. 245–248; and Lin Grensing-Pophal, "A Pension Formula That Pays Off," *HR Magazine* (February 2003): 58–62.

123. Many employers are considering terminating their plans, but most employers are considering instead either ceasing benefits accruals for all participants or just for future participants. Michael Cotter, "The Big Freeze: The Next Phase in the Decline of Defined Benefit Plans," *Compensation & Benefits Review* (March/April 2009): 44–53.

124. Nancy Pridgen, "The Duty to Monitor Appointed Fiduciaries under ERISA," *Compensation & Benefits Review* (September/October 2007): 46–51; "Individual 401(k) Plan Participant Can Sue Plan Fiduciary for Losses, Justices Rule," *BNA Bulletin to Management* (February 20, 2008): 65.

125. Jack VanDerhei, "The Pension Protection Act and 401(k)s," *Wall Street Journal* (April 20, 2008): A12. The Bureau of Labor Statistics reports that about half of companies automatically enrolled employees into defined contribution benefit plans. "Nearly Half of Employers Automatically Enrolled Employees," *BNA Bulletin to Management* (October 6, 2009): 316.

126. "New Pension Law Plus a Recent Court Ruling Doom Age-Related Suits, Practitioners Say," *BNA Bulletin to Management* 57, no. 36 (September 5, 2006): 281–282; and www.dol.gov/ebsa/FAQs/faq_consumer_cashbalanceplans.html, accessed January 9, 2010.

127. www.pbgc.gov/news/press/releases/pr12-07.html, accessed March 11, 2012.

128. Joseph O'Connell, "Using Employee Assistance Programs to Avoid Crises," *Long Island Business News* (April 19, 2002): 10. The Mental Health Parity Act of 1996 (as amended in 2008) sets minimum mental health-care benefits; it also prohibits employer group health plans from adopting mental health benefits limitations without comparable limitations on medical and surgical benefits. "Mental-Health Parity Measure Enacted as Part of Financial Rescue Signed by Bush," *BNA Bulletin to Management* (October 7, 2008): 321.

129. "EAP Providers," *Workforce Management* (July 14, 2008): 16.

130. Richard Buddin and Kanika Kapur, "The Effect of Employer-Sponsored Education on Job Mobility: Evidence from the U.S. Navy," *Industrial Relations* 44, no. 2 (April 2005): 341–363; see also Michael Laff, "US Employers Tighten Reins on Tuition Reimbursement," *Training and Development* (July 2006): 18.

131. See, for example, "Compressed Workweeks Gain Popularity, but Concerns Remain about Effectiveness," *BNA Bulletin to Management* (September 16, 2008): 297.

132. Brian O'Connell, "No Baby Sitter? Emergency Child Care to the Rescue" (May 2005), www.SHRM.org/rewards/library, accessed December 23, 2006; Kathy Gurchiek, "Give Us Your Sick," *HR Magazine* (January 2007): 91–93.

133. "Employers Gain from Elder Care Programs by Boosting Workers Morale, Productivity," *BNA Bulletin to Management* 57, no. 10 (March 7, 2006): 73–74.

134. Sue Shellenbarger, "The Mommy Drain: Employers Beef Up Perks to Lure New Mothers Back to Work," *Wall Street Journal* (September 28, 2006): D1.

135. "Making Up for Lost Time: How Employers Can Curb Excessive Unscheduled Absences," *BNA Human Resources Report* (October 20, 2003): 1097. See also W. H. J. Hassink et al., "Do Financial Bonuses Reduce Employee Absenteeism? Evidence from a Lottery," *Industrial and Labor Relations Review* 62, no. 3 (April 2009): 327–342.

136. Timothy Judge et al., "Work Family Conflict and Emotions: Effects at Work and at Home," *Personnel Psychology* 50, no. 9 (2006): 779–814.

137. Farrokh Mamaghani, "Impact of Information Technology on the Workforce of the Future: An Analysis," *International Journal of Management* 23, no. 4 (2006): 845–850; Jessica Marquez, "Connecting a Virtual Workforce," *Workforce Management* (September 20, 2008): 1–3.

138. Ann Pomeroy, "The Future Is Now," *HR Magazine* (September 2007): 46–52.

139. Scott Harper, "Online Resources System Boosts Worker Awareness," *BNA Bulletin to Management* (April 10, 2007): 119.

140. See, for example, Patricia Zingheim and Jay Schuster, "The Next Decade for Pay and Rewards," *Compensation & Benefits Review* (January/February 2005): 29; Patricia Zingheim and Jay Schuster, "What Are Key Pay Issues Right Now?" *Compensation & Benefits Review* (May/June 2007): 51–55; and "A Framework for Understanding New Concepts in Compensation Management," *Benefits & Compensation Digest* 46, no. 9 (September 2009): front cover, 13–16.

141. Another dubious trend is that U.S. wage disparities are rising. Those with high salaries have seen their pay rise much faster in the past 20 or so years than have

those at the bottom. Increased demand for the skills that come through education (for instance, for more skilled workers as manufacturing facilities became computerized) explains much of this. The wage gap has not grown as much in Europe, in part because "unions in Europe were and are still more powerful and able to keep up [workers'] wages." Thomas Atchison, "Salary Trends in the United States and Europe," *Compensation & Benefits Review* (January/February 2007): 36.

142. See, for example, Hai-Ming Chen et al., "Key Trends of the Total Reward System in the 21st Century," *Compensation & Benefits Review* (November/December 2006): 64–70, and Frank Giancola, "Skill-Based Pay: Fad or Classic?" *Compensation & Benefits Review* 43, no. 4 (2011): 220–226.

143. See, for example, Robert Henneman and Peter LeBlanc, "Development of an Approach for Valuing Knowledge Work," *Compensation & Benefits Review* (July/August 2002): 47.

144. Martocchio, *Strategic Compensation*, p. 168. See also B. Lokshin et al., "Crafting Firm Competencies to Improve Innovative Performance," *European Management Journal* 27, no. 3 (June 2009): 187–196.

145. Bobby Watson Jr. and Gangaram Singh, "Global Pay Systems: Compensation in Support of Multinational Strategy," *Compensation & Benefits Review* (January/February 2005): 33–36.

146. "The New Talent Equation," www.accenture.com/NR/rdonlyres/7438E440-F7D5-4F81-B012-8D3271891D92/0/Accenture_Outlook_The_New_Talent_Equation.pdf, accessed November 9, 2010.

147. "Five Rules for Talent Management in the New Economy," www.towerswatson.com/viewpoints/2606, accessed November 9, 2010.

148. www.msnbc.msn.com/id/15219832/ns/business-corporate_scandals/t/mcafeeousts-execs-after-stock-options-probe, accessed June 1, 2011.

149. Mark Poerio and Eric Keller, "Executive Compensation 2005: Many Forces, One Direction," *Compensation & Benefits Review* (May/June 2005): 34–40.

150. The federal government also recently introduced new compensation disclosure rules, and these are affecting executive compensation. For example, corporations must now list a single dollar figure to represent an executive's total pay, including salary, bonus, perquisites, long-term incentives, and retirement benefits. They must also be more diligent in listing all executive perquisites. The net effect of this greater transparency will probably be to pressure employers to increasingly link their executives' pay with the company's performance. See Brent Longnecker and James Krueger, "The Next Wave of Compensation Disclosure," *Compensation & Benefits Review* (January/February 2007): 50–54.

151. Ibid.

Chapter 8

1. Keith Winstein, "Suit Alleges Pfizer Spun Unfavorable Drug Studies," *Wall Street Journal* (October 8, 2008): B1.

2. "What Role Should HR Play in Corporate Ethics?" *HR Focus* 81, no. 1 (January 2004): 3. See also Dennis Moberg, "Ethics Blind Spots in Organizations: How Systematic Errors in Person Perception Undermine Moral Agency," *Organization Studies* 27, no. 3 (2006): 413–428.

3. Kevin Wooten, "Ethical Dilemmas in Human Resource Management: An Application of a Multidimensional Framework, A Unifying Taxonomy, and Applicable Codes," *Human Resource Management Review* 11 (2001): 161. See also Sean Valentine et al., "Employee Job Response as a Function of Ethical Context and Perceived Organization Support," *Journal of Business Research* 59, no. 5 (2006): 582–588.

4. Manuel Velasquez, *Business Ethics: Concepts and Cases* (Upper Saddle River, NJ: Prentice Hall, 1992), p. 9. See also Joel Lefkowitz, "The Constancy of Ethics amidst the Changing World of Work," *Human Resource Management Review* 16 (2006): 245–268.

5. The following discussion, except as noted, is based on Velasquez, *Business Ethics*, pp. 9–12. See also O. C. Ferrell, John Fraedrich, and Linda Ferrell, *Business Ethics* (Boston: Houghton Mifflin, 2008).

6. Velasquez, *Business Ethics*, p. 9.

7. This discussion is based on Velasquez, *Business Ethics*, pp. 12–14.

8. Velasquez, *Business Ethics*, p. 12. For further discussion, see Kurt Baier, *Moral Points of View*, abbr. ed. (New York: Random House, 1965), p. 88. See also Milton Bordwin, "The 3 R's of Ethics," *Management Review* (June 1998): 59–61.

9. Carroll Lachnit, "Recruiting Trouble for Tyson," *Workforce, HR Trends and Tools for Business Results* 81, no. 2 (February 2002): 22.

10. Richard Osborne, "A Matter of Ethics," *Industry Week* 49, no. 14 (September 4, 2000): 41–42.

11. This list based on Linda K. Treviño, Gary R. Weaver, and Scott J. Reynolds, "Behavioral Ethics in Organizations: A Review," *Journal of Management* 32, no. 6 (2006): 951–990.

12. R. Bergman, "Identity as Motivation: Toward a Theory of the Moral Self," in D. K. Lapsley & D. Narvaez (Eds.), *Moral Development, Self and Identity* (Mahwah, NJ: Lawrence Erlbaum, 2004), pp. 21–46.

13. M. E. Schweitzer, L. Ordonez, and B. Douma, "Goal Setting as a Motivator of Unethical Behavior," *Academy of Management Journal* 47, no. 3 (2004): 422–432.

14. N. M. Ashkanasy, C. A. Windsor, and L. K. Treviño, "Bad Apples in Bad Barrels Revisited: Cognitive Moral Development, Just World Beliefs, Rewards, and Ethical Decision Making," *Business Ethics Quarterly* 16 (2006): 449–474.

15. Gary Weaver and Linda Treviño, "The Role of Human Resources in Ethics/Compliance Management: A Fairness Perspective," *Human Resource Management Review* 11 (2001): 115.

16. Michelle Donovan et al., "The Perceptions of Fair Interpersonal Treatment Scale: Development and Validation of a Measure of Interpersonal Treatment in the Workplace," *Journal of Applied Psychology* 83, no. 5 (1998): 683–692.

17. Rudy Yandrick, "Lurking in the Shadows," *HR Magazine* (October 1999): 61–68. See also Helge Hoel and David Beale, "Workplace Bullying, Psychological Perspectives and Industrial Relations: Towards a Contextualized and Interdisciplinary Approach," *British Journal of Industrial Relations* 44, no. 2 (June 2006): 239–262.

18. Bennett Tepper, "Consequences of Abusive Supervision," *Academy of Management Journal* 43, no. 2 (2000): 178–190. See also Samuel Aryee et al., "Antecedents and Outcomes of Abusive Supervision: Test of a Trickle-Down Model," *Journal of Applied Psychology,* no. 1 (2007): 191–201.

19. Wendy Boswell and Julie Olson-Buchanan, "Experiencing Mistreatment at Work: The Role of Grievance Filing, Nature of Mistreatment, and Employee Withdrawal," *Academy of Management Journal* 47, no. 1 (2004): 129–139. See also Samuel Aryee et al., 2007, op. cit.

20. Bennett Tepper et al., "Abusive Supervision and Subordinates' Organization Deviance," *Journal of Applied Psychology* 93, no. 4 (2008): 721–732.

21. "Facebook Harassment: Social Websites May Prompt Need for New Policies, Procedures," *BNA Bulletin to Management* (July 20, 2010): 225.

22. Eugene Kim and Teresa Glomb, "Get Smarty-Pants: Cognitive Ability, Personality, and Victimization," *Journal of Applied Psychology* 95, no. 3 (2010): 889–901.

23. Ibid.

24. Weaver and Treviño, "Role of Human Resources," p. 117.

25. Suzanne Masterson, "A Trickle-Down Model of Organizational Justice: Relating Employees' and Customers' Perceptions of and Reactions to Fairness," *Journal of Applied Psychology* 86, no. 4 (2001): 594–601.

26. Insubordinate and gross conduct acts based on Kenneth Sovereign, *Personnel Law* (Upper Saddle River, NJ: Prentice Hall, 1999), p. 150.

27. This list is from www.legaltarget.com/employee_ rights, accessed January 3, 2008.

28. Basically, common law refers to legal precedents. Judges' rulings set precedents that then generally guide future judicial decisions.

29. Sovereign, *Personnel Law,* p. 192.

30. Lester Bittel, *What Every Supervisor Should Know* (New York: McGraw-Hill, 1974), p. 308; see also Paul Falcone, "The Fundamentals of Progressive Discipline," *HR Magazine* (February 1997): 90–92;

and Thomas Salvo, "Practical Tips for Successful Progressive Discipline," SHRM White Paper (July 2004), www.shrm.org/hrresources/whitepapers_ published/CMS_009030.asp, accessed January 5, 2008.

31. David Mayer et al., "When Do Fair Procedures Not Matter? A Test of the Identity Violation Effect," *Journal of Applied Psychology* 94, no. 1 (2009): 142–161. For fair discipline guidelines, see Lester Bittel, *What Every Supervisor Should Know* (New York: McGraw Hill, 1972), p. 308; Paul Falcone, "Fundamentals of Progressive Discipline," *HR Magazine* (February 1997): 90–92; and "How to Discipline and Fire Employees," www .entrepreneur.com/article/79928, accessed May 3, 2012.

32. Nonpunitive discipline discussions based on David Campbell et al., "Discipline Without Punishment—At Last," *Harvard Business Review* (July/August 1995): 162–178; "Positive Discipline Replaces Punishment," *BNA Bulletin to Management* (April 27, 1995): 136.

33. "After Employer Found Liable for Worker's Child Porn, Policies May Need to Be Revisited," *BNA Bulletin to Management* (March 21, 2006): 89. Rita Zeidner, "Keeping E-Mail in Check," *HR Magazine* (June 2007): 70–74.

34. See "Twitter Is Latest Electronic Tool to Pose Challenges and Opportunities for Employers," *BNA Bulletin to Management* (June 16, 2009): 185. See also Sean Valentine et al., "Exploring the Ethicality of Firing Employees Who Blog," *Human Resource Management* 49, no. 1 (January/February 2010): 87–108.

35. Zeidner, "Keeping E-Mail in Check."

36. Fredric Leffler and Lauren Palais, "Filter Out Perilous Company E-Mails," *Society for Human Resource Management Legal Report* (August 2008): 3. A recent survey of 220 large U.S firms suggests that about 38% of them have people reading or otherwise analyzing employees' outgoing e-mail. Dionne Searcey, "Some Courts Raise the Bar on Reading Employee E-Mail," *Wall Street Journal* (November 19, 2009): 817.

37. Bill Roberts, "Stay Ahead of the Technology Use Curve," *HR Magazine* (October 2008): 57–61.

38. "Do You Know Where Your Workers Are? GPS Units Aid Efficiency, Raise Privacy Issues," *BNA Bulletin to Management* (July 22, 2004): 233.

39. "Time Clocks Go High Touch, High Tech to Keep Workers from Gaining the System," *BNA Bulletin to Management* (March 25, 2004): 97.

40. One attorney notes that problems can arise with the Federal Stored Communications Act if the employer uses illicit or coercive means to access the employees' private social media accounts. *BNA Bulletin to Management* (July 20, 2009): 225.

41. Some employers, such as Eastman Kodak, are appointing chief privacy officers to ensure that the human resource management and other departments don't endanger the company by conducting inappropriate investigations of job applicants or employees. Rita

Zeidner, "New Face in the C-Suite," *HR Magazine* (January 2010): 39.

42. "Surveillance of Employees," *BNA Bulletin to Management* (April 25, 1996): 136.

43. "Telephone and Electronic Monitoring: A Special Report on the Issues and the Law," *BNA Bulletin to Management* (April 3, 1997): 2.

44. *Quon* v. *Arch Wireless Operating Co.*, 529f.3d 892 (Ninth Circuit 2008); "Employers Should Re-examine Policies in Light of Ruling," *BNA Bulletin to Management* (August 12, 2008): 263.

45. Many employees probably assume that their communications using the corporate e-mail system are open to review, but that e-mails they send via the employer's system but using their personal e-mail accounts (such as Gmail) aren't subject to review. Recently, courts in New York and New Jersey have supported this assumption, although on a limited basis. It's still not an entirely clear-cut situation, but at a minimum the employer should take steps to make it clear that no employee has a reasonable expectation that any e-mails he or she sends using the employer's systems are private. Dionne Searcey, "Some Courts Raise the Bar on Reading Employee E-Mail," *Wall Street Journal* (November 19, 2009): 817.

46. A recent U.S. Federal Trade Commission decision may even make employers liable for deceptive endorsements that employees post on their own blogs or on social media sites such as Facebook, even if the employers didn't authorize the statements. "FTC Rules May Make Employers Liable for Worker Web Conduct," *BNA Bulletin to Management* (January 19, 2010): 23.

47. "When Can an Employer Access Private E-Mail on Its System?" *BNA Bulletin to Management* (July 14, 2009): 224.

48. *Vega-Rodriguez* v. *Puerto Rico Telephone Company*, CAL 962061, April 8, 1997; discussed in "Video Surveillance Withstands Privacy Challenge," *BNA Bulletin to Management* (April 17, 1998): 121.

49. "Secret Videotaping Leads to $200,000 Settlement," *BNA Bulletin to Management* (January 22, 1998): 17.

50. Andrea Poe, "Make Foresight 20/20," *HR Magazine* (February 20, 2000): 74–80. See also Nancy Hatch Woodward, "Smoother Separations," *HR Magazine* (June 2007): 94–97.

51. Robert Lanza and Morton Warren, "United States: Employment at Will Prevails Despite Exceptions to the Rule," *Society for Human Resource Management Legal Report* (October–November 2005): 1–8.

52. Ibid.

53. Joseph Famularo, *Handbook of Modern Personnel Administration* (New York: McGraw-Hill, 1982), pp. 63–65. See also Carolyn Hirschman, "Off Duty, Out of Work," *HR Magazine*, www.shrm.org/hrmagazine/articles/0203/0203hirschman.asp, accessed January 1, 2008.

54. Connie Wanberg et al., "Perceived Fairness of Layoffs among Individuals Who Have Been Laid Off: A Longitudinal Study," *Personnel Psychology* 52 (1999): 59–84. See also Nancy Hatch Woodward, "Smoother Separations," *HR Magazine* (June 2007): 94–97.

55. Michael Orey, "Fear of Firing," *Business Week* (April 23, 2007): 52–54.

56. Paul Falcon, "Give Employees the (Gentle) Hook," *HR Magazine* (April 2001): 121–128.

57. Sovereign, *Personnel Law*, p. 185.

58. "Fairness to Employees Can Stave Off Litigation," *BNA Bulletin to Management* (November 27, 1997): 377.

59. Adrienne Fox, "Prune Employees Carefully," *HR Magazine* (April 1, 2008), http://findarticles.com/p/articles/mi_m3495/is_4_53/ai_n25358109/?tag=content;col1, accessed April 14, 2010.

60. Ibid.

61. Ibid. Also "Severance/Retention Practices: 2002; Pension Benefits," October 2002, p. 11; "Severance Pay," July 2007; Culpepper Compensation & Benefits Surveys.

62. Ibid.

63. Terry Baglieri, "Severance Pay," www.SHRM.org, accessed December 23, 2006.

64. "Severance Decisions Swayed by Cost, Legal, Morale Concerns," *BNA Bulletin to Management* (May 12, 2009): 151.

65. Edward Isler et al., "Personal Liability and Employee Discipline," *Society for Human Resource Management Legal Report* (September–October 2000): 1–4.

66. "One More Heart Risk: Firing Employees," *Miami Herald* (March 20, 1998): C1, C7.

67. Based on James Coil III and Charles Rice, "Three Steps to Creating Effective Employee Releases," *Employment Relations Today* (Spring 1994): 91–94. See also Martha Frase-Blunt, "Making Exit Interviews Work," *HR Magazine* (August 2004): 9–11; "Severance Pay: Not Always the Norm," *HR Magazine* (May 2008): 28.

68. Paul Brada, "Before You Go...," *HR Magazine* (December 1998): 89–102.

69. Peter Hom et al., "Challenging Conventional Wisdom about Who Quits: Revelations from Corporate America," *Journal of Applied Psychology* 93, no. 1 (2008): 1–34.

70. "Workers Hit by Mass Layoffs Rose to 143,977 in February," *BNA Bulletin to Management* (April 3, 2007): 109.

71. Joseph Zarandona and Michael Camuso, "A Study of Exit Interviews: Does the Last Word Count?" *Personnel* 62, no. 3 (March 1981): 47–48.

72. Leon Grunberg, Sarah Moore, and Edward Greenberg, "Managers' Reactions to Implementing Layoffs: Relationship to Health Problems and Withdrawal Behaviors," *Human Resource Management* 45, no. 2 (Summer 2006): 159–178.

73. See also Rodney Sorensen and Stephen Robinson, "What Employers Can Do to Stay Out of Legal Trouble

When Forced to Implement Layoffs," *Compensation & Benefits Review* (January/February 2009): 25–32.

74. "Mass Layoffs at Lowest Level Since July 2008, BLS Says," *BNA Bulletin to Management* (January 12, 2010): 13.

75. Ibid.

76. Roderick Iversen and Christopher Zatzick, "The Effects of Downsizing of Labor Productivity: The Value of Showing Consideration for Employees' Morale and Welfare and High Performance Work Systems," *Human Resource Management* 50, no. 1 (January–February 2011): 29–44.

77. Ibid., p. 40.

78. "Adopting Laid-Off Alternatives Could Help Employers Survive, Even Thrive, Analysts Say," *BNA Bulletin to Management* (February 20, 2009): 57.

79. See, for example, "Cushioning the Blow of Layoffs," *BNA Bulletin to Management* (July 3, 1997): 216; "Levi Strauss Cushions Blow of Plant Closings," *BNA Bulletin to Management* (November 20, 1997): 370. In one recent year, U.S. employers implemented about 1,300 mass layoffs, involving a total of almost 133,000 workers. "Layoffs: 133,914 Workers Idled by Mass Layoffs in April, BLS Says," *BNA Bulletin to Management* (June 3, 2008): 181.

80. "Calling a Layoff a Layoff," *Workforce Management* (April 21, 2008): 41.

81. Ibid.

82. See, for example, www.nobscot.com/survey/index.cfm and www.bls.gov/jlt/, both accessed April 27, 2011.

83. Jean Phillips and Stanley Gulley, *Strategic Staffing* (Upper Saddle River, NJ: Pearson Education, 2012).

84. The following example is based on Barbara Hillmer, Steve Hillmer, and Gale McRoberts, "The Real Costs of Turnover: Lessons from a Call Center," *Human Resource Planning* 27, no. 3 (2004): 34–41. See also Rosemary Batt and Alexander Colvin, "An Employment Systems Approach to Turnover: Human Resources Practices, Quits, Dismissals, and Performance," *Academy of Management Journal* 54, no. 4 (2011): 695–717.

85. www.worldatwork.org/waw/adimLink?id=17180, accessed April 27, 2011.

86. Phillips and Gulley, *Strategic Staffing*, p. 329.

87. Stephen Robbins and Timothy Judge, *Organizational Behavior* (Upper Saddle River, NJ: Pearson, 2011), p. 81. See also Eric Krell, "Five Ways to Manage High Turnover," *HR Magazine* (April 2012): 63–65.

88. Phillips and Gulley, *Strategic Staffing*, p. 328.

89. Max Messmer, "Employee Retention: Why It Matters Now," *CPA Magazine* (June/July 2009): 28; and "The Employee Retention Challenge," Development Dimensions International, 2009.

90. Messmer, "Employee Retention."

91. Ibid.

92. David Wilson, "Comparative Effects of Race/Ethnicity and Employee Engagement on Withdrawal Behavior," *Journal of Managerial Issues* 21, no. 2 (Summer 2009): 165–166, 195–215.

93. Paul Eder and Robert Eisenberger, "Perceived Organizational Support: Reducing the Negative Influence of Coworker Withdrawal Behavior," *Journal of Management* 34, no. 1 (2008): 55–68.

94. Wilson, "Comparative Effects of Race/Ethnicity and Employee Engagement."

95. Lisa Hope Pelled and Katherine R. Xin, "Down and Out: An Investigation of the Relationship between Mood and Employee Withdrawal Behavior," *Journal of Management* 25, no. 6 (1999): 875–895.

96. Ibid.

97. Ibid.

98. Ibid.

99. For an examination of this, see ibid.

100. See for example, Margaret Shaffer and David Harrison, "Expatriates' Psychological Withdrawal from International Assignments: Work, Nonwork, and Family Influences," *Personnel Psychology* 51, no. 1 (Spring 1998): 87–118; Karl Pajo, Alan Coetzer, and Nigel Guenole, "Formal Development Opportunities and Withdrawal Behaviors by Employees in Small and Medium-Sized Enterprises," *Journal of Small Business Management* 48, no. 3 (July 2010): 281–301; and P. Eder et al., "Perceived Organizational Support: Reducing the Negative Influence of Coworker Withdrawal Behavior," *Journal of Management* 34, no. 1 (February 2008): 55–68.

101. Adrienne Facts, "Raising Engagement," *HR Magazine* (May 2010): 35–40. See also Michael Christian, Adela Garza, and Jerel Slaughter, "Work Engagement: A Quantitative Review and Test of its Relations with Task and Contextual Performance," *Personnel Psychology* 60, no. 4 (2011): 89–136.

102. Except as noted, this is based on Kathryn Tyler, "Prepare for Impact," *HR Magazine* 56, no. 3 (March 2011): 53–56.

103. Rosa Chun and Gary Davies, "Employee Happiness Isn't Enough to Satisfy Customers," *Harvard Business Review* 87, no. 4 (April 2009): 19. See also Claudio Fernandez-Araoz, Boris Groysberg, and Nitin Nohria, "How to Hang Onto Your High Potentials," *Harvard Business Review* (October 2011): 76–83.

104. As another example, one recent study distinguished among physical engagement ("I work with intensity on my job," "I exert my full effort to my job," and so on), emotional engagement ("I am enthusiastic in my job," "I feel energetic at my job," and so on), and cognitive engagement ("at work, my mind is focused on my job," and "at work, I pay a lot of attention to my job"). Bruce Louis Rich et al., "Job Engagement: Antecedents and Effects on Job Performance," *Academy of Management Journal* 53, no. 3 (2010): 617–635.

105. Ibid. See also Kathryn Tyler, "Prepare for Impact," *HR Magazine* (March 2011): 53–56.

106. Paula Ketter, "What's the Big Deal about Employee Engagement," *Training & Development* (January 2008): 47–48. See also Michael Tucker, "Make Managers Responsible," *HR Magazine* (March 2012): 75–78.

107. David Gebler, "Is Your Culture a Risk Factor"? *Business and Society Review* 111, no. 3 (Fall 2006): 337–362.

108. John Cohan, "'I Didn't Know' and 'I Was Only Doing My Job': Has Corporate Governance Careened out of Control? A Case Study of Enron's Information Myopia," *Journal of Business Ethics* 40, no. 3 (October 2002): 275–299.

109. Ibid.

110. Facts adapted from Bureau of National Affairs, Bulletin to Management (September 13, 1985): 3.

Chapter 9

1. www.bls.gov/news.release/union2.nr0.htm, accessed June 5, 2011.

2. Ibid.; and "Union Membership Rises," *Compensation & Benefits Review* (May/June 2008): 9.

3. Joseph Adler, "The Past as Prologue? A Brief History of the Labor Movement in the United States," *International Personnel Management Association for HR* 35, no. 4 (Winter 2006): 311–329. As of 2009, for the first time most of those union members (7.6%) are in the public sector, as opposed to the private sector (7.2%). Stephen Greenhouse, "Most US Union Members Are Working for the Government, New Data Shows," *New York Times* (January 23, 2010): B1–B5.

4. www.bls.gov/news.release/union2.t03.htm, accessed March 13, 2012.

5. Eric Krell, "The Rebirth of Labor Relations," *HR Magazine* 54, no. 2 (February 2009): 57–60.

6. Paul Monies, "Unions Hit Hard by Job Losses, Right to Work," *Daily Oklahoman* (via Knight Ridder/Tribune Business News) (February 1, 2005).

7. Ann Zimmerman, "Pro-Union Butchers at Wal-Mart Win a Union Battle But Lose War," *Wall Street Journal* (April 11, 2000): A14. See also Steven Greenhouse, "Report Assails Wal-Mart over Unions," *New York Times* (May 1, 2007): C3.

8. Donna Buttigieg et al., "An Event History Analysis of Union Joining and Leaving," *Journal of Applied Psychology* 92, no. 3 (2007): 829–839.

9. Robert Grossman, "Unions Follow Suit," *HR Magazine* (May 2005): 49.

10. Ibid., p. 836; see also Lois Tetrick et al., "A Model of Union Participation: The Impact of Perceived Union Support, Union Instrumentality, and Union Loyalty," *Journal of Applied Psychology* 92, no. 3 (2007): 820–828.

11. Benjamin Taylor and Fred Witney, *Labor Relations Law* (Upper Saddle River, NJ: Prentice Hall, 1992), pp. 157–184. See also Arthur Sloane and Fred Witney, *Labor Relations* (Upper Saddle River, NJ: Prentice Hall, 2007), pp. 335–336.

12. Taylor and Witney, *Labor Relations Law,* pp. 170–71. See also www.dol.gov/whd/state/righttowork.htm, accessed June 5, 2010.

13. "Unions Hit Hard by Job Losses, Right to Work," *Daily Oklahoman* (via Knight Ridder/Tribune Business News) (February 1, 2005); and www.dol.gov/esa/programs/whd/state/righttowork.htm, accessed January 13, 2008.

14. www.dol.gov/esa/programs/whd/state/righttowork.htm, accessed January 13, 2008.

15. www.seiu.org/our-union/, accessed June 1, 2011.

16. http://articles.moneycentral.msn.com/Investing/Extra/CostcoTheAntiWalMart.aspx?page=1, accessed June 29, 2011.

17. Ibid.

18. Ibid.

19. The following material is based on Arthur Sloane and Fred Witney, *Labor Relations* (Upper Saddle River, NJ: Prentice Hall, 2001), pp. 63–120. See also www.nlrb.gov/what-we-do/investigate-charges, accessed March 13, 2012.

20. Sloane and Witney, *Labor Relations*, p. 106.

21. Karen Robinson, "Temp Workers Gain Union Access," *HR News, Society for Human Resource Management* 19, no. 10 (October 2000): 1.

22. Michael Carrell and Christina Heavrin, *Labor Relations and Collective Bargaining* (Upper Saddle River, NJ: Pearson, 2004), p. 180.

23. Ibid., p. 179.

24. Sloane and Witney, *Labor Relations*, 102–106.

25. William Fulmer, "Step by Step Through a Union Election," *Harvard Business Review* 60 (July/August 1981): 94–102. For an interesting description of contract negotiations, see Peter Cramton and Joseph Tracy, "The Determinants of U.S. Labor Disputes," *Journal of Labor Economics* 12, no. 2 (April 1994): 180–209. Sloane and Witney, *Labor Relations*, p. 29.

26. Sloane and Witney, *Labor Relations,* p. 29.

27. Jonathan Segal, "Expose the Union's Underbelly," *HR Magazine* (June 1999): 166–176.

28. "Some Say Salting Leaves Bitter Taste for Employers," *BNA Bulletin to Management* (March 4, 2004): 79. For a management lawyer's perspective, see www.fklaborlaw.com/union_salt-objectives.html, accessed May 25, 2007.

29. For more information on the Starbucks Workers Union, go to www.starbucksunion.org, accessed January 14, 2008.

30. The union must file a petition for an election within 30 days after the start of picketing, the firm cannot already be lawfully recognizing another union, and there cannot already have been a valid NLRB election during the past 12 months.

31. Fulmer, "Step by Step Through a Union Election," p. 94.

32. Frederick Sullivan, "Limiting Union Organizing Activity Through Supervisors," *Personnel* 55 (July/

August 1978): 55–65. See also Edward Young and William Levy, "Responding to a Union-Organizing Campaign: Do You and Your Supervisors Know the Legal Boundaries in a Union Campaign?" *Franchising World* 39, no. 3 (March 2007): 45–49.

33. See, for example, www.powelltrachtman.com/CM/Publications/pps_unions.ppt, accessed September 30, 2010.

34. Jonathon Segal, "Unshackle Your Supervisors to Stay Union Free," *HR Magazine* (June 1998): 62–65. See also www.nlrb.gov/workplace_rights/nlra_violations.aspx, accessed January 14, 2008.

35. Whether employers must give union representatives permission to organize on employer-owned property at shopping malls is a matter of legal debate. The U.S. Supreme Court ruled in *Lechmere, Inc.* v. *National Labor Relations Board* that employers may bar nonemployees from their property if the nonemployees have reasonable alternative means of communicating their message to the intended audience. However, if the employer lets other organizations like the Salvation Army set up at their workplace, the NLRB may view discriminating against the union organizers as an unfair labor practice. See, for example, "Union Access to Employer's Customers Restricted," *BNA Bulletin to Management* (February 15, 1996): 49; "Workplace Access for Unions Hinges on Legal Issues," *BNA Bulletin to Management* (April 11, 1996): 113.

36. Edwin Arnold et al., "Determinants of Certification Election Outcomes in the Service Sector," *Labor Studies Journal* 25, no. 3 (Fall 2000): 51.

37. "2008 Union Win Rate Rose to 66.8%; Number of Elections Increased, Data Show," *BNA Bulletin to Management* (May 12, 2009): 145–152.

38. "Union Decertifications Up in First Half of 1998," *BNA Bulletin to Management* (December 24, 1998): 406. See also www.nlrb.gov/nlrb/shared_files/brochures/rpt_september2002.pdf, accessed January 14, 2008.

39. Carrell and Heavrin, *Labor Relations and Collective Bargaining*, pp. 120–121.

40. Terry Leap, *Collective Bargaining and Labor Relations* (Upper Saddle River, NJ: Prentice Hall, 1995). See also www.nlrb.gov/nlrb/shared_files/brochures/basicguide.pdf, accessed January 14, 2008.

41. Leap, *Collective Bargaining and Labor Relations*, pp. 307–309.

42. Ibid., p. 308.

43. Kathryn Tyler, "Good-Faith Bargaining," *HR Magazine* (January 2005): 52. For an interesting insight into negotiating tactics, see Marwan Sineceure, et al., "Hot or Cold: Is Communicating Anger or Threats More Effective in Negotiation?" *Journal of Applied Psychology* 96, no. 5 (2011): 1019–1032.

44. Bargaining items based on Reed Richardson, *Collective Bargaining by Objectives* (Upper Saddle River, NJ:

Prentice Hall, 1997), pp. 113–115; see also Sloane and Witney, *Labor Relations*, pp. 180–217.

45. Sloane and Witney, *Labor Relations*, pp. 192–220.

46. Preceding items based on Reed Richardson, *Collective Bargaining by Objectives* (Upper Saddle River, NJ: Prentice-Hall, 1977), p. 150; see also D. Scott DeRue et al., "When Is Straightforwardness a Liability in Negotiations? The Role of Integrative Potential and Structural Power," *Journal of Applied Psychology* 94, no. 4 (2009): 1032–1047.

47. www.thedeal.com/corporatedealmaker/2009/11/us_airways_pilots_seek_federal.php, accessed November 17, 2009.

48. Jonathan Kramer and Thomas Hyclak, "Why Strikes Occur: Evidence from the Capital Markets," *Industrial Relations* 41, no. 1 (January 2002): 80–93.

49. This is based on Sloane and Witney, *Labor Relations*, p. 213.

50. Ibid., p. 213.

51. Micheline Maynard and Jeremy Peters, "Northwest Airlines Threatens to Replace Strikers Permanently," *New York Times* (August 26, 2005): C3.

52. For a discussion, see Herbert Northrup, "Union Corporate Campaigns and Inside Games as a Strike Form," *Employee Relations Law Journal* 19, no. 4 (Spring 1994): 507–549. See also Rachel Feintzeig, "Teamsters Act Tough with Twinkies Maker," *The Wall Street Journal* (February 14, 2012): b-4.

53. Melanie Evans, "Labor Pains: As Membership Slides, Unions Have Turned to Provocative Corporate Campaigns," *Modern Health Care* 34, no. 26 (December 6, 2004): 26.

54. Matthew Dolan, "UAW Targets Foreign Car Plants in US," *Wall Street Journal* (December 23, 2010): B3.

55. Northrup, "Union Corporate Campaigns and Inside Games as a Strike Form."

56. Ibid., p. 518.

57. "The Owners Take a Punt," *The Economist* (March 12, 2011): 40. See also James Hagerty and Caroline Van Hasselt, "Lockout Tests Union's Clout," *The Wall Street Journal* (January 30, 2012): B-1.

58. The NLRB held in 1986 in Charter Equipment, Inc. 280 NLRB No. 71, that an employer could lawfully hire temporary replacements during the course of a lockout, in the absence of proof of specific antiunion motivation, in order to bring economic pressure to bear upon a union to support a legitimate bargaining position.

59. Clifford Koen Jr., Sondra Hartmen, and Dinah Payne, "The NLRB Wields a Rejuvenated Weapon," *Personnel Journal* (December 1996): 85–87; and D. Silverman, "The NLRA at 70: A New Approach to Processing 10(j)s [NLRA at Seventy conference in New York City, 2005]," *Labor Law Journal* 56, no. 3 (Fall 2005): 203–206.

60. http://sports.espn.go.com/nfl/news/story?id= 4508545, accessed November 17, 2009.

61. Duncan Adams, "Worker Grievances Consume Roanoke, VA, Mail Distribution Center," *Knight Ridder/Tribune Business News* (March 27, 2001): Item 1086009.

62. Walter Baer, *Grievance Handling: 101 Guides for Supervisors* (New York: American Management Association, 1970); M. Newport, *Supervisory Management*; Mark Lurie, "The Eight Essential Steps in Grievance Processing."

63. See M. Gene Newport, *Supervisory Management* (St. Paul, MN: West Group, 1976), p. 273, for an excellent checklist. See also Mark Lurie, "The Eight Essential Steps in Grievance Processing," *Dispute Resolution Journal* 54, no. 4 (November 1999): 61–65.

64. See, for example, Jo Blandon et al., "Have Unions Turned the Corner? New Evidence on Recent Trends in Union Recognition in UK Firms," *British Journal of Industrial Relations* 44, no. 2 (June 2006): 169–190; Mark Schoeff Jr., "Labor on the March," *Workforce Management* (February 2010): 1, 18–19; and "With Membership Bottoming Out, What Does the Future Hold for Unions?" *BNA Bulletin to Management* (March 1, 2011): 65–66.

65. "Unions Using Class Actions to Pressure Nonunion Companies," *BNA Bulletin to Management* (August 22, 2006): 271. Some believe that today, "long-term observers see more bark than bite in organized labor's efforts to revitalize." See, for example, Robert Grossman, "We Organized Labor and Code," *HR Magazine* (January 2008): 37–40.

66. Kris Maher, "Specter Won't Support Union-Backed Bill," *Wall Street Journal* (March 20, 2009): A3.

67. "Unions Using Class Actions to Pressure Nonunion Companies," *BNA Bulletin to Management* (August 22, 2006): 271.

68. Dean Scott, "Unions Still a Potent Force," *Kiplinger Business Forecasts* (March 26, 2003).

69. "Contracts Call for Greater Labor Management Teamwork," *BNA Bulletin to Management* (April 29, 1999): 133.

70. Jennifer Schramm, "The Future of Unions," *Workplace Visions,* Society for Human Resource Management (2005): 6.

71. Mei Fong and Kris Maher, "US Labor Chief Moves into China," *Wall Street Journal Asia* (June 22–24, 2007): 1.

72. Steven Greenhouse, "Steelworkers Merge with British Union," *New York Times* (July 3, 2008): C4.

73. Matthew Dolan and Neil Boudette, "UAW to Send Activists Abroad," *Wall Street Journal* (March 23, 2011): B2.

74. Carol Gill, "Union Impact on the Effective Adoption of High Performance Work Practices," *Human Resource Management Review* 19 (2009): 39–50. See also Thomas Kochan, "A Jobs Compact for America's Future," *Harvard Business Review* (March 2012): 64–70.

75. Chris Purcell, "Rhetoric Flying in WGA Talks," *Television Week* 26, no. 30 (July 20, 2007): 3, 35; Peter Sanders, "In Hollywood, a Tale of Two Union Leaderships," *Wall Street Journal* (January 7, 2008): B2.

76. Purcell, "Rhetoric Flying in WGA Talks."

77. Ibid.

78. James Hibberd, "Guild Talks Break with No Progress," *Television Week* 26, no. 38 (October 8–15, 2007): 1, 30.

79. Ibid.

80. "DGA Deal Sets the Stage for Writers," *Television Week* 27, no. 3 (2008): 3, 33.

81. "WGA, Studios Reach Tentative Agreement," *UPI News Track* (February 3, 2008).

82. Raymond Hilgert and Cyril Ling, *Cases and Experiential Exercises in Management* (Upper Saddle River, NJ: Prentice Hall, 1996), pp. 201–203.

Chapter 10

1. Michael Wilson, "Manslaughter Charge in Trench Collapse," *New York Times* (June 12, 2008): B1.

2. Figures for 2009. www.bls.gov/iif/oshwc/cfoi/cfch0008.pdf, accessed June 1, 2011.

3. All data refer to 2009. www.bls.gov/news.release/archives/osh_10212010.pdf, accessed June 1, 2011.

4. "Workers Rate Safety Most Important Workplace Issue," *EHS Today* (October 2010): 17.

5. Katherine Torres, "Stepping into the Kitchen: Food Protection for Food Workers," *Occupational Hazards* (January 2007): 29–30.

6. Based on *All About OSHA*, rev. ed. (Washington, DC: U.S. Department of Labor, 1980); www.OSHA.gov, accessed January 19, 2008.

7. "OSHA Hazard Communication Standard Enforcement," *BNA Bulletin to Management* (February 23, 1980): 13. See also William Kincaid, "OSHA vs. Excellence in Safety Management," *Occupational Hazards* (December 2002): 34–36. Flow diagram based on *What Every Employer Needs to Know about OSHA Recordkeeping* (Washington, D.C.: U.S. Department of Labor, 1978), p. 3.

8. "What Every Employer Needs to Know about OSHA Record Keeping," U.S. Department of Labor, Bureau of Labor Statistics (Washington, DC), report 412–13, p. 3; and www.osha.gov/recordkeeping/index.html, accessed October 26, 2011.

9. "Supreme Court Says OSHA Inspectors Need Warrants," *Engineering News Record* (June 1, 1978): 9–10; W. Scott Railton, "OSHA Gets Tough on Business," *Management Review* 80, no. 12 (December 1991): 28–29. Steve Hollingsworth, "How to Survive an OSHA Inspection," *Occupational Hazards* (March 2004): 31–33.

10. osha.gov/as/opa/oshafacts.html, accessed January 19, 2008; Edwin Foulke Jr., "OSHA's Evolving Role in Promoting Occupational Safety

and Health," *EHS Today* (November 2008): 44–49. Some believe that under the new Democratic administration of President Obama, OSHA may move from voluntary programs back to increased attention on inspections. See, for example, Laura Walter, "Safety Roundtable: The View from the End of an Era," *EHS Today* (December 2008): 30–31.

11. Lisa Finnegan, "Industry Partners with OSHA," *Occupational Hazards* (February 1999): 43–45. OSHA instituted a pilot Voluntary Protection Program (VPP) for companies with exemplary safety practices. On-site VPP evaluation teams evaluate such things as supervisory safety training and safety and health communications programs. VPP certification removes a facility from OSHA's routine inspection list. Sara Escborn and Mary Giddings, "The Ripple Effect of Fluor's Corporate VPP Status," *EHS Today* (February 2009): 44–45.

12. www.osha.gov/Publications/osha2098.pdf+ OSHA+inspection+priorities&hl=en&ct=clnk&cd= 1&gl=us, accessed January 19, 2008.

13. www.OSHA.gov, accessed May 28, 2005; and http://osha.gov/pls/oshaweb/owadisp.show_document?p_table=NEWS_RELEASES&p_id=14883, accessed January 19, 2008. "OSHA Sends 15,000 Letters to Employers with High Injury Rates and Offers Assistance," *BNA Bulletin to Management* (March 16, 2010): 83.

14. Patricia Poole, "When OSHA Knocks," *Occupational Hazards* (February 2008): 59–61.

15. For example, OSHA recently settled with Murphy Oil USA with Murphy paying just over $179,000 in OSHA fines for a variety of violations such as activated alarms, and OSHA recently proposed a penalty of $195,200 against a masonry contractor with a total of 21 violations. See "Enforcement Briefs," *Occupational Hazards* (March 2008): 13.

16. www.osha.gov/Publications/osha2098.pdf+ OSHA+inspection+priorities&hl=en&ct= clnk&cd=1&gl=us, accessed January 19, 2008.

17. For a discussion of how to deal with citations and proposed penalties, see, for example, Michael Taylor, "OSHA Citations and Proposed Penalties: How to Beat the Rap," *EHS Today* (December 2008): 34–36. Employers with high injury rates may also be subject to additional monitoring. For example, OSHA recently sent about 15,000 letters to employers telling them that their injury and illness rates were much higher than the national average. "OSHA Sends 15,000 Letters to Employers with High Injury Rates and Offers Assistance," *BNA Bulletin to Management* (March 16, 2010): 83.

18. Jim Lastowka, "Ten Keys to Avoiding OSHA Liability," *Occupational Hazards* (October 1999):

163–70; and www.osha.gov/Publications/osha2098 .pdf+OSHA+inspection+priorities&hl=en&ct=clnk&c d=1&gl=us, accessed January 19, 2008.

19. Robert Grossman, "Handling Inspections: Tips from Insiders," *HR Magazine* (October 1999): 41–50.

20. Arthur Sapper, "The Oft-Missed Step: Documentation of Safety Discipline," *Occupational Hazards* (January 2006): 59.

21. Asking employees what is prompting their resistance may head off the problem. See J. Heitman, "Gaining Their Trust," *Occupational Health & Safety* 71, no. 5 (May 2002): 22, 24.

22. Don Williamson and Jon Kauffman, "From Tragedy to Triumph: Safety Grows Wings at Golden Eagle," *Occupational Hazards* (February 2006): 17–25.

23. "A Safety Committee Man's Guide," *Aetna Life and Casualty Insurance Company*, Catalog 872684. See also Todd Nighswonger, "Get a Grip on Slips," *Occupational Hazards* (September 2000): 47–50.

24. For a discussion of this, see David Hofmann and Adam Stetzer, "A Cross-Level Investigation of Factors Influencing Unsafe Behaviors and Accidents," *Personnel Psychology* 49 (1996): 307–308.

25. David Hofman and Barbara Mark, "An Investigation of the Relationship between Safety Climate and Medication Errors as Well as Other Nurse and Patient Outcomes," *Personnel Psychology* 50, no. 9 (2006): 847–869.

26. List of unsafe acts from "A Safety Committee Man's Guide," *Aetna Life and Casualty Insurance Company*.

27. Robert Pater and Robert Russel, "Drop That Accident Prone Tag: Look for Causes beyond Personal Issues," *Industrial Safety and Hygiene News* 38, no. 1 (January 2004): 50.

28. Discussed in Douglas Haaland, "Who's the Safest Bet for the Job? Find Out Why the Fun Guy in the Next Cubicle May Be the Next Accident Waiting to Happen," *Security Management* 49, no. 2 (February 2005): 51–57.

29. "Thai Research Points to Role of Personality in Road Accidents," *Asia and Africa Intelligence Wire* (February 23, 2005); Donald Bashline et al., "Bad Behavior: Personality Tests Can Help Underwriters Identify High-Risk Drivers," *Best's Review* 105, no. 12 (April 2005): 63–64.

30. See, for example, Michael Christian et al., "Workplace Safety: A Meta-Analysis of the Roles of Person and Situation Factors," *Journal of Applied Psychology* 94, no. 5 (2009): 1103–1127.

31. Michael Frone, "Predictors of Work Injuries among Employed Adolescents," *Journal of Applied Psychology* 83, no. 4 (1998): 565–576.

32. Benjamin Mangan, "Lockout/Tagout Prevents Workplace Injuries and Saves Lives," *Occupational Hazards* (March 2007): 59–60; Jimi Michalscheck, "The Basics of Lock Out/Tag Out Compliance:

Creating an Effective Program," *EHS Today* (January 2010): 35–37.

33. Mike Carlson, "Machine Safety Solutions for Protecting Employees and Safeguarding against Machine Hazards," *EHS Today* (July 2009): 24.

34. James Nash, "Beware the Hidden Eye Hazards," *Occupational Hazards* (February 2005): 48–51. A combustible dust explosion at a sugar refinery recently killed 14 employees and injured dozens of others, many with serious burns. The employers subsequently required all employees and visitors to the manufacturing areas to wear fire-resistant clothing. But if that requirement had been in effect *before* the explosion, many burns might have been avoided. Laura Walter, "FR Clothing: Leaving Hazards in the Dust," *EHS Today* (January 2010): 20–22.

35. You can find videos about new personal protective products at "SafetyLive TV" at www.occupational hazards.com, accessed March 14, 2009.

36. James Zeigler, "Protective Clothing: Exploring the Wearability Issue," *Occupational Hazards* (September 2000): 81–82; Sandy Smith, "Protective Clothing and the Quest for Improved Performance," *Occupational Hazards* (February 2008): 63–66.

37. "The Complete Guide to Personal Protective Equipment," *Occupational Hazards* (January 1999): 49–60. See also Edwin Zalewski, "Noise Control: It's More than Just Earplugs: OSHA Requires Employers to Evaluate Engineering and Administrative Controls before Using Personal Protective Equipment," *Occupational Hazards* 68, no. 9 (September 2006): 48; and Judy Smithers, "Use OSHA's Compliance Directive to Evaluate Your PPE Program," *EHS Today* (January 2012): 43–45.

38. Sandy Smith, "Protecting Vulnerable Workers," *Occupational Hazards* (April 2004): 25–28. In addition to millions of women in factory jobs, about 10% of the construction industry workforce is female, and there are almost 200,000 women in the U.S. military. Women also represent almost 80% of health care workers, where puncture- and chemical-resistant gloves are particularly important. David Shutt, "Protecting the Hands of Working Women," *EHS Today* (October 2009): 29–32.

39. Donald Groce, "Keep the Gloves On!" *Occupational Hazards* (June 2008): 45–47.

40. See, for example, Laura Walter, "What's in a Glove?" *Occupational Hazards* (May 2008): 35–36.

41. J. P. Sankpill, "A Clear Vision for Eye and Face Protection," *EHS Today* (November 2010): 29.

42. Linda Tapp, "We Can Do It: Protecting Women Workers," *Occupational Hazards* (October 2003): 26–28.

43. Katherine Torres, "Don't Lose Sight of the Older Workforce," *Occupational Hazards* (June 2008): 55–59.

44. Robert Pater, "Boosting Safety with an Aging Workforce," *Occupational Hazards* (March 2006): 24.

45. Michael Silverstein, M.D., "Designing the Age Friendly Workplace," *Occupational Hazards* (December 2007): 29–31.

46. Elizabeth Rogers and William Wiatrowski, "Injuries, Illnesses, and Fatalities among Older Workers," *Monthly Labor Review* 128, no. 10 (October 2005): 24–30.

47. www.osha.gov/Publications/osha3071.pdf, accessed April 21, 2011.

48. www-ns.iaea.org/reviews/op-safetyreviews.asp, accessed March 14, 2012.

49. Robert Pater and Ron Bowles, "Directing Attention to Boost Safety Performance," *Occupational Hazards* (March 2007): 46–48.

50. F. Scott Geller, "The Thinking and Seeing Components of People-Based Safety," *Occupational Hazards* (December 2006): 38–40.

51. "Feds Ordered, Contractors Urged, Not to Text While Driving," *BNA Bulletin to Management* (October 6, 2009): 314. See also "DOT Final Rule Bans Cell Phone Use by Commercial Bus Drivers, Truckers," *BNA Bulletin to Management* (December 6, 2011): 387.

52. "Thai Research Points to Role of Personality in Road Accidents," *Asia and Africa Intelligence Wire* (February 23, 2005); Donald Bashline et al., "Bad Behavior: Personality Tests Can Help Underwriters Identify High-Risk Drivers," *Best's Review* 105, no. 12 (April 2005): 63–64.

53. S. Laner and R. J. Sell, "An Experiment on the Effect of Specially Designed Safety Posters," *Occupational Psychology* 34 (1960): 153–169; Ernest McCormick and Joseph Tiffin, *Industrial Psychology* (Upper Saddle River, NJ: Prentice Hall, 1974), p. 536.

54. See also Josh Cable, "Erring on the Side of Caution," *Occupational Hazards* (February 2007): 21–22; and Shel Siegel, "Incentives: Small Investments Equal Big Rewards," *Occupational Hazards* (August 2007): 42–44.

55. See, for example, Ron Bruce, "Online from Kazakhstan to California," *Occupational Hazards* (June 2008): 61–65.

56. Michael Blotzer, "PDA Software Offers Auditing Advances," *Occupational Hazards* 63, no. 12 (December 2001): 11. See also Eric Anderson, "Automating Health & Safety Processes Creates Value," *Occupational Hazards* (April 2008): 53–63.

57. Laura Walter, "Surfing for Safety," *Occupational Hazards* (July 2008): 23–29.

58. John Rekus, "Is Your Safety Training Program Effective?" *Occupational Hazards* (August 1999): 37–39. See also www.osha.gov/Publications/osha2254.pdf, accessed October 25, 2011.

59. Laura Walter, "Surfing for Safety," *Occupational Hazards*, July 2008, pp. 23–29.

60. Michael Burke et al., "The Dread Factor: How Hazards and Safety Training Influence Learning and Performance," *Journal of Applied Psychology* 96, no. 1 (2011): 46–70.

61. James Nash, "Rewarding the Safety Process," *Occupational Hazards* (March 2000): 29–34.

62. J. Nigel Ellis and Susan Warner, "Using Safety Awards to Promote Fall Prevention," *Occupational Hazards* (June 1999): 59–62. See also William Atkinson, "Safety Incentive Programs: What Works?" *Occupational Hazards* (August 2004): 35–39.

63. Don Williamson and Jon Kauffman, "From Tragedy to Triumph: Safety Grows Wings at Golden Eagle," *Occupational Hazards* (February 2006): 17–25.

64. Quoted in Josh Cable, "Seven Suggestions for a Successful Safety Incentives Program," *Occupational Hazards* 67, no. 3 (March 2005): 39–43. See also J. M. Saidler, "Gift Cards Make Safety Motivation Simple," *Occupational Health & Safety* 78, no. 1 (January 2009): 39–40.

65. John Dominic, "Improve Safety Performance and Avoid False Reporting," *HR Magazine* 49, no. 9 (September 2004): 110–119; see also Josh Cable, "Safety Incentives Strategies," *Occupational Hazards* 67, no. 4 (April 2005): 37; and See also, "Are Traditional Incentive Programs Illegal?" *EHS Today* (April 2012): 12.

66. See also Kelly Rowe, "OSHA and Small Businesses: A Winning Combination," *Occupational Hazards* (March 2007): 33–38.

67. One study recently concluded that, "Employee perceptions of the extent to which managers and supervisors are committed to workplace safety likely influence employee safety behavior and, subsequently, injuries." Jeremy Beus et al., "Safety Climate and Juries: An Examination of Theoretical and Empirical Relationships," *Journal of Applied Psychology* 95, no. 4 (2010): 713–727.

68. Willie Hammer, *Occupational Safety Management and Engineering* (Upper Saddle River, NJ: Prentice Hall, 1985), pp. 62–63. See also "DuPont's 'STOP' Helps Prevent Workplace Injuries and Incidents," *Asia Africa Intelligence Wire* (May 17, 2004).

69. James Nash, "Weyerhaeuser Fires Plant, Safety Managers for Record-Keeping Abuses," *Occupational Hazards* (November 2004): 27–28.

70. In a similar case, in 2008, the owner of a Brooklyn, New York, construction site was arrested for manslaughter when a worker died in a collapsed trench. Michael Wilson, "Manslaughter Charge in Trench Collapse," *New York Times* (June 12, 2008): B1.

71. "A Safety Committee Man's Guide," pp. 17–21.

72. Dov Zohar, "A Group Level Model of Safety Climate: Testing the Effect of a Group Climate on Students in Manufacturing Jobs," *Journal of Applied Psychology* 85, no. 4 (2000): 587–596. See also Steven Yule, Rhona Flin, and Andy Murdy, "The Role of Management and Safety Climate in Preventing Risk-Taking at Work," *International Journal of Risk Assessment and Management* 7, no. 2 (December 20, 2006): 137.

73. For a discussion of developing a safety climate survey, see Sara Singer et al., "Workforce Perceptions of Hospital Safety Culture: Development and Validation of the Patient Safety Climate in Healthcare Organizations Survey," *Health Services Research* 42, no. 5 (October 2007): 1999. Items discussed based on Sandy Smith, "Breakthrough Safety Management," *Occupational Hazards* (June 2004): 43.

74. Jennifer Nahrgang et al., "Safety at Work: A Meta-Analytic Investigation of the Link between Job Demands, Job Resources, Burnout, Engagement, and Safety Outcomes," *Journal of Applied Psychology* 96, no. 1 (2011): 86.

75. Howard Street, "Getting Full Value from Auditing and Metrics," *Occupational Hazards* (August 2000): 33–36.

76. Thomas Krause, "Steps in Safety Strategy: Executive Decision-Making & Metrics," *EHS Today* (September 2009): 24.

77. Sandy Smith, "Zero Isn't Good Enough at AMEC Earth & Environmental," *EHS Today* (November 2009): 26; Laura Walter, "Safety Evolves at the Concrete Pipe Division of Cemex US Operations," *EHS Today* (November 2009): 27.

78. See the BP case in the Comprehensive Cases Appendix for further discussion, and see also Sandy Smith, "Deep Water Horizon: Production Rewarded, Safety Ignored," *EHS Today* (October 2011): 66–68.

79. This is based on Paul Puncochar, "The Science and Art to Identifying Workplace Hazards," *Occupational Hazards* (September 2003): 50–54.

80. Ibid., p. 52.

81. Gareth Evans, "Wireless Monitoring for a Safe Indoor Environment," *EHS Today* (December 2010): 35–39.

82. Based on the report *Workplace Screening & Brief Intervention: What Employees Can and Should Do about Excessive Alcohol Use,* in "Report Says Employee Alcohol Abuse Closely to Companies," *BNA Bulletin to Management* (June 10, 2008): 101.

83. "15% of Workers Drinking, Drunk, or Hung Over While at Work, According to New University Study," *BNA Bulletin to Management* (January 24, 2006): 27. By some estimates, employee alcoholism costs U.S. employees about $226 billion per year. Samuel Bacharach et al. "Alcohol Consumption and Workplace Absenteeism: The Moderating Effect of Social Support," *Journal of Applied Psychology* 95, no. 2 (2010): 334–348.

84. "Employers Can Play Key Role in Preventing Painkiller Abuse, But Many Remain Reluctant," *BNA Bulletin to Management* (February 15, 2011): 49.

85. Bacharach et al. "Alcohol Consumption and Workplace Absenteeism."

86. See for example, L. Claussen, "Can You Spot the Meth Addict?" *Safety & Health* 179, no. 4 (April 2009): 48–52.

87. CAGE is an acronym for the first letters of four of its questions: **C**ut Down, **A**nnoyed, **G**uilty, and **E**ye Opener. MAST is the Michigan Alcoholism Screening Test.

88. Gopal C. Pati and John I. Adkins Jr., with Glenn Morrison, *Managing and Employing the Handicapped: The Untapped Potential* (Lake Forest, IL: Brace-Park, Human Resource Press, 1981); see also Commerce Clearing House, "How Should Employers Respond to Indications an Employee May Have an Alcohol or Drug Problem?" *Ideas and Trends* (April 6, 1989): 53–57; and "The Employer's Role in Alcoholism Assistance," *Personnel Journal* 62, no. 7 (July 1983): 568–572.

89. Beth Andrus, "Accommodating the Alcoholic Executive," *Society for Human Resource Management Legal Report* (January 2008): 1, 4.

90. "New Jersey Union Takes on Mandatory Random Drug Tests," *Record* (Hackensack, NJ) (January 2, 2008): p. NA.

91. William Current, "Pre-Employment Drug Testing," *Occupational Hazards* (July 2002): 56. See also William Current, "Improving Your Drug Testing ROI," *Occupational Health & Safety* 73, no. 4 (April 2004): 40, 42, 44.

92. Diane Cadrain, "Are Your Employees' Drug Tests Accurate?" *HR Magazine* (January 2003): 41–45; and Sally Roberts, "Random Drug Testing Can Help Reduce Accidents for Construction Companies; Drug Abuse Blamed for Heightened Risk in the Workplace," *Business Insurance* 40 (October 23, 2006): 6.

93. Frank Lockwood et al., "Drug Testing Programs and Their Impact on Workplace Accidents: A Time Series Analysis," *Journal of Individual Employment Rights* 8, no. 4 (2000): 295–306.

94. Teresa Long, "Intexicated Drivers and Employer Liability," *EHS Today* (September 2009): 22–23.

95. The research is quite clear that work stress increases alcohol use among normal drinkers, and this has several implications for employers. Employers and supervisors should take steps to reduce stressful daily work experiences such as interpersonal conflicts at work, role ambiguity, and excessive workloads as way to reduce stress. Songqi Liu et al., "Daily Work Stress and Alcohol Use: Testing the Cross Level Moderation Effects of Neuroticism and Job Involvement," *Personnel Psychology* 60, no. 2 (2009): 575–597.

96. www.OSHA.gov, accessed May 28, 2005.

97. "Few Employers Addressing Workplace Stress, Watson Wyatt Surveys Find," *Compensation & Benefits Review* (May/June 2008): 12.

98. Eric Sundstrom et al., "Office Noise, Satisfaction, and Performance," *Environment and Behavior* 2 (March 1994): 195–222; and "Stress: How to Cope with Life's Challenges," *American Family Physician* 74 no. 8 (October 15, 2006).

99. "The Dawning of a New Era," *Workforce Management* (December 2010): 3.

100. Tara Parker-Pope, "Time to Review Workplace Reviews?" *New York Times* (May 18, 2010): D5.

101. Michael Manning, Conrad Jackson, and Marcelline Fusilier, "Occupational Stress, Social Support, and the Costs of Health Care," *Academy of Management Journal* 39, no. 3 (1996): 738–50; "Failing to Tackle Stress Could Cost You Dearly," *Personnel Today* (September 12, 2006); and www.sciencedaily.com/releases/2007/06/070604170722.htm, accessed November 3, 2009.

102. "Stress, Depression Cost Employers," *Occupational Hazards* (December 1998): 24. See also Patricia B. Gray, "Hidden Costs of Stress," *Money* 36, no. 12 (December 2007): 44.

103. Sabine Sonnentag et al., "'Did You Have a Nice Evening?' A Day-Level Study on Recovery Experiences, Sleep, and Affect," *Journal of Applied Psychology* 93, no. 3 (2008): 674–684.

104. See, for example, Elizabeth Bernstein, "When a Coworker Is Stressed Out," *Wall Street Journal* (August 26, 2008): B1, B2.

105. Karl Albrecht, *Stress and the Manager* (Upper Saddle River, NJ: Prentice Hall, 1979), pp. 253–55; "Stress: How to Cope with Life's Challenges," *American Family Physician* 74, no. 8 (October 15, 2006); http://familydoctor.org/familydoctor/en/prevention-wellness/emotional-wellbeing/mental-health/stress-how-to-cope-better-with-lifeschallenges.html, accessed April 11, 2012; www.mayoclinic.com/health/coping-with-stress/SR00030/NSECTIONGROUP=2, accessed April 11, 2012; www.cdc.gov/violenceprevention/pub/coping_with_stress_tips.html, accessed April 11, 2012.

106. "Meditation Gives Your Mind Permanent Working Holiday; Relaxation Can Improve Your Business Decisions and Your Overall Health," discussed in *Investor's Business Daily* (March 24, 2004): 89. See also "Workplace Yoga, Meditation Can Reduce Stress," *EHS Today* (September 2009): 21.

107. "Meditation Helps Employees Focus, Relieve Stress," *BNA Bulletin to Management* (February 20, 2007): 63.

108. "Going Head to Head with Stress," *Personnel Today* (April 26, 2005): 1.

109. Ibid.

110. William Atkinson, "Turning Stress into Strength," *HR Magazine* (January 2011): 51.

111. See, for example, Christina Maslach and Michael Leiter, "Early Predictors of Job Burnout and Engagement," *Journal of Applied Psychology* 93, no. 3 (2008): 498–512.

112. Ibid.

113. Sabine Sonnentag et al., "Staying Well and Engaged When Demands Are High: The Role of Psychological

Detachment," *Journal of Applied Psychology* 95, no. 5 (2010): 965–976.

114. Andy Meisler, "Mind Field," *Workforce Management* (September 2003): 58.

115. "Employers Must Move from Awareness to Action in Dealing with Worker Depression," *BNA Bulletin to Management* (April 29, 2004): 137.

116. Sandy Smith, "SARS: What Employers Need to Know," *Occupational Hazards* (July 2003): 33–35.

117. "CDC Recommends N95 Respirators in Revised H1N1 Flu Guidance for Healthcare Workers," *BNA Bulletin to Management* (October 20, 2009): 329–336; Pamela Ferrante, "H1N1: Spreading the Message," *EHS Today* (January 2010): 25–27.

118. Diane Cadrain, "Smoking and Workplace Laws Ensnaring HR," *HR Magazine* 49, no. 6 (June 2004): 38–39.

119. "Smoking Succession Plans Aimed at Curbing Health Care Costs," *BNA Bulletin to Management* (October 20, 2009): 343.

120. However, note that some experts believe that in some circumstances the EEOC might see a smoking addiction as similar to use of illegal drugs, and thus possibly covered by the ADA. "Policies to Not Hire Smokers Raise Privacy, Bias Issues," *BNA Bulletin to Management* (December 14, 2010): 399. See also Joan Deschenauxh, "Is a 'Smoke-Free' Workplace Right for You?" *HR Magazine* (July 2011): 43–45.

121. Leonard Berry et al., "What's the Hard Return on Employee Wellness Programs?" *Harvard Business Review* (December 2010): 105.

122. Steve Bates, "Where There Is Smoke, There Are Terminations: Smokers Fired to Save Health Costs," *HR Magazine* 50, no. 3 (March 2005): 28–29.

123. Susan Wells, "Does Work Make You Fat?" *HR Magazine* (October 2010): 28.

124. J. A. Savage, "Are Computer Terminals Zapping Workers' Health?" *Business and Society Review* (1993) 41–43; www.ninds.nih.gov/disorders/repetitive_motion/repetitive_motion.htm, accessed February 28, 2010.

125. www.OSHA.gov, accessed May 28, 2005. See also www.cdc.gov/od/ohs/Ergonomics/compergo.htm, accessed May 26, 2007.

126. Anne Chambers, "Computer Vision Syndrome: Relief Is in Sight," *Occupational Hazards* (October 1999): 179–184; and www.OSHA.gov/ETOOLS/computerworkstations/index.html, accessed May 28, 2005.

127. "Worker Opens Fire at Ohio Jeep Plant," *Occupational Hazards* (March 2005): 16.

128. Gus Toscano and Janice Windau, "The Changing Character of Fatal Work Injuries," *Monthly Labor Review* (October 1994): 17. See also Robert Grossman, "Bulletproof Practices," *HR Magazine* (November 2002): 34–42; Chuck Manilla, "How to Avoid Becoming a Workplace Violence Statistic," *Training & Development* (July 2008): 60–64.

129. "Bullies Trigger 'Silent Epidemic' at Work, but Legal Cures Remain Hard to Come By," *BNA Bulletin to Management* (February 24, 2000): 57.

130. Jennifer Laabs, "Employees Sabotage," *Workforce* (July 1999): 33–42; see also "Workplace Violence Takes a Deadly Toll," *EHS Today* (December 2009): 17.

131. Paul Viollis and Doug Kane, "At Risk Terminations: Protecting Employees, Preventing Disaster," *Risk Management Magazine* 52, no. 5 (May 2005): 28–33.

132. Jean Thilmany, "In Case of Emergency," *HR Magazine* (November 2007): 79–82; Chuck Manilla, "How to Avoid Becoming a Workplace Violence Statistic," *Training & Development* (July 2008): 60–64.

133. See also "Creating a Safer Workplace: Simple Steps Bring Results," *Safety Now* (September 2002): 1–2; L. Claussen, "Disgruntled and Dangerous," *Safety & Health* 180, no. 1 (July 2009): 44–47.

134. Florida recently passed a law giving employees the right to carry guns in cars parked at work. See "Right to Carry Guns in Cars Parked at Work Becomes Loaded Issue in Florida, Elsewhere," *BNA Bulletin to Management* (May 13, 2008): 153.

135. M. Sandy Hershcovis et al., "Predicting Workplace Aggression: A Meta-Analysis," *Journal of Applied Psychology* 92, no. 1 (2007): 228–238.

136. Alfred Feliu, "Workplace Violence and the Duty of Care: The Scope of an Employer's Obligation to Protect Against the Violent Employee," *Employee Relations Law Journal*, 20, n. 3, (Winter 1994–95), 401–402; Fay Hansen, "Burden of Proof," *Workforce Management* 89, no. 2 (February 2010), pp. 27–28, 30, 32–33.

137. Ibid.

138. See, for example, James Thelan, "Is That a Threat?" *HR Magazine* (December 2009): 61–63.

139. Paul Viollis and Doug Kane, "At Risk Terminations: Protecting Employees, Preventing Disaster," *Risk Management* 52, no. 15 (May 2005): 28–33.

140. Kenneth Diamond, "The Gender-Motivated Violence Act: What Employers Should Know," *Employee Relations Law Journal* 25, no. 4 (Spring 2000): 29–41; and "Bush Signs 'Violence against Women Act'; Funding Badly Needed Initiatives to Prevent Domestic & Sexual Violence, Help Victims," *America's Intelligence Wire* (January 5, 2006).

141. www.cdc.gov/ncipc/dvp/ipv_factsheet.pdf, accessed February 28, 2010.

142. "Employers Battling Workplace Violence Might Consider Postal Service Plan," *BNA Bulletin to Management* (August 5, 1999): 241.

143. Lloyd Newman, "Terrorism: Is Your Company Prepared?" *Business and Economic Review* 48, no. 2 (February 2002): 7–10.

144. Li Yuan et al., "Texting When There's Trouble," *Wall Street Journal* (April 18, 2007): B1.

145. Sources of *external* risk include legal/regulatory, political, and business environment

(economy, e-business, etc.). *Internal* risks sources include financial, strategic, operational (including safety and security) and integrity (embezzlement, theft, fraud, etc.). William Atkinson, "Enterprise Risk Management at Wal-Mart," www.rmmag. com/MGTemplate.cfm?Section=RMMagazine& NavMenuID=128&template=/Magazine/ DisplayMagazines.cfm&MGPreview=1&Volume= 50&IssueID=205&AID=2209&ShowArticle=1, accessed April 1, 2009.

146. Unless otherwise noted, the following including the six matters to address is based on Richard Maurer, "Keeping Your Security Program Active," *Occupational Hazards* (March 2003): 49–52. See also Sandy Smith, "Are You Prepared?" *EHS Today* (March 2012): 33–36.

147. Maurer, op. cit., p. 50.

148. Lisbeth Claus, "International Assignees at Risk," *HR Magazine* (February 2010): 73. Employers should even probably take precautions to protect workers who might be at risk for developing blood clots, for instance in their legs, as a result of sitting sedentary or flying long distances. "Employees Who Are Sedentary or Take Long Trips May Be at Risk for Blood Clot Disorder," *BNA Bulletin to Management* (March 2, 2010): 65.

149. Cynthia Ross, "How to Protect the Aging Workforce," *Occupational Hazards* (January 2005): 38–42; and Cynthia Ross, "How to Protect the Aging Workforce," *Occupational Hazards* (February 2005): 52–54.

150. "Importance of Taking Precautions for Overseas Operations Underscored by Mumbai Attacks," *BNA Bulletin to Management* (January 6, 2009): 1–8.

151. Ibid.

152. Ibid., p. 52.

Module A

1. Daren Dahl, "Recruiting: Tapping the Talent Pool . . . without Drowning in Resumes," *Inc.* 31, no. 3 (April 2009): 121–122.

2. Ibid.

3. Ibid.

4. Ibid.

5. Except as noted, this section is quoted from or paraphrased from http://eeoc.gov/laws/practices/index .cfm, accessed October 31, 2011.

6. This is based on John Drake, *Interviewing for Managers: A Complete Guide to Employment Interviewing* (New York, AMACOM, 1982).

7. Ibid.

8. From Stephen Covey, "Small Business, Big Opportunity," *Training* 43, no. 11 (November 2006): 40.

9. Paul Harris, "Small Businesses Bask in Training's Spotlight," *T + D* 59, no. 2 (Fall 2005): 46–52.

10. Ibid.

11. Ibid.

12. Gina Ruiz, "Smaller Firms in Vanguard of Flex Practices," *Workforce Management* 84, no. 13 (November 21, 2005): 10.

13. Ibid.

14. These are from Ty Freyvogel, "Operation Employee Loyalty," *Training Media Review* (September–October 2007).

15. Ibid.

16. Ibid.

17. Based on Bob Nelson, *1001 Ways to Reward Employees* (New York: Workmen Publishing, 1994), p. 19. See also Sunny C. L. Fong and Margaret A. Shaffer, "The Dimensionality and Determinants of Pay Satisfaction: A Cross-Cultural Investigation of a Group Incentive Plan," *International Journal of Human Resource Management* 14, no. 4 (June 2003): 559(22).

18. Jeffrey Marshall and Ellen Heffes, "Benefits: Smaller Firm Workers Often Getting Less," *Financial Executive* 21, no. 9 (November 1, 2005): 10; and www.irs.gov/ retirement/sponsor/article/0%2C%2Cid=139831%2C00 .html, accessed May 15, 2012.

19. Kristen Falk, "The Easy Retirement Plan for Small Business Clients," *National Underwriter* 111, no. 45 (December 3, 2007): 12–13.

20. Ibid.

21. Jack Griffin, *How to Say It at Work* (Paramus, NJ: Prentice Hall Press, 1998), p. 178.

22. Ibid.

23. Joyce Osland, David Kolb, and Irwin Rubin, eds., *The Organizational Behavior Reader* (Upper Saddle River, NJ: Prentice Hall, 2001), pp. 185–95. The Active Listening Checklist is adapted from Paula J. Caprioni, *The Practical Coach: Management Skills for Everyday Life* (Upper Saddle River, NJ: Prentice Hall, 2001), p. 86.

24. For a more complete list, see, for example, Sondra Servais, *Personnel Director* (Deerfield Beach, FL: Made E-Z Products, 1994); and www.hoovers.com/business-forms/—pageid_16436—/global-mktg-index.xhtml?cm_ ven=PAID&cm_cat=GGL&cm_pla=FRM&cm_ite= employment_contract_forms, accessed July 20, 2008.

25. See for example, www.officemax.com/office-supplies/ business-forms/human-resource-forms? position=1&prodPage=91&cm_mmc=Google-_- 2012+Awareness+-+OFSU+-+Business+ Forms-_-Human+Resource+Forms+-_-employment+ application+form_Phrase&002= 2539317&004=4595778581&005=83482931&006= 18978753461&007=Search&008=, accessed May 15, 2012; and www.officedepot.com/a/products/431415/ Socrates-Media-Small-Business-Employment-Forms/; jsessionid=0000XiY0hwZThX8srXlLhy4eXsY: 13ddpq53l, accessed May 14, 2012.

26. www.ihrim.org/index.php?option=com_mtree& Itemid=176, accessed May 15, 2012.

NAME/ORGANIZATION INDEX

Note: page numbers with *n* indicate notes.

SUBJECT INDEX

Notes: page numbers with *f* indicate figures; those with *t* indicate tables.